THE TIBETAN BOOK
OF THE
GREAT LIBERATION

OR THE METHOD OF
REALIZING *NIRVĀṆA* THROUGH
KNOWING THE MIND

THE GREAT *GURU* PADMA-SAMBHAVA

Described on pages xv–xvi

THE TIBETAN BOOK
OF THE
GREAT LIBERATION

OR THE METHOD OF REALIZING *NIRVĀṆA*
THROUGH KNOWING THE MIND

PRECEDED BY AN
EPITOME OF PADMA-SAMBHAVA'S BIOGRAPHY
AND FOLLOWED BY
GURU PHADAMPA SANGAY'S TEACHINGS

According to English Renderings by
Sardar Bahādur S. W. Laden La, c.b.e., f.r.g.s.
and by the Lāmas Karma Sumdhon Paul
Lobzang Mingyur Dorje, and
Kazi Dawa-Samdup

Introductions, Annotations and Editing by
W. Y. EVANS-WENTZ, M.A., D.Litt., D.Sc.
Jesus College, Oxford
Author of *The Tibetan Book of the Dead*
Tibet's Great Yogī Milarepa
Tibetan Yoga and Secret Doctrines, &c.

With Psychological Commentary by
DR. C. G. JUNG

OXFORD UNIVERSITY PRESS
London   Oxford   New York

OXFORD UNIVERSITY PRESS

London   Oxford   New York
Glasgow   Toronto   Melbourne   Wellington
Cape Town   Ibadan   Nairobi   Dar es Salaam   Lusaka   Addis Ababa
Delhi   Bombay   Calcutta   Madras   Karachi   Lahore   Dacca
Kuala Lumpur   Singapore   Hong Kong   Tokyo

First published by Oxford University Press, London, 1954
First issued as an Oxford University Press paperback, 1968
This reprint, 1972
Printed in the United States of America

IN GRATEFUL REMEMBRANCE OF
THE *GURUS*
WHO INSPIRED THE
TRANSMISSION OF THIS BOOK AND
THE TWO PRECEDING BOOKS
IN THIS SERIES
TO THE PEOPLES OF THE
WESTERN WORLD

DEDICATED
TO THOSE
SEEKING WISDOM

Bondage and Liberation

I: BONDAGE

Upon Ignorance dependeth *karma*;
Upon *karma* dependeth consciousness;
Upon consciousness depend name and form;
Upon name and form depend the six organs of sense;
Upon the six organs of sense dependeth contact;
Upon contact dependeth sensation;
Upon sensation dependeth desire;
Upon desire dependeth attachment;
Upon attachment dependeth existence;
Upon existence dependeth birth;
Upon birth depend old age and death, sorrow, lamentation, misery, grief, and despair. Thus doth this entire aggregation of misery arise.

II: LIBERATION

But upon the complete fading out and cessation of Ignorance ceaseth *karma*;
Upon the cessation of *karma* ceaseth consciousness;
Upon the cessation of consciousness cease name and form;
Upon the cessation of name and form cease the six organs of sense;
Upon the cessation of the six organs of sense ceaseth contact;
Upon the cessation of contact ceaseth sensation;
Upon the cessation of sensation ceaseth desire;
Upon the cessation of desire ceaseth attachment;
Upon the cessation of attachment ceaseth existence;
Upon the cessation of existence ceaseth birth;
Upon the cessation of birth cease old age and death, sorrow, lamentation, misery, grief, and despair. Thus doth this entire aggregation of misery cease.

The Buddha, *Samyutta Nikāya*, xxii. 90[16]
(based upon H. C. Warren's Translation).

PLATE II

THE TRANSLATORS AND THE EDITOR
Described on page xvii

PREFACE

IN this volume, the fourth of my Tibetan Series, I have placed on record, in a manner intended to appeal equally to the learned and to the unlearned, to the philosopher and to the scientist, some of the most recondite teachings of Oriental Sages. In doing so, I have had the right guidance of an original text, heretofore unknown to Europe, the authorship of which is attributed to Tibet's Precious *Guru* Padma-Sambhava, the illustrious master of the Tantric Occult Sciences, of whose life-history an epitome is herein presented.

Inasmuch as this volume sets forth the very quintessence of the Great Path, the Māhāyana, it not only supplements the three previous volumes, but is, in some respects, the most important member of the Series. At the time of the publication of *Tibetan Yoga and Secret Doctrines*, I did not, however, foresee that it was my destiny to be the transmitter of this additional volume.

In the General Introduction and the textual annotations there have been incorporated, to serve as a very necessary commentary, complementary teachings which were orally transmitted through a long line of *Gurus* of the Kargyütpa School to my own Tibetan *Guru*, the late Lāma Kazi Dawa-Samdup. Also, in Book III, the teachings of the *Guru* Pha-dampa Sangay supplement those of the other *Gurus*.

Thanks to the kindly assistance of Lāma Karma Sumdhon Paul and Lāma Lobzang Mingyur Dorje, the first two successors of the late Lāma Kazi Dawa-Samdup in the University of Calcutta, Book II, the essential part of this volume, has been rendered into English.

All who read this volume will join with me in offering homage to the late Sardar Bahādur S. W. Laden La, whom I had the great joy of assisting, in my capacity as scribe and editor, when he translated the excerpts from the Lotus-Born One's Biography, upon which the epitome of it, comprising Book I, is based.

I am especially grateful to Dr. C. G. Jung, the distin-

guished dean of Western psychologists, for his erudite Foreword, which serves as a bridge between the best thought of
Occident and Orient. Today, even more than in the days of
the Greek philosophers, East and West not only are meeting,
but are recognizing their inherent and inseparable oneness.
Only the vulgar notice and advocate racial and religious differentiation. To the clear-seeing, Humanity is One Family,
eternally transcending geographical demarcations, national
limitations, and every fettering concept born of the unenlightened mind.

To the late Dr. R. R. Marett, Rector of Exeter College, and
formerly Reader in Social Anthropology in the University of
Oxford, whose encouragement of my anthropological research
is well known to readers of other books bearing my name, I
am indebted for his having critically examined the matter
herein contained before it took final shape. I owe a similar
debt to Dr. F. W. Thomas, Emeritus Boden Professor of
Sanskrit in the University of Oxford, more particularly for
his assistance with certain of the Tibetan transliterations and
place-names; and to Mr. E. T. Sturdy, translator of the
Nārada Sūtra, for his no less timely help with the Sanskrit
transliterations. I am, also, very greatly indebted to Mr.
R. F. C. Hull, translator of the forthcoming Collected Edition
of the works of Dr. C. G. Jung, for having constructively read
the proofs of this book as a whole.

My thanks are likewise due to each of the translators who
in Germany and in France have made the results of my
Tibetan studies available in their several languages. In this
connexion I cannot omit the names of Madame Marguerite
La Fuente, of Paris, who, under the extreme stress of
economic conditions, arranged for the production of *Le Yoga
Tibétain et les Doctrines Secrètes* (Paris, 1938); and of Miss
Constant Lounsbery, author of *Buddhist Meditation in the
Southern School* and also President of *Les Amis du Bou-
dhisme*, of Paris, who aided Madame La Fuente in the arduous
task of making the translation.

I acknowledge, too, the encouragement and aid rendered
by many other helpers, friends, and correspondents hail-

ing from all the continents—who, like myself, are earnestly striving to overthrow every barrier born of Ignorance that separates race from race, nation from nation, and religion from religion.

May this book afford added courage and strength to those many helpers and friends. May that Universal Good Will of the Great Teachers of Wisdom, such as is herein set forth, speedily prevail, so that mankind may recognize their divine at-one-ment.

W. Y. E.-W.

SAN DIEGO, CALIFORNIA
All Saints' Day, 1952

It Were Better to Live One Single Day

'It were better to live one single day in the development of a good life of meditation than to live a hundred years evilly and with undisciplined mind.

'It were better to live one single day in the pursuit of understanding and meditation than to live a hundred years in ignorance and unrestraint.

'It were better to live one single day in the commencement of earnest endeavour than to live a hundred years in sloth and effortlessness.

'It were better to live one single day giving thought to the origin and cessation of that which is composite than to live a hundred years giving no thought to such origin and cessation.

'It were better to live one single day in the realization of the Deathless State than to live a hundred years without such realization.

'It were better to live one single day knowing the Excellent Doctrine than to live a hundred years without knowing the Excellent Doctrine.'

The Buddha, from the *Dhammapada*, vv. 110–15
(based upon N. K. Bhagwat's Translation).

CONTENTS

BOOK I

AN EPITOME OF THE LIFE AND TEACHINGS OF TIBET'S GREAT *GURU* PADMA–SAMBHAVA

Introduction, *p.* 103; Buddha's Prophecy of Birth of Padma-Sambhava, 105; King Indrabodhi, 105; King's Despondency, 106; Avalokiteshvara's Appeal, and Amitābha's Response, 106; King's and Priests' Dreams, 107; Prophecy of Amitābha's Incarnation, 107; Wish-granting Gem, 108; Discovery of Lotus-Born, 108; Child Taken to Palace, 109; As Prince, Athlete, and King, 110; Coming of *Arhants*, 112; Plan to Marry Padma, 112; Marriage to Bhāsadhara, 113; Renunciation, 114; Parting, 115; *Karmic* Taking of Life, 116; Exile, 117; God of the Corpses, 118; Overthrow of the Irreligious, 119;

BOOK II

THE *YOGA* OF KNOWING THE MIND, THE SEEING OF REALITY, CALLED SELF–LIBERATION

BOOK III

THE LAST TESTAMENTARY TEACHINGS OF THE *GURU* PHADAMPA SANGAY

The Buddha's Sermon on What is True Blessedness?

Praise be to the Blessed One, the Holy One, the Author of all Truth.

Thus I have heard. On a certain day dwelt the Blessed One at Srāva-stī, at the Jetavana Monastery, in the Garden of Anathapindaka. And when the night was far advanced, a certain radiant celestial being, illuminating the whole of Jetavana, approached the Blessed One and saluted Him, and standing aside, and remaining so, addressed Him with these words: 'Many gods and men, yearning after good, have held diverse things to be blessings; declare Thou, What is true blessedness?'

'To serve wise men rather than fools, to give honour to whom honour is due; this is true blessedness.

'To dwell in a pleasant land, to have done virtuous deeds in a former existence, to have a heart filled with right desires; this is true blessedness.

'Much wisdom and much science, the discipline of a well-trained mind, and right speech; this is true blessedness.

'To wait on father and mother, to cherish wife and child, to follow a peaceful calling; this is true blessedness.

'To give alms, to live piously, to protect kinsfolk, to perform blameless deeds; this is true blessedness.

'To cease doing evil, to abstain from strong drink, to persevere in right conduct; this is true blessedness.

'Reverence and humility, contentment and gratitude, the hearing of the Law of Righteousness at due seasons; this is true blessedness.

'Patience and pleasing speech, association with holy men, to hold religious discourse at fitting moments; this is true blessedness.

'Penance and chastity, discernment of the Four Noble Truths and the realization of peace; this is true blessedness.

'A mind unshaken by the vicissitudes of this life, inaccessible to sorrow, passionless, secure; this is true blessedness.

'They that observe these things are invincible on every side, on every side they walk in safety; yea, their's is the true blessedness.'— *Maṅgala Sūtra.*[1]

---

[1] A recension by the Editor, based on Professor Childer's Translation and on that by Irving Babbitt in *The Dhammapāda* (Oxford University Press, New York and London, 1936), page 76.

DESCRIPTION OF ILLUSTRATIONS

I. THE GREAT *GURU* PADMA-SAMBHAVA   *Frontispiece*

A photographic reproduction (about one-fifth of the original size) of a modern Tibetan painting in colour, on cotton cloth, acquired in Nepal, representing Padma-Sambhava, robed in his royal robes as a King of Sahor, India, sitting in kingly posture on a lotus-lunar throne. The *dorje* (described on p. 107[1]), in his right hand, is held in the posture (or *mudrā*) called in Tibetan the *Dorje Dik-dzup* (*Rdo-rje-sdigs-mdzub*), i.e. the Indomitable (or *Vajra*) Finger-pointing *Mudrā*, to guard against all evils which might affect the *Dharma*, and to place the Three Realms of Existence (described on p. 205[1]) under his dominion. The human-skull cup in his left hand is filled with the nectar of immortality (Skt. *amrita*); and superimposed upon the nectar is the urn of longevity and immortal life, also filled with the ambrosia of the gods, of which his devotees are privileged to drink. The skull cup itself symbolizes renunciation of the world. The trident-pointed staff (Skt. *trishūla*) which he holds in the folds of his left arm is highly symbolical. The trident at the top symbolizes the Three Realms of Existence (in Sanskrit, the *Trailokya*), and suggests his dominion over them and over the three chief evils, lust, anger (or ill will), and sloth (or stupidity). It also symbolizes the Three Times, the past, present, and future. The flames emanating from the middle point of the trident are the Flames of Divine Wisdom which consume Ignorance (Skt. *avidyā*). The skull underneath the trident symbolizes the *Dharma-Kāya*; the first of the two human heads below the skull symbolizes the *Sambhoga-Kāya*, and the second the *Nirmāṇa-Kāya*. (The Three *Kāyas* are described on pp. 3–4, 178[1]). The golden urn below the heads is filled with the essence of transcendent blessings and perfections. The golden double-*dorje* below the urn is described by the *lāmas* thus: the southern (or lower) point represents Peace; the western point Multiplicity; the northern (or upper) point (hidden by the urn) Initiatory Power; the eastern point Fearfulness; and the centre the at-one-ment of all spiritual endowments and perfections. The white silk ribbon-like banner below the double-*dorje*, resembling a Banner of Victory, of which it is an abbreviated form, symbolizes the Great *Guru*'s Victory over the *Sangsāra*. The staff itself symbolizes the Divine *Shakti*.

The Great *Guru* wears as his head-dress what Tantrics call the lotus-cap. The crescent moon and the sun, on the front of it, signify, as does the lotus-cap itself, that he is crowned with all initiatory powers. The feather surmounting the lotus-cap being that of a vulture, regarded as the highest and mightiest of fliers among birds, symbolizes that his Doctrine of the Great Perfection is the most aspiring, noblest, and loftiest of spiritual doctrines. His blue and purple and priestly yellow inner dress is the dress of a Tibetan *Nyag-pa* (*Sngags-pa*), or one who is a Master of Tantric Occultism.

Kneeling on a smaller lotus-lunar throne, to the left of the Great *Guru*, is the figure of Bhāsadhara, his Queen when he was the King of Sahor, offering to him *amrita* in a bowl made of a human skull; and on his right, similarly enthroned and kneeling and making a like offering, that of Mandāravā, his most faithful and beloved disciple.

Immediately above the head of the Great *Guru* is shown the Buddha Shākya Muni, sitting in *Padmāsana*, or Buddha posture, on a lotus-lunar throne, holding in His left hand the begging-bowl, symbolical of His being a religious mendicant, and with His right hand touching, and thus calling, the Earth to bear witness to the truth of His Doctrine. The Buddha is so placed above the Great *Guru* because He is his spiritual Predecessor and Ancestor; the Great *Guru* representing on Earth the Tantric, or Esoteric, Emanation of the Buddha.

On either side of the Buddha, posed as He is, but on the simpler throne of a disciple or *Bodhisattva*, are two *Arhants*, each holding a mendicant's begging-bowl and alarm-staff. The Sun (red) to the left and the Moon (white) to the right of the Buddha, the clouds, the blue sky, the land and mountains and waters below, the blossoms and the fruits, signify, as in other of the Illustrations, the *Sangsāra*, and, therefore, that the Teachers are still active therein and ever striving for the salvation of mankind.

The Great *Guru*, the Buddha, and the two *Arhants* are enhaloed in rainbow-like radiance: The Great *Guru* and the Buddha have nimbi of green, indicating the eternity of the Bodhic Essence manifested through Them. The nimbi of the other four figures are orangered, suggestive of their possessors not yet being wholly free from worldly or *sangsāric* bondage.

Directly below the Great *Guru* are the insignia of the Five Objects of Enjoyment, offerings made to him by his devotees: (1) luscious food substances, symbolical of pleasing taste, in the blue receptacle at the centre surmounted by a red *chorten*; (2) the white conch-shell filled with perfume, symbolical of pleasing smell, resting on two sweet-smelling fruits; (3) the mirror on the opposite side, symbolizing pleasing form or sight; (4) the pair of cymbals (resting against the mirror), symbolical of pleasing sound or hearing; and (5) the red Chinese silk (binding the two cymbals together), symbolical of pleasing touch or feelings. In the Hindu system, whence they appear to have been derived, these Five Objects of Enjoyment correspond in symbolism, in their order as here given, to the Sanskrit *Rasa* (Taste), *Gandha* (Smell), *Rūpa* (Form or Sight), *Shabda* (Sound or Hearing), and *Sparsha* (Touch or Feelings).

II. THE TRANSLATORS AND THE EDITOR   *facing p.* vii

Upper: A reproduction of a group photograph, showing the Editor in the centre, in Tibetan dress, holding a copy of the *Bardo Thödol* block-print series of texts containing the text employed in producing the translation of the ' *Yoga* of Knowing the Mind in Its Nakedness ' ; to the Editor's right the Lāma Karma Sumdhon Paul, and to the Editor's left the Lāma Lobzang Mingyur Dorje. This photograph was taken during October 1935 in front of the Temple of the coming Buddha Maitreya, which appears in the background and forms a part of the Ghoom Monastery, Darjeeling. Three Tibetan prayer-flags (*Dhar-chok*), mounted on tall poles, appear to the left of the Temple. Such prayer-flags, made of cotton cloth printed on both sides with Tibetan prayers and *mantras*, usually bear verses ending with 'May the Doctrine of the Buddha prosper'.

Lower: A reproduction of a photograph of the late Sardar Bahādur S. W. Laden La, of Darjeeling, in the yellow silk dress of a Tibetan Peer (*Dzasa*) and wearing the black travelling-hat called *Chhok-sed* (*Mchhog-sred*) and some of the insignia of the various high honours conferred upon him by the British Government and the Government of Tibet.

Brief biographies of the late Sardar Bahādur and of the two Lāmas are given on pages 86–92.

III. MAÑJUSHRĪ'S BOOK OF DIVINE WISDOM   *facing p.* xxiii

A reproduction of a photograph of a rare manuscript copy of the *Phak-pa-Jam-pal-gi-Tsa-way-Gyud* (*Hphags-pa-Hjam-dpal-gyi-Rtsa-wahi-Rgyud*): Skt. *Ārya Mañjushrī Mūla Tantra*: Eng. 'The Original [or Root] Treatise [or Book] of the God of Wisdom', concerning the Kālachakra Doctrine as taught originally by the Lord Buddha, and forming a part of the *Kanjur* (*Bkah-'gyur*), ' The Translated Commandments', the canon of Tibetan Buddhism. The exposition and guardianship of this Doctrine, because of its profound esotericism, is entrusted to the Tashi Lāma, who is otherwise known, among the Tibetans, as 'The Precious Great Doctor', or 'Great Gem of Learning' (*Pan-chen Rin-po-ch'e*), and also as 'The Precious Lordly Victor' (*Kyap-gön-Rin-po-ch'e*). The text is written in gold and silver on lacquered Tibetan-made paper, each folio of which measures $25\frac{3}{8}$ inches by $6\frac{1}{8}$ inches. The first page of the text is shown underneath the volume.

In order to safeguard it, the manuscript was given over to the custody of one of the officials accompanying the late Tashi Lāma at the time His Holiness fled from Tibet. It was then seized, along with other goods of the fleeing Tashi Lāma, by the Tibetan Government and sold, and afterwards came into the possession of Mr. Tharchin, editor of *The Tibetan Newspaper*, Kalimpong, from whom we acquired it. The manuscript was probably one of the Tashi Lāma's most treasured books that he wished to carry with him and, as the incarnate guardian of its secret teachings, to preserve inviolate.

The manuscript, which is about two hundred years old, was examined by Lāma Lobzang Mingyur Dorje, who submitted to the Editor the following report. 'This, rightfully, is the Book which Mañjushrī holds on the lotus blossom. According to tradition, the King of Shambhala having been the chief listener when the Kālachakra Doctrine was taught by the Buddha, committed the Doctrine to writing for the first time; and, inasmuch as he was the incarnation of Mañjushrī, it is said that Mañjushrī himself was its compiler. In the Sam-bha-la-hi-Lam-yik, or Journey to Shambhala, is contained the prophecy that the twenty-fifth Tashi Lāma will be the incarnation of the King of Shambhala and attain dominion over the whole world.'

The Book is largely astrological; and no one save a master of classical Tibetan and an adept in the esotericism and initiatory mantras of Mañjushrī could intelligibly translate it as a whole. There is no treatise in Tibet, or elsewhere among men, more sacred and occult. Lāma Karma Sumdhon Paul has rendered the text of the page shown, as follows:

'In the Sanskrit language [this treatise is called] Ārya Mañjushrī Mūla Tantra; in the Tibetan language, Phak-pa-Jam-pal-gi-Tsa-way-Gyud (Hphags-pa-Hjam-dpal-gyi-Rtsa-wahi-Rgyud).

'Homage I render to all the Buddhas and Bodhisattvas.

'Thus have I heard: Once upon a time, the Bhagavat, in the celestial pure region above, where the Bodhisattvas, in their own ineffable excellent various maṇḍalas [or divine conclaves], had assembled, preached [this doctrine] to the sons of the gods of that pure realm in the following manner: "O ye sons of the divine ones, give ear to me".'

The Kālachakra (Tib. Dus-kyi Khor-lo: pron. Dü-kyi Khor-lo), meaning 'Circle of Time', is an esoteric system of yoga, to which tradition assigns a primeval origin antedating the advent of the Buddha Gautama and therefore associates it with the Ādi (or Primordial)-Buddha. The prophecy, that the King of Shambhala, who is sometimes called the Chief of the Secret Tibetan Brotherhood of Initiates of the Occult Sciences, shall govern mankind, implies the coming of a Golden Age and the enthronement of Divine Wisdom on Earth. Further reference to the Kālachakra and to Shambhala is made on pages 59, 122³, 117, following.

Initiates consider the Kālachakra to be the most important doctrine contained in the Kan-jur, wherein it is expounded in the first of the twenty-two volumes of Tantra. The mention made by the editors of the Peking edition of The Voice of the Silence (excerpts by H. P. Blavatsky from The Book of the Golden Precepts), that they were presented by the late Tashi Lāma 'with a small treatise in Tibetan on the Kālachakra, entitled *The Communion of Mystic Adepts* (Tü Kor-la *deṅ-pä la-mä niṅ-jor*)',[1] suggests the deeply esoteric character of this Tantric doctrine, the teaching of which is a prerogative of the Tashi Lāma Dynasty of *Gurus*.

IV. MAÑJUSHRĪ, THE GOD OF DIVINE WISDOM   *facing p.* lxiv

A photographic reproduction (about one-quarter of the original size) of an old monastic painting in colour, on heavy cotton cloth, painted in Lhāsa (or 'The Place of the Divine One'). The central figure represents the princely and youthful *Bodhisattva* Mañjushrī (Tib. *Hjam-dpal*: pron. *Jam-pay*), the 'Gently Beautiful One', also called, in Sanskrit, Mañjughosha, or, in Tibetan, Jam-yang (*Hjam-dyang*), the 'Melodious Voiced One'. Quite in musical keeping with this character of Mañjughosha is his mellifluous *mantra*: '*Om! a-ra-pa-ca-na-ḍhi!*' As the 'God of Divine Wisdom' (Tib. *Shes-rab-kyi-lha*) he is the Secret Presence presiding over this volume, especially over Book II. His worship confers Divine Wisdom, mastery of the *Dharma*, retentive memory, mental perfection, and eloquence; even by uttering his *mantras* one attains enlightenment. He is the third of the *Dhyānī Bodhisattvas*. According to the Nepalese *Svayambhū Purāna*, Mañjushrī came from the Five-peaked Mountain in China (mentioned, herein, in Book I), and with his sword cleft asunder the southern barrier of hills in Nepal, and the water rushed out, and the broad fertile valley of Nepal emerged. Thus he appears to have been a Chinese culture hero who brought culture to Nepal.[2] In his right hand he holds aloft the all-victorious flaming Sword of Wisdom and Light, with which he cuts off Ignorance and Darkness. In his left hand he holds, on a blue lotus blossom, the Book of Divine Wisdom,[3] shown in Illustration III and described above, by virtue of which his devotees attain the Great Liberation of the Other Shore.

In the Tibetan canonical *Kanjur* more books or treatises are dedicated to Mañjushrī, as the Divine Protector of the *Dharma*, than to any other *Bodhisattva*; and the *lāmas* place him first in the list of *Bodhisattvas*. He is, in some of the *Tantras*, the listener, or one receiving the *yogic* instruction. There are attributed to him discourses with the Buddha, and a discussion with Shāriputra on the problem of how the world came to exist.

Esoterically, Mañjushrī is the *Logos*, which, in the Wisdom Teachings of ancient Egypt, was personified as Thoth, a form of Hermes. In ancient Greece he was the beautiful young sun-god Apollo, who

[1] Cf. *The Voice of the Silence*, edited with notes and comments by Alice Cleather and Basil Crump (Peking, 1927), p. 105.

[2] Cf. B. Bhattacharyya, *Indian Buddhist Iconography* (Oxford University Press, 1924), pp. 15–16.

[3] It is sometimes said that this Book represents the *Prajñā-Pāramitā* (or 'Transcendental Wisdom'), referred to on pp. 129, 157[2], following.

enlightened the mind of those initiated into the Mysteries; or, under another manifestation, the youthful Mercury, with winged feet, bearing the mystic staff of intertwined serpents, who, being the messenger of the gods, brought to men the Heavenly Wisdom.

In the earliest Mahāyāna Buddhism, Mañjushrī is the only Tantric deity represented without a *shakti* (or feminine counterpart), in signification of his perfect state of *brahmachāri* (or sexual continence) and adeptship of the occult sciences. In later Mahāyāna Buddhism there was assigned to him as his *shakti* the Hindu Goddess of Learning, Sarasvati.

Mañjushrī also presides over the law of righteousness; and all knotty problems of law he cuts with his sword. He is particularly associated with Astrology; and astrologers make him their chief tutelary and patron. There are a number of special forms or aspects of Mañjushrī, some of which receive mention in the Biography of Padma-Sambhava. Various Sages, too, in India, Nepal, Tibet, and China have been regarded as incarnations of Mañjushrī. Among these is Ātisha (A.D. 980–1052), who, in the year 1038, when almost sixty years of age, set out for Tibet from the Vikramashīla Monastery in Maghada to begin his great pioneer reformation of Lāmaism which resulted in the Gelugpa or Established Church. Tsong-Khapa, who, at the beginning of the fifteenth century, went to Tibet from the Amdo Province, China, and completed Ātisha's work of establishing the Gelugpa Order, in A.D. 1417, is believed to be another of these incarnations, and, as such, the reincarnation of Ātisha. In Sikkim, the founder of the present dynasty of kings has also been canonized as one of Mañjushrī's earthly manifestations.

In his ordinary aspect, Mañjushrī is a deity of the Peaceful Order (Tib. *Zhi-wa*). When represented as of the Wrathful Order (Tib. *Tho-wo*), he is Bhairava-Vajra, or 'The Awesome Thunderbolt One'.

In this Illustration, Mañjushrī sits in the Buddha posture on a lotus-lunar throne. His loose-flowing garments of silk, his bodily adornments of gold inset with precious gems, and his richly bejewelled golden head-dress indicate that he is a royal prince. His body emanates a rainbow-hued halo; and his nimbus, of the mystic colour green edged with dark crimson, indicates his immutable and everlasting spirituality.

At the bottom of the painting is depicted the Jewel Lake of Wisdom. The radiance of the jewels emanates from the water; and on either corner of the upper shore are the Three Jewels, or Three Values (Skt. *Tri-Ratna*), of the Buddhist Faith, symbolizing the Buddha, the Doctrine, and the Priesthood. A miniature figure, amidst the lotus leaves above the lake, represents the deceased devotee of Mañjushrī in whose honour the painting was made by command of the devotee's surviving relatives, and, as a votive offering, dedicated to Mañjushrī.

In the upper corner, above Mañjushrī's sword, is the figure of the Dhyānī Buddha Amitābha, the 'One of Boundless (or Incomprehensible) Light', of whom the Tashi Lāmas are believed to be incarnations. His colour, being red, symbolizes his likeness to the Sun, which visibly illuminates the world; but Amitābha's own enlightening influence, being invisible, is symbolized by the Sun's Secret Essence (referred to on p. 215[2]). Amitābha presides over the Western Paradise known as Devachān. He sits in the Buddha posture on a lotus-lunar throne, and holds in his hands a bowl filled with immortality-conferring *amrita*.

In the opposite upper corner is the figure of the Dhyānī Buddha Vajra-Sattva, the 'Divine Heroic-Minded Being', who presides over the Eastern Direction. He holds the *dorje* (Skt. *vajra*), the symbol of his immutability, in his right hand, and a bell, the symbol of his divine transcendent heroism, in his left hand. He, too, sits in Buddha posture on a lotus-lunar throne; and, like Amitābha and Mañjushrī, radiates an encircling rainbow-like aura and a nimbus. His colour is white, the colour associated with the Eastern Direction. (For further details concerning both Vajra-Sattva and Amitābha see *The Tibetan Book of the Dead*, pp. 108–10, 112–15.)

In this painting, the three deities represent a Divine Trinity; and, as such, symbolize the *Tri-Kāya*, or 'Three Bodies' (described on pp. 3–4, 178[1]), by which, as here, the Buddha Essence is personified, Amitābha being associated with the *Dharma-Kāya*, Vajra-Sattva with the *Sambhoga-Kāya*, and Mañjushrī with the *Nirmāṇa-Kāya*. Another aspect of the *Tri-Kāya* is shown by Illustration VII. According to *maṇḍala*, school, and degree of initiation conferred, the personifications of the *Tri-Kāya* differ; but, in essentiality, all the personifications are one.

V. THE EIGHT *GURUS*   .   .   .   . *facing p.* 100

A photographic reproduction (about one-fourth of the original size) of an old monastic painting in colour, on heavy cotton cloth, painted in Shigatse, Tibet, representing the Great *Guru* in his manifestations in eight personalities, or minds, or powers, known to the Tibetans as the *Guru-tshan-gye*, or 'The Eight Worshipful Forms of the *Guru*'.

In royal guise, as the King of Sahor, the figure of the *Guru* Padma Jungnay, 'The *Guru* Born of a Lotus', otherwise called 'He Who Leadeth all Beings of the Three Realms of Existence to Happiness',[1] occupies the central position here as in the frontispiece; and in the description of the frontispiece this manifestation of the Great *Guru* is described in detail.

[1] This appellation, and those herein given of the other Eight *Gurus*, are contained in *The Brief Precepts Composed by Padma-Sambhava of Urgyān* (*U-rgyan Pad-mas Msad-pahi Bkah-thang Bsdus-pa*), according to the translation made by Lāma Karma Sumdhon Paul, assisted by the Editor.

In the upper corner to the left of the *Guru* Padma Jungnay is shown the *Guru* Shākya Seṅg-ge, 'The *Guru* Who is the Lion of the Shākya Clan', otherwise called 'The Eight Incarnations in One Body', as a Buddha sitting on a lotus-lunar throne in the Buddha posture (Skt. *Buddhāsana*), also known as the Lotus posture (Skt. *Padmāsana*), his body bent slightly to the right as is customary among Tibetan *yogins* who are his followers, his right hand in the Earth-touching *mudrā*, his left hand holding a begging-bowl filled with food.

In the opposite corner is the representation of the *Guru* Padma-Sambhava, 'The Lotus-born *Guru*', otherwise called 'The Great King of the *Dharma*, the Patron of Religion', as a young *Bhikṣhu*, likewise posed on a lotus-lunar throne, holding in his right hand, in the attitude of bestowing benediction, a *dorje*, in his left hand a human-skull bowl of *amrita* as an offering to all deities, and in the folds of his left arm the symbolic trident staff.

Directly above the *Guru* Padma Jungnay is the figure of the *Guru* Nyima Hodzer, 'The Sunbeam *Guru*' (or 'The Sunlight One'), otherwise known as 'He Who Embraceth all Doctrines as the Sky Embraceth all Space', in the guise of a *Herukapa*, or 'Unclad One', of the Order of Great Masters of *Yoga*. His colour is that of the Sun. In his left hand he holds, by a filament of light, a sun; and in his right hand the trident-pointed staff. Being a *Heruka*, he wears human-bone ornaments, to signify his world renunciation. His head-dress of human skulls indicates his triumph over *sangsāric* existence. The tiger-skin loin-covering is a further sign of his *yogic* powers. He sits in *Bodhisattvic* posture on a lotus-sun throne. (See the description of the *Heruka* in *Tibet's Great Yogī Milarepa*, pp. xvi–xvii.)

Directly below the *Guru* Padma-Sambhava is the figure of the *Guru* Lōden Chog-se, 'The *Guru* Possessing Wisdom and Best Desires', also called 'The Transmitter of Wisdom to all Worlds',[1] in the guise of a king, sitting on a lotus-lunar throne, with his right leg extended in what is known among Tibetans as the kingly dancing pose (Tib. *Gyal-po-rolpai-tak*). In his right hand he holds a mirror, symbolical of the mirage-like or reflected (as in a mirror) nature of all *sangsāric* things; and, in his left hand, a human-skull bowl filled with the nectar of immortality, symbolical of his immunity to old age and death.

Directly below the *Guru* Shākya Seṅg-ge is the figure of the *Guru* Padma Gyalpo, 'The Lotus King *Guru*', otherwise known as 'The One Untouched by Faults, [the Representative of] the *Tri-Piṭaka* (or Three Collections of Buddhist Scriptures)', sitting on a lotus-lunar throne, with his left leg extended in the kingly dancing posture, here the same as the *Bodhisattvic* posture. In his right hand he holds aloft a double-drum (Tib. *damāru*), symbolical of his mastery of *mantric* sound; and, in his left hand, a human-skull cup filled with gems, sym-

[1] Cf. L. A. Waddell, *The Buddhism of Tibet* (Cambridge, 1934), p. 379.

bolical of his having discovered, by means of *yoga*, the Precious Gems of the *Dharma*.

In the lower corner to the right of the *Guru* Padma Jungnay is the figure of the *Guru* Seṅg-ge Dradog, 'The *Guru* Who Teacheth with the Voice of a Lion', otherwise known as 'The One Who Proclaimeth the *Dharma* to all the Six Classes of Beings' (enumerated on p. 205[2]), standing in the wrathful mood of a Tantric deity on a lotus-lunar throne, his right foot upon the breast of a human form, signifying the treading underfoot of all *sangsāric* existences. Being a Great *Yogī*, he wears a tiger-skin loin-covering and around his body a lion skin, the lion head of which appears above his head-dress and the claws appear on either side of him. In his right hand he holds, in an attitude menacing to evil demons who oppose the spread of the *Dharma*, a *dorje*, symbolical of his dominion over them; and in his left hand a bell, symbolical of his adeptship in *mantra yoga* and of his *yogic* power to control all classes of spiritual beings throughout the *Sangsāra*. He is enhaloed in the mystic Flames of Wisdom which consume the evils of the world. His colour is dark blue, which signifies, like that of the sky, the all-pervading and everlasting characteristic of the *Dharma*, of which he is the Guardian as well as the Disseminator. It was in this very occult manifestation that the Great *Guru*, like a supreme Saint Michael, overthrew the Forces of Darkness and enabled the Forces of the Light to prevail.

In the opposite lower corner is the figure of the *Guru* Dorje Drōlō, 'The Immutable *Guru* with Loose-hanging Stomach', otherwise called 'The One in Whose Body all Happiness Culminateth', and also known as 'The Changeless Comforter of all Beings'.[1] He, too, is shown in the wrathful mood of a Tantric deity and enhaloed in Flames of Wisdom, standing on a tigress (symbolical of the *shakti*). The treading underfoot by the tigress of a prostrate human form has the same significance as that by the *Guru* Seṅg-ge Dradog. In his right hand he holds, in the menacing attitude, a *dorje*, symbolizing almighty spiritual power, and in his left hand a magical demon-exorcising *phurbu*. His colour is red, in symbol of his power to fascinate and so discipline *sangsāric* beings. On his forehead—as on that of the *Guru* Seṅg-ge Dradog— appears the third eye of divine vision, signifying intuitive insight into Reality. It was in Bhutan, at the famous Monastery of *Pato-tak-tshang* (the 'Lion's Den of Pato'), that the Great *Guru* is said to have manifested himself as Droje Drōlō, for the purpose of disciplining the people and winning them from their practices of black magic, and to exorcise the demoniacal beings of Bhutan and establish the *Dharma* there. Similarly, each of the other Eight Manifestations was employed in accordance with need and circumstances, in order

---

[1] Cf. L. A. Waddell, op. cit., p. 379.

that to all sentient creatures there should be revealed the Path of the Great Liberation.

Directly below the *Guru* Padma Jungnay, as in the frontispiece, are shown the Five Objects of Enjoyment offered to him, the last (next to the cymbals) being the Chinese silk in two scroll-like rolls.

The *Guru* Padma Jungnay and the five *Gurus* above him, except the *Guru* Nyima Hodzer (whose bodily aura is deep blue), are enhaloed in rainbow-like radiance. The colour of the nimbi of all the six is green.

VI. EMANATION .   .   .   .   . *facing p.* 106

A photographic reproduction (about one-eighth of the original size) of a remarkable Chinese monastic painting in colour, on a gauze-faced paper scroll, acquired by Mr. H. Sussbach, a German student, when in China in 1936, and said to date from the end of the Ming (or 'Bright') dynasty (A.D. 1368–1661). Its origin is uncertain, Mr. Sussbach having been told that it came from central China. An inscription on its back indicates that it belonged to the Yama temple of a Tantric monastery.

· At the top are the figures of two *Bodhisattvas* in super-human realms. Each is emanating from the crown of his head a light-ray (of the character described in Book I) and thereby manifesting in the world a Tantric aspect of his own *Bodhic* essence. On the light-shaft emanated from the tip of the third finger of the deity beneath the lower *Bodhisattva* is inscribed in Chinese, 'In the South-east: the *Bodhisattva* Ākāshagarbha[1] emanating the form of the Wrathful, Resplendent, Great Laughing King of Wisdom'.[2] On the similar light-shaft, emanated from the tip of the second finger of the deity below the higher *Bodhisattva*, is inscribed in Chinese, 'In the East: the *Bodhisattva* Sarvanīvaraṇa-Vishkambhin[3] emanating the form of the Wrathful, Resplendent, Exalted, Immutable King of Wisdom'.

The Ākāshagarbha emanation is three-faced, like a Brahma-Vishnu-Shiva deity, which signifies that in him the Three Divine Bodies (Skt. *Tri-Kāya*) are one. The right face is white (symbolical of purity and compassion); the middle face, like the deity himself, is blue (symbolical, like the blue sky, of the eternal nature of his *Bodhic* essence);

[1] The Sanskrit term *Ākāshagarbha* (Chinese: *Hsü K'ung Tsang*) is translatable as 'Essence of the Void Space (or Sky) above', and its Tibetan equivalent (*Nam-mkhahi Snying-po*) as 'Matrix of the Sky', or 'Womb of Space', or 'Receptacle of the Void'.
[2] 'King of Wisdom' is in the Chinese *Ming Wang*, corresponding to the Sanskrit *Vidyā-Rāja*.
[3] The Sanskrit term *Sarvanīvaraṇa-Vishkambhin* (Chinese: *Ch'u Kai Chang*) is translatable as 'Bar against all Impediments', and its Tibetan equivalent (*Sgrib-pa [Thams-cad] Rnam-par-sel-ba*) as 'That which clears away the Darknesses (or Delusions)'.

the left face is red (symbolical of his fascinating power). The two bells, in his first pair of hands, symbolize the Voidness of which he, as 'The Essence of the Void Space above', is the Tantric personification. The handle of the bell in his right hand is surmounted by a trident, indicating his supremacy over the Three Realms and that he has conquered the three cardinal evils, lust, ill will, and stupidity, which are the chief causes of rebirth. His next pair of hands and arms support a spear, suggestive of the spear of the Five *Ḍākinī* in the *yogic* exorcising dance of the *Chöd* Rite (described in *Tibetan Yoga and Secret Doctrines*, p. 306), and also suggestive of the Tibetan *phurbu*, both alike being symbols of dominion over demoniacal and elemental beings, one of which, of a green hue, crouches to the left of the spear's point. In three of the other four hands he holds a spiked staff (symbolical of triumph over the *Sangsāra*), a large gold ring inset with a gem, on the crown of it, and seven smaller gems (probably symbolical of the Jewels of the *Dharma*), and a golden object resembling a lotus bud. From the middle finger of the other hand he emanates the light-shaft. As he dances the *yogic* dance of supremacy over *sangsāric* existence, he treads underfoot, as do the wrathful two of the Eight *Gurus*, human beings, with parallel significance. His diadem of two human skulls indicates his triumph over death.

The Bar-against-all-Impediments (or Clearer-away-of-Delusions) Emanation appears to represent a wrathful Tantric aspect of Mañjushrī, for in his first two hands, held aloft, he holds a Book of Wisdom and the lotus blossom associated with it, and, in the second of his right hands, the Sword of Wisdom. From a gem, probably a type of the wish-granting gem (Skt. *Chintāmaṇi*) referred to in various parts of this volume, held between the thumb and middle finger of his fourth hand, he emanates three insects and a raven-like bird, signifying the sub-human kingdoms. The bird emanates, from the lower part of its mammalian-like mouth, the green demon. The lotus breastplate and other lotus adornments, over his abdomen and shoulders and on his first pair of arms, suggest that he belongs to the Lotus Order of *Herukas*. The less prominently placed lotus adornments worn by the other Emanation signify that he, likewise, is of the same Order of Great Masters of *Yoga*. The Sarvanīvaraṇa-Vishkambhin Emanation is also three-faced, the right face being red, the left white; and the central face, being green, like his body, indicates his perennial youthfulness and the generative or creative power which he is exercising. His lotus diadem, as befits a Mañjushrī, is that of a royal prince. As he dances his *yogic* dance, he treads underfoot a demon monster with three monkey-like faces, symbolical of the power, which he confers upon his devotees, of overcoming brutish propensities, he being the *Bodhisattva* who prevents or overcomes all hindrances, or delusions.

From the head of each deity radiates a flame-like aura, apparently representing, in Chinese manner, Flames of Wisdom. After the style of a Shiva, the Supreme Patron of *yogins*, both deities wear serpents around their arms and legs, in symbol of Wisdom, they being, as Kings of Wisdom, Enlightening Deities. This is emphasized by their prominent third eye.

These two deities, Tantric personifications of the Enlightening Power of the *Dharma*, appertain to a group of Eight *Dhyānī Bodhisattvas*, known as the Eight Spiritual Sons of the Buddha, the other six being Maitreya, Avalokiteshvara, Samantabhadra, Mañjushrī, Vajra-Pāṇi, and Kshitigarbha.

In this tentative interpretation of a most unusual and very rare Chinese Tantric painting, the Editor has been guided by the symbology of Tibetan Tantricism. He gratefully acknowledges the indispensable assistance of Mr. Wang Wei-Chang, Spalding Lecturer in Chinese Philosophy and Religion in the University of Oxford, and of Mr. Yu Dawchyuan, Lecturer in the School of Oriental Studies, University of London.

VII. THE *TRI-KĀYA*, OR THREE DIVINE BODIES

facing p. 192

A photographic reproduction (about one-half of the original size) of a painting in colour, on heavy cotton cloth, painted in the Ghoom Monastery, Darjeeling, during October 1935 for the Editor, by the Tibetan artist, Lharipa Jampal Trashi (who was then painting the frescoes in the Ghoom Temple of Maitreya), to illustrate the *Tri-Kāya* of the *Bardo Thödol* Series of *yogic* treatises to which Book II appertains.

The uppermost figure is a symbolic personification of the Ādi-Buddha Samanta Bhadra (Tib. *Kun-tu Bzang-po*), the 'One of All Good', representing the *Dharma-Kāya*. His nudity signifies that the *Dharma-Kāya*, being the Unqualified, Unpredicable Thatness, is the Naked Reality. The blue colour of his body indicates that even as the blue sky is all-pervading, immutable, and eternal, so is the Primordial (Skt. *Ādi*) Buddha Essence. He sits on a lotus-lunar throne in the Buddha posture with his hands in the pose, or *mudrā*, of profound meditation.

The figure below, on the Ādi-Buddha's right, represents the four-armed form of the Great *Bodhisattva* Avalokiteshvara (Tib. *Spyan-ras-gzigs*: pron. *Chen-rä-zi*), the 'Keen-seeing Lord', who is also called the 'Great Pitier and Lord of Mercy' (Skt. *Mahākarunā*), sitting in the Buddha posture on a lotus-lunar throne. He is the spiritual son of the Dhyānī Buddha Amitābha, and incarnate in the Dalai Lāma; and the most spiritually powerful of all the *Bodhisattvas*. His dress and adornments show him to be a royal prince. His colour is white, symbolical of his immaculate nature and all-embracing mercy. His two inner hands are held palm to palm in attitude of devotion. In his right outer hand he holds a crystal rosary, symbolical of *yogic* meditation; and, in his left outer hand, a lotus, symbolical of the spiritual perfection and beauty of the *Dharma*, of which he is the Protector. He personifies the *Sambhoga-Kāya*.

The third figure represents *Guru* Rinpoch'e, the 'Precious *Guru*', one of the Tibetan appellations of Padma-Sambhava; and the description is the same as that of the Great *Guru* shown by the frontispiece. He is the personification of the *Nirmāṇa-Kāya*.

Underneath each of the three figures, written in Tibetan, is the appellation. And in the lower corner, outside the margin, below the Great *Guru*, the artist has written his own name.

VIII. BODHIDHARMA   .   .   .   .   *facing p.* 194

A photographic reproduction, one-quarter reduced, of the illustration in *Truth and Tradition in Chinese Buddhism* depicting Bodhidharma, made and published by kind permission of the Rev. Dr. K. L. Reichelt, the author, and of The Commercial Press Limited, Shanghai, the publishers of the said work, which is referred to in our General Introduction. It shows Bodhidharma (of whom account is given in the Introduction to Book II) in meditation, seated on a meditation mat of leaves, three books of scripture behind him and incense burning in a bronze Chinese urn on his right.

IX. MAITREYA, THE COMING BUDDHA   .   *facing p.* 240

A photographic reproduction (about one-half of the original size) of an old Tibetan painting in colour, on cotton cloth, of Maitreya (Pali: *Metteya*; Tib. *Byams-pa*: pron. *Jham-pa*), the 'Loving One', the Buddhist Messiah, who will regenerate the world by the power of divine love, and inaugurate a New Age of Universal Peace and Brotherhood. He is at present in the Tushita Heaven, whence He will descend and be born among men and become the future Buddha, to reveal anew, as did Gautama and the long Dynasty of past Buddhas, the Path leading to the Great Liberation.[1]

Maitreya sits on a lotus-lunar throne posed and robed as a Buddha. His right hand is in the *mudrā* of preaching the *Dharma*; and on its palm and on each sole of His feet appears the mystic stigmata of a double-*dorje*, like a Greek cross, formed by a golden dot inscribed by a golden circle, the symbol of the Sun, and by twelve other golden dots arranged in four groups of three each, thereby constituting, in all, the sacred number thirteen, symbolical of the thirteen degrees of enlightenment leading to the Great Liberation of *Nirvāṇa*. In His left

---

[1] In the Pāli Canon (*Digha Nikāya*, xxvi) the Buddha Shākya Muni is reported as having said: 'An Exalted One, named Metteya, will arise. . . . His followers will number thousands, whereas mine number hundreds' (cf. Warren's *Buddhism in Translation*, pp. 481–6).

hand He holds a vessel of gold, filled with the essences of purity, regeneration, and salvation for all living creatures. The dot between His eyebrows symbolizes, as does the like dot in other *Bodhic* Beings, the third eye of Divine Wisdom and Transcendent Insight and Vision. His nimbus is green; and the aura surrounding His body is dark blue, indicative of the eternal, ever-present, and all-embracing Buddha Essence. And beneath His throne are shown, as in the other Illustrations, the Five Objects of Enjoyment offered to Buddhas incarnate on Earth. They symbolize the five senses representing the physical man.

The Five Hindrances

'There are these five hindrances in the Discipline of the Noble One, which are called "veils", and are called "hindrances", and are called "obstacles", and are called "entanglements":
'The hindrance of lustful desire,
The hindrance of malice,
The hindrance of sloth and idleness,
The hindrance of pride, and self-righteousness,
The hindrance of doubt.'

The Buddha, *Tevigga Suttanta*, i. 30
(according to the translation in *The Library of Original Sources*, i,
edited by Oliver J. Thatcher).

PLATE III

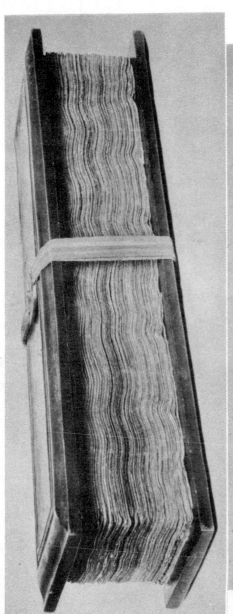

MAÑJUSHRI'S BOOK OF DIVINE WISDOM

Described on pages xvii–xix

THE TIBETAN BOOK OF THE GREAT LIBERATION

PSYCHOLOGICAL COMMENTARY

By C. G. JUNG

I. THE DIFFERENCE BETWEEN EASTERN AND WESTERN THINKING

DR. EVANS-WENTZ has entrusted me with the task of commenting on a text which contains an important exposition of Eastern 'psychology'. The very fact that I have to use inverted commas shows the dubious applicability of this term. It is perhaps not superfluous to mention that the East has produced nothing equivalent to what we call psychology, but rather philosophy or metaphysics. Critical philosophy, the mother of modern psychology, is as foreign to the East as to medieval Europe. Thus the word 'mind', as used in the East, has the connotation of something metaphysical. Our Western conception of mind has lost this connotation since the Middle Ages, and the word has now come to signify a 'psychic function'. Despite the fact that we neither know nor pretend to know what 'psyche' is, we can deal with the phenomenon of 'mind'. We do not assume that the mind is a metaphysical entity or that there is any connexion between an individual mind and a hypothetical Universal Mind. Our psychology is, therefore, a science of mere phenomena without any metaphysical implications. The development of Western philosophy during the last two centuries has succeeded in isolating the mind in its own sphere and in severing it from its primordial oneness with the universe. Man himself has ceased to be the microcosm and eidolon of the cosmos, and his 'anima' is no longer the consubstantial *scintilla*, or spark of the *Anima Mundi*, the World Soul.

Psychology accordingly treats all metaphysical claims and assertions as mental phenomena, and regards them as statements about the mind and its structure that derive ultimately from certain unconscious dispositions. It does not consider them to be absolutely valid or even capable of establishing a metaphysical truth. We have no intellectual means of ascertaining whether this attitude is right or wrong. We only know that there is no evidence for, and no possibility of proving, the validity of a metaphysical postulate such as 'Universal Mind'. If the mind asserts the existence of a Universal Mind, we hold that it is merely making an assertion. We do not assume that by such an assertion the existence of a Universal Mind has been established. There is no argument against this reasoning, but no evidence, either, that our conclusion is ultimately right. In other words, it is just as possible that our mind is nothing but a perceptible manifestation of a Universal Mind. Yet we do not know, and we cannot even see, how it would be possible to recognize whether this is so or not. Psychology therefore holds that the mind cannot establish or assert anything beyond itself.

If, then, we accept the restrictions imposed upon the capacity of our mind, we demonstrate our common sense. I admit it is something of a sacrifice, inasmuch as we bid farewell to that miraculous world in which mind-created things and beings move and live. This is the world of the primitive, where even inanimate objects are endowed with a living, healing, magic power, through which they participate in us and we in them. Sooner or later we had to understand that their potency was really ours, and that their significance was our projection. The theory of knowledge is only the last step out of humanity's childhood, out of a world where mind-created figures populated a metaphysical heaven and hell.

Despite this inevitable epistemological criticism, however, we have held fast to the religious belief that the organ of faith enables man to know God. The West thus developed a new disease: the conflict between science and religion. The critical philosophy of science became as it were negatively metaphysical—in other words, materialistic—on the basis of an error in judgement; matter was assumed to be a tangible and recognizable reality. Yet this is a thoroughly metaphysical concept hypostatized by uncritical minds. Matter is an hypothesis. When you say 'matter', you are really creating a symbol for something unknown, which may just as well be 'spirit' or anything else; it may even be God. Religious faith, on the other hand, refuses to give up its pre-critical *Weltanschauung*. In contradiction to the saying of Christ, the faithful try to *remain* children instead of becoming *as* children. They cling to the world of childhood. A famous modern theologian confesses in his autobiography that Jesus has been his good friend 'from childhood on'. Jesus is the perfect example of a man who preached something different from the religion of his forefathers. But the *imitatio Christi* does not appear to include the mental and spiritual sacrifice which he had to undergo at the beginning of his career and without which he would never have become a saviour.

The conflict between science and religion is in reality a misunderstanding of both. Scientific materialism has merely introduced a new hypostasis, and that is an intellectual sin. It has given another name to the supreme principle of reality and has assumed that this created a new thing and destroyed an old thing. Whether you call the principle of existence 'God', 'matter', 'energy', or anything else you like, you have created nothing; you have simply changed a symbol. The materialist is a metaphysician *malgré lui*. Faith, on the other hand, tries to retain a primitive mental condition on merely sentimental grounds. It is unwilling to give up the primitive, childlike relationship to mind-created and hypostatized figures; it wants to go on enjoying the security and confidence of a world still presided over by powerful, responsible, and kindly parents. Faith may include a *sacrificium intellectus* (provided there is an intellect to sacrifice), but certainly not a sacrifice of feeling. In this way the faithful *remain* children instead of becoming *as* children, and they do not gain their life because they have not lost it. Furthermore, faith collides with science and thus gets its deserts, for it refuses to share in the spiritual adventure of our age.

Any honest thinker has to admit the insecurity of all metaphysical positions, and in particular of all creeds. He has also to admit the unwarrantable nature of all metaphysical assertions and face the fact that there is no evidence whatever for the ability of the human mind to pull itself up by its own boot-strings, that is, to establish anything transcendental.

Materialism is a metaphysical reaction against the sudden realization that cognition is a mental faculty and, if carried beyond the human plane, a projection. The reaction was 'metaphysical' in so far as the man of average philosophical education failed to see through the implied hypostasis, not realizing that 'matter' was just another name for the supreme principle. As against this, the attitude of faith shows how reluctant people were to accept philosophical criticism. It also demonstrates how great is the fear of letting go one's hold on the securities of childhood and of dropping into a strange, unknown world ruled by forces unconcerned with man. Nothing really changes in either case; man and his surroundings remain the same. He has only to realize that he is shut up inside his mind and cannot step beyond it, even in insanity; and that the appearance of his world or of his gods very much depends upon his own mental condition.

In the first place, the structure of the mind is responsible for anything we may assert about metaphysical matters, as I have already pointed out. We have also begun to understand that the intellect is not an *ens per se*, or an independent mental faculty, but a psychic function dependent upon the conditions of the psyche as a whole. A philosophical statement is the product of a certain personality living at a certain time in a certain place, and not the outcome of a purely logical and impersonal procedure. To that extent it is chiefly subjective; whether it has an objective validity or not depends on whether there are few or many persons who argue in the same way. The isolation of man within his mind as a result of epistemological criticism has naturally led to psychological criticism. This kind of criticism is not popular with the philosophers, since they like to consider the philosophic intellect as the perfect and unconditioned instrument of philosophy. Yet this intellect of theirs is a function dependent upon an individual psyche and determined on all sides by subjective conditions, quite apart from environmental influences. Indeed, we have already become so accustomed to this point of view that 'mind' has lost its universal character altogether. It has become a more or less individualized affair, with no trace of its former cosmic aspect as the *anima rationalis*. Mind is understood nowadays as a subjective, even an arbitrary, thing. Now that the formerly hypostatized 'universal ideas' have turned out to be mental principles, it is dawning upon us to what an extent our whole experience of so-called reality is psychic; as a matter of fact, everything thought, felt, or perceived is a psychic image, and the world itself exists only so far as we are able to produce an image of it. We are so deeply impressed with the truth of our imprisonment in, and limitation by, the psyche that we are ready to admit the existence in it even of things we do *not* know: we call them 'the unconscious'.

The seemingly universal and metaphysical scope of the mind has thus been narrowed down to the small circle of individual consciousness, profoundly aware of its almost limitless subjectivity and of its infantile-archaic tendency to heedless projection and illusion. Many scientifically-minded persons have even sacrificed their religious and philosophical leanings for fear of uncontrolled subjectivism. By way of compensation for the loss of a world that pulsed with our blood and breathed with our breath, we have developed an enthusiasm for *facts*—mountains of facts, far beyond any single individual's power to survey. We have the pious hope that this incidental accumulation of facts will form a meaningful whole, but nobody is quite sure, because no human brain can possibly comprehend the gigantic sum-total of this mass-produced knowledge. The facts bury us, but whoever dares to speculate must pay for it with a bad conscience—and rightly so, for he will instantly be tripped up by the facts.

Western psychology knows the mind as the mental functioning of a psyche. It is the 'mentality' of an individual. An impersonal Universal Mind is still to be met with in the sphere of philosophy, where it seems to be a relic of the original human 'soul'. This picture of our Western outlook may seem a little drastic, but I do not think it is far from the truth. At all events, something of the kind presents itself as soon as we are confronted with the Eastern mentality. In the East, mind is a cosmic factor, the very essence of existence; while in the West we have just begun to understand that it is the essential condition of cognition, and hence of the cognitive existence of the world. There is no conflict between religion and science in the East, because no science is there based upon the passion for facts, and no religion upon mere faith; there is religious cognition and cognitive religion.[1] With us, man is incommensurably small and the grace of God is everything; but in the East man is God and he redeems himself. The gods of Tibetan Buddhism belong to the sphere of illusory separateness and mind-created projections, and yet they exist; but so far as we are concerned an illusion remains an illusion, and thus is nothing at all. It is a paradox, yet nevertheless true, that with us a thought has no proper reality; we treat it as if it were a nothingness. Even though the thought be true in itself, we hold that it exists only by virtue of certain facts which it is said to formulate. We can produce a most devastating fact like the atom bomb with the help of this ever-changing phantasmagoria of virtually non-existent thoughts, but it seems wholly absurd to us that one could ever establish the reality of thought itself.

'Psychic reality' is a controversial concept, like 'psyche' or 'mind'. By the latter terms some understand consciousness and its contents, others allow the existence of 'dark' or 'subconscious' representations. Some include instincts in the psychic realm, others exclude them. The vast majority consider the psyche to be a result of biochemical processes in the brain cells. A few conjecture that it is the psyche that makes the cortical cells function. Some identify 'life' with psyche. But only an insignificant minority regards the psychic phenomenon as a category of existence *per se* and draws the necessary conclusions. It is indeed paradoxical that *the* category of existence, the indispensable *sine qua non* of all existence, namely the psyche, should be treated as if it were only semi-existent. Psychic existence is the only category of existence of which we have *immediate* knowledge, since nothing

[1] I am purposely leaving out of account the modernized East.

can be known unless it first appears as a psychic image. Only
psychic existence is immediately verifiable. To the extent
that the world does not assume the form of a psychic image,
it is virtually non-existent. This is a fact which, with few
exceptions—as for instance in Schopenhauer's philosophy—
the West has not yet fully realized. But Schopenhauer was
influenced by Buddhism and by the *Upanishads*.

Even a superficial acquaintance with Eastern thought is
sufficient to show that a fundamental difference divides
East and West. The East bases itself upon psychic reality,
that is, upon the psyche as the main and unique condition of
existence. It seems as if this Eastern recognition were a psychological or temperamental fact rather than a result of
philosophical reasoning. It is a typically introverted point of
view, contrasted with the equally typical extraverted viewpoint of the West.[1] Introversion and extraversion are known
to be temperamental or even constitutional attitudes which
are never intentionally adopted in normal circumstances. In
exceptional cases they may be produced at will, but only
under very special conditions. Introversion is, if one may so
express it, the 'style' of the East, an habitual and collective
attitude, just as extraversion is the 'style' of the West. Introversion is felt here as something abnormal, morbid, or otherwise objectionable. Freud identifies it with an auto-erotic,
'narcissistic' attitude of mind. He shares his negative position with the National Socialist philosophy of modern Germany,[2] which accuses introversion of being an offence against
community-feeling. In the East, however, our cherished extraversion is depreciated as illusory desirousness, as existence
in the *sangsāra*, the very essence of the *nidāna*-chain which
culminates in the sum of the world's sufferings.[3] Anyone with
practical knowledge of the mutual depreciation of values
between introvert and extravert will understand the emotional conflict between the Eastern and the Western standpoint. For those who know something of the history of

[1] *Psychological Types*, definitions 19 and 34, pp. 542 ff. and 567 ff.
[2] Written in the year 1939.
[3] *Saṃyutta-nikāya* 12, *Nidāna-saṃyutta*.

European philosophy the bitter wrangling about 'universals' which began with Plato will provide an instructive example. I do not wish to go into all the ramifications of this conflict between introversion and extraversion, but I must mention the religious aspects of the problem. The Christian West considers man to be wholly dependent upon the grace of God, or at least upon the Church as the exclusive and divinely sanctioned earthly instrument of man's redemption. The East, however, insists that man is the sole cause of his higher development, for it believes in 'self-liberation'.

The religious point of view always expresses and formulates the essential psychological attitude and its specific prejudices, even in the case of people who have forgotten, or who have never heard of, their own religion. In spite of everything, the West is thoroughly Christian as far as its psychology is concerned. Tertullian's *anima naturaliter christiana* holds true throughout the West—not, as he thought, in the religious sense, but in the psychological one. Grace comes from elsewhere; at all events from outside. Every other point of view is sheer heresy. Hence it is quite understandable why the human psyche is suffering from undervaluation. Anyone who dares to establish a connexion between the psyche and the idea of God is immediately accused of 'psychologism' or suspected of morbid 'mysticism'. The East, on the other hand, compassionately tolerates those 'lower' spiritual stages where man, in his blind ignorance of *karma*, still bothers about sin and tortures his imagination with a belief in absolute gods, who, if he only looked deeper, are nothing but the veil of illusion woven by his own unenlightened mind. The psyche is therefore all-important; it is the all-pervading Breath, the Buddha essence; it is the Buddha Mind, the One, the *Dharma-Kāya*. All existence emanates from it, and all separate forms dissolve back into it. This is the basic psychological prejudice that permeates Eastern man in every fibre of his being, seeping into all his thoughts, feelings, and deeds, no matter what creed he professes.

In the same way Western man is Christian, no matter to what denomination his Christianity belongs. For him man is small inside, he is next to nothing; moreover, as Kierkegaard says, 'before God man is always wrong'. By fear, repentance, promises, submission, self-abasement, good deeds, and praise he propitiates the great power, which is not himself but *totaliter aliter*, the Wholly Other, altogether perfect and 'outside', the only reality. If you shift the formula a bit and substitute for God some other power, for instance the world or money, you get a complete picture of Western man—assiduous, fearful, devout, self-abasing, enterprising, greedy, and violent in his pursuit of the goods of this world: possessions, health, knowledge, technical mastery, public welfare, political power, conquest, and so on. What are the great popular movements of our time? Attempts to grab the money or property of others and to protect our own. The mind is chiefly employed in devising suitable 'isms' to hide the real motives or to get more loot. I refrain from describing what would happen to Eastern man should he forget his ideal of Buddhahood, for I do not want to give such an unfair advantage to my Western prejudices. But I cannot help raising the question of whether it is possible, or indeed advisable, for either to imitate the other's standpoint. The difference between them is so vast that one can see no reasonable possibility of this, much less its advisability. You cannot mix fire and water. The Eastern attitude stultifies the Western, and vice versa. You cannot be a good Christian and redeem yourself, nor can you be a Buddha and worship God. It is much better to accept the conflict, for it admits only of an irrational solution, if any.

By an inevitable decree of fate the West is becoming acquainted with the peculiar facts of Eastern spirituality. It is useless either to belittle these facts, or to build false and treacherous bridges over yawning gaps. Instead of learning the spiritual techniques of the East by heart and imitating them in a thoroughly Christian way—*imitatio Christi!*—with a correspondingly forced attitude, it would be far more to the point to find out whether there exists in the unconscious an introverted tendency similar to that which has become the guiding spiritual principle of the East. We should then be in a position to build on our own ground with our own methods. If we snatch these things directly from the East, we have merely indulged our Western acquisitiveness, confirming yet again that 'everything good is outside', whence it has to be fetched and pumped into our barren souls.[1] It seems to me that we have really learned something from the East when we understand that the psyche contains riches enough without having to be primed from outside, and when we feel capable of evolving out of ourselves with or without divine grace. But we cannot embark upon this ambitious enterprise until we have learned how to deal with our spiritual pride and blasphemous self-assertiveness. The Eastern attitude violates the specifically Christian values, and it is no good blinking this fact. If our new attitude is to be genuine, i.e. grounded in our own history, it must be acquired with full consciousness of the Christian values and of the conflict between them and the introverted attitude of the East. We must get at the Eastern values from within and not from without, seeking them in ourselves, in the unconscious. We shall then discover how great is our fear of the unconscious and how formidable are our resistances. Because of these resistances we doubt the very thing that seems so obvious to the East, namely, the *self-liberating power of the introverted mind*.

This aspect of the mind is practically unknown to the West, though it forms the most important component of the unconscious. Many people flatly deny the existence of the unconscious, or else they say that it consists merely of instincts, or of repressed or forgotten contents that were once part of the conscious mind. It is safe to assume that what the East calls 'mind' has more to do with our 'unconscious' than with mind as we understand it, which is more or less identical with consciousness. To us consciousness is inconceivable without an ego; it is equated with the relation of contents to an ego. If

---

[1] 'Whereas who holdeth not God as such an inner possession, but with every means must fetch Him from without . . . verily such a man hath Him not, and easily something cometh to trouble him.' Meister Eckhart (*Büttner*, vol. ii, p. 185).

there is no ego there is nobody to be conscious of anything. The ego is therefore indispensable to the conscious process. The Eastern mind, however, has no difficulty in conceiving of a consciousness without an ego. Consciousness is deemed capable of transcending its ego condition; indeed, in its 'higher' forms, the ego disappears altogether. Such an ego-less mental condition can only be unconscious to us, for the simple reason that there would be nobody to witness it. I do not doubt the existence of mental states transcending consciousness. But they lose their consciousness to exactly the same degree that they transcend consciousness. I cannot imagine a conscious mental state that does not refer to a subject, that is, to an ego. The ego may be depotentiated—divested, for instance, of its awareness of the body—but so long as there is awareness of something, there must be somebody who is aware. The unconscious, however, is a mental condition of which no ego is aware. It is only mediately and by indirect means that we eventually become conscious of the existence of an unconscious. We can observe the manifestation of unconscious fragments of the personality, detached from the patient's consciousness, in insanity. But there is no evidence that the unconscious contents are related to an unconscious centre analogous to the ego; in fact there are good reasons why such a centre is not even probable.

The fact that the East can dispose so easily of the ego seems to point to a mind that is not to be identified with our 'mind'. Certainly the ego does not play the same role in Eastern thought as it does with us. It seems as if the Eastern mind were less egocentric, as if its contents were more loosely connected with the subject, and as if greater stress were laid on mental states which include a depotentiated ego. It also seems as if Hathayoga were chiefly useful as a means for extinguishing the ego by fettering its unruly impulses. There is no doubt that the higher forms of *yoga*, in so far as they strive to reach *samādhi*, seek a mental condition in which the ego is practically dissolved. Consciousness in our sense of the word is rated a definitely inferior condition, the state of *avidyā* (ignorance), whereas what we call the 'dark background of

consciousness' is understood to be a 'higher' consciousness.[1]
Thus our concept of the 'collective unconscious' would be the
European equivalent of *buddhi*, the enlightened mind.

In view of all this, the Eastern form of 'sublimation'
amounts to a withdrawal of the centre of psychic gravity from
ego-consciousness, which holds a middle position between the
body and the ideational processes of the psyche. The lower,
semi-physiological strata of the psyche are subdued by *askesis*,
i.e. exercises, and kept under control. They are not exactly
denied or suppressed by a supreme effort of the will, as is
customary in Western sublimation. Rather, the lower psychic
strata are adapted and shaped through the patient practice
of Hathayoga until they no longer interfere with the development of 'higher' consciousness. This peculiar process seems
to be aided by the fact that the ego and its desires are checked
by the greater importance which the East habitually attaches
to the 'subjective factor'.[2] By this I mean the 'dark background' of consciousness, the unconscious. The introverted
attitude is characterized in general by an emphasis on the
a priori data of apperception. As is well known, the act of
apperception consists of two phases: first the perception of
the object, second the assimilation of the perception to a pre-
existing pattern or concept by means of which the object is
'comprehended'. The psyche is not a nonentity devoid of all
quality; it is a definite system made up of definite conditions
and it reacts in a specific way. Every new representation, be
it a perception or a spontaneous thought, arouses associations
which derive from the storehouse of memory. These leap immediately into consciousness, producing the complex picture
of an 'impression', though this is already a sort of interpretation. The unconscious disposition upon which the quality of
the impression depends is what I call the 'subjective factor'.
It deserves the qualification 'subjective' because objectivity

[1] In so far as 'higher' and 'lower' are categorical judgements of consciousness, Western psychology does not differentiate unconscious contents in
this way. It appears that the East recognizes subhuman psychic conditions,
a real 'subconsciousness' comprising the instincts and semi-physiological
psychisms, but classed as a 'higher consciousness'.

[2] *Psychological Types*, pp. 472 ff.

is hardly ever conferred by a first impression. Usually a rather laborious process of verification, comparison, and analysis is needed to modify and adapt the immediate reactions of the subjective factor.

The prominence of the subjective factor does not imply a *personal subjectivism*, despite the readiness of the extraverted attitude to dismiss the subjective factor as 'nothing but subjective'. The psyche and its structure are real enough. They even transform material objects into psychic images, as we have said. They do not perceive waves, but sound; not wavelengths, but colours. Existence is as we see and understand it. There are innumerable things that can be seen, felt, and understood in a great variety of ways. Quite apart from merely personal prejudices, the psyche assimilates external facts in its own way, which is based ultimately upon the laws or patterns of apperception. These laws do not change, although different ages or different parts of the world call them by different names. On a primitive level people are afraid of witches; on the modern level we are apprehensively aware of microbes. There everybody believes in ghosts, here everybody believes in vitamins. Once upon a time men were possessed by devils, now they are not less obsessed by ideas, and so on.

The subjective factor is made up, in the last resort, of the eternal patterns of psychic functioning. Anyone who relies upon the subjective factor is therefore basing himself on the reality of psychic law. So he can hardly be said to be wrong. If by this means he succeeds in extending his consciousness downwards, to touch the basic laws of psychic life, he is in possession of that truth which the psyche will naturally evolve if not fatally interfered with by the non-psychic, i.e. the external, world. At any rate, his truth could be weighed against the sum of all knowledge acquired through the investigation of externals. We in the West believe that a truth is satisfactory only if it can be verified by external facts. We believe in the most exact observation and exploration of nature; our truth must coincide with the behaviour of the external world, otherwise it is merely 'subjective'. In the same way that the East turns its gaze from the dance of *prakṛti* (physis) and from the multitudinous illusory forms of *māyā*, the West shuns the unconscious and its futile fantasies. Despite its introverted attitude, however, the East knows very well how to deal with the external world. And despite its extraversions the West, too, has a way of dealing with the psyche and its demands; it has an institution called the Church, which gives expression to the unknown psyche of man through its rites and dogmas. Nor are natural science and modern techniques by any means the invention of the West. Their Eastern equivalents are somewhat old-fashioned, or even primitive. But what we have to show in the way of spiritual insight and psychological technique must seem, when compared with *yoga*, just as backward as Eastern astrology and medicine when compared with Western science. I do not deny the efficacy of the Christian Church; but, if you compare the *Exercitia* of Ignatius Loyola with *yoga*, you will take my meaning. There is a difference, and a big one. To jump straight from that level into Eastern *yoga* is no more advisable than the sudden transformation of Asian peoples into half-baked Europeans. I have serious doubts as to the blessings of Western civilization, and I have similar misgivings as to the adoption of Eastern spirituality by the West. Yet the two contradictory worlds have met. The East is in full transformation; it is thoroughly and fatally disturbed. Even the most efficient methods of European warfare have been successfully imitated. The trouble with us seems to be far more psychological. Our blight is ideologies—they are the long-expected Anti-Christ! National Socialism comes as near to being a religious movement as any movement since A.D. 622. Communism claims to be paradise come to earth again. We are far better protected against failing crops, inundations, epidemics, and invasions from the Turk than we are against our own deplorable spiritual inferiority, which seems to have little resistance to psychic epidemics.

In its religious attitude, too, the West is extraverted. Nowadays it is gratuitously offensive to say that Christianity implies hostility, or even indifference, to the world and the flesh. On the contrary, the good Christian is a jovial citizen, an enterprising business man, an excellent soldier, the very best in every profession there is. Worldly goods are often interpreted as special rewards for Christian behaviour, and in the Lord's Prayer the adjective ἐπιούσιος, *supersubstantialis*,[1] referring to the bread, has long since been omitted, for the real bread obviously makes so very much more sense! It is only logical that extraversion, when carried to such lengths, cannot credit man with a psyche which contains anything not imported into it from outside, either by human teaching or divine grace. From this point of view it is downright blasphemy to assert that man has it in him to accomplish his own redemption. Nothing in our religion encourages the idea of the self-liberating power of the mind. Yet a very modern form of psychology—'analytical' or 'complex' psychology—envisages the possibility of there being certain processes in the unconscious which, by virtue of their symbolism, compensate the defects and anfractuosities of the conscious attitude. When these unconscious compensations are made conscious through the analytical technique, they produce such a change in the conscious attitude that we are entitled to speak of a new level of consciousness. The method cannot, however, produce the actual process of unconscious compensation; for that we depend upon the unconscious psyche or the 'grace of God'— names make no difference. But the unconscious process itself hardly ever reaches consciousness without technical aid. When brought to the surface, it reveals contents that offer a striking contrast to the general run of conscious thinking and feeling. If that were not so, they would not have a compensatory effect. The first effect, however, is usually a conflict, because the conscious attitude resists the intrusion of apparently incompatible and extraneous tendencies, thoughts, feelings, &c. Schizophrenia yields the most startling examples of such intrusions of utterly foreign and unacceptable contents. In schizophrenia it is, of course, a question of pathological distortions and exaggerations, but anybody with the slightest

[1] This is not the unacceptable translation of ἐπιούσιος by Hieronymus, but the ancient spiritual interpretation by Tertullian, Origen, and others.

knowledge of the normal material will easily recognize the sameness of the underlying patterns. It is, as a matter of fact, the same imagery that one finds in mythology and other archaic thought-formations.

Under normal conditions every conflict stimulates the mind to activity for the purpose of creating a satisfactory solution. Usually—i.e. in the West—the conscious standpoint arbitrarily decides against the unconscious, since anything coming from inside suffers from the prejudice of being regarded as inferior or somehow wrong. But in the cases with which we are here concerned it is tacitly agreed that the apparently incompatible contents shall not be suppressed again, and that the conflict shall be accepted and suffered. At first no solution appears possible, and this fact, too, has to be borne with patience. The suspension thus created 'constellates' the unconscious—in other words, the conscious suspense produces a new compensatory reaction in the unconscious. This reaction (usually manifested in dreams) is brought to conscious realization in its turn. The conscious mind is thus confronted with a new aspect of the psyche, which arouses a different problem or modifies an old one in an unexpected way. The procedure is continued until the original conflict is satisfactorily resolved. The whole process is called the 'transcendent function'.[1] It is a process and a method at the same time. The production of unconscious compensations is a spontaneous *process*; the conscious realization is a *method*. The function is called 'transcendent' because it facilitates the transition from one psychic condition to another by means of the mutual confrontation of opposites.

This is a very sketchy description of the transcendent function, and for details I must refer the reader to the literature mentioned in the footnotes. But I had to call attention to these psychological observations and methods because they indicate the way by which we may find access to the sort of 'mind' referred to in our text. This is the image-creating mind, the matrix of all those patterns that give apperception its peculiar character. These patterns are inherent in the un-

[1] *Psychological Types*, pp. 601 ff., s.v. Symbol, definition 51.

conscious 'mind'; they are its structural elements, and they alone can explain why certain mythological motifs are more or less ubiquitous, even where migration as a means of transmission is exceedingly improbable. Dreams, fantasies, and psychoses produce images to all appearances identical with mythological motifs of which the individuals concerned had absolutely no knowledge, not even indirect knowledge acquired through popular figures of speech or through the symbolic language of the Bible.[1] The psychopathology of schizophrenia, as well as the psychology of the unconscious, demonstrate the production of archaic material beyond a doubt. Whatever the structure of the unconscious may be, one thing is certain: it contains an indefinite number of motifs or patterns of an archaic character, in principle identical with the root ideas of mythology and similar thought-forms.

Because the unconscious is the matrix mind, the quality of creativeness attaches to it. It is the birthplace of thought-forms such as our text considers the Universal Mind to be. Since we cannot attribute any particular form to the unconscious, the Eastern assertion that the Universal Mind is without form, the *arūpaloka*, yet is the source of all forms, seems to be psychologically justified. In so far as the forms or patterns of the unconscious belong to no time in particular, being seemingly eternal, they convey a peculiar feeling of timelessness when consciously realized. We find similar statements in primitive psychology: for instance, the Australian word *aljira*[2] means 'dream' as well as 'ghostland' and the 'time' in which the ancestors lived and still live. It is, as they

---

[1] Some people find such statements incredible. But either they have no knowledge of primitive psychology, or they are ignorant of the results of psychopathological research. Specific observations occur in:

C. G. Jung, *Psychology of the Unconscious*, passim (new and revised edition in preparation under the title *Symbols of Transformation*), and *Psychology and Alchemy* (also in preparation), Part II ; J. Nelken, *Analytische Beobachtungen über Phantasien eines Schizophrenen*, Jahrbuch f. psychoanal. u. psychopath. Forschung, vol. iv. pp. 504 ff. ; S. Spielrein, *Ueber den psychol. Inhalt eines Falles von Schizophrenie*, ibid., vol. iii, pp. 329 ff. ; C. A. Meier, *Spontanmanifestationen des kollektiven Unbewussten*, Zentralblatt f. Psychotherapie, Bd. II, H. 4, 1939.

[2] L. Lévy-Bruhl, *La Mythologie primitive*, 1935, pp. xxiii ff.

say, the 'time when there was no time'. This looks like an obvious concretization and projection of the unconscious with all its characteristic qualities—its dream manifestations, its ancestral world of thought-forms, and its timelessness.

An introverted attitude, therefore, which withdraws its emphasis from the external world (the world of consciousness) and localizes it in the subjective factor (the background of consciousness) necessarily calls forth the characteristic manifestations of the unconscious, namely, archaic thought-forms imbued with 'ancestral' or 'historic' feeling, and, beyond them, the sense of indefiniteness, timelessness, oneness. The extraordinary feeling of oneness is a common experience in all forms of 'mysticism' and probably derives from the general contamination of contents, which increases as consciousness dims. The almost limitless contamination of images in dreams, and particularly in the products of insanity, testifies to their unconscious origin. In contrast to the clear distinction and differentiation of forms in consciousness, unconscious contents are incredibly vague and for this reason capable of any amount of contamination. If we tried to conceive of a state in which nothing is distinct, we should certainly feel the whole as one. Hence it is not unlikely that the peculiar experience of oneness derives from the subliminal awareness of all-contamination in the unconscious.

By means of the transcendent function we not only gain access to the 'One Mind' but also come to understand why the East believes in the possibility of self-liberation. If, through introspection and the conscious realization of unconscious compensations, it is possible to transform one's mental condition and thus arrive at a solution of painful conflicts, one would seem entitled to speak of 'self-liberation'. But, as I have already hinted, there is a hitch in this proud claim to self-liberation, for a man cannot produce these unconscious compensations at will. He has to rely upon the possibility they *may* be produced. Nor can he alter the peculiar character of the compensation: *est ut est aut non est*. It is a curious thing that Eastern philosophy seems to be almost unaware of this highly important fact. And it is precisely this

fact that provides the psychological justification for the
Western point of view. It seems as if the Western mind had
a most penetrating intuition of man's fateful dependence
upon some dark power which must co-operate if all is to be
well. Indeed, whenever and wherever the unconscious fails
to co-operate, man is instantly at a loss, even in his most
ordinary activities. There may be a failure of memory, of co-
ordinated action, or of interest and concentration; and such
failure may well be the cause of serious annoyance, or of a
fatal accident, a professional disaster, or a moral collapse.
Formerly, men called the gods unfavourable; now we prefer
to call it a neurosis, and we seek the cause in lack of vitamins,
in endocrine disturbances, overwork, or sex. The co-operation
of the unconscious, which is something we never think of and
always take for granted, is, when it suddenly fails, a very
serious matter indeed.

In comparison with other races—the Chinese for instance
—the White Man's mental equilibrium, or, to put it bluntly,
his brain, seems to be his tender spot. We naturally try to get
as far away from our weaknesses as possible, a fact which may
explain the sort of extraversion that is always seeking security
by dominating its surroundings. Extraversion goes hand in
hand with mistrust of the inner man, if indeed there is any
consciousness of him at all. Moreover, we all tend to under-
value the things we are afraid of. There must be some such
reason for our absolute conviction that *nihil sit in intellectu
quod non antea fuerit in sensu*, which is the motto of Western
extraversion. But, as we have emphasized, this extraversion
is psychologically justified by the vital fact that unconscious
compensation lies beyond man's control. I know that *yoga*
prides itself on being able to control even the unconscious
processes, so that nothing can happen in the psyche as a
whole that is not ruled by a supreme consciousness. I have
not the slightest doubt that such a condition is more or less
possible. But it is possible only at the price of becoming identical with the unconscious. Such an identity is the Eastern
equivalent of our Western fetish of 'complete objectivity',
the machine-like subservience to one goal, to one idea or cause,

at the cost of losing every trace of inner life. From the Eastern point of view this complete objectivity is appalling, for it amounts to complete identity with the *sangsāra*; to the West, on the other hand, *samādhi* is nothing but a meaningless dream-state. In the East, the inner man has always had such a firm hold on the outer man that the world had no chance of tearing him away from his inner roots; in the West, the outer man gained the ascendancy to such an extent that he was alienated from his innermost being. The One Mind, Oneness, indefiniteness, and eternity remained the prerogative of the One God. Man became small, futile, and essentially in the wrong.

I think it is becoming clear from my argument that the two standpoints, however contradictory, each have their psychological justification. Both are one-sided in that they fail to see and take account of those factors which do not fit in with their typical attitude. The one underrates the world of consciousness, the other the world of the One Mind. The result is that, in their extremism, both lose one half of the universe; their life is shut off from total reality, and is apt to become artificial and inhuman. In the West, there is the mania for 'objectivity', the asceticism of the scientist or of the stockbroker, who throw away the beauty and universality of life for the sake of the ideal, or not so ideal, goal. In the East, there is the wisdom, peace, detachment, and inertia of a psyche that has returned to its dim origins, having left behind all the sorrow and joy of existence as it is and, presumably, ought to be. No wonder that one-sidedness produces very similar forms of monasticism in both cases, guaranteeing to the hermit, the holy man, the monk or the scientist unswerving singleness of purpose. I have nothing against one-sidedness as such. Man, the great experiment of nature, or his own great experiment, is evidently entitled to all such undertakings—if he can endure them. Without one-sidedness the spirit of man could not unfold in all its diversity. But I do not think there is any harm in trying to understand both sides.

The extraverted tendency of the West and the introverted

tendency of the East have one important purpose in common: both make desperate efforts to conquer the mere naturalness of life. It is the assertion of mind over matter, the *opus contra naturam*, a symptom of the youthfulness of man, still delighting in the use of the most powerful weapon ever devised by nature: the conscious mind. The afternoon of humanity, in a distant future, may yet evolve a different ideal. In time, even conquest will cease to be the dream.

II. Comments on the Text

Before embarking upon the commentary proper, I must not omit to call the reader's attention to the very marked difference between the tenor of a psychological dissertation and that of a sacred text. A scientist forgets all too easily that the impartial handling of a subject may violate its emotional values, often to an unpardonable degree. The scientific intellect is inhuman and cannot afford to be anything else; it cannot avoid being ruthless in effect, though it may be well-intentioned in motive. In dealing with a sacred text, therefore, the psychologist ought at least to be aware that his subject represents an inestimable religious and philosophical value which should not be desecrated by profane hands. I confess that I myself venture to deal with such a text only because I know and appreciate its value. In commenting upon it I have no intention whatsoever of anatomizing it with heavy-handed criticism. On the contrary, my endeavour will be to amplify its symbolic language so that it may yield itself more easily to our understanding. To this end, it is necessary to bring down its lofty metaphysical concepts to a level where it is possible to see whether any of the psychological facts known to us have parallels in, or at least border upon, the sphere of Eastern thought. I hope this will not be misunderstood as an attempt to belittle or to banalize; my aim is simply to bring ideas which are alien to our way of thinking within reach of Western psychological experience.

What follows is a series of notes and comments which should be read together with the textual sections indicated by the titles.

The Obeisance

Eastern texts usually begin with a statement which in the West would come at the end, as the *conclusio finalis* to a long argument. We would begin with things generally known and accepted, and would end with the most important item of our investigation. Hence our dissertation would conclude with the sentence: 'Therefore the *Tri-Kāya* is the All-Enlightened Mind itself.' In this respect, the Eastern mentality is not so very different from the medieval. As late as the eighteenth century our books on history or natural science began, as here, with God's decision to create a world. The idea of a Universal Mind is a commonplace in the East, since it aptly expresses the introverted Eastern temperament. Put into psychological language, the above sentence could be paraphrased thus: The unconscious is the root of all experience of oneness (*dharma-kāya*), the matrix of all archetypes or structural patterns (*sambhoga-kāya*), and the *conditio sine qua non* of the phenomenal world (*nirmāṇa-kāya*).

The Foreword

The gods are archetypal thought-forms belonging to the *sambhoga-kāya*.[1] Their peaceful and wrathful aspects, which play a great role in the meditations of *The Tibetan Book of the Dead*, symbolize the opposites. In the *nirmāṇa-kāya* these opposites are no more than human conflicts, but in the *sambhoga-kāya* they are the positive and negative principles united in one and the same figure. This corresponds to the psychological experience, also formulated in Lao-Tzu's *Tao Te Ching*, that there is no position without its negation. Where there is faith, there is doubt; where there is doubt, there is credulity; where there is morality, there is temptation. Only saints have diabolical visions, and tyrants are the slaves of their *valets de chambre*. If we carefully scrutinize our own character we shall inevitably find that, as Lao-Tzu says, 'high stands on low', which means that the opposites condition one another, that they are really one and the same thing. This can easily be seen in persons with an inferiority

[1] Cf. the *Shrī-Chakra-Sambhara Tantra*, in *Tantric Texts*, vol. vii.

complex: they foment a little megalomania somewhere. The fact that the opposites appear as gods comes from the simple recognition that they are exceedingly powerful. Chinese philosophy therefore declared them to be cosmic principles, and named them *yang* and *yin*. Their power increases the more one tries to separate them. 'When a tree grows up to heaven its roots reach down to hell', says Nietzsche. Yet, above as below, it is the same tree. It is characteristic of our Western mentality that we should separate the two aspects into antagonistic personifications: God and the Devil. And it is equally characteristic of the worldly optimism of Protestantism that it should have hushed up the Devil in a tactful sort of way, at any rate in recent times. *Omne bonum a Deo, omne malum ab homine* is the uncomfortable consequence.

The 'seeing of reality' clearly refers to Mind as the supreme reality. In the West, however, the unconscious is considered to be a fantastic irreality. The 'seeing of the Mind' implies self-liberation. This means, psychologically, that the more weight we attach to unconscious processes the more we detach ourselves from the world of desires and of separated opposites, and the nearer we draw to the state of unconsciousness with its qualities of oneness, indefiniteness, and timelessness. This is truly a liberation of the self from its bondage to strife and suffering. 'By this method, one's mind is understood.' Mind in this context is obviously the individual's mind, that is, his psyche. Psychology can agree in so far as the understanding of the unconscious is one of its foremost tasks.

Salutation to the One Mind

This section shows very clearly that the One Mind is the unconscious, since it is characterized as 'eternal, unknown, not visible, not recognized'. But it also displays positive features which are in keeping with Eastern experience. These are the attributes 'ever clear, ever existing, radiant and unobscured'. It is an undeniable psychological fact that the more one concentrates on one's unconscious contents the more they become charged with energy; they become vitalized, as if illuminated from within. In fact they turn into something like a substitute reality. In analytical psychology we make methodical use of this phenomenon. I have called the method 'active imagination'. Ignatius Loyola also made use of active imagination in his *Exercitia*. There is evidence that something similar was used in the meditations of alchemical philosophy.[1]

The Result of Not Knowing the One Mind

'Knowledge of that which is vulgarly called mind is widespread.' This clearly refers to the conscious mind of everybody, in contrast to the One Mind which is unknown, i.e. unconscious. These teachings 'will also be sought after by ordinary individuals who, not knowing the One Mind, do not know themselves.' Self-knowledge is here definitely identified with 'knowing the One Mind', which means that knowledge of the unconscious is essential for any understanding of one's own psychology. The desire for such knowledge is a well established fact in the West, as evidenced by the rise of psychology in our time and a growing interest in these matters. The public desire for more psychological knowledge is largely due to the suffering which results from the disuse of religion and from the lack of spiritual guidance. 'They wander hither and thither in the Three Regions . . . suffering sorrow.' As we know what a neurosis can mean in moral suffering, this statement needs no comment. This section formulates the reasons why we have such a thing as the psychology of the unconscious today.

Even if one wishes 'to know the mind as it is, one fails'. The text again stresses how hard it is to gain access to the basic mind, because it is unconscious.

The Results of Desires

Those 'fettered by desires cannot perceive the Clear Light'. The 'Clear Light' again refers to the One Mind. Desires crave for external fulfilment. They forge the chain that fetters man to the world of consciousness. In that condition he naturally cannot become aware of his unconscious contents. And indeed there is a healing power in withdrawing from the conscious world—up to a point. Beyond that point, which varies with individuals, withdrawal amounts to neglect and repression.

[1] C. G. Jung, *Psychology and Alchemy*, Part III.

Even the 'Middle Path' finally becomes 'obscured by desires'. This is a very true statement, which cannot be dinned too insistently into European ears. Patients and normal individuals, on becoming acquainted with their unconscious material, hurl themselves upon it with the same heedless desirousness and greed that before had engulfed them in their extraversion. The problem is not so much a withdrawal from the objects of desire, as a more detached attitude to desire as such, no matter what its object. We cannot compel unconscious compensation through the impetuousness of uncontrolled desire. We have to wait patiently to see whether it will come of its own accord, and put up with whatever form it takes. Hence we are forced into a sort of contemplative attitude which, in itself, not rarely has a liberating and healing effect.

The Transcendent At-one-ment

'There being really no duality, pluralism is untrue.' This is certainly one of the most fundamental truths of the East. There are no opposites—it is the same tree above and below. The *Tabula Smaragdina* says: 'Quod est inferius est sicut quod est superius. Et quod est superius est sicut quod est inferius, ad perpetranda miracula rei unius.'[1] Pluralism is even more illusory, since all separate forms originate in the indistinguishable oneness of the psychic matrix, deep down in the unconscious. The statement made by our text refers psychologically to the subjective factor, to the material immediately constellated by a stimulus, i.e. the first impression which, as we have seen, interprets every new perception in terms of previous experience. 'Previous experience' goes right back to the instincts, and thus to the inherited and inherent patterns of psychic functioning, the ancestral and 'eternal' laws of the human mind. But the statement entirely ignores the possible transcendent reality of the physical world as such, a problem not unknown to Saṇkhya philosophy, where *prakṛti* and *purusha*—so far as they are a polarization of Universal Being—form a cosmic dualism that can hardly be

[1] Cf. J. Ruska, *Tabula Smaragdina: Ein Beitrag zur Geschichte der Hermetischen Literatur*, 1926, p. 2.

circumvented. One has to close one's eyes to dualism and pluralism alike, and forget all about the existence of a world, as soon as one tries to identify oneself with the monistic origin of life. The question naturally arises: 'Why should the One appear as the Many, when ultimate reality is All-One? What is the cause of pluralism, or of the illusion of pluralism? If the One is pleased with itself, why should it mirror itself in the Many? Which after all is the more real, the one that mirrors itself, or the mirror it uses?' Probably we should not ask such questions, seeing that there is no answer to them.

It is psychologically correct to say that 'At-one-ment' is attained by withdrawal from the world of consciousness. In the stratosphere of the unconscious there are no more thunderstorms, because nothing is differentiated enough to produce tensions and conflicts. These belong to the surface of our reality.

The Mind in which the irreconcilables—*sangsāra* and *nirvāṇa*—are united is ultimately our mind. Does this statement spring from profound modesty or from overweening hybris? Does it mean that the Mind is 'nothing but' our mind? Or that our mind is the Mind? Assuredly it means the latter, and from the Eastern point of view there is no hybris in this; on the contrary, it is a perfectly acceptable truth, whereas with us it would amount to saying 'I am God'. This is an incontestable 'mystical' experience, though a highly objectionable one to the Westerner; but in the East, where it derives from a mind that has never lost touch with the instinctual matrix, it has a very different value. The collective introverted attitude of the East did not permit the world of the senses to sever the vital link with the unconscious; psychic reality was never seriously disputed, despite the existence of so-called materialistic speculations. The only known analogy to this fact is the mental condition of the primitive, who confuses dream and reality in the most bewildering way. Naturally we hesitate to call the Eastern mind primitive, for we are deeply impressed with its remarkable civilization and differentiation. Yet the primitive mind is its matrix, and this is particularly true of that aspect of it which stresses the validity of psychic phenomena, such as relate to ghosts and spirits. The West has simply cultivated the other aspect of primitivity, namely, the scrupulously accurate observation of nature at the expense of abstraction. Our natural science is the epitome of primitive man's astonishing powers of observation. We have added only a moderate amount of abstraction, for fear of being contradicted by the facts. The East, on the other hand, cultivates the psychic aspect of primitivity together with an inordinate amount of abstraction. Facts make excellent stories but not much more.

Thus, if the East speaks of the Mind as being inherent in everybody, no more hybris or modesty is involved than in the European's belief in facts, which are mostly derived from man's own observation and sometimes from rather less than his observation, to wit, his interpretation. He is, therefore, quite right to be afraid of too much abstraction.

The Great Self-Liberation

I have mentioned more than once that the shifting of the basic personality-feeling to the less conscious mental sphere has a liberating effect. I have also described, somewhat cursorily, the transcendent function which produces the transformation of personality, and I have emphasized the importance of spontaneous unconscious compensation. Further, I have pointed out the neglect of this crucial fact in *yoga*. This section tends to confirm my observations. The grasping of 'the whole essence of these teachings' seems also to be the whole essence of 'self-liberation'. The Westerner would take this to mean: 'Learn your lesson and repeat it, and then you will be self-liberated.' That, indeed, is precisely what happens with most Western practitioners of *yoga*. They are very apt to 'do' it in an extraverted fashion, oblivious of the inturning of the mind which is the essence of such teachings. In the East, the 'truths' are so much a part of the collective consciousness that they are at least intuitively grasped by the pupil. If the European could turn himself inside out and live as an Oriental, with all the social, moral, religious, intellectual, and aesthetic obligations which such a course would involve, he might be able to benefit by these teachings. But you cannot be a good Christian, either in your faith or in your morality or in your intellectual make-up, and practise genuine *yoga* at the same time. I have seen too many cases that have made me sceptical in the highest degree. The trouble is that Western man cannot get rid of his history as easily as his short-legged memory can. History, one might say, is written in the blood. I would not advise anyone to touch *yoga* without a careful analysis of his unconscious re- actions. What is the use of imitating *yoga* if your dark side remains as good a medieval Christian as ever was? If you can afford to seat yourself on a gazelle skin under a Bo-tree or in the cell of a *gompa* for the rest of your life without being troubled by politics or the collapse of your securities, I will look favourably upon your case. But *yoga* in Mayfair or Fifth Avenue, or in any other place which is on the telephone, is a spiritual fake.

Taking the mental equipment of Eastern man into account, we may suppose that the teaching is effective. But unless one is prepared to turn away from the world and to disappear into the unconscious for good, mere teaching has no effect, or at least not the desired one. For this the union of opposites is necessary, and in particular the difficult task of reconciling extraversion and introversion by means of the transcendent function.

The Nature of Mind

This section contains a valuable piece of psychological information. The text says: 'The mind is of intuitive ("quick- knowing") Wisdom.' Here 'mind' is understood to be iden- tical with immediate awareness of the 'first impression' which conveys the whole sum of previous experience based upon instinctual patterns. This bears out our remarks about the essentially introverted prejudice of the East. The formula also draws attention to the highly differentiated character of Eastern intuition. The intuitive mind is noted for its disre- gard of facts in favour of possibilities.[1]

----

[1] Cf. *Psychological Types*, definition 36, pp. 641 ff.

The assertion that the Mind 'has no existence' obviously refers to the peculiar 'potentiality' of the unconscious. A thing seems to exist only to the degree that we are aware of it, which explains why so many people are disinclined to believe in the existence of an unconscious. When I tell a patient that he is chock full of fantasies, he is often astonished beyond all measure, having been completely unaware of the fantasy-life he was leading.

The Names given to the Mind

The various terms employed to express a 'difficult' or 'obscure' idea are a valuable source of information about the ways in which that idea can be interpreted, and at the same time an indication of its doubtful or controversial nature even in the country, religion, or philosophy to which it is indigenous. If the idea were perfectly straightforward and enjoyed general acceptance, there would be no reason to call it by a number of different names. But when something is little known, or ambiguous, it can be envisaged from different angles, and then a multiplicity of names is needed to express its peculiar nature. A classical example of this is the philosopher's stone; many of the old alchemical treatises give long lists of its names.

The statement that 'the various names given to it (the Mind) are innumerable' proves that the Mind must be something as vague and indefinite as the philosopher's stone. A substance that can be described in 'innumerable' ways must be expected to display as many qualities or facets. If these are really 'innumerable', they cannot be counted, and it follows that the substance is well-nigh indescribable and unknowable. It can never be realized completely. This is certainly true of the unconscious, and a further proof that the Mind is the Eastern equivalent of our concept of the unconscious, more particularly of the collective unconscious.

In keeping with this hypothesis, the text goes on to say that the Mind is also called the 'Mental Self'. The 'self' is an important item in analytical psychology, where much has been said that I need not repeat here. I would refer the interested

reader to the literature given below.¹ Although the symbols
of the 'self' are produced by unconscious activity and are
mostly manifested in dreams,² the facts which the idea covers
are not merely mental; they include aspects of physical existence as well. In this and other Eastern texts the 'Self' represents a purely spiritual idea, but in Western psychology the
'self' stands for a totality which comprises instincts, physio-
logical and semi-physiological phenomena. To us a purely
spiritual totality is inconceivable for the reasons mentioned
above.³

It is interesting to note that in the East, too, there are
'heretics' who identify the Self with the ego.⁴ With us this
heresy is pretty widespread and is subscribed to by all those
who firmly believe that ego-consciousness is the only form of
psychic life.

The Mind as 'the means of attaining the Other Shore'
points to a connexion between the transcendent function and
the idea of the Mind or Self. Since the unknowable substance
of the Mind, i.e. of the unconscious, always represents itself
to consciousness in the form of symbols—the self being one
such symbol—the symbol functions as a 'means of attaining
the Other Shore', in other words, as a means of transformation. In my essay on *Psychic Energy* I said that the symbol
acts as a transformer of energy.⁵

My interpretation of the Mind or Self as a symbol is not
arbitrary; the text itself calls it 'The Great Symbol'.

It is also remarkable that our text recognizes the 'potentiality' of the unconscious, as formulated above, by calling
the Mind the 'Sole Seed' and the 'Potentiality of Truth'.

The matrix-character of the unconscious comes out in the
term 'All-Foundation'.

¹ C. G. Jung, *Two Essays on Analytical Psychology*, p. 268; *Psychological Types*, def. 16, p. 540; *Psychology and Alchemy*, Part II; *Psychology and Religion*, passim.
² One such case is described in Part II of *Psychology and Alchemy*.
³ This is no criticism of the Eastern point of view *in toto*; for, according to the *Amitāyus Dhyāna Sutra*, Buddha's body is included in the meditation.
⁴ Cf., for instance, *Chāndogya Upanishad*, viii. 8.
⁵ *Contributions to Analytical Psychology*, 1928, p. 54.

The Timelessness of Mind

I have already explained this 'timelessness' as a quality inherent in the experience of the collective unconscious. The application of the '*yoga* of self-liberation' is said to reintegrate all forgotten knowledge of the past with consciousness. The motif of ἀποκατάστασις (restoration, restitution) occurs in many redemption myths and is also an important aspect of the psychology of the unconscious, which reveals an extraordinary amount of archaic material in the dreams and spontaneous fantasies of normal and insane people. In the systematic analysis of an individual the spontaneous re-awakening of ancestral patterns (as a compensation) has the effect of a restoration. It is also a fact that premonitory dreams are relatively frequent, and this substantiates what the text calls 'knowledge of the future'.

The Mind's 'own time' is very difficult to interpret. From the psychological point of view we must agree with Dr. Evans-Wentz's comment here. The unconscious certainly has its 'own time' inasmuch as past, present, and future are blended together in it. Dreams of the type experienced by J. W. Dunne,[1] where he dreamed the night before what he ought logically to have dreamed the night after, are not infrequent.

Mind in its True State

This section describes the state of detached consciousness[2] which corresponds to a psychic experience very common throughout the East. Similar descriptions are to be found in Chinese literature, as, for instance, in the *Hui Ming Ch'ing*:

A luminosity surrounds the world of spirit.
We forget one another when, still and pure, we draw strength from
        the Void.
The Void is filled with the light of the Heart of Heaven . . .
Consciousness dissolves in vision.[3]

---

[1] J. W. Dunne, *An Experiment with Time*, 1927.
[2] I have explained this in *The Secret of the Golden Flower*, pp. 21 ff.
[3] Translated from *Hui Ming Ch'ing*, Chinesische Blätter, ed. R. Wilhelm, vol. i, no. 3.

The statement 'Nor is one's own mind separable from other minds' is another way of expressing the fact of 'all-contamination'. Since all distinctions vanish in the unconscious condition, it is only logical that the distinction between separate minds should also disappear. Wherever there is a lowering of the conscious level we come across instances of unconscious identity,[1] or what Lévy-Bruhl calls 'participation mystique'.[2] The realization of the One Mind is, as our text says, the 'at-one-ment of the *Tri-Kāya*'; in fact it creates the at-one-ment. But we are unable to imagine how such a realization could ever be complete in any human individual. There must always be somebody or something left over to experience the realization, to say 'I know at-one-ment, I know there is no distinction'. The very fact of the realization proves its inevitable incompleteness. One cannot know something that is not distinct from oneself. Even when I say 'I know myself', an infinitesimal ego—the knowing 'I'—is still distinct from 'myself'. In this as it were atomic ego, which is completely ignored by the essentially non-dualist standpoint of the East, there nevertheless lies hidden the whole unabolished pluralistic universe and its unconquered reality.

The experience of 'at-one-ment' is one example of those 'quick-knowing' realizations of the East, an intuition of what it would be like if one could exist and not exist at the same time. If I were a Moslem, I should maintain that the power of the All-Compassionate is infinite, and that He alone can make a man to be and not to be at the same time. But for my part

---

[1] *Psychological Types*, def. 25, p. 552.

[2] Cf. L. Lévy-Bruhl, *Les Fonctions mentales dans les sociétés inférieures*. Recently this concept as well as that of the *état prélogique* have been severely criticized by ethnologists, and moreover Lévy-Bruhl himself began to doubt their validity in the last years of his life. First he cancelled the adjective 'mystique', growing afraid of the term's bad reputation in intellectual circles. It is rather to be regretted that he made such a concession to rationalistic superstition, since 'mystique' is just the right word to characterize the peculiar quality of 'unconscious identity'. There is always something numinous about it. Unconscious identity is a well-known psychological and psychopathological phenomenon (identity with persons, things, functions, roles, positions, creeds, &c.), which is only a shade more characteristic of the primitive than of the civilized mind. Lévy-Bruhl unfortunately having no psychological knowledge was not aware of this fact, and his opponents ignore it.

I cannot conceive of such a possibility. I therefore assume that, in this point, Eastern intuition has overreached itself.

Mind is Non-Created

This section emphasizes that as the Mind is without characteristics, one cannot assert that it is created. But then, it would be illogical to assert that it is non-created, for such a qualification would amount to a 'characteristic'. As a matter of fact you can make no assertion whatever about a thing that is indistinct, void of characteristics and, moreover, 'unknowable'. For precisely this reason Western psychology does not speak of the One Mind, but of the unconscious, regarding it as a thing-in-itself, a noumenon, 'a merely negative borderline concept', to quote Kant.[1] We have often been reproached for using such a negative term, but unfortunately intellectual honesty does not allow a positive one.

The Yoga of Introspection

Should there be any doubt left concerning the identity of the One Mind and the unconscious, this section certainly ought to dispel it. 'The One Mind being verily of the Voidness and without any foundation, one's mind is, likewise, as vacuous as the sky.' The One Mind and the individual mind are equally void and vacuous. Only the collective and the personal unconscious can be meant by this statement, for the conscious mind is in no circumstances 'vacuous'.

As I have said earlier, the Eastern mind insists first and foremost upon the subjective factor, and in particular upon the intuitive 'first impression', or the psychic disposition. This is borne out by the statement that 'All appearances are verily one's own concepts, self-conceived in the mind'.

The Dharma Within

Dharma, law, truth, guidance, is said to be 'nowhere save in the mind'. Thus the unconscious is credited with all those faculties which the West attributes to God. The transcendent function, however, shows how right the East is in assuming

[1] Cf. *The Critique of Pure Reason*, section i, Part I. 2, 3.

that the complex experience of *dharma* comes from 'within', i.e. from the unconscious. It also shows that the phenomenon of spontaneous compensation, being beyond the control of man, is quite in accord with the formula 'grace' or the 'will of God'.

This and the preceding section insist again and again that introspection is the only source of spiritual information and guidance. If introspection were something morbid, as certain people in the West opine, we should have to send practically the whole East, or such parts of it as are not yet infected with the blessings of the West, to the lunatic asylum.

The Wondrousness of These Teachings

This section calls the mind 'Natural Wisdom', which is very much the same expression that I used in order to designate the symbols produced by the unconscious. I called them 'natural symbols'.[1] I chose the term before I had any knowledge of this text. I mention this fact simply because it illustrates the close parallelism between the findings of Eastern and Western psychology.

The text also confirms what we said earlier about the impossibility of a 'knowing' ego. 'Although it is Total Reality, there is no perceiver of it. Wondrous is this.' Wondrous indeed, and incomprehensible; for how could such a thing ever be *realized* in the true sense of the word? 'It remains undefiled by evil' and 'it remains unallied to good'. One is remined of Nietzsche's 'six thousand feet beyond good and evil'. But the consequences of such a statement are usually ignored by the emulators of Eastern wisdom. While one is safely ensconced in one's cosy flat, secure in the favour of the Oriental gods, one is free to admire this lofty moral indifference. But does it agree with our temperament, or with our history, which is not thereby conquered but merely forgotten? I think not. Anyone who affects the higher *yoga* will be called upon to prove his professions of moral indifference, not only as the doer of evil but, even more, as its

---

[1] *Psychology and Religion*, 1938, 'Dogma and Natural Symbols', and 'A Natural Symbol'.

victim. As psychologists well know, the moral conflict is not to be settled merely by a declaration of superiority bordering on inhumanity. We are witnessing today some terrifying examples of the Superman's aloofness from moral principles.

I do not doubt that the Eastern liberation from vices, as well as from virtues, is coupled with detachment in every respect, so that the *yogī* is translated beyond this world, and quite inoffensive. But I suspect every European attempt at detachment of being mere liberation from moral considerations. Anybody who tries his hand at *yoga* ought therefore to be conscious of its far-reaching consequences, or else his so-called quest will remain a futile pastime.

The Fourfold Great Path

The text says: 'This meditation [is] devoid of mental concentration.' The usual assumption about *yoga* is that it chiefly consists in intense concentration. We think we know what concentration means, but it is very difficult to arrive at a real understanding of Eastern concentration. Our sort may well be just the opposite of the Eastern, as a study of Zen Buddhism will show.[1] However, if we take 'devoid of mental concentration' literally, it can only mean that the meditation does not centre upon anything. Not being centred, it would be rather like a dissolution of consciousness and hence a direct approach to the unconscious condition. Consciousness always implies a certain degree of concentration, without which there would be no clarity of mental content and no consciousness of anything. Meditation without concentration would be a waking but empty condition, on the verge of falling asleep. Since our text calls this 'the most excellent of meditations' we must suppose the existence of less excellent meditations which, by inference, would be characterized by more concentration. The meditation our text has in mind seems to be a sort of Royal Road to the unconscious.

The Great Light

The central mystical experience of enlightenment is aptly

[1] Cf. D. T. Suzuki, *Essays in Zen Buddhism.*

symbolized by Light in most of the numerous forms of
mysticism. It is a curious paradox that the approach to a
region which seems to us the way into utter darkness should
yield the light of illumination as its fruit. This is, however, the
usual *enantiodromia per tenebras ad lucem*. Many initiation
ceremonies[1] stage a κατάβασις εἰς ἄντρον (descent into the
cave), a diving down into the depths of the baptismal water,
or a return to the womb of rebirth. Rebirth symbolism simply
describes the union of opposites—conscious and unconscious
—by means of concretistic analogies. Underlying all rebirth
symbolism is the transcendent function. Since this function
results in an increase of consciousness (the previous condition
augmented by the addition of formerly unconscious contents),
the new condition carries more insight, which is symbolized
by more light.[2] It is therefore a more enlightened state compared with the relative darkness of the previous state. In
many cases the Light even appears in the form of a vision.

The Yoga of the Nirvāṇic Path

This section gives one of the best formulations of the
complete dissolution of consciousness, which appears to be
the goal of this *yoga*: 'There being no two such things as action
and performer of action, if one seeks the performer of action
and no performer of action be found anywhere, thereupon the
goal of all fruit-obtaining is reached and also the final consummation itself.'

With this very complete formulation of the method and its
aim, I reach the end of my commentary. The text that follows, in Book II, is of great beauty and wisdom, and contains nothing that requires further comment. It can be translated into psychological language and interpreted with the
help of the principles I have here set forth in Part I and
illustrated in Part II.

[1] As in the Eleusinian mysteries and the Mithras and Attis cults.
[2] In alchemy the philosopher's stone was called, among other things, *lux
moderna, lux lucis, lumen luminum*, &c.

PLATE IV

MAÑJUSHRĪ THE GOD OF DIVINE WISDOM
Described on pages xix–xxi

GENERAL INTRODUCTION

'To attain the Good, we must ascend to the highest state, and, fixing our gaze thereon, lay aside the garments we donned when descending here below; just as, in the Mysteries, those who are admitted to penetrate into the inner recesses of the sanctuary, after having purified themselves, lay aside every garment, and advance stark naked.'   Plotinus (I. vi. 6)

I. REALITY ACCORDING TO THE MAHĀYĀNA

HEREIN, in Book II, in the 'Yoga of Knowing the Mind in Its Nakedness', otherwise known as the doctrine which automatically liberates man from bondage to appearances, is set forth, in aphorisms, an epitome of the root teachings of Mahāyānic transcendentalism concerning Reality.

In common with all Schools of the Oriental Occult Sciences, the Mahāyāna postulates that the One Supra-Mundane Mind, or the Universal All-Pervading Consciousness, transcendent over appearances and over every dualistic concept born of the finite or mundane aspect of mind, alone is real. Viewed as the Voidness (known in Sanskrit as the Shūnyatā), it is the Unbecome, the Unborn, the Unmade, the Unformed, the predicateless Primordial Essence, the abstract Cosmic Source whence all concrete or manifested things come and into which they vanish in latency. Being without form, quality, or phenomenal existence, it is the Formless, the Qualityless, the Non-Existent. As such, it is the Imperishable, the Transcendent Fullness of the Emptiness, the Dissolver of Space and of Time and of sangsāric (or mundane) mind, the Brahman of the Rishis, the Dreamer of Māyā, the Weaver of the Web of Appearances, the Outbreather and the Inbreather of infinite universes throughout the endlessness of Duration.

Plotinus, the Platonic inheritor of this ancient oriental teaching, has concisely summarized it: 'The First Principle, being One, is transcendent over measure or number. . . . The Supreme Principle must be essentially unitary, and simple, while essences [derived therefrom] form a multitude.'[1] The

[1] Cf. Plotinus, Ennead V, Book V, 11; Book IX, 14. These renderings from Plotinus, and all hereinafter contained, are recensions, based upon translations contained in *Plotinos' Complete Works*, by K. S. Guthrie, as published in London in 1929, a work to which grateful acknowledgement is

Great *Guru*, Padma-Sambhava, the author of our present treatise, in Book II, page 207, sets forth the same doctrine from the Mahāyānic point of view: 'The whole *Sangsāra* [or the phenomenal Universe of appearances] and *Nirvāṇa* [the Unmanifested, or noumenal state], as an inseparable unity, are one's mind [in its natural, or unmodified primordial state of the Voidness].' In like manner, the Buddha Himself teaches that *Nirvāṇa* is a state of transcendence over 'that which is become, born, made, and formed'.[1] Accordingly, *Nirvāṇa* is the annihilation of appearances, the indrawing of the Web of the *Sangsāra*, the blowing out of the flame of bodily sensuousness, the Awakening from the Dream of *Māyā*, the unveiling of Reality.

The Buddha, and, after Him, Nāgārjuna, who compiled the *Prajñā-Pāramitā*, the chief Mahāyāna treatise on Transcendental Wisdom, aimed to avoid in their teachings the extreme of superstition on the one hand and of nihilism on the other; and so their method is that of the Middle Path, which, under Nāgārjuna, became known as the Mādhyamika. Prior to Nāgārjuna, Buddhist metaphysicians were divided into two schools of extremists, one school teaching of a real existence, the other of an illusory existence. Nāgārjuna showed that nothing can be said to exist or not to exist, for so long as the mind conceives in terms of dualism it is still under *sangsāric* bondage, and fettered by the false desire for either personal immortality or annihilation. Reality, or the Absolute, or Being *per se*, is transcendent over both existence and non-existence, and over all other dualistic concepts. According to Nāgārjuna, it is the Primordial Voidness, beyond mental conception, or definition in terms of human experience.

here made. Frequent reference is herein made to Plotinus, because he is the outstanding exponent in the West of the same *yogic* doctrines as those which form the basis of this volume. He was an eminently successful disciple of the Oriental Sages, no less than of his European *Guru* Plato; by Plotinus, these doctrines were put to the test of practice, with far-reaching results to the whole Christian world. In Plotinus, East and West cease to be twain and become one, as in reality they always have been and will be increasingly, when the Sun of the approaching New Renaissance, which shall be world-wide, rises, and waxes in brilliance and power, and dissipates the darkness of Ignorance.

[1] *Udāna*, viii. 1, 4, 3; cf. *The Tibetan Book of the Dead*, p. 68.

The Mādhyamika maintains that the World is to be renounced not as the Theravāda teaches, because of its pain and sorrow, but because it is as non-real as are dreams; it, being merely one of the many dream-states comprising the *Sangsāra*, is wholly unsatisfying. Man should strive to awaken from all the dream-states of the *Sangsāra* into the State of True Awakening, *Nirvāṇa*, beyond the range of all the glamorous illusions and hypnotic mirages of the *Sangsāra*; and thus become, as is the Buddha, a Fully-Awakened One.

This Doctrine of the Voidness is the essential doctrine of the Mahāyāna; it represents in Northern Buddhism what the *Anātmā* (or Non-Soul) Doctrine does in Southern Buddhism. Accordingly, as our treatise implies, no existing thing or being has other than an illusory existence, nor has it separate or individualized existence apart from all other beings.

As set forth in the *Avatamsaka Sūtra*, attributed to Nāgārjuna, the essentiality, or the true essence, behind all *sangsāric* things or beings is likened to a dust-free mirror, which is the basis of all phenomena, the basis itself being permanent, or non-transitory, and real, the phenomena being evanescent and unreal. And, just as the mirror reflects images, so the True Essence embraces all phenomena; and all things and beings exist in and by it. It is this True Essence which comes to fruition in the Buddhas; and is everywhere present throughout the manifested cosmos, which is born of it, and eternally present, unmanifested, throughout limitless space. There is no place throughout the Universe where the Essentiality of a Buddha is not present. Far and wide throughout the spaces of space the Buddha Essence is present and perpetually manifested.[1]

This Universal Essence manifests itself in three aspects, or modes, symbolized as the Three Divine Bodies (Skt. *Tri-Kāya*). The first aspect, the *Dharma-Kāya*, or Essential (or True) Body, is the Primordial, Unmodified, Formless, Eternally Self-Existing Essentiality of *Bodhi*, or Divine Beingness. The second aspect is the *Sambhoga-Kāya*, or Reflected *Bodhi*,

---

[1] Cf. S. Beal, *A Catena of Buddhist Scriptures from the Chinese* (London, 1871), pp. 124-5.

wherein, in heaven-worlds, dwell the Buddhas of Meditation (Skt. *Dhyānī-Buddhas*) and other Enlightened Ones while embodied in superhuman form. The third aspect is the *Nirmāṇa-Kāya*, or Body of Incarnation, or, from the standpoint of men, Practical *Bodhi*, in which exist Buddhas when on Earth.

In the Chinese interpretation of the *Tri-Kāya*, the *Dharma-Kāya* is the immutable Buddha Essence, the Noumenal Source of the Cosmic whole. The *Sambhoga-Kāya* is, as phenomenal appearances, the first reflex of the *Dharma-Kāya* on the heavenly planes. In the *Nirmāṇa-Kāya*, the Buddha Essence is associated with activity on the Earth plane; it incarnates among men, as suggested by the Gnostic Proem to the Gospel of St. John, which refers to the coming into the flesh of the 'Word', or 'Mind' (see herein Book II, p. 217[1]).[1]

In its totality, the Universal Essence is the One Mind, manifested through the multitudinous myriads of minds throughout all states of *sangsāric* existence. It is called 'The Essence of the Buddhas', 'The Great Symbol', 'The Sole Seed', 'The Potentiality of Truth', 'The All-Foundation'. As our text teaches, it is the Source of all bliss of *Nirvāṇa* and of all sorrow of the *Sangsāra*. Mind in its microcosmic aspect is variously described by the unenlightened, some calling it the ego, or soul.

Complete realization of the essential and undifferentiated oneness of the *Sangsāra* and *Nirvāṇa*, which, according to the Mahāyāna, are the Ultimate Duality, leads to that Deliverance of the Mind taught by the Enlightened One as being the aim and end of the *Dharma*, as it is of all systems of *yoga* and of all Schools of Buddhism and of Hinduism.[2]

II. *NIRVĀṆA*[3]

Nirvāṇa, the State Transcendent Over Sorrow, and, thus, over the *Sangsāra*, is a state of vacuity, of the Voidness of the

[1] For fuller interpretation of the Chinese view of the *Tri-Kāya*, the student is referred to the Rev. K. L. Reichelt's *Truth and Tradition in Chinese Buddhism* (Shanghai, 1934), pp. 357-9.

[2] See *Tibetan Yoga and Secret Doctrines*, pp. 6-7.

[3] This part of the Introduction is supplementary to the more technical exposition of *Nirvāṇa* presented in the General Introduction to *Tibetan Yoga and Secret Doctrines*, pp. 7-9, and should be read in connexion therewith.

Mahāyāna, for it is empty of all conceivable things, or qualities, which are of the *Sangsāra*, the opposite of *Nirvāna*.
Nirvāna, as the Buddha teaches, neither is nor is not; is
neither existence nor non-existence, being nor non-being, all
of which are, as Nāgārjuna shows, illusory dualities. *Nirvāna*,
being thus beyond all *sangsāric* concepts, transcends all
human predication.

Nirvāna cannot be intellectually realized, because it is
beyond intellect. Not being relative to any thing, it transcends
relativity; and, being beyond conception, is of the Voidness.

All dualities depend upon the human intellect, which, in its
turn, is a reflex, in the realm of appearances, of the Thatness,
of the True State, of *Nirvāna*. The Sun gives forth light and
energy, but is transcendent over both. *Nirvāna*, as the Voidness, is the Source of *sangsāric* existence, yet transcends it.
Even as the Sun remains unchangedly the Sun, notwithstanding its emanations of light and energy, so *Nirvāna* remains the
Quiescent, although the ultimate initiator of mundane activities. Man, mundane mind, life, energy, are illusorily individualized aspects, or manifestations, of That, which is the unique
and indivisible At-one-ment of All Things; they are, as our
treatise teaches, of the One Mind. Man *per se* is and has been
eternally immersed in the One Mind, in the Voidness.

The True State, *Nirvāna*, as the Voidness, like the Sun,
shines unceasingly. Man by his involution in the realm of
appearances, without Right Guidance, misinterprets the
world; he strives after illusion rather than reality, the
evanescent rather than the permanent, the unreal rather
than the Real. His mind loses its primitiveness; it becomes
learned in Ignorance, puffed up with pride in its own perishable creations; from the Sea of Appearances rise up the mists
and clouds of *Māyā* which hide from man the splendour of
the Radiance of the Real. Through the *Māyā*, illuminated by
the Radiance beyond it, man on Earth receives the feeble
light of the mundane mind; he gropes in the shadows, and
cannot perceive the Perfect Truth. The Buddhas are those
who have penetrated Ignorance, risen above the shadows and
mirages of life by the power of *yoga*, and standing, as it were,

upon the summit of an exceedingly high mountain, above the clouds and mists obscuring the world of men, who prefer the valleys to the mountains, have beheld the unclouded Sun.

The process of spiritual unfoldment, to which mankind either consciously or unconsciously are parties, is a process of dissipating the *Māyā*. *Māyā* literally means 'illusion'. To a Buddha, *Māyā* is the manifestation, as the *Sangsāra*, of that creative energy inherent in the Cosmos and spoken of in the *Tantras* as the Universal Mother, or *Shakti*, through whose womb embodied beings come into existence. When this energy is latent, there is no Creation and hence no *Māyā*. Transcendence over *Māyā*, or a going out of the realm of illusion, implies transcendence over differentiation (or separateness) and transitoriness, or, in other words, a return to primordial at-one-ment, the realization, such as our text teaches, of the One Mind (or Cosmic Consciousness), the re-union of the part with the whole, emancipation from the limitations of time, space, and causation, a rising out of conditioned existence into unconditioned Being *per se*, Buddhahood. The disciple must, accordingly, view the phenomenal Universe not as something to be escaped from, but as being the very essence, in symbol, of that almighty and ineffable essence of the One Mind in eternal evolution, as do those who tread the path of the Yogāchāra. Then, indeed, does life here on this planet Earth become, as the Teachers declare, the greatest good fortune that can ever fall to the lot of sentient beings, the Supreme Opportunity. And 'Who', they ask, 'save the deluded, would prefer Ignorance to Divine Wisdom?' 'The Ten Great Joyful Realizations', as set forth in the 'Precepts of the *Gurus*' (in Volume III of this Tibetan Series), make joyous this initiation into the Mystery of *Māyā*, joyous the Pilgrimage, joyous the returning from the Other Shore, joyous the guiding of others to the Great Liberation.

The Mahāyāna maintains that not only man, but all sentient creatures throughout the *Sangsāra*, will, ultimately, thus reach the end of this evolutionary process. For the *yogin*, however, the normal process is too wearisome, too long and painful. As did Tibet's great *Yogī* Milarepa, he strives to

attain the Supreme Goal in a single lifetime, that he may the
sooner become a worker for world-betterment; for he is
vowed, with the vow of the *Bodhisattva*, not to attain
Nirvāṇa for himself alone, but chiefly that he may be empowered to return to the *māyā*-shrouded valleys and lead
their inhabitants to the Supreme Height, to salute the Sun.

III. TIME AND SPACE

Involved in this Doctrine of Reality is the ancient Indian
view of time, as set forth in the treatise, namely, that 'past',
'present', and 'future' are merely concepts of the limited
sangsāric mind, that in the True State of the unlimited Supra-
Mundane Mind there is no time, just as there is no thing. In
the True State, the *yogin* realizes that even as time is, in its
essentiality, beginningless and endless duration, incapable of
division into past, present, and future, so space is dimension-
less, and divisionless, and non-existent apart from the One
Mind, or the Voidness. In other words, in the True State,
Mind is the container of matter and form as of time and space.

Simultaneously with the birth of the Cosmos, time is born,
and ceases with the cessation of the Cosmos. Or time is the
illusory life or duration of the *Sangsāra*; and when the *Sangsāra* ceases, so does time. It is not movement that begets
time; for time is merely indicated by movement, as by the
movement of the hands of a clock or by that of the heavenly
bodies. Time is, therefore, as Plotinus (III. vii. 11–12) also
teaches, nothing more than the measure of movement.

Time, being thus a *sangsāric* concept of mind in its finite
or mundane manifestation, has only a relative, not a true,
existence. In like manner, 'beginning and ending of time' is
merely a dualistic concept, employed by unenlightened men
who are under the domination of illusion (Skt. *māyā*). There
is timelessness, the unending present, eternal duration, but
not past and future, for these are merely another *sangsārically*
conceived duality. All things having been completely immersed in the Voidness from beginningless timelessness, are,
in their essentiality, as this *yoga* shows, inseparable from it,

their True State being, as the Enlightened One taught, Perfect Quiescence, transcendent over time, space, and duration. When Brahman remains quiescent in dreamless sleep there is no Universe, no multiplicity of anything, there are no minds, no consciousnesses; there is but the One Mind (or Consciousness). Time and space have vanished like the indrawn web of the spider. When Brahman passes from dreamlessness to dreaming, all things come forth in this Dream.

To Brahman the Quiescent there is only the beginninglessness and endlessness of duration which is timelessness; to Brahman the Dreamer there are past, present, and future, time, and space. In that True State of Quiescence, Mind is One, or Consciousness is One; but when Mind illusorily ceases to be the Thatness, or the One of all things, and appears to be the Many, then there arise the various states of *sangsāric* consciousness which men call states of sleeping, dreaming, waking, of being born, of living, of dying, and of after-death.

The illusory character of all these *sangsārically*-conceived concepts is clearly set forth in our ' *Yoga* of Knowing the Mind in Its Nakedness', as in the correlative *Yogas* expounded by the Doctrines of the Illusory Body, and of Dreams, in *Tibetan Yoga and Secret Doctrines*. There is, as therein taught, no fixed standard of time. The waking-state conception of time is quite different from that of the dream-state, wherein, in one night or even one moment of waking-state time, the dreamer may go through years, centuries, aeons of experiences, as 'real' in the dream-state as are experiences in the waking-state. Then, again, one dream-state may be superimposed on another dream-state, and that upon another, *ad infinitum*. These demonstrable facts of human experience are for the *yogin* incontrovertible proof of the illusoriness and unfixableness of what men call time. And he deduces therefrom, as he advances in *yoga*, that every conceivable state, of the dream-world, of the waking-world, of the after-death-world, and of the *Sangsāra* as a whole, is unreal. Then, as he wakes up from all of them, he is truly the Awakened One, transcendent over time and space.

Thus the Great Sages of India and of Tibet long ago under-

stood the occult truths concerning time and space, of which
European thinkers are only now, in the twentieth century of
the Occident's as yet unbroken Dark Age, beginning to catch
glimpses.

IV. The Nature of Mind

Correlatively, a few of the more adventurous of those who
indomitably battle against Ignorance in the occidental world
are prepared to postulate as scientific another of the long-
accepted axioms of their oriental brethren in scientific research,
namely, that mind and matter are, in their final analysis,
indistinguishable, matter being, as the ' *Yoga* of Knowing the
Mind' also implies, merely what may be called a crystalline or
illusory aspect of mind concretely manifested.[1] Of mind *per se*,
concerning which the Occident has no clear, if any, conception whatsoever, our text teaches:

In its true state [of unmodified, unshaped primordialness], mind
is naked, immaculate; not made of anything, being of the Voidness; clear, vacuous, without duality, transparent; timeless, uncompounded, unimpeded, colourless [or devoid of characteristic];
not realizable as a separate thing, but as the unity of all things,
yet not composed of them; of one taste [i.e. of the Voidness,
Thatness, or Ultimate Reality], and transcendent over differentiation.

From the standpoint of Western Science, particularly of
dynamics and physics, the One Mind is the unique root of
energy, the potentiality of potentialities, the sole dynamo
of universal power, the initiator of vibrations, the unknown
source, the womb whence there come into being the cosmic
rays and matter in all its electronic aspects, as light, heat,
magnetism, electricity, radio-activity, or as organic and inorganic substances in all their manifold guises, visible and
invisible, throughout the realm of nature. It is thus the maker
of natural law, the master and administrator of the Universe,
the architect of the atom and the builder therewith of world
systems, the sower of nebulae, the reaper of harvests of

[1] See *Tibetan Yoga and Secret Doctrines*, pp. 16-17.

universes, the immutable store-house of all that has been, is now, and ever shall be.

The One Mind, as Reality, is the Heart which pulsates for-ever, sending forth purified the blood-streams of existence, and taking them back again; the Great Breath, the Inscrut-able Brahman, the Eternally Unveiled Mystery of the Mys-teries of Antiquity, the Goal of all Pilgrimages, the End of all Existence.

When, as the text teaches, mind attains its True State, divested of its robes of illusion, and is naked, it is, like the Brahman, the Quiescent. Then, as temporarily in dreamless sleep or in *samādhi*, like a child that has cast aside its toys, it is transcendent over appearances, over the Cosmos as a whole. For mind in its nakedness, the world, dissolved like a dream by the Full Awakening, ceases to exist. Hence it is that when the world ceases to exist, so do time and space, they being of the same illusory nature as is the mundaneness of mind. Even as in the *Sangsāra*, time is illusorily divided into past, present, and future, or is seen severally rather than as a unity, so mind is divided into the multiplicity of finite minds. Although the Sun may shine in each of a thousand rooms of a palace, its unity is not affected; although the One Mind illuminates the innumerable myriads of finite minds, it remains inseparably a unit. Nor does the One Mind contain any thought such as men know. Although it contains all things, yet it is no thing. It comprises all existences, but has no existence.

If the One Mind partook of the essence of time, it would be subject to transitoriness and dissolution. If it partook of the essence of thought, it would not be the Quiescent. If it were a thing, it would not be the transcendent totality of things. If it were of the essence of existences, it would be subject to birth and death.

It is, therefore, the intellectually Unknowable, the Essen-tiality, or Thatness, of which the *Sangsāra* partakes and by virtue of which it has illusory, or relative, but not real existence.

The microcosmic mind, being the offspring of the Macro-cosmic Mind, may, by process of *yoga*, attain ecstatic consciousness of its parental source and become one with it in essence. The drop may merge in the ocean. Whether the drop ceases to be a drop, whether the ocean is to be regarded as being constituted of individualized drops or as being one undifferentiated mass of water, no man can tell until the at-one-ment has come; and then, being no longer man, for him, or for that microcosmic fraction of consciousness through which he once manifested as man, the Cosmos has ceased to exist, has vanished like a dream or like a mirage.

Concerning this ultimate problem, the *Guru* Prince Shri Singha, of ancient Pegu in Burma, declared to his disciple Padma-Sambhava, 'No one yet hath discovered either the Primary Cause or the Secondary Cause. I myself have not been able to do so; and thou, likewise, thou Lotus-Born One, shalt fail in this.'[1]

How then can man, so long as he is man, solve the riddle of existence? The wisest of the *Gurus*, the Buddhas, tell us that it is only by transcending human existence, by rising above the mists of appearances into the Clear Light of Reality, and *sangsārically* ceasing to exist. Man cannot solve the problem of why he is fettered to existence until he recovers consciousness of the preceding state of freedom. If, like a prisoner long immured to a prison, he has no desire to attain freedom, he will continue in bondage indefinitely. If he no longer remembers anything of a preceding state of freedom, and, therefore, believes that there is no such state, he will continue to fix his hopes upon a worldly Utopia until suffering and disillusionment have, after long ages, performed their purpose and stirred in him that Divine Wisdom, that 'true Light, which lighteth every man that cometh into the world'. Then, like one who has lost his way in a wilderness, he will regain the Path.

Paradoxically, as every Great Teacher has taught, it is only by losing one's life that one finds life more abundantly; it is only by ceasing to exist that one transcends existence; it is only when the microcosmic becomes one with the macrocosmic that existence and the cause of existence are knowable.

[1] Cf. the Epitome, p. 134.

In the same metaphorical language which the late Sri Ramana Mahārshi of Tiruvannamalai employed to describe the quest of the Absolute, or Transcendent *Ātman*, of the Brāhmins, the parallel quest of the Absolute of the Mahāyāna may also be described: 'Just as a pearl-hunter, aided by heavy stones tied to his feet, dives to the bottom of the ocean and secures the precious pearl, so should man, aided by indomitable will, dive deep within himself and secure the most precious of all jewels.'[1]

Realization of the One Mind, through introspectively attaining understanding of the true nature of its macrocosmic aspect innate in man, is equivalent to the attainment of the Brāhmanical *Moksha* (or *Mukhti*), the Mahāyāna *Nirvāṇa*, the Full Awakening of Buddhahood.

V. INDIVIDUALIZED AND COLLECTIVE MIND

Unenlightened man, being far from the Full Awakening, believes himself to be possessed of an individualized mind uniquely his own; and this illusion-based belief has given rise to the doctrine of soul. But the Tibetan Teachers declare that the One Cosmic Mind alone is unique; that, on each of the incalculable myriads of life-bearing orbs throughout space, the One Cosmic Mind is differentiated only illusorily, by means of a reflected, or subsidiary, mind appropriate to, and common to, all living things thereon, as on the planet Earth.

Though there be but a single speaker, his voice may be broadcasted to all the millions of Earth's inhabitants and be heard by each of them individually. Though there be but a single power-house, everywhere throughout the wide confines of a metropolitan city there are electric lights. Though there be but a single sun of a planetary system, innumerable are its rays, giving light and vitality to every one of the multitudinous living things on all its planets. From one cloud fall countless drops of rain.

---

[1] See pp. 71–72, following; also *Who Am I?* (p. 10) there referred to. The Editor had the privilege of residing in the Mahārshi's *Āshrama* at Tiruvannamalai for a time during the early part of the year 1936 and of daily sitting at his feet then. Grateful acknowledgement is here made of the Mahārshi's kindly assistance.

Similarly, mankind are a unit of mental illusions. If men were not mentally one, there would be no collective hallucination of the world. If each microcosmic manifestation of mind in each apparently individualized being were a separate mind, it would have its own distinctive illusory world; no two men would see the world the same. It is because mankind's minds, or consciousnesses, are collectively one that all mankind see the same world of phenomenal appearances, the same mountains, the same rivers and oceans, the same clouds and rainbows, the same colours, hear the same sounds, smell the same odours, taste the same tastes, and feel the same sensations.

Thus, there is the illusory one mind, conscious and unconscious, common to all human beings, and in which all sub-human creatures of the Earth share. Upon this collectivity of mind, man's sciences are based; it gives uniformity and continuity to all human knowledge.

This illusory one mind, common to all mankind, in its conscious and unconscious aspects, directs mankind's activities and shapes all mankind's concepts. In its unconscious motivation, it controls the unitary instinct governing the life of a beehive, or of an ant colony, or flock of birds, or herd of wild animals. In its lower, or brutish, aspects, it manifests itself in the oneness of the irrational thinking and behaviour of a rioting mob.

Earth's multitude of human and sub-human creatures, each of them like a single cell, collectively constitute the body of one multicellular organism, mentally illuminated by the One Cosmic Mind. We are, as St. Paul perceived, all members of One Body; or, as the Mahāyāna likewise teaches, other and self are identical. It is because of what the Buddha designates as Ignorance, or lack of right seeing into the facts of incarnate being, that mankind fail to practise the Golden Rule. Instead of mutual helpfulness, or co-operation, we behold man's inhumanity to man, his wars amongst the members of his own body, against himself.

It is only by transcending man's collective hallucination, the hereditary and racial Ignorance which fetters man to the

illusory, the transitory and the lowly, that the Seers behold
the absolute at-one-ment not only of mankind and of every
living thing here on the planet Earth, but of the Cosmos, as a
whole. Behind all these illusory appearances, behind all personality, behind all mind and matter, man should seek the
undifferentiated Thatness, the Unborn, the Unshaped, the
Qualityless, the Non-Cognizable, the Unpredicable, beyond
what those fettered to Ignorance know as soul, or consciousness, or existence.

Nāgājuna and Ashvaghosha, the Patriarchs of the Mādhyamika School, named this beyond-Nature Reality the Voidness
(Skt. *Shūnyatā*); Asaṅga, the founder of the Yogāchāra
School, called it the Basic (or Root) Awareness (Skt. *Ālaya-
Vijñāna*), the all-transcendent consciousness of the One Cosmic Mind. To realize it is to attain *Nirvāṇa*, the omniscience
of One Fully Awakened from the Dream of Ignorance.

As our treatise on the Knowing of the One Mind teaches, it
is by knowing himself in the sense implied by the Delphic
Oracle that man *yogically* merges his microcosmic mundane
consciousness in the supra-mundane All-Consciousness; ceasing to be man, he becomes Buddha: the circumscribed becomes the uncircumscribed, the universalized, the cosmic.

So long as the dew-drop is individualized, it is subject to
many vicissitudes. It is petty, weakly, and without protection; its very existence is wholly precarious. The sunshine
may dry it up, the wind may disperse it, the soil may absorb
it, and it may cease to be. But once united with all other dewdrops, it attains the durability and mightiness of an ocean.
As the Guardians of the Great Path proclaim,

So long as the Sages have separate being, separate ideas, and
separate functions, they have but finite intelligence, and profit
only a small number of creatures; for they have not penetrated
into Buddhahood. But once entered into Buddhahood, they have
but one being, but one . infinite intelligence, but one unified
function, and they render service to multitudes of creatures
forever.[1]

---

[1] Cf. *Mahāyāna Sūtralamkara*, Levi's trans., p. 92; or J. B. Pratt, *The
Pilgrimage of Buddhism* (New York, 1928), p. 258.

VI. Wisdom Versus Knowledge

Before entering the path of the higher evolution leading to Buddhahood, the disciple must learn to differentiate Wisdom from Knowledge, the real from the unreal, the transitory from the non-transitory, the *Nirvāṇic* from the *Sangsāric*; and to this end the 'Yoga of Knowing the Mind [or Divine Wisdom] in its Unobscured Reality [or Nakedness]' is a guide. Mastery of its *yogic* precepts produces not contempt for the world of appearances, but understanding of it; not the egoism of Knowledge, whose realm is the *Sangsāra*, but the selflessness of Wisdom; not desire for self-salvation, but for the enlightenment of all sentient beings.

Accordingly, Tibetan Buddhism teaches that the lower knowledge, or worldly wisdom, is born of the bodily senses in their unenlightened *sangsāric* aspect, and that the higher knowledge, or supramundane wisdom, lies deep hidden in man, beneath its illusive reflections through mundane sensuousness, awaiting the magic touch of the wand of the *Dharma* to awaken. Thus worldly wisdom is imperfect wisdom, even as the moonlight is imperfect sunlight.

The *Kanjur* teaches that there are Eight Treasures of Learning: (1) the treasure of ever-present or innate learning, which, like its ineffable receptacle, the One Mind, cannot be lost, because indestructible; (2) the treasure of *yogic* learning, which develops the mundane mind; (3) the treasure of *yogic* reflection and meditation; (4) the treasure of learning to be retained in the mind after having been heard or understood, sometimes, as in our treatise, in the form of precepts or *yogic* formulae; (5) the treasure of fortitude in learning; (6) the treasure of secret, or initiatory, learning, or knowledge of the Doctrine; (7) the treasure of a *Bodhisattva's* saintly heart, born of indomitable faith in the *Tri-Kāya*; and (8) the treasure of spiritual perfection. The Absolute, or Divine, Wisdom (Tib. *Shes-rab*: pron. *Shey-rab*) itself is, according to the Mahāyāna, manifested or acquired in three ways: through listening to the *Dharma*, through reflecting upon the *Dharma*, and through meditating upon the *Dharma*. It is the *Dharma*, or Truth, which, transcendent over learning, teaches Wisdom, and trains the disciple to discern the true from the false, the evanescent from the everlasting, the urges of the finite human mind or intellect from the divine intuition of the supramundane consciousness, the eye-doctrine from the heart-doctrine.

Self-praise, born of pride of worldly learning, the disciple must avoid, knowing it to be one of Māra's poisoned arrows. The disciple should seek the Bread of Wisdom, of which the immortals partake; worldly learning is but the husk of the Wheat of Gold. Such knowledge as the world can give is transitory; it concerns only the external, the phenomenal. Divine Wisdom comes from the *Hridaya*, the Secret Heart; it concerns only the internal, the invisible *Sat*, the Real, the Noumenal, the Source. Knowledge is of the existent, Wisdom of the non-existent.

Wisdom dissipates the mists of illusion. Like its receptacle, the One Mind, Wisdom knows neither past nor future; it is timeless and eternal. Being of the Secret Essence of the Sun, it conquers the darkness of Ignorance. The Night flees before Wisdom, and the Day dawns. The wise reject Knowledge, but the ignorant hold it fast. Wisdom is treasured by the few, Knowledge by the multitude.

It is by the alchemy of Wisdom that the gold of life is separated from the dross. Knowledge nurtures the illusory, Wisdom the transcendent. Knowledge is treasured by those who, although alive, are dead, Wisdom by the Awakened Ones. Knowledge teaches of the Shadows and Obscurations, Wisdom of the Shadowless and the Unobscured. Knowledge appertains to the Mutable, Wisdom to the Immutable.

Those who tread the Wisdom Path transcend all the illusions of the world. To pleasure and to pain they are indifferent, knowing them to be but the two extremes of a dualism. They seek to exhaust their *karmic* attachment to Knowledge and to Ignorance of the Law. As one who was a disciple of the Tibetan *Gurus* has taught: 'Be humble if thou wouldst attain to Wisdom. Be humbler still when Wisdom thou hast mastered.'

Those who have possessed Wisdom have been the Teachers

of Men and the Directors of Culture. Those who have possessed only Knowledge have been the war-lords of nations and the creators of Dark Ages.

The aspirant for Wisdom must not become fettered by the false learning of men. The senses, the source of all the sorrow of the *Sangsāra*, must be *yogically* disciplined, and all misleading mental concepts be dominated. Personality must be impersonalized. Neither praise nor blame, success nor failure, good nor evil, are to be allowed to turn one from the course of those right actions constituting the Noble Eightfold Path. As the treatise itself teaches, the treader of the Path must pass beyond illusion's realm and reach that true state of immutableness personified by the Dhyāni Buddha Vajra-Sattva.

Apart from their all-embracing categories of Reality, wherein Knowledge and Wisdom were a unity, the Oriental Sages of old possessed no such classification of phenomenal appearances as that of modern Occidental Science. But today, understanding of the external world, with which our scientists are chiefly concerned, has come to be called Knowledge in contradistinction to that understanding called Wisdom with which the masters of *yoga* are concerned.

Knowledge is differentiable; Wisdom, transcendentally conceived, as partaking of the One Mind, is a homogeneous whole, incapable of differentiation. Knowledge is essentially utilitarian and mundane; Wisdom transcends utilitarianism and the concrete. Knowledge may be racial, or national, and is ever limited; Wisdom is universal, or catholic. Knowledge, being wholly dependent upon transitory phenomena, is fallible and illusory; it is the offspring of the Great Mother *Māyā*; it deludes man, and veils from him Reality. Its characteristics are, therefore, dependence and incompleteness; whereas those of Wisdom are independence and completeness; for Wisdom is the unique root and the at-one-ment of all understanding. It is Wisdom which enables the Sages to apply Knowledge wisely.

Knowledge, like human life itself, if employed aright, becomes, for occidental man, a pathway to the all-complete Wisdom; for him it serves as a light on the quest for

self-realization. But for the oriental *yogin*, the Pathway of
Knowledge is too full of pitfalls, too wearisome and long; by
what the Tibetan *Gurus* call the 'Short Path', he attains to
Wisdom first, and then, as from the heights of a great mountain, surveys the Kingdom of *Māyā*, which is the Kingdom
of Knowledge. Comprehension of noumena automatically
produces knowledge of phenomena. 'Who', the Tibetan
Sages ask, 'would be so foolish as to prefer a pellet of goat's
dung to the Wish-Granting Gem?'

As set forth above, it has ever been necessary for the aspirant after Wisdom to renounce Knowledge, to cleanse his mind
of all intellectualism preparatory to the incoming tide of that
knowing which, as Plotinus teaches, is above intellect. Unguided by Wisdom, Knowledge ever leads to bitter disillusionment, even as life leads to death.

Knowledge, being the product of utilitarianism, is the
foundation of the world's educational systems, designed
chiefly to prepare mankind for the parasitic exploitation of
the riches of nature and thus to enhance their own *sangsāric*
sensuousness. But Wisdom, as the Buddhas and Wise Ones
have taught, being born of world renunciation, of selflessness,
leads not to worldliness, but to *Bodhisattvic* Altruism.

Fettered to the Wheel of Knowledge, the race of men pass
from disillusionment to disillusionment unceasingly. Misled
by the will-o'-the-wisps of *sangsāric* sensuousness, few there
are among the millions of incarnate beings who escape the
quagmires and the mirages of worldly existence. Steeped in
Knowledge, unguided by Wisdom, they are overwhelmed by
pride; and not until myriads of lifetimes have been frittered
away in the worthless doings of *Māyā*'s Kingdoms do they
become humbled and seek for freedom. Then there enter
into the darkness of their animal nature the first rays of the
New-born Sun.

It is for those who have been aroused by the Light of Dawn,
who now hunger after Wisdom, and are prepared to put
Knowledge aside as being of no further use on the Pilgrimage,
that this book has been written.

Abuse of worldly learning leads to that destructiveness and

retrogression of which we who live in this century are the witnesses. Many of the forces discovered by Western Science have been harnessed more to the degradation than to the upliftment of man. Until Knowledge shall be transmuted into Wisdom by the alchemy of spiritual understanding, which sees that all things are one and that the outer laws of Nature are no more than emanations or reflexes of inner laws, man will remain, as he is now, in bondage to *Māyā* and Ignorance. The chief purpose of Science should not be to exploit for purely selfish and uninspiring utilitarian ends the forces of the phenomenal universe, but to investigate and so come to know and apply for social betterment the far mightier forces of the Atom of Atoms, present in man himself.

It is in Wisdom, not in Knowledge, that in future time man will, at last, discover Right Law, Right Society, Right Government. When his age-long quest for happiness in Knowledge shall have been abandoned as futile, he will find transcendence over sorrow in Wisdom. He will then have realized that in Wisdom alone is there true power; that Wisdom is the sole source of true progress; that Knowledge is the creator of Iron Ages and Wisdom the creator of Golden Ages.

The problem herein presented is a problem not for Europe and America alone; it must be faced by every Oriental who has grown intoxicated with the wine of westernization, by commercialized and Knowledge-loving oriental nations, as by all in Hindustan who have allowed the world-obsessing demons of politics and hankerings after the perishable comforts and pleasures afforded by Western Science to become their tutelary deities. In the Acquarian Age, as in this New Age now being entered upon, India, if she remains faithful to those Great Masters of Wisdom who have preserved her since prehistoric times, who have enabled her to witness the passing of Egypt and Babylon, of Greece and Rome and Spain, shall once more, phœnix-like, arise from the ashes of the present and, strengthened by realization of the failure of Knowledge, retain the spiritual leadership of the world. If she chooses Knowledge and ceases to cherish Wisdom, then shall history record her temptation and her fall. Then shall the whole

Earth, as never before in the annals of time, be conquered by
Ignorance and Darkness. The progress of humanity will be
retarded for centuries, perhaps for millenniums. Its great
cities, the strongholds of Knowledge, will become the grave-
yards of their builders. Barbarism will have conquered not a
race, a continent, or an empire, but the whole man-bearing
Planet. And not until those who seek to guide, but who
cannot guide when guidance is refused, send a new Messenger,
a new Culture Hero, shall the Sacred Fire be rekindled in the
hearts of men.

VII. ILLITERACY AND UTILITARIANISM

The subject-matter of the ' Yoga of Knowing the Mind in Its
Nakedness ' ends with the statement, 'Even a cowherd [or
an illiterate person] may by realization attain Liberation'. The
Great Guru himself, like the Buddha, having exhausted
literacy, and ascertained, as have all Sages, its non-essen-
tiality, did not insist upon it in his disciples. One of the most
successful of these was the illiterate cowherd Hūṃ-Kāra, of
whom our Epitome tells. Nor have all Prophets and Teachers
been scholars. Eminent Moslem authorities believe that
Mohammed was unable to read and write, and that he dictated the Koran under angelic inspiration. In his youth, he,
too, had been a shepherd boy, tending his flocks in the wild
mountains of Arabia, where he meditated and practised yoga,
and so attained divine insight. Although the boy Jesus taught
in the synagogue and confounded the learned, his training
was that of a carpenter ; and there is no evidence that He was
literate apart from the uncertain passage in the Gospel of St.
John (viii. 8), wherein it is said that with His finger He
'wrote on the ground'—whether in symbols, letters, or
meaninglessly is unknown.

Milarepa, Tibet's Great Yogī, when confronted by a proud
pandit, representative of the worldly arrogance of the intellectually learned, addressed him thus:

Accustomed long to meditating on the Whispered Chosen Truths,
I have forgot all that is said in written and in printed books.

Accustomed, as I've been, to study of the Common Science,
Knowledge of erring Ignorance I've lost.

·   ·   ·   ·   ·

Accustomed long to keep my mind in the Uncreated State of
    Freedom,
I have forgot conventional and artificial usages.

·   ·   ·   ·   ·

Accustomed long to know the meaning of the Wordless,
I have forgot the way to trace the roots of verbs and source of
    words and phrases;
May thou, O learned one, trace out these things in standard
    books.[1]

To most Occidentals, illiteracy is regarded as a most fright-
ful evil. This is due, in large measure, to their bondage to
appearances, their educational systems being almost wholly
utilitarian and directed to the production of material things
—many of which are quite unnecessary for true progress
—and to the exploitation of the Earth's natural resources
rather than to the knowing of man *per se*. Oriental thinkers,
who long ago realized the short-comings of literacy un-
directed by spiritual insight, have always maintained that
one need not be able to read and write or hold academic
degrees in order to attain the truly Higher Education. The
Editor, in his own world-wide study of humanity, has found
many of the noblest and wisest men and women wholly illiterate. He has intimately known illiterate peasants in remote
parts of Eire, in the western Hebrides, on the Continent of
Europe, in Egypt, Ceylon, India, Tibet, and China who were
better thinkers and more cultured than most graduates of
colleges and universities. The two French peasant girls, Joan
of Arc, and Bernadette Soubirous to whom the Lady of Lourdes
appeared, are illustrations, out of many in all ages and faiths,
of how spiritual power is transcendent over what men proudly
call 'education' and 'culture'. St. Catherine of Siena, too,
was an illiterate daughter of the people, who attained spiritual
illumination after three years of *yogic* retreat and meditation

---

[1] For the full narrative, see *Tibet's Great Yogī Milarepa* (pp. 244 ff.),
which illustrates, as a whole, the remarkable results of the practical application of the teachings set forth in our present volume.

and then returned to the world and dominated the political life of Italy.

The Occident is as misdirected educationally as it is socially and economically. The chief purpose of occidental education and government appears to be to foster economic prosperity by continually increasing unnecessarily the wants of the people, and thus to keep factories occupied. Naturalness, and that dignified simplicity of the Simple Way of Lao-tze, which Thoreau, Lao-tze's American disciple, taught, without any apparent effect other than academic upon Americans, survive only in inaccessible regions of 'lost horizons', and largely among such as are illiterate cowherds and peasants.

Education, as conceived in the Occident, results in not much more than an increase of international economic competitiveness, more and more utilitarianly applied science, largely directed to destructiveness and war, and mechanical devices intended to increase animal comfort. And occidental progress implies ever new creation of fresh fetterings to appearances, to *māyā*, to unreality.

Occidental 'education', whether called 'higher' or 'lower', is, in fact, as the *Gurus* maintain, merely training for the purpose of gaining a living, and, as such, should be regarded as the lowest; the truly Higher Education is directed to the one end of transcending appearances, to attaining a more satisfactory state than the human state of being. But until Occidentals believe that such a superior state is attainable, they will continue to exploit one another, and to strive after purely materialistic standards of 'education' and 'living' called 'higher'.

Unless Science, like Philosophy, is directed chiefly to human betterment, to raising the spiritual, along with the material, standard of life on Earth, it is not, in the oriental view, worthy the name Science. Thus, the true concern of chemistry should be, as it was when it was known as alchemy, the quest for the elixir of life in the occult sense, for the philosopher's stone which transmutes the human into the divine, and not for purely utilitarian ends, fostering selfishness rather than altruism. An astronomy concerned merely with the physics and mechanics of the Universe or with the calculation of celestial distances and the cataloguing of stars, and wholly neglectful of the application of astronomical knowledge to the end that man may be better understood in his relation to the heavenly bodies, as in astrology, is equally utilitarian and spiritually fruitless.

When, on the contrary, the Great *Guru* studied the science of the stars in its original form of astrology, he applied it to understanding man. Similarly, instead of undertaking any such intellectual pursuit as that which is entailed by the study of dogmatic theology, he practised the applied psychological science of *yoga*. He applied himself to arts and crafts not in order to win worldly wealth, but to acquire a better understanding of the worldly activities of men. His study of linguistics was not directed to philology, but to the comprehension of human mentalities, and to the reading of the riddle of existence by confabulating with gods and demons and other sentient creatures throughout the *Sangsāra*. He did not study systems of philosophy and *yoga* in order to become a *pandit*, but to master life. And, like Milarepa's, Padma-Sambhava's goal, in all that he studied under his many *gurus* on Earth and in non-human worlds, was not simply knowledge of the mundane, but, more especially, of the Divine Wisdom of the Supra-mundane. The Great *Guru* sought not intellectual power, but insight into Reality, beyond the *Sangsāra*, in the True State, in the vacuity of the Voidness.

Here again the late Mahārshi of Tiruvannamalai contributed independent confirmatory testimony: 'There may come a time when one shall have to forget all that one has learnt. Rubbish that is swept together and heaped up is to be thrown away. No need is there to make any analysis of it.'[1]

On behalf of Europe, Plotinus likewise testifies to the same truth, which, being realizable, and thus capable of proof, has been expounded by Seers during all epochs, in all nations, races, and faiths, in parallel manner:

Our comprehension of the One cometh to us neither by scientific knowledge, nor by thought, as doth the knowledge of other

[1] This recension is based upon *Who Am I?* (cf. p. 14).

intelligible things, but by a presence which is superior to science. When the knowing-principle in man acquireth scientific knowledge of something, it withdraweth from unity and ceaseth to be entirely one; for science implieth discursive reason and discursive reason implieth manifoldness. We must, therefore, transcend science, and never withdraw from what is essentially One; we must renounce science, the objects of science, and every other intellectual pursuit. Even Beauty must be put aside, for beauty is posterior to unity, being derived therefrom, as is the light of the day from the Sun. Accordingly, Plato saith that Unity is unspeakable and indescribable. Nevertheless, we speak and write of it only to stir our higher natures thereby, and so direct them towards this Divine Vision, just as we might point out the road to someone who desireth to traverse it. The teaching itself goeth only so far as is requisite to point out the Path and to guide one thereon; the attaining of the Vision is the task of each one alone who seeketh it.[1]

Plotinus thus demonstrates that Beauty, or Art (conceived as an emanation of the One Mind), is not of a primary nature, as is sometimes assumed in aesthetics, but of secondary nature and importance. This accords with the *yogic* view, as set forth herein in Section IX, entitled 'Good and Evil'.

It is not commonly recognized among Occidentals that there are methods of imparting culture other than through literacy, which, according to the *Gurus*, is the least efficient of all. Four methods are employed in the Orient: (1) through telepathy, or psychic osmosis; (2) through abstract symbols, such as *mudrās* made by the various members of the body, and *maṇḍalas* inscribed on the earth or painted on paper, cloth or wood; and also through concrete symbols, which may be geometrical forms, images, living animals and their effigies, the celestial bodies, and magically produced forms; (3) through sound, as in music or audibly expressed *mantras*, or spoken words, which are often whispered into the ear of the neophyte in initiations; (4) through written words, setting forth the secret doctrines, usually in symbolical and very abstruse technical and metaphorical style. The first method is the highest, the fourth is the lowest method of imparting the Higher Learning.

[1] Cf. Plotinus, VI. ix. 4.

VIII. THE GREAT *GURU*

In the following presentation of Padma-Sambhava, the
Great *Guru* and Culture Hero, there is no need to consider,
save in passing, sectarian criticism of him. Although some
who are of the Gelugpa, or Reformed School, which grew out
of the Nyingmapa School founded by Padma-Sambhava, may
be his critics, he is, nevertheless, reverenced by all sects of
Tibetan Buddhism ; and on Yellow-Cap altars, both in temples
and private homes, as on those of the Red Caps, and in all the
chief Gelugpa monasteries such as Sera, Drepung, and Ganden,
his image occupies a place of prominence, sometimes alongside that of the Buddha. In the Yellow Cap, or Gelugpa,
Monastery at Ghoom, in Darjeeling, for instance, while the
Editor was living just outside it, the Gelugpa artist, then
painting frescoes of various members of the Buddhist pan-
theon, took quite as much delight in painting the figure of
Padma-Sambhava on one wall as of Tsong-Khapa, the founder
of the Gelugpa School, in a corresponding position of prominence on the opposite wall. The criticism vulgarly directed
against the character of the Great *Guru* is considered at some
length in the Section entitled 'Good and Evil' which immediately follows, and that relating to his Tantricism receives
consideration in the next Section entitled 'Tantric Buddhism'.

The historic fact, that during the latter part of the eighth
century A.D. Padma-Sambhava was recommended to the King
of Tibet by some of India's most famous scholars as being the
greatest master of the occult sciences then known, is sufficient
attestation of the high esteem in which the Great *Guru* was
held by his contemporaries.

The King, Thī-Srong-Detsan, who reigned from A.D. 740 to
786, having accepted the recommendations, invited Padma-
Sambhava to Tibet to help in the re-establishment of Buddhism.
The Biography tells of the *Guru's* acceptance of the royal
invitation and of his departure from Bōdh-Gayā in December
of the year 746, and of his arrival in Tibet early in the spring
of the following year. The *Guru* spent a number of years in
Tibet; the Biography, typically oriental in its exaggeration

of numbers, states that he passed III years there. At all
events, he supervised the building of the first Buddhist
monastery in Tibet, that at Sāmyé, overthrew the ancient
ascendency of Tibet's shamanistic pre-Buddhist religion
known as the Bön (or Bön-pa), and firmly established the
Tantric or deeply esoteric form of Tibetan Buddhism. As
a direct result of Padma-Sambhava's efforts, the people
of Tibet were elevated from a state of barbarism to a state of
unsurpassed spiritual culture. He is, therefore, truly one of
the greatest of the world's Culture Heroes.

His less critical devotees generally regard the strange stories
told of him in the Biography as being literally and historically
true; the more learned interpret them symbolically. And the
anthropologist observes that the historic Padma-Sambhava,
like the historic King Arthur, is barely discernible amidst the
glamour of legend and myth. As a master of miracles, Padma-
Sambhava resembles the famous Pythagorean, Apollonius of
Tyana (who died about A.D. 96); and there appears to be no
good reason for doubting the adeptship in magic of either hero.
Precisely like Apollonius, Padma is credited with having
understood the languages of men and of beasts, and with
ability to read their most secret thoughts. Both heroes alike
dominated demons, resuscitated the dead, and, in all their
supernormal deeds, strove to deliver the unenlightened from
Ignorance. Having been white magicians, their aim was
always altruistic and productive of good. There is probably
no miracle attributed to Jesus or the Apostles which Apollonius, like Padma, could not perform.[1] Greek and Roman

---

[1] As the late Lāma Kazi Dawa-Samdup contended, Christian theology
is open to criticism for its insistence upon the paramount importance of
miracles in the life of Jesus, whom the Lāma regarded as being a Great
Yogī and *Bodhisattva*. Partly because of this insistence, modern sages of the
Orient say that Christianity, as interpreted by Church Councils, is representative of a purely exoteric religion. In this connexion they refer to its
animistic teachings concerning the soul, its range of vision limited to the
Sangsāra (i.e. to Earth, Heaven, and Hell), and its lack of any doctrine (such
as Gnostic Christianity, which it has decreed to be heretical, did hold) concerning transcendence over this purely *sangsāric* eschatology comparable
with the Brāhmanical *Moksha* or the Buddhist *Nirvāṇa*. And in their view,
the performance of miracles—as Jesus Himself implied by saying that His
followers would do greater things than He had done—is no proof, as it is

accounts of moving and speaking images find parallels in the Biography.[1] Even the striking of a rock with a staff, resulting in the immediate issuance of water, quite after the manner of the water-miracle performed by Moses, is credited to Padma. According to trustworthy tradition and accounts of modern travellers who have visited the place, the water continued flowing and still issues from the rock to this very day.

The date of the Great *Guru's* appearance, as a babe in the midst of the lotus on the Dhanakosha Lake, cannot be stated with historical accuracy. One of the prophecies, mentioned in our Epitome of the Biography, would make the date to be twelve years after the Buddha's passing, while other prophecies recorded in the Biography name various irreconcilable dates. On folio 333 of our text of the Biography, Padma himself is quoted as having said it was eight years after the passing. The Biography takes for granted the belief that Padma, having been immune to illness, old age, and death, is still alive and preaching the *Dharma* to non-human beings, that he flourished in the human world from the unrecorded time of his supernormal birth, presumably soon after the death of the Buddha, in the fifth century B.C., to the time of his departure for the land of the *Rākṣhasas*, 111 years after the date of his arrival in Tibet, or in A.D. 858.[2] The Biography attributes to Padma the statement that he had been alive for three thousand years; and in *The Prophecies of Guru Pema Jungnay* he is reported as having said, 'I uncovered the Chosen Truths, and, turning the sacred wheel of the

vulgarly assumed to be, of spiritual greatness; it is merely the *sangsāric* exercise of powers of magic, which is quite as capable of evil as of good. It was this miraculous aspect of Christianity which converted St. Augustine and proved to be the chief attraction for the emotional and irrational slave converts throughout the spiritually decadent Roman Empire.

[1] An adept in *yoga* can accumulate energy in his own body and, by a sort of wireless radiation, infuse it into an inanimate object, causing that object to move as he wills, just as an electric current, either with or without a connecting wire from an electric accumulator, can be conveyed to a machine and set it in motion. It is in like manner that a far distant *guru* transmits a current of psychic energy to encourage and aid a disciple.

[2] According to Tibetan chronicles, Padma-Sambhava resided in Tibet for about fifty years, and announced his approaching departure in A.D. 802. Cf. L. A. Waddell, *The Buddhism of Tibet* (Cambridge, 1934), p. 32[1].

Dharma, I made India happy; and there I lived for 3,600 years'.[1]

Learned *lāmas*, both of the Reformed and Unreformed Sects, believe that when the Buddha was dying He said, 'I will take rebirth as Padma-Sambhava for the special purpose of preaching the Esoteric *Dharma*'. This belief appears to be based upon a passage in the *Kanjur*, or the Tibetan Canon, to the effect that the Buddha when about to pass away was asked why He had not taught the Tantric Mysteries, and made reply that, having been born of a human womb, He was unfitted to do so, that He needed to attain superhuman birth in order to enjoy the pure body through which alone the Secret Doctrine of the *Tantras* can be revealed. He added, 'In the Heaven-Worlds I will convoke a vast assembly of the Great Ones, from the Ten Directions, and decision shall be taken as to whether or not the Tantric Mysteries are to be taught'. Accordingly, when the Buddha had passed on, the divine convocation was called together by Him; and the Buddhas of past aeons and many Great *Bodhisattvas* assembled and reached a favourable decision. And thus, as Tibetan Buddhists believe, the Buddha Gautama once more took birth on Earth, as Padma-Sambhava; and the tenth day of the fifth month of the Tibetan calendar is sacred to this coming into incarnation of the Great *Guru*.[2]

The supernormal birth of Padma-Sambhava from a lotus blossom signifies immaculate birth, that is, birth unsullied by a human womb. Such birth, so the *Kanjur* account implies, is essential to a Tantric incarnation or emanation of the Buddha Essence. Lotus birth is normal among *devas* in the

----

[1] This excerpt comes from fragmentary translations of the said work by the late Lāma Kazi Dawa-Samdup which the Editor recently discovered in the Lāma's notebooks.

[2] Although the Great *Guru's* day of birth is held to be the tenth of the fifth month of the Tibetan calendar, the birthday celebration has been shifted to the fifteenth day, because that is the full-moon day. This day, the fifteenth, is called by the Great *Guru's* devotees '*Jamling Chisang*', or 'The Blessed Day for the World'. Also the tenth day of the fifth month, the true birthday, and, correlatively, the tenth day of every month of the Tibetan calendar, are observed as the Great *Guru's* Day, and the Tibetans call it '*Tse-chu*', which means 'The Tenth'.—Lāma Karma Sumdhon Paul.

various *deva* worlds; and, although Padma-Sambhava is not the only one of humankind said to have been born of a lotus blossom, his devotees believe him to be the only Buddha so far born in that manner. Another marked characteristic of the Great *Guru*, as suggested by Illustration V, was his exercise of the *yogic* power, said to be still practised in Tibet, of shape-shifting, multiplication and invisibility of bodily form.[1] The description of the Illustration tells of the Eight

[1] The Tibetan belief concerning this *yoga* of dominion over bodily form may be summarized as follows:

Through transcendental direction of that subtle mental faculty, or psychic power, whereby all forms, animate and inanimate, including man's own form, are created, the human body can either be dissolved, and thereby be made invisible, by *yogically* inhibiting the faculty, or be made mentally imperceptible to others, and thus equally invisible to them, by changing the body's rate of vibration. When the mind inhibits emanation of its radioactivity, it ceases to be the source of mental stimuli to others, so that they become unconscious of the presence of an adept of the art, just as they are unconscious of invisible beings living in a rate of vibration unlike their own. Inasmuch as the mind creates the world of appearances, it can create any particular object desired. The process consists of giving palpable being to a visualization, in very much the same manner as an architect gives concrete expression in three dimensions to his abstract concepts after first having given them expression in the two dimensions of his blue-print. The Tibetans call the One Mind's concretized visualization the *Khorva* (*Hkhorva*), equivalent to the Sanskrit *Sangsāra*; that of an incarnate deity, like the Dalai or Tashi Lāma, they call a *Tul-ku* (*Sprul-sku*), and that of a magician a *Tul-pa* (*Sprul-pa*), meaning a magically produced illusion or creation. A master of *yoga* can dissolve a *Tul-pa* as readily as he can create it; and his own illusory human body, or *Tul-ku*, he can likewise dissolve, and thus outwit Death. Sometimes, by means of this magic, one human form can be amalgamated with another, as in the instance of the wife of Marpa, *guru* of Milarepa, who ended her life by incorporating herself in the body of Marpa.

Madame Alexandra David-Neel, who investigated these magical matters among the Tibetans, states that 'a phantom horse trots and neighs. The phantom rider who rides it can get off his beast, speak with travellers on the road, and behave in every way like a real person. A phantom house will shelter real travellers, and so on.' See *With Mystics and Magicians in Tibet* (London, 1931, p. 316, and throughout chapter viii), a work to which the Editor gratefully acknowledges assistance. Similarly, a master magician, such as the Great *Guru* was, can multiply his own or any other illusory form. Madame David-Neel herself, after some months' practice, succeeded in creating the form of a monk which followed her about and was seen by others. She lost control of it, whereupon it grew inimical; and only after six months of difficult psychic struggle in concentration was she able to dissipate it (cf. ibid., pp. 314–15). In like manner, 'mediums' in the Occident can, while entranced, automatically and unconsciously create materializations which are much less palpable than the consciously produced *Tul-pas*, by exuding 'ectoplasm' from their own bodies. Similarly, as is suggested by

Bodily Manifestations which were employed by him, according to need, to make most fitting appeal when preaching the *Dharma* to various types of men, gods, and demons. In the *Great Crown Sutra*, according to a version prepared by the late Mr. Dwight Goddard, the Buddha urges all Great *Bodhisattvas* and *Arhants* to choose to be reborn in the last *kalpa* (or creation period), and to employ all manner of bodily transformations for the sake of emancipating sentient beings. In the Biography itself the Great *Guru* is represented as being able to assume every conceivable shape, animate and inanimate. Our frontispiece, in colour, represents the Great *Guru* in his more ordinary form, as the royal Prince or King of Sahor. In *The Scripture Concerning Ti-ts'ang's Fundamental Promises* (Chinese: *Ti-ts'ang Pen-yüan Ching*) the Buddha says, as He blesses the multitudinous forms in which the *Bodhisattva* Ti-ts'ang, for the sake of saving others, has incarnated during many *kalpas*:

I constantly take various forms and make use of countless different methods to save the unfortunate. I change myself into a heavenly god like Brahma, into a god of transformations, into a king, a minister, or a relative of a minister. I manifest myself as a nun, as a man who devotes himself to Buddhism in the quiet of his own house, as a woman who gives herself to meditation in the stillness of home. I do not hold obstinately to my Buddha body. I take upon myself all the above-mentioned bodily forms in order to be able to rescue all [beings].[1]

As will be seen in the Epitome of the Biography, Padma-Sambhava was ever active, even as a child. His early life as a royal prince and his renunciation resemble those of the Buddha. In the beginning of his religious career he is the pupil rather than the teacher; he exhausts the learning of every type of human and non-human *guru*, and receives numerous initiations and initiatory names. Afterwards, in company with his *shakti* and chief disciple, Mandāravā, he is

instances of phantasms of the living reported by psychic research, a thought-form may be made to emanate from one human mind and be hallucinatorily perceived by another, although possessed of little or no palpableness.

[1] Cf. K. L. Reichelt, op. cit., p. 109.

shown practising *yoga*. More often he is represented preaching the *Dharma*. His mission in the human world takes him to all parts of India, to Persia, China, Nepal, Bhutan, Sikkim, and Tibet. At other times he is in non-human worlds, either being taught by Buddhas or teaching gods, demons, unhappy ghosts, and inhabitants of the hells.

In short, as stated in other words in the Introduction to the Epitome, around Padma-Sambhava are centred, like systems of worlds around a Central Sun, legends, mythologies, doctrinal systems, hierarchies of deities, and the root teachings of Mahāyāna Buddhism, aureoled by all the gorgeous glamour of oriental imagery. His field of action is the Cosmos; his religious mission embraces every sentient creature, in all worlds, paradises, and hells. Master of all human arts and crafts and systems of philosophy, an initiate of all schools of the occult sciences, perfect in *yoga*, transcendent over good and evil, immune to illness, old age and death, and not subject to birth, and thus greater than the Buddha Gautama, he is the idealized exponent of the Divine Wisdom practically applied.

So viewed, Padma-Sambhava is the world's supreme Culture Hero. Osiris, Mithras, Odin, Odysseus, Arthur, Quetzalcoatl, and the others equal him in some things, but not in all.

Much of the Biography is written in symbolical language, which, to interpret fully, would require one who has had complete initiation in all schools, exoteric and esoteric, of Tantric Buddhism, such as no known Occidental has had. The section entitled 'Tantric Buddhism' will illustrate this in more detail.

Consideration of the general and by far the most serious criticism directed against the Great *Guru* by those who disapprove of his Tantric doctrines, namely, that he advocates disregard for all commonly recognized standards of right and wrong, is reserved for the special Section entitled 'Good and Evil', where this charge is met at the necessary length. Consideration may here be given to the related and equally serious charge that the Great *Guru* was a slave to strong drink and that he advocated the use of wine among his followers.

Devotees of the Great *Guru* with whom the Editor discussed this charge, have replied:

Yes; it is true that the Precious *Guru* did drink to the point of
intoxication, and taught his disciples to do likewise. But the
liquor was the ambrosia of the gods, the elixir of life, the nectar of
immortality. They who quaff deeply of it become so intoxicated
that they lose all consciousness of the world of appearances.

In most images and paintings of Padma-Sambhava, as in
the frontispiece of this volume, he is shown holding in his left
hand a cup made of a human skull, symbolical of renunciation
of the *Sangsāra*, filled with this divine liquor, which he offers
to all who choose him as their *Guru*, bidding them drink of it
and so attain the Great Liberation. In Sūfism, as illustrated
by the symbolical poem of Omar Khayyām, wine-drinking
and intoxication have the same esoteric significance.

Parallel criticism is directed against modern Hindu Tantrics of Bengal. There are those of them who are of the Inner
Circle and those who are of the Outer Circle. To the former,
the latter are the uninitiated, the immature, awaiting enlightenment. Those who are of the Outer Circle, the exotericists, drink real wine, eat real flesh, and have real *shakta* and
shakti sexual union. But to those who are fully initiated, all
these things are done symbolically; for to them it is given to
know the Mysteries, but to them that are without it is not
given.[1] When the Great *Guru* was accused of conjugal irreg-

---

[1] Cf. Arthur Avalon (Sir John Woodroffe) *Tantra of the Great Liberation*
(London, 1913), pp. cxv–cxix. The aim of Tantric worship is union with the
Brahman; and, men's propensities being such as they are, this is dependent
upon the special treatment prescribed by the *Tantras*. Woman must be
recognized as the image of the Supreme Shakti, the Great Mother, and worshipped with the symbolic elements, by use of which the Universe itself is
employed as the article of worship. Wine signifies the power (*shakti*) which
produces all fiery elements; meat and fish symbolize all terrestrial and
aquatic creatures; *mudrā* (in this symbolism, parched grain) symbolizes all
vegetable life, and *maithuna* (sexual union) symbolizes the will (*ichchha*),
action (*kriyā*), and knowledge (*jñāna*), in relation to the Shakti of the
Supreme Prakriti (or matrix of Nature), whence arises that keen pleasure
which accompanies the process of creation. Thus there is offered to the
Great Mother the restless life of Her Universe.

'Wine' is said to be 'that intoxicating knowledge acquired by *yoga* of the
Parabrahman, which renders the worshipper senseless as regards the

ularities (as set forth on page 161, following) he forgave his critic, and thought to himself, 'Inasmuch as this fellow is ignorant of the inner significance of the Mahāyāna and of the *yogic* practices appertaining to the three chief psychic nerves, I should pardon him.'

Thus the age-old conflict between esotericism and exotericism still disturbs Buddhism and Hinduism. Islam, too, with its 'heretical' Sūfīs, the esotericists, and its orthodox exotericists, is disturbed by it. In Christianity it completely disrupted the primitive church. The Christian exotericists, derived largely from uncultured slave populations, inaugurated a religious revolution against the Christian esotericists, the cultured and well-born followers of the Gnosis; and, the revolt being successful, the exotericists used the church councils to anathematize the esotericists as a whole. Thus that form of Christianity which was shaped by the church councils of the triumphant revolutionaries, and which today dominates

external world'. Meat (*māngsa*) is not any fleshly thing, but the act whereby the *sādhaka* [or devotee] consigns all his acts to Me (*Mām*). *Matsya* (fish) is that *sattvika* [or pure] knowledge by which, through the sense of 'mineness', the worshipper sympathizes with the pleasure and pain of all beings. *Mudrā* is the act of relinquishing all association with evil which results in bondage; and *maithuna* is the union of the Shakti Kuṇḍalinī with Shiva in the body of the worshipper. This, the *Yoginī Tantra* says, is the best of all unions for those who have already controlled their passions (*yati*). According to the *Agamasāra*, wine is the *somadhārā*, or lunar ambrosia, which drops from the *brāhmarandra*. *Māngsa* (meat) is the tongue (*mā*), of which its parts (*angsha*) are speech; the *sādhaka*, by 'eating' it, controls his speech. *Matsya* (fish) are those which are constantly moving in the two rivers of *Idā* and *Pingalā*. He who controls his breath by *prānāyāma*, 'eats' them by *kumbhaka* [retention of breath in *prānāyāma*]. *Mudrā* is the awakening of knowledge in the pericarp of the Great *Sahasrāra* Lotus, where the *Atmā*, like mercury, resplendent as ten thousand suns, and deliciously cool as ten million moons, is united with the Devi Kuṇḍalinī. The esoteric meaning of *Maithuna* is thus stated by the *Āgama* to be 'the union on the purely *sāttvika* plane, which corresponds on the *rājasika* plane to the union of Shiva and Shakti in the person of their worshipper'. This union of Shiva and Shakti is a true *yoga*, from which, as the *Yāmala* says, arises that joy known as the Supreme Bliss (ibid., pp. cxv–cxix).

Thus the use of all these elements is sacramental, and their abuse is sacrilege. It is easy to see how they can be misused and result in orgies, as with those hypocrites who follow the 'left-hand path', in Bengal and elsewhere. But there are also those, less in evidence, who follow the 'right-hand path', for whom the Tantric method is a support to a life of virtual abstinence and, indeed, of asceticism.

Christendom, represents chiefly the popular or exoteric tradition.[1]

Modern Christians, both within and without the Churches, who favour or follow the Gnostic tradition, are inclined to view much of the New Testament esoterically, the Gospel of St. John being for them evidence of the esotericism originally underlying Christianity as a whole.[2] Accordingly, holding to the symbology of the Mysteries of Antiquity, which was also that of the Gnostics, they interpret the wine-drinking of the

[1] Cf. G. R. S. Mead, *Fragments of a Faith Forgotten* (London, 1931), passim. The Editor is well aware of the contention of the Christian exotericists that Gnosticism is derived from pre-Christian sources and that its Christianized forms are essentially non-Christian. The same argumentation can be employed against exoteric Christianity itself, as St. Augustine has suggested; for there is no fundamental doctrine of the Christian Faith which is uniquely Christian, or without pagan parallel. Some of the outstanding elements or practices associated with the teachings of the Gnostics (or 'Knowing Ones'), suggestive of the esotericism which distinguishes 'heretical' Christianity from 'orthodox' Christianity, may be briefly outlined as follows:

(1) The view that the *Christos*, made manifest in the flesh in Jesus, is the mystical archetype of the Primal Man, the *Ā-dām*; that the *Christos* is innately present in all men and capable of being realized by them. In the '*Yoga* of Knowing the Mind', the Buddha, too, is said to be similarly innate and realizable.

(2) The doctrines of unerring cause and sequence in regard to thought, word, and deed (*karma*), and rebirth based upon these.

(3) A doctrine concerning divine hierarchies that constitute an unbreakable chain of being, of which man is a link; and the corollary teaching that ultimately all living creatures, members of One Body, will attain Deliverance by virtue of knowing the Mysteries of the *Gnosis*.

(4) A doctrine of emanations, or of the descent of the divine into generation, comparable to that of the Mahāyāna; and thus a doctrine of pre-existence, such as the learned Origen of Alexandria held to be Christian and for belief in which he was anathematized.

(5) A highly evolved mystical symbology.

(6) The use of *mantras*, or words of power.

(7) And particularly an eschatology (elsewhere referred to herein in another context) which, unlike that of exoteric Christianity, is supra-*sangsāric*; the exoteric Christian eschatology being entirely *sangsāric* because of the exoteric teachings that the human principle of consciousness does not pre-exist before man's birth, that man lives but one life on Earth, that after death man is destined to pass an endless eternity either of blissfulness in Heaven or of suffering in Hell.

[2] Cf. G. R. S. Mead, *The Gnostic John the Baptizer* (London, 1924), pp. 123–6, excerpts from which are incorporated in the annotations to Book II (p. 217[1]).

Lord's Supper in much the same manner as would Sūfis and the Tantric devotees of Padma-Sambhava. Many, if not all, of the miracles attributed to Jesus they also interpret Gnostically, including the wine-making miracle, which nowadays is often cited, when viewed exoterically, to justify the traffic in alcoholic beverages throughout Christendom, and the manufacture and sale for ecclesiastical revenue of rare liquors and fine wines by Christian monks.

It is, therefore, essential to a right understanding of the Great *Guru* that he be judged not from the viewpoint of his critics, whether these be of the Outer Circle or complete exotericists, but from his own viewpoint, which, as we are well aware, the overwhelming majority of those occidentally-minded will be prompted by their own peculiar social and religious psychology to question, if not reject outright.

In concluding this Section, the Editor quotes from matter dictated to him by one of his *gurus*:

It is unnecessary to give overmuch consideration to the opinions of the vulgar concerning the Precious *Guru*. The self-evident fact is that no one save a Great Master of *Yoga* could have written the ' *Yoga* of Knowing the Mind in Its Nakedness', the authorship of which is accepted as being his. No man of uncontrolled appetites and passions could have conceived such a supreme teaching. When, too, there is taken into account the historic fact that Padma-Sambhava, as the specially invited guest of King Thī-Srong-Detsan, was the first great teacher of the Doctrine of the Enlightened One to the people of Tibet, that he lifted them socially from crude barbarism to unsurpassed religious insight, that all sects of Tibetan Buddhists revere him, the Precious *Guru* cannot but be regarded as being one of the chief Culture Heroes and Enlighteners of our common humanity.

IX. Good and Evil

Padma-Sambhava, like all other Culture Heroes, Prophets and Teachers, has not been immune to the criticism, and, even in our own times, to condemnation by the unenlightened, as has been mentioned above. This has been due almost entirely to his utter disregard of social, moral, and dogmatic religious conventionalities or established codes of conduct based upon mankind's limited conceptions of good and evil, instances of which are very common throughout the Biography and our epitome of it. In order, therefore, that the Great *Guru* may be understood by his own standards of right and wrong, adequate consideration should herein be given to the Vedāntic, and, more particularly, the Tantric, view of Good and Evil.

As Krishna teaches in the *Bhagavad-Gītā*, life is a conflict between two opposing forces, good and evil; or, as the *Mahābhārata* esoterically implies, between light and darkness, between Kuruvas and Pāndavas. The *Rāmāyana*, the other of India's two great epics, also tells of the same aeon-old struggle, between *Dharma* (or Righteousness), personified in the *Avatāra* Rāma, and *Adharma* (or Unrighteousness), personified in the demon-king Rāvana. In ancient Egypt the same teaching was set forth in the symbolical story of the slaying of the divine Osiris by his demon brother Set. The Great Mother Isis, viewing this mysterious tragedy inherent in the Cosmos itself, made dire lamentation. A parallel account of this conflict, in which all living things are *karmically* engaged, was dramatically represented in the Orphic Mysteries by the slaying of Dionysus Zagreus, symbol of life and regeneration, by his Titan brethren, symbol of death and destruction.

Or life is like a shuttle moving from right to left and from left to right unceasingly, carrying the thread of being with which is woven on the warp and woof of sensuousness, by each microcosmic consciousness, the *karmic* pattern. The Buddha, too, saw this continuous oscillation, this heart-throb of Nature, this Dance of Shiva, the Destroyer and Regenerator, and of Vishnu, the Restorer and Sustainer, and the state beyond both, personified by Brahma. The Supreme State, the state of at-one-ment, is the supra-mundane state of transcendent equilibrium, wherein negative and positive become undifferentiated, wherein the two opposing charges constituting the atom merge in primordial unity, wherein neither good nor evil exists.

The Buddhist Tantricism of Padma-Sambhava, like Hindu
Tantricism, postulates, in harmony with these more ancient
teachings underlying all Tantric Schools, that good and evil
are inseparably one; that good cannot be conceived apart
from evil; that there is neither good *per se* nor evil *per se*. This
doctrine is expounded in the ' *Yoga* of Knowing the Mind in
Its Nakedness', particularly in the section entitled 'The *Yogic*
Science of Mental Concepts'. Therein it is said that 'the various views concerning things are due merely to different
mental concepts. . . . The unenlightened externally see the
externally-transitory dually. . . . As a thing is viewed, so it
appears.'

Hence, as the Great *Guru* himself teaches in the treatise,
life, being a fabric of correlative, interdependent, interacting
dualities, cannot be understood without knowing both aspects
of the dualities; and the Great Liberation is consequent upon
attaining that state of transcendence wherein all dualities
become undifferentiated Wisdom. Impartial judgement cannot be reached without knowing both sides of a question; and
evil must be philosophically understood and tested along with
good if man is to see life steadily and see it whole. No chemist
or physicist would fail to test every possibility of a chemical
compound or substance or of an energy. Much has been argued,
often unwisely, about white magic and black magic; and yet
all magic is alike; it is merely the way in which magical power
is employed that makes its usage good or bad. The supreme
law of the inseparableness, as set forth in this volume, of good
and evil, of white and black, of negative and positive, is too
often forgotten or else not recognized; and its non-recogni-
tion constitutes Ignorance (in Sanskrit, *Avidyā*).

Tantricism, in its higher esoteric reaches, of which Europeans have but little knowledge, propounds, as do all philoso-
phies, ancient and modern, based upon the occult sciences,
that the ultimate truth (at least from the viewpoint of man)
is neither this nor that, neither the *Sangsāra* nor *Nirvāṇa*, but
at-one-ment, wherein there is transcendence over all opposites, over both good and evil. From the One proceed all
dualities, and in the One they dissolve in undifferentiation;

and thus, ceasing to exist as dualities, they are realized by the *yogin* to be phantasmagoria, will-o'-the-wisps of the mind, children of *Māyā*.

It is perhaps not generally recognized that all Enlightened Seers, throughout the ages, teach essentially the same *yogic* doctrine as that of our present treatise. As Sri Ramana Mahārshi, the recently deceased sage of Tiruvannamalai, south India, taught, 'All scriptures, with one voice, declare that control of the mind is absolutely necessary for the attainment of salvation. Hence, control of the mind is the goal to be aimed at.'[1] And the Mahārshi summarized the *yogic* doctrine of good and evil thus:

There are no two such things as a good mind and an evil mind. It is one and the same mind. *Vāsanās* (tendencies) cause desires and attractions which may be at times good and at other times bad. The mind when influenced by good *vāsanās* is, for the time being, considered good, and, when under the influence of evil *vāsanās*, bad. However bad some may seem to be at times, they ought not to be disliked, nor should we conceive prejudice in favour of those that seem for the time being friendly and benefi-cent to us. Shun both likes and dislikes.[2]

Here, then, is a master of *yoga*, living until quite recently in south India, who had no knowledge whatsoever of our treatise, setting forth, as a direct result of his own life-long *yogic* re-search and ultimate realization, precisely the same para-mount conclusions as those reached by Padma-Sambhava nearly twelve centuries ago in north India.

Plotinus, too, teaches that evil is quite as necessary as good. 'Even evil', he says, 'is useful in certain ways, and can produce many beautiful things; for instance, it leadeth to useful inventions, it forceth men to prudence, and preventeth them from falling asleep in an indolent security.'[3]

So long as men are held in the bondage of appearances, so long will they use such terms as moral and immoral, right and wrong, good and evil, and enact laws to preserve virtue and

---

[1] Cf. *Who Am I?* (p. 13), a booklet summarizing the Mahārshi's teachings, published by his *Āshrama* in Tiruvannamalai, in 1932.

[2] Cf. ibid., p. 15.

[3] Cf. Plotinus, II. iii. 18.

to destroy vice; not knowing that all sentient beings are members of one body, even as the Christian seer St. Paul perceived; and that, therefore, whatever punishment be meted out to the one part cannot but affect all parts of the social organism. In this connexion the writer recalls how, when a student under the late Professor William James, he was taught that if even the most inconspicuous Eskimo within the Arctic Circle were to suffer pain or misfortune, it would inevitably affect, although unconsciously, every other human being on the planet. And the eminent psychologist illustrated his teaching by pointing out that if the tiniest pebble were picked up and placed elsewhere, even at a very short distance from its original resting place, the whole centre of gravity of the Earth would be shifted.

For these reasons, none of the Fully Enlightened Teachers have advocated, as do the unenlightened multitude, the infliction of suffering and death upon others. Throughout uncounted millenniums, even as now, the unenlightened, the world-fettered, have maintained that this doctrine of the Enlightened Ones is impracticable, that if society is to be held together there must be the jungle law of eye for eye, tooth for tooth. Because of man's failure to rewrite his legal codes in the light of Divine Wisdom, the world today is probably more given to serious crime, particularly in the legalized form of war, than at any epoch in known history. And, notwithstanding that humanly instituted laws have failed to make man good or brotherly or wise after all these millenniums, Ignorance remains unshaken. Inevitably, as the Great *Gurus* teach, what men sow in law-courts or on battle-fields produces ever new harvests; and the sowing will continue until they recognize, individually and collectively, the Higher Law of the Divine At-one-ment of mankind, irrespective of nationality, race, religion, or social status, and, equally, of everything that lives.

It was in order to show to mankind the method of overcoming their bondage to appearances, to mentally-fettering concepts of dualism, that the Buddha expounded the *Dharma*. He has been called the Fully Awakened One, because, as He sat under the Bodhi-Tree at Bōdh-Gayā, His spiritual insight was awakened from latency and He saw life as a fabric of dream illusions upon which men fix their gaze and become fascinated as though in a hypnotic trance. Among His disciples were those who had been murderers, bandits, harlots; and to none, no matter what their past deeds may have been, did He refuse guidance.[1]

When a certain youthful disciple was unable to attain mental concentration because of the haunting features of a beautiful maiden, regarded by him as the most beautiful of all maidens in the world of men, the Buddha, soundly scientific in His applied psychology, had the disconsolate disciple brought face to face with the still more beautiful maidens of the *deva* worlds; and, in the end, the disciple, guided by *yoga*, became thoroughly disillusioned, and recognized, as should all human beings, male and female alike, the folly of being mentally perturbed by illusory appearances.

Similarly, a modern *guru*, in India, had a disciple distracted by longing for a courtesan, who, being much sought after by the influential and wealthy, was quite beyond the disciple's reach. The *guru* prepared a special *mantra* containing the courtesan's name, and, going to the love-sick disciple, said, 'My son, I advise thee to enter into solitary retreat; and then, fixing thy mind upon the courtesan to the exclusion of all else, to repeat this *mantra* incessantly by day and by night.' After some days the *guru* went to see how the disciple was progressing, and found him to be completely cured; the disciple had attained the ecstatic vision of the at-one-ment of all living things and realized that he and the courtesan were, in fact, one and inseparable, beyond name and form.

Thus, by understanding, and sublimation if needs be, not by suppression uncontrolled by philosophy, the *yogin* is to

[1] The late Mahārshi of Tiruvannamalai, also unattached to good and evil, taught, 'Let a man's sins be great and many; yet he should not weep and wail saying "I am a sinner, and how can a sinner attain salvation?" Let him cast away all thoughts of being a sinner, and take to *Swarūpa-dhyāna* [a *yogic* practice of introspection like that set forth in our treatise and in the "Yoga of the Great Symbol"] with zeal; he will soon be perfect.' (Cf. *Who Am I?*, p. 10.)

attain indomitable control of mind. As the *Guru* Phadampa
Sangay concisely teaches,

Draw strength from the Unobstructed; let the Stream flow
naturally;
No suppression, no indifference should there be.[1]

The opposite and wrong method, as modern psycho-analysts
have lately discovered, leads to mental, physical, and psychic
disorders.

It is only by philosophically tasting life in its many aspects,
good and bad alike, that the wise man attains, through experience, the power, born of understanding and consequent
disillusionment, to transcend life. No *yogin*, Tantricism
teaches, should ever experiment with life unless guided by
Divine Wisdom.

A libertine is one who has neither any such guidance nor
any consciousness of the true purpose of human existence;
like a ship at sea without compass and rudder he fails to
reach the Other Shore. And, being a prey to the whims of
animal passion, he retards his super-animal, or spiritual, unfoldment and increases his bondage. If, on the contrary, he
were guided in all his acts, good and bad, by philosophy, he
would extract from life's experiences the Nectar of Immortality; and, at last, when the complete disillusionment and
awakening came, he would claim his freedom.

Discipline and self-control of mind and body must never
be abandoned. The *yogin's* aim should be to increase, day by
day, life by life, their efficiency, until all dualities disappear
from his mental vision of the world. Neither should he prefer
unrighteousness to righteousness; for, as the Noble Eightfold
Path suggests, it is easier for man, while striving after that
Nirvāṇic state wherein both good and evil are recognized as
nothing more than mental concepts, products of *māyā*, to
overcome the wrong by adhering to the right. But if, through
lack of right guidance, man has strayed into evil, he is neither
to be made an outcast nor put to death on that account; for,
no matter what his human character may be, he is inseparably
a part of the whole, and until all parts attain Enlightenment

[1] See the annotation to this aphorism on p. 247 following.

there can be no Perfect, or Complete, Enlightenment for any. The inseparableness of all living things is as natural as it is inescapable. When the devotee has realized this law of being, all striving for self-interest, even for self-salvation, is abandoned; and, in the Great Awakening, he automatically becomes one of the Order of Infinite Compassion, vowed to the sole purpose of helping to overcome Ignorance.

Viewing life on Earth in this wise, as a state wherein to know and so transcend both good and evil, and all opposites, the neophyte must neither be elated by success nor dejected by failure, for these, too, are merely another duality. Seeking nothing for himself alone, but striving for the upliftment of all creatures, he must follow the Middle Path, without attachment either to good or to evil, knowing them to be of the two extremes. As our text teaches, he must attain this transcendent state of at-one-ment wherein there is neither defilement by evil nor alliance with good.

Error will be inevitable, for he is still in the imperfect human state, far below the status of Buddhahood; and yet, having attained the human state, which is much in advance of the sub-human states, he must not live the brutish life but the life of the aspirant for Enlightenment. Deliberate choice of the life of animal sensuousness leads not merely to a stoppage of progress on the Path, but to retrogression which may require many lifetimes of *karmically* imposed suffering to overcome, if degenerative disintegration of the human personality is to be avoided. But should it be the neophyte's *karmic* lot to taste of evil that he may transcend it by knowing its illusory and, therefore, wholly unsatisfactory character, he must not become attached to it. Attachment to evil for its own sake results in criminality; and criminality is one of the most terrible of all impediments on the Path. Likewise, attachment to good because of fear of the fruits of evil-doing is also an impediment.

The Middle Path goes to neither extreme. The Buddha accepted the hospitality of a courtesan as graciously as He did that of a virtuous king; and He awakened both from their Ignorance. He knew that it is not external appearances, not

Ignorance-born attachment to evil or to good, not a state of sensuality or a state of virtue which really matter, the Goal to which He directs being the Deliverance of the Mind.

Not only actions, but thoughts, too, as emphasized in the *Bardo Thödol*, must be dominated. By keeping to the Middle Path of non-attachment, no thought appertaining to either extreme can take root and grow. On any other Path, thoughts, becoming fixed on evil, turn into an army of demons who make the pilgrim a captive slave, and for ages all spiritual progress may cease.

Although the pilgrim is already fettered to sensuousness, he should face it fearlessly, then understand it and dominate it, and transmute it. With all thoughts concentrated on the Pilgrimage and the Goal, every impediment can be surmounted. If habits born of ignorance-directed actions of the past, whether moral or immoral, exist, they will continue to be fetters until killed out. Vice cannot be conquered by acquiescing in it or weakly giving way to it, but by realizing its unsatisfactoriness, its purely *sangsāric* nature, its power to impede one's progress towards supra-mundaneness. Once recognized to be a barrier on the Path, vice becomes an incentive to the removal of the barrier and thereby a stepping-stone to a higher than human consciousness. Accordingly, vice dominated by Wisdom is equivalent to good giving insight into evil.

As suggestively set forth in the ' *Yoga* of Knowing the Mind in Its Nakedness', unless all ignorance-created barriers, whether regarded as resulting from good or from evil actions or thoughts, are removed through the exercise of Divine Wisdom, the pilgrim, unable to pass on, grows confused, and another incarnation ends in failure. Once again the icy winds of Ignorance have blighted the promise of the Springtime; and a new Springtime must be awaited beyond the Winter of death before new efforts can be put forth.

The external Universe, as a whole, with its hypnotic glamour, its sensuous enticements of sights and sounds, odours and other *sangsāric* stimuli, which result in what mankind call good and evil sensations, thoughts and actions, must be transcended; and the pilgrim must live in the inner silence of neutrality.

Even art, called a good by the multitude, whether pictorial, sculptural, musical, or dramatic, becomes an impediment if allowed to create sensuous attachment to the world. For this reason, the Prophet of Arabia, more completely than any other Teacher, prohibited all images or representations of the Supreme. Men, being spiritually unenlightened, degrade the supra-*sangsāric* by visualizing and depicting it in unreal *sangsāric* form; and thus, in the view of Mohammed, men by venerating or worshipping or even aesthetically enjoying the creations of their own unenlightened minds tighten not only their own fetters to the *Sangsāra*, but the fetters of the vulgar multitude who see the untruthful and misleading images and presentations. The Buddha similarly taught that it is not productive of enlightenment, but fettering, for mankind to take part in or witness worldly shows or spectacles or to be enamoured of music and dancing; and to the *Sangha*, in particular, He prohibited all such sensuous pleasures.

In this relationship, as in that of good and evil and of all dualism as a whole, the popular or accepted consensus of opinion is not to be followed by the neophyte. He is bidden to ponder such teachings as are set forth in 'The Precepts of the *Gurus*', and to realize that the Great Man differs in every thought and action from the multitude.[1]

The conception of death as an evil and the conception of life as a good, illustrate better than most other dualities the illusoriness of all mental concepts and of all dualism; for there is for the enlightened neither death *per se* nor life *per se*. The illusory phenomena of what the unenlightened call death and life are only moods or aspects of something which is *sangsārically* indescribable, that indestructible essence, microcosmically innate in man, capable of transcending both death and life and attaining what has been called *Nirvāṇa*. In other

---

[1] See *Tibetan Yoga and Secret Doctrines*, Book I. In this connexion, the Editor directs attention to Dr. Jung's sound and timely warning (set forth above, on p. lxii) concerning those who, ignorantly practising *yoga* in the Occident, fail, like the worldly, to attain that supreme moral indifference implied in *yogic* undefilement by evil and non-alliance with good.

words, death and life are, as concepts, modifications of consciousness in its finite or mundane manifestation, and in the state of the supra-mundane consciousness, or *Nirvāṇa*, they, like good and evil and all other *sangsārically*-conceived dualities, have no existence. It is, therefore, only mind in its limited finiteness that conceives of death as being an evil and of life as being a good.

Man dies daily when he sleeps, and yet he is not dead; and that death which comes at the end of every lifetime is merely a longer sleep than that which comes at the end of every day. The content of the nightly dream-state is, in large measure, and commonly, the product of the day-time waking-state; the content of the dream-state of death is, in similar degree, the product of the waking-state of life. And neither death nor life are either good or evil save as their percipient conceives and makes them to be so. Both equally are dream-states of the same *sangsāric* character and content, wholly illusory and unsatisfying. Whether alive or dead, unenlightened man is continually enwrapped in the Sleep of Ignorance; and it is the sole purpose of the Great *Guru*, transcendent over all dualities, as shown in his teachings in the 'Yoga of Knowing the Mind in Its Nakedness', to cause man to awaken.

No master of *yoga*, such as the Great *Guru* was, does anything merely to accord with the conventional standards of good and evil; for he knows that it is not the external aspect of an act, but the internal intention initiating it, which makes an act right or wrong. For illustration, an officer appointed to enforce law may be obliged to commit the same acts as those for which the common citizen is punished; in order to punish theft, society steals from the thief his personal liberty; in order to punish the practice of slavery, the state itself makes the practitioner a slave, condemning him to penal servitude without other wage than his bare maintenance, precisely as in illegal slavery; in order to punish murder, the state itself commits murder. In some instances, as in the employment of 'stool-pigeons' in the United States, agents of the state decoy suspects to commit punishable offences in order to arrest and convict them; or the 'third degree' method may be employed to extort confession, with excessive cruelty to the person, comparable to that of the Spanish Inquisition in its enforcement of ecclesiastical law. Thus, the acts of those who wilfully break the law are regarded as evil, and the same acts when performed by law-enforcement officers are regarded as good, the incentive behind the several acts being the determinant.

Speaking from the viewpoint of social psychology and anthropology, there is no socially, religiously, or traditionally fixed standard of morality historically known. What one age or religion or society has deemed right in morals another has decreed to be wrong. The history of European morals since the days of Plato (427–345 B.C.) records very violent oscillations from one extreme to another. And, seeing that man's progressive evolution from the animal status to that of the super-animal is far from completion, no moral standard among those so far tried by one society or another appears to be fixable. In illustrative substantiation of this, the instances which follow are applicable.

King Solomon, regarded by his contemporaries as the very incarnation of wisdom and justice, 'had seven hundred wives, princesses, and three hundred concubines'.[1] Polygamy was thus legal in his time among the Jews; and although, as the same text adds, 'his wives turned away his heart' [from the Lord], there is no account of Jehovah's having denounced the institution of polygamy itself. It is still legal among the Moslems, whose faith is based upon and evolved out of that of the Jewish people. Today, in most occidental countries, polygamy, or bigamy, is punishable by long years of imprisonment. When, in the deserts of Utah, the Church of Mormon of Latter Day Saints arose and began to practise polygamy after the fashion of the great men of the Old Testament, their fellow countrymen, who worshipped the same God, speedily enacted a constitutional amendment outlawing polygamy;

[1] 1 Kings xi. 3. There is, too, the esoteric interpretation which makes the 700 wives and 300 concubines to be personifications of human attributes such as feelings, passions, and occult powers, the Kabalistic numbers seven and three being taken to be the keys. 'Solomon, himself, moreover, being simply the emblem of Sol'.—H. P. Blavatsky, in *Lucifer* (London, Nov. 1888).

and now no immigrant is allowed entry into the United States of America if he favours or advocates a plurality of wives. In Buddhist Tibet, a plurality of husbands is legally allowable; in Christian England, a woman who claims more than one husband is chargeable with crime. Throughout Europe and the two Americas, adultery, though frequently sworn to in divorce courts and found very useful, goes unpunished; in Arabia it receives capital punishment.

In ancient Greece, by far the most cultured society yet evolved in the Occident, pæderasty was not only tolerated and legalized, as in Athens where contracts based upon it were recognized in courts of law, but it was regarded as having spiritual value, and attempts were made to apply it to social good. In the Dorian States and among the Spartans it was established as a martial institution. Throughout the Greek Empire it acquired religious sanction, as suggested by the symbolical sun-myth of Ganymede and Zeus and similar myths. It was widely sung by poets, and the great dramatists, Aeschylus and Sophocles, made it a subject of drama.[1] Then, about seven centuries later, Europe began to experiment with another theory of good and evil; and under Constantine (A.D. 288?–337) pæderasty became punishable with death. In A.D. 538, Justinian, believing that pæderasty was the direct cause of plagues, famines, and earthquakes, accepted Constantine's precedent as being thoroughly Biblical and Christian, and also decreed pæderasty to be a capital offence.[2] It remained so in most states of Europe until the time of Napoleon (1769–1821) who crystallized in the Napoleonic Code a revulsion of feeling against the inhumane codes of the Christian Emperors; and again there was change of moral standard. In the year 1889 Italy, too, adopted that part of the Napoleonic law relating to pæderasty, which, in England

---

[1] Cf. J. A. Symonds, *A Problem in Greek Ethics* (London, 1901), passim.

[2] Cf. J. A. Symonds, *A Problem in Modern Ethics* (London, 1896), p. 131, and passim. Justinian in the preamble to his *Novella* (77) states: 'It is on account of such crimes that famines and earthquakes take place, and also pestilence.' This serves as one, out of many interesting instances, of the unscientific influences which have shaped so much of modern European criminal procedure.

and the United States and a few other countries still under the influence of the older scientifically unsound codes, remains a felony punishable by long years of imprisonment or even penal servitude for life.

Thus, concomitant with change of religious, and, sometimes, social or political, outlook, standards of morality, or at least certain categories of them, also change. Given time enough, the change may be as much from left to right or from right to left as in parliamentary governments; and whether the change be designated as being towards right or towards left depends, as in politics or religion, upon party or church affiliation. Changes of this nature, as illustrated in our own generation by Soviet Russia, may be dependent, when religious and ordinary political influences are inoperative, upon personal opinions of governing factions, who arbitrarily, like ecclesiastical factions when in power, impose their opinions upon the governed. For instance, in the first enthusiasm for social reform immediately after the Revolution, the old ecclesiastically formulated laws governing sex relationships were abolished, even those penalizing homosexuality. Then, quite recently, there was a regression, parallel to that after the French Revolution; and what at first was regarded as right and legal became wrong and illegal.

Not only is there no one world-wide standard of right and wrong under which mankind live, but much the greater part of mankind are subject to two standards of right and wrong, that of their religion or church and that of their nation; and between the ecclesiastical and the civil codes of law there exist irreconcilable and far-reaching differences. Then, again, as between one canon law and another, such as that of Islam, of Hinduism, and of Christendom, there are far greater conflicts. Even within a single religious jurisdiction, where if nowhere else uniformity might be expected, there are numerous serious divergences, as, for example, between the canon law of the Church of Rome and that of the various non-Roman Churches of Christendom. This condition also prevails among antagonistic Islamic sects; and, to a certain extent, in Hinduism, as between one caste or religious school and another.

Thus, according to the moral standard of the Church of Rome, and also of that of the Established Church of Holland, marriage performed outside the pale of the Church is invalid, and the issue therefrom illegitimate. When the Dutch held Ceylon, their Church socially ostracized all Singhalese who were not communicants and declared them ineligible for public office and their children without legal status. In Spain, when the standard of good and evil of the Church of Rome was practically applied, with the Holy Inquisition as the enforcement agency, the effect on society was even more marked, for those who persisted in adhering to any other moral standard were legally liable to torture, mutilation, and death. Should the same standard of good and evil be applied today, in like manner, in any Protestant country, such as England or the United States of America, there would result a most disastrous moral-standard warfare.

Throughout Christendom itself there are three standards of morality, that of the secular state, that of the churches, and that of the Sermon on the Mount and the Golden Rule of the New Testament. The first, being based upon the law codes of the Roman Empire, is pagan; the second, being based upon worldly expediency and rulings of church councils and synods, is ecclesiastical; the third, being based upon the teachings of the Founder of Christianity, is Christian. Any one of these three standards of morality is incapable of being reconciled with another. In India, for instance, there is even greater disagreement as to what is right and wrong; for there are not only the three quite irreconcilable standards of the Christian community, but similarly conflicting standards of other religions, such as those of Hinduism, Islam, Buddhism, Parseeism, Judaism, and primitive Animism.

A still more striking illustration of the remarkable inconsistency between the theory and practice of what men call right and wrong, presents itself in the social phenomenon of war. In times of peace, the state penalizes forgery, perjury, theft, arson, destruction of another's property, assault and battery, and murder, and even threats to commit any of these acts; but in times of war it compels each of its militarily trained citizens, under penalty of death, to commit, wherever necessary for victory, any or all of them. It trains its cleverest young men and women to practise every act of deceit and dishonesty which may be required to obtain military secrets from neighbouring states, employing, when needed, any of the variants of eroticism and prostitution, including homo-sexuality ;[1] but if it apprehends similarly trained foreign citi-zens within its own territory, it either imprisons or shoots them. There appears to be no crime known to the underworld which a nation's secret service will not sanction, especially in time of war, for the purpose of outwitting an enemy nation. War, being an abrogation of ethical and cultural systems, recognizes no standard of good and evil.

If, as the *Gurus* teach, men would seriously consider these things, the illogical and impracticable nature of the moral standards of the unenlightened multitude would be self-evident, and human society would speedily advance beyond the mental status of brute creatures and transcend the law of the jungle.

Plato, the greatest of Greek Sages, spent many years in an attempt to define Justice, or what the Hindu Sages call *Dharma*. He recognized the evils of democratic governments, wherein it is not the right, or justice, which always prevails, but the will of the philosophically untrained vulgar majority ; and that it is fallacious to assume that the minority are always wrong. It is with these conditions in view that the *Gurus* teach that the great man is he who differs in every thought and action from the multitude. Accordingly, it has ever been the lone pioneers of thought, the sowers of the seed of new ages, the Princes of Peace, rather than the Lords of War, and the minorities (who may be the disciples of the Sages), that have suffered martyrdom and social ostracism at the hands of the majority, who impose their standards of good and evil upon the helpless minority.

It is, therefore, very unwise to accept without question, as is nowadays customary in many modern states where un-

---

[1] Cf. Dr. Magnus Hirschfeld, *The Sexual History of the World War* (New York, 1941), pp. 125, 239, 252, 258–64.

sound moral standards prevail, the verdict of the people, whether expressed by a jury in a court of law or through the ballot box, as to what is justice, right or wrong, good or evil. So long as mankind are more selfish than altruistic, the majority are unfit to dominate the minority, who may be much the better citizens. As both Plato and the Wise Men of the East teach, the democratic-majority standard of judgement as to what is moral and immoral conduct is unreliable.[1]

As the word *morals*, in the sense of *custom*, indicates, moral conduct, or morality, is that which any particular society has grown used to and so accepted as being customary. Accordingly, for certain societies infanticide, or head-hunting, or killing of the physically unfit and aged are a good, and for other societies an evil; and until all peoples agree upon uniform customs there can be no one moral standard. Without taking into account the motive initiating an act and the social environment in which the act is done, no right judgement can be reached as to whether any act is good or bad.

Mankind's various standards of aesthetics (which in many respects are inseparable from the standards of morality), in art as in everyday life, are as chaotic as those of good and evil. For instance, in classical Greece the consensus of philosophical opinion declared the human male form the most beautiful of all forms in nature; and now, in the Occident, it is, according to vulgar opinion, the female form which is held to be the most beautiful. Throughout India, naked holy men wander about in public, as the Great *Guru* did when so inclined, and are venerated; in Canada, when the devout Russian Doukhobors (or 'Spirit-Wrestlers') publicly appear in their natural state, they are forcibly clothed and hurried off out of sight to prisons. Images of Osiris in his phallic aspect, as Lord of Fertility, still stand in their original shrines

[1] It is not, however, suggested that the alternative is the modern dictatorial state, but rather a social order inspired and directly guided by altruistically minded leaders of divine insight and training in the science of right government, somewhat after the type of the Governors of Plato's *Republic*, transcendent over racial, national, religious, and traditional limitations, and ever striving for the federation rather than the dismemberment of the world.

along the Nile; the *lingam* (or imaged generative organ) of
Shiva is worshipped by Hindus today; and their temples
depict in sculptured stone what the *Kama Shastra* (or 'Treatise on Sensual Love') describes in words; and in the various
countries where Tantricism prevails, including Tibet, imaged
or painted representations of the *Shakta* and *Shakti* in *yab-
yum* posture (or father–mother embrace) are sacred. But were
any such products of oriental art to be permitted entry into
occidental countries, they would be kept under lock and key
and capable of being seen only *in camera*, and books describing them in language of the multitude would be labelled porno-
graphic, and not be available without apologetic request or
perhaps written permission from some superior person.
Marbles in the nude, from the classical age of Greece, which
adorn the Vatican Library and Art Gallery, at present wear
Italian-made plaster-of-Paris fig-leaves.

Those who pride themselves on their own peculiar racial or
religious standards of virtue and vice, right and wrong, good
and evil, thinking them alone infallible, resemble certain
members of the Younghusband military expedition to Lhāsa,
who wrote down in their diaries, and possibly still believe,
that the people of Lhāsa welcomed them with hand-clapping.
The people did clap their hands as the foreign invaders entered
the Holy City, but not to welcome them. Unknown to most
Europeans, handclapping is never by custom employed in
Tibet to signify appreciation; it is only so employed magically
to exorcize evil spirits and demons.

A very large part of the world's troubles is due to these conflicting standards of aesthetics and of morals. The soundest
standard of judgement of human conduct appears to be the
Great *Guru's*, based upon the intention of thought and action.

The theory that a good end justifies evil means is, as all the
Gurus hold, fallacious, because it assumes that good alone is
desirable, whereas that which is really desirable is neither
good nor evil, but transcendence, in the *yogic* sense, over both.
In the realm of nature, the negative is quite as necessary as the
positive. No universe could be constituted of absolute positive-
ness; if the atom lost its negativeness, it would not be an

atom. And thus, as Plotinus says, 'without the evils in the Universe, the Universe would be imperfect'.[1]

It ought now to be clear that, instead of there being, as is sometimes carelessly assumed, a fixed standard of morality or of aesthetics, even in any one nation or religious jurisdiction, there is universally a condition of chaotic confusion as to what mankind should or should not do or believe to be proper and right. Accordingly, it is incumbent upon the critics of the Great *Guru*, firstly to state from the standpoint of what moral standard they judge him, and, secondly, to show wherein that standard is preferable to each of the many other moral standards which govern human society at the present time or have governed it in past ages.

Criticism may very fairly be directed against Padma-Sambhava, as it is, by Buddhists who are not of his School, on the ground that a number of the strange deeds attributed to him in the Biography, or by tradition, are at variance with the Noble Eightfold Path and the Ten Precepts. His more learned devotees reply that the stories therein representing him in such light being wholly legendary and symbolical, as some if not all of them clearly are, really emphasize rather than oppose the teachings of the Buddha, as shown, for instance, by the humorous account of the slaying of the butchers, and that of the wine-drinking *Heruka* (on pages 138, 162, following).

It is, of course, not germane to this discussion of good and evil to consider the contention of the Southern Buddhists that their Pāli Canon is the only true canon, and that, therefore, the Tibetan Canon and all Buddhist *Tantras* are largely heretical. In the same way, it is not necessary to consider the similar charge of the modern Christian Churches that the Canon of Gnosticism is heretical, as they have decreed it to be. The devotees of the Great *Guru* do maintain, however, as the *Kanjur* account of the prophesied incarnation of the Lotus-Born One suggests, that he, being a Tantric manifestation of the Buddha Essence, teaches a more transcendental doctrine than did the Buddha Gautama; and that the

[1] Cf. Plotinus, ii. iii. 18.

Pāli Canon expounds a purely exoteric Buddhism, intended for the multitude, whereas the Tibetan Canon, which is largely Tantric, expounds, in addition, a purely esoteric Buddhism, intended for higher initiates. Hence, the moral standard of the Great *Guru* is also transcendental, although in strict accord with the *Dharma*, when viewed both exoterically and esoterically.

Evil, otherwise viewed, is that which impedes self-realization; it is that which inhibits man from transcending Ignorance and attaining the full enlightenment of Buddhahood. Accordingly, Evil has been personified as the Devil, as Māra, as the Tempter who makes the illusory so enticingly glamorous that, by a sort of hypnosis, he who beholds the deceptive glamorousness loses self-control, and is, as long as the spell remains unbroken by Wisdom, fettered to appearances, and incapable of extricating himself from the meshes of the *sangsāric* Web of *Māyā*.

The natural, or uncreated and primordial state, the *Nirvānic* state, being a state of at-one-ment with all that is, whatever prevents its realization is Evil and whatever fosters its realization is Good. But neither Evil nor Good being absolute, or real in itself, each is no more than a state of consciousness, the one making for attachment to the transitory, the other making for freedom from the transitory. When this freedom has been attained, both Good and Evil have lost their purpose and become inoperative; they are transcended, and the freed one has attained the state beyond Good and Evil, beyond all opposites, which exist and operate only in the *Sangsāra*.

Because Evil is an impediment and Good an assistance to the attainment of the Full Awakening, all Great Teachers have taught of the need for virtuous conduct, not as an end in itself, any more than the mere physical training of an athlete is an end in itself, but only as a means to an end far greater than itself. And just as chastity is essential to the gaining of spiritual insight into reality, although, likewise, only a means to that end, it, too, is inculcated for all disciples who would tread the path to freedom from *sangsāric* existence, from the lowly condition of attachment to the world and animal sensuousness; and is, in this aspect, Good, while licentiousness is, for the opposite reasons, Evil.

The Noble Eightfold Path, or the Sermon on the Mount, or any other system of right conduct, is not merely a category of so many apparently restrictive rules, but an efficient and long-tested method for evolving beyond the human state and attaining the *Nirvāṇic* state. A boat is necessary only so long as there is a body of water to be traversed, and spiritual disciplines are necessary only so long as there is Enslavement; when Emancipation has been attained, there is no longer any path to be trodden nor any commandments to be kept: one more pilgrim has reached the Other Shore.

If he who dwells in the Valley of Ignorance should aspire to climb to the summit of the Mountain of Enlightenment, he must begin at the mountain's base, and, laboriously, step by step, enduring fatigue and perhaps despondency, advance to the goal. And once he stands on the summit, the compass, which guided him through the mists and clouds, and the Alpine staff, which supported his footsteps and gave to him assurance against dangers, may be cast aside; these were, at the outset, necessary, now they have become unnecessary. When the end has been attained, the means may be discarded. So it is with Good, or Virtue, or rules of right conduct when the Great Consummation of incarnate existence on Earth has been realized.

Good and Evil are the two-forked trunk of the Tree of Life, sprung from a single Seed. Each fork alike has its support in the root-system of the One Tree. The same sap flows to and nourishes both forks equally.

Or Good and Evil may be viewed as being like twins, offspring of one Father–Mother. They are compensatory, the one to the other, like the right and left ventricles of the heart. They are the two hands doing the work of the Cosmic Body, the two feet by which humanity traverses the Highway of Life leading to the City of *Nirvāṇa*. If either be amputated, there is crippling. Virtue of itself leads to good results, vice to evil results. The Sage who knows both Good and Evil to be one and inseparable is transcendent over both. It is only in the *Sangsāra* that opposition is operative. In the Beyond-Nature, in the Voidness, there is but the Unmodified, the Primordial, the Unformed, the Unmade, the Unborn, the All-Embracing Womb whence comes forth into being the manifested Universe. The *Dharma*, or the Supra-mundane Law of the Cosmos, enthroned upon the Immutable Throne of *Karma*, crowned with the Double Crown of the Two Opposites, holding the Sceptre of At-one-ment, robed in the gold and purple robes of Justice, guides all sentient creatures to Understanding and Wisdom by means of Good and Evil.

This Section, which is necessarily the longest and in some respects the most important part of this Introduction, will be fittingly concluded by summarizing in a tenfold category the essentialities of the moral standard of the Oriental Sages, by which alone the Great *Guru* should be judged:

(1) Good and Evil, when viewed exoterically, are a duality, neither member of which is conceivable or capable of mentally existing independently of the other. Being thus inseparable, Good and Evil, when viewed esoterically, are intrinsically a unity.

(2) A thing is considered to be either good or evil in accordance with the mental state in which it is viewed, the state itself being determined by racial, social, or religious environment and heredity. Otherwise stated, as by Shakespeare, 'there is nothing either good or bad, but thinking makes it so'.[1]

(3) There being nothing which has other than an illusory existence in the mundane mind, nothing can be said to be either good or evil *per se*.

(4) Inasmuch as it is the motive and intent initiating an act which determines its character, no act, in itself, can be either good or evil; for the same act when performed independently by two persons, one with altruistic the other with selfish motive and intent, becomes both good and evil.

---

[1] Cf. *Hamlet*, II. ii. 245.

(5) There being nothing which is good *per se* or evil *per se*, Good and Evil, like all dualities, are hallucinatory concepts of the *sangsārically* constituted mind of their percipient. As such, like the world of appearances (which is merely a conglomerate of *sangsāric* concepts), they have only a relative, not an absolute, or true, existence.

(6) Hence, doctrines concerning a state of absolute evil called Hell and a state of absolute good called Heaven, being based entirely upon *sangsārically*-born concepts, are also entirely relative and illusory; *Nirvāṇa* is beyond good and evil.[1]

(7) Accordingly, all standards of morality founded upon any such doctrines are unstable; and, like the *Sangsāra* itself, by which they are circumscribed, from which they arise, and upon which they are dependent for their illusoriness, they are ever-changing and transitory, like the mundane mind of their creators and advocates, and, therefore, unsatisfactory and unfixable.

(8) Not until mankind shall transcend dualism and phenomenal appearances, and realize the natural at-one-ment of all living creatures, will they be able to formulate a sound standard of morality.

(9) Such a standard will be based entirely, not partially, as are prevailing standards of morality, upon world-wide *Bodhisattvic* altruism.

(10) Its Golden Rule may be stated thus: 'Do unto others and to yourself only that which fosters Divine Wisdom and will guide every sentient being to the *Bodhi* Path of transcendence over the *Sangsāra* and to the Final Goal of Deliverance from Ignorance.'[2]

---

[1] This is suggested also by Dr. Jung's Commentary, pp. l–li, above.

[2] The teaching, that men should do unto others what they would that others should do unto them, is capable of misconstruction, or misapplication, notwithstanding that its intent is obviously right. For so long as men are fettered to the *Sangsāra* and misled by its delusive glamorous mirages, and thus in bondage to Ignorance, they are quite incapable of knowing in what right action, either to themselves or to others, consists,

X. TANTRIC BUDDHISM

Padma-Sambhava, having come to be regarded by his many devotees throughout Tibet, Mongolia, China, Nepal, Kashmir, Bhutan, and Sikkim as being peculiarly a Tantric emanation or reincarnation of the Buddha Gautama, exercised a very profound influence on the shaping of Mahāyāna Buddhism; and this influence, in its own sphere of Tantricism, was probably as far-reaching as was that of Nāgārjuna in the shaping of the Doctrine of the Voidness, as set forth in the canonical *Prajñā-Pāramitā*.

Tantricism itself, in its two aspects, Hindu and Buddhist, is as yet too little investigated to make possible, at this time, incontrovertible or exhaustive statements concerning its origin, which, however, seems to have been exceedingly complex. According to some scholars who have looked into the problem more or less superficially, the Yogāchāra School, which originated under Asaṅga, a Buddhist monk of Gandārā (now Peshawar), in north-west India, presumably about A.D. 500, appears to have leavened the Mahāyāna as a whole. In other words, the method of attaining ecstatic union with the One Mind (or Absolute Consciousness), known as *yoga* (which Patanjali in his *Yoga Sutras* first systematized about the year 150 B.C.), being the basis of the Yogāchāra, *yoga* is, undoubtedly, one of the chief roots of Tantricism. From this point of view, we should, perhaps, be justified in defining Tantricism as being a school of eclectic esotericism based fundamentally upon *yoga* practically applied, both to esoteric Brāhmanism and to esoteric (or Mahāyāna) Buddhism.

Another of the peculiarities of Tantricism, which distinguishes it from all other living cults, is its personification of the dual aspects of the procreative forces in nature, the *shakta* representing the male (or positive) aspect and the *shakti* representing the female (or negative) aspect. As a direct outcome of this, there appear to have developed, within the Mahāyāna, the Vajrayāna and Mantrayāna Schools, which represent a blending with the earlier Yogāchāra School. By the middle of the seventh century A.D., when Tantricism was well established in India, both in its Shaivaic (or Hindu) and its Buddhistic form, the many Buddhas and *Bodhisattvas*, and corresponding Hindu deities and saints, were already being imaged there, each with an appropriate female energy or *shakti*; and that peculiar esotericism which is inseparable from Tantricism was already highly evolved. It was this form of Tantric Buddhism which Padma-Sambhava introduced into Tibet during the second half of the eighth century.

Then, as is believed, early in the second half of the tenth century, the Kālachakra form of Tantricism was more or less developed in northern India, Kashmir, and Nepal. The Kālachakra doctrine is said to have originated in the mysterious secret land of Shambhala.[1] According to the late Sarat Chandra Dās, Shambhala was 'a city said to have been located near the river Oxus in Central Asia'; and the Kālachakra had become a distinctly Buddhistic system by the eleventh century, and introduced the cult of the Ādi (or Primordial)-Buddha. In India, varieties of the cult assigned to Shiva or to Gaṇesha (as the Hindu God of Wisdom) the position of Ādi-Buddha.[2]

Possibly, as we venture to suggest, one source, if not the most primitive source, of the Kālachakra system may yet be discovered to have been in the ancient pre-Buddhistic Bön religion of Tibet. If so, the seed of the system already lay in the Tibetan mind and found in Padma-Sambhava's form of Tantricism a favourable environment, long before the time when the Kālachakra, as a distinct School of Buddhism, is believed to have arisen in countries adjacent to Tibet. The association of the Kālachakra system with Shambhala, which

[1] Cf. L. A. Waddell, *The Buddhism of Tibet* (Cambridge, 1934), pp. 13–17, a work to which the Editor is much indebted, although he cannot agree with its author's opinion that Tantric Buddhism's 'mysticism became a silly mummery of unmeaning jargon'. Although this may be a common opinion among non-initiated Europeans, it is, as the late Sir John Woodroffe once remarked to the Editor, no more than their opinion. Sir John was himself a Tantric initiate, and the foremost occidental authority on Tantricism of our epoch. To his works, mostly published under the pseudonym 'Arthur Avalon', students are referred for right understanding of Tantricism. In *The Tibetan Book of the Dead* (pp. 213–20) there is a brief exposition of Tantricism, based chiefly upon Sir John's works, which will serve as a supplement to our present more historical exposition.

[2] Cf. S. C. Dās, *Tibetan–English Dictionary* (Calcutta, 1902), p. 632.

many *lāmas* say is somewhere unknown in Tibet or to the north of Tibet, is significant in this connexion. Furthermore, and of greater importance, is the documentary evidence from original Tibetan sources, as set forth in the *Bardo Thödol*, and in the text of the *Chöd* Rite (presented in Book V of *Tibetan Yoga and Secret Doctrines*) that, long before the rise of Tibetan Tantric Buddhism, the ancient Bön faith of Tibet propounded a highly developed cult of wrathful demons, of which the *To-wo* and *Drag-po* (corresponding to the *Bhairava* and *Heruka* of Hindu Tantricism) are outstanding representatives. And within the very elaborate demonology of the Bön faith probably lie the prototypes not only of the Wrathful but also of the Peaceful Deities of Tibetan Tantricism.

In the Kālachakra system, the inscrutable powers which work through nature, bringing into manifestation universes and then absorbing them, and causing men to live and to die, are personified not only in their dual aspect by the *Shakta* and *Shakti* as in the older Tantricism, but also in their dual functions of preservation (represented in Hinduism by Vishnu) and destruction (represented in Hinduism by Shiva). Thus there came into Tantricism two new groupings of deified personifications, one being the order of Peaceful Deities, personifying the powers making for preservation, the other being that of the Wrathful Deities, personifying the powers making for destruction. And, as will be observed throughout the Epitome of the Biography, in Tibetan Buddhism, all Buddhas, *Bodhisattvas*, gods and goddesses and lesser deities are visualized or represented in both the peaceful and wrathful aspect. Today, the form of Tantricism most prominent in Tibet is the Vajrayāna, or 'Path of the Indomitable Thunderbolt of the Gods'.

If the compilation of the Biography be really that of Padma's disciple, the Tibetan lady Yeshey Tshogyal, who was contemporaneous with him, then, as the Biography's internal evidence indicates, the Vajrayāna form of Tantricism was already highly developed by the latter half of the eighth century and also the Kālachakra system, into which the Mantrayāna and Vajrayāna practices were eventually incorporated. If, on the other hand, the Biography is of later date than the colophon assigns to it, and the presumption that the Kālachakra system was unknown to Tantricism prior to the tenth century is sound, the Tantricism of the Biography must, therefore, be taken to be of a form more highly developed than that introduced into Tibet by Padma-Sambhava himself. The true date of the Biography will, no doubt, eventually be established; and then, when the Biography and similar biographical records of the Great *Guru* have been critically examined, much new evidence will be adduced to clarify our present uncertainties concerning Tantricism's origin.

Whatever be the origin or age of Tantricism, it has unquestionably been an influence of the first importance throughout the whole empire of Mahāyāna Buddhism. Our Illustration of the Chinese Tantric representation of Mañjushrī in wrathful aspect is significant of this influence in China, and that of Mañjushrī in peaceful aspect is significant of this influence in India, Tibet, Nepal, and other of the Himalayan regions culturally related thereto.

Philosophically viewed, Tantricism, Hindu as well as Buddhist, aims to interpret human nature pragmatically. For this reason, the *Tantra Shāstra*, historically the latest of the *Shāstras*, is held to be the *Shāstra* best fitted for the *Kali-Yuga*, the present age.

Unlike most other faiths, Tantricism teaches understanding and sublimation of the chief force active in humanity, namely, the reproductive force, and opposes the more prevalent and scientifically unsound teaching concerning the forcible suppression of it. By that all-important force in nature, birth is balanced with death; the current of the *Prānic* River of Life, whereby all worlds and suns are sustained, is kept flowing, and the growth from higher to lower states of consciousness, even to the Final Emancipation of Buddhahood, is made possible. Thus it is that Tantricism propounds a science of sex, such as the late Sir John Woodroffe (pseudonym, Arthur Avalon) suggested in *The Tantra of the Great Liberation*, in *The Serpent Power*, and in *Shakti and Shakta*.

Even our own Occidental Science has now discovered, as the scientists of the Orient discovered long ago, that there is direct relationship between the highest mental and psychic powers in mankind and the secretions of the sex glands, and that physical youthfulness and efficiency are dependent upon conservation of the reproductive essences. All religions likewise, even the most primitive, have recognized that there is inseparableness between the sex-energy and spiritual growth. In the early Christian church, the ruling that a sexually incomplete man could not fittingly serve the church as a priest was made a basis for deposing the learned and saintly Origen of Alexandria from presbyterial status. Having applied literally rather than esoterically the New Testament command referring to the cutting off of an offending member of the physical body, Origen, at the age of 21, had made himself a eunuch physically rather than spiritually. Similarly, Indian *gurus* now teach that to attain the bliss of *samādhi* the sexual power must be complete and active, yet sublimated, and under as complete control as an aeroplane is by its pilot. In the Occident, the Society of Jesus, equally, insists that candidates for its priesthood must have attained dominion over their sexuality. But, for the oriental *yogin*, mastery of the 'serpent power' does not imply celibacy in the Christian monastic sense, for many of the Great *Rishis* of India had offspring. And today, as in the time of Padma-Sambhava, Tantric priests or *lāmas* may or may not marry, celibacy for them being optional; but it is only the Ngag-pas (Skt. *Mandar*) among the Nyingmapa *lāmas* of Padma-Sambhava's School who commonly marry.[1] Marpa, the *guru* of Milarepa, for example, was married and had a son. The *Bodhisattva* Gautama, too, before he became the Buddha, was married and had a son; and both the son and the wife became faithful disciples of the Enlightened One.

It is because sex plays so large a part in the various accounts of Padma-Sambhava which have been handed down that he

---

[1] Ngag-pa *lāmas*, being reputed to be expert magicians, are employed by Tibetans of all sects to bring about rain in times of drought or to protect growing crops from destructive hail.

is looked upon, by many who misunderstand Tantricism, as the very antithesis of what a holy man should be. The standards by which such critics judge the Great *Guru* are those of the unenlightened, and usually those of the Occident. In his own time such critics were not lacking, as the episode (recorded on page 161, following) concerning the suspicions of one who had professed to be his friend shows. Therefore, without at least some general comprehension of Padma-Sambhava's Tantricism, such as the present Section affords, this volume as a whole is apt to be misinterpreted.

XI. ASTROLOGY

The Biography makes it clear that astrology was quite as influential in the life of Padma-Sambhava as it is known to have been in the lives of many other, if not all, of the Sages of the Mahāyāna, and as it still is in the life of every Oriental who has remained true to his or her wisdom-born ancestral heritage.

Learned Indian astrologers maintain that astrology *per se* is of all sciences the most important, because there can be no true art of living apart from it. In so viewing astrology, they exclude, as being unworthy the name astrology, almost all of that which passes for astrology in the Occident and the greater part of that which is popularly called astrology in the Orient.

Astrology regards man as being not only a microcosm of the macrocosm, but as being, like all *sangsāric* things, a product of multitudinous astral and cosmic influences; for in him they find focus, and shape his physical, mental, and psychic environment. Astrology does not, however, imply fatalism; for the master of *yoga* is also the master of astrological influences, and, by knowing them, is enabled scientifically to chart the course of his Vessel of Salvation across the Sea of Existence in such manner as to avoid hidden reefs and shallows, and be prepared for tempests and contrary currents and, at last, attain the safety of the Other Shore. Notwithstanding that his body and mental tendencies and environment are shaped by astrological influences, the Sage thus remains the master of his own fate despite them. Similarly, a ship on the high seas is the product of man's labour and inventive skill, and no matter what inherent weaknesses or imperfections it may possess, or whether it be of one shape or another, great or small, the captain has free will to direct its course in any direction, and bring it through all dangers to the port desired.

Each moment in time is as much different from another as one leaf on a tree is different from all the other leaves, because the effects of these innumerable astrological influences are never for two consecutive moments exactly the same. Owing to the incessant movements of the heavenly bodies and of the Earth, the angle of the focus, and correlatively the character of the influences, unceasingly change. It is upon this premise that astrology is founded.

Accordingly, all visible and invisible things, organic and inorganic, man, beast, plant, crystal, and every material, aqueous or gaseous substance, being responsive to these influences, are branded by them in terms of *sangsāric* time. This is very curiously illustrated by the practice of wine-tasting, and also, in lesser degree, by that of tea-tasting. A master wine-taster, although totally ignorant of the source and age of a certain vintage, can, by tasting it, determine with mathematical exactitude where the grapes were grown, their quality and species, and when they were pressed.[1] Ultimately, when fully developed, the practice of tea-tasting should result in the taster being able to determine not only the quality, but also the exact origin of the tea and the date of its production and curing.

As taste is a very subtle thing, totally invisible and knowable only by experience, it is, in this sense, comparable to something psychic; we might even call it the essential psychic quality or flavour of a living organism. It is precisely in this way, astrology maintains, that every organic and inorganic substance has its own peculiar astrological characteristic or taste; and an astrologer is a taster or calculator of the astro-

[1] For this very suggestive reference to wine-tasting, the Editor is personally indebted to Dr. Jung, who contributed it to a discussion which touched upon astrology at a luncheon in Balliol College, during the time of the Tenth International Congress for Psychotherapy held in Oxford in the summer of 1938.

logical quality of a given moment in the transitory cycle of time. By knowing the astrological influences operative at any given moment of nativity, it is thus possible to ascertain the physical, mental, and psychic characteristic or taste of a human being; and, also, how another and unlike combination of influences, radionic, magnetic, psychic, and physical, emanating from Moon and Sun, Stars and Cosmic Spaces, will affect those already stamped upon the individual at the moment of birth.

Sufficient scientific data are available to suggest that the study of these astrological influences would be of fundamental importance also to botanists and zoologists. The Editor recalls how an old Yankee schoolmaster used to demonstrate to him, in schoolboy days, proofs, derived from experiments, that each phase of the moon has a definite effect not only, as is popularly believed, upon the growth of vegetation and the maturing of seeds, but also upon the fertility of domestic animals. Similarly, in Ceylon, horary astrology is so highly evolved that astrologers there have assured me that if the seed of a mango be planted at the exact moment when there is a certain rare combination of astrological influences, the seed will speedily sprout and fruit be produced as soon as three or four leaves have appeared on the young tree.

Likewise, some of the most fascinating phenomena elicited by biological research appear to merit astrological explanation. For illustration, the Great Barrier Reef Expedition of 1928–9 found that the pearl oyster has annually two breeding seasons, six months apart, 'at the full-moon in May and in November'.[1] The coral *Pocillopora bulbosa*, in the shallow pools on Low Isles, Australia, was found to have three reproductive periods, the first period occurring at about the time of new moon during the months of December to April, the second period at about the time of the full moon in July and August, and the third in May and June, when there is a transitional period from new moon to full moon.[2] The marine Palolo worms (*Palolo viridis*), used as food by the natives of Samoa

---

[1] Cf. T. A. Stephenson, in *Nature* (London, 6 May 1933), p. 665.
[2] Ibid. (London, 29 Apr. 1933), p. 622.

and Fiji, leave their homes in the fissures of the coral reefs and swarm to the shores of these islands in countless myriads at two fixed periods annually, in October and in November, on two successive days, which are, 'at dawn on the day on which the moon is in her last quarter and at dawn on the day before'.[1] Thirteen lunations occur between the appearances of the Palolo every third year, or, in other words, the Palolo adjusts itself, in the long run, to solar time. Mr. S. J. Whitmee, who made this suggestive discovery, says, 'A most remarkable compensation for the difference between *lunar* and *solar* time is made by some natural process in the development of 'this little annelid. I am not at present prepared to give an opinion as to how this can be effected'.[2]

There might also be cited parallel biological phenomena showing a definite connexion between the phases of the moon and periodicity in the life-cycles of other marine creatures, as, for illustration, the spawning time of fish, when the fish pass from the depths of the oceans to the shallows of the shores or to the fresh waters of estuaries and rivers, or, again, the run of herring on the coasts of Britain or of cod on the Grand Banks of Newfoundland. The season of rut in wild animals, and of the monogamous mating followed by the communal migration of birds and butterflies, are also suggestive of astrological influences. Thus, each year, on the nineteenth day of March the famous swallows (*Hirundo erythrogaster*) of the San Juan Capistrano Mission in California return to their nests after their winter outing in the lands to the south; and they take their departure from the Mission, quite as regularly, on the twenty-third day of October. Records of their annual arrival and departure have been kept by the Mission fathers for many years, and never yet have the swallows failed to arrive and depart at these fixed dates, even in leap years;[3]

[1] Cf. A. Sedgwick, *A Student's Text-Book of Zoology* (London, 1898), p. 481; *The Cambridge Natural History*, vol. ii (London, 1910), p. 297.
[2] Cf. S. J. Whitmee, *Proceedings of the Zoological Society of London*, 1875, pp. 496–502.
[3] The Editor is indebted to the late Rev. A. J. Hutchinson, Custodian of the Mission, for this information, contained in a letter dated 19 September 1938.

for, like the Palolo worms, they adjust their cyclic movements to solar rather than terrestrial time.

Here, of course, we approach the problem of instinct, which also, in the last analysis, is claimed by astrologers to be the evolutionary outcome of astrological fixation, or what otherwise may be termed astrological periodicity, as shown in breeding seasons. In the view of some learned astrologers, even the origin and mutation of species, and the law of biological evolution as a whole, are best explained astrologically.

Although there are the ordinary external stimuli which are obviously and generally effective in the determination of breeding seasons, such as temperature, latitude, light, and rainfall, not all birds and animals are invariably responsive to them, as Dr. John R. Baker, of the University of Oxford, demonstrates in his essay, 'The Evolution of Breeding Seasons'.[1] Other influences must be considered. Also, 'Internal rhythm can never account wholly for the timing of breeding seasons, for it would get out of step with the sun in the course of ages, but it is likely that it plays its part in making many species quick to respond to the external factors.'[2] Some interesting instances are cited by Dr. Baker of the lack of response to the terrestrial environmental stimuli.

'Some species of birds have quite different breeding seasons on the two sides of Ceylon, and it is thus certain that length of day does not control them. It is possible that intensity of visible or ultra-violet illumination is the cause.'[3] Despite severe cold, the *Nestor notabilis* parrot of the Nelson Province of New Zealand breeds in mid-winter.[4] Even where there is a constant temperature, as in the tropics, it is usual for birds to have breeding seasons, as the Oxford University Expedition to the New Hebrides discovered. 'The climax was presented by the insectivorous bat, *Miniopterus australis*, the adult females of which all become pregnant once a year about the beginning of September, despite the constancy of climate and the fact that they hang all day in a dark and almost ther-

[1] A Reprint from *Evolution Essays* presented to E. S. Goodrich, ed. by G. R. De Beer (Clarendon Press, Oxford, 1938).
[2] J. R. Baker, ibid., p. 166.   [3] Ibid., p. 168.   [4] Ibid., p. 169.

mostatic cave.'[1] Thus temperature, too, does not appear to be the determining influence. Some birds seem almost insensitive to latitude as well.[2] Rainfall (which is itself the direct result of astrological influences, according to astrologers), although a far more important factor, is not always the determining cause of the breeding seasons of certain animals.[3]

Man and domesticated animals appear to be less susceptible than animals in the state of nature to all such obvious external stimuli, and, as the astrologers maintain, to invisible astrological stimuli also. The lower the organism and more primitive the environment—as in the instances of the pearl oyster, coral and marine worms—the more direct is the response. In inorganic substances, as research in radio-activity may some day discover, the response is said to be entirely automatic.

Astronomical data, too, have already been accumulated pointing to the reasonableness of at least some of the postulates of astrology. And more and more, as astronomers advance in their quest, very recently begun, for the source of cosmic rays, and physicists in their related quest concerning radio-activity, both alike will enter the realm claimed by astrology. Then, as they begin to study the effects of these radiations upon the Earth and upon living things, there will be laid foundations for an occidental science of astrology.

No person of intelligence nowadays doubts the effect of sunspots on the Earth's magnetic and climatic conditions, nor that the Moon, aided by gravitational forces, causes tides in oceans and in the apparently immovable land surfaces of continents. It is only in the Occident that the far more important effect of all such astrological influences on man himself is either denied or arrogantly ignored or left to the exploitation of ignorant charlatans who make scientists averse to inquiry. The well-established law of gravitation alone contributes additional scientific evidence tending to give validity to certain of the claims of oriental astrology. Until quite recently, Western Science has been far more concerned with the external visible Universe than with the internal invisible

[1] J. R. Baker, *Evolution Essays*, ed. G. R. De Beer (Clarendon Press, Oxford, 1938), p. 163.   [2] Ibid., p. 164.   [3] Ibid., p. 172.

universe in man; but, fortunately for man, Western Science appears to be destined to become more and more anthropocentric.

Quite unlike scientists, many eminent occidental philosophers and poets, among whom were Roger Bacon and Shakespeare, have been keenly interested in astrology. Nor has Christianity itself escaped its influence, as the Christianized story of the coming of the Wise Men from the East guided by the star over Bethlehem shows. In an earlier and historic version of this astrological story, concerning the birth of the *Bodhisattva* Gautama, the Wise Men were astrologers, who came and cast the horoscope of the royal babe and thus foretold how he was destined to become either a universal emperor or a Buddha. And on the babe's body they saw the thirty-two signs of his coming greatness, as astrological time-markings, cumulatively inherited from many previous incarnations.

Astrology is, of course, historically and scientifically, a subject far too vast to consider at further length here. The Biography itself will contribute much to the present discussion. Our sole purpose in discussing astrology, even in this rather superficial manner, is to suggest that it may yet prove to be, for occidental scientists, the source of a new science— apart from astronomy, which has sprung from it—even as alchemy was the source of chemistry and modern psychology. Then, eventually, if occidental civilization endures sufficiently long, an age may come when the universities of Europe and of the two Americas will see fit to follow the illustrious tradition of the far-famed Buddhist and other universities of the Orient, such as Nālanda, the Oxford of ancient India, and institute chairs and departments of astrology. Even today, in all the chief monastic schools of Tibet, astrology is inferior in importance only to religion and metaphysics; and in modern India there still survive colleges of astrology. In our view, it is unreasonable to assume that a people so practical as the Chinese or so scientifically religious as the Hindus and Tibetans have been foolishly deluded in their age-long faithfulness to astrology.[1]

[1] The interested student is directed to the discussion of astrology

XII. The *Yoga*

The '*Yoga* of Knowing the Mind in Its Nakedness' is *Jñāna Yoga* in purest form. Thus, quite unlike the many complex and often dangerous *yogas* dependent upon breathings and ordinary meditations, it can be safely practised without a *guru*, providing the practitioner leads a normal and well-regulated life. A living *guru* is, nevertheless, desirable, not only in solving the many *yogic* problems which are certain to arise, but chiefly to safeguard one from error and to supervise one's progress personally. Still, if a trustworthy *guru* is not available, the *yogin* need not hesitate to proceed alone, remembering always the aphorism, 'When the disciple is ready, the master will appear'. Those best fitted to profit by this *yoga* are, consequently, *yogins* who have gone beyond, either in this or some previous life, preliminary *yogic* practices.

The author of our treatise, whether Padma-Sambhava, as stated in the Colophon, or some person unknown, was, as internal evidence suggests, an adept in *yoga* with most unusual insight into Reality. There is, however, no sound evidence at present available which would tend to discredit the Colophon's assertion that the Great *Guru* himself wrote it as a direct outcome of his own realization.

Its concise perceptual teachings must be meditated upon one by one, with unlimited patience, and exhaustively. Otherwise, the only result will be an intellectual comprehension of them. This *yoga* is, therefore, apt to make little or no appeal to those of whom it has been said, 'It is as easy to teach them philosophy as to eat custard with a spoon'. Nor is it likely to attract the attention of those who are striving for worldly riches, comfort, and fame rather than for Freedom. A treatise such as this purports to be, the very quintessence of the Mahāyāna expounded in few words, cannot but be addressed to those already in possession of that profound insight which is the fruit of disciplined mind.

The goal of this *yoga* is the attainment of *Nirvāṇa*, or of

contained in *Tibetan Yoga and Secret Doctrines* (pp. 286–7), to which this present discussion is complementary.

complete awakening from the *Sangsāra*, simultaneously with which comes the Supreme Realization that both *Nirvāṇa* and the *Sangsāra* are eternally indistinguishably one. And this constitutes the Great Liberation.

Nirvāṇa being eternally at the basis of all existence, its attainment is dependent upon the *yogic* process of transmuting the mundane mind into the Supra-mundane Mind, success in which is equivalent to winning the philosopher's stone of the medieval alchemists, or to mastering their occult teaching concerning the transmutation of base metal into gold. The process is normally threefold. Firstly, through study and research, comes intellectual comprehension of Divine Wisdom. Secondly, the aspirant advances to intuitional insight. Thirdly, he stands face to face with the Nakedness.

It will assist and encourage the practitioner to have placed before him or her, for comparative study here, a brief outline of this same system of *Jñāna Yoga* from the Brāhmanical viewpoint, as expounded by a recently living Master of it, the late Mahārshi of Tiruvannamalai:

Right inquiry (Skt. *vichāra*) is the only efficacious method of tranquillizing the mind. Although the mind may be brought and kept under control by other means, such, for example, as breath regulation (Skt. *prāṇāyāma*), it invariably rebounds again and again. So long as the breath is restrained, the mind remains tranquil, but the moment the restraint is relaxed, the mind bounds up, and is tossed about by its inherent tendencies (Skt. *vāsanās*) resulting from past deeds (Skt. *karma*).

Both the mind and the vital force (Skt. *prāṇa*) have a common source. Thoughts are the manifestations of the mind. The thought 'I' is the root-thought which first springs from the mind, and this is egoism (Skt. *aham-kāra*). *Prāṇa* also arises from the same source as egoism. Therefore, when *prāṇa* is controlled, the mind, too, is controlled; and when the mind is controlled the breathing is brought under control. Breath (or *prāṇa*) is considered to be the gross expression or index (Skt. *sthūla*) of the mind. During one's lifetime the mind keeps the *prāṇa* within the body, and at the moment of death the mind and *prāṇa* depart from the body simultaneously.

Prāṇāyāma may help to bring under control, but not to

annihilate, the thought-process. Similarly, meditation upon a form (Skt. *mūrti-dhyānam*), repetition of a formula (Skt. *mantra-japam*), accompanied by food-discrimination, are no more than intermediate steps towards mind-control. The mind becomes fixed on a single object by *mūrti-dhyānam* or *mantra-japam*, just as the restless trunk of an elephant when given a chain to hold remains steady and makes no attempt to catch hold of any other object.

Each thought by itself is extremely weak, because the mind is distracted by countless and ever varying thoughts. The more the thoughts are restrained the more the mind concentrates and, consequently, gains strength and power. Success is assured if the mind is trained in *ātmā-vichāra* [or right inquiry into Reality].

Of all disciplines, food-discrimination, i.e. partaking of only *sāttvic* [or pure, vegetarian food], and in moderate quantities, is the most important. By means of this, the mind is rendered more and more *sāttvic* [or pure], and *ātmā-vichāra* more and more effective.

Countless *vāsanās*, or tendencies caused by past *karma*, reside in the mind. These have accumulated, from time immemorial, during untold past lives. Like waves upon the ocean, they rise on the mind, one after another.

As progress is made in *swarūpa-dhyāna* [or meditation on Truth, or the Real], these *vāsanās* are suppressed and vanish, no matter how old and deep they are. One should become firm and steady in *swarūpa-dhyāna* and allow no room for any doubt whether all the accumulated *vāsanās* can ever be extinguished and the mind can ever be transmuted into *Ātmā-Swarūpam* [or the Ultimate Truth, or Thatness]. . . .

So long as *vāsanās* adhere to the mind, one should pursue the quest of 'Who am I?' Continuing on this quest, one should suppress each thought as soon as it arises in the mind. Freedom from all attraction of every extraneous thing is called *Vairāgyam*, or desirelessness; and clinging to *Ātmā-Swarūpam* unswerved is *Jñānam*, or Wisdom, i.e. true understanding. Both *Vairāgyam* and *Jñānam* ultimately lead to the same goal.[1]

The *yogin* is to recognize that there are aspects of mind as innumerable as are the various modes of its manifestation, not only in human and sub-human creatures on Earth, but in

---

[1] This matter as quoted is the Editor's recension of matter contained in *Who Am I?* (pp. 7-10).

all other sentient beings throughout the *Sangsāra*. He is not
to regard the Universe, in the manner of Christian theology,
as being centred in man, but in mind. The *Abhidharma* makes
four general classifications of mind: (1) mind manifested
through animal sensuousness (Skt. *kāma-vicāra*); (2) mind
manifested through living organisms or forms (*rūpa-vicāra*);
(3) mind manifested independently of form (*arūpa-vicāra*);
and (4) mind in its primordial, unmodified condition of nakedness (*lokottara-vicāra*). Mind is further divisible in accordance
with its *sangsāric* manifestations. Or we may say that there
are two chief aspects of mind, *sangsāric* and *nirvāṇic*; mind
per se, or unmodified consciousness (*chit*), transcends both.

So long as there is mind *sangsārically* manifested, there is
suffering, for suffering is inherent in transitoriness, in illusion,
in Ignorance (*Avidyā*). Not until *sangsāric* mind is transcended
can there be an end of suffering.

All things, bodily forms, sensations, perceptions, concepts,
subjective differentiation, mind, or consciousness, in their
sangsāric aspects are unreal in the sense that they are merely
illusive reflections of Reality, as the One in the Many. The
moonlight is not truly moonlight, it is only a reflex of sunlight;
it illusorily appears to be what it is not, and is in that way
unreal. Similarly, all *sangsāric* things appear to be real, like
images seen reflected on the calm surface of a pool. If one is
to know the Real, and not its pale illusory reflections, one
must attain the Real; if one seeks the source of the light of
the Sun itself, it is not to be found in the Moon. Likewise, the
One Mind, or the Ultimate Consciousness in its primordiality,
can be known only by itself alone, not by its *sangsāric* manifestations. In the words of Plotinus, 'Seek not to see this
Principle by the aid of external things; otherwise, instead of
seeing It itself, thou shalt see no more than its image'.[1]

Thus the essential objective of the *yogin* is *yogic* understanding of his own microcosmic aspect of mind, in order that
mind may be realized in its true state. In speaking of this
process, Professor D. T. Suzuki, the eminent authority on
Zen Buddhism, with which our present '*Yoga* of Knowing the

[1] Cf. Plotinus, v. v. 10.

Mind in Its Nakedness' has much in common, describes it as the seeing the [One] Mind within the inner nature of one's own being, in accordance with the teachings of Bodhidharma, the Founder of Zen Buddhism, known in Japan as Daruma.[1] As our text emphasizes, the Microcosmic Mind is inseparable from the Macrocosmic Mind, both alike being of the One Essence of the Supra-mundane Mind. 'Nor is one's own mind separable from other minds.' The *yogin's* whole aim is to yoke the microcosmic aspect of mind, innately shining, yet hidden beneath the dense mists of Ignorance, with its parental source, the macrocosmic mind, and so attain transcendency over all dualities and all illusory appearances, the constituents of the *Sangsāra*.

Plotinus describes the process thus:

We must, therefore, meditate upon the mind in its divinest aspect in order to discover the nature of intellect. This is how we may proceed: from man, that is from thyself, strip off the body; then lay aside that subtle power which fashioneth the body; then separate thyself from sensuousness, hankering, and anger, and each of the lower passions that incline thee towards worldly things. What remaineth afterwards in the consciousness is what we call the 'image of intelligence', which emanateth from the mind, as from the mighty orb of the Sun emanateth the surrounding sphere of luminosity. Above intellect, we shall meet That which is called the 'nature of the Good'. The Good, which is transcendent over the Beautiful, is the source and essentiality of the Beautiful. Man must amalgamate himself with the Principle that he possesseth innately. Then, from the manyness that he was, he will have become one.[2]

Accordingly, it is by deep introspective meditation, and not by purely intellectual means, that this *yoga*, like Buddhism itself, can be comprehended. In the words of the Buddha, 'Without knowledge there is no meditation; without meditation there is no knowledge. He who hath both knowledge and meditation is near unto *Nirvāṇa*.'[3]

[1] Cf. D. T. Suzuki, *The Message of Bodhidharma*, in 'The Aryan Path' (Bombay, Jan. 1936).
[2] Cf. Plotinus, v. iii. 9; I. vi. 9; vi. ix. 3.
[3] *The Dhammapāda*, aphorism 372, as translated by Irving Babbitt (Oxford University Press, New York and London, 1936).

XIII. The Problem of Self (or Soul)

In the process of introspectively meditating upon the aphoristic teachings concerning the One Mind, the disciple will inevitably come face to face with the age-old problem of what man is. He will intuitively ask himself, Why am I? What am I? Am I a something, a self, a soul, eternally separate and different from each of the countless myriads of similarly constituted beings I see round about me in various states of existence? Is the glamorous world of appearances real? Are all these inanimate objects and all these living, breathing creatures, in the midst of which I find myself, real? Or are they, as the Buddhas declare, no more than the content of a *karmic* mirage, the stuff composing the dream of life?

When the truth begins to come from within, very feebly at first, like the consciousness of a man awakening from the torpor of a drugged sleep, or like the first traces of dawn coming forth in an eastern sky, the disciple will realize gradually that only by transcending the realm of separateness and attaining super-consciousness of the immutable at-one-ment of all things, organic and inorganic, can the age-old problem be solved. The more the disciple meditates upon what the self has in common with other selves, the more he will discover the impersonal self common to all selves. Thence he will reach the conclusion 'that if one and the same factor is the core of each individual's selfhood, no individual in its true essence has individuality. There would be nothing like *my* self; there would be only the Self.'[1]

As the Sages have repeatedly emphasized by means of paradoxical aphorisms, it is only by losing oneself that one finds oneself, it is only by self-surrender that one attains self-victory, it is only by dying on the Cross of the *Sangsāra* that one attains life more abundantly, and becomes a Light in the Darkness. It is by impersonalizing the personality, by self-extinction, by realizing the voidness of every objective ap-

---

[1] The Editor here acknowledges indebtedness to the clear and concise thinking set forth by Dr. Edward Conzé in his booklet entitled *Contradiction and Reality* (London, 1939), pp. 13-14.

pearance throughout the Universe, that the disciple reaches that understanding of self to which the text directs him.

To tread this path successfully, the *karmically*-inherited tendency to emphasize the self through attachment to the results of worldly activities must be neutralized; self-aggrandizement, self-glorification, must give place to self-diminution and complete passivity.[1] Then all opposition between the self and the world of appearances will subside, even as the waves on a sea subside when the wind has ceased. It is in this state that

the self loses itself and all measure, sinks into a measureless being that is without limitations, foundations, and determinations. It is devoured by being, in which no more one thing is opposed to another. In consequence, there is nothing to which the person opposes himself. This is achieved by identification with all things and events as they come along, and as they are. The self relaxes and becomes empty. The entrance of reality is no longer barred by predilections of one's own which, being peculiar to the individual, could act as a distorting medium. Things are experienced as they are, as one sees the bottom of a lake through clear and quiet water.[2]

Expositions of the Buddhist doctrine of non-self, or non-soul, frequently exhibit looseness of thinking and misleading argumentation, sometimes by Buddhists themselves. The Buddha did not teach that there is no self, or soul; He taught that there is no self, or soul, that is real, non-transitory, or possessed of unique and eternally separate existence. In Buddhism, salvation is not of a self, or soul; it is entirely dependent upon what the Buddha declared to be the deliverance of the mind from the *sangsāric* bondage imposed by Ignorance (Skt. *Avidyā*), from the erroneous belief that appearances are real and that there are individualized immortal selves, or souls.

When there is no longer a clinging to selfhood, when all the

---

[1] This teaching of the Clear-Seeing Ones, the Conquerors of Self, the supra-*sangsāric* Supermen, who are humanity's true guides, is quite the antithesis of that of men who are fettered to the *Sangsāra* and enamoured of the tyrannizing passions and the warfare of the animal-man.

[2] Cf. Edward Conzé, op. cit., pp. 16–17.

external play of *sangsāric* energies is allowed to subside, because there is no longer attachment to any of them, then there is that state of absolute quiescence of mental activities which our text refers to as the natural state of the mind. When the human consciousness of illusory appearances has been swallowed up in the supra-mundane consciousness of the *Arhant*, then the Path leading to Limitless Understanding and Divine Wisdom, to transcendence over the limitations *karmically* imposed by existence in the *Sangsāra*, has, indeed, been entered upon. On that Path, the aspirant advances to the state beyond self; he loses himself; the purified drop reunites with the Cosmic Ocean of Being. The illusory microcosmic mind dissolves; there is only the One Mind; there is Final Emancipation, Perfect Buddhahood.

Only when Ignorance has been done away with, only when the limited self, or soul, has been alchemically resolved into its *karmic* constituents, and the littleness of the man has become the greatness of a Buddha, is the Goal reached.

Among all the Buddha's teachings, that of non-soul (Skt. *anātma*: Pāli *anattā*) is of supreme importance,

for therein, having discarded personality and permanent substance, He preached a moral law, without anyone or anything on which the law would be binding, and proclaimed a salvation to be attained by a great endeavour, which apart altogether from the existence of somebody entitled to reach the goal, consisted not in a blissful, eternal survival in a heaven or some such abode of joy, but merely in a quiescence from the things that men generally value in life.[1]

Thus, by successful practice of the *Yoga* of the One Mind, the aspirant realizes that the illusory separateness of things camouflages reality, that Ignorance is the price paid for illusorily enjoying distinctness and the sense of selfhood. This supreme realization will receive further exposition, from the viewpoints of Psychology and Therapy, in the Section which immediately follows.

[1] Cf. *The Buddhist Doctrine of Anattā* by Dr. G. P. Malalasekara, in the Vaisaka Number of *The Mahā-Bodhi* (Calcutta, May and June 1940), pp. 222–3.

XIV. The Psychology and the Therapy

Psychologically considered, the ' *Yoga* of Knowing the Mind in Its Nakedness' is a system of practically applied transcendental sublimation of life, in keeping with that of the Noble Eightfold Path, which is itself entirely a process of greater and greater sublimation. As study of the mind of children shows, there is a natural inborn tendency in man to transcend the external world of non-homogeneity and to seek a state of homogeneity, such as that of the supra-mundane at-one-ment which results from the *yogic* knowing of mind in its unobscured naturalness. It is out of a realm of nothingness, metaphorically akin to the philosophical Voidness of the Mahāyāna, that the child creates its own world of fantasy, which, like the state of *Nirvāṇa*, being a state of homogeneity, is harmonious and blissful.

The quest for homogeneity is common not only to children, but to mature humanity of all races and times. In the more primitive societies, it manifests itself in myths and wonder-tales of faerie, where everything normally impossible becomes realizable in a homogeneous state of all-embracing transcendent magic. In the most culturally advanced societies it manifests itself in dreams of an ideal commonwealth like that of Plato's or a world utopia such as that conceived by a Sir Thomas More or a Karl Marx, or the Heaven on Earth of the Christians, or the Paradise of Islam.[1]

Likewise, there appears to be deep-hidden in the unconscious, awaiting favourable opportunity to come forth into the conscious, a transcendent geometrical symmetry, like that referred to by the Greek philosophers in such aphorisms as 'God geometrizes', or 'The Universe is founded on number'; and, also, a divine beauty and perfect harmony. Here, too, there lie in embryo, awaiting to be born into the lives of men,

---

[1] We gratefully acknowledge in this connexion the help of the very fruitfully suggestive paper by Dr. A. Groeneveld, of Holland, entitled 'Early Childhood and its Mechanisms: Isotropism (Homotropism) and Canontropism', and that by Dr. F. Künkel, of Germany, entitled 'Das "Wir" als Faktor in der Heilpaedogogik', which were read on 30 July 1938 in Oxford, before the Tenth International Medical Congress for Psychotherapy.

unwavering constancy, indomitable will, and power to transform the world.

Dr. C. G. Jung, the eminent psychologist, in his presidential address concluding the proceedings of the Tenth International Medical Congress of Psychotherapy, held in Oxford from 29 July to 2 August 1938, emphasized the importance of a philosophical preparation for understanding primitive thought. The soundness of this contention cannot be questioned. As a direct result of our own researches, we found that the more primitive, or more unfettered by civilization's inhibitions, a society is, the more natural it is. Accordingly, then, the mind of primordial man must have been the freest from illusion (Skt. *māyā*), and the mind of twentieth-century man in London, New York, Paris, or Berlin, the most fettered to illusion. What is today known as social progress is essentially movement away from primitive naturalness. As has been suggested in Section VII above, it is in the study of unsophisticated or so-called primitive societies that the psychologist, equally with the anthropologist, will make the nearest external approach to that state referred to in our treatise as the seeing of mind in its nakedness. In other words, the 'uncivilized' man is a clearer percipient and thus a sounder interpreter of life than the 'civilized' man. This I discovered during my four years of research among the Celtic peasantry of Ireland, Scotland, Isle of Man, Wales, Cornwall, and Brittany, and set forth in *The Fairy-Faith in Celtic Countries*.[1]

The more 'civilized' and utilitarianly educated the man, the less fitted he is to understand himself in the sense of the well-known Greek aphorism, Γνῶθι Σεαυτόν, 'Know Thyself'. The child, like the primitive man and the illiterate peasant, is much nearer the True Vision. There have been no more profound psychologists than the Great Teachers, who, with unanimity, have proclaimed that the neophyte must become as a little child before he can enter into the Realm of Truth.

[1] This, the Editor's first important work, has long been out of print. The new edition of it, now being prepared, should appeal to readers of our Tibetan Series, wherein the *ḍākinī* and various other orders of fairy-like beings receive, as they do in this volume of the Tibetan Series, much attention.

Here, then, is the psychological reason why the *Gurus* teach renunciation of the world, the putting aside of the intellectualisms of men, the need of being born again to a higher perception; and why the wisdom of babes is greater than that of scholars.

Animal instincts, whereby the multitude are chiefly guided and through which they are controlled by the state, must be transcended. The transcendent sublimation through knowing the mind in its nakedness cannot be brought about by exercise of lowly brutish propensities, which also are inherent in man's nature, but by virtue of the ascendency of the higher propensities latent in the unconscious, even of the unborn child. Self-control and indomitable will are preliminary prerequisites for one who would master the divine alchemical science of mind. Apart from self-control, there can be no dominion over the animal in man; apart from indomitable will, there can be no sublimation of life.

Although psychology, as we know it, is peculiarly occidental, particularly in its terminology and methods, there is a psychology which by contrast is essentially transcendental, far older and more mature, known to Orientals as *yoga*. In order, therefore, to understand the psychology of the teachings set forth in this volume there must be adequate understanding of *yoga* itself; and the student is directed to the three previous volumes of this Tibetan Series, wherein *yoga* in its various aspects has been expounded. The two preceding Sections of this Introduction are complementary thereto.

As will be observed, the *yogic* doctrine of concepts set forth in our present treatise parallels that of the *Bardo Thödol* concerning the mental content of the percipient of the after-death state. During countless ages, mind, in its mundane reflex, has been experiencing *sangsāric* sensuousness. Like blotting-paper incorporating ink, it has absorbed concepts. In its primordial condition it was as colourless and clear as pure water. Like drops of various coloured fluids, some almost transparent and colourless, others black as soot, so many varying concepts have been received by it that its natural transparency and colourlessness have been lost. It is this condition of cloudiness or obscuration, called Ignorance, which now prevails in the mind, that *yoga* is intended to eliminate.

The first step in the process of removing the ink from the blotting-paper and the foreign substances from the water is dependent upon recognition of the illusory and non-real character of concepts. The *yogin* must come to realize that the world of human concepts is merely a product of the micro-cosmic mind even as the Cosmos is the product of the macro-cosmic mind. He must be able to control the mechanism of his mind as completely as a master engineer does that of an engine; he must be able at will to bring the thought-process to a dead stop.

When Mind is the Quiescent, and there is no thought-process, it is the One; when it emanates intelligence, intelligence thinks beings, and causes them to exist, and is the beings. According to Plotinus, 'Considered in its universality, Intelligence containeth all entities as the genus containeth all species, as the whole containeth all parts. Intelligence resideth within itself, and by possessing itself quiescently, is the eternal fullness of all things.' But thought does not itself think:

It is the cause which maketh some other being to think. The cause, however, cannot be identified with that which is caused. So much more reason is there then to say that the cause of all these existing things cannot be any of them. Accordingly, this Cause must not be conceived as being the good it emanateth, but as the good in a higher sense, that Good which transcendeth all other goods. Inasmuch as the One containeth no difference, It is eternally present; and we are eternally present in the One, as soon as we contain no more difference.

He who would attain to this state of non-differentiation, must practise psychic analysis of himself: 'Withdraw within thyself, and analyze thyself.'[1]

The writer is frequently asked, 'What purpose is served by concentrating the mind upon some external object or by attaining mental one-pointedness?' The answer is that the *yogin* thereby gains control of his thinking-process, very much after the manner of a man attaining control of an engine by

[1] Cf. Plotinus, v. ix. 6, 8; vi. ix. 6, 8; i. vi. 9.

studying its mechanism. The finite aspect of mind, undominated by *yoga*, is as unruly as a wild horse. It must be caught, as Milarepa teaches, and tied up. Not until it is tied up with the rope of one-pointedness can it be tamed and put in a corral for close observation.

The whole aim of the *yogin*, in this particularly psychological *yoga*, is research into the origin, nature, and powers of the dynamo, the mind, the energy of which runs his body. When, eventually, he becomes able *yogically* to dissect or take it to pieces, then only will he know it, and by knowing it know himself.

One of the most remarkable aphorisms of oriental psychology is, 'To whatever the mind goeth (or is attached), that it becometh.'[1] For illustration, it is by fixing the mind upon agriculture that a man becomes an agriculturist, or upon chemistry a chemist, or upon evil a criminal, or upon good a saint. The agriculturist is merely the outcome of his accumulating, by will power, mental concepts called agriculture, and so on for the chemist, the criminal, and the saint; each has become that to which his or her mind has gone. As the *Maitri Upanishad* (vi. 34) teaches,

> The *Sangsāra* is no more than one's own thought.
> With effort one should therefore cleanse the thought.
> What one thinketh, that doth one become.
> This is the eternal mystery.[1]

This psychology is clearly brought out in the *Bardo Thödol*. The character of the after-death existence, as it teaches, is dependent upon the character of the mental content of the deceased, precisely as the character of human existence is determined by the mental content of its experiencer. There is, however, this difference: the after-death state is passive, that is, digestive of the experiences of the human state; the human state is a state of activity, of the storing up of concepts as mental content. Immediately mind in its *sangsāric* aspect is divested of its grosser physical integument, which enabled it to accumulate concepts, it automatically relaxes, the mental

[1] According to a translation privately made by Mr. E. T. Sturdy.

tension born of the activities of life on Earth having been removed by death. Like a clock which has been wound up, it then begins to run mechanically, impelled by *karma*, and it runs so until it is run down, whereupon there is rebirth to store up fresh energy. The winding up results from the activities of the human existence just ended, the running results from the burning up in the after-death state of passivity of the stored-up energy derived from those activities, and the consequent release of their *karmic* potentialities. Similarly, vegetative activities result in coal, and the burning of the coal releases, in the form of heat, light, and gases, the stored-up energy derived from the vegetative activities.

As the teachings set forth in our treatise imply, the ultimate aim of the *yogin* is to put an end to this perpetual and monotonous oscillation of mind between the latency of the after-death state and the activeness of the human state. But he cannot do so until he stops the dynamo of mind from accumulating ever fresh energy with which to keep running its bodily machine. At the outset of his efforts to accomplish this supreme task, he must apply the *yoga* expounded by the precepts in a thorough psychological self-analysis.

There then ensue very definite and classifiable mental states, which may be enumerated as follows: (1) the initial comprehension that the finiteness of mind is due to aeons of misdirected concept-forming; (2) after the necessary halting of the thought-process has been accomplished, the *yogic* psychic analysis of the mental content; (3) the discovery of the purely illusory character of the concepts forming the mental content; (4) the inevitable disillusionment concerning the world of apparent reality; (5) the resultant birth of an indomitable resolve to purge the mind of its Ignorance, and thereby restore it to its primordial naturalness; (6) the realization of the psychic inseparableness and at-one-ment of all things and minds, equivalent to the realization of that native homogeneity innate in man and postulated by occidental psychologists as being more clearly discernable in the mind of the child; (7) the Ineffable Union with the One Mind, which is the transcendent fruit of *Yoga*, or divine yoking of the microcosmic with the macrocosmic, the complete Sublimation of Life, the Transmutation of Ignorance into Wisdom.

In this psychological *yoga* lie the fundamentals of true therapy, to which a few of the pioneer scientists of the Occident are now, rather belatedly, beginning to give serious attention. There cannot be Health so long as Ignorance remains uncured ; there cannot be Sanity so long as there is belief that the world of appearances is real or that there exists the eternal separateness and pluralism implied by the doctrine of soul.

The technique of this Higher Medicine—as suggested by Dr. Jung's Foreword-Commentary—rather than being dependent upon knowledge merely of mental phenomena, as these are understood by occidental psychology, with its concentration upon fact-collecting, is more akin to that of the analytical psychologist. The Buddha, like the Christ, has been very rightly called the Great Physician. But His method of treatment is not imposed from without; it is applicable only by the patient himself, through *yogic* introspection, as has been more fully explained herein elsewhere.

The Cure is dependent upon the elimination from the conscious mind of all seeds, both active and latent, of desire, of all elements of Ignorance. Until this elimination is accomplished, man cannot enjoy mental health ; he cannot see things as they are, for his eyes are *sangsārically* jaundiced; he remains obsessed with innumerable fantasies, mere will-o'-the-wisps of the mind; he is, in the Buddhistic sense, irrational, even to the point of insanity, as regards Reality. Like a mad man, he goes from birth to birth repeatedly; and, becoming a menace to every sentient creature, wherever he wanders he incessantly sows warfare and selfishness. Only when the mind attains what our text calls the Natural State is there Deliverance from Delusion and from Insanity.

This, then, is Right Psychology and Right Therapy, the knowing of and the transcendence over the conscious psyche, the ego of illusoriness. It is the '*Yoga* of Knowing the Mind in Its Nakedness', the Clear Seeing of Reality. It is that Deliverance of the mind which the Enlightened One proclaims to be the Goal of the *Dharma*. It is the Great Liberation.

XV. ORIGIN OF THE TEXT

The original Tibetan text of the ' *Yoga* of Knowing the Mind
in Its Nakedness', which constitutes the Great Liberation,
belongs to the *Bardo Thödol* series of *yogic* treatises concerning various methods of attaining transcendence over Ignorance. This will be obvious upon making comparison of its
transliterated title with that of the *Bardo Thödol* itself in
The Tibetan Book of the Dead. The whole series appertains to
the Tantric School of the Mahāyāna, and is believed to have
been first committed to writing during the eighth century A.D.
The authorship of our present treatise is attributed to Padma-
Sambhava himself. The text is said to have been hidden and
subsequently recovered by the *tertön* (or taker-out of hidden
treasures of sacred writings) Rigzin Karma Ling-pa.[1]

The Block-Print employed contains sixteen such treatises,
corresponding to the first sixteen of the cycle of seventeen
enumerated in *The Tibetan Book of the Dead* (pp. 71–72) ; and
the ' *Yoga* of Knowing the Mind in Its Nakedness' is the tenth
of the series. The last sentence of the Block-Print reads: 'The
block-types [of this Block-Print] belong to the Tan-gye-ling
Monastery'. This monastery is situated in the northern quarter
and within the walls of the city of Lhāsa; and its abbot, one
of the four *lāma-tulkus*, or grand *lāmas* who successively
reincarnate, bears the title Demo Rinpoch'e, the 'One of
Precious Peace.' He is said to be the incarnation of the illustrious Tibetan King Srong-Tsan-Gampo's minister of state,
Lon-po Gar.[2]

[1] See *The Tibetan Book of the Dead*, pp. 73–77.

[2] Each of the other three *lāma-tulkus*, upon reincarnating, becomes the
abbot of one of the three other of the four chief monasteries of Lhāsa, which
are, Kundeling, Ts'omoling, and Ts'ech'ogling. The Government of
Tibet being controlled by these four monasteries, called 'The Four *Lings*
(or Places)', the Regent, when the Dalai Lāma is dead or until he attains his
majority at the age of 18, is always the eldest of these four *lāma-tulkus*, who
then rules as the King of Tibet. (Cf. L. A. Waddell, op. cit., pp. 253–4.) The
reincarnations of all four of these abbots are discovered and chosen in much
the same manner as is the reincarnation of the Dalai Lāma. Lāma Karma
Sumdhon Paul, the chief of the two translators of our text, described to me
the installation of the present Demo Rinpoch'e, which he witnessed in Lhāsa
on 13 Oct. 1909, at the Tangyeling Monastery. The 'One of Precious Peace'
was then a bright-faced boy of about 13 or 14 years of age. All the high

The history of the Block-Print text of the Biography of Padma-Sambhava is given at the end of our Epitome of it; and that of the manuscript text of *Guru* Phadampa Sangay's Teachings on the title-page of Book III, herein.

XVI. THE TRANSLATORS

The translator of the excerpts upon which our 'Epitome of the Life and Teachings of Tibet's Great *Guru* Padma-Sambhava' is based, the late Sardar Bahādur S. W. Laden La, C.B.E., F.R.G.S., A.D.C., I.P., passed away in Kalimpong on 26 December 1936, less than a year after the time of the completion of the translation. Of ancient Tibetan ancestry, he was born on 16 June 1876 in Darjeeling, and there received his education. In 1898 he joined the corps of the Darjeeling Police, and soon attained official rank. In 1903–4 he was deputed to the Staff of the Tibetan Mission of Colonel Younghusband. After this he was an assistant to Colonel O'Connor in connexion with His Holiness the Tashi Lāma's tour throughout India. In 1906 he assisted the British Government when the question of an important treaty with Tibet and of indemnity had to be discussed with the Tibetan Minister. In 1907 he founded the General Buddhist Association, of the Darjeeling District, and was its first President. In 1909 he became the Founder-President of the Himalayan Children's Advancement Association which has already educated and placed over 600 orphans and poor boys. It is said that he spent out of his own pocket over Rs.25,000 in this noble work. In 1910 his

dignataries of the Lhāsa Government attended the installation, which is a very important affair of state; and for a number of days the Holy City abandoned itself to religious festivities. Differences having arisen between the late Dalai Lāma and the previous Demo Rinpoch'e, the late Dalai Lāma took over the administration of the wealth and income of Tangyeling and decreed that no more of the incarnations of the Demo Rinpoch'e would be recognized. The Demo Rinpoch'e made reply, saying that he would next incarnate in the Dalai Lāma's own family and compel the Dalai Lāma to recognize him. Accordingly, soon after the Demo Rinpoch'e's decease, a son was born to the Dalai Lāma's sister with every physical and mental characteristic of the late Demo Rinpoch'e; and the Dalai Lāma, being obliged to admit that the boy really was the reincarnated Demo Rinpoch'e, permitted his installation as the head of Tangyeling and cancelled the decree against him.

services were requisitioned by the Political Department of the Indian Government in connexion with the journey of His Holiness the Dalai Lāma to visit the Viceroy and make pilgrimage to the Buddhist Holy Places of India. Later, he was deputed to Tibet to settle terms between the Chinese and Tibetans as a representative of the British Government; and part of his duty consisted in helping to lead the Chinese Amban, Lien-Yu, and General Chung and the Chinese troops out of Tibet, whilst Colonel Willoughby held the Indian frontier.

It was said that the Tibetans were then much incensed against the Sardar Bahādur because of his services with the Younghusband Mission. According to rumour, at the time of the Mission, in 1904, the Tibetan Government had offered a reward of Rs.10,000 for his head and hands. But, after some years, all this was overlooked, and he was appointed by the Tibetan Government to accompany to England four carefully chosen Tibetan boys of good family, who were sent there at their Government's expense to acquire a modern technical and scientific education and return to Tibet to train their fellow countrymen. And he went to England also entrusted with credentials as envoy of His Holiness the Dalai Lāma, and, as such, carried letters and presents to Their Majesties in Buckingham Palace. In 1914, after his return, he attended the Tibetan–Chinese Conference at Simla, and thence accompanied the Prime Minister of Tibet to Sikkim.

During the First World War the Sardar Bahādur assisted in raising war loans and in recruiting the hill tribes. He was mentioned in dispatches, and in 1917 received the military title of Sardar Bahādur. Then, in 1921, when Sir Charles Bell went to Lhāsa with the object of cementing the friendly relationship with the Tibetan Government, the Sardar Bahādur was appointed his personal assistant.

In 1923 the Tibetan Government again enjoyed the Sardar Bahādur's services, for which they had been asking the Government of India for two years. This time, he organized a Police Force in Lhāsa and, also, the Tibetan Army. During the following year, in recognition, the Dalai Lāma conferred upon him the highest distinction in Tibet by raising him to the rank of a *Dzasa* or Tibetan Peer. Previously, in 1912, when some misunderstanding existed between His Holiness the Dalai Lāma and His Holiness the Tashi Lāma, the Sardar Bahādur succeeded in bringing about a friendly agreement between them. For this good service, His Holiness the Dalai Lāma conferred upon the Sardar Bahādur the title of *De-Pon* (or General) and a Premier Class Gold Medal of the Order of the Golden Lion, the first of its kind struck in Tibet, which is a massive gold nugget bearing the name of the Dalai Lāma. His Holiness the Tashi Lāma presented to the Sardar Bahādur a gold medal and conferred upon him the title of *Deo-nyer-chhem-Po* or Lord Chamberlain of the Court of Tashi Lhunpo.

The Sardar Bahādur, who was the most active of Tibetan Buddhist laymen in the maintenance and support of the *Dharma* among his Himalayan peoples along the Indian–Tibetan frontier, was the President and Patron of ten Buddhist monasteries, among which are those at Ghoom, Kurseong, Darjeeling, and Lopchu. Owing almost wholly to his financial assistance, the Ghoom Monastery was reconstructed, and then, after the disastrous earthquake of 1934, repaired, and its Mahāyāna Chapel built.

In 1927 he was made a Chevalier of the Order of Leopold II by the King and Queen of Belgium. In the midst of winter, in January 1930, he was sent to Lhāsa by the Indian Government in connexion with a very serious disagreement between Tibet and Nepal; and by his tactful and diplomatic intervention prevented war between the two countries. For this outstanding service he was made a Commander of the British Empire. Later on in the same year, 1930, he made his last visit to Lhāsa. This was for the purpose of personally presenting Colonel Weir, the Political Officer of Sikkim, and Mrs. Weir to the Dalai Lāma, Mrs. Weir thereby becoming the first English lady to be honoured by an introduction at the Court of His Holiness the Dalai Lāma at Lhāsa.

In June 1931 the Sardar Bahādur, after thirty-three years of public life, retired from Government Service; but to the day of his death he gave himself, in the true *Bodhisattvic* spirit, to the good of others. Thus, in the same year, he accepted the Presidency of the Hillmen's Association; he was active in the Boy Scouts' Clubs; in 1923 he was elected Vice-Chairman of the Darjeeling Municipality, and became vested with the full authority of a Chairman; and for his many educational, religious, and philanthropic activities he was probably the most beloved citizen of Darjeeling, as indicated by his mile-long funeral procession to the Ghoom Monastery, where his body was cremated. He was an Honorary Aide-de-camp to His Excellency the Governor of Bengal; and it was in grateful recognition of the voluntary services which the Sardar Bahādur rendered in connexion with the three Mount Everest Expeditions that he was elected a Fellow of the Royal Geographical Society.[1] The Sardar Bahādur was one of the really true Buddhists of our generation, who not only fostered but also practically applied the Precepts of the Enlightened One. Of the Great *Guru* Padma-Sambhava he was a fervent devotee. He had scholarly command of ten languages, English, Tibetan, Hindustani, Kyathi, Bengali, Nepalese, Lepcha, and other Himalayan tongues. Save for his assistance, Book I of this volume would never have been written. As to a *Guru*, and a *Bodhisattva* far advanced on the Great Path, the Mahāyāna, the Editor here acknowledges with profound gratitude his own personal indebtedness to the Sardar Bahādur. And all who read this book are, in like manner, the Sardar Bahādur's debtors.

There now follows a brief biographical account of the two translators of Book II.

Lāma Karma Sumdhon Paul was born in Ghoom on 4 September 1891 of Tibetan ancestry. As a boy, his education commenced, and continued for three years, under the learned Mongolian Lāma Sherab Gyatsho, of the Ghoom Monastery. Later, he entered the Darjeeling High School with a government scholarship and there completed his studies at the age

---

[1] For a large part of this biographical matter the Editor is indebted to *The Darjeeling Times* of 2 Jan. 1937 wherein there appears a special article concerning the death of the Sardar Bahādur, entitled 'The passing of a Truly Great Man', covering four pages.

of sixteen. His first post was as a government employee in the Deputy Commissioner's Office, Darjeeling.

During 1905–6 he was attached to the staff of the Tashi Lāma as an interpreter and accompanied His Holiness on a tour of India and afterwards to the Monastery of Tashi Lhunpo ('Heap of Blessings'). For about seven months he resided in this monastery of the Tashi Lāma, in intimate personal contact with His Holiness. 'My own impression', he said in reply to the Editor's query, 'is that His Holiness the Tashi Lāma really regarded himself as being an incarnation of the Buddha Amitābha. His officials told me that His Holiness possessed many unusual psychic powers, and the Tibetan Priesthood, as a whole, recognized in him the Supreme Head of the Esoteric Doctrines.'

Of the daily activities of His Holiness, the Lāma added:

He arose before dawn, prayed, and performed his personal religious duties. At about 5.30 a.m. he partook of tea and light refreshments. The early morning was taken up chiefly with receiving visiting officials of the Church. At about 10 a.m. he took a regular meal. Afterwards, he would attend the temples, bless pilgrims, and see visitors. I always left his presence soon after sunset, and went to my own apartments; but I was told that His Holiness retired late, after a very long day's work.

In India, at Bōdh-Gayā, Benares, and Taxila, His Holiness gave many religious discourses and blessed the people by touching their head. In public blessings he generally held an arrow to which were attached various coloured Tibetan scarfs, and with these he touched the head of those he blessed. In bestowing blessings privately he used his hands alone. He taught us especially concerning the coming Buddha, Maitreya, and read texts referring to Him and made prayers to Him.

In 1908 the Lāma Karma Sumdhon Paul went to Lhāsa and remained there for almost one year, visiting temples and monasteries and making pilgrimages. At that epoch the Dalai Lāma was absent in China. After returning to Darjeeling the Lāma became the headmaster of the Ghoom Middle English School. In 1924 he became the first successor to the late Lāma Kazi Dawa-Samdup in the Department of Tibetan Studies of the University of Calcutta. Very successfully he occupied that post for about ten years, retiring in 1933, whereupon he was appointed Head Lāma of the Government High School, Darjeeling, as he is, in 1935. There appeared in 1934 his translation into English of the *Dri-med-Kun-lDen's Namthar*, or *Birth-Story of Sarva-Vimala, King of Religion*, published by the Calcutta University.

Lāma Lobzang Mingyur Dorje, too, was born in Ghoom of Tibetan parentage, in the year 1875, and also had as his *guru* the same venerable abbot Lāma Sherab Gyatsho, who had come from Mongolia some years previously and founded the Ghoom Monastery. His discipleship under this learned Lāma began at the age of 10 and continued for fifteen years, and then, at the age of 25, he left the Monastery and, as his first scholarly work, aided the late Rai Bahādur Sarat Chandra Dās to compile his *Tibetan–English Dictionary* (Calcutta, 1902), now the standard treatise of its kind. At this task of compilation, Lāma Lobzang Mingyur Dorje worked for almost five years; and, although it was due to him, assisted by his *guru* in the Ghoom Monastery, more than to the Rai Bahādur that the Dictionary was accurately arranged, unfortunately no credit was given to him or to his *guru* in its preface.

Soon after the Dictionary was completed, the Lāma was appointed Head Lāma of the Government High School, Darjeeling. He held this post with great honour for thirty years, and then, as is customary, retired on a pension. But he was still a vigorous man; and, being a true scholar, he made this retirement an opportunity for yet wider social service. First we see him at the Urusvati Himalayan Roerich Research Institution, where he worked for four years on another Tibetan–English Dictionary and in experimenting with Tibetan methods of treating cancer and other diseases, with valuable results. Then, on 1 August 1935 he was appointed to the Tibetan Instructorship for Research in Tibetan in the University of Calcutta, becoming the late Lāma Kazi Dawa-Samdup's second successor.

These two Lāmas, the translators of Book II, did much to raise the standard of Tibetan studies not only in the Darjeeling High School but in the University of Calcutta as well, and both were intimately acquainted with the late Lāma Kazi Dawa-Samdup.

Of the late Lāma Kazi Dawa-Samdup's *Guru* Norbu (of whom some account is recorded in *Tibetan Yoga and Secret Doctrines*, pp. 105–7), Lāma Lobzang Mingyur Dorje said to the Editor, in the year 1935:

> I met him in Buxaduar more than twenty years ago, and found him to be a most excellent Lāma of the Kargyüd (*Dkar-brgyud*) Sect. The Director of Public Instruction of Bengal deputed me to inspect his monastic school, for the Government was making him a grant-in-aid. He had about twenty disciples. I remained with the *Guru* for two days, and made a very favourable report.

XVII. THE TRANSLATING AND EDITING

In its original Block-Print form, the treatise translated as Book II consists of 143 lines of Tibetan text divided into 395 metrically constructed verses written on fifteen folios, or thirty pages counting the title-page, of Tibetan-made paper, each measuring 14½ by 3½ inches. Of the 395 verses, 389 are in a regular nine-syllable metre.[1] Of the other verses, consisting of *mantras*, three are of six, one of three, and two of two syllables each. There are, on an average, nine words in each of the 143 lines, or a total of about 1287 words. The metre of the 389 regular nine-syllable verses is illustrated by the following transliteration of verses 37 and 38:

> *Kri-yog bsnyen bsgrub mthah la zhen pas bsgribs.*
> *Ma-hā a-nu dbyings rig zhen pas bsgribs.*
> (*pron. Kri-yog nyen drub thah la zhen pe drib.*
> *Ma-hā ah-nu ying rig zhen pe drib*).

The translation is on page 206, following.

In order to make the words fit the metre, many of them throughout the text are abbreviated, like the first two here given, *Kri-yog* being a shortened form of the Sanskrit *Kriyā-Yoga*. Some of the verses are merely so many words or

---

[1] See *Tibetan Yoga and Secret Doctrines*, pp. 278–80, where Tibetan versification is discussed.

syllables without verbal or other connexion. Owing to this abbreviated style of diction and to the epigrammatic character of the aphoristic text as a whole, all the skilled ability of the two translators and of the Editor was required to produce a rendering which would be true both to the highly philosophical and classical Tibetan, with its many technical and idiomatic expressions, and to the requirements of literary English. No such translation can be expected to be entirely free from error, more especially in our actual pioneering stage of Tibetan studies. The translators and the Editor believe, however, that the rendering herein contained faithfully conveys the real meanings which an educated *lāma* would derive from a careful study of the treatise in its original form.

No attempt has been made in the English translation to conform to the metrical structure of the Tibetan text. Nor has a strictly literal rendering always been considered desirable; and frequently a rather free rendering has been found necessary to bring out in the English the inner significance of the Tibetan idioms, in particular those peculiarly Tantric.

The same methods were employed in translating the excerpts from the Block-Print text of the Biography of Padma-Sambhava by the late Sardar Bahādur S. W. Laden La, ably assisted by Lāma Sonam Senge, a graduate in Tibetan Grammar of the Sakya Monastery, Tibet, and by the Editor. The work of translating these excerpts was begun in Darjeeling on 22 November 1935 and completed in Calcutta on 21 January 1936. The Block-Print which was used consisted of 397 large folios, or 794 pages inclusive of the title-page.

The translation of the text of the ' *Yoga* of Knowing the Mind in Its Nakedness' was started on 4 September 1935, the forty-fourth birthday of the Lāma Karma Sumdhon Paul, in the bungalow then occupied by the Editor, just outside the entrance to the Ghoom Monastery, Darjeeling. The first rough draft of the translation was in manuscript form on the second day of the following month; and the various revisions of the translation were completed, there in Ghoom, about five weeks later.

Although the ' *Yoga* of Knowing the Mind in Its Nakedness', like the 'Yoga of the Great Symbol' set forth in *Tibetan Yoga and Secret Doctrines*, is not strictly a *Tantra*, it is, nevertheless, a product of Tantricism.

The Epitome of the Biography is, necessarily, a brief synopsis of the very extensive and frequently verbose mass of matter comprised within the 794 large pages of the original text, which contains not only textual inconsistences, such as are inseparable from a collection of semi-historical traditions, but much mythology, as in its first chapters, that has no more than remote bearing on the life-history of Padma-Sambhava. Thus, the Epitome opens with the Buddha's prophecy of Padma's birth, on folio 40, where the Biography properly begins, and thence continues to the end of the Tibetan text. No critical examination of the material, historical or philosophical, has been attempted; for our purpose in presenting it is essentially anthropological. This task of criticism remains for scholars of the future, when a translation of the Biography as a whole will have been made.

The version of the *Guru* Phadampa Sangay's teachings contained in Book III is based upon a translation made by the late Lāma Kazi Dawa-Samdup in the year 1919, from a manuscript text, the history of which is given in the annotation on the title-page of Book III.

So far as is consistent with soundness of method, the use of square brackets has been avoided, especially in Book II. But wherever they appear they usually indicate an interpolation intended to bring out the meaning of an abbreviated or concise aphorism or phrase, or of an idiomatic, technical, or obscure expression. Sometimes they are used, in translated texts, parenthetically.

The examination of the textual matter of all three Books has been anthropological, in the strict sense of Anthropology, the Knowing, or Knowledge, of Man. Its critical examination from the viewpoint of history, philosophy, and philology remains for specialists in those respective fields of scholarship. As to the validity of the doctrines presented, the right attitude is that of the rationalist, so well stated by the Buddha when He admonished His disciples not to believe or accept anything, even though contained in Bibles and taught by Sages, until tested *yogically* and found to be true.

Up to the present time, occidental research concerning Padma-Sambhava and the very voluminous mass of material treating of him, chiefly in Tibetan, Mongolian, and Chinese, has been quite pioneer and limited. Save for our present treatise there is no work in English chiefly devoted to the Great *Guru*. Brief accounts concerning him are contained in *The Buddhism of Tibet*, by Dr. L. A. Waddell, to which frequent reference is made herein, in *Tibetan Literary Texts and Documents Concerning Chinese Turkestan*, by Dr. F. W. Thomas, and in works on Tibet by Sir Charles Bell and other writers, including the three preceding volumes of our own Tibetan Series.[1]

XVIII. Englishing

The English language, itself an importation into Great Britain from the European Continent, has attained pre-eminence by virtue of its unsurpassed power of absorbing the words of other languages. Its original Anglo-Celtic vocabulary was fundamentally Germanic. Under the Romans, the long

---

[1] In German, the chief works concerning Padma-Sambhava are, by E. Schlagintweit, *Die Lebensbeschreibung von Padma-Sambhava, dem Begründer des Lāmaismus (Aus dem Tibetischen übersetzt)*, and by A. Grünwedel, *Padmasambhava und Verwandtes* (Leipzig u. Berlin, 1912); those concerning the *Padma-thaṅ-yig* are by A. Grünwedel, *Drei Leptscha Texte; Mit Auszügen aus dem Padma-thaṅ-yig und Glossar* (Leiden, 1896), *Flucht des Padmasambhava aus dem Hause seines königlichen Pflegevaters Indrabhuti* (Leipzig, 1902), and *Ein Kapitel des Ta-se-sun* (Berlin, 1896). Other matter concerning Padma-Sambhava are: by A. Grünwedel, *Padmasambhava und Mandarava* (Leipzig, 1898); by S. H. Ribbach, *Vier Bilder des Padmasambhava und seiner Gefolgschaft* (Hamburg, 1917); by B. Laufer, *Die Bru-ža Sprache und die historische Stellung des Padmasambhava (T'oung Pao,* Ser. II, Vol. 9, 1908), and *Btsun-mo-bkai-thaṅ-yig* (Leipzig, 1911). In French, the outstanding work is *Le Dict de Padma* (Paris, 1933), a translation from the Tibetan of the *Padma Thang Yig MS. de Lithang*, by Gustave-Charles Touissaint, concerning the 'History of the Existences of the Guru Padma-Sambhava', the matter of which parallels in a general way although not in fullness of detail that of the *Unabridged Biography* epitomized herein in Book I. Each of these two biographical works consist of 117 chapters and both have the same three titles in the colophons. The chapters of the one work do not, however, correspond with those of the other work as to content.

process of word-absorption from classical sources, more especially from Latin, began, and attained great momentum with the coming of Christianity. When the Norman conquerors made French the court language, fresh impetus was given to the latinization. The Renaissance brought in many more classically derived words. Then, after the discovery of America, generation by generation, as England became more and more the seat of empire, English laid under tribute all the languages of England's far-flung possessions. In modern times, the demand of the physical sciences for new terminologies has been satisfied by further recourse to the languages of Greece and Rome.

The words now anglicized are so numerous that they constitute at least three-quarters and perhaps four-fifths of the vocabulary of English as a whole. Eventually, if the ever widening process of word-absorption continues, as it appears destined to continue, English, by realizing in itself the at-one-ment of all the languages of mankind, will become the universal world language.

Ever since the British occupation of India, especially during the last quarter of the nineteenth century, and with accelerating rapidity since the beginning of the twentieth century, English has been absorbing an immense number of entirely new words expressive of the transcendent things of the spirit, from Sanskrit sources. Whilst Science, Commerce, and Techniques have been creating their own particular vocabularies chiefly from French, Latin, and Greek, the New Philosophy, based upon the Ancient Higher Psychology of the Sages, now reshaping the thought of the Occident far more profoundly than during the fifteenth-century Renaissance, has been establishing another vocabulary, of immeasurably greater value to Occidental man. Words such as *Buddha*, *Nirvana*, *karma*, *yoga*, *guru*, *rishi*, *tantra*, *mantra* are already fully naturalized and appear as English in the Oxford *New English Dictionary*. In order that this process of naturalization may be quickened, it is incumbent upon those who are students of the Supreme Science, the Divine Wisdom, rather than professional philologists (to whom philological exactitude is essential) to employ such transliterations from the Sanskrit as are most in keeping with vernacular English phonetics and therefore the easiest to anglicize. For illustration, *Nirvāṇa* appears in the *New English Dictionary* bereft of the two diacritical marks (which for the purpose of exact scholarship are indispensable) because it has become anglicized and is, strictly speaking, no longer Sanskrit.

Accordingly, the Editor has made choice of a middle path, which avoids the two extremes, of philological exactitude and of complete anglicization; and, therefore, all Sanskrit, Tibetan, and other transliterations from oriental and foreign languages have been italicized and diacritical marks have been added for the purpose of conforming to the parallel usage in the previous volumes of this Series. But, favouring the anglicization process, the Editor has preferred to write *Shiva* as an English word, rather than *Şiva* as a Sanskrit word; and, similarly, *Ashoka* and *Upanishad* rather than *Aşoka* and *Upaniṣad*; the Bengali-Sanskrit *Sangsāra* (favoured, as, for instance, in *The Tantra of the Great Liberation*, p. cxvi, by the late Sir John Woodroffe) rather than *Saṃsāra* (or *Saṃsāra*), and so on. Preference has been given to such forms derived from the Tibetan as *Nyingma* instead of *Ñingma*, *Thī-Srong-Detsan* instead of *Thī-Sroṅ-Detsan*, and so on. The result being inconsistent with either of the two extremes is, of course, open to the criticism of scholars. It is, however, intended to represent a transitional stage in the anglicization process; and this is its justification in a popularly written treatise of this character.

After all, the chief social consideration is not phonetic exactness of the form anglicized, but its acceptance as a word symbol of very definite import. In the end, it is popular usage, not exactitude of spelling or pronunciation, that determines the formation of standard speech. Words being, as the Buddhas teach, merely *sangsāric* means of expounding the *Dharma*, it matters not how they are written or spoken so long as they convey the meaning intended, and thus assist mankind to attain the Great Liberation.

XIX. CRITICISM BY CRITICS

This Introduction is intended to serve as a commentary to the two chief texts upon which this volume is based, the text of the Biography, summarized in our Epitome, and the text of the 'Yoga of Knowing the Mind In Its Unobscured Reality [or Nakedness]'. Book III serves as an independent commentary to Book II. The annotations to the texts are supplementary to this Introduction as a commentary. A certain amount of repetition, each time in a different context or from a different viewpoint, has been allowed, somewhat after the style employed by the Gurus to produce emphasis upon essentials; this appears to be quite necessary in presenting to the Occident these most recondite of oriental doctrines.

The yogic treatise itself, presented by Book II, is, essentially, and as critics may fairly point out, a series of suggestive deductions in aphorisms unaccompanied by proof. No treatise on Reality can be other than intellectually stated. Nevertheless, if it be, as it purports to be, based upon realizable truths, the proof must lie in the putting its teachings to the test of practical application in a strictly scientific manner. If one wishes to sustain his body he must eat and digest food for himself; no one else can do this for him. Or, otherwise stated, in keeping with the Piers Plowman philosophy of fourteenth-century England, 'It is not what a man eats, but what he digests that makes him strong'. Similarly, it is not what a critic may think or believe to be true which is always true, or necessarily true because he thinks it is; but only what he proves empirically to be true. Accordingly, if any one desires to criticize, let him do so only after having applied the 'Yoga of Knowing the Mind in Its Nakedness' exhaustively.

Padma-Sambhava, to whom the authorship of the treatise is attributed, may be taken to be, on the basis of historically verifiable data concerning him, one who has proved for himself, by actual realization, the assertions therein contained. This is clear from the passage at the end of the treatise concerning the tasting of honey. A chemical formula, even one of the simplest, such as H_2O (or water), cannot be scientifically, or chemically, stated except in language common to all chemists, and none but chemists can interpret it fully. Likewise, recondite supra-mundane doctrines cannot be conveyed in written form without employing written words; and if written in the symbolical formulae of the esoteric science of alchemy, the transcendent chemistry, none but students of the occult sciences are fitted to study, much less interpret and criticize them.

XX. Conclusion

In concluding this Introduction there arises in the mind of him who writes these words the teaching, the most practically important of all the teachings of the *Gurus*, that whosoever hears and applies the *Dharma* must continually recollect that human life is transient and fleeting, and that the human body, although the 'Vessel of Salvation', is no more than a *karmic* aggregate productive of suffering. Attachment to life and form, and to *sangsāric* sensuousness will thereby be avoided. But, at the same time, the disciple must not fail to take good care of his or her bodily instrument, not for the purpose of enjoying worldly pleasures, but for the sole end of attaining the Great Liberation.[1]

Having obtained this pure and difficult-to-obtain, free, and endowed human body, it would be a cause of regret to die an irreligious and worldly man.

This human life in the Age of Darkness, the *Kali Yuga*, being so brief and uncertain, it would be a cause of regret to spend it in worldly aims and pursuits.

The mind, imbued with love and compassion in thought and deed, ought ever to be directed to the service of all sentient beings.[2]

---

[1] In similar language, the same teaching is set forth at more length in *Homeless Brothers*, based upon *Buddha, Truth and Brotherhood*, a translation from the Japanese of an epitomized version of a number of Buddhist Scriptures prepared by Prof. S. Yamabe of Kyoto, and incorporated in *A Buddhist Bible* (pp. 625–33), compiled and published by Dwight Goddard, at Thetford, Vermont, U.S.A. *A Buddhist Bible* will be found of much assistance to all students of our Tibetan Series.

[2] *The Precepts of the Gurus*, whence these three (I. 2–3; II. 9) come, contained in Book I of *Tibetan Yoga and Secret Doctrines*, are all-sufficient to guide the *yogin* and to serve as a *guru* to the *yogin* who desires a *guru*.

Nāgārjuna, one of the most illustrious of the Great *Gurus*, in his *Epistles* to his friend King De-chöd Zang-po, wrote:

There are those who pass from light to light, those who pass from darkness to darkness, those who pass from light to darkness, and those who pass from darkness to light. Of these four, be thou the first. . . .

The Teacher hath called Faith, Chastity, Charity, Learning, Sincerity united with Modesty, Avoidance of Wrong Action, and Wisdom the Seven Divine Riches. Know that other riches cannot aid thee. . . .

He who would misuse the boon of human life is far more stupid than he who would employ a gold vessel inlaid with precious gems as a receptacle for filth. . . .

The Buddha hath said that association with holy men is the root of all virtue. . . .

Right Views, Right Livelihood, Right Endeavour, Right Recollection, Right Meditation, Right Speech, Right Intentions, and Right Judgement are the Eight Parts of the Path. By meditating upon them one attaineth Peace.[1]

And, like the faithful folk of Tingri, Tibet, may each reader of this volume comprehend the full import of the words of their *Guru* Phadampa Sangay (whose Last Testament of Teachings is set forth herein, in Book III) when he sang,

Like the sunshine from a clear space twixt the clouds the *Dharma* is. Know that now there is such Sunshine; use it wisely, Tingri folk.

---

[1] These excerpts are recensions from an English rendering of the *Epistles*, entitled in Tibetan *Bshes-pahi-hphrin-yig* (Skt. *Suttri* [da] *Lekha*, 'Friendly Letters'), prepared by the late Lāma Kazi Dawa-Samdup in the year 1919 and now in the Editor's possession.

PLATE V

THE EIGHT *GURUS*

Described on pages xxi-xxiv

BOOK I

AN EPITOME OF
THE LIFE AND TEACHINGS OF
TIBET'S GREAT *GURU*
PADMA-SAMBHAVA

ACCORDING TO THE BIOGRAPHY BY HIS CHIEF DISCIPLE
THE TIBETAN LADY YESHEY TSHOGYAL
INCARNATION OF SARASVATI
GODDESS OF LEARNING[1]

Based upon Excerpts rendered into English by the late
Sardar Bahādur S. W. Laden La, C.B.E., F.R.G.S.,
assisted by Lāma Sonam Senge

---

[1] The various titles given to the Biography are set forth herein, both in
Tibetan and English translation, in the Colophon, on pages 191–2. The more
general title, on the first folio of the Block-Print text, is as follows:
 'Herein is contained the Unabridged Biography of the Urgyān *Guru*
 Padma-Sambhava: "The Gold Rosary [of Teachings] Illuminating the
 Path of Liberation" (*U-rgyān Guru Pad-ma Hbyung-gnas gyi Rnam-
 thar Rgyas-pa Gser-gyi Phreng-ba Thar-lam Gsal-byed Bzhug-so*).'

A Fully Enlightened One

'Know, Vasettha, that from time to time a Tathāgata is born into the world, a Fully Enlightened One, blessed and worthy, abounding in wisdom and goodness, happy, with knowledge of the world, unsurpassed as a guide to erring mortals, a teacher of gods and men, a Blessed Buddha. He, by Himself, thoroughly understandeth, and seeth, as it were face to face, this Universe—the world below, with all its spiritual beings, and the worlds above, of Māra and Brahma—and all creatures, Samanas and Brāhmins, gods and men; and He then maketh His knowledge known to others. The Truth doth He proclaim, both in its letter and in its spirit, beautiful in its origin, beautiful in its progress, beautiful in its consummation; the Higher Life doth He reveal, in all its purity and in all its perfectness.'

The Buddha, *Tevigga Suttanta*, I, 46
(based upon the translation in *The Library of Original Sources*, i, edited by Oliver J. Thatcher).

THE INTRODUCTION

In this Book, Padma-Sambhava is presented as the divine personification of Tibetan idealism, a Culture Hero greater than even the Buddha Gautama. The wonders of oriental myth, the mysteriousness of the secret doctrines of the Mahāyāna, and the marvels of magic enhalo him. Like the Celtic Arthur and Cuchullain, the Scandinavian Odin and Thor, the Greek Orpheus and Odysseus, or the Egyptian Osiris and Hermes, the Lotus-Born One is of superhuman lineage, transcendent over the pomp and circumstance and the conventionalities of the world.

In the *Saga of Gesar*, the Iliad of Central Asia, Padma-Sambhava's heroic characteristics are similarly emphasized.[1] While Gesar, the supernormally gifted warrior-king puts down violence and injustice, the Great *Guru's* mission is to overthrow unrighteousness and establish the *Dharma*.

Probably nowhere in the sacred literature of mankind is there to be found a more remarkable parallelism than that existing between the accounts of the extraordinary characteristics attributed to Padma-Sambhava and to Melchizedek. Each was a King of Righteousness and a King of Peace, and a high priest. Each, as is said of Melchizedek, was 'without father, without mother, without genealogy, having neither beginning of days nor end of life' and 'abideth a priest continually'.[2] Both alike, being of the Succession of Great Teachers, founded an occult spiritual fraternity, that of Melchizedek traditionally dating from as early as the sixth century B.C., and that of Padma-Sambhava dating from the middle of the eighth century A.D. Nothing is known either of the origin or of the end of these two Heroes. According to tradition, both of them are believed never to have died.[3]

To the historian and student of religious origins, no less than to anthropologists, this Epitome of the Great *Guru's*

[1] Cf. *The Superhuman Life of Gesar of Ling*, by Alexandra David-Neel and Lāma Yongden (London, 1933).
[2] Cf. Hebrews vii. 2–3.
[3] Ibid. vi. 20; vii. 17.

Biography should prove to be of unique value. Not only does it illustrate the process of deification of one who undoubtedly was an historical character, but it also affords glimpses into the remarkable cultural state of India twelve centuries ago, and sets forth certain far-reaching deductions arrived at by a succession of Sages of the Mahāyāna School concerning the supreme problem of Reality.

Quite apart from the myths, the folk traditions, and the lore of the *Gurus*, the Biography contains much that should be of more than ordinary interest to Buddhists of all Schools. This is clearly indicated by the sections of the Epitome about the ordination of Padma by Ānanda, the story of the unfaithful monk, how Ānanda was chosen chief disciple, Ānanda's testimony concerning the Buddha and the Scriptures, and the remarkable account of the defeat of the non-Buddhists at Bōdh-Gayā in controversy and magic. Whether the Theravāda Buddhist sees fit to give credence or not to these Mahāyāna accounts relating to the life and teachings of the Buddha, they at least show that in Buddhism, as in Christianity and other religions, there is an apocryphal literature. In themselves, they are of value in the study of Buddhist origins.

Of the strange incidents and various doctrines described in the Epitome, each of its readers must be the judge. In it, undoubtedly, the rational and the irrational blend, and so do the esoteric and the exoteric. But underlying the Biography of the Great *Guru* when seen as a whole there is discernible the Right Intention of the illustrious Tibetan lady Yeshey Tshogyal, who, as the colophon of the Tibetan text records, compiled it in manuscript form some twelve hundred years ago, and then hid it in a cave in Tibet, where it remained until the time came for its recovery and transmission to our age. And each reader of the Epitome, which now follows, is indebted to her, as the faithful disciple is to the preceptor.

THE EPITOME OF THE GREAT *GURU'S* BIOGRAPHY

THE BUDDHA'S PROPHECY OF THE BIRTH OF PADMA-SAMBHAVA

When the Buddha was about to pass away at Kushinagara,[1] and His disciples were weeping, He said to them, 'The world being transitory and death inevitable for all livings things, the time for my own departure hath come. But weep not; for twelve years after my departure, from a lotus blossom on the Dhanakosha Lake,[2] in the north-western corner of the country of Urgyān,[3] there will be born one who will be much wiser and more spiritually powerful than Myself. He will be called Padma-Sambhava,[4] and by him the Esoteric Doctrine will be established.'

THE KING INDRABODHI

In the country of Urgyān (or Udyāna), westward from Bōdh-Gayā, there was the great city of Jatumati, containing a palace called 'Emerald Palace' wherein dwelt King Indrabodhi. Although possessed of vast worldly wealth and power and blessed with five hundred queens and one hundred Buddhist and one hundred non-Buddhist ministers, Indrabodhi was blind; and his subjects called him 'the wealthiest king without eyes'. When his only son and heir died and famine immediately thereafter weakened his kingdom, Indrabodhi wept, overcome with misfortune. Consoled by a *yogī*, the King called together the priests, and they made offerings to the gods and read the sacred books. Then the King took oath to give in charity all his possessions; and his treasury

---

[1] Kushinagara, the place of the Buddha's *Pari-Nirvāṇa*, is about thirty-five miles east of the modern Gorakpur. Kushinagara means 'Town (or Place) of Kusha-Grass', a grass sacred to *yogins* (see p. 152[1]).

[2] According to some accounts, the Dhanakosha Lake, or, as it is otherwise called, the Lotus Lake (Tib. *Tsho-Padma-chan*), is placed near Hardwar, in the United Provinces of India, although it is usually stated to be in the country of Urgyān (or Udyāna).

[3] Urgyān (or Udyāna) is said to have corresponded to the country about Gazni, to the north-west of Kashmir. (Cf. L. A. Waddell, op. cit., p. 26.)

[4] Or the 'Lotus-Born'. See pp. 131, 173.

and granaries were emptied. In the end, his subjects were so impoverished that they were obliged to eat the young un-ripened crops and even flowers.

THE KING'S DESPONDENCY

Oppressed with the thought of being heirless, the King made offerings and prayers to the deities of all the prevailing faiths, but, no son being vouchsafed to him, he lost confidence in every religion. Then, one day, he went to the roof of his palace and beat the summoning drum; and, when all the people had come, he addressed the assembled priests thus: 'Hear me, each of you! I have made prayer to the deities and to the guardian spirits of this land and offerings to the Trinity,[1] but I have not been blessed with a son. Religion is, therefore, devoid of truth; and I command that within seven days ye destroy every one of these deities and guardian spirits. Other-wise, ye shall know my punishment.'

AVALOKITESHVARA'S APPEAL TO AMITĀBHA

The priests, in their consternation, hurriedly collected materials for the performance of a ceremony of burnt offer-ings. The deities and guardian spirits, filled with anger, sent storms of wind, hail, and blood; and throughout Urgyān the inhabitants were as frightened as fish are when taken from the water and placed upon dry sand. In great pity, Avalo-kiteshvara made appeal to the Buddha Amitābha, in the Sukhāvatī Heaven, to protect the suffering people.

AMITĀBHA'S RESPONSE AND EMANATION

Thereupon, the Buddha Amitābha thought, 'Let me take birth in the Dhanakosha Lake'; and there went forth from His tongue a ray of red light, which, like a meteor, entered the centre of the lake. Where the ray entered the water, there appeared a small island covered with golden-coloured grass, whence flowed three springs of the colour of turquoise; and from the centre of the island there sprang forth a lotus

---

[1] Namely, the Buddha, the *Dharma* (or Scriptures), and the *Saṅgha* (or Brotherhood of the Priests of the Buddhist Order).

PLATE VI

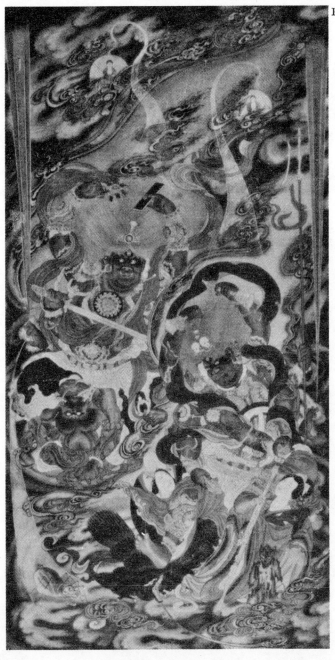

EMANATION

Described on pages xxiv–xxvi

blossom. Simultaneously, the Buddha Amitābha, with great radiance, emitted from His heart a five-pointed *dorje*,[1] and the *dorje* fell into the centre of the lotus blossom.

THE KING'S AND THE PRIESTS' DREAMS

Being appeased by this, the deities and guardian spirits ceased harming the people of Urgyān, and circumambulated the lake, making obeisance and offerings. The King dreamt that he held in his hand a five-pointed *dorje* which emitted radiance so great that all the kingdom was illuminated. Upon awakening, the King was so happy that he worshipped the Trinity; and the deities and guardian spirits appeared and made humble submission to him. The Buddhist priests, too, had an auspicious dream, which perturbed the non-Buddhist priests: they beheld a thousand suns illuminating the world.

THE PROPHECY OF AMITĀBHA'S INCARNATION

Then, whilst the King was piously circumambulating a *stūpa* of nine steps which had miraculously sprung forth from a pond in front of his palace, gods appeared in the heavens and prophesied: 'Hail! Hail! the Lord Amitābha, Protector of Mankind, shall take birth as a Divine Incarnation from a lotus blossom amidst the Jewel Lake ;[2] and he will be worthy to become thy son. Suffer no harm to befall Him and give Him thy protection. Thereby, every good will come to thee.'

The King reported this prophecy to his minister of state Triguṇadhara and requested him to search for the promised

---

[1] The Tibetan *dorje* (Skt. *Vajra*), being one of the chief ritual objects of Tibetan Buddhism, has come to be called the *lāmas'* sceptre. Esoterically, the word *dorje* has many meanings. It is applied to Buddhas and deities, to Tantric initiates, to specially sacred places, to texts and philosophical systems. For instance, *Vajrayāna*, meaning 'Path of the *Vajra*', is the name of one of the most esoteric of the schools of Northern Buddhism. *Dorje*, or *Vajra*, is applied to anything of an exalted religious character which is lasting, immune to destruction, occultly powerful and irresistible. *Dorje Lopon*, referring to the high initiate presiding at Tibetan Tantric rites, is a further illustration of its usage. On the cover of this volume is depicted a double *dorje*, which is like a Greek cross. In *The Tibetan Book of the Dead*, facing page 137, appears an illustration of the single *dorje*, which, rather than the double *dorje*, is the form commonly used.

[2] Or the Dhanakosha Lake.

son. The minister went to the lake at once, and saw at the centre of the lake a very large lotus full blown and seated in its midst a beautiful boy child, apparently about one year of age. Perspiration beaded the child's face, and an aura encircled him. Doubtful of the wisdom of having the King adopt so unusual a child, that might not be of human origin, the minister decided to postpone reporting the discovery.

The Wish-granting Gem

The kingdom being impoverished, the King called his ministers together for advice. Some suggested increase of agriculture, some increase of trade, and others declared for the making of war and the plundering of the property of others. Rather than adopt any policy not in accord with the precepts of the *Dharma*, the King decided to risk his own life for the good of his people and obtain from the *Nāgas*, who dwelt beneath the waters of the ocean, a wondrous wish-granting gem. 'When I return with the gem', he said, 'I shall be able to feed all my subjects and all the mendicants.'

Then the King went to the palace of the *Nāgas*, and the wish-granting gem was presented to him by their princess. As soon as the gem was placed in the hand of the King he wished for sight in his left eye and the sight came.

The King's Discovery of the Lotus-Born Child

On his return to the Urgyān country, just as the minister Triguṇadhara approached and greeted him, the King noticed a rainbow of five colours over the Dhanakosha Lake, although there were no clouds and the sun was shining brightly. And the King said to the minister, 'Please go and ascertain what there is in that lake yonder'.

'How is it that thou, being blind, canst see this?' asked the minister. 'I appealed to the wish-granting gem and my sight was restored', replied the King. Thereupon the minister revealed his discovery of the wonderful babe, saying, 'I dared not report the matter to thee previously', and he begged the King to go to the lake and see for himself. 'Last night', responded the King, 'I dreamt that from the sky there came into my hand a nine-pointed *dorje*, and before that I dreamt that from my heart issued a sun, the light of which shone over the whole world.'

The King and his minister went to the lake and, taking a small boat, reached the place over which the rainbow shone. There they beheld a fragrant lotus blossom, the circumference of which exceeded that of one's body and circled arms, and seated at the centre of the blossom a fair rosy-cheeked little boy resembling the Lord Buddha, holding in his right hand a tiny lotus blossom and in his left hand a tiny holy-water pot, and in the folds of the left arm a tiny three-pronged staff.

The King felt much veneration for the self-born babe; and, in excess of joy, he wept. He asked the child, 'Who are thy father and mother, and of what country and caste art thou? What food sustaineth thee; and why art thou here?' The child answered, 'My father is Wisdom and my mother is the Voidness. My country is the country of the *Dharma*. I am of no caste and of no creed. I am sustained by perplexity; and I am here to destroy Lust, Anger, and Sloth.' When the child had ceased speaking, the King's right eye was no longer blind. Overwhelmed with joy, the King named the child 'The Lake-born *Dorje*', and he and the minister made obeisance to the child.

THE CHILD IS TAKEN TO THE PALACE

The King asked the child if he would come to him, and the child said, 'I will, for I have entered the world to benefit all sentient creatures, to dominate those that are harmful, and for the good of the Doctrine of the Buddhas'. Then the lotus opened more fully and the child leapt, like a discharged arrow, to the shore of the lake. At the spot where the child touched the earth a lotus blossom immediately sprang up, and in it the child seated himself, whereupon the King named him 'The Lotus-Born', and thought to himself, 'He will be my heir and my *guru*'. Then the King severed the lotus blossom from its stem and lifted it up with the child sitting therein and with the minister set out for the palace.

The cranes and the wild ducks were overwhelmed with

grief at the loss of the child. Some perched on the child's shoulders. Some flew in front and bowed down their heads. Some fell to the earth and lay there as if dead. Some circled round and round the lake wailing. Some placed their beaks in the earth and wept. Even the trees and bushes bent over towards the child in their sadness. Magpies and parrots, peacocks and other birds flew to the fore of the procession and placed their wings tip to tip in an effort to halt the procession. Vultures and kites struck the King and the minister with their beaks. The small birds gave vent to their cries. Lions, tigers, bears, and other ferocious animals ran about on all sides in a threatening attitude trying to disrupt the procession. Elephants, buffaloes, and asses came out of the jungle and joined with the other animals in protest. The guardian spirits and the genii of the locality were greatly perturbed and caused thunder, lightning, and hail.

When the procession reached the villages all the villagers joined it. There happened to be an old man sitting by the wayside fishing; and the Lotus-Born One, seeing him, thought to himself, 'This is a sign that if I become the King of this country I shall suffer even as the fish do'. Shortly afterwards, the Lotus-Born One, upon seeing a crow chasing a partridge, which took refuge under a raspberry bush and escaped, thought to himself, 'The raspberry bush represents the kingdom, the crow represents the king, and the partridge represents myself; and the significance is that I must gradually abdicate from the kingship'.

The Lotus-Born One as Prince, Athlete, and King

When the procession reached the palace, the King took the wish-granting gem and wished a throne made of seven sorts of precious gems surmounted by a royal umbrella. The throne appeared instantaneously, and on it he seated the child and acknowledged him as son and heir. The Lotus-Born One became known as the *Bodhisattva*[1] Prince, and was proclaimed

---

[1] A *Bodhisattva*, or Enlightened Being, is one who is far advanced on the path to Buddhahood. Gautama, for example, was a *Bodhisattva* up to the moment of His supreme Illumination, attained while sitting in meditation under the Bodhi-Tree, whereupon he became a Buddha.

king. When he was thirteen years of age, as he sat on a throne of gold and turquoise and priests were performing religious ceremonies for the prosperity of the kingdom, the Buddha Amitābha, Avalokiteshvara, and the Guardian Gods of the Ten Directions[1] came and anointed him with holy water and named him 'The Lotus King'.[2]

The Lotus King established a new legal code based upon the Ten Precepts.[3] The kingdom prospered and the people were happy. He studied and became learned, and excelled in poetry and philosophy. In wrestling and sports none could equal him. He could shoot an arrow through the eye of a needle. He could send forth thirteen arrows, one directly after another, so quickly that the second arrow hit the first and forced it higher, and the third the second, and so on to the thirteenth. The force with which he discharged an arrow was so great that the arrow would penetrate seven doors of leather and seven doors of iron; and when he shot an arrow upward, no one could see how high it went. So the people called him 'The Mighty Athletic Hero-King'.

Once he picked up a stone as big as a yak[4] and threw it so far that it was barely visible. He could take nine anvils in a sling and cast them against a great boulder and overthrow it. With one breath he could run around the city thrice, with the speed of an arrow. He surpassed the fish in swimming. He

---

[1] These are the ten gods who, like door-keepers at an initiatory assembly, guard the world, one in each of the ten directions, which are the four cardinal and intermediate points of the compass, the nadir, and zenith.

[2] Tib. *Padma Gyalpo*, one of the eight manifestations, or personalities, assumed by the Great *Guru*, and described on page xxii.

[3] The Ten Precepts (*Dasha-Shīla*), or Prohibitions, of the Buddhist Moral Code are: (1) Kill not; (2) Steal not; (3) Commit not adultery; (4) Lie not; (5) Drink not Strong Drink; (6) Eat no Food except at the stated times; (7) Use no Wreaths, Ornaments, or Perfumes; (8) Use no High Mats or Thrones [to sit or sleep upon]; (9) Abstain from Dancing, Singing, Music, and Worldly Spectacles; (10) Own no Gold or Silver and accept none. Of these the first five (the *Panca-Shīla*) are binding upon the laity; the whole ten are binding upon members of the Order only, but sometimes laymen take a pious vow to observe, on certain fast days, one or more of those numbered 6 to 9. (Cf. L. A. Waddell, *The Buddhism of Tibet*, Cambridge, 1934, p. 134.)

[4] The *yak* is the Tibetan long-haired animal of the bovine family, the male being used as a beast of burden and in agricultural work, the female as a milch cow.

could lasso a flying hawk. He was also a master musician. Now he was named 'The Undefeated Lion King'.

THE COMING OF THE *ARHANTS*

One day he went unaccompanied to the 'Sorrowful Forest', which lay about two miles from the palace, to meditate. As he sat there in the Buddha posture, *Arhants*,[1] who were passing by overhead in the firmament, descended and praised him saying, 'Hail! Hail! Thou art the undoubted Lotus King, Thou art the second Buddha, heralding a new era, who shalt conquer the world. Though we were to possess hundreds of tongues and go from *kalpa* to *kalpa*,[2] we would not be fortunate enough to enjoy even a fraction of thy vast learning.' After circumambulating him seven times, they ascended and disappeared.

THE PLAN TO FETTER PADMA BY MARRIAGE

The King Indrabodhi and the ministers, seeing the Prince's inclination towards the meditative life, feared that eventually he would renounce the kingdom, so they assembled in council and decided to find for him a wife. The Prince knew that the chief purpose of the plan was to fetter him to the household state; and he refused to choose any of the many maidens who were carefully selected from all parts of Urgyān. The King Indrabodhi insisted that the Prince make choice and marry within seven days. After due consideration, the Prince decided not to disobey the old King who, like a father, had safe-guarded and reared him, and he gave to the King in writing a description of the sort of a maiden he would accept.

The written description was handed over to the minister

---

[1] An *Arhant*, literally 'Worthy One', is a Buddhist saint, often indistinguishable from a *Bodhisattva*, and comparable to the Hindu *Rishi*, who has attained the goal of the Noble Eightfold Path, and, at death, is fitted for *Nirvāṇa*. If the *Arhant* renounces his right to enter *Nirvāṇa*, in order to work for the salvation of the unenlightened, he automatically becomes a perfected *Bodhisattva*.

[2] A *kalpa* is a Day of Brahma, or the period of a thousand *yugas*, or ages, in which the Cosmos endures before being dissolved again in the Night of Brahma.

Triguṇadhara with the King's command to find such a maiden without delay. The minister immediately set out for Singala, where, at a religious festival in honour of the Lord Buddha, he saw a most attractive girl, one of a group of five hundred maidens. Questioning the girl, he ascertained that her name was Bhāsadhara ('The Light-Holder'), that she was the daughter of King Chandra Kumār and already betrothed to a prince.[1] The minister hurriedly returned to his King and reported that he considered Bhāsadhara entirely suitable.

THE CHOICE OF BHĀSADHARA AND THE MARRIAGE CEREMONY

On the pretext that he wished to give them valuable gifts, the King Indrabodhi invited Bhāsadhara and her four hundred and ninety-nine companions to his palace. When the Prince saw Bhāsadhara he was pleased with her; he handed to her the wish-granting gem and she wished that she might become his queen. Bhāsadhara and all the maidens returned to Singala, and a letter was sent to King Chandra Kumār requesting that he give Bhāsadhara in marriage to the Lotus-Born Prince. King Chandra Kumār replied that although he would be glad to meet the request he was unable to do so, for even then Bhāsadhara's marriage to a prince of Singala was about to take place.

When informed of this reply, the Lotus-Born Prince said, 'She alone is suitable, and I must have her'. The King Indrabodhi, calling in a *yogī* and informing him of the matter, commanded him to proceed to Singala, saying, 'Go to the palace

[1] The late Gustave-Charles Toussaint in his *Le Dict de Padma* (Paris, 1933), p. 491, considers this reference to 'Singala' (commonly regarded as being synonymous with Ceylon) to refer to a continental country not far from Udyāna (or Urgyān) and substitutes for it the name 'Siṁhapura'. Dr. L. A. Waddell, in *The Buddhism of Tibet* (Cambridge, 1934), p. 381[4], being of like opinion, says: 'This is probably the Siṅhapura of Hiuen Tsiang, which adjoined Udayāna, or Udyāna; or it may be Sagāla.' The late Sardar Bahādur S. W. Laden La remarked, as we translated this passage, that 'Singala' may have been what is now the Gantour District of the Madras Presidency rather than Ceylon. All of this and very much more that the Biography will present, as we proceed, touch complex problems of geography and history, the detailed consideration of which is beyond the scope of our present essentially anthropological study.

where the marriage procession is to halt for a night, and place under the tips of the girl's finger-nails iron dust moistened with water'.[1]

After the *yogī* had set out on the mission, the King went to the roof of the palace and raising aloft, on a banner of victory,[2] the wish-granting gem and, bowing to the four cardinal directions, prayed that Bhāsadhara with all her attendant maidens should be brought there before him ; and, as if by a wind, they were brought.

The King ordered that preparations for the marriage of the Lotus-Born Prince and Bhāsadhara be made at once. Bhāsadhara was bathed, arrayed in fine garments and jewels, and placed on a seat beside the Lotus-Born Prince ; and they were married. One hundred thousand women of Urgyān proclaimed Bhāsadhara Queen.[3] Then the four hundred and ninety-nine other maidens were married to the Prince, for it was customary for a King of Urgyān to have five hundred wives. Thus for five years the Prince experienced worldly happiness.

THE RENUNCIATION

Then the Dhyānī Buddha Vajra-Sattva appeared and announced to the Prince that the time had come to renounce both the married state and the throne. And the King Indra-bodhi dreamt that the Sun and Moon set simultaneously, that the palace was filled with lamentation and that all the ministers were weeping. When the King awoke, he was overcome with forebodings and sadness. Shortly afterwards, the Prince, with his ministers, went for a walk to the 'Sorrowful Forest' where he had been visited by the *Arhants* ; and there appeared in the southern heavens the various emblems of the Buddhist Faith, to signify that the Prince was about to become a world

---

[1] Iron, the world over, is commonly taboo to evil spirits, and prevents spells from taking effect. Its use here seems to be precautionary, neutralizing any magical power which might be exercised to prevent the spiriting-away of Bhāsadhara.

[2] Such a banner is shown in *Tibet's Great Yogī Milarepa*, opposite p. 30.

[3] In ancient India it was customary in some kingdoms, as in Urgyān, for women to proclaim the accession of a queen and for men to proclaim the accession of a king.

emperor. Accordingly, one after another, many kings made submission to him.

Thus having attained the heights of worldly power and of sensuous enjoyment, the Lotus-Born One realized the illusory and unsatisfactory nature of all worldly things. And, thinking of the Great Renunciation of the Lord Buddha, he announced to the King–Father his intention to abdicate and enter the Order. Faced by the King–Father's opposition, he said to him, 'If thou dost not permit me to embrace religion, I will die here in thy very presence'; and he struck his right side with a dagger, seemingly with intent to do away with himself. Fearful lest the Prince carry out the threat, the old King thought, 'It is preferable that I allow him to enter the Order than for him to die'. Neither the entreaties of the ministers of state, nor the special pleading of the King's bosom friend, 'Golden Light', who was fetched from Singala especially, nor the lamentations of the five hundred queens, moved the Lotus-Born One from his fixed purpose. Therefore he was named 'The Irresistible *Dorje* King'.

THE PARTING

The Queens, in tears, said to the Lotus-Born One as he was taking leave of them, 'Thou, our Lord, art like the eyes below our forehead. Not for a moment can we be parted from thee. Shalt thou abandon us as though we were corpses in a cemetery? Wherever thou goest, invite us to join thee; otherwise we shall resemble ownerless dogs. Hast thou no pity for us?'

The Lotus-Born One replied, 'This worldly life is transitory, and separation is inevitable. As in a market-place, human beings come together and then separate. Why, therefore, be troubled about separation? This is the Wheel of the World; let us renounce it and fix our thoughts upon attaining Liberation. I am determined to follow the religious career; and I will prepare the way for your own salvation, so that ye may join me hereafter. For the present, remain here.' Because, as he left, he promised to return to them when he had attained the Truth, they named him 'The King Who Keepeth One in Mind'.

THE *KARMIC* TAKING OF LIFE

In another part of Urgyān, to which the Lotus-Born One went, there happened to be a man born with organs of generation all over his body, because in his previous life he, having been a priest, violated the vow of celibacy by living with a courtesan. The courtesan was reborn as the son of a king ; and the man, assuming the form of a fly, alighted on the infant son's forehead. The Lotus-Born One threw a pebble at the fly with such force that the pebble not only killed the fly but penetrated to the child's brain, carrying the fly with it ; and both the fly and the child died.

When charged with the crime, the Lotus-Born One explained that in a former life he had been a contemporary of the courtesan and been known as Gautama, that Padma Tsalag, the courtesan's paramour, in a fit of jealousy had killed her when informed, by her own maid-servant, of her secret acceptance of a rival who was a merchant named Hari, and that, Padma Tsalag having falsely accused Gautama of the murder, Gautama was put to death. Inasmuch as the fly was Padma Tsalag[1] and the king's son the courtesan, the Lotus-Born One was impelled by *karma* to commit the deed. He said, 'Had it not been for the *karma*, the pebble could not have killed both the fly and the child'. The Lotus-Born One requested the King Indrabodhi to allow the law of the realm to take its course, and was imprisoned in the palace.

The royal city was then besieged by ten thousand evil spirits who sought to prevent the Lotus-Born One from becoming a great and learned priest and destroying their prestige and power. The gates both of the city and palace being closely guarded because of the siege, the Lotus-Born One considered

---

[1] There are both the exoteric or vulgar interpretation of the rebirth doctrine, such as this folk-tale illustrates, and the esoteric interpretation of the initiates which does not sanction the wide-spread popular belief in transmigration from the human to sub-human forms. See *The Tibetan Book of the Dead*, pp. 39–61. While the many, the exotericists, may accept this strange folk-tale literally, the more spiritually advanced of the Great *Guru's* devotees interpret it symbolically, as they do very much else in the Biography as a whole, the fly being to them significant of the undesirable characteristics of the unbridled sensuality associated with Padma Tsalag.

how he might escape. And, putting off his garments, he placed on his naked body magical ornaments made of human bone, and, taking with him a *dorje* and a *trishūla*,[1] went to the roof of the palace and danced like a mad man. He let both the *trishūla* and the *dorje* fall below; the prongs of the *trishūla*, striking the breast of the wife of one of the ministers of state, pierced her heart, and the *dorje*, striking the head of her infant son, penetrated to the brain, and both died.

THE GOING INTO EXILE

The ministers advised that the Lotus-Born One be put to death by hanging, but the King said, 'This son is not of human origin; and, inasmuch as he may be an incarnate divinity, capital punishment cannot be inflicted upon him. Accordingly, I decree that he be exiled.'

The King summoned the Lotus-Born One and told him that the decree would come into force after three months. The Lotus-Born One explained that, as in the case of the slaying of the infant and the fly, there existed a *karmic* reason for the slaying of the minister's wife and son. The minister's son had been in that former life the courtesan's maid-servant who had betrayed to Padma Tsalag the clandestine relationship between the courtesan and the merchant Hari; and the minister's wife was the reincarnation of this merchant Hari. Though unrepentant, the Lotus-Born One bore no ill will towards any one.

Different parts of India, also China, Persia, and the mysterious country called Shambhala were considered as places of exile for the Prince, but the King told him that he might go wherever he liked. 'To me', said the Prince, 'all countries are pleasant; I need only undertake religious work and every place becometh my monastery.'

Secretly, the King presented the Prince with the wish-granting gem, saying, 'This will satisfy all thy wants'. The Prince handed it back, saying, 'Whatever I behold is my

---

[1] The *trishūla* is a three-pronged staff like that held by him in the Frontispiece. It is employed in Tantric rituals, and symbolizes mastership of occult powers.

wish-granting gem'; and when the King, in response to the Prince's request, extended his hand opened, the Prince spat in it, and instantaneously the spittle became another wish-granting gem.

Bhāsadhara, weeping, caught the Prince by the hand and pleaded to be allowed to go with him into exile. Then she appealed to the King not to let him be exiled. Meanwhile, the Prince departed and went to a garden whence he addressed the multitude that followed him:

'The body is impermanent; it is like the edge of a precipice.[1] The breath is impermanent; it is like the cloud. The mind is impermanent; it is like the lightning. Life is impermanent; it is like the dew on the grass.'

Then the Guardian Kings of the four cardinal directions with their attendant deities appeared and prostrated themselves before the Prince and praised him. The Four Ḍākinī[2] also came with music and song; and they placed the Prince on a celestial horse and he disappeared into the heavens, in a southerly direction. At sunset he descended to earth and went to a cave where he engaged in worship and prayer for seven days, and all the Peaceful Deities[3] appeared to him as in a mirror and conferred upon him transcendency over birth and death.

The God of the Corpses

Thence he proceeded to the 'Cool Sandal-Wood' Cemetery,[4]

---

[1] Even as the body leads one to death, so does the edge of a precipice.

[2] These are four chief ḍākinī, namely, the Divine (or *Vajra*) Ḍākinī, associated with the eastern direction, in a *maṇḍala*; the Precious (or *Ratna*) Ḍākinī, of the southern direction; the Lotus (or *Padma*) Ḍākinī, of the western; and the Action (or *Karma*) Ḍākinī, of the northern direction. The centre, or central position, is assigned to the Ḍākinī of Enlightenment, or the Buddha Ḍākinī.

[3] In Tantric cults the principal deities, including the Buddhas, are symbolically represented in the dualistic moods of peacefulness and wrathfulness, as illustrated throughout *The Tibetan Book of the Dead*.

[4] This cemetery (Tib. *Bsil-ba-tshal*), wherein the Buddha is said to have delivered some of His Mahāyāna teachings, is one of the Eight Cemeteries of ancient India, in all of which, one after another, the Lotus-Born One practised the *yoga* of sosānika. Sosānika (or 'frequenting of cemeteries') is one of the twelve observances incumbent upon a *bhikṣhu*. It is intended to impress upon him the three chief *sangsāric* phenomena, namely, transitoriness, suffering (or sorrow), and vacuity (or illusoriness), by witnessing the funerals,

about ten miles from Bōdh-Gayā. Using corpses for his seat, he remained there five years practising meditation. His food was the food offered to the dead[1] and his clothing the shrouds of the corpses. People called him 'The God of the Corpses'. It was here that he first expounded, to the *ḍākinī*, the nine progressive steps on the Great Path.

When a famine occurred, a multitude of corpses was deposited in the cemetery without food or shrouds; and Padma, as we shall now call the Great *Guru*, transmuted the flesh of the corpses into pure food and subsisted upon it, and the skin of the corpses served him for raiment. He subjugated the spiritual beings inhabiting the cemetery and made them his servitors.

THE OVERTHROW OF THE IRRELIGIOUS

Indrarāja, a petty king of the Urgyān country, having become inimical to religion, and his subjects, following his example, likewise, Padma went there in the guise of one of the Wrathful Deities and deprived the king and all the men among the unbelievers of their bodies, or means of sowing further evil *karma*; and, magically transmuting the bodies, he drank the blood and ate the flesh.[2] Their consciousness-principles[3] he liberated and prevented from falling into the hells.[4] Every woman whom he met he took to himself, in order to purify

the grieving relatives, the combats of beasts of prey for the remains, and by smelling the stench of the decaying corpses. The Buddha, too, is said to have practised *sosānika*. (Cf. L. A. Waddell, op. cit., p. 381[6].)

[1] It was then customary for the surviving relatives when depositing a corpse in a cemetery (or cremation ground, or place of corpses) to put with it a large earthenware pot full of cooked rice.

[2] Apparently this magical transmutation is to be regarded as being the reverse of that whereby, according to pagan beliefs of antiquity, wine may be transmuted into blood and bread into flesh.

[3] The term 'soul', as understood in the Occident, has no equivalent in Buddhist thought, Buddhism denying the existence of an unchanging personal entity. Here, as elsewhere, the term consciousness-principle (Tib. *pho*, and *nam-she*) is preferable. Cf. *The Tibetan Book of the Dead*, pp. 86[n], 92[3].

[4] This legend, in the eyes of the Tibetans, shows that it is right for a Great *Yogī* to cut short the career of an evil-doer by depriving him of his body and directing his consciousness-principle (which is quite different from the 'soul' in occidental theology) in such manner that it will be reborn in a religious environment. But to take life without the *yogic* power so to direct the consciousness-principle is a most henious sin.

her spiritually and fit her to become the mother of religiously minded offspring.[1]

THE YOUTHFUL ESCAPED DEMON

The queen of King Ahruta having died in pregnancy, her corpse was deposited in a cemetery where Padma was meditating. From the womb of the corpse, Padma recovered a female child which was still alive. As there existed a *karmic* relationship from a past life between the child and Padma, he decided to rear it. King Ahruta sent soldiers to attack Padma, and King Warma-Shrī sent a mighty warrior famed for prowess in arms to aid the attackers. Padma shot the warrior with an arrow and escaped; and thus he acquired the name, 'The Youthful Escaped Demon'.

After erecting a *stūpa*[2] of repentance, Padma took up residence in the 'Cemetery of Happiness', where the Wrathful *Ḍākinī* known as the 'Subjugator of Demons' came and blessed him. Afterwards, he sat in meditation in the Sosaling Cemetery, to the south of the Urgyān country, and received the blessings of the *ḍākinī* of the Peaceful Order.

THE SUBMISSION OF THE *ḌĀKINĪ* OF THE LAKE

Thence, going to the Dhanakosha Lake, where he was born, he preached the Mahāyāna to the *ḍākinī* in their own lan-

[1] Like many other Culture Heroes, Padma-Sambhava makes natural use of his masculinity, as in this instance, for eugenic good. It is pointed out in our General Introduction that conventional concepts of sex morality are completely ignored by him. Under other circumstances, that which has been called his Tantric dalliance with females, both human and of the *ḍākinī* order, is regarded by the Nyingmapas as being one of his many religious acts which has esoteric significance and results in benefit to the religion. The act itself is called in Tibetan *Dze-pa*.

[2] The Tibetan *Ch'orten*, literally meaning 'receptacle for offerings', corresponds to the *stūpa* (*caitya*, or *tope*) of Indian Buddhism. A *stūpa* is usually a conical masonry structure containing, like a tumulus, whence it was probably derived, a central chamber intended to hold reliques such as charred bits of bones from the funeral pyre of a saint, precious objects like images, and texts of scriptures. From a few of the ancient Indian *stūpas* authentic reliques of the Buddha have been recovered. As in this textual instance, a *stūpa* may be a *stūpa* of repentance. Other *stūpas*, like many at Bōdh-Gayā, are votive *stūpas*. Generally, a *stūpa* is a cenotaph in memory of the Buddha or a great Buddhist *Arhant* or *Bodhisattva*. See *Tibet's Great Yogī Milarepa*, wherein a *stūpa* is shown and its symbolism expounded, opposite p. 269.

guage.[1] He brought them and other deities of the locality under the sway of his *yogic* power; and they vowed to give to him their aid in his mission on Earth.

THE BLESSING BY VAJRA-VARĀHĪ

Padma's next place of abode was the 'Very Fearful Cemetery', where Vajra-Varāhī[2] appeared and blessed him. The four orders of male *ḍākinī* and the *ḍākinī* of the Three Secret Places—which are underneath, upon, and above the Earth—also appeared; and, after conferring upon him the power to overcome others, named him 'Dorje Dragpo'.[3]

THE DECISION TO SEEK *GURUS*

Padma now went to Bōdh-Gayā,[4] and worshipped at the Temple. Practising shape-shifting, he multiplied his body so that sometimes it appeared like a vast herd of elephants and sometimes like a multitude of *yogīs*. Asked by the people who he was and what *guru* he had, he replied, 'I have no father, no mother, no abbot, no *guru*, no caste, no name; I am the self-born Buddha'. Disbelieving him, the people said, 'Inasmuch as he hath no *guru*, may he not be a demon?'[5] This

---

[1] This is one of the secret languages of Tibet, which, as the late Lāma Kazi Dawa-Samdup told me, is nowadays known only by a very few highly initiated *Lāmas*.

[2] Vajra-Varāhī (Tib. *Dorje-Phag-mo*) is believed by the Tibetans to be incarnate successively in each abbess of the Yam-dok Lake monastery, Tibet. The name, literally meaning 'Indestructible (*Vajra*) Sow (*Varāhī*)', suggests, like other names of Vajra Deities of the Vajra-yāna School, high initiatory powers.

[3] Or 'Indomitable Wrathful One', a *Drag-po* being a demoniacal deity of the most terrific type, tantrically symbolizing nature's destructive forces. Members of the *Drag-po* (Skt. *Bhairava*) Order are chiefly defenders of Buddhism.

[4] Text: *Rdorje-gdan* (pron. *Dorje-dān*): Skt. *Vajrāsana*, meaning, with reference to the place, or seat, where the Buddha sat in meditation and attained Enlightenment, Indestructible (or Immutable, or Diamond-like) Throne. Bōdh-Gayā is also written, but incorrectly, Buddha-Gayā.

[5] This query would be put today by the pious multitudes of India to the millions in the Occident who pride themselves on having no *guru*, no wise guide to the science of life and the art of living and of dying. None in India or Tibet save the occidentalized are without religion; and today every boy and girl, even among the outcastes, still receives religious instruction and has a *guru*. Aware of the worldly effects of Westernization, so marked in America, the Tibetans, like the Nepalese, maintain a policy of watchful

remark aroused in Padma the thought, 'Although I am a self-born incarnation of the Buddha and therefore do not need a *guru*, it will be wise for me to go to learned *pandits* and make a study of the Three Secret Doctrines,[1] seeing that these people and those of coming generations need spiritual guidance'.

PADMA'S MASTERY OF ASTROLOGY, MEDICINE, LANGUAGES, ARTS, AND CRAFTS

Accordingly, Padma went first to a saintly *guru* who was a *Loka-Siddha*,[2] at Benares, and mastered astrology. He was taught all about the year of the conception of the Buddha, the year in which the mother of the Buddha dreamt that a white elephant entered her womb, the year of the Buddha's birth, and how these esoterically significant periods have correspondence with the Tibetan calendar. He was also taught how the Sun and Moon eclipse one another. And now he was called 'The Astrologer of the Kālachakra'.[3]

Having mastered astrology, Padma mastered medicine under the son of a famous physician, known as 'The Youth Who Can Heal'. Thus Padma became known as 'The Life-Saving Essence of Medicine'.

---

aloofness. The Tibetans have a proverb which may be rendered thus: 'Inasmuch as men and beasts are alike in eating, sleeping, and copulating, if men be without religion, which alone differentiates them from beasts, they become indistinguishable from beasts.' The applicability of this to present world conditions is self-evident.

[1] The Three Secret Doctrines are, briefly, the teachings conveyed by initiation, concerning the External (or Exoteric), the Internal (or Esoteric), and the Transcendental (or Non-Dualistic, i.e. Non-Exoteric and Non-Esoteric) aspects of Truth, or Reality. The essentiality of the Hīnayāna represents the first; the essentiality of the Mahāyāna, the second; and the Doctrine of the Voidness (Skt. *Shūnyatā*), as set forth in the *Prajñā Pāramitā*, represents the third.

[2] A *Loka-Siddha*, or 'World *Siddha*', is one who has attained all *yogic* accomplishments, or powers over human existence, both physical and psychical, and, as in this instance, is also an adept in the astrological sciences.

[3] Tib. *Dus-kyi-Khorlo*, or 'Circle of Time', one of the most esoteric of Tantric doctrines. (See p. xviii, above.) The Kālachakra Doctrine includes what the Lāma Sonam Senge designates as 'the science of all kinds of Astrology and Astronomy'. 'The Kālachakra Doctrine itself', he added, 'has been known in Tibet for a thousand years or more.'

Padma's next teacher was a *yogī*, the most learned in orthography and writing, who taught him Sanskrit and related vernacular languages, the language of demons, the meaning of signs and symbols, and the languages of gods and of brute creatures, and of all the other beings of the Six States of Existence.[1] Altogether, Padma mastered sixty-four forms of writing and three hundred and sixty languages. And the name he was given was 'The Lion *Guru* of Speech'.

Then, placing himself under the guidance of a great artist, named Vishvakarma, who was eighty years of age, Padma became expert in working with gold and gems, silver, copper, iron, and stone, in the making of images, in painting, clay-modelling, engraving, carpentry, masonry, rope-making, boot-making, hat-making, tailoring, and in all other arts and crafts. A beggar women taught him to mould and glaze clay pots. And the name given him was 'The Learned Master of All Applied Arts'.

THE *GURU* PRABHAHASTI (OR 'ELEPHANT OF LIGHT')

In his wanderings shortly afterwards, Padma encountered two ordained monks on their way to their *guru*. Making obeisance to them, he requested of them religious instruction. Frightened at his being armed and at his uncouth appearance, they took him to be one of the order of demons who eat human flesh, and ran away. He called to them, saying, 'I have relinquished evil actions and taken to the religious life. Be good enough to instruct me in religion.' At their request, he handed over to them his bow and quiver of iron arrows and accompanied them to their *guru*, Prabhahasti, an incarnate emanation of the Ādi-Buddha, who lived in a wooden house with nine doors.[2] After bowing down before the *guru*, Padma addressed him thus: 'Hail! Hail! be good enough to give ear to me, thou noble *guru*. Although I am a prince, born in the

---

[1] The Six States of Existence are the realms of the gods, of titans, of men, of brutes, of ghosts, and of dwellers in various hells.

[2] This passage is an example of the esotericism underlying many of the legends, the 'nine doors' being the nine apertures of the human body, namely, the two apertures of the eyes, the two of the nose, the two of the ears, the mouth, anus, and aperture of the organ of sex.

country of Urgyān, I sinfully killed the demon son of a minister and was exiled. I am without worldly possessions; and I fear that I have done wrong in coming here without a gift to offer to thee.[1] Nevertheless, condescend to teach me all that thou knowest.'

The *guru* replied, 'Hail! Hail! thou wondrous youth! Thou art the precious vessel into which to pour the essence of the religious teachings. Thou art the incarnate receptacle for the Mahāyāna; I will instruct thee in the whole of it.'

Padma responded, 'First of all, please confer upon me the state of *brahmacharya*.'[2] And the *guru* said, 'I understand the *yoga* systems; and if thou desirest instruction in them as forming a part of the Mahāyāna, I will so instruct thee, but I cannot confer upon thee the state of *brahmacharya*.[3] For this thou shouldst go to Ānanda at the Asura Cave. Meanwhile, and before I instruct thee in the Mahāyāna, receive my blessing.'

Accordingly, Prabhahasti taught Padma the means of attaining Buddhahood, of avoiding spiritual retrogression, of gaining mastery over the Three Regions,[4] and concerning the *Pāramitās*[5] and *yoga*. Although Padma could remember and master anything he had been taught once, this *guru*, in order to cleanse Padma of his sins, made him review each of the teachings eighteen times.

PADMA'S ORDINATION BY ĀNANDA

Afterward, at the Asura Cave, in the presence of Ānanda, Padma took the vow of celibacy and received ordination into

[1] It is customary for a disciple when first presenting himself to a *guru* to make the *guru* a gift, thereby signifying his desire for spiritual guidance. See *Tibet's Great Yogī Milarepa*, pp. 65, 68, 77, 103.

[2] The state of *brahmacharya*, or sexual continence, is one of the essentials for success in practically applied *yoga*.

[3] As will presently be seen, Padma was destined to take the vow of celibacy before Ānanda, the cousin and chief disciple of the Buddha, at the Asura Cave, and to receive from him ordination into the Order. The instructions which Prabhahasti gave to Padma appear to have been more or less exoteric or preliminary to those given by Ānanda later, and may, therefore, be called intellectual rather than applied. In this connexion, it is significant that Prabhahasti does not initiate, but merely blesses, Padma.

[4] See p. 205[1], following.　　　　　[5] See pp. 173[2], 234[3], following.

the Order; and Ānanda made Padma a regent of the Buddha. The Earth Goddess came carrying a yellow robe; and, as she robed Padma in it, all the Buddhas of past aeons appeared in the firmament from the ten directions and named Padma 'The Lion of the Shakyas, Possessor of the Doctrine'.

PADMA'S QUESTIONING CONCERNING ĀNANDA'S PRE-EMINENCE

Being a fully ordained monk, and possessed of the power of the Mahāyāna to destroy the evils of the world, Padma, like the previous Buddhas, went forth and taught the Doctrine and discussed it with *Bodhisattvas*. Then, having become a *Bodhisattva* himself, he returned to Ānanda; and, at a time when Ānanda was discussing the *Dharma*, asked him how he had become the Lord Buddha's chief disciple. Ānanda replied that his pre-eminence was due to his having faithfully practised the precepts; and, in illustration, told the following story:

THE STORY OF THE UNFAITHFUL MONK

A monk at Bōdh-Gayā, named 'Good Star' (*Legs-pahi-Skarma*) had memorized twelve volumes of the precepts, but practised none of them, so the Lord Buddha admonished him, saying, 'Although thou canst recite all these precepts from memory, thou failest to practise them. Thou canst not, therefore, be considered a man of learning.' At this, the monk grew exceedingly angry, and retorted, 'There are only three things that make Thee different from me: Thy thirty-two illustrious names, Thine eighty good examples, and Thine aura the breadth of Thine outstretched arms. I, too, am learned. Despite my having served Thee for twenty-four years, I have not discovered any knowledge in Thee the size of a *til*-seed.'[1] Then, the monk's temper increasing, he shouted at the top of his voice, 'I refuse to serve Thee any longer, thou worthless beggar; I am much superior to Thee in understanding of the Doctrine, Thou scoundrel who hath run away from Thine own kingdom'. And, still shouting angrily, the monk went off.

---

[1] The Indian *til*-seed, like a mustard seed, is very small.

How Ānanda was chosen Chief Disciple

The Lord Buddha called together the disciples and said to them, ' "Good Star" became very angry and left me. I desire to ascertain who will serve me in his stead.' All the disciples together bowed down and offered themselves, each one saying, 'I desire to serve; I desire to serve'. He asked, 'Why do ye desire to serve me, knowing that I am now grown old?' And the Lord Buddha not choosing any of them, they entered into silent meditation; and Moggallāna at once saw that Ānanda was the most suitable to select. Accordingly, the assembly, composed of five hundred learned monks, many of them *Bodhisattvas*, chose Ānanda. The Lord Buddha smiled, and said, 'Welcome!' and Ānanda said, 'Although I am quite unfitted to serve Thee, nevertheless, if I must serve Thee, I desire Thee to make to me three promises. The first promise is that I be allowed to provide mine own food and clothing; the second is, that Thou shalt give to me whatever [religious guidance] I may beg of Thee; and the third is, that Thou shalt not give out a [new] doctrine at a time when I am not present.'

The Buddha again smiled, and made reply, 'Very well; very well; very well'.

The Buddha Foretells the Unfaithful Monk's Death

Ānanda's first request of the Lord was for information concerning 'Good Star'; and, thereupon, the Lord prophesied that 'Good Star' would die within seven days and become an unhappy ghost in the monastic garden. When told of the prophecy by Ānanda, 'Good Star', somewhat perturbed, said, 'Occasionally His lies come true. If I am alive after seven days, I shall have some more things to say about Him. Meanwhile I shall remain here.'

On the morning of the eighth day Ānanda found 'Good Star' dead and his ghost haunting the garden. Thereafter, whenever the Lord Buddha was in the garden expounding the *Dharma*, the ghost turned its face away from the Lord and placed its hands over its ears.

Ānanda's Testimony concerning the Buddha

Ānanda said it was because of all these things that he had
served the Lord faithfully for twenty-one years. Then he told
how the Buddha had attained Buddhahood at Bōdh-Gayā in
His thirty-fifth year; how He set the Wheel of the Law in
motion at Sarnath, near Benares, by teaching to His disciples
the Four Noble Truths: Sorrow, the cause of Sorrow, the
Overcoming of Sorrow, and the method (or Path of Salvation) whereby Sorrow may be overcome. Ānanda also told
how, continuing to preach at Sarnath for seven years less two
months, the Buddha taught the Truths contained both in the
twelve volumes of precepts which 'Good Star' had memorized
and in ten other volumes. The contents of each of these ten
volumes, Ānanda described as follows: volume 1 expounded
the doctrine of good and evil; volumes 2, 3, 4, the one-hun-
dred religious duties; volume 5, the method of practising these
duties; volume 6, the theories of self; volume 7, *yoga*; volume
8, recompense for kindness; volume 9, Wisdom; and volume
10, mind and thought. There were also a number of other
teachings, concerning lust, anger and sloth, priestly precepts, *guru* and *shishya*, methods of preaching, the Voidness,
the fruits of practising the precepts, and the method of
attaining Deliverance.[1]

During the second period of His mission, extending over
about ten years, the Lord preached the Mahāyāna in Magadha,
at Gridhrakūta, Jetavana, and elsewhere. He also preached to
Maitreya, Avalokiteshvara and other *Bodhisattvas* in heaven-
worlds, and to gods and demons, the essence of the *Dharma*
as set forth in various Scriptures; and told of His visit to
Ceylon.

The third period of the Buddha's preaching extended over
thirteen years, and was chiefly to gods, *nāgas*, *arhants*, and
various orders of spiritual beings. During the fourth period,
of seven years, He taught Tantric doctrines, but only exoterically.

[1] Tibetan Buddhists regard the teachings given out by the Buddha at
Sarnath as being of the Hīnayāna (or Theravāda) and those delivered afterwards in other places as being of the Mahāyāna.

The Buddha directed and empowered Vajra-Pāṇi[1] to teach the esoteric aspects of the *Tantras*, and said to him, 'In the same country and epoch there cannot be two Buddhas of Bōdh-Gayā[2] preaching the Doctrine. If there be another Buddha, He can come only after the departure of the present Buddha.'

It was at this time and until His eighty-second year, when He passed away into *Nirvāṇa*, that the Lord Buddha preached the *Vinaya*, *Sūtra*, and *Abhidharma Piṭaka*,[3] and the *Getri*.[4]

PADMA'S STUDIES UNDER ĀNANDA

Padma was much pleased with this lengthy discourse of Ānanda's [which has here been summarized], and he remained with Ānanda for five years and mastered the twelve volumes of precepts comprising the *Getri*, which 'Good Star' had memorized.

When his studies under Ānanda were nearing completion, Padma, seeing the limitations of the exoteric exposition of the Doctrine, thought to himself, 'By means of the teachings concerning the Voidness and the Divine Wisdom I must discover a more perfect path'.[5]

---

[1] Vajra-Pāṇi (Tib. *Phyag-na-Rdo-rje*: pron. Chhak-na-Dorje; or *Phyag-Rdor*: pron. *Chhak-Dor*) 'Wielder of the *Vajra* (or Thunderbolt of the Gods)', is assumed to be a Tantric personification of the force personified as Indra by the Hindus, Zeus by the Greeks, Jupiter by the Romans, and Jehovah by the Hebrews. He is the spiritual son of Akṣhobhya, the second of the Five Dhyānī Buddhas. Cf. L. A. Waddell, op. cit., p. 356. As Chhak-Dor he is the ruling deity in the Tantric system.

[2] That is to say, there can be no two Buddhas incarnate at the same time who have attained Enlightenment as Gautama did at Bōdh-Gayā.

[3] These three *Piṭaka* (or collections) comprise the canon of Southern Buddhism. The *Vinaya Piṭaka* consists of rules for the government of the priesthood; the *Sūtra Piṭaka*, of discourses of the Buddha; the *Abhidharma Piṭaka*, of the psychology and metaphysics.

[4] See note 1 on p. 204, following. The Tibetan tradition here set forth concerning various periods of the Buddha's teaching suggests the theory formulated by the Chinese monk Chih-chē (who lived during the last half of the sixth century A.D.) that the sermons and utterances of the Buddha point to five great periods in His life. The student is referred to K. L. Reichelt, op. cit., pp. 43–45.

[5] The translated text of the 'Yoga of Knowing the Mind', contained herein in Book II, sets forth in epitomized form the results of this far-reaching decision of the Great *Guru* to discover the Ultimate Truth. The Scriptures of all religions are designed to guide the unenlightened multitude towards the

ĀNANDA'S TESTIMONY CONCERNING THE SCRIPTURES

He asked Ānanda, 'For how long have the *Sūtras* and *Mantras*[1] been recorded; and, if counted, how many volumes of them are there, and where are the texts to be had?' Ānanda replied, 'Ever since the Lord's passing away into *Nirvāṇa*, all that He said hath been recorded. If carried by the Elephant of Indra,[2] there would be five hundred loads of these writings.' A dispute arose between the *Devas* and the *Nāgas*, the *Devas* wishing to have the Scriptures in their world and the *Nāgas* to have them in theirs. The volumes of the *Boom*[3] were hidden in the realm of the *Nāgas*; the *Prajñā-Pāramitā* was hidden in Indra's heaven; most of the *Sūtras* were hidden in Bōdh-Gayā; the *Abhidharma Piṭaka* was hidden in the Nālanda Monastery; the greater part of the Mahāyāna texts were hidden in Urgyān. Other texts were deposited in the *stūpa* at Nālanda. And all of these writings were secured against the ravages of insects and of moisture.

PADMA'S TEACHINGS AND VARIOUS STUDIES

Upon completing his studies under Ānanda, Padma went to a cemetery, wherein dwelt the Tantric deity Mahākāla,[4]

Higher Teachings. Guidance by priests, even by the wisest *gurus*, is for the purpose of fitting the disciple to be a lamp and a refuge unto himself, as the Buddha taught. The Path may be pointed out, leading from the obscuring darkness of worldly existence to the unobscured radiance of the *Nirvāṇic* Goal. But the pilgrim must by his own efforts travel the route of the Pilgrimage to its very end; no one else can do it for him.

[1] The *Mantras* are the special Scriptures of the Mantrayāna School of Northern Buddhism.

[2] A mythical elephant of supernormal strength, commonly referred to in the literature of India, as here, figuratively, to emphasize oriental exaggeration.

[3] The *Boom*, or *'Bum* (Skt. *Sata Sahasrikā*), meaning '100,000 [shlokas of Transcendental Wisdom]', consists of the first twelve of the twenty-one volumes of the Tibetan canonical *S'er-p'yin* (pron. *Sher-chin*), as translated from the original Sanskrit *Prajñā-Pāramitā* (which corresponds to the *Abhidharma* of the Southern School of Buddhism). (See *Tibetan Yoga and Secret Doctrines*, pp. 343–9.)

[4] Mahākāla ('Great Black One') is the Tantric personification of the masculine, or *shakta*, aspect of the disintegrating forces of the Cosmos, of which Kāli ('Black Female One') is the feminine, or *shakti*, aspect. As such, Mahākāla is the Lord of Death, synonymous with Dharma-Rāja. And he is the wrathful manifestation of Avalokiteshvara (Tib. *Chenrazee*) of whom the Dalai Lāma is the incarnate representative on Earth.

who had the body of a yak, the head of a lion, and legs like serpents. The cemetery contained a *stūpa* made of precious gems, against which Padma was accustomed to rest his back as he expounded the *Dharma*; and there for five years he occupied himself with teaching the *ḍākinī*, and was called 'The Sun-rays One'.[1]

Desirous of finding a doctrine capable of being expounded in few words of vast import and which, when applied, would be immediately efficacious, even as the Sun once it has arisen is immediately efficacious in giving light and heat, Padma went to the Ādi-Buddha in the 'Og-min Heaven, and was taught the Doctrine of the Great Perfection.[2] And then Padma was called Vajra-Dhāra in the esoteric aspect.[3]

After this, Padma went to the Cemetery of 'Expanded Happiness', in Kashmir. There, for five years, Padma taught the *Dharma* to the demoness Gaurima and to many *ḍākinī*; and he was named 'The Transmitter of Wisdom to all Worlds'.[4] Thence he went to Vajra-Sattva in His heaven-world, and acquired proficiency in *yoga* and in Tantric doctrines;[5] and was named Vajra-Dhāra in the exoteric aspect.

Padma also dwelt for a period of five years in the 'Self-Created Peak' Cemetery in Nepal, where, after teaching and subjugating various classes of spiritual beings, including

[1] Tib. *Nyi-ma Hod-zer*, one of the eight forms, or personalities, in which Padma-Sambhava manifested himself. (See Illustration V and its description on p. xxii, above.)

[2] The Doctrine of the Great Perfection is the root doctrine of mystical insight of the Nyingma School founded by Padma-Sambhava. (See *Tibetan Yoga and Secret Doctrines*, pp. 277-8.)

[3] Vajra-Dhāra ('Holder of the Vajra, or *Dorje*') is the super-human Teacher of the Secret Doctrine upon which the Vajrayāna and Mantrayāna are based. He is associated with the Ādi (or Primordial)-Buddha, personification of the One Cosmic Mind, and with the *Dharma-Kāya* ('Body, or Essentiality, of the *Dharma* or Truth'), symbolical of Reality. As such, Vajra-Dhāra is the Divine *Guru* of the Nyingma School.

[4] Tib. *Lōden Chog-se*, another of the eight personalities in which Padma manifested himself.

[5] Vajra-Sattva is the *Sambhoga-Kāya* aspect, or reflex of the *Dharma-Kāya* aspect, of the Dhyānī Buddha Akṣhobhya associated with the Eastern Realm of Pre-eminent Happiness, as in *The Tibetan Book of the Dead* (p. 108). Exoterically He manifests the Universe, esoterically He comprises all deities. He, like Shiva, being the Great Master of *Yoga*, is, in this School, the Tutelary of all aspirants for success in *yoga*.

demons, and acquiring dominion over the Three Regions of conditioned existence, he was called 'He Who Teacheth with the Voice of a Lion'.[1]

In the heaven of the Ādi-Buddha, Padma was completely instructed in the Nine Vehicles, or Paths,[2] in twenty-one treatises on *Chitti-Yoga*,[3] and in everything appertaining to the *Mantras*, and *Tantras*; and was called 'The Completely Taught One'.

It was in the 'Lanka-Peak' Cemetery, in the Sahor country, after he had preached to and disciplined many fearful demons, that he was named 'The One Born of a Lotus'.[4]

In the 'God-Peak' Cemetery, of the land of Urgyān, Padma remained five years, and received instruction from one of the ḍākinī of the Vajra-Yoginī Order[5] on the secret Tantric method of attaining liberation. It was after he had taught the ḍākinī in the 'Lotus-Peak' Cemetery that Padma became known as 'The Eternal Comforter of all [Beings]'.[6]

PADMA'S INITIATION BY A ḌĀKINĪ

Padma's next teacher was an ordained ḍākinī, who dwelt in a sandal-wood garden, in the midst of a cemetery, in a palace of skulls. When he arrived at the door of the palace he found it closed. Then there appeared a servant woman

---

[1] Or *Seṅg-ge Dra-dog*, which is yet another of the names given to the eight personifications, or forms, assumed by Padma.

[2] These consist of nine methods of attaining Enlightenment, such as those represented by the *Mahāyāna*, *Hīnayāna*, *Vajrayāna*, *Mantrayāna*, and *Yogā-chāra* (based upon the *Five Books of Maitreya*, the coming Buddha). Similarly, in Hinduism there are the Six Schools (Skt. *Shad-Darshanas*) of Philosophy, or Visions, or Means of attaining Liberation, namely, the *Nyāya*, *Vaisheshika*, *Sānkhya*, *Mimāngsa*, *Yoga*, and the *Vedānta* systems.

[3] Or *Yoga* appertaining to the mind in its True Nature, as expounded in our treatise.

[4] The Tibetans say that this cemetery was inhabited by many water-born creatures who compared their birth with that of the lotus and correlatively with that of the Great *Guru*. Hence they named him 'The One Born of a Lotus' (Skt. *Padma-Sambhava*).

[5] The order of Vajrayāna *devatas* is collectively personified in Vajra-Yoginī, the chief tutelary goddess associated with many esoteric practices of Tibetan Tantric *yoga*. (See *Tibetan Yoga and Secret Doctrines*, Illustration V and description of Vajra-Yoginī on pp. 173–5.)

[6] Or, more literally, *Dorje Drō-lō*, the name of another of Padma's eight personalities. (See p. xxiii, above.)

carrying water into the palace; and Padma sat in meditation so that her water-carrying was halted by his *yogic* power. Thereupon, producing a knife of crystal, she cut open her breast, and exhibited in the upper portion of it the forty-two Peaceful Deities and in the lower portion of it the fifty-eight Wrathful Deities.[1] Addressing Padma, she said, 'I observe that thou art a wonderful mendicant possessed of great power. But look at me; hast thou not faith in me?' Padma bowed down before her, made apology, and requested the teachings he sought. She replied, 'I am only a maid-servant. Come inside.'

Upon entering the palace, Padma beheld the *ḍākinī* enthroned on a sun and moon throne, holding in her hands a double-drum[2] and a human-skull cup,[3] and surrounded by thirty-two *ḍākinī* making sacrificial offerings to her. Padma made obeisance to the enthroned *ḍākinī* and offerings, and begged her to teach him both esoterically and exoterically. The one hundred Peaceful and Wrathful Deities then appeared overhead. 'Behold', said the *ḍākinī*, 'the Deities. Now take initiation.' And Padma responded, 'Inasmuch as all the Buddhas throughout the aeons have had *gurus*, accept me as thy disciple'.

Then the *ḍākinī* absorbed all the Deities into her body. She transformed Padma into the syllable *Hūṃ*.[4] The *Hūṃ* rested on her lips, and she conferred upon it the Buddha-Amitābha blessing. Then she swallowed the *Hūṃ*; and inside her stomach Padma received the secret Avalokiteshvara initiation. When the *Hūṃ* reached the region of the *Kuṇḍalinī*, she conferred upon him initiation of body, speech, and mind;

---

[1] These constitute the Tantric *maṇḍala* of One Hundred Deities. (See *The Tibetan Book of the Dead*, p. 217.)

[2] The Tibetan *damāru*, or ritual drum. (See Illustration V.)

[3] Such as that held by Padma-Sambhava in the Frontispiece.

[4] The *mantra* syllable *Hūṃ* of the Tibetans, when properly intoned by an initiate of the Mantrayāna, is said to be one of the most efficacious of all *mantras*, like the *Aum* (or *Om*) of the Hindus. It plays a very important role in all Tantric rituals of Tibet, and is associated with the psychic centres (Skt. *chakra*) of the lower part of the body, and thus with the *Mūlādhāra-chakra*, at the base of the spinal column, wherein the Serpent Power of the Goddess Kuṇḍalinī resides, the awakening of which, under wise guidance, is essential to successful initiation.

and he was cleansed of all defilements and obscurations. In secret, she also granted to him the Hayagrīva initiation,[1] which gives power to dominate all evil spiritual beings.

THE WISDOM-HOLDER *GURU*

A Wisdom-Holder[2] of 'Og-min, the highest of the Buddha heavens, afterwards taught to Padma all that was known concerning magic, rebirth, worldly knowledge, hidden treasure, power over worldly possessions, and longevity, both exoterically and esoterically.

THE ZEN-LIKE METHODS OF A BURMESE *GURU*

This Wisdom-Holder directed Padma to Pegu,[3] in Burma, to acquire from Prince Shrī Singha, who dwelt in a cave, the essence of all Schools of Buddhism, without differentiating one teaching from another. When Padma requested the *guru* Shrī Singha to teach him this, the *guru* pointed to the heavens and said, 'Have no desire for what thou seest. Desire not; desire not. Desire; desire. Have no desire for desire; have no desire for desire. Desire and deliverance must be simultaneous. Voidness; voidness. Non-voidness; non-voidness. Non-obscuration; non-obscuration. Obscuration; obscuration.[4] Emptiness of all things; emptiness of all things. Desire above, below, at the centre, in all directions, without differentiation.' When all of this had been explained in detail, and the *guru* had assured Padma that he would realize the essentiality of all doctrines, Padma praised the *guru*.[5]

[1] This initiation consists in the transference of such occult power as will enable the initiate to employ with mastery the cosmic forces personified by the Tantric deity Hayagrīva (Tib. *Rta-mgrin*: pron. *Tam-ding*), the Horse-headed One, and manifested through evil spirits and otherwise as forces of destruction or disharmony.

[2] Tib. *Rig-hdzin* (pron. *Rig-zin*), a highly advanced being, such as a *Bodhisattva*.

[3] Text: *Ser-ling*, the ancient Pegu, in Burma, where Buddhism flourished in the ninth and tenth centuries A.D.

[4] Or Ignorance (Skt. *Avidyā*).

[5] This *guru's* method of teaching resembles that of the *gurus* of the Zen School, and is intended to stir the disciple to deep meditative introspection, to the end that he will be enabled to answer his own questions and solve his own problems. The Zen School, precisely like the ' *Yoga* of Knowing the Mind in its Nakedness', teaches the futility of seeking outside oneself, in Scriptures or through *gurus*, deliverance from Ignorance.

Then Padma asked him, 'What is the difference between Buddhas and non-Buddhas?' And Shrī Singha replied, 'Even though one seek to discern a difference, there is no difference.[1] Therefore be free of doubt concerning external things. To overcome doubt concerning internal things, employ the perfect absolute Divine Wisdom. No one yet hath discovered either the Primary Cause or the Secondary Cause. I myself have not been able to do so; and thou, likewise, thou Lotus-Born One, shalt fail in this.'

THE SUPERNORMAL ORIGIN OF MAÑJUSHRĪ

Padma's next great *guru* was the *Bodhisattva* Mañjushrī, residing on the Five-Peaked Mountain, near the Sītā-sara River, in the Shanshi Province of China. Mañjushrī's origin, like that of Padma, was supernormal:

The Buddha once went to China to teach the *Dharma*, but instead of listening to Him the people cursed Him. So He returned to Gṛidhrakūta, in India.[2] Considering it to be useless to explain the higher truths to the Chinese, He decided to have introduced into China the conditional truths,[3] along with astrology. Accordingly, the Buddha, while at Gṛidhrakūta, emitted from the crown of His head a golden yellow light-ray which fell upon a tree growing near a *stūpa*, one of five *stūpas*, each of which was on one of the peaks of the Five-Peaked Mountain. From the tree grew a goitre-like excrescence, whence there sprang a lotus blossom. And from this

[1] Understanding of this paradoxical assertion implies understanding of the teaching that all living things, sub-human as well as human, are potentially Buddhas, or, in the Gnostic Christian sense, Christs. Accordingly, the *guru* goes on to suggest that what men call differences are merely differences of illusory external appearances. Innately all things are the One, and, thus, in essence, indistinguishable. Hui-neng, one of the Chinese teachers of the Zen School, similarly declares, 'The only difference between a Buddha and an ordinary man is that the one realizeth that he is a Buddha and the other doth not'. And as Bodhi-dharma, the first of the Zen teachers, taught, all things contain the Buddha nature from beginningless time.

[2] According to Tibetan tradition, it was at Gṛidhrakūta that the Buddha taught the Mahāyāna. Gṛidhrakūta, or the 'Vulture's Peak', is the highest of five mountains surrounding Rājagriha, where the first great Buddhist Council was held in 477 B.C.

[3] That is, the more exoteric aspects of the *Dharma*, which are preliminary or subordinate to the esoteric aspects.

lotus blossom Mañjushrī was born, holding in his right hand the Sword of Wisdom and in his left hand a blue lotus blossom, supporting the Book of Wisdom; and the people spoke of Him as having been born without a father and mother.

THE GOLDEN TORTOISE AND MAÑJUSHRĪ'S ASTROLOGICAL SYSTEMS

From Mañjushrī's head there issued a golden tortoise. The tortoise entered the Sītā-sara River, and from a bubble there came forth two white tortoises, male and female, which gave birth to five sorts of tortoises.[1]

At about this time the Lord Buddha emitted from the crown of His head a white light-ray which fell upon the Goddess of Victory. The Goddess went to Mañjushrī; and he, taking in his hand the golden tortoise, said, 'This is the great golden tortoise'. Then he instructed and initiated the Goddess in seven astrological systems; and she studied under him a total of 84,000 treatises. Of these, 21,000 treated of astrology as applied to living human beings, 21,000 of astrology as applied to the dead,[2] 21,000 of astrology as applied to marriage, and 21,000 of astrology as applied to land and agriculture.[3]

PADMA RESTORES MAÑJUSHRĪ'S ASTROLOGICAL TEACHINGS TO MANKIND

When these astrological teachings, known as the teachings which issued from the head of the most holy Mañjushrī, had

[1] The Chinese employ the tortoise, symbolical of the Cosmos, for purposes of divination, as suggested by the *Si-pa-Khor-lo (Srid-pa-Hkhor-lo)*, a Tibetan astrological and divinatory chart of Chinese origin, presided over by Mañjushrī transformed into a tortoise, on the different parts of whose body Sanskrit letters are placed in a magical sequence.

[2] In Tibet, astrology is employed to ascertain the auspicious day and hour for a funeral, and the time, place, and circumstances of a deceased person's rebirth, the moment of death being made the basis of calculation. (See *The Tibetan Book of the Dead*, p. 193[n].)

[3] Throughout India, Ceylon, Tibet, China, and other lands of the Orient, all the chief activities of one's earthly career, all agricultural operations such as ploughing, sowing, and harvesting crops, and the determining of the characteristics of land and of places are subject to astrological calculations. In Ceylon, where horary astrology is still a flourishing science, the exact moment for initiating the construction of a house, a fence, or gate, for felling a tree, digging a well, and for all similar operations, is fixed by astrology.

spread all over the world, the people gave so much attention
to them that the *Dharma* of the Lord Buddha was neglected.
So Mañjushrī placed all the texts containing the teachings in
a charmed copper box and hid it in a rock on the eastern side
of the Five-Peaked Mountain. Deprived thus of astrological
guidance, mankind suffered dire misfortunes: diseases, short-
ness of life, poverty, barrenness of cattle, and famine.

Upon learning of these misfortunes, Avalokiteshvara went
to Padma-Sambhava and said, 'I have renovated the world
thrice; and, thinking that all beings were happy, returned to
Ripotāla.[1] But now, when I look down, I behold so much
suffering that I weep.' And Avalokiteshvara added, 'Assume
the guise of Brahma; and, for the good of the creatures of the
world, go and recover these hidden treasures [of texts]'.

Having assumed the guise of Brahma, Padma went to
Mañjushrī and said, 'Although not really a part of the *Dharma*
of the Lord Buddha, astrology is, nevertheless, of vast benefit
to worldly creatures. Therefore, I beg of thee to take out the
hidden texts and instruct me in them.' And Mañjushrī took
out the hidden texts and instructed and initiated Padma in
all of them.[2]

OTHER *GURUS* OF PADMA

After completing his training is astrology under Mañjushrī,
Padma received further instruction in religion from the Ādi-
Buddha. Then, by various human *gurus*, each of whom gave
him a new name, he was initiated in eight doctrines, concerning the Peaceful and Wrathful Deities, the demons of the
Three Realms of Existence, offering of hymns of praise, male-
dictions, the best of all religious essences, and the essentiality
of consecration; and the corresponding deities appeared
before him. He constructed a *stūpa* of thirteen steps and in it
hid the texts of these eight doctrines.

[1] Text: *Ripotāla*, the heavenly residence of Avalokiteshvara: Skt.
Potāla, the name by which the palace of the Dalai Lāma (The incarnation
of Avalokiteshvara) is known outside of Tibet.
[2] The many titles of these astrological treatises are given in a long list on
folios 105–6 of our Tibetan text.

PADMA'S RECOVERY OF HIDDEN TEXTS

Then there appeared to Padma a *ḍākinī* who, after having saluted him as 'the incarnation of the Mind of the Buddha Amitābha', declared that the time was ripe for him to take out the hidden texts of the Lord Buddha's teachings. And Padma gathered together the texts, some from the heaven-worlds, some from the *nāga*-world, and some from the human-world;[1] and, upon mastering their contents, Padma was called 'The Powerful Wealthy One of the World'.[2]

YOGIC ARTS MASTERED BY PADMA

Padma now went to Gṛidhrakūta and mastered the *yogic* art of extracting essences for producing health and longevity; the power of supernormal seeing, hearing, feeling, smelling, and tasting, by drinking only water and abstaining from food, and of retaining healthfulness and bodily warmth without wearing clothing;[3] and the method of acquiring clearness of mind, lightness of body, and fleetness of foot through breath-control, and of prolonging life and of acquiring learning as limitless as the sky through fasting and application of the teachings concerning the Voidness.[4] And by practising all penances, Padma became inured to all hardships. His name at this time was 'The Enjoyer of Greatest Bliss'.

Padma also mastered the *yogic* art of extracting elixir from pebbles and sand, and of transmuting filth and flesh of human corpses into pure food. Another accomplishment was expert-ness in acrobatics. He was then called 'The Kingly Enjoyer of Food'.

Other *yogic* arts in which Padma acquired proficiency were the prolonging of life by taking essence of gold, the preventing

[1] The names of these texts are given on folio 107 of our Tibetan text.

[2] As is the wise custom of the East, one is said to be powerful and wealthy not in worldly things, but in Wisdom. The name here applied to Padma is commonly applied to Avalokiteshvara.

[3] This suggests the practice of *Tummo*, a translated text of which is contained in Book III of *Tibetan Yoga and Secret Doctrines*.

[4] In this series of accomplishments (Skt. *siddhi*), *yogic* power over the Five Elements (earth, water, fire, air, ether) is symbolically implied. The essences symbolize earth; the drinking, water; the clothing, fire; the breath-control, air; the Voidness, ether.

of disease by taking essence of silver, the walking on water by taking essence of pearl, the neutralizing of poison by taking essence of iron, the acquiring of clear vision by taking essence of lapis-lazuli.[1] Now he was named 'The Lotus Essence of Jewels'.

Padma mastered the practice of one thousand such essences, and promulgated them for the benefit of mankind. The texts of some of them he wrote on paper and hid.

The Buddha of Medicine appeared before Padma, and, giving to him a pot of *amrita*,[2] requested him to drink of it. Padma drank one half of it for the prolongation of his life and the other half he hid in a *stūpa*; and now he was called 'Padma the One of Accomplishment'.[3]

Brahma, Lord of *Rishis*, accompanied by twenty-one Great *Rishis*, appeared before Padma, and showered flowers on him and sang his praises. Brahma addressed him, and said, 'Thou art an emanation of the mind of Amitābha, and wert born of a lotus. Thou hast mastered the arts appertaining to medicine, to the neutralizing of poison, to the Five Elements, and to the prolongation of life.'

PADMA'S DESTRUCTION OF THE BUTCHERS

There happened to be at one of the extremities of India a town inhabited by butchers; and Padma, in order to dominate and destroy them, incarnated as one of their sons named Kati, the Evil-Handed Outcaste. To Kati, being by profession a butcher, it made no difference whether he killed and ate a beast or a man; and so he began killing the butchers and eating their flesh. When he took to the habit of cutting off bits of his own flesh and eating it, the people cursed him and drove him away.[4]

[1] Text: *bai-dur-ya*: Skt. *vaidūrya*, referring to malachite or chrysolite, of which there are three varieties, the yellow, green, and white lapis-lazuli. The chief of the Medical Buddhas, the Bedūriya Buddha, is named after this curative mineral substance.

[2] *Amrita* is the nectar of the gods, which confers upon men the boon of long or immortal life.

[3] Or 'Padma the *Siddha*'.

[4] All living things being one's kin, the eating of the flesh of the lower animals is, to the strict Buddhist, essentially the same as eating one's own flesh.

Kati went off and made the acquaintance of a butcher named Tumpo,[1] who was quite as wicked as himself, and said to him, 'Both of us live the same sort of a life and we should be quite good company for one another.' Kati furnished Tumpo with bows and arrows and snares, and said to him, 'Now keep on killing the butchers with all thy might and I with all my might will send their consciousness-principles to the abodes of the gods'. In this way all the butchers were killed off.[2]

PADMA'S CONQUEST OF ALL EVILS AND OF ALL DEITIES

Padma's next exploit was the subjugation and conversion of heretics and demons, who vowed to give their life to help him establish the *Dharma*. He wrote a book on how to subjugate and convert demons, and hid it in a rock.

Then Padma thought, 'I cannot very well spread the Doctrine and aid sentient beings until I destroy evil'. He returned to the 'Cool Sandal-Wood' Cemetery near Bōdh-Gayā, and there constructed of human skulls a house with eight doors, and inside it a throne whereon he sat like a lion and entered into meditation. The god Tho-wo-Hūṃ-chen[3] appeared before Padma and making obeisance to him said, '*Hūṃ*! O thou, the *Vajra*-bodied One, Holder of the Shākya Religion, who, like a lion, sittest on thy throne, being self-born, self-grown, the conqueror of birth, old age, and death, eternally youthful, transcendent over physical weakness and infirmities, thou art the True Body.[4] Victorious thou art over the demon born of the bodily aggregates, over the demon of suffering and disease,

[1] This name refers to a fierce-looking individual who is a member of a barbarous tribe regarded as being outside of caste.

[2] Although this tale is, apparently, to be taken as a legendary fable to emphasize the Buddhist precept prohibiting, as the Emperor Ashoka did by law, the taking of life, whether human or sub-human, the Tibetans who accept it literally maintain that the Great *Guru*, by killing the butchers and sending their consciousness-principles to the heaven-worlds and thus saving them from the sufferings of the hells, wherein otherwise they would have fallen, acted wisely and humanely. The text goes on to say that he also closed the doors to their rebirth in states lower than human.

[3] A deity of the Wrathful Order under whose protection are placed temples and places of pilgrimage.

[4] That is, the Body of Truth, the *Dharma-Kāya*.

over death and the messenger of the Lord of Death,[1] and over the god of lust. O thou Hero, the time hath come for thee to subjugate all these evils.'

Then Padma came out of his meditation. Mounting to the roof of the house, he hoisted eight victory-banners, spread out human hides from the corpses of the cemetery and thereon danced in wrathful mood various dances. He assumed a form with nine heads and eighteen hands. He intoned mystic *mantras* while holding a rosary of beads made of human bones. In this wise he subjugated all these demons and evil spirits, slew them, and took their hearts and blood in his mouth. Their consciousness-principles he transmuted into the syllable *Hūṃ* and caused the *Hūṃ* to vanish into the heaven-worlds. He was now called 'The Essence of the *Vajra*'.

Transforming himself into the King of Wrathful Deities, Padma, while sitting in meditation, subjugated the gnomes. In the same manner he brought under his control all women who had broken solemn vows, and, destroying their bodies, sent their consciousness-principles to the heavens of the Buddha.[2] Now he was called 'The Subjugator of Gnomes'.

Assuming the form of Hayagrīva, the horse-headed deity, Padma performed magical dances on the surface of a boiling poisonous lake, and all the malignant and demoniacal *nāgas* inhabiting the lake made submission to him; and he was named 'The Subjugator of *Nāgas*'.

Assuming the forms of other deities, he subjugated various kinds of demons, such as those causing epidemics, diseases, hindrances, hail, and famine. In the guise of the Red Mañjushrī,[3] Padma brought all the gods inhabiting the heavens presided over by Brahma under his control, by uttering their

[1] Otherwise known as Dharma-Rāja, the Lord of Truth, Judge of the Dead, King of the Lower Regions; and also as Yama, the Lord of Death. (See *The Tibetan Book of the Dead*, p. 35.)

[2] Since these women had broken their vows and were, according to Tibetan belief, *karmically* destined to be reborn among the gnomes, Padma conferred immeasurable good upon them by saving them from their fate and sending their consciousness-principles to Buddha realms.

[3] Mañjushrī is represented in many aspects, most of the countries where Northern Buddhism prevails having their own special Mañjushrī. See description of Illustration IV, p. xix, above.

mantras.[1] And, in other guises, Padma conquered all the most furious and fearful evil spirits, and 21,000 devils, male and female.

As Halā-halā,[2] Padma dominated all good and bad demons controlling oracles in Tibet.[3] As the Body of the Thirty-two Wrathful Swastikas, Padma dominated the Nine Planets, the Sun, Moon, Mars, Mercury, Venus, Jupiter, Saturn, Rahu, and Khetu,[4] and all things under their influence. As the six-faced Yama, the Lord of Death, Padma dominated all the Lords of Death under Yama. Similarly, Padma conquered Pe-har, the King of the Three Realms of Existence,[5] subdued all haughtiness, gained ascendency over Mahādeva,[6] Pashu-patī,[7] and other deities of the Brāhmins, and also over the chief deities of the Jains. And the god Mahākāla,[8] and the goddesses Remati[9] and Ekadzati,[10] appeared before Padma

[1] Each living thing, in all states of existence, possesses a bodily form attuned to a certain frequency of vibration. A *mantra* is a syllable or series of syllables of the same frequency as the thing or being (usually an invisible spiritual being, god or demon) to which it appertains; and an expert magician who knows the *mantra* of any deity or order of lesser beings can, by intoning it properly, invoke the deity or dominate the lesser beings. (See *The Tibetan Book of the Dead*, pp. 220–2.)

[2] Halā-halā is a Tantric six-faced manifestation of Avalokiteshvara.

[3] Some of the demons of this order control the 'spirit-mediums' officially appointed as oracles in Tibet, and are believed to be vengeful spirits of deceased *lāmas* who, when in human bodies, practised black magic and thus failed spiritually. The Tibetans call them *Btsan*.

[4] The Nine Planets are described in *Tibetan Yoga and Secret Doctrines*, p. 287.

[5] It was Pe-har whom Padma afterwards made the guardian deity of the famous Monastery of Sāmyé.

[6] Text: *Wang-chuk Chen-po*: Skt. *Mahādeva* ('Great Deva'). Mahādeva, who in various forms and aspects is worshipped by Tibetans and by Hindus, dwells on Mount Kailās, the goal of the Pilgrimage, in western Tibet.

[7] Text: *Gu-lang*: Skt. *Pashupatī*, a goddess chiefly of the Nepalese. As Gulang, this deity is propitiated by all mothers in Tibet who have living children.

[8] Text: *Gon-po-Nag-po*: Skt. *Mahākāla* ('Great Black One'), or *Kālānātha* ('Black Lord'), a form of the Hindu Shiva, is one of the chief Tantric deities of the Tibetans.

[9] Text: *Re-ma-ti*, a form of the Hindu Kālī, and a deity of great significance both to the Reformed (or Gelugpa) and Unreformed (Ningmapa) sects of Tibetan Buddhism, is commonly chosen as the tutelary by highly advanced *yogins*, and is associated with Tantric secret doctrines.

[10] Text: *E-ka-dza-ti*, a one-eyed goddess of the mystic cults, the single-eye symbolizing the single (or non-dualistic) eye of Wisdom.

and praised him for thus having conquered all evils and all deities.

THE RESUSCITATION OF THE SLAIN EVIL BEINGS AND THE INCULCATION OF THE *DHARMA*

Padma so far had employed *mantras* and magic to conquer evil; but now, desiring to attain Absolute Knowledge of Truth, he went to Bōdh-Gayā to subjugate all untruth by employing the power of the *Sūtras*; and there he sat in meditation. By uttering the *Hrī-Hūm-Ah mantra*, Padma resuscitated all the evil spirits, *nāgas*, and demons he had slain, taught them the *Dharma*, initiated them,[1] and made them to serve the cause of religion. Returning to Gṛidhrakūta in order to ascertain if there were any more beings in need of special religious teachings, he found none.

After this, he preached the *Dharma*, both exoterically and esoterically, to the *ḍākinī*, especially to the four chief *ḍākinī*[2] at the Dhanakosha Lake where he was born. Vajra-Varāhī,[3] together with these *ḍākinī*, made submission to him. He likewise taught the gods of the Eight Planets.

THE BIRTH AND GIRLHOOD OF MANDĀRAVĀ

Padma went to the city of Sahor,[4] in the north-western corner of the country of Urgyān, where King Arshadhara reigned. The King had 360 wives and 720 ministers of state. Padma beholding the King and his principal wife, the Queen Haukī, in union, caused a light-ray to enter the Queen's

[1] That is, he gave them 'Power' (text: *Wang*). This *mantra* appertains chiefly to Avalokiteshvara.

[2] See *Tibetan Yoga and Secret Doctrines*, p. 306.

[3] The Tibetans sometimes call Vajra-Varāhī 'The Most Precious Power of Speech, the Female Energy of All Good' (cf. L. A. Waddell, op. cit., p. 275). Her association here with these *ḍākinī* of the lake indicates that she, too, is of their order.

[4] Sahor (or Zahor), signifying a city or town, is sometimes thought to have been situated in what is now Mandi, a small principality in the Punjab between the rivers Byas and Ravi, where there is a lake sacred as a place of Hindu pilgrimage. (Cf. S. C. Dās, op. cit., p. 1089.) Tibetan Buddhists also make pilgrimages to the lake, believing it to be the very lake which miraculously appeared on the site of the pyre underneath which Padma was tied to a stake and condemned to death by burning, as our narrative will presently tell.

womb, and she dreamt that one hundred suns rose simultaneously, that their heat parched the Sahor country, and
that from the crown of her head sprang forth a flower of
turquoise. Gods and goddesses overshadowed the Queen during her pregnancy. A daughter being born, to the consternation of the royal household, the Queen called in a *yogī* and
showed to him the girl and narrated the dream. The *yogī*
bathed the girl with perfume, placed her so that half her body
was in sunshine and half in shade. After having carefully
examined the babe, the *yogī* announced that she possessed
the 32 signs of a Buddha,[1] that she was the daughter of a god
and could not, therefore, be given in marriage, and that she
would renounce the world and become a *yoginī*; and he named
her Mandāravā.[2]

The girl grew up rapidly, growing as much in one day as a
normal child would in a month. By the time she was thirteen,
she was regarded by everybody as really being an incarnate
goddess. Chinese princes, Hindu, Moslem, and Persian kings
were among her forty royal suitors. When she refused all of
them, the King commanded her to choose one of them within
three days. Thinking over her past lives, she told the King she
must devote her life to religion. The King, much angered at
her decision, placed a guard of 500 servants over her and
refused her exit from the palace, and told the guards that he
would put all of them to death if they allowed Mandāravā to
commit suicide.

The Queen's own servants having failed to find meat such
as the Queen desired, the Queen secretly sent Mandāravā out
to find some. The markets were over for the day and Mandāravā found no meat for sale; so she cut off flesh from a child's
corpse which she discovered on her way back to the palace

[1] There are 32 signs of physical, moral, psychic, and spiritual potentialities of Buddhahood, which appear on the bodies of *Bodhisattvas* about to
become Buddhas.

[2] Mandāravā, whose full name was Mandāravā Kumāri Devi, is said to
have been the sister of the Indian monk Shānta-Rakshita, the family priest
of Thī-Srong-Detsan, King of Tibet, who, at the monk's suggestion, invited
Padma-Sambhava to Tibet to re-establish Buddhism. Padma-Sambhava
made Shānta-Rakshita the first abbot of Sāmyé Monastery. (Cf. L. A.
Waddell, op. cit., pp. 24[5], 28.)

and gave it to her mother, who ordered her to make a stew of it, and Mandāravā did so. Upon partaking of the stew, the King was levitated from his seat and felt as though he could fly; and taking the meat to be that of a Brāhmin seven times born,[1] sent Mandāravā to fetch the remainder of the corpse. The King took the corpse, had it turned into magical pills, and had these buried in a box in a cemetery under the guardianship of the *ḍākinī*.

Mandāravā's Escape to the Jungle and Ordination

Mandāravā, accompanied by a maid-servant, escaped from the palace through a secret passage-way and, going into the jungle, discarded her garments of silk and her jewellery, and prayed that she might become a sister of the Order and not a bride. She pulled out her hair and scratched her face with her finger-nails in order to destroy her beauty so that no suitors would desire her, and entered into silent meditation.

The maid-servant, in consternation, hurriedly returned to the palace and made report to the King. The King dismissed Mandāravā's suitors, saying that she had joined the Sisterhood; and he had her and her 500 maid-sevants ordained, and built for them a palatial monastery where they entered upon the religious life.

Padma's Arrival and Instruction of Mandāravā

Knowing that the time had come to instruct Mandāravā, Padma flew on a cloud from the Dhanakosha Lake to Mandāravā's religious retreat. Mandāravā and her followers, who were out in their garden, beheld a smiling youth sitting in a rainbow. The air was filled with the sound of cymbals and the odour of incense. Overcome with joy and wonder, Mandāravā and her followers swooned. Padma revived them by emanating red, white, and blue light rays.[2] He landed in the garden and

---

[1] Text: *Kewa-dun*. The translator told me, as we translated this passage, that he recalled seeing, as a boy, a dried bit of such flesh brought to his mother and described as having been found by a *tertön* (or taker-out of hidden books and treasures) amidst a cache of hidden books in Tibet.

[2] The red ray symbolizes the speech-principle; the white, the body-principle; the blue, the mind-principle.

all the nuns bowed down before him. Then Mandāravā invited him into the monastery to expound the Doctrine.

Mandāravā having questioned Padma concerning his parentage and country, he replied, 'I have no parents. I am a gift of the Voidness. I am the essentiality of Amitābha and of Avalokiteshvara, born of a lotus in the Dhanakosha Lake; and, being of the same essence as the Ādi-Buddha, Vajra-Dhāra, and the Buddha of Bōdh-Gayā, I am the Lotus miraculously produced from all These. I will aid all beings. I am the master of the Eight Fathers of Generation, of the Eight Mothers of Birth, of the Eight Places of Travel, of the Eight Places of Abode, of the Eight Cemeteries for Meditation, of the Eight Kinds of *Gurus*, of the Eight Classes of Wisdom, of the Eight Highest *Lāmas* [or Directors of Religion], of the Eight Classes of Magical Illusion, of the Eight Sorts of Garments, of the Eight Tantric Deities Difficult to Propitiate, of the Eight Parts of *Yogic* Dress in Cemeteries, of the Eight Past and Eight Future [Events?], of the Eight Classes of Past Error and of the Eight Classes of Future Error. I have collected all perfection doctrines, and I know the past, present, and future in completeness. I will plant the banners of the Truth in the Ten Directions throughout this World. I am the matchless [Teacher] of all.'

Padma instructed Mandāravā and her 500 followers in the Three *Yogas*[1] first; and they practised these *yogas*.

MANDĀRAVĀ'S IMPRISONMENT AND PADMA'S BURNING AT THE STAKE

A cowherd having observed the coming of Padma and how he was taken inside the monastery by the nuns, went to the door and listened, and, hearing him talking to them, reported that Mandāravā was living with a youthful *brahmachāri* and was not so virtuous as they took her to be. When the King heard this accusation, he offered a reward for anyone able to prove it; and the cowherd claimed the reward. The King

[1] These comprise the *Ati*, *Anu*, and *Chitti* systems of *Yoga*, of the *Yogāchāra* (or 'Contemplative') School of the Mahāyāna, founded by Asaṅga, which developed into the *Mantrayāna*, or 'Path of the *Mantra*', about A.D. 700. (Cf. L. A. Waddell, op. cit., p. 128.)

ordered that the monastery be forcibly entered and that the youth be seized if found within; and Padma was taken and bound with ropes.

The King commanded, 'Collect *til*-seed oil from the villagers and burn the youth. To punish Mandāravā, confine her naked in a pit filled with thorns for twenty-five years. Put a cover over the pit so that she cannot see the blue sky. Imprison the two chief nuns in a dungeon; and confine all the other nuns to the monastery in such manner that they can never more hear the voice of a man.'

Soldiers took Padma, stripped him naked, spat upon him, assaulted him and stoned him, tied his hands behind his back, placed a rope around his neck, and bound him to a stake at the junction of three roads. The people to the number of 17,000 were ordered each to fetch a small bundle of wood and a small measure of *til*-seed oil. A long roll of black cloth was soaked in the oil and then wrapped around Padma. Then there were heaped over him leaves of the *tala*-tree and of the *palmyra* palm. Upon these the wood was placed and the *til*-seed oil poured over it. The pyre was as high as a mountain; and when fire was put to it from the four cardinal directions the smoke hid the sun and the sky. The multitude were satisfied and dispersed to their homes.

A great sound was heard as of an earthquake. All the deities and the Buddhas came to Padma's aid. Some created a lake, some cast aside the wood, some unrolled the oil-soaked cloth, some fanned him. On the seventh day afterwards the King looked forth and, seeing that there was still smoke coming from the pyre,[1] thought to himself. 'This mendicant may have been, after all, some incarnation;' and he sent ministers to investigate. To their astonishment, they saw a rainbow-enhaloed lake where the pyre had been and surrounding the lake all the wood aflame, and at the centre of the lake a lotus blossom upon which sat a beautiful child with an aura, apparently about eight years of age, its face covered with a dew-like perspiration. Eight maidens of the same appearance as Mandāravā attended the child.

[1] The pyre should have been already reduced to ashes.

When the King heard the ministers' report, he took it all to be a dream. He himself went to the lake and walked around it rubbing his eyes to be sure he was awake; and the child cried out, 'O thou evil King, who sought to burn to death the Great Teacher of the past, present and future, thou hast come. Thy thoughts being fixed upon the things of this world, thou practisest no religion. Thou imprisonest persons without reason. Being dominated by the Five Poisons—lust, anger, sloth, jealousy, selfishness—thou doest evil. Thou knowest naught of the future. Thou and thy ministers are violators of the Ten Precepts.' The King made humble repentance, recognized in Padma the Buddha of the past, present, and future, and offered himself and his kingdom to him. In accepting the King's repentance, Padma said, 'Be not grieved. My activities are as vast as the sky. I know neither pleasure nor pain. Fire cannot burn this inexhaustible body of bliss.'

Mandāravā refused to come out of the thorn-filled pit when the King sent for her. Not until the King in person went to her and explained everything did she return to the palace. Then she sang her *guru's* praises and Padma in his turn sang hers. The King clad Padma in royal garments, placed jewels upon him and a crown-like head-dress, and gave to him both the kingdom and Mandāravā.

PADMA'S METHOD OF PREVENTING WAR

The old suitors of Mandāravā made war against the King for giving Mandāravā to Padma. Mahāpāla brought up his army first. Obtaining from the demi-gods enormous all-victorious bows and arrows, Padma dispatched them on an elephant along with a message carried by two gigantic heroes. When Mahāpāla beheld the bows and arrows and learned that Padma and the two heroes could handle them, and fearing lest Padma had a thousand such heroes and arms, he withdrew his army. It being rumoured that no one could possibly use such mighty bows and arrows, Rāhula,[1] at Padma's command, took up one of the bows and arrows and hit a horn

---

[1] A personification of the God of the Planet Rāhula.

target at a distance from which a man would barely have been visible; and all the kings withdrew their armies.

THE SAHOR KING'S INITIATION

The Sahor King, taking Padma as his *guru*, begged him for adequate instruction in the doctrines of the *Mantras*, *Tantras*, and *Sūtras*, that he might attain *Nirvāṇa*; and Padma said, 'O King, difficult is it for thee when immersed in worldly affairs to practise the Precepts. Wert thou to be taught the secret doctrines appertaining to the *Mantras* and *Tantras* without initiation, it would be like pouring water into an earthen pot before the pot has been fired.'[1] But, after receiving the necessary *yogic* training, the King and twenty-one of his followers were duly initiated; and the King became a teacher of the *Dharma*.

MANDĀRAVĀ'S QUESTIONS AND PADMA'S ANSWERS

One day Mandāravā put to Padma a series of doctrinal questions, which, with Padma's replies, were as follows:

'How do the *Sūtras* differ from the *Mantras* and *Tantras*?'

'The *Sūtras* are the seed, the *Mantras* and *Tantras* are the fruit.'

'What difference is there between the Greater Path and the Lesser Path?'[2]

'The difference is twofold; that between the ordinary significance and the implied significance.'[3]

'What difference is there between the conditional and the unconditional truth?'

'The difference is that between the non-truth and the truth.'[4]

'What is the difference between ritual and Divine Wisdom?'[5]

---

[1] Even as an unfired earthen pot will not retain water, so the untrained and uninitiated disciple cannot retain Truth in its fullness. The Jungian interpretation would be that the Truth often produces an inflation and disruption of the personality.

[2] Or 'between the Mahāyāna and the Hīnayāna'.

[3] Or 'between the exoteric and the esoteric'.

[4] Or 'between the partial truth and the full truth'.

[5] Or 'between exoteric religious observances and intuitive insight'.

'The difference is that between non-having and having.'

'What is the difference between the *Sangsāra* and *Nir-vāna*?'

'The difference is that between Ignorance and Wisdom.'

When Mandāravā asked Padma concerning her past and future lives, he replied that the answer would be too long to give then. To her query, 'Who was my father in my previous incarnation?' Padma answered, 'Thy father was the prince of a *yogī* king of Kalinga. He became an ordained monk of the Lord Buddha at Benares. He converted the Jains and Hindus to Buddhism. The monastery of Vikramashīla was under his jurisdiction. He fought the non-Buddhists and slew many, and because of this sin he returned to *sangsāric* birth, being conceived in the womb of the Queen of King Arti. The Queen died; and in the cemetery I cut open the womb and took out the child, which died and was reborn as your father the King.'

'What fate awaiteth my father in his next births?'

'He will first be born as Akara-mati-shīla in the Monkey-land of Tibet;[1] then in the country of the *Rākṣhasas*;[2] then as a prince of the King of Kotāla; then among the demi-gods, and I shall be his *guru*; then as Deva Akarachandra, son of a monk, in Nepal. Then, after being taught by Avalokitesh-vara in His heaven, he will take birth as prince Lhaje, son of King Mu-thī-tsan-po of Tibet. He will encounter me in Tibet, and once more I shall tell him of his future. After twenty generations he will be reborn in the Sahor country, now as a virtuous king, now as a very learned man (or *pandit*), now in lower conditions, but through my kindness he shall never see the hell-worlds. All this thou shalt keep secret.' Padma instructed Mandāravā in the Precepts and the Doctrine. And

---

[1] When in ancient times travellers from India first visited Tibet, the Tibetans were in a state of barbarism, and observing their faces reddened, as today, with cold-resisting ochre-coloured ointment, their apparently ferocious mien, their bodies covered with hairy animal skins and their uncouth manners, the travellers took them to be a species of apes. There is also a legend of Tibetan origin, that the progenitor of the Tibetans was a monkey. Tibet is known to the people of Tibet as the *Bod-kyi-yul*, the Country of Bhot. Before it accepted Buddhism, Tibet was known as the country of the red-faced cannibals (or savages)—*Dong-mar-can-gyi-yul*.

[2] A non-human land, sometimes fancifully taken to be Ceylon.

he remained in the Sahor country for 200 years and established
the Faith.

PADMA'S AND MANDĀRAVĀ'S MEDITATION IN CAVES

Thinking the time ripe to preach the *Dharma* throughout
India, China, Tibet, Nepal, and non-Buddhist countries,
Padma told Mandāravā of his imminent departure. She requested that he first instruct her in *Kuṇḍalinī Yoga*; and he
said, 'I am going to Ripotāla to the east. On the third night
after I am gone face the east and make earnest supplication
to me, and I will come to thee.' Padma, sitting on a seat
formed of crossed *dorjes*, was conveyed by four goddesses to
the heavenly palace of Avalokiteshvara whence he went to a
cave and sat in meditation.

Overcome with loneliness and sad at heart, Mandāravā fled
weeping from the Sahor palace. Padma appeared before her
and said, 'Thou canst not control thyself, yet askest all the
doctrines of me. Renounce all worldly things and centre thy
mind on religion.' Padma took her to the cave in Avalokiteshvara's heaven, and for three months and seven days made
prayer and offerings to the Buddha of Long Life.[1] Then
Amitāyus appeared, placed the urn of boundless life on the
heads of Padma and Mandāravā, gave them to drink of the
nectar of immortality, initiated them, and conferred upon
them immunity from death and birth until the end of the
kalpa. Padma was transformed into Hayagrīva and Mandāravā into Vajra-Vārāhī.[2] Both possessed the *siddhi* of
transformation into a rainbow and of invisibility. After
this, Padma and Mandāravā descended to the human world
and dwelt in the Cave of the 'High Slate Mountains' in the
country of Kotāla, between Sahor and the rest of India,
where they remained for twelve years practising *yoga*, the
King of Kotāla giving them maintenance.

[1] That is, Amitāyus ('The One of Boundless Life'), the Buddha invoked
for the obtaining of longevity, especially in the celebration of the Tibetan
eucharist. He is represented as holding on his lap a vase of life-giving
ambrosia, the nectar of the immortals.
[2] See pp. 121[2] and 142[3], above.

THE PRINCESS GIVES HER BODY TO FEED THE
STARVING BEASTS

Padma, in a *yogic* vision, beheld a cemetery wherein the animals which fed on the flesh of the dead were starving because of a dearth of new corpses. Feeling great compassion for the animals, Padma went to the cemetery and offered to them his own body for food. But his body was a body of invisibility,[1] and the animals could not eat it.

[1] That is to say, a non-fleshy, subtle body, such as is attained by success in *yoga.* Psychic research in Europe and America has accumulated much data tending to support the hypothesis of an etheric body as being the normally invisible framework sustaining the body of flesh. Two American physicians found, by weighing a dying person before and a moment after death, that the death-process resulted in a loss of weight of from two to three ounces, which have been credited to the withdrawn etheric body. Colonel de Rochas, Professor of the Polytechnic at Paris, proved that when the etheric body is exteriorized by hypnotizing the subject, sensation no longer exists in the physical body, but is removed thence to a distance of two or three metres. Madame de Esperance, a trance 'medium', dematerialized her legs; and Baron de Meck also reports the case of a man who could dematerialize at will to such a degree that lights could be seen through his body. The Baron himself experimentally ascertained that where a physical limb had been amputated from a living human organism the etheric limb is still present. (Cf. Baron de Meck's Lecture as reported in *The Two Worlds*, London, 16 Dec. 1938, p. 794.) Similarly, as oriental masters of *yoga* maintain, when the fleshly form as a whole is amputated by the high surgery of death, the etheric counterpart (which the Tibetans call the 'rainbow body' because of its auric radiances) continues to exist, possessed not only of the normal sense faculties of the Earth-plane body, but also of the super-normal faculties of the body of the after-death plane (known in Tibetan as the *Bardo*, or state intervening between the complete dematerialization produced by the death-process and the complete rematerialization produced by the birth-process). The translated text in *The Tibetan Book of the Dead*, pp. 158–9, describes the *Bardo*-body of the after-death state as follows:

Addressing the deceased, the Officiant says, 'Thou mayst have been, when living, blind of the eye, or deaf, or lame, yet on this After-Death Plane thine eyes will see forms, and thine ears will hear sounds, and all other sense-organs of thine will be unimpaired and very keen and complete. . . . Thy present body being a desire-body—thine intellect having been separated from its seat [the human body]—is not a body of gross matter, so that now thou hast the power to go right through any rock-masses, hills, boulders, earth, houses, and Mt. Meru itself without being impeded. . . . Or thou canst instantaneously arrive in whatever place thou wishest; thou hast the power of reaching there within the time which a man taketh to bend, or to stretch forth his hand. . . . None is there [of the various psychic powers of illusion and of shape-shifting] which thou mayst desire which thou canst not exhibit. The ability to exercise them unimpededly existeth in thee now.'

The *lāmas* maintain that all these miraculous powers, if developed on the Earth-plane through *yogic* practices, can be exercised either in the fleshly or

In order to ascertain what he should do to save the animals, Padma entered into meditation ; and discovering thereby that the late King of Sahor had reincarnated as the princess of the King of Kotāla, considered how the flesh of this princess might be given to the animals. Padma transformed himself into a pair of hawks, and they built a nest and laid eggs in it. The princess happening to go out to gather *kusha* grass,[1] saw the eggs, and placed leaves over the nest to shelter the eggs, and stones at the corners of the nest to prevent it from being blown away. The male hawk assisted her. Pity was thus aroused in her ; and, deciding to adopt the religious life, she went to Padma and Mandāravā at the cave seeking religious guidance. Padma said to the princess, 'If thou desirest to become a woman of religion, realize first the sufferings of all the animals in the cemetery ; then go and offer to them thy body. By devouring thy body, all these animals will be reborn as human beings, and become thy disciples when thou thyself, after some lives, shalt be born as King Srong-Tsan-Gampo in the Land of Snow.[2] He will send envoys to bring the image of Avalokiteshvara to Tibet. At that time the animals will take

in the *Bardo*-body at will, as they were by the Great *Guru*, to whom journeys in the subtle (or etheric) body to extra-terrestrial states of existence are reported in the Biography as having been as commonplace as journeys in the fleshly form are among ordinary men.

A 'body of invisibility', or, following our Tibetan text more literally, a 'body capable of vanishing', is a concept quite similar to that of the alchemist's '*lapis* (or *corpus*) *invisibilitatis*', to which frequent reference is made by Dr. Jung in *Psychology and Alchemy* and other of his writings.

[1] A grass peculiar to India, used by *yogins* for making mats and cushions upon which to sit when meditating. It also affords feed for cattle. *Lāmas* make brooms of it for temple use and also employ it as an altar decoration, associated with the sacred peacock feathers, in holy-water vases. It is prized as a sacrificial grass by Hindus and by Buddhists on account of its having formed the cushion upon which the *Bodhisattva* Gautama sat under the Bodhi-Tree when He became the Buddha.

[2] Text: *Kha-wa-chen*, 'Land of Snow', a name given to Tibet. Srong-Tsan-Gampo, who flourished in the first half of the seventh century A.D. and died about 650, was the first Buddhist king of Tibet, and, being a great patron of learning, is justly the most famous and popular of Tibetan rulers. He was canonized as an incarnation of Avalokiteshvara, the Lord of Mercy and Compassion, and thus prepared the way for the line of Dalai Lāmas. He is believed to have reincarnated in 1077 as Dvag-po Lharje, the direct apostolic successor of Milarepa, and became known as the Great *Guru* Gampopa, dying in 1152.

human birth, some in the east of India, some in Singala; they will build two hundred monasteries and be servitors of the Buddha, the *Dharma* and the *Saṅgha*.¹ Then the image of the eleven-faced Avalokiteshvara will be taken to Tibet, and the Children of the Monkey shall have opportunity of worshipping Him.'

The princess at once handed over to Padma her garments and ornaments, and, going to the cemetery, offered her body to the animals and they devoured it.

When the King learned from Padma of the wondrous pity of the princess, he, too, sought religious guidance of him; and Padma went to the palace and preached the Mahāyāna of self-sacrifice and universal altruism, for all living things.

PADMA'S CONDEMNATION BY KING ASHOKA

Then after having visited each of the Eight Great Cemeteries of India, and other places, Padma went to Pataliputra,² where lived King Ashoka,³ who, after having incited feuds between the older and younger monks, had the latter put to death and the former beaten and left to die. The King had also made war against a rival king and captured him, and was now holding him prisoner.

In order to subdue Ashoka, Padma transformed himself into a *bhikṣhu*⁴ and went to Ashoka's palace and begged alms. 'This man', said Ashoka, 'is come to show contempt of me', and he ordered Padma to be imprisoned. As a punishment, Padma was cast into a vat of boiling oil. 'Boil him until he is dissolved', commanded the King. On the following day the

---

¹ Literally, the Body, the Mind, the Speech, which are Tibetan equivalents for the Buddha, the *Dharma*, the *Saṅgha*.

² Pataliputra, 'The City of Sweet Scented Flowers', known to the ancient Greeks as 'Palibothra', situated near the modern Patna on the Ganges, was the capital of Ashoka's empire, where, during the ninth year of his reign, or in 261 B.C., he adopted Buddhism as the state religion. (Cf. L. A. Waddell, op. cit., p. xx.) Previously, in 245 B.C., a special Buddhist council was held at Pataliputra, but, inasmuch as only the stricter wing of the monastic orders was represented, the Chinese Buddhists do not recognize this council's decisions. (Cf. K. L. Reichelt, op. cit., p. 23.)

³ This legendary story concerns the Ashoka who, after his subsequent conversion to Buddhism, became the famous Buddhist Emperor of India.

⁴ A *Bhikṣhu* is an ordained monk of the Buddhist Order. *Bhikṣhu* is Sanskrit, the Pāli form being *Bhikkhu* and the Tibetan, *Ge-long* (*Dge-sloṅ*).

King went to the vat to see how well the sentence had been carried out ; and he beheld a lotus blossom growing out of the vat and the *bhikṣhu* sitting amidst the blossom. Overcome with wonder, Ashoka immediately recognized his error, and, bowing down before the *bhikṣhu* in repentance, said, 'Owing to sloth, I have committed a great sin ; O Lord, tell me how I may atone for it'. And Padma replied, 'If thou build ten million[1] *stūpas* in one night and make surpassingly great charitable gifts to the poor, only thus canst thou wipe away thy sin'.

The King said, 'It is easy to make such gifts to the poor, but difficult to build so many *stūpas* in one night. Perhaps thy words imply that I shall be unable to wipe away my sin.' Padma replied, 'Thou art come into the world in fulfilment of the Lord Buddha's prophecy.[2] If thou go and make prayer before the Bodhi-Tree at Bōdh-Gayā, thou shalt succeed in building so many *stūpas*.'

The King went to the Bodhi-Tree and prayed, 'If it be true that I am come into the world in fulfilment of the Lord Buddha's prophecy, may I be empowered to build so many millions of *stūpas* in one night'; and, to his astonishment, this came to pass. And in the City of Maghadha[3] the King gave surpassingly great alms to the poor.

PUBLIC EXAMINATION OF TWO RIVAL PRINCES IN MEDICINE

Now Padma took up residence in a cemetery in the country of Baidha,[4] where lived a *yogī* King named Balin, who was

[1] This is a typical example of oriental exaggeration to emphasize greatness of number.

[2] This prophecy would refer to the historic fact that King Ashoka became the Great Buddhist Emperor of India. As such, he has been called the Buddhist Constantine. In order to signify his sincere conversion to Buddhism and his deep remorse at the appalling loss of human life and the widespread suffering which his bloody conquest of Kaliṅga, in southern India, had caused, he changed his name from Ashoka, or 'The Sorrowless One', to 'The Compassionate One' (*Piye-dasi* in the Indian vernacular and *Priya-darsin* in Sanskrit). In his edicts he is also called 'The One Beloved of the Gods', *Devanam-priya*. (Cf. L. A. Waddell, op. cit., p. xxi.)

[3] By some authorities the City of Maghadha is believed to have occupied the site of the modern Allahabad ; others have associated it with the modern Patna, or Patalipūtra.

[4] According to the *Kah-gyur* version, Baidha was the birth-place of the

very learned in medicine. Balin had two wives and each had
given him a son. To the son of the elder wife, Balin secretly
taught all of his medical knowledge, but to the son of the
younger wife he taught nothing of it. One day, the King
announced that he intended to ascertain by means of an
examination which son had a better head for studying medicine. The mother of the younger son thinking that the King
was planning thereby to choose one of the sons as heir to the
throne, wept bitterly because her son knew nothing of medical
science. Her son told her not to lament; and, going to Padma
in the cemetery, mastered the five higher systems of medicine.
When the time approached for the examination, the King
made public proclamation that whichever son showed greater
proficiency in medical knowledge would be chosen to succeed
to the kingship.

Publicly the two sons were examined. The elder son showed
proficiency in three hundred medical treatises; but the
younger son showed much greater proficiency, and, in addition to his exposition of them, set forth the Doctrine of the
Buddha so wonderfully that *devas*, *nāgas*, and demons appeared and made obeisance to him.

'Without having been taught, thou hast mastered everything', said the King, and he bowed down before the son and
set the son's feet on his head. In anger, the elder wife cried,
'Although thou hast secretly instructed mine own son, to the
son of the younger queen thou hast conveyed the very essence
of medical science. Had they been taught together my son
would have been the victor. And now thou hast disgraced him
in public. Unless thou divide the kingdom equally between the
two, I will put an end to my life here and now.' To this pro-
posal of dividing the kingdom the King agreed, whereupon
the younger son said, 'I will embrace the religious career'.
And the victorious son, becoming Padma's disciple, mastered

Prince Vishantara, whose incarnation represents the last and greatest of
the Ten Great [Former] Births (or *Mahājātaka*) preceding the birth in
which the *Bodhisattva* Gautama attained Buddhahood. Tibetans believe
Baidha (or Biddha) to be the ancient Videha, which they identify, probably
erroneously, with the modern Bettiah is northern Bengal. (Cf. L. A.
Waddell, op. cit., p. 543[8].)

the *Sūtras*, the *Tantras*, and the *Mantras*, and wrote many treatises on religion and medicine, and was named Siddhi-Phala.[1]

THE SUN *YOGĪ* SETS FIRE TO THE VIKRAMASHĪLA MONASTERY

During this epoch a Sun-*Siddha*[2] was preaching non-Buddhist doctrines. He practised a *yoga* intended to draw the Sun's vital energy into his own body, so that when he opened his eyes fire came forth and set aflame the Buddhist monastery of Vikramashīla [in Magadhā]. In the conflagration, many of the *Abhidharma* scriptures were destroyed. As a result of this destruction, the *nāga* King Muchilinda became very ill.[3] Nanda, another King of the *nāgas*, foresaw that Muchilinda would die unless a human physician were summoned at once. Two *nāgas* fetched the *Bhikṣhu* Siddhi-Phala, who cured Muchilinda. As a reward, the King presented the *bhikṣhu* with the greater part of the text of the *Boom*, which Ānanda, the chief disciple of the Buddha, had hidden in the realm of the *nāgas*. The part of the *Boom* which the *nāga* King withheld was his security for the *bhikṣhu's* promise to return to the *nāgas'* kingdom. And this *bhikṣhu*, after his return to the human world with the *Boom*, became known as Ārya Nāgārjuna.

THE SUPERNORMAL BIRTH OF ĀRYA-DEVA, DISCIPLE OF NĀGĀRJUNA

Padma now went to a cemetery in the country of Singala. The King of Singala, Shrī Phala, became his patron and

[1] A Sanskrit appellation meaning 'Fruit of *Siddhi*', or 'Fruit of *Yogic* Accomplishments'.

[2] A Sun-*Siddha* (Skt. *Sūrya-Siddha*) is a *yogī* proficient in *yogic* practices relating to the Sun, as the matter which follows shows. The Editor recalls having encountered on the banks of the upper Ganges, near Rikhikesh, a *yogī* who practised similarly. Daily the *yogī* sat in practice with his gaze fixed on the unclouded disk of the tropical Sun, with no protection whatsoever to his eyes. If not done with utmost care, the practice may result in total blindness, but this practitioner enjoyed unusually keen vision and was in robust health. His exact purpose in so practising he never made quite clear to me.

[3] This illness was due to pollution of the air and water (which *nāgas* inhabit) by the burning of the monastery and scriptures (of which the *nāga* King had been made the custodian).

disciple. Padma by his supernormal vision beheld the non-Buddhists bring up their army, and complete the destruction of the Vikramashīla Monastery and re-establish the non-Buddhist religion. After Padma had seen this vision, the King's gardener noticed in a pond of the palace garden an immense lotus blossom which never folded its petals at night. When the King and Queen went to see the lotus blossom they beheld in it a beautiful child, apparently about eight years old, with perspiring face.[1] The King's chief priest, being'called to explain what the child was, said, ' He is the incarnation of Shākya Mitra. He is destined to defeat Maticitra, the arch-enemy of Buddhism, whose tutelary deity is Mahādeva. Take him into the palace and care for him.' And the King took the child and cared for him; and Padma initiated the child and instructed him in the *Dharma*; and the child was called Ārya-Deva. The child begged Padma for ordination into the Order, but Padma, refusing to ordain him, said, 'Thou art to be ordained by Nāgārjuna.'[2] And Padma remained in Baidha and Singala nearly two hundred years,[3] and converted the people to Mahāyāna Buddhism.

THE ESTABLISHING OF BUDDHISM IN BENGAL

In eastern Bengal a youthful non-Buddhist King was ruling. His palace was surrounded by six moats and had eight doors.

[1] The appearance of the child following Padma's vision suggests that Padma exercised his *yogic* powers to bring about the lotus-birth of the child, and the parallelism between the perspiring face of this child and of Padma's when found in a lotus points to a spiritual relationship between them or may even imply that this child is one of the Great *Guru's* emanations.

[2] Nāgārjuna was the greatest of the Fathers of the Māhāyāna, having been (*c.* A.D. 150) the thirteenth, or according to some the fourteenth, in the direct succession of the Buddhist Patriarchs. He is believed to have been the reincarnation of Ānanda, the Buddha's illustrious disciple. As has been suggested above, Nāgārjuna was the transmitter of the *Prajñā-Pāramitā*. (See *Tibetan Yoga and Secret Doctrines*, pp. 344–6.) Ārya-Deva did receive ordination at the hands of Nāgārjuna and was his most learned disciple and successor to the Buddhist hierarchical chair at Nālanda, the Oxford of ancient India.

[3] This Biography represents the Great *Guru* as having flourished in India and elsewhere in the human world for many centuries. He, being a Master of *Yoga*, lived, as has been already suggested above, in a non-fleshy body, immune to illness, old age, and death. He is thus the idealized living exponent of Buddhism practically applied and, in this respect, a Buddha greater than the Buddha Gautama, as the Tibetan Buddhists believe.

He possessed a cat with a thousand eyes, and a magical light-giving gem. His subjects were many, his power great, but his rule was harmful.

Padma, upon setting out to subdue this King, placed Mandāravā on a main highway and directed her to transform herself into a cat-faced being. By means of magic, Padma collected an army of 81,000 men and armed them with bows and arrows. The King was slain and his kingdom conquered. The Five Goddesses of Sensual Pleasure, who were the King's chief deities, were converted. Assuming the guise of the Ādi-Buddha, Padma caused the consciousness-principles of all who had been killed in the war to go to the paradises. The living he converted to Buddhism. He aided the poor, and comforted the brute creatures. The country prospered and the people were happy.

The Vikramashīla Monastery having been rebuilt, King Houlagou of Persia came with a large army and destroyed the twelve buildings comprising the Monastery and a part of the *Abhidharma* scriptures of the Mahāyāna School. Two learned *bhikṣhus*, Thok-me[1] and Yik-nyen,[2] transformed themselves into ordained nuns; and they introduced and established the Five Doctrines of Maitreya, the Eight Kinds of *Prakaraṇa*[3] and the *Abhidharma-Kosha*.

PADMA ATTAINS TO BUDDHAHOOD AT BŌDH-GAYĀ

Padma went to Bōdh-Gayā and in the presence of the *Guru* Singha constructed the *Maṇḍalas* of the Wrathful Deities associated with *Ati-Yoga, Chitti-Yoga,* and *Yangti-Yoga*; and, by this means, demonstrated to the *Guru* the methods where-by, in virtue of doctrine and conduct, one may, step by step, attain *Nirvāṇa*.[4] When the verbal part of the exposition was

[1] This is the Tibetan equivalent of Āryasangha (or Asaṅga), the founder of the Yogāchāra School. He is also known as the Sage of Ajanta, with reference to the famous Caves of Ajanta, which in his day were known as Achintapuri Vihara. He is said to have lived 150 years.

[2] A Tibetan name meaning 'Precious-Stone Helper'.

[3] The Eight *Prakaraṇa* are eight metaphysical treatises appertaining to the Hīnayāna School.

[4] As this passage suggests, these three *yogas*, appertaining to the Yogā-chāra School, are directly associated with the *Nirvāṇic* Path. (See p. 145[1], above.)

completed, Padma levitated himself and rose into the air so high that he could no longer be seen, and then reappeared in various supernormal forms and exhibited various supernormal powers. He returned to the earth and there constructed a *stūpa* of precious stones and consecrated it.

Many learned *pandits* who happened to witness Padma's magical performances, requested that he teach to them the Doctrine; and he expounded to them the *Sūtras*, *Tantras*, *Mantras*, *Vinaya Piṭaka*, *Abhidharma*, and medical sciences in detail; and they named him 'The Great *Pandit*'. Then Padma taught them the system of *Kriyā Yoga*[1] in its completeness; and they named him 'The *Dorje* without Imperfection' [or 'The *Dorje* Lacking in Nothing']. Everything that Padma taught to the *pandits*, they wrote down. Then they placed all the manuscripts in a box made of precious gems, tied the box to a banner of victory, and raised the banner over the ruins of the Vikramashīla Monastery. They now named Padma 'The Enlightened One [or Buddha], the Victory Banner of the Doctrine'. Immediately afterwards there was a fall of rain for seven days, all diseases disappeared, and the thirteen lucky signs appeared. Thus Padma really became a Buddha at Bōdh-Gayā; and from the roof of the palace there he roared like a lion. The non-Buddhists were much agitated; and he converted them; and they named him '*Guru* Sèng-ge-Dradog'.[2]

PADMA'S MISSION TO EIGHT COUNTRIES

Padma considered that the time had come to go on to eight other countries to establish the Doctrine, and he went first to the country of Jambu-mala to the east of Urgyān, where grew many *jambu* [*eugenia jambolans*] trees, and taught the *Vajrāyāna* form of Buddhism. Next he went to the country of Par-pa-ta, to the south, where the prevailing cult was of the Black Mañjushrī;[3] and there he taught concerning the

---

[1] See p. 206[2], following.

[2] That is, 'The Lion-roaring *Guru*', the name of one of the eight chief forms assumed by Padma. (See Illustration V and its description, p. xxiii.)

[3] Or Mañjushrī in wrathful aspect: Tib. *Dorje-Jig-je*: Skt. *Vajra-Bhairava*, 'Immutable Wrathful One', one of the most important deities of the

peaceful and the wrathful aspects of Mañjushrī. Then he went to the country of Nāgapota, to the west, where the people were devotees of Hayagrīva in Lotus Aspect; and to them Padma taught concerning the peaceful and wrathful aspects of Avalokiteshvara.[1] Thence he went to the country of Kasha-kamala, to the north, where the cult of the *Phurbu*, or Magical Dagger,[2] prevailed; and Padma amplified this worship. From here, he went to the country known as Trang-srong,[3] to the southeast, where the people worshipped the Mother Goddesses; and Padma amplified their worship by teaching them how to invoke these goddesses. Going thence to the country of the flesh-eating *Rākṣhasas*, to the southwest, ruled by a king of the Ten-headed Dynasty of Lanka (or Ceylon), where the people worshipped Vishnu, he taught the Kālachakra Doctrine to convert them. Padma's next mission was to the country of Lung-lha,[4] to the northwest, peopled by devotees of Mahādeva; and to them he taught concerning *sangsāric* offerings with hymns of praise.[5] In the eighth of the countries, called Kekki-ling, or 'Place of Heroes', to the northeast, where the people practised black magic, Padma introduced one of the eight systems for propitiating deities.

Now Padma went to the Dhanakosha Lake, at the centre of the Urgyān country,[6] and found the people prospering and the Mahāyāna doctrines flourishing. He entered into meditation and ascertained that the time was not yet come to convert all other countries; and he returned to Bengal and lived with Mandāravā in a cemetery, where the two practised *yoga*.

Gelugpa, or Established Church of Tibetan Buddhism. (See Illustration VI.) Mañjushrī in peaceful aspect is the Guardian of Divine Wisdom. (See Illustration IV.)

[1] Avalokiteshvara represents the peaceful and Hayagrīva the wrathful aspect of the Lord of Mercy, of whom the Dalai Lāma is the incarnate representative on Earth.

[2] The Tibetan *phurbu* is a symbolical dagger with a triangular-shaped blade, used for the ceremonial exorcising, or slaying, of demons.

[3] A Tibetan place-name equivalent to the Sanskrit *Krisi*, or *Suni*, meaning 'Reciter of Sacred Hymns'.

[4] This Tibetan term, meaning 'Wind God' (Skt. *Marut*), refers to the storm god presiding over the North-west Quarter of the heavens.

[5] Text: *Jik-ten Choe-toe*, with reference to the eight gods difficult to propitiate, of the Nyingma School. (See S. C. Dās, op. cit., p. 325.)

[6] As will be noted, each of the eight countries last above named was in

PADMA'S SUSPICIOUS FRIEND

One of Padma's friends having visited Padma and Man-dāravā in their cemetery retreat and suspecting that the two were living together as husband and wife, said to Padma, 'What a wonderful man thou art! Thou hast left thy lawful wife Bhāsadhara in thy palace in the Urgyān country; and this is quite disgraceful!' And notwithstanding that the friend slighted Padma by refusing to invite him to his home, Padma thought to himself, 'Inasmuch as this fellow is ignorant of the inner significance of the Mahāyāna and of the *yogic* practices appertaining to the three chief psychic nerves,[1] I should pardon him.'

THE ONE SEVEN TIMES BORN A BRĀHMIN

Transforming himself into the son of a Brāhmin, Padma went to the Khasar-Pāṇi[2] Temple and made obeisance before a Brāhmin possessed of divine prescience. 'Why dost thou make obeisance to me?' asked the Brāhmin. And Padma replied, 'In order that I may aid the creatures of the world, I require the flesh of one who hath been born a Brāhmin seven times successively.[3] If thou canst not provide me with any now, please do so at the hour of thy decease.'

The Brāhmin said, 'While in this world, one ought not to relinquish one's life before the time hath come; but as soon as I am dead thou mayst have my flesh'; and then Padma took leave of the Brāhmin.

Five years afterwards, the Brāhmin died. A great *pandit* named Dhombhi Heruka immediately appeared to claim the body. Many wolves attacked the *pandit*, but, exercising *yogic* powers, he drove them away by looking at them; and, placing

one of the Eight Directions, the Dhanakosha Lake in the Urgyān country being central to all of them. Thus they constitute a vast geometrical *maṇḍala*-like symbolic figure.

[1] These are, according to *Kuṇḍalinī Yoga*, the median-nerve, in the hollow of the spinal column, and the right and left psychic nerves coiled around the spinal column. (See *The Tibetan Book of the Dead*, p. 215.)

[2] Khasar-Pāṇi is a form of Avalokiteshvara.

[3] One so born is believed to possess the power of seeing into the future, as did this Brāhmin. Similarly, in the Occident, a seventh son is believed to be endowed with 'the sight'.

the body on his lap, mounted a tiger. He used serpents for the bridle, girth, and crupper of the tiger, wore on his body ornaments of human bone, and, carrying a three-pronged staff,[1] went to the Moslem city of De-dan. There he rode round about announcing that he would make a gift of the body to anyone who could come and take it.[2] A passer-by remarked, 'Look at this *yogī* who is talking nonsense. He would not be riding the tiger had he not given it honey, nor making use of the serpents had he not given them musk.'[3]

THE WINE-DRINKING *HERUKA* WHO PREVENTED THE SUN FROM SETTING

Then the *Heruka* went to a tavern kept by a woman named Vinasā and ordered wine. 'How much?' asked the woman. 'I wish to buy as much as thou hast', he replied. 'I have five hundred jars', she said; and the *Heruka* said, 'I will pay the price at sunset'.

The *Heruka* not only drank all the wine which the woman had, but kept her busy fetching wine from other shops. When the Sun was about to set, the *Heruka* placed his *phurbu*[4] half in sunshine, half in shadow, and the Sun could not set; and he kept it there so long that the country became parched, the grass dried up and the trees died. For seven days the *Heruka* sat there drinking wine, and all the while the *phurbu* remained half in sunshine, half in shadow, and the Sun continued shining.

The people complained bitterly to their King, saying that

[1] Such as that (shown in Illustration I) commonly held by Padma-Sambhava, of whom Dhombhi Heruka is an emanation or metamorphosis. The term *heruka* refers to the wrathful manifestations of the chief Tantric deity, Samvara (Tib. *Demchog*), and is applied only to great masters of Tantric *yoga*. One aspect of Demchog is believed to be successively incarnate in the hierarchical line of the Chief Lāma resident in Peking.

[2] *Yogīs* commonly practise gift-making, in order to accumulate spiritual merit, in accordance with the precept, 'It is better to give than to receive'.

[3] According to popular Tibetan belief, a tiger can be tamed by feeding it on honey, and a serpent kept at a distance by the odour of musk. As Tibetans are accustomed to carry musk on their person, it is said that they are never bitten by serpents. The translator told me he had never known of a Tibetan to die from snake-bite.

[4] A *phurbu* is usually carried by a Tibetan *yogin* concealed on his person for use in *yogic* ceremonial practices.

a mendicant who was sitting in a tavern drinking wine might be the source of their dire misfortune.[1] So, on the morning when the seven days of the *Heruka's* wine-drinking were ended, the King went to the *Heruka* and said, 'O thou mendicant who shouldst be doing good to all creatures, why art thou drinking in this fashion?' And the *Heruka* answered, 'O King, I am without money to pay for the wine which I have drunk'. And when the King promised to settle the account, the *Heruka* took up the *phurbu* and the Sun set.

After this, the *Heruka* went to the Cave of Kuru-kullā and made it his abode. Vinasā, the wine-seller, who had unbounded faith in the *Heruka*, paid a visit to him, taking with her, on an elephant, wine and food and presented them to him, and requested that he accept her as his disciple, which he did. He favoured her with full instructions in *yoga*; and she attained the *siddhi* of immunity to drowning in water, of flying through the air, and of passing through solid substances.

How the Urgyān King was Cured of Snake Bite

The King of the Urgyān country, having gone to a cemetery, was bitten by a venomous serpent. When the most learned Brāhmins, mendicants, and physicians failed to cure him, they decided that the only hope lay in water from the bottom of the ocean. Such water was speedily procured, but the bearer, while fetching it, encountered a youth weeping and, upon asking the youth why he wept, the youth said that the King was dead. Much perturbed, the bearer threw away the water and hurried to the palace and found the King still alive.[2]

Vinasā, now the learned disciple of the *Heruka*, was sent for; and she, succeeding in fetching water taken from the depths of the ocean, cured the King; and the King, in gratitude, made her his spiritual adviser.

---

[1] No *yogin* is expected to enter a tavern where intoxicants are sold, much less to drink alcoholic liquor; and seeing that the *Heruka* had not the least regard for these prohibitions, the people suspected that their misfortunes were the direct result of his evil actions.

[2] The serpent which bit the King was the incarnation of an evil *nāga*, and the youth was a form which this *nāga* assumed in order to prevent the cure of the King.

Vinasā being a woman of low caste, the wives of the King objected to her presence. Vinasā was quite willing to quit the post, but the King would not hear of it. Seeing how difficult it was for her to get away from the palace, Vinasā magically produced a child, and pretending that it had been born to her in the normal manner, presented it to the King, saying that it was to be his *guru* in place of herself. The King accepted the child and reared it, and the child became a most learned saint, known as Saint La-wa-pa.

Padma and Mandāravā are Burned at the Stake in Urgyān

The time having come, as Padma foresaw, to discipline the people of Urgyān, four *ḍākinī* appeared with a palanquin and placed Padma and Mandāravā in it and transported them by air to the land of Urgyān. Appearing there as mendicants, Padma and Mandāravā begged their food from house to house. Eventually Padma was recognized, and when the ministers of the King heard of it they said, 'This is the man who ignored the Queen Bhāsadhara and killed the wife and son of the minister; and now he is living with a beggar woman. Formerly he broke the law of the realm; and he hath returned to do further harm to us.'

Without the King's knowledge, the ministers had Padma and Mandāravā seized. The pair were tied together, and then wrapped in oil-saturated cloth and fettered to a stake. Wood was piled around them, oil poured over the wood, and fire set to the pyre from each of the four cardinal directions. Even on the twenty-first day afterwards the pyre still gave off smoke,[1] and a rainbow enhaloed it. When the King inquired about the cause of the phenomenon, and no one volunteered an explanation, Bhāsadhara said, 'My husband, having entered the Order, abandoned me and the kingdom for the sake of religion. Then, having recently returned to live with a beggar woman, he was condemned by the ministers and burnt to death.' Angry at not having been consulted concerning the

---

[1] Usually such a pyre ceases smoking by the seventh day after having been fired.

condemnation, the King said, 'If he were an incarnation he could not have been burnt'; and, going to the place where the pyre had been, he beheld a lake, in the centre of which stood an enormous lotus blossom, and Padma and Mandāravā sitting together in the lotus blossom, enhaloed in auras so radiant that one could hardly look upon them. The Earth-Goddess, accompanied by other divinities, appeared, and in songs of praise told of Padma's deeds in the world. The King and the ministers and the multitudes also offered praise and asked Padma's forgiveness; and the King invited Padma to be his *guru* until the *kalpa* should end, and to diffuse the Doctrine. Padma said, 'The Three Worlds are a prison-house; even though one be born a *Dharma-rāja*,[1] one cannot escape from worldly pleasures. And even though one be possessed of the *Dharma-Kāya*[2] and know not how to govern one's own mind, one cannot break the chain of miseries of *sangsāric* existence. O King, make pure thy mind and attain clear vision; and thou shalt attain Buddhahood.'[3]

The King's mind was at once changed; and he and his ministers and followers entered the Order. Padma was escorted to the palace, and the King placed him upon the royal seat, and obeisance and offerings were made to him. For thirteen years Padma remained in the Urgyān land, disciplining the people and establishing the Faith.

MANDĀRAVĀ AND THE ABANDONED FEMALE BABE

Mandāravā went to the Sacred *Heruka* Cave of the *Ḍākinī*, and there became the *ḍākinī's* abbess. Sometimes she assumed the form of a *ḍākinī*, sometimes that of a jackal or tigress, sometimes that of a small boy or girl. By such means she advanced the Doctrine, and converted the various types of beings.

---

[1] A *Dharma-rāja*, or 'King of the *Dharma*', is the highest type of an ideal monarch.

[2] The *Dharma-Kāya*, or 'Body of the *Dharma*', symbolizes the *Nirvāṇic* state in which a Buddha exists. (See *The Tibetan Book of the Dead*, pp. 10–15.)

[3] This doctrine is strictly Buddhistic, the Buddha having emphasized that the whole aim of His teaching is to deliver the mind from its bondage to the *Sangsāra*. This, too, is the purpose of the teaching set forth in our treatise which follows. (Cf. *Tibetan Yoga and Secret Doctrines*, pp. 5–6.)

There lived in the City of Pal-pang-gyu a man and his wife who were weavers. The wife died in giving birth to a female child; and the father, thinking the child could not survive without a mother, deposited both the child and the mother's corpse in a cemetery. Mandāravā, in her tigress transformation, went to the cemetery to eat of the flesh of corpses and saw the child sucking the breast of the dead mother, and, feeling infinite compassion, suckled the child and nurtured it with her own milk. Day by day the tigress ate of the mother's corpse and fed bits of the flesh to the child.

When the child was sixteen, she was as pretty as a goddess, and Mandāravā left her to shift for herself. Padma, seeing that the hour had come to convert the girl, assumed the guise of a *bhikṣhu* and initiated her into the *Maṇḍala* of Vajra-Sattva.[1]

The Cowherd *Guru*

A cowherd, who had been supplying the pair with milk, also became Padma's disciple, and, after having been initiated by Padma into the same *Maṇḍala*, attained the *siddhi* of Vajra-Sattva. There having appeared on the cowherd's forehead, as a result of this *siddhi*, the *mantric* syllable *Hūṃ*, Padma named him *Hūṃ-kāra*. Then Padma taught the cowherd the Doctrine of the Long *Hūṃ*;[2] and he also conferred upon him the *siddhi* of fast-walking,[3] so that he had the power of walking thus, levitated one cubit above the ground.[4] As a

---

[1] See *The Tibetan Book of the Dead*, pp. 108–10, 220.

[2] This Doctrine, which appertains to the Wisdom of the Five Dhyānī Buddhas, is set forth in detail in *Tibetan Yoga and Secret Doctrines*, Book VI.

[3] Text: *Rkang-mgyogs* (pron. *Kang-gyok*), literally meaning 'fast feet', or 'fleetness of foot'.

[4] The late Sardar Bahādur Laden La told me that he had once seen a Tibetan *yogī* transporting himself in this manner. It was in Tibet about the year 1931. 'I had sent him', he said, 'to carry a message to a great *lāma* named Pha-pong-kha living in Lhāsa; and he traversed a distance of twelve miles in about twenty minutes.' A master of this art of fast-walking, called in Tibetan a *lung-gom-pa*, was once encountered, while exercising this art, in the wilds of northern Tibet by Madame Alexandra David-Neel, the explorer of Tibetan mysticism. Apparently the man was in a meditative trance, his eyes wide open and gaze fixed on some invisible far-distant object; and she was told that to stop him in his fast-walking would probably

psychic result of so much progress in *yoga*, a protuberance resembling the head of the Horse-headed Hayagrīva appeared on the cowherd's head above the aperture of Brahma.[1] Then, as the cowherd progressed further in *yoga*, the outline of a single *dorje* appeared on his body over the heart and that of a double *dorje* on his forehead, and from each of his nine bodily apertures light radiated.[2]

After having attained these *siddhi*, the cowherd, driving his cattle home at nightfall, was seen by his master as Vajra-Sattva; and the master exalted the cowherd on a specially arranged seat and bowed down before him. 'Why', asked the cowherd, 'art thou bowing down before me, thy servant? People will look down upon thee for doing so.' And the master replied, 'Thou art Vajra-Sattva; canst thou tell me where my cowherd is?' And the master and the people assembled and declared the cowherd to be their *guru*; and the cowherd expounded the Doctrine and made many converts.

---

kill him. He did not run, but 'seemed to lift himself from the ground, proceeding by leaps. He looked as if he had been endowed with the elasticity of a ball and rebounded each time his feet touched the ground. His steps had the regularity of a pendulum. He wore the usual monastic robe and toga, both rather ragged. His left hand gripped a fold of the toga and was half hidden by the cloth. The right hand held a *phurbu* (magic dagger). His right arm moved slightly at each step, quite as though the *phurbu*, whose pointed extremity was far above the ground, had touched it and were actually a support.' Observed from a distance, he 'seemed as if carried on wings'. (Cf. A. David-Neel, *With Mystics and Magicians in Tibet*, London, 1931, pp. 201–4.) Reference to this art is also made above (on p. 137), where Padma is represented as having mastered the method of acquiring 'fleetness of foot'.

[1] This is the aperture whence the consciousness-principle departs from the body at death, called in Sanskrit the *Brāhmarandhra*. (See *The Tibetan Book of the Dead*, pp. xxix, 18, 87[3].)

[2] Thus the cowherd attained five perfections or *yogic* accomplishments (Skt. *siddhi*): the perfection of body, resulting in fast-walking (Tib. *Kang-gyok-thar-phyin-pa*); the perfection of speech, or vast *yogic* learning (Tib. *Sung-thar-phyin-pa*); the perfection of mind, or mastery of mental processes (Tib. *Thuk-thar-phyin-pa*); the perfection of efficiency in spiritual work, or mastery of the teachings (Tib. *Thin-le-thar-phyin-pa*); and the perfection of excellence, or adeptship in *yoga* (Tib. *Yon-ten-thar-phyin-pa*). As a result of the second perfection, the Hayagrīva-like protuberance appeared; of the third, the single *dorje*; of the fourth, the double *dorje*; of the fifth, the radiance from the nine bodily apertures (Tib. *Ne-gu*), which are the two apertures of the eyes, the two of the nose, the two of the ears, and those of the mouth, anus, and generative organ.

THE STORY OF SHĀKYA SHRĪ MITRA

A brief biography of Shākya Shrī Mitra is set forth as follows: Dharma-Bhitti, daughter of King Dharma Ashoka, was asleep in a garden and dreamt that a white-complexioned man in a rainbow aura placed before her a vessel of *amrita*, and poured holy water on her head so that it entered her body through the aperture of Brahma and made her feel most tranquil. Ten months afterward she gave birth to a boy child. Feeling great shame, she exposed the child, and it was lost in the sand. A dog belonging to a vassal of the King of the Urgyān country discovered the child, which was still alive, and brought it to the King; and the child was reared in the royal household. When the boy was five years old he expressed his desire to become a *bhikṣhu*, but, being too young for ordination, was sent to the Shrī Nālanda Monastery, where, under Padma-Karpo,[1] he became learned in the Five Classes of Knowledge.[2] The great *Pandit* Shrī Singha named the youth Vimala Mitra; and then the abbot of Nālanda named him Shākya Shrī Mitra, and admitted him to the fellowship of the five hundred *pandits* of Nālanda.

THE NON-BUDDHISTS' DEFEAT AT BŌDH-GAYĀ IN CONTROVERSY AND MAGIC

Exercising his power of prescience, Padma saw that he should return to Bōdh-Gayā. First he went to the Cemetery of Jalandhar[3] to meditate. Meanwhile, a non-Buddhist King, known as 'The All-pervading Demi-god', having collected his army, sent four high non-Buddhist priests, each accom-

---

[1] Probably the Padma-Karpo who established Buddhism in Bhutan, and became one of the *Gurus* of the Kargyütpa School. (See *Tibetan Yoga and Secret Doctrines*, p. 251[5].)

[2] The Five Classes of Knowledge are: Knowledge of Medicine, of Languages, of Dialects, of Physics and Mechanical Arts, and of the *Tri-Piṭaka*, comprising, as in the Southern School, the Buddhist Scriptures.

[3] At Jalandhar, in north India, about the end of the first century A.D., under the auspices of King Kanishka, the great Buddhist council was held which caused the schism into what has come to be called 'Northern' and 'Southern' Buddhism. Today, Southern Buddhism prevails in Ceylon, Burma, Thailand, and Cambodia, and Northern Buddhism in Tibet, Sikkim, Bhutan, Nepal, Ladak, Mongolia, Tartary, China, and Japan.

panied by nine *pandits* and five hundred followers, to Bōdh-Gayā, to prepare the way for the overthrow of Buddhism. Each of the four high priests approached Bōdh-Gayā from one of the four cardinal directions and challenged the Buddhists there to public debate, saying, 'If ye be defeated by us, it shall be incumbent upon you to join our Faith; and, if ye defeat us, we will become Buddhists'. The four chief scholars of the Buddhists said among themselves, 'Although we can defeat them in controversy, we cannot overcome their occult powers'.

When the Buddhists were assembled in the royal palace at Bōdh-Gayā discussing the coming debate, a woman with a blue complexion, carrying a broom in her hand, suddenly appeared and said, 'If ye compete with the non-Buddhists, ye will not be successful. There is one, my brother, who can defeat them.' They replied, 'What is thy brother's name, and where doth he live?' She answered, 'His name is Padma Vajra,[1] and he is at present living in the Jalandhar Cemetery'. The Buddhists wishing to know how they might invite him, she said, 'Ye cannot invite him. Assemble at the Temple of the Bodhi-Tree,[2] make many offerings and prayer, and I will go and fetch him.'

The strange woman vanished as suddenly as she had appeared; and the Buddhists, doing as she had advised, made prayer to Padma Vajra to come and vanquish the non-Buddhists. Next morning at dawn, Padma arrived at the palace, coming down through the branches of the trees like a great bird, and at once entered into meditation; and, while Padma was meditating, the Buddhists sounded their religious drums. As the drums were sounding, the spies of the non-Buddhists listened to what the Buddhists were saying. The spy on the east side reported how the Buddhists said that the non-Buddhists, whose brains were like those of foxes, would be defeated. The spy on the south side reported the Buddhists

[1] Meaning 'Diamond (or Indestructible or Adamantine) Lotus'. The strange woman herself was a *ḍākinī* in disguise.
[2] Referring to the Temple of Bōdh-Gayā, built at the side of the Bodhi-Tree under which Gautama attained Buddhahood.

as having said that the followers of Ganesha and their army would be subdued. The spy on the west side reported having heard that the mischievous non-Buddhists with their followers would be annihilated, and the spy on the north side that all the black assembly would be crushed.

When the Sun rose, Padma assumed the guise of a *Dharma-Rāja* and flew over Bōdh-Gayā. The King of Bōdh-Gayā, seeing him thus manifesting magical power, doubted his intellectual ability, and said to him, 'O thou, a mere boy of eight years, pretending to be a *pandit*, thou art not fitted to defeat the non-Buddhists'. Padma replied, 'O my lord, I am an old man of three thousand years; and who is it that is saying I am only eight years of age? Thou brainless one, why presume to compete with me?'

The King made no response, but on his telling the non-Buddhists what Padma had said, they requested, 'O King, be good enough to call in now that inferior monk who caused our hairs to stand on end this morning. Should we fail to nip him in the bud our religion may suffer; we must subdue him.'

Then all the most learned non-Buddhists, possessed of magical powers, assembled. Padma emanated four personalities resembling his own personality, one in each of the four directions, while he himself remained in meditation; and these four personalities debated the religious subjects with the non-Buddhists; and the Buddhists, winning, clapped their hands, shouting that the non-Buddhists were defeated. Similarly, the Buddhists came off victorious in the miracle-performing contest which followed.

In the next competition, which consisted in producing magical fire, the non-Buddhists were better by ten flames; and, as the non-Buddhists were applauding, Padma cried, 'Wait! wait!' Then, placing his hand on the ground, a lotus blossom sprang up and from it went forth a flame that reached to the top of the world. Thereupon, the four chief priests of the non-Buddhists with a few followers flew up into the sky. Padma pointed at them, and fire went round and round and over them; and, filled with fear, they descended to their places, shouting to Padma, 'Thou hast defeated us, both in argumentation and in magic; prepare to meet thy death within seven days'. Going off into the jungle, they practised black magic in order to kill Padma. All their 500 followers, who were left behind, embraced Buddhism.[1]

Padma then made thank-offerings to the *ḍākinī*; and, next morning at dawn, the *ḍākinī* called 'Subduer of Evil' appeared and gave to him a leather box bound with iron nails, saying, 'Hold in check the demons and the non-Buddhists'. Upon opening the box, Padma found in it manuscripts of secret doctrines explaining how to produce thunder, lightning, and hail within seven days of commencing appropriate magical ceremonies.[2] No sooner had the four non-Buddhist priests completed the magical rites which were intended to cause Padma's death and had returned to their home city, than thunder and lightning came and killed them and set the city afire so that all its non-Buddhist inhabitants perished.

Padma went to the roof of the palace in Bōdh-Gayā and, exercising his power of roaring like a lion, all non-Buddhists who heard him fell down in great fear and embraced the Doctrine. Religious drums and gongs and conch shells were sounded from the palace roof. The chief Buddhists carried Padma aloft on their heads and named him 'The Most Exalted Lion Roarer'.[3] Neighbouring kings invited Padma to their kingdoms, and Buddhism spread widely. The converted non-Buddhists at Bōdh-Gayā called him 'The All-Subduing Victorious One'.

THE MARRIAGE OF THE DEFORMED PRINCE

In the non-Buddhist Ser-ling country there was born to the King a deformed prince. The child's face was bony and of a

---

[1] In similar fashion, on the Hill of Tara, Ireland, St. Patrick and the Druids, in the Irish King's presence, competed in producing magical fire and other of the phenomena herein described; and, St. Patrick, being victorious, converted the pagan Irish to Christianity even as Padma converted the non-Buddhists to Buddhism.

[2] Milarepa, too, studied these secret doctrines and practised them. (See *Tibet's Great Yogī Milarepa*, pp. 68, 77–79, 117–18.)

[3] Text: *Phak-pa Seṅg-ge Dradog*, 'Arya (or Most Exalted) Lion-Roarer'. Formerly Padma was given a similar but lesser appellation, Seṅg-ge Dradog; see p. 159, above.

bluish colour and very ugly, one eye was blind, the left leg
lame, the right hand crippled, and the body emitted an offensive odour like rotting hide. The King and Queen, ashamed of
the child, kept him secreted in the palace. When the prince
grew up and wished to marry and live as a layman, they said
to him, 'Thou art too deformed and ugly; no bride would marry
thee. It would be better for thee to enter the Order and allow
us to supply thy needs.' The prince replied, 'Religion is empty
within and luxurious without. If ye, my parents, do not pro-
cure me a bride, I shall set the palace afire and then do away
with myself, or I shall kill both of you.' The prince, having
procured a lighted torch, came rushing at the King and
Queen; so, in fear of the prince, they married him to the princess of the King of Baidha, relinquished the palace and lived
apart from him. The princess exhibited such great displeasure
of her royal husband that he was fearful lest she run away.

Padma, sitting in meditation, saw the trouble between the
newly married pair; and, going to the court-yard of the palace
and exhibiting magical powers, produced many men and
women wearing ornaments of human bone, and dancing. The
princess wished to go out to see the magical performance, but
the prince would not allow her. Looking out of a window, she
caught sight of Padma, and exclaimed, 'Oh! if only I had a
husband like that man how happy I should be!'

Padma hearing her, replied, 'If a [married]¹ woman love
another man, she suffereth such anguish of heart that the two
cannot be comrades. If a man love a woman [against her will],¹
harm resulteth, as from evil spirits, and preventeth their
comradeship. If husband and wife be socially unequal, lack of
mutual respect, like that attributed to Ara,² ariseth, and this
also preventeth comradeship.'

The prince and princess were so deeply affected by these
remarks that they went out to Padma and bowed down and

¹ These two interpolations are necessary to bring out the sense implied
by the Tibetan, Padma's remarks here being in the nature of a reprimand
to the princess for expressing love for him, and to the prince for living with
the princess against her will.
² Ara was a famous bandit who had no respect for anybody, whether of
high or low birth.

made offerings before him, and embraced Buddhism. The King, recalling Padma's former exploits in the Baidha country, was much displeased, and said, 'This little beggar killed my priest and destroyed my palace.' Then Padma was seized and placed in an enclosure of bricks over which straw was heaped and set afire. Next morning, at the place where Padma had been enclosed and the fire set, there stood a *stūpa* of gold. And the King and Queen and all their subjects made public repentance and became Buddhists.

THE FORMAL GIVING OF THE NAME PADMA-SAMBHAVA

After this, Padma preached the *Dharma* to gods, *nāgas*, *dākinī* and demons in their own respective languages and realms; and to men in many parts of the human world—in China, Assam, Ghasha,[1] Trusha [near Simla], and elsewhere in India, and in Persia. He built many temples and monasteries, 824 of them in Tibet. In Devachān, the heaven of Avalokiteshvara,[2] he constructed a *stūpa* of crystal. Because

---

[1] Or Gharsha (*Gharsha-kha-dō-ling*, 'Country of the *Dākinī*'), the present Lahoul, above Kulu.

[2] Avalokiteshvara being the spiritual offspring of Amitābha, the Buddha of Boundless (or Immeasurable) Light, resides in Amitābha's Western Paradise, known to Tibetans as *Deva-chān* ('Abode of the *Devas*') and in Sanskrit as *Sukhāvatī* ('Realm of Happiness'). For the pious Mahāyāna Buddhist who is far below the evolutionary status of Buddhahood, Sukhāvatī is the heaven-world wherein he aspires to dwell during the interval between two incarnations. Sukhāvatī is attained as a *karmic* result of altruistic service done in the name of Amitābha and of Avalokiteshvara, the all-merciful *Bodhisattva* who has renounced the right to enter *Nirvāna* in order to help guide mankind to the Great Liberation. It is for making direct appeal to Avalokiteshvara that use is made of his *mantra*: *Om Mani Padme Hūm!* ('*Om!* The Jewel in the Lotus! *Hūm!*')

Esoterically, it is said that Amitābha, the fourth of the Five Buddhas of Meditation, represents the Buddha Essence innate in man, and that to be born in his paradise implies the awakening of this Buddha Essence; and that Avalokiteshvara, Amitābha's celestial *Bodhisattvic* reflex, is the 'personification of the self-generative cosmic force', the *Om* (or *Aum*) of his *mantra* being its symbol. (Cf. *A Brief Glossary of Buddhist Terms*, by the Buddhist Lodge, London, 1937, pp. 8, 14.)

Thus the Mahāyāna consists of three Paths. The first Path, trodden by the unevolved multitude, leads to the highest of the paradises. A second Path, that of the *Pratyeka* (i.e. self-evolved, or solitary non-teaching) Buddhas, leads to *Nirvāna*. The third and most glorious Path is that of the *Bodhisattvas*, leading to Perfect Buddhahood. On the first Path, the aspirant practises piety; on the second, philosophy; on the third, the Six *Pāramitā*

of having done all these things, he was given the name Padma-Sambhava.

THE BRĀHMIN BOY THAT BECAME THE KING OF BŌDH-GAYĀ

While sitting in meditation in Avalokiteshvara's heaven, Padma perceived that Bōdh-Gayā had been taken and sacked by a non-Buddhist King named 'Vishnu of the *Nāgas*'. The temple and palace had been reduced to ruin, the monks set to doing worldly works and the people were suffering greatly because of the King's tyranny. And Padma foresaw that the son of a certain Brāhmin's daughter and a fish were destined to overthrow the King.

One day this Brāhmin's daughter was out watching her cattle when rain came on and she took shelter in a cave and fell asleep. She dreamt that Padma as a beautiful youth came and cohabited with her and initiated her. After some days she told her brother's wife about the dream, saying that she was pregnant and wished to kill herself. The brother, hearing of this, said he would look after the child; and the girl gave birth to a boy. The family astrologer declared that the child had been born under a good sign and the child was named 'Sambhāra of the Essence of Time'.

When the boy was about eight years old, he asked his mother, 'Who was my father?' The mother wept and said, 'Thou hast no father'. Then he asked, 'Who is the King of this country, and who is his priest [or *guru*]?' The mother replied, 'His name is "Vishnu of the *Nāgas*," and he hath many non-Buddhist priests'. The boy said, 'It is not right to support a son who hath no father. So permit me to go to Bōdh-Gayā.'

And the boy went to Bōdh-Gayā, and sought to enter a non-Buddhist monastery, but, being too young for admission, he found employment in the King's kitchen.

The King having the habit of eating raw fish, the boy transformed himself into a fish in a stream and was caught by a

(or Transcendental Virtues), and, delaying his own entrance into *Nirvāṇa*, the Supra-*saṅgsāric* State, dedicates himself to teaching a suffering world the means of crossing, in the Ship of the *Dharma*, the Sea of *Saṅgsāric* Existence to the Other Shore.

fisherman and given to the King to eat. As the King was
about to bite off a bit of the fish, it slipped from his grasp and
went into his stomach where it caused him severe pain. When
all the priests had been called to the palace to offer aid, the
boy reappeared in his natural shape, and, taking advantage
of the commotion, set fire to the palace, opened its windows
and locked its doors, and all who were within it perished.
Then the boy went to the city of Sahor and was ordained a
Buddhist priest, and attained many spiritual perfections.

Now that Bōdh-Gayā was once more under Buddhist control, the Buddhists there decided to rebuild the Temple and
the old palace and restore Buddhist rule. For a whole year
search was made for one suitable to become the king, and no
one was found.

The boy, assuming the guise of a beggar, went to the market-place and sat down there. That very day, the party of
Buddhists who were making search for a suitable candidate
for the kingship, took an elephant to the market-place and
announced that he to whom the elephant should go and offer
a vase as a crown would be regarded as the king. As soon as
the elephant was set free, it ran, with trunk and tail straight
out, direct to the boy and placed the vase on his head. And
the boy became the King of Bōdh-Gayā.

Later on, when the boy met his mother, she refused to
believe that he, the King, was her son, saying that her son
had died in the last Bōdh-Gayā fire. So the King made prayer
that a fish should be born under a wooden plank, saying to
his mother, 'If this prayer be granted, thou must believe that
I am thy son'. The fish was thus found and the mother
believed. And under this virtuous Buddhist King, 'Sambhāra
of the Essence of Time', the Faith spread and the country
prospered.

PADMA'S FURTHER EXPLOITS

Padma now revisited Bōdh-Gayā, consecrated the restored
Temple and palace, had many *stūpas* constructed and the lost
scriptures re-written, and revived the Faith as a whole. He
also went to the country of asafoetida in Khoten, where he

remained 200 years and established the *Sūtra*, the *Mantra*, and the *Mahāyāna* forms of Buddhism.[1] Then he proceeded to a hill on the frontier of India and Nepal and entered into meditation. Seven huntsmen came with barking dogs and Padma magically stopped the barking. The huntsmen, overcome with fear, reported this to the king and the king ordered Padma to quit the place.

THE MONKEY-REARED GIRL AND PADMA'S INTERRUPTED MEDITATION

Thence Padma went to the temple of Shankhu. The Queen of King Ge-wa-dzin of Nepal having died when giving birth to a female child, the child, along with the Queen's corpse, was deposited in the cemetery. A monkey, finding the child, adopted it; and the child grew up, feeding on fruits. When the girl was ten years old, her hands were webbed like the feet of a duck, but she was very beautiful. Padma went to the cemetery and initiated the girl and named her Shākya-devi. Then, taking her to a cave for further instruction, he formed a *maṇḍala* of nine lighted lamps; and, as he sat there with her in *yogic* meditation, three impediments arose. Firstly, in the evening, lightning interrupted their meditation, but ceased when they broke their meditation. As a result of this, drought prevailed for three years. Secondly, at midnight, the chief of the *māras*[2] appeared and, after disturbing the meditation, vanished. As a result of this, all over India and Nepal famine prevailed. Thirdly, in the morning before dawn a bird interrupted the meditation; and, as a result, the evil spirits of India, Nepal, and Tibet brought epidemics upon men and cattle.

Because of all these things, Padma sought advice of those who had been his *gurus*; and they consulted together and

---

[1] Khoten, or eastern Turkestan, as recent archaeological research confirms, was once a very flourishing centre of Mahāyāna Buddhism; and is commercially noted for its production of asafoetida, which Tibetans employ in treating colds and 'winds' in the heart.

[2] The *māras* are demons who seek to prevent human beings from attaining Enlightenment, as in the classic instance of the *Bodhisattva* Gautama when He sat under the Bodhi-Tree on the point of attaining Buddhahood.

advised him to study the *Dorje-Phurbu* teachings[1] under Pandit Prabhahasti.

Accordingly, Padma wrote to this *pandit* and the *pandit* dispatched to Padma a *phurbu* text, which was so heavy that a man could hardly carry it. As soon as the text reached Padma in the cave, the evil spirits that had caused the impediments disappeared and Padma and Shākya-devi were able to continue their *yogic* practices without molestation. And Padma said, 'I am like the lotus blossom. Although it groweth out of the mud, no mud adhereth to it'. Making a copy of the text, he secreted it in the cave. Vapour arose from the sea, clouds formed in the sky, rain fell, flowers blossomed and fruits ripened. All famine and disease disappeared and people were happy. And after Padma had established the Doctrine in the region of the cave he was called 'Padma, the Victorious Tutelary of the *Ḍākinī*'.[2]

PADMA'S MANY MAGICAL GUISES

Padma, assuming numerous guises, continued to subdue evil. Sometimes he appeared as a common beggar, sometimes as a boy of eight years, sometimes as lightning, or wind, sometimes as a beautiful youth in dalliance with women, sometimes as a beautiful woman in love with men, sometimes as a bird, an animal, or insect, sometimes as a physician, or rich almsgiver. At other times he became a boat and wind on the sea to rescue men, or water with which to extinguish fire. He taught the ignorant, awakened the slothful, and dominated jealousy by heroic deeds. To overcome sloth, anger, and lust in mankind, he appeared as the Three Chief Teachers, Avalokiteshvara, Mañjushrī, and Vajra-Pāṇi; to overcome arrogance, he assumed the Body, the Speech, and the Mind of the

---

[1] These teachings concern magical methods of dominating demons and overcoming their evil influences. The Tibetan *dorje* (or thunderbolt of the gods) and the *phurbu* (or magical dagger), being ritual objects used for controlling and exorcizing evil spirits, lend their names to the magical teachings.

[2] The *ḍākinī*, an exalted class of fairy-like spiritual beings, themselves commonly chosen as tutelaries by neophytes in Tibet, appear from this appellation to have chosen Padma as their own tutelary by virtue of his mastery over gods, demons, and men.

Buddha;[1] and, to overcome jealousy, the fifth of the 'Five Poisons',[2] he transformed himself into the Five Dhyāni Buddhas.[3] He was now called 'The Chief Possessor of Magical Dances [or of Shape-Shifting]'. In short, to accomplish his mission to all sentient creatures, human, super-human, and sub-human, Padma assumed the guise most suitable to the occasion.

TEXTS AND TREASURES HIDDEN BY PADMA

The many books which he wrote he hid in the world of men, in heaven-worlds, and in the realm of the *nāgas* under the waters of seas and lakes, in order that there might be preserved for future generations the original uncorrupted teachings. For this reason the *dākinī* called him 'The One Possessed of Power over Hidden Treasures [of Texts].' Many of these hidden texts were written on tala-palm leaves, on silk, and on blue [or lacquered] paper in ink of gold, silver, copper, iron, and malachite, and enclosed in gold-lined boxes, earthen pots, stone receptacles, skulls, and precious stones. All that he taught was recorded and hidden. Even the teachings of the Lord Buddha in their purity he hid, so that the non-Buddhists might not interpolate them. No one save the *tertöns* [or takers-out of hidden texts] would have power to discover and bring forth the secreted writings.[4]

[1] The Body of the Buddha is the *Dharma-Kāya*; the Mind, the *Sambhoga-Kāya*; the Speech, the *Nirmāṇa-Kāya*. These Three *Kāyas* are the three forms in which the Buddha Essence is mystically personified. The first is the True Body, wherein all Buddhas in *Nirvāṇa* are in inconceivable at-one-ment; the second is the Reflected Body of glory where dwell, in the heaven-worlds, the Dhyāni Buddhas and all Buddhas and *Bodhisattvas* within the *Sangsāra* when not incarnate on Earth; the third is the Body of Incarnation in which all Buddhas and *Bodhisattvas* dwell when working among men. (See *The Tibetan Book of the Dead*, pp. 10–17.)

[2] These are lust, hatred (or anger), stupidity (or sloth), egotism (or arrogance), and jealousy. (See *Tibet's Great Yogī Milarepa*, pp. 195[1], 260.)

[3] These, the Buddhas of Meditation, are Vairochana, Vajra-Sattva, Ratna-Sambhava, Amitābha, and Amogha-Siddhi. (See *The Tibetan Book of the Dead*, pp. 105–18.)

[4] These *tertöns*, some of whom have appeared, are said to be reincarnations of certain of Padma's disciples, or else emanations of Padma himself. The text of our present treatise, like that of the *Bardo Thödol*, is believed by the Tibetans to have been among these texts thus written and hidden by Padma and subsequently taken out by a *tertön*. (See *The Tibetan Book of the*

Padma placed the hidden texts under the guardianship of the *ḍākinī* and Wisdom-Holders; and he blessed the texts so that none of them should fall into the hands of one who, lacking the merit born of good deeds done in a past incarnation, was undeserving. Thus there could be no diminution of the Doctrine, nor of initiation, nor of priestly succession through reincarnation, nor of the practice of religion.

Between the Khang-kar-te-say Mountains [near the Nepal frontier in southern Tibet] and Tri-shi-trik in China, Padma hid 108 large works, 125 important images, five very rare essences [of secret doctrines], the sacred books of Buddhism and of the Bönpos,[1] and books on medicine, astrology, arts, and crafts. Similar caches were made by Padma in Nepalese caves and temples. Along with the texts, he buried such worldly treasures, magical weapons, and food as would afford support to the *tertöns* who should take out the texts and give them to the world. Altogether, Padma is credited with having hidden away texts and accessory objects to the number of ten million.[2]

THE HIDDEN TREASURES AND PERSONS FITTED TO DISCOVER THEM

After explaining to Shākya-devi, in answer to her question why, as already set forth above, so many texts and treasures had been hidden, Padma added, 'Ārya-devā and Nāgārjuna will take out one of the hidden treasures and thereby subdue the non-Buddhists'.

Then Shākya-devi asked, 'O Great *Guru*, if the number of the treasures is so great how did they originate, and why call them treasures? Who shall have the merit of a previous incarnation to profit by them? Who shall possess the power to take

Dead, pp. 75–77.) According to the Nyingma School, sacred texts have been found by *tertöns* in forty-nine different places in Tibet.

[1] The Bönpos are the followers of the pre-Buddhistic religion of Tibet called Bön, which Padma dominated, taking over certain of its teachings and incorporating them in his Tantric Buddhism, as illustrated in *Tibetan Yoga and Secret Doctrines*, Book V.

[2] This, of course, is another typical oriental figurative exaggeration, expressive of multitude, but without precise numerical significance.

out the treasures? And how will the discoverer of such a treasure take birth? Please explain all this to me.'

Padma replied, 'Be good enough to give ear, O thou, of
meritorious birth. It was after the destruction of the Demon
Thar-pa Nag-po[1] that the treasures originated. From his mind
sprang the Eight Cemeteries.[2] His skin represents the paper;
his hands and legs represent the pen; the watery fluid which
he exuded from the four apertures of his body[3] represents the
ink. Out of these three [the skin, bodily limbs, and watery
fluid] came the "Five Poisons"; and from the "Five Poisons"
came the alphabet of letters. His skull, mouth, and nose became the receptacles for containing the treasures. His internal
organs, toes, and fingers represent the places of the treasures.
The Six Receptacles of the Doctrine[4] will declare who shall
possess the power to discover the treasures. From the five
chief organs [the heart, liver, lungs, stomach, and intestines]
will come the Blessed Ones.[5] From the five sensory organs [the
tongue, nostrils, ears, eyes, and organs of touch including
those of sex] will come the "Five Powers",[6] and also the
"Five Elements";[7] and from the "Five Elements", the Body
[the *Dharma-Kāya*], the Mind [the *Sambhoga-Kāya*], and the
Speech [the *Nirmāṇa-Kāya*].'

'If classified, there would be eighteen kinds of treasures.
The mad finder[8] of the chief treasure shall be known as the

[1] A Tibetan name of a *rudra*, or demon, meaning 'Black Salvation', who
obstructed the progress of Buddhism in Tibet. Padma subjugated him and
enlisted his powerful services in the spread of the *Dharma*. After Thar-pa
Nag-po died he reincarnated as a *Mahākala*.

[2] These are the well-known Eight Great Cemeteries (or Cremation
Grounds) of ancient India in which Padma lived and meditated at various
times.

[3] These are the mouth, nose, anus, and sex organ.

[4] These are probably six of the chief patriarchs of the Mahāyāna such as
Nāgārjuna, Ārya-devā (mentioned by Padma above), otherwise known as
Kana-devā, and their immediate successors.

[5] The Teachers of the *Dharma*, the Buddhas, *Bodhisattvas*, and Great *Gurus*.

[6] The Five Powers are: the Power of religious faith, the Power of diligent
application, the Power of memory, the Power of profound meditation, and
the Power of ingenuity or wit.

[7] Namely, Earth, Water, Fire, Air, Ether.

[8] It is customary among *gurus* and *yogīs* to refer euphemistically to one
of high spiritual accomplishments as being mad. (Cf. *Tibetan Yoga and
Secret Doctrines*, p. 269.)

balls of the eyes, and those inferior *tertöns* shall be known as the skin of the eyes. If any of the *tertöns* be called an eunuch,[1] he shall be like the discharge from the nose [of the Demon]; one of higher life and blissfulness shall be like the consciousness and mind. Anyone who may be called a *tertön* of average spirituality shall be like the liver and bile. And from all these examples thou shouldst be able to recognize the discoverers.'

These hidden treasures, as Padma, at great length, proceeded to explain, cannot all be found simultaneously. One after another, when needed for the advancement of mankind, they will be discovered. Just as the *udambara*[2] is rare so are *tertöns*. Whenever a *tertön* is born, the *udambara* will appear. If the birth be among the *kshatriya*, the blossom's colour will be white; if among *brāhmins*, the blossom will be red; if among *vaishyas*, it will be yellow; and if among *shūdras*,[3] blue. The birth of a *tertön* is immediately followed by the death of either the mother or father of the *tertön*. Two or more *tertöns* cannot be born simultaneously [or in the same generation], for only one *tertön* incarnates at a time. The power to find the hidden treasures will be given chiefly to six persons, who will be born one after another and succeed each other; there will be five *tertöns* of lesser degree.[4] Kings, persons of worldly fortune, laymen, and those attached to property will not have this power.

THE SCORPION *GURU*

After completing other missions, in the valley of Nepal, and in Kosala,[5] Padma went to the Cave of Phūllahari where

[1] This whole passage being esoterically symbolical, the appellation eunuch is symbolic also, and probably refers to a *yogin* who has made himself, not literally, but figuratively in the Biblical sense, an eunuch to attain righteouness.

[2] The *udambara* (*ficus clonerata*) is a mythical lotus of immense size which is commonly represented in oriental literature as blooming only when a great spiritual being like a Buddha is born on Earth.

[3] The *kshatriya*, or warrior class, the *brāhmins*, or spiritually learned class, the *vaishyas*, or merchant class, and the *shūdras*, or labouring class, constitute the four castes of the Hindu social organization.

[4] In Padma's *Abridged Testament*, the full Tibetan title of which is given in *The Tibetan Book of the Dead*, on p. 76, Padma mentions eight *tertöns* who are to be his own incarnations.

[5] Kosala was a part of the ancient Oudh.

Vajra-pāṇi appeared to him and foretold how Padma would
attain a certain *siddhi* in the great cemetery near Rājagir.
Padma, upon reaching the cemetery, beheld an enormous
scorpion having nine heads and eighteen horns and three eyes
on each head. Padma made obeisance to the scorpion, and it
requested him to come on the morrow for the *siddhi*. Accordingly, Padma kept the appointment; and the scorpion took
out from under a rock a triangular-shaped stone box containing manuscript texts of the *Phurbu* Doctrine,[1] and Padma at
once understood the texts. And each of the eyes and each of
the horns of the scorpion gave out one *yāna*.[2]

PADMA'S JOURNEY TO TIBET

Padma returned to Bōdh-Gayā at the request of the King
Nyima Singha; and while he was there strengthening the Doctrine the thought came to Padma that the time had come for
him to proceed to Tibet to establish Tibetan Buddhism more
firmly than it had been established originally by King Srong-
Tsan-Gampo and thereafter re-established by King Thī-Srong-
Detsan, the incarnation of Mañjushrī.[3]

King Thī-Srong-Detsan had tried to build a monastery at
Sāmyé, but the site not having been properly consecrated,
evil spirits prevented the construction; no sooner was a wall
built than it was thrown down.[4] Some of the King's priests
declared that a priest of superior powers was needed to subdue
the evil spirits; and the King dispatched messengers to India
and to China to find such a priest. As a result, the Great *Paṇḍita
Bodhisattva*, who was teaching in Nālanda, went to Tibet at
the King's invitation; and the King met the *Bodhisattva* at
Sang-phor [near Sāmyé]. Although the *Bodhisattva* conse-

---

[1] See pp. 160, 177[1], above, for explanation.

[2] A *yāna* is a doctrinal method or path for attaining spiritual powers.

[3] Srong-tsan-Gampo died in A.D. 650, and Thī-Srong-Detsan reigned
from A.D. 740 to 786. During the ninety years separating the two reigns,
Buddhism suffered a decline and almost disappeared, the immediate successors of Srong-Tsan-Gampo having apostatized to the old pre-Buddhist
Bön religion.

[4] Although the external visible cause of this was probably earthquakes,
the Tibetans considered the hidden cause to be demoniacal. At all events,
according to Tibetan historical records, as soon as the site had been exor-
cized by Padma, no more walls were thrown down.

crated and exorcised the site of the Sāmyé Monastery, the evil spirits were not overcome; and he advised the King that Padma-Sambhava, then at Bōdh-Gayā, was the only one able to subdue the evil spirits, and the King invited Padma-Sambhava to come to Tibet.[1]

Padma, accepting the invitation, set out for Tibet on the fifteenth day of the eleventh month according to the Tibetan calendar.[2] On the thirtieth of the same month he reached Nepal. Padma said that he would proceed, stage by stage, as he subdued the demons of one place after another. He remained in Nepal three months as the guest of King Vasudhari, preaching the Doctrine. When he was about to quit Nepal, after having subdued many evils, the *ḍākinī* and other spiritual beings who had befriended and aided him, begged him not to go; and he said, ' I must go; the time hath come to subdue the evil spirits of Tibet'.

THE WATER MIRACLE

Padma then travelled on towards Tibet subduing demoniacal beings all along the route; and his first resting place was at Tod-lung [about twelve miles from Lhāsa]. The Tibetan King sent the two chief ministers of state to meet Padma, with letters and presents and 500 mounted followers. The King's own horse, saddled with a golden saddle, was sent to fetch Padma. When this numerous delegation met Padma

[1] Certain scholars in the Occident have stated that Padma-Sambhava was a professor in the Buddhist University of Nālanda at the time the Tibetan King invited him to Tibet (e.g. Dr. L. A. Waddell, op. cit., p. 24); and the Editor having accepted this statement repeated it in his own publications (as in *The Tibetan Book of the Dead*, p. 74). Now it appears from this original textual account that it was the Great *Paṇḍita Bodhisattva*, and not Padma-Sambhava, who was the professor in Nālanda; and, as our text shows later, the *Bodhisattva* was undoubtedly a personage quite distinct from Padma-Sambhava. The Tibetan King, for instance, on the occasion of Padma's public reception at Sāmyé, placed Padma on a golden throne and the *Bodhisattva* on a silver throne. Furthermore, the *Bodhisattva* is shown herein to have died at about the same time as the King Thī-Srong-Detsan. Apparently, therefore, because of erroneous reading of the Tibetan text, the *Bodhisattva* and Padma have been taken to be one and the same person.

[2] The Tibetan year, which is lunar, begins in February with the rise of the new moon. Thus the eleventh month would be December of the year A.D. 746. His arrival in Tibet was about three and a half months later, or in A.D. 747, at the beginning of springtime.

they were suffering from lack of water, and no water being available at the place, Padma, taking a long stick, struck a rock with it and water flowed forth, and men and beasts quenched their thirst. The place is called Zhon-pa-hi-lha-chhu.[1]

THE ROYAL RECEPTION OF PADMA AND THE FIRE MIRACLE

The King with his party went to Zung-khar, near the Haopori Pass [seven to eight miles from Lhāsa], to meet Padma. The people had assembled there in vast numbers to greet Padma; and he was taken in procession, to the accompaniment of music and dancing by masked dancers, to Lhāsa, where great festivity ensued.

When Padma and the King met, Padma failed to bow down before the King, and seeing that the King expected him to do so, even as the *Bodhisattva* at the time of his reception had done, Padma said to the King, 'Thou wert born of a mother's womb; I was born of a lotus, and am a second Buddha'. Then, after having referred to his *yogic* powers and learning, Padma said, 'O King, inasmuch as I have come for thy good, thou shouldst bow down before me'. And Padma pointed his fingers at the King and fire issued from the tips of the fingers and burnt the King's garments, and there came thunder and an earthquake. Thereupon, the King and his ministers and all the people bowed down before Padma.

THE CONSTRUCTION OF THE SĀMYÉ MONASTERY

On the first day of the eighth Tibetan month Padma visited Sāmyé. The King escorted Padma to the Palace at Sāmyé and placed him on a gold throne and the *Bodhisattva* on a silver throne and made religious offerings; and Padma foretold what he was to do in Tibet.

Padma cast treasures in the lakes to win the goodwill of the

---

[1] A Tibetan place-name meaning 'Nectar of the Gods for the Cavalry', with reference to the water which Padma miraculously produced there for the King's mounted followers. The late Sardar Bahādur S. W. Laden La, when we translated this passage, told me that he had visited the place and that the water still flows in a stream of about 1 inch out of solid rock at a height of approximately 8 feet from the ground.

nāgas. Little by little he subdued the gods and goddesses and evil spirits throughout Tibet; and performed many miracles.

On the eighth day of the eighth month of the earth-male-tiger year the work of building the Sāmyé Monastery was begun, Padma having consecrated the site and appeased the evil spirits by teaching to them the Precepts.[1] Padma appointed Brahma and Indra directors-in-chief of the building operations, the Four Kings of the Four Directions he made overseers, and the gods and evil spirits and the local genii and guardian deities he employed as labourers. Men carried on the work by day and the spiritual beings carried it on by night, so that progress was rapid.

THE TALE OF PADMA'S SUBJECTION OF THE *NĀGA* KING

Padma, seeing that the King of the *Nāgas* remained unsubdued, went to the Chhim-phug Cave near Sāmyé and entered into meditation for the purpose of overcoming the *Nāga* King. Just at that time the King Thī-Srong-Detsan was having much difficulty in procuring lumber for the building of the monastery; and the *Nāga* King, assuming the guise of a white-complexioned man, went to the Tibetan King and said, 'I will supply all the wood needed, provided thou breakest, as I request thee to do, Padma's meditation'.[2] The Tibetan King vowed to carry out the request, and the man promised to provide the lumber.

The Tibetan King went to the cave; but instead of seeing

---

[1] Sāmyé, the first Buddhist monastery built in Tibet after the Potāla at Lhāsa, is situated about thirty miles southeast of Lhāsa, near the north bank of the Tsang-po River, at an altitude of about 11,430 feet. Its full name translated into English means 'Academy for Obtaining the Heap of Unchanging Meditation'. Sāmyé, as it is today, comprises a large temple, four important colleges, and several other buildings, enclosed in a lofty circular wall about a mile and a half in circumference with gates facing the four cardinal points. Its large image of the Buddha, over ten feet high, is called 'The King of Sāmyé'. The monastic library is said to contain many rare manuscripts which were brought from India. (For fuller details see L. A. Waddell, op. cit., pp. 266–8.)

[2] Tibet being a country of very scanty timber resources, one can imagine the problem of finding suitable and adequate lumber which faced the Tibetan King, and how great was the temptation to grant the *Nāga* King's request.

Padma he beheld a huge *garuḍa*[1] holding in its claws an enormous serpent which it had almost swallowed; only a small
portion of the serpent's tail remained unswallowed. The King
said, 'Be gracious enough to break thy meditation, for we are
about to attain a great *siddhi*'; whereupon the serpent freed
itself, and the *garuḍa* became Padma, who asked, 'What
siddhi is it?'

After the King had made explanation, Padma said, 'Whereas I have completely subdued all other evil spirits, I have only
subdued the *Nāga* King's body and not his mind. Had I subdued his mind, the lumber would have come of itself. Hereafter, owing to thine action, the *Nāga* King will dominate
Tibet and send upon the people eighteen kinds of leprosy; and
the wrathful *nāgas* will be thine enemies.'

The Tibetan King returned to Sāmyé to ascertain whether
or not the white-complexioned man had kept his vow, and
found the wood already there; and this wood was utilized in
the construction of the monastery.

Now the Tibetan King inquired of Padma if there was not
still some way by which to subdue the *Nāga* King; and Padma
replied, 'The only way is for the King of Tibet and the King
of the *Nāgas* to become friends'. So Padma went to the
Malgro Lake, near Sāmyé, wherein the *Nāga* King dwelt. The
Tibetan King with his ministers hid themselves in a valley, as
Padma had advised; and Padma pitched a small white tent
on the shore of the lake and meditated there for three nights.[2]
On the third night, a beautiful maiden appeared before Padma
and asked, 'What art thou doing here, and what dost thou

[1] A *garuḍa* is a mythical creature, with eagle head, human-bird body, two
human-like arms, and eagle wings and feet, symbolizing energy and aspiration. It is analogous to the classical phoenix and to the thunder-bird of the
North American Red Men. In a more esoteric sense, the Tibetans, like the
Chinese, regard it as symbolizing the Earth and its cosmic environment, its
head representing the heavens, its eyes the Sun, its back the crescent Moon,
its wings the wind, its feet the Earth itself, its tail the trees and plants. Like
the adjutant, or stork, popularly called by the Hindus *garuḍa*, it is the
enemy and devourer of serpents, as in our text. (Cf. L. A. Waddell, op. cit.,
pp. 395–6.)

[2] During these three nights, as the pitching of the tent suggests, Padma
probably celebrated a form of the *Chöd* Rite (which is fully expounded in
Book V of *Tibetan Yoga and Secret Doctrines*).

seek?' Padma answered, 'I desire the King of Tibet and the King of the *Nāgas* to become friends. The treasury of the Tibetan King having become empty through the building of the monastery, I have come to ask for wealth from the *Nāgas*. And I wish thee to convey this message to thy King.'

Then the maiden disappeared; and next morning a very large serpent emerged from the lake and stirred up the water; and gold flooded all the shores. Thus the treasury was replenished and the building of the monastery continued. Some of the gold was applied to the making of images and frescoes for the monastery, which had thirty-two entrances and required five years to complete.

Padma placed the monastery under the guardianship of the Wrathful Deity Pe-har.[1] The monastery was consecrated on the fifteenth day of the eleventh month of the male-water-horse year. The *Bodhisattva* himself consecrated it thrice. Then Padma meditated for one day, and initiated the King of Tibet into the Doctrine of Sarasvati.[2]

THE MIRACLES ATTENDING THE CONSECRATION

Comprised within the monastery there were one hundred and eight temples [or shrines]; and Padma manifested him-

[1] Pe-har (usually pronounced *Pé-kar*) belongs to the kingly group of Wrathful Protectors, and is the chief of the Four Great Kings who guard the four quarters of the Universe. Although Pe-har appears to be a non-Hindu deity, he has sometimes been identified with the Hindu deity Veda, or the Chinese Wei-to, whom the Chinese Buddhists invoke as a protector of monasteries. Hence *Pe-har* is believed by some scholars to be a corruption of the Sanskrit *Vihar* ('Monastery'). It is believed that Pe-har successively incarnates in each of the living oracles represented by 'The Religious Noble' (*Ch'ō-je*), the actual State Oracle of Tibet known as the Nä-ch'uṅ Oracle. Pe-har is said to inspire also the Karma-s'ar Oracle in Lhāsa. (Cf. L. A. Waddell, op. cit., pp. 371, 478–81.) Each Tibetan monastery is under the guardianship of some such deity of the Wrathful Order of Tantric Guardians; and so are all Tibetan temples, sacred mountains, rivers, lakes, places of pilgrimage, and natural deposits of precious metals or gems. Similarly, each field and dwelling-house in Tibet is under the guardianship of a beneficent spiritual being, as are cattle and crops; and each individual Tibetan, man, woman, and child, has a tutelary, or directing and guardian deity, comparable to the guardian angel of Christians.

[2] Sarasvati, the Goddess of Learning, is sometimes, as she seems to be here, the *shakti*, or feminine complement, of Mañjushrī, the God of Divine Wisdom; and, accordingly, it appears that the King was initiated into the secret Tantric doctrines associated with the Sarasvati-Mañjushrī *maṇḍala*.

self in one hundred and eight bodies, each body like his own, and simultaneously performed the consecration ceremony. When, in three of these temples, he was scattering the blossoms used in the ceremony, the images descended from the altars and circumambulated their own temples thrice. The images of the other temples came out of their temples and moved their hands. The King was afraid, and doubted that the images would go back to their temples. Padma snapped his fingers, and each of the images returned to its own place. From the painted flames of fire in the haloes of the frescoes depicting the Wrathful Guardian Deities by the doors, real flames of fire issued. Again the King was afraid; and Padma threw flowers on the flames and the flames subsided, and from the petals of the flowers sprang up lotus blossoms.

The deities assembled in the sky overhead, and witnessed the consecration ceremony; and there was a rain of flowers, accompanied by other phenomena. The thousands of people present were witnesses to all these miracles.

The Bönpos's Defeat in Public Debate and their Expulsion from Tibet

Later on, the Buddhists and Bönpos in Tibet publicly debated; and, the Bönpos being defeated, the King expelled most of those who would not embrace Buddhism, to the deserts of the north, to Nepal, Mongolia, and other sparsely populated countries. Buddhism was introduced into all parts of Tibet. The *Kanjur* and *Tanjur* and other Mahāyāna works were translated from the Sanskrit into Tibetan. So also were the exoteric and esoteric *Tantras* and *Mantras*, and treatises on medicine and astrology.

The Authoress and Origin of the Biography

Folio 288[b] gives an account of the origin of the incarnate *ḍākinī* Ye-she-Tsho-gyal,[1] who, having been one of Padma's

[1] A Tibetan name meaning 'Victorious [One] of the Ocean of Wisdom'. The late Sir John Woodroffe (Arthur Avalon) in an article entitled 'Origin of the *Vajrayāna Devatas*', reprinted from the *Modern Review* for June 1916 and based on work which he and the late Lāma Kazi Dawa-Samdup did together, states, on p. 2: '*Guru* Padma-Sambhava, the so-called founder of "Lāmaism", had five women disciples who compiled several accounts of

most intimate disciples from the age of sixteen, compiled the matter contained within the Biography.

THE HIDING OF THE MANUSCRIPT TEXT OF THE BIOGRAPHY

When Ye-she-Tsho-gyal had finished writing down, on yellow paper, at Padma's dictation, the matter of this Biography, Padma said to her, 'Before thou diest, bury this manuscript in the Cave situated about eighteen yards from a solitary tree growing over a rock shaped like a lion in Boom-thang.[1] The Cave, into which no light penetrateth, can be entered only from above, by sliding down a rope. I have already buried the *Long-sal-nyi-mai-gyud*[2] therein, and this manuscript should be preserved along with that.' He admonished her that if the hiding of the manuscript was not kept secret, the *ḍākinī* would trouble her.

TERTÖNS, DEATH OF THE *BODHISATTVA* AND THE KING, AND SUMMARY

From folio 303[b] to folio 332[a] directions are given for finding hidden texts and their accompanying treasures, together with the names of *tertöns*, and the auspicious times and omens which guide the *tertöns*.

Folios 332[b] and 333 contain accounts of the death of the *Bodhisattva* from Nālanda, who preceded Padma to Tibet, and of the passing of King Thī-Srong-Detsan, whose death occurred at about the same time as that of the *Bodhisattva*. To King Mu-thī-tsan-po, who succeeded to the Tibetan throne, Padma, speaking of himself, declared that he had been born

the teachings of their Master and hid them in various places for the benefit of future believers. One of these disciples, Khandro [or *Ḍākinī*] Yeshe Tshogyal, was a Tibetan lady who is said to have possessed such a wonderful power of memory that if she was told a thing only once she remembered it for ever. She gathered what she had heard from her *Guru* into a book called the *Padma Thangyig Serteng*, or Golden Rosary of the history of her *Guru*, who was entitled the Lotus-born (Padma-Sambhava). The book was hidden away and was subsequently revealed under inspiration some five hundred years ago by [a] *Tertön*.' *Padma Thangyig Serteng* is another title for the Biography of the Great *Guru* herein epitomized.

[1] Boom-thang is about fourteen miles northeast of Lhāsa.

[2] Text: *Klong-gsal-nyi-mahi-rgyud* (pron. *Long-sal-nyi-mai-gyud*), meaning 'A Clear Treatise on the *Tantra* of *Sūrya*, the Sun.'

in the eighth year after the passing of the Buddha, from a lotus blossom in the Dhanakosha Lake.[1]

Afterwards comes a summarized account of Padma's activities and of the places he visited, which included Persia, Sikkim, Bhutan, China, Ceylon, and all parts of Tibet and India. And there is the statement that Padma remained in Tibet one hundred and eleven years.

PADMA'S DEPARTURE FROM TIBET

Having decided to depart from Tibet, Padma said to the King, 'The time is ripe to subjugate the *Rākṣhasas*; and only the Lotus-Born can subjugate them. If I do not subjugate them now, they will devour all mankind, and the Earth will be devoid of human beings.' Of the country of the *Rākṣhasas*, which is triangular like a shoulder blade, and contains five large cities, Padma gives a lengthy description. 'These cities are not far from the Urgyān country.'[2] Each of these five cities is composed of five hundred villages. Padma's purpose was not to destroy the *Rākṣhasas*, but to convert them to Buddhism.

As Padma was about to depart from Tibet, he said, 'Hereafter, the Doctrine will be disseminated by Avalokiteshvara.'[3]

[1] If one were inclined to seek reconciliation between this account of Padma-Sambhava having been born eight years after the passing of the Buddha and that of the Buddha's prophecy given on p. 105, above, it would be necessary to assume that Padma-Sambhava did not begin his active mission in the world until his fortieth year; but a biography such as this of the Great *Guru*, wherein historical facts and legendary stories are inextricably interwoven, cannot be expected to exhibit correlation or common unity of its many diverse parts.

[2] This passage, literally quoted from the text, recalls one theory among other theories, advanced by the late Sardar Bahādur S. W. Laden La, that Urgyān, Padma's native country, was probably in Southern India and not, as is commonly assumed, 'the country about Ghazni to the northwest of Kashmir' (cf. L. A. Waddell, op. cit., p. 26) or, as others have thought, a part of what is now Afghanistan. The supposition that the country of the *Rākṣhasas* is Ceylon, tends to support the theory. Sometimes, too, the country of the *Rākṣhasas* has been supposed to be Java.

[3] This probably refers to the Dalai Lāma, the incarnation of Avalokiteshvara, as being the future guardian and teacher of the *Dharma* in Tibet, of whom the first historical representative was the Grand (Dalai) Lāma Geden-ḍub (A.D. 1391–1475), the nephew of Tsong-Khapa, the founder of the Gelugpa Order. (Cf. L. A. Waddell, op. cit., pp. 38 and 233.)

The King and the ministers of state and the attendants, mounted on horses, accompanied Padma to Gung-thang-la,[1] where all the party halted for the night.

In the morning, after Padma had given his parting good wishes to the King and everyone present, there appeared out of the heavens, in the midst of rainbow radiance, a blue horse fully saddled. Celestial music was heard, and a concourse of deities also appeared. Padma mounted the horse and the horse rose upward. Then, after Padma had pronounced his final blessings, in the name of the Buddha, the *Dharma*, and the *Saṅgha*, he and the deities following him disappeared on the sun-rays.

PADMA'S ARRIVAL IN THE COUNTRY OF THE *RĀKSHASAS* AND THEIR SUBJECTION

Certain *lāmas* entered into deep *yogic* meditation and watched Padma pass over the Urgyān country and afterward come down in the country of Singala[2] and take shelter under a magnolia tree; and they saw the blue horse rolling in the golden sands of Singala. Later they beheld Padma surrounded by *Rākṣhasa* maidens, whom he was teaching, and then that he had transformed himself into the King of the *Rākṣhasas* and subjugated all the *Rākṣhasas*.

Here Chapter 116 ends on folio 393. Chapter 117 contains the Tibetan King's lamentations about Padma's departure.

THE COLOPHON OF THE BIOGRAPHY

On folio 394 the Colophon begins, and is as follows:

'This Book was written down [or compiled] by Ye-she-Tsho-gyal, the incarnation of Yang-chen,[3] in order to benefit the creatures of coming generations and to prevent its contents from being lost to their memory.

'The name of this Book is *Padma Ka-ḥi-thang-yig* [or *Padma's Precepts*].[4] It is also called *Ke-raḥ Nam-thar Gye-pa*

---

[1] Gung-thang-la, meaning 'High Plain Pass', is in Mangyul, on the northern confines of Tibet.

[2] Text: *Singa-la*, is here presumed to refer to Ceylon.

[3] Or, in Sanskrit, Sarasvati, Goddess of Learning.

[4] Tib., *Padma-bkaḥi-thang-yig*.

[or *Complete Birth-History*].[1] Another of its titles is *Thī-Srong-Detsan Ka-chem* [or *Thī-Srong-Detsan's Testament*].[2]

'This well-detailed [account of the Book's] origin has been recorded in writing and buried [along with the Book] like a precious gem.

'May this [Book] be met with by persons of great meritorious deeds.

'This hidden treasure was taken out from the large Mirror Cave of Pourī by the *Guru* Sang-gye Ling-pa.

'[It was in the form of] a scroll written in Sanskrit,[3] and translated into Tibetan without the omission of a word.

'For the good of the beings of the world, the Nam-gyal-Duk-pa[4] carved the blocks of type under the supervision of the reigning Pum-thang family of Bhutan, by command of Ngag-ki-Wang-po.'[5]

The last folio, 397, ends with good wishes to all sentient beings and with praises of Padma.

[The translation, of which this Epitome is the fruit, was completed on the twenty-first day of January 1936.]

---

[1] Tib., *Skyes-rabs-rnam-thar-rgyas-pa*.

[2] Tib., *Khri-srong-ldehu-btsan-gyi-bkaḥ-chems* (or *kha-chems*).

[3] According to Tibetan tradition, Ye-she-Tsho-gyal had acquired from Indian *pandits* a sound knowledge of Sanskrit before she compiled this Biography.

[4] Meaning 'Ever Victorious Bhutanese'.

[5] Meaning 'The One Powerful of Speech', probably the name of a *Dharma-Rāja* (or 'Religious King') of Bhutan.

PLATE VII

THE *TRI-KĀYA* OR THREE DIVINE BODIES

Described on pages xxvi–xxvii

BOOK II

HERE FOLLOWS THE [*YOGA* OF] KNOWING THE MIND, THE SEEING OF REALITY, CALLED SELF-LIBERATION, FROM 'THE PROFOUND DOCTRINE OF SELF-LIBERATION BY MEDITATION UPON THE PEACEFUL AND WRATHFUL DEITIES'[1]

ACCORDING TO LĀMA KARMA SUMDHON PAUL'S AND LĀMA LOBZANG MINGYUR DORJE'S ENGLISH RENDERING

[1] Text: ZAB-CHÖS ZHI-KHRO DGONGS-PA RANG-GRÖL LAS RIG-PA NGO-SPRÖD GÇER-MTHONG RANG-GRÖL SHES-BYA-WA BZHUGS-SO (pron.: ZAB-CHÖ SHI-HTO GONG-PA RANG-DÖL LAY RIG-PA NGO-TÖD CHER-THONG RANG-DÖL SHAY-JHA-WA ZHUG-SO).

Another rendering might be: HEREIN IS CONTAINED THE [ART OF] KNOWING THE MIND, THE SEEING OF [MIND IN ITS] NAKEDNESS, CALLED SELF-LIBERATION, FROM 'THE PROFOUND DOCTRINE OF SELF-LIBERATION BY MEDITATING UPON THE PEACEFUL AND WRATHFUL DEITIES'.

Wakefulness

'Wakefulness is the path to immortality; heedlessness is the path to death. Those who are wakeful die not; the heedless are as if dead already.

'The wise, those who have realized this efficacy of wakefulness, rejoice in wakefulness, and are drawn to such spheres of activity as engage the Noble Ones.

'Such sages, ever meditative, ever putting forth strong effort, attain the incomparable security of *Nirvāṇa*.

'Continually increasing is the glory of him who is wakeful, who hath aroused himself and is ever alert, who performeth blameless deeds, and acteth with becoming consideration, who restraineth himself, and leadeth a righteous life.

'Let such an one, rousing himself to wakefulness by self-restraint and self-subjugation make for himself an island which no flood can overwhelm.

*   *   *

'As a man of discernment, standing on a rocky eminence, beholdeth those who are below and in distress, so doth the sage, who by his wakefulness hath put to flight his ignorance, look down upon suffering mankind from the Heights of Wisdom which he hath attained.

'Wakeful amidst the heedless, keenly vigilant amidst the sleeping ones, the wise man forgeth ahead, even as a charger outdistanceth a horse of lesser strength.'

The Buddha, from the *Dhammapada*, vv. 21–25, 28–29
(based upon N. K. Bhagwat's Translation).

PLATE VIII

BODHIDHARMA

Described on page xxvii

INTRODUCTION

As the Biography in the preceding Book has shown, Padma-Sambhava spent many years as a disciple under various wise teachers in India, Burma, Afghanistan, Nepal, and other lands. He practised the different *yogas*. Having lived in India at a time when India was still comparatively free from disrupting foreign influences and the good life was that of the philosopher, he was able to collect, like a honey-bee, the nectar from the rarest of blossoms in the Orient's vast garden of philosophical and psychic research. And here, in this *yogic* treatise, he has transmitted to us the results, which are, intrinsically, of more value than all the gold and precious gems of the world.

Even as Bodhidharma, the twenty-eighth of the Buddhist Patriarchs, was the great pioneer teacher of the Dhyāna School of Buddhism to the people of China, where he went by sea from India and arrived in Canton in A.D. 527[1] and gave direction to the enlightening spiritual influences that made Buddhism an integral part of Chinese culture, so was Padma-Sambhava the great pioneer teacher of the Tantric School of Buddhism to the people of Tibet, where he arrived from India in A.D. 747, by invitation of the Tibetan King, and, under royal patronage, made Tibet Buddhistic. Both teachers taught that Right Meditation is the indispensable means of attaining the Goal of the Buddha's *Nirvāṇic* Path. Accordingly, Bodhidharma founded the Meditation (Skt. *Dhyāna*) School in China known as the Ch'an, whence arose the Zen School of Japan; and Padma-Sambhava founded in Tibet the Nyingma School, of which the more esoteric teachings are set forth in the Ādi-Yoga System, otherwise known as the Doctrine of the Great Perfection (Tib. *Rdzogs-Ch'en*), whence arose the Western Branch of the Chinese Esoteric Sect known as the Tibetan Esoteric Sect (Chinese, *Tsang Mi Tsung*) or the Lotus Division (Chinese *Lien Hua Pu*). Although

---

[1] Cf. J. Blofeld, *The Jewel in the Lotus* (London, 1948), p. 128. The exact date of Bodhidharma's arrival in China is uncertain. Other dates, e.g. A.D. 520 and 526, have been assigned to the event.

the Eastern Branch of this Sect arose in China independently of the direct personal influence of Padma-Sambhava, it was inspired by the same Yogāchāra School of India that inspired his teachings in Tibet, and its founders, Vajrabodhi and Amoghavajra, who reached China together in A.D. 719, had been his fellow students in Bengal.[1]

Our present treatise, attributed to Padma-Sambhava, which expounds the method of realizing the Great Liberation of *Nirvāṇa* by *yogic* understanding of the One Mind, appertains to the Doctrine of the Great Perfection of the Dhyāna School. Between it and the *Treatise on Achieving Pure Consciousness* (Chinese, *Ch'eng Wei Shih Lun*), upon which the Pure Consciousness Sect (Chinese, *Wei Shih Tsung*) of China is based,[2] there is a very close doctrinal relationship. Research may even establish direct historical relationship. Both treatises alike set forth the doctrine that the only reality is mind or consciousness and that no living thing has individualized existence but is fundamentally in eternal and inseparable at-one-ment with the universal all-consciousness.

Of the Doctrine of the Great Perfection itself, the *Guru* Marpa says to the neophyte Milarepa (who subsequently became Tibet's most beloved *Mahātma*) as he is about to initiate him into it,

It is excellent alike in its root, in its trunk, and in its branches. . . . He who meditateth upon it in the day is delivered in the course of that day; and the like happeneth to him who meditateth upon it in the night. . . . This is a doctrine for those intellects that are most highly developed.[3]

This introductory eulogy by the *Guru* Marpa may also, very fittingly, be applied to 'The *Yoga* of Knowing the Mind'.

In order to grasp intellectually the significance of this *yoga* of *yogas*, the student should make careful study not only of occidental psychology, but, more especially, of the psychologically-based philosophy of the Orient; and no better guidance therein can be found than the teachings concerning

---

[1] Cf. J. Blofeld, *The Jewel in the Lotus* (London, 1948), pp. 150–1.
[2] Ibid., pp. 161–2.
[3] Cf. W. Y. Evans-Wentz, *Tibet's Great Yogī Milarepa*, pp. 4, 85–86, and *Tibetan Yoga and Secret Doctrines*, pp. 277–8.

the Illusory Body and Dreams, forming part of *The Six Doctrines*, in *Tibetan Yoga and Secret Doctrines*, together with Dr. Jung's Psychological Commentary, the Foreword of this volume. It will also be found helpful, in this connexion, to re-read Sections IV and V of our General Introduction above.

This *yogic* treatise, like the Gospel of St. John, teaches that one needs only to look within oneself to find Truth, for Truth is not—as the mind in its true state is not—a subject of the Kingdom of Time and Space and *Māyā*. The ancient teaching that the Universe is the product of thought, that Brahma thinks the Universe and it is—as Jehovah thought light and there was light—will, when meditated upon, lead the meditant to the realization that the only reality is Mind, the One Mind, of which all the microcosmic minds throughout the Cosmos are illusorily parts, that everything conceivable is, at root, idea and thought, and thus the offspring of Mind.

The idea and the thought and the object are inseparable; and all three have their origin in mind. It was Plato's belief that ideas pre-exist in the mind, and that, being transcendent over all mundane concepts relating to past, present, and future, they are of that timelessness to which our text makes reference.

Tibetan Masters of *Yoga*, by projecting a mental image, and, through *yogic* power of will, giving to it a form as palpable as that which builders give to the blue-print of an architect, have demonstrated how all external appearances, even the most solid-appearing objective things, are mind-made. This *yogic* method of materialization is referred to at some length above, on page 29[1].

We must not think of mind as something tangible, as the misguided materialists do when they confuse brain substance with mind. In its human manifestation, mind is an invisible energy capable of setting into activity the visible physical brain, just as an invisible vibration sets into activity a radio. The brain thus activated gives off thought, and the radio sound. The sound is merely the product of the vibratory impulse to which the radio responds. Likewise, the thought produced by the brain is the product of the vibratory impulse imparted to the brain by an invisible consciousness, which is *per se* unknowable. If Brahma fails to think the Universe, there is no Universe ; and if there be no thought, there cannot be such a thing as that which men call a material object. Unless an inventor thinks, and then gives substance to an invention, there will be no invention. As taught in our text, the One Mind, the cosmic focus of consciousness, is all-in-all ; there is nothing other than it, no thought other than its thought, no object or universe independent of it.

According to *The Six Doctrines*, all states of consciousness —the waking, the sleeping, the hypnotic, that at death and after death and at rebirth—are not, primordially viewed, true states, being only illusory emanations of the microcosmic mind. Our apparently solid planet is, accordingly, no more solid or real than the world of the dream-state. A stone is as hard in a dream as in the waking-state, because the stone and the hardness are mental concepts. Thus, substance *per se* having no existence apart from mind, the thesis of materialism is fallacious.

Wherever there is law, as there is in every manifested aspect and kingdom of nature, from the atom to the cosmos, there is mind. Mind itself, having neither place nor form, is measureless. As our text repeatedly emphasizes, mind is of the uncreated, timeless, spaceless, all-embracing Reality.

Evolution is a purely mental process. The microcosmic mind of man fashions for itself ever new mansions ; and, in the process of evolution, there is continuous expansion of mind until at-one-ment with the One Mind has been attained. The many illusorily re-become the One, the One illusorily re-becomes the many ; and thereby is made manifest the heart-throb of the cosmos, the pulsation of existence, the inbreathing and the outbreathing by Brahma of the cosmic Whole, the eternal tidal rhythm of the Great Ocean. Just as we speak of an expanding physical universe when the tide in the Great Ocean is rising, so must we think of an expanding human mind during this Day of Brahma. From the reservoir of Cosmic Consciousness there now flows through the microcosmic mind of man a tiny trickle. As evolution proceeds, this trickle will grow into a rivulet, the rivulet into a deep broad river, and, at last, this river will become an infinite sea. The rain-drop will have been merged in its Source.

The Conquerors of Life and Death vow not to enter *Nirvāṇa* until all things are restored to the divine at-one-ment; for They know it is only when They and all beings have awakened from the Earth-Dream and from the dreaming in the after-death and rebirth states that Complete Buddhahood can be attained. Though They themselves have gained the Goal, it cannot be fully enjoyed until all other sentient creatures, who, along with Them collectively form the Whole, have gained the Goal also.

Mind may be regarded from our human viewpoint as being composed of concepts, or ideas, its function being to think, and its products being thoughts; and, correlatively, we may mentally resolve the visible Universe into ideas, and these into mind, the One Mind, which our Teachers assert is the Sole Reality. So viewed, life is no more than an experience of mind.

When we know mind, we also know matter, for matter is mind; and there is nought else conceivable save mind, as this *yoga* postulates. In the One Mind is the summation of the whole of consciousness, the ineffable at-one-ment of all the One Mind's microcosmic aspects. In transcending the micro-cosmic mind of the human ego, man transcends himself; he becomes a conscious participator in the all-embracing Univer-sal Mind, the Over-Mind, the Cosmic Consciousness.

The Dream of Existence is for the purpose of enabling the dreamer to attain the Wisdom born of the Full Awakenment of Buddhahood. Ignorance gives way to understanding, illu-sion to disillusion, the state of sleep to the state of waking, the unreal to the real. *Sangsāric* consciousness is compounded of dualities; and beyond the dualism of the dreaming and the waking lies That which is beyond both.

Through knowing the microcosmic self, his own illusory little self, man attains knowledge of the selfless self, beyond self, the Self of All, the One Mind, beyond mind. This supreme attainment, being possible only when existence itself, as man knows existence, has been transcended, must forever remain, for the unenlightened, mentally incomprehensible, as our text suggests when enumerating the various names men apply to it.

So it is that the paths of the lower *yogas* merge into the Great Path, whereon the pilgrim relinquishes ego and self and even life. The Masters of the Mahāyāna declare that all verbal and symbolic methods of transmitting their teachings are directed to the one end of leading the disciple to that Great Path itself. Nevertheless, the disciple must first have exhausted the lesser paths; initially there must be the seed, then the growth, then the blossoming, and then the fruition. The acorn is not an oak as soon as it sprouts.

In this supreme system of realizing Truth in its undivided unity, by the aeon-old method of knowing the self in the sense implied by the Ancient Oracles and Mysteries, all the ordinary *yogic* practices or techniques, postures, breathings, exercises, and use of concentration-points are transcended. The 'Yoga of Knowing the Mind in its Nakedness' is, in fact, as the text proclaims, 'the most excellent of *yogas*'.

Those who are treading any of the lesser paths are unaware, unless under the guidance of a perfected *guru*, that they are on a lesser path. With very rare exceptions, the various teachers of *yoga* have unknowingly deemed some particular system of conventionalized *yoga* to be all-sufficient in itself, whereas it is, according to our text, no more than a preparation for the truly *Mahāyāna* or Great Path.

Thus the teachings herein set forth are presented as being the very quintessence of all *yogas*; and the Great Path leads from the mundane to the supramundane, from that which is formed and manifested to that which is beyond form and manifestation, from the created, the mind-projected, to the uncreated, the mind-contained, from the phenomenal to the noumenal, from the many to the One, from the *Sangsāra* to *Nirvāṇa*.

Similarly, the *Bhagavad-Gītā* teaches that the *yoga* of divine understanding is paramount, and leads to liberation. Since man, as the Greek Sages declared, is the measure of all things, he sees beyond the illusion of the world and of the self once he has attained understanding of what he intrinsically and transcendentally is.

This *yoga* teaches that mind and the world are inseparable, that without mind there would be no world, that the world is the child of mind, that, as the *Rishis* taught ages ago, Mind is the source of all that man perceives as time and space and the Universe. The *Sangsāra* being the dream-product of the One Mind, its illusory reality is entirely relative; when the One Mind no longer sustains its Creation, its Creation ceases to be.

The time approaches rapidly when occidental scientists, too, will realize that all their so-called exact knowledge is knowledge not of reality, but of an ever-changing, evanescent mirage. Instead of studying the real, they are studying the unreal, the phenomenal instead of the noumenal, appearances rather than the cause of appearances. In the True State of the One Mind, the pluralistic Universe has no existence; and therein man, as man, together with his mind-begotten world of sensuousness and all his mundane sciences, will have vanished into the Voidness.

[PART I. THE INTRODUCTORY PRELIMINARIES]

[*THE OBEISANCE*]

To the Divine Ones, the *Tri-Kāya*,[1] Who are the Embodiment of the All-Enlightened Mind Itself, obeisance.

[*THE FOREWORD*]

This treatise appertains to 'The Profound Doctrine of Self-Liberation by Meditating upon the Peaceful and Wrathful Deities'.[2]

It expounds the *Yoga* of Knowing the Mind, the Seeing of Reality, Self-Liberation.

By this method, one's mind is understood.

[*THE* GURU'S *FIRST CHARGE TO THE DISCIPLES AND THE INVOCATION*]

O blessed disciples,[3] ponder these teachings deeply.

Samayā; gya, gya, gya.[4]

E-ma-ho![5]

---

[1] Text: *Sku-gsum* (pron. *Kū-sūm*), the three states in which the Buddhas, the All-Enlightened Ones, exist, namely (1) the humanly incomprehensible, transcendent at-one-ment of the *Dharma-Kāya* ('Divine Body of Truth'), the primordial, unmodified, unshaped Thatness, beyond the realm of descriptive terms, and knowable solely by realization; (2) the celestial state of the *Sambhoga-Kāya* ('Divine Body of Perfect Endowment'), the reflex or modified aspect of the *Dharma-Kāya*; and (3) the state of divinely pure human embodiment, the *Nirmāṇa-Kāya* ('Divine Body of Incarnation'). The personifications of the *Tri-Kāya* vary according to sect or specialized doctrine. Amitābha, the Dhyānī Buddha of Boundless Light, Who presides over the Western Paradise of Sukhāvatī, very often personifies the *Dharma-Kāya*. In the *Bardo Thödol* series of texts, to which this text belongs, Samanta-Bhadra, the Primordial Buddha of the Nyingma School, personifies the *Dharma-Kāya*, Avalokiteshvara the *Sambhoga-Kāya*, and Padma-Sambhava the *Nirmāṇa-Kāya*, as in Illustration VII.

[2] By comparing this title with that of the translated text of *The Tibetan Book of the Dead*, known as the *Bardo Thödol*, it will be observed that both texts belong to the same *yogic* doctrine concerning self-liberation, or the attaining of *Nirvāṇa*.

[3] Literally '[spiritual] sons', i.e. disciples of a *guru*, or spiritual preceptor. According to the Mahāyāna School, Mañjushrī, Avalokiteshvara, Vajra-Pāṇi, and other Great *Bodhisattvas* are spiritual sons of Gautama the Buddha.

[4] This *mantra* indicates that the teachings about to be given are too profound and esoteric to be taught to, or comprehended by, any save *yogically*

---

[5] See p. 203.

[*SALUTATION TO THE ONE MIND*]

All hail to the One Mind[1] that embraces the whole *Sangsāra* and *Nirvāṇa*,

That eternally is as it is, yet is unknown,

That although ever clear and ever existing, is not visible,

That, although radiant and unobscured, is not recognized.

[*THESE TEACHINGS SUPPLEMENT THOSE OF THE BUDDHAS*]

These teachings are for the purpose of enabling one to know this Mind.

All that has been taught heretofore by the Buddhas of the Three Times,[2] in virtue of Their having known this Mind, as

purified and disciplined disciples. The reference to the disciples as being blessed, or *karmically* fortunate, confirms this. The treatise before us may, therefore, be regarded as appertaining to the Secret Lore of the *Gurus*. In the eyes of initiated Tibetans of this School, the *mantra* itself is equivalent to a seal of secrecy placed upon these teachings. Sometimes, in some of the esoteric manuscripts, the seal of secrecy takes the form of a carefully drawn double *dorje*, perhaps in colour, such as appears on the cover of this volume. A text like the text here translated ought never to be given publicity without authoritative permission, such as the late Lāma Kazi Dawa-Samdup obtained from his *guru* and then gave to the Editor, with respect to the *Bardo Thödol* series of texts as a whole. (See *Tibetan Yoga and Secret Doctrines*, pp. 105–7; also *The Tibetan Book of the Dead*, pp. 79–80.) The Sanskrit *Samayā* of our text corresponds to the Tibetan form *Tog-pa* (*Rtogs-pa*), meaning 'thorough perception', 'infallible knowledge', 'complete realization of Truth'. It also means 'self-realization', or 'self-knowledge'. *Tog-pa* cannot be thoroughly comprehended without practice of *yoga*. The first step consists in comprehending *Tog-pa* intellectually; the second, in deepening or expanding this comprehension by study; the third, in meditating upon *Tog-pa*; and the fourth, in fully comprehending it, such complete comprehension being equivalent to the realization of Buddhahood, or *Nirvāṇa*. The thrice-repeated *gya* (*rgya*) is a Tibetan expression literally translatable as 'vast'. The *mantra* may, therefore, be rendered as 'Vast, vast, vast is Divine Wisdom'.

[5] *E-ma-ho!* is an interjection, commonly occurring in the religious literature of Tibet, expressive of compassion for all living creatures. In this context, it is to be regarded as being the *guru's* invocation addressed to the Buddhas and *Bodhisattvas* in super-human realms that They may telepathically bestow upon the disciples Their divine grace and guidance. The Christian doctrine of divine grace is similar. An interesting illustration of this is supplied by the Latin inscription round the arched entrance of the chapel of the Editor's College in Oxford: *Ascendat Oratio; Descendat Gratia.*

[1] Text: *Sems-gchik-po* (pron. *sem-chik-po*), 'One Mind'.

[2] The Buddhas of the Three Times are: Dīpamkara ('The Luminous

recorded in 'The Door of the *Dharma*', consisting of the Eighty-Four Thousand *Shlokas*,[1] and elsewhere, remains incomprehensible.[2]

The Conquerors[3] have not elsewhere taught anything concerning the One Mind.

Although as vast as the illimitable sky, the Sacred Scriptures contain but a few words relating to knowledge of the mind.

This, the true explanation of these eternal teachings of the Conquerors, constitutes the correct method of their practical application.

[*THE* GURU'S *SECOND CHARGE TO THE DISCIPLES*]

Kye![4] Kye! Ho!
Blessed disciples, harken.

One'), of the past time-cycle ; Shākya Muni ('The Sage of the Shākya Clan'), of the present time-cycle ; and Maitreya ('The Loving One'), of the future time-cycle.

[1] These 84,000 *shlokas* contain the essentials of Buddhist teachings, and are, therefore, commonly known among Tibetan Buddhists as 'The Door of the *Dharma*', or 'Entrance into the *Dharma*', or, vernacularly, as the *Getri*.

[2] That is to say, incomprehensible by one of *yogically* untrained mind, as are all fundamentally esoteric teachings.

[3] The Conquerors (Skt. *Jina*) are the Buddhas, Who are the Conquerors of *sangsāric*, or conditioned, existence. In the Occident there prevails the view that oriental ascetics who renounce the world invariably do so to escape the burdens of social existence. Although this may be true of certain orders of monks in the Occident who do not accept the doctrines of *karma* and rebirth, it is not true of those Hindu and Buddhist monks who, sincere in their renunciation, look forward to the time, even though it be after numerous lifetimes on Earth, when they, too, like the Buddhas, shall have won the spiritual power to live in the midst of society, and, in helping men towards Liberation, shall conquer the world. To those who hold to the one-life-on-Earth theory and renounce the world in the hope of escaping from it for ever into a paradisal after-death state, there can be no desire or opportunity to return to the world to work for social betterment ; and they alone may rightly be regarded as escapists. On the other hand, the candidates for Buddhahood, like the Gnostic candidates for Christhood, are the ones of iron will and indomitable purpose, who, like an athlete in training, bide the hour of their Victory. Such an ideal as that exemplified by the *Bodhisattva* cannot but make for greater and greater strength of mind and a desire to meet face to face and conquer every evil of human society in the glorious spirit of a Saint George, whose spear of righteousness transfixes the Dragon.

[4] Text: *Kye*, a vocative, known in Tibetan as the word of invocation or calling (or, as here, charge to the disciples), which may be translated as 'O!'

[*THE RESULT OF NOT KNOWING THE ONE MIND*]

Knowledge of that which is vulgarly called mind is widespread.

Inasmuch as the One Mind is unknown, or thought of erroneously, or known one-sidedly without being thoroughly known as it is, desire for these teachings will be immeasurable. They will also be sought after by ordinary individuals, who, not knowing the One Mind, do not know themselves.

They wander hither and thither in the Three Regions,[1] and thus among the Six Classes of beings,[2] suffering sorrow.

Such is the result of their error of not having attained understanding of their mind.

Because their suffering is in every way overpowering, even self-control is lacking to them.

Thus, although one may wish to know the mind as it is, one fails.

[*THE RESULTS OF DESIRES*]

Others, in accordance with their own particular faith and practice, having become fettered by desires,[3] cannot perceive the Clear Light.[4]

---

[1] The Three Regions (Tib. *Khams-gsum*: Skt. *Trailokya*) into which Buddhists divide the *Sangsāra*, or realm of conditioned existence, known to men as the Cosmos or Universe, are: (1) The Region of Desire (Skt. *Kāma-dhātu*), which is the lowest, comprising the six heavens of the *devas*, or gods, and the Earth; (2) the Region of Form (Skt. *Rūpa-dhātu*), comprising the purer heavens, wherein form is free from sensuality, called the sixteen worlds of Brahma, which are divided into four realms of meditation (Skt. *dhyāna*); (3) the Region of Formlessness (Skt. *Arūpa-dhātu*), comprising the four highest Brahma heavens, whence the Fully Awakened One passes into the unconditioned state of *Nirvāṇa*. (Cf. L. A. Waddell, op. cit., pp. 84–85.)

[2] These are: (1) the Gods (Tib. *Lha*: Skt. *Sura* or *Deva*); (2) Titans (Tib. *Lha-ma-yin*: Skt. *Asura*); (3) Man (Tib. *Mi*: Skt. *Nara*); (4) Beasts (Tib. *Du-do*: Skt. *Tiryak*); (5) Ghosts (Tib. *Yi-dvag*: Skt. *Preta*); (6) Dwellers in Hells (Tib. *Nyal-kham*: Skt. *Naraka*). Thus the Six Classes of sentient beings are those of the Six States of Existence within the *Sangsāra*. The various Hells or states of *karmic* purgation, unlike the Hell of the Semitic Faiths, are, for the fallen ones who enter them, of but limited duration, like all other *sangsāric* states, the unconditional supra-*sangsāric Nirvāṇic* State alone being eternal, and transcendent over time.

[3] Commonly, unsound religious beliefs and practices result in increased

[4] See p. 206.

They are overwhelmed by suffering, and are in darkness because of their suffering.

Although the Middle Path contains the Twofold Truth,[1] because of desires it finally becomes obscured.

Desires likewise obscure *Kriyā-Yoga*[2] and *Seva-Sādhanā*,[3] and even the greatest and sublimest states of mind.

[THE TRANSCENDENT AT-ONE-MENT]

There being really no duality, pluralism is untrue.[4]

Until duality is transcended and at-one-ment realized, Enlightenment cannot be attained.

sangsāric bondage. There may be, for instance, strong desire to escape distasteful duties which are inseparable from the station in life assigned to one by *karma*, and, in consequence, an overpowering longing for death and for some after-death paradise. This merely results, as the *Bardo Thödol* teaches, in exchanging one state of illusion for another. *Karma* cannot possibly be escaped; it must be faced eventually and, no matter how terrible, experienced, if not in one lifetime then in another. There is no place to which one can go to get away from oneself, or from the results of one's actions. Very often, too, prayer may be made for purely worldly benefits rather than for emancipation from the bondage to appearances.

⁴ For those who are attracted to religions which, not affording true guidance, tend to enhance the *karmic* predilections of the unenlightened to create ever new fetters, the Clear Light of Reality remains obscured by the darkness of *Avidyā* (Ignorance of Truth).

¹ Text: *Bden-gnyis* (pron. *Den-nyi*), 'Two Truths', or 'Twofold Truth': namely, the ordinary truth, such as that of science, which concerns all things and phenomena observable in nature; and the transcendental, or metaphysical, truth, as set forth in the teachings of the Buddha.

² Text: *Kri-yog*, an abbreviated form of the Sanskrit *Kriyā-Yoga*, the *yoga* concerned with religious observances and worship (*kriyā*).

³ *Seva-Sādhanā*, the Sanskrit equivalent of the Tibetan *bsnyen-bsgrub* (pron. *nyen-drub*) of the text, literally means 'Service-Worship', with reference to a *yogic* practice of regarding all one's duties to society and the world as sacred, to the end that every act of life on Earth shall be performed with religious reverence.

⁴ In the words of Plotinus, 'The Primordial [or First Principle] is neither all things that imply duality, nor any of them; it containeth no duality whatsoever' (v. vi. 6). It is said that Plotinus attained ecstatic realization of the divine at-one-ment, here symbolized by the One Mind. At the age of 39 he followed in the wake of the army of the Roman Emperor Gordian III in the expedition against Persia, and came into direct contact with Persian and Hindu *gurus*. We have, therefore, made Plotinus our chief occidental witness to the Truth expounded in this Mahāyāna text. In essentials, the Platonic philosophy, which Plotinus greatly enriched, is an efflorescence in the Occident of the more ancient Brāhmanical philosophy; and this accounts for the remarkable parallelisms, set forth in annotations, between the two Schools.

The whole *Sangsāra* and *Nirvāṇa*, as an inseparable unity, are one's mind.[1]

[THE GREAT SELF-LIBERATION]

Owing to worldly beliefs, which he is free to accept or reject, man wanders in the *Sangsara*.[2]

Therefore, practising the *Dharma*, freed from every attachment, grasp the whole essence of these teachings expounded in this Yoga of Self-Liberation by Knowing the Mind in its Real Nature.

The truths set forth herein are known as 'The Great Self-Liberation'; and in them culminates the Doctrine of the Great Ultimate Perfection.[3]

---

[1] This aphorism expounds most succinctly the ultimate teaching of the Mahāyāna. To comprehend it intellectually, a thorough understanding of the doctrine of the Voidness, the *Shūnyatā*, is necessary. (In our General Introduction, pp. 1–4, the doctrine has been set forth at some length.) The One Mind being the Cause of All Causes, the Ultimate Reality, every other aspect of the Whole, visible and invisible, and all states or conditions of consciousness, are inseparably parts of the One Mind. Every duality, even the Final Duality, the *Sangsāra* and *Nirvāṇa*, is, in the last analysis, found to be a unity. Therefore, both pluralism, or the belief that the Cosmos is primordially and eternally a plurality rather than a unity, and dualism, or the belief that all things conceivable are divided into indissoluble dualities, are untrue.

[2] Many of human kind believe in animism, in a 'soul', as being a principle of personal consciousness separately existing, apart from all other 'souls', eternally. Some animists believe that such a 'soul' repeatedly incarnates. Others hold that it dwells in a fleshly body on Earth only once prior to its final reincarnation at the time of a general resurrection and judgement of the dead, and thereafter for an endless eternity continues to exist as a personal entity either in a *sangsāric* state of sensuous blissfulness or in a *sangsāric* state of suffering of the most terrible character humanly imaginable. Again, there are vast multitudes who maintain that no part or principle of man survives death; and such as these, not having developed by *yogic* training that intuitive insight innately common to all men, are spiritually asleep and fettered by Ignorance (Skt. *Avidyā*). Inasmuch as all beliefs of this character fetter man to the *Sangsāra*, he is, so long as he remains unawakened to Truth, chained Prometheus-like to the Wheel of Life. Ignorance of human law·cannot be used as a plea to escape the law's penalty; and ignorance of the Law of Truth (Skt. *Dharma*) causes man to suffer interminably, or until he breaks his fetters and claims his birthright to Freedom.

[3] Text: *Rdzogs-pa ch'en-po* (pron. *Dzog-pa ch'en-po*) = *Rdzog-ch'en*, 'Most Perfect', or 'Most Complete', or 'Great Ultimate Perfection', with reference to the chief doctrine known as the Great Perfection of the Nyingma School founded by Padma-Sambhava. In this doctrine, of which our present

[*THE* GURU'S *THIRD CHARGE TO THE DISCIPLES*]

Samayā; gya, gya, gya.

[*THE NATURE OF MIND*]

That which is commonly called mind is of intuitive[1] Wisdom.

Although the One Mind is, it has no existence.[2]

Being the source of all the bliss of *Nirvāṇa* and of all the sorrow of the *Sangsāra*, it is cherished like the Eleven *Yānas*.[3]

[*THE NAMES GIVEN TO THE MIND*]

The various names given to it are innumerable.

Some call it 'The Mental Self'.[4]

Certain heretics[5] call it 'The Ego'.[6]

treatise is the quintessence, all doctrines reach their culmination, or fruition, which is emancipation from *sangsāric*, or conditioned, existence and the attainment of the non-conditioned supra-*sangsāric* state of *Nirvāṇa*.

[1] Or literally, 'quick-knowing'. Intuitive Wisdom is known to the Mahāyāna as *Prajñā*, the awakening of which, by practice of meditation, in relation to the doctrine of Enlightenment, is the aim of Zen Buddhism. As taught in the *Saddharma-Pundarika*, the *Dharma*, 'the true law understood by the Tathāgata, cannot be reasoned, is beyond the pale of reasoning'. Cf. D. T. Zuzuki, *Essays in Zen Buddhism* (New York, 1949), p. 71.

[2] Or, 'it has no existence [*sangsārically*]', that is to say, 'it has no conditioned existence'. As Plotinus teaches, 'above existence, therefore, is the One' (v. i. 10).

[3] Text: *Theg-pa bchu-gchig* (pron. *Theg-pa chu-chig*), 'Eleven *Yānas* (or Paths)', with reference to eleven schools of Buddhist philosophy or doctrine, of which the Mahā-Yāna and Hīna-Yāna are the two chief primary divisions. There is also a threefold primary division: (1) the Hīna-Yāna, or Shravaka-Yāna; (2) the Pratyeka-Buddha-Yāna, or Pradecika-Yāna; and (3) the Bodhisattva-Yāna, which is the Mahā-Yāna or Eka-Yāna. Then, again, the Mahā-Yāna has been sub-divided into the Mantra-Yāna and the Vajra-Yāna, which expound an esoteric Buddhism. The Mantra-Yāna is itself divided into the Hetu-Yāna, based on the Doctrine of Cause (Skt. *Hetu*) and the Phala-Yāna, based on the Doctrine of Effect (Skt. *Phala*); and each of these Schools is sub-divided into four, as illustrated by the Great Perfection sect of the Nyingma School of Padma-Sambhava. (Cf. S. C. Dās, op. cit., pp. 585–7.) Taking, with some uncertainty, the ten sub-divisions of the Mahā-Yāna here enumerated together with the Hīna-Yāna as a whole, we arrive at the Eleven *Yānas* of our text.

[4] Text: *sems-nyid* (pron. *sem-nyi*), literally, 'mind-self', or 'mental self'.

[5] According to the Mahāyāna, heresy, or the holding of wrong views concerning Truth, is of two sorts: (1) denial of reincarnation, denial that charity,

[6] See p. 209.

By the Hīnayānists it is called 'The Essentiality of Doctrines'.[1]

By the Yogāchāra[2] it is called 'Wisdom'.[3]

Some call it 'The Means of Attaining the Other Shore of Wisdom'.[4]

Some call it 'The Buddha Essence'.[5]

Some call it 'The Great Symbol'.[6]

Some call it 'The Sole Seed'.[7]

Some call it 'The Potentiality of Truth'.[8]

Some call it 'The All-Foundation'.[9]

Other names, in ordinary language, are also given to it.

self-sacrifice, and righteousness produce good *karma*, and denial both of unrighteousness and of Divine Wisdom; (2) the assertion that happiness and misery are arbitrarily allotted to human beings by a deity rather than as a direct result of the individual's past deeds, and that all things are either permanent or real, and that there is no *Nirvāṇic* Reality as their root or essentiality.

[6] Text: *bdag* (pron. *dag*), 'self', 'ego', 'I': Skt. *ātman*.

[1] Text: *gdams-ngag gdams-ngag* (pron. *dam-ngag dam-ngag*), literally 'precept (or religious teaching) precept', or 'precept of precepts', i.e. essentiality of doctrines (or teachings).

[2] The Yogāchāra is a system of Mahāyāna metaphysics, based on *yoga*, and developed by Āryasangha.

[3] Text: *sems* (pron. *sem*), 'mind', 'consciousness', 'Wisdom', &c.

[4] Text: *Shes-rab pha-rol phyin-pa* (pron. *Shay-rab pha-rol chin-pa*) = the short form, *Sher-phyin* (pron. *sher-chin*): Skt. *Prajñā-Pāramitā*, 'Divine Wisdom', known to Tibetan Buddhists as 'the means of arriving at the Other Shore of Wisdom'. It is also referred to as 'the Ship of Salvation', or 'the Vessel which conducts man to *Nirvāṇa* (or the Other Shore)'.

[5] Text: *Bde-gshegs snyings-po* (pron. *De-sheg nying po*), 'Sugatas' (i.e. Buddhas') Essence'.

[6] Text: *Phyag-rgya Ch'en-po* (pron. *Chag-gya Chen-po*): Skt. *Mahā-Mudrā*, 'Great Hand-Gesture', or 'Great Symbol'. The technical *yogic* meaning of *Mahā-Mudrā* is *Anuttara*, the highest and final doctrine. *Mahā-Mudrā*, the method of practically applying the *Dharma*, is also known as *Dharma Karma*. *Phyag* refers to knowledge of the Shūnyatā, or Voidness, and *rgya* conveys the meaning of liberation from worldliness; and *Ch'en-po* signifies the at-one-ment of these two all-important teachings. (Cf. S. C. Dās, op. cit., p. 831.) The *Yoga* of the Great Symbol is set forth in detail in *Tibetan Yoga and Secret Doctrines* (pp. 115–54).

[7] Text: *Thig-lé nyag-gchig* (pron. *Thig-lé nyag-chig*), 'Sole (or Unique) Seed'. *Thig-lé* = Skt. *Bindu*, 'Seed', 'Point', &c.

[8] Text: *Chōs-kyi-dvyings* (pron. *Chō-kyi-ing*): Skt. *Dharma-Dhātu*, 'Seed (or Potentiality) of Truth', equivalent to the *Dharma-Kāya*, the Shape (which is Shapelessness) of the Divine Body of Truth regarded as the all-pervading Voidness. (See *The Tibetan Book of the Dead*, pp. 10–15.)

[9] Text: *Kun-gzhi* (pron. *Kun-zhi*), 'All-Foundation'.

[PART II. THE PRACTICAL APPLICATION]
[*THE TIMELESSNESS OF MIND*]

If one knows how to apply in a threefold manner[1] this knowing of the mind, all past knowledge lost to memory becomes perfectly clear, and also knowledge of the future, thought of as unborn and unconceived.

In the present, when the mind remains as it is naturally,[2] it is ordinarily comprehended by its own time.[3]

[1] It is customary among Tibetan Buddhist *gurus* to assign to all things a threefold aspect. The Cosmos itself is divided into the Three Regions; the Voidness, into the Three Voids; the Buddha Essence is manifested in the Three Divine Bodies; the chief perfections are threefold, namely, of the body, speech, and mind; there are three principal psychic centres, namely, of the brain, of the throat, and of the heart. Doctrines themselves are threefold, those of the two extremes and those of the Middle Path. Accordingly, this *Yoga* of Knowing the Mind is to be applied in a threefold manner to the end that the *yogin* may, like the Buddhas, become a Master of Everything— of the Three Regions, of the Three Divine Bodies, of the Three Perfections, of the Three Psychic Centres, and of all doctrines. To the one who thus attains understanding of his or her own limited *sangsāric* and illusory self, the 'soul' of animists, and correlatively realizes the True Essence of Mind, which is 'soul'-less and impersonal, there is no past and future, but only timelessness, as the next aphorism sets forth.

[2] Mind *per se*, in its true or natural state, is unmodified, primordial quiescence. By virtue of successful application of such *yogic* practices as are expounded in the text of the Great Symbol, in *Tibetan Yoga and Secret Doctrines* (Book II), the current of the thought-process, born of *sangsāric* existence, is inhibited and the True State realized. Then, there being no longer past or future, mind *per se* is comprehended by its own time, which is timelessness. As the great Buddhist Patriarch Ashvaghosha taught, during the first century A.D., 'While the essence of mind is eternally clean and pure, the influence of ignorance makes possible the existence of a defiled mind. But in spite of the defiled mind the mind [*per se*] is eternal, clear, pure, and not subject to transformation. Further, as its original nature is free from particularization, it knows in itself no change whatever, though it produces everywhere the various modes of existence. When the one-ness of the totality of things (*dharmadhātu*) is not recognized, then ignorance as well as particularization arises, and all phases of the defiled mind are thus developed. But the significance of this doctrine is so extremely deep and unfathomable that it can be fully comprehended by Buddhas and by no others.' (Cf. Prof. Suzuki's translation of Ashvaghosha's *The Awakening of Faith*, Chicago, 1900, pp. 79–80.)

[3] The sense here may be brought out by making comparison with the well-known aphorism in Milton's *Paradise Lost* (I. 254–5):

> The mind is its own place, and in itself
> Can make a Heaven of Hell, a Hell of Heaven.

Paraphrasing Milton, one may say that the mind is its own time, and of itself can make the past the present and the future the present. In other

[*MIND IN ITS TRUE STATE*]

When one seeks one's mind in its true state, it is found
to be quite intelligible, although invisible.

In its true state, mind is naked, immaculate; not made of
anything, being of the Voidness; clear, vacuous, without
duality, transparent; timeless, uncompounded, unimpeded,
colourless; not realizable as a separate thing, but as the
unity of all things, yet not composed of them; of one taste,[1]
and transcendent over differentiation.[2]

words, mind, in its pure, primordial, unmodified, natural condition, is
transcendent over what *sangsāric* man calls time. As implied above, in the
aphorisms that the One Mind embraces the whole *Sangsāra* and *Nirvāṇa*
and all other dualities, mind *per se* also transcends space. For, as the
Mahāyāna teaches, space is merely a mode of particularization. Therefore,
space *per se* has no existence any more than has time *per se*, it being impossible to think of space apart from the variety of things illusorily existing in
space. In this sense, then, space and objects of space are merely another
dualism. Time *per se* being timelessness, space *per se* is spacelessness. Neither
time nor space, *sangsārically* conceived, exists apart from relationship to the
sangsāric particularizing consciousness; and thus both have only a relative,
not an absolute existence.

Mind, being in its abstract or potential condition non-*sangsāric*, has innate
power (while it 'remains as it is naturally', that is, in its unmodified, or
primordially *Nirvāṇic*, true state) to view, by its own standard of timelessness, the past, the present, and the future as an inseparable homogeneous
unity. And this *yogic* power can be made operative in this world or in any
region of the *Sangsāra* by the devotee who masters the *yoga* herein expounded. In this connexion, reference may very profitably be made to *An
Experiment with Time* and *The Serial Universe*, by J. W. Dunne.

The One Mind, as Eternity, is the eternal present, but is neither past nor
future. Time, as Plotinus teaches, is the measure of movement. In its
naturalness, the One Mind, as the Quiescent, is the Immutable, the Motionless. Time begins with motion, with the initiation of thought; when the
mind attains the transcendent at-one-ment, by concentration upon unity,
and the thought-process is inhibited, simultaneously with the cessation of
thought, time ceases, and there is only timelessness.

[1] The expression, 'of one taste', occurs throughout Buddhist literature
to indicate, as here, homogeneity, undifferentiated at-one-ment, qualityless
or supramundane unity. The Buddha frequently uses it in this sense when
speaking of the single purpose of the Doctrine, which is to lead mankind to
Freedom, to *Nirvāṇa*. Even as the Great Waters are of one taste, the taste
of salt, so the One Mind is really One, and incapable of being divided, or of
being differentiated from any of the microcosmic aspects of the Thatness,
the Ultimate Reality.

[2] In similar language, Plotinus teaches that the One, 'possessing no
[geometrical] magnitude, is indivisible in its power. . . . We must also
insist that the One is infinite, not as would be a mass of a magnitude which

Nor is one's own mind separable from other minds.

To realize the quintessential being of the One Mind is to realize the immutable at-one-ment of the *Tri-Kāya*.

The mind, being, as the Uncreated and of the Voidness, the *Dharma-Kāya*, and, as the Vacuous and Self-Radiant, the *Sambhoga-Kāya*, and, as the Unobscured, shining for all living creatures, the *Nirmāṇa-Kāya*, is the Primordial Essence wherein its Three Divine Aspects are One.[1]

If the *yogic* application of this Wisdom be thorough, one will comprehend that which has just been set forth above.

[*MIND IS NON-CREATED*]

Mind in its true nature being non-created and self-radiant, how can one, without knowing the mind, assert that mind is created?

There being in this *yoga* nothing objective upon which to meditate, how can one, without having ascertained the true nature of mind by meditation, assert that mind is created?

Mind in its true state being Reality, how can one, without having discovered one's own mind, assert that mind is created?[2]

could be examined serially, but by the incommensurability of its power. Even though it be conceived as being of intelligence or divinity, it is still higher. If it be thought of as being the most perfect unity, it is still higher. Shouldst thou form for thyself an idea of a divinity by rising to what in thy comprehension is most unitary [the One is still simpler]; for it dwelleth within thee, and containeth nothing which is dependent' (VI. ix. 6).

[1] Plotinus's doctrine of the ultimate Unity parallels this doctrine of the At-one-ment of the *Tri-Kāya*: 'Inasmuch as Unity is the nature that begetteth all things, Unity cannot be any of them. It is, therefore, neither any particular thing, nor quantity, nor quality, nor intelligence, nor soul, nor what is movable, nor what is stable; nor doth it partake of place or time. But it is the uniform in itself, or rather it is the formless; for it is above all form, movement, and stability' (VI. ix. 3). 'The One cannot be enumerated along with anything, nor even with uniqueness, nor with aught else. The One cannot be enumerated in any way because It is measure without itself being measured' (V. v. 4).

[2] In the True State, the State of Reality, mind and matter in their *sangsāric*, or mundane, or temporally illusory aspects are inseparably one. Ashvaghosha teaches, 'there is no distinction between mind and matter; it is on account of the finite in the round of life and death that these distinctions appear [*sangsārically*]'. Eternally all things 'are neither mind nor matter, neither infinite wisdom nor finite knowledge, neither existing nor

Mind in its true state being undoubtedly ever-existing, how can one, without having seen the mind face to face, assert that mind is created?[1]

The thinking-principle being of the very essence of mind, how can one, without having sought and found it, assert that mind is created?

Mind being transcendent over creation, and thus partaking of the Uncreated, how can one assert that mind is created?

Mind being in its primordial, unmodified naturalness non-created,[2] as it should be taken to be, and without form, how can one assert that it is created?

Inasmuch as mind can also be taken to be devoid of quality, how can one venture to assert that it is created?[3]

non-existing, but are after all inexpressible'. Although words must be employed to convey thought, so that mankind may be led to discover Reality for themselves, 'the best human thought of all things is only temporary and is not Truth Absolute'. (Cf. Ashvaghosha's *Awakening of Faith*, as translated by the late Rev. Timothy Richard, Shanghai, 1907, pp. 26–28.) It is only quite recently that occidental scientists have discovered, as the Sages of the Mahāyāna did very many centuries ago, that matter, formerly believed by a now obsolete materialism to be inert, is, as indicated by the electronic character of the atom, the very quintessence of energy. Moreover, Western Science is beginning to suspect that the Universe is wholly a mental phenomenon; or, as the Wise Men of the East teach, that it is the product of One Cosmic Mind; or, in a theological sense, that it is the Thought of an Incommensurable Intelligence.

[1] Mind or consciousness in its true state being Reality, and ever-existing, is of the Uncreated; and, being uncreated, is primary in Nature. Accordingly, matter is derived from mind or consciousness, and not mind or consciousness from matter.

[2] Literally rendered, this passage would read, 'Mind being in its own place [i.e. in its primordial, unmodified naturalness] non-created'. This is one more illustration of the desirability of departing from a strictly literal rendering.

[3] Although the mind, in its mundane aspect, is the root of all quality, in its natural or true state of primordial non-createdness it is *per se* devoid of all quality and thus beyond the realm of predication. Being undifferentiated voidness, vacuity, or *no thing*, it transcends *sangsāric* attributes. As Ashvaghosha teaches, all phenomena throughout the *Sangsāra* are mind-made. 'Without mind, then, there is practically no objective existence. Thus all existence arises from imperfect notions in our mind. All differences are differences of the mind. But the mind cannot see itself, for it has no form. We should know that all phenomena are created by the imperfect notions in the finite mind; therefore all existence is like a reflection in a mirror, without substance, only a phantom of the mind. When the finite mind acts, then all kinds of things arise; when the finite mind ceases to act, then all kinds of things cease.' (Cf. Ashvaghosha's, *The Awakening of Faith*,

The self-born, qualityless mind, being like the Three Voids[1] undifferentiated, unmodified, how can one assert that mind is created?

Mind being without objectivity and causation, self-originated, self-born, how can one, without having endeavoured to know mind, assert that mind is created?

Inasmuch as Divine Wisdom dawns in accordance with its own time,[2] and one is emancipated, how can opponents of these teachings assert that it is created?

Mind being, as it is, of this nature, and thus unknowable,[3] how can one assert that it is created?

[*THE* YOGA *OF INTROSPECTION*]

The One Mind being verily of the Voidness and without any foundation, one's mind is, likewise, as vacuous as the

Richard's translation, p. 26.) The object of our present *yoga* is to arrive at that right understanding of mind which is attainable only when the finite activities, the thought-processes, of the mundane mind are stilled. Then the world of objectivity vanishes. When an electric current is cut off, the external or visible manifestation of electricity as kinetic energy ceases and no longer exists; there is then only electricity *per se* in its natural or unmodified state of potentiality. To know mind, one must know it in its true state.

[1] Apart from its threefold aspect, the Voidness is further divided by the *lāmas* into eighteen degrees, which may be extended to seventy. (Cf. L. A. Waddell, op. cit., pp. 125–6.)

[2] The Divine Wisdom, or the *yogic* knowing of mind, is attained in the true state of timelessness, which is the mind's or Divine Wisdom's own time. The One Mind, not having had an origin at any time, will not have an ending at any time; being really eternal, it cannot be known or conceived in terms of time.

[3] Mind in its finite or mundane aspect cannot know mind in its infinite, supramundane aspect. By virtue of *yogic* discipline the finite mind is purged of Ignorance (Skt. *Avidyā*). 'As Ignorance is thus annihilated, the mind [i.e. the *ālaya vijñāna*] is no more disturbed so as to be subject to individuation. As the mind is no more disturbed, the particularization of the surrounding world is annihilated. When in this wise the principle and the condition of defilement, their products, and the mental disturbances are all annihilated, it is said that we attain to *Nirvāṇa* and that various spontaneous displays of activity are accomplished.' (Ashvaghosha's *The Awakening of Faith*, Suzuki's translation, op. cit., pp. 86–87.) The same passage in Richard's rendering (op. cit., p. 17), is as follows: 'As Ignorance disappears, then false ideas cease to arise. As these false ideas do not arise, the former objective world also ends. As the forces cease to exist, then the false powers of the finite mind cease to exist, and this [state] is called *Nirvāṇa*, when the natural forces of the True Reality alone work.' These passages suggest the *yogic* process of transmuting the finite aspect of mind into the infinite, supramundane aspect.

sky.[1] To know whether this be so or not, look within thine own mind.

Being of the Voidness, and thus not to be conceived as having beginning or ending, Self-Born Wisdom has in reality been shining forever, like the Sun's essentiality,[2] itself unborn. To known whether this be so or not, look within thine own mind.

Divine Wisdom is undoubtedly indestructible, unbreakable, like the ever-flowing current of a river. To know whether this be so or not, look within thine own mind.

Being merely a flux of instability like the air of the firmament, objective appearances are without power to fascinate and fetter.[3] To know whether this be so or not, look within thine own mind.[4]

All appearances are verily one's own concepts, self-conceived in the mind, like reflections seen in a mirror.[5] To

[1] The finite aspect of mind being a microcosmic reflex of the One Mind, and, in the last analysis, inseparable from the One Mind, it partakes of its vacuous and foundationless nature. Only in the highest trance state of *samādhi*, or divine at-one-ment, is the truth of this realizable; it cannot be demonstrated intellectually, in the state in which mundane mind acts. This *yoga* is the *yoga* of introspection.

[2] Text: *snying-po* (pron. *nying-po*), pith, heart, essence, or essentiality, with reference to the secret essence of the Sun as known to the occult sciences, and thus suggestive of doctrines concerning the Sun *per se*, which, like the Mind *per se*, is of the Unborn, Unshaped, Unmodified Thatness, synonymous with the Voidness.

[3] As a result of successful practice of the *yoga* of knowing the mind in its true state, the *yogin*, having realized the wholly illusory and unsatisfactory nature of all mundane things, is no longer fettered by them. Mechanical gadgets, bodily luxuries, fashionable clothing, worldly conventionalities, the pomp and circumstance of men, even the intellectualisms of the world, have lost their hypnotic power to fascinate and fetter him, as they still do the ignorant multitudes, who, like long-immured prisoners rejoicing in their bondage, consider themselves 'progressive' and the *yogin* an unpractical visionary, and desire not Freedom.

[4] Again Plotinus's teaching is parallel: 'We must advance into the sanctuary, penetrating into it, if we have the strength to do so, closing our eyes to the spectacle of terrestrial things. . . . Whoever would let himself be misled by the pursuit of those vain shadows, mistaking them for realities, would grasp only an image as fugitive as the fluctuating form reflected by the waters, and would resemble that foolish youth [the ravishingly beautiful Narcissus] who, wishing to grasp that image of himself [seen in a stream], according to the fable, disappeared, carried away by the current' (I. vi. 8).

[5] Ashvaghosha and many other of the expounders of the esotericism of the Mahāyāna employ this simile of images seen reflected in a mirror to

known whether this be so or not, look within thine own mind.

Arising of themselves and being naturally free like the clouds in the sky, all external appearances verily fade away into their own respective places.[1] To know whether this be so or not, look within thine own mind.

[*THE* DHARMA *WITHIN*]

The *Dharma*[2] being nowhere save in the mind, there is no other place of meditation than the mind.

explain, as far as it is possible to do so in words, the unreality of all phenomenal appearances, the sum total of which constitutes the *Sangsāra*. Similarly, occidental science has arrived at the assumption that the true essence of things is not visible phenomena, but invisible noumena. The abstract and the potential manifest themselves as the concrete and kinetic. Behind the abstract and potential there is what Plato has called the realm of Ideas, and what the Mahāyānists call the One Mind, the homogeneous at-one-ment of all things conceivable, abstractly or concretely, potentially or kinetically, the undifferentiated, unpredicable *Shūnyatā*, or Voidness. 'The True Reality is originally only one, but the degrees of Ignorance are infinite. . . . There are unruly thoughts more numerous than the grains of sand of the Ganges, some arising from ignorant conceptions and others arising from ignorance of senses and desires. Thus all kinds of wild thoughts arise from Ignorance; and have, first and last, infinite differences, which the Tathāgata alone knows.' (Cf. Ashvaghosha's *The Awakening of Faith*, Richard's translation, op. cit., p. 18, upon which our version is based.)

[1] This philosophical assertion is in amplification of the last. The comparing of the arising and passing away of appearances, born of unruly mental concepts, to that of clouds is very apt. As has been already suggested in our annotations and introductions, when the darkness of Ignorance is dissipated by the light of Divine Wisdom, all appearances vanish as does the fog of the night after the Sun has risen. It is the false concept in the mundane mind that the world is real which gives to the world its illusory aspect of being real. When this concept is transcended by realization of the true nature of mind, and the at-one-ment of the microcosmic mind with the Macrocosmic Mind is attained, the Universe and all apparent things of the phenomenal realm of the *Sangsāra* vanish, and there is only undifferentiated, primordial Vacuity, which is the natural, or native, place of every thing and of every appearance. And here, again, the testimony from realization by the recently deceased Sage of Tiruvannamalai, Sri Ramana Mahārshi, parallels this of the Great *Guru*: 'After all, the world is merely an idea or thought. When the mind ceases to think, the world vanishes, and there is bliss indescribable. When the mind begins to think, immediately the world reappears and there is suffering.' (Cf. *Who Am I?* p. 12.)

[2] According to the Mahāyāna, the *Dharma*, the Law of Being, the Truth, the Divine Wisdom, the Guide to the Science and Art of Living, is in its true nature the unpredicable Voidness.

The *Dharma* being nowhere save in the mind, there is no other doctrine to be taught or practised elsewhere.

The *Dharma* being nowhere save in the mind, there is no other place of truth for the observance of a vow.

The *Dharma* being nowhere save in the mind, there is no *Dharma* elsewhere whereby Liberation may be attained.

Again and again look within thine own mind.[1]

---

[1] Herein is set forth in a Buddhistic manner the ancient aphorism which Christianity, too, adopted and expressed: 'And the light shineth in darkness; and the darkness comprehended it not. . . . That was the true Light, which lighteth every man that cometh into the world.' St. John, i. 5, 9.

To serve as a Gnostic commentary to this 'Yoga of Knowing the Mind', there is here added the following excerpts from a translation made by the late G. R. S. Mead of the original Greek of the Proem of the Gospel of St. John, and contained in *The Gnostic John the Baptizer* (published by John M. Watkins, London, 1924), pp. 123–6:

1. In the Beginning was Mind; and Mind was with God.
2. So Mind was God. This was in Beginning with God.
3. All kept coming into existence through it; and apart from it came into existence not a single [thing].
4. What hath come into existence in it was Life; and Life was the Light of the [true] Men.
5. And the Light shineth in the Darkness; and the Darkness did not emprison it. . . .
6. It was the True Light, which enlighteneth every Man who cometh into the world.
7. It was in the world; and the world kept coming into existence through it.
8. And the world did not know it. It came unto its own; and its own did not receive it.
9. And as many as received it, to them it gave power to become children of God,—
10. To those who have faith in his name,—Who was brought to birth, not out of [blending of] bloods,
11. Nor of urge of flesh, nor urge of a male,—but out of God.
12. So Mind became flesh and tabernacled in us,—
13. And we beheld its glory,—glory as of [? an] only-begotten Father,—full of Delight and Truth.

The following comments are made: To verse 4, 'The true Men who have the Light of Life are the Prophets and Perfect'. To verse 5, 'emprison' may otherwise be rendered, 'hold back', 'detain'. Between verses 5 and 6 comes a paragraph which 'seems clearly to be an interpolation into, or overworking of, his original "source" by the writer, or perhaps part-compiler, of the fourth gospel': 'There was a Man sent by God,—his name Yōánes. This [Man] came for bearing witness, that he might bear witness about the Light, in order that all [men] might have faith through it. That [Man] was not the Light, but [came] in order that he might bear witness about the Light.' To verse 6, 'Man' is equivalent to 'Prophet' or 'Divine Messenger'. Verse 10,

When looking outwards into the vacuity of space,[1] there is no place to be found where the mind is shining.[2]

When looking inwards into one's own mind in search of the shining, there is to be found no thing that shines.

One's own mind is transparent, without quality.[3]

Being of the Clear Light of the Voidness, one's own mind is of the *Dharma-Kaya*; and, being void of quality, it is comparable to a cloudless sky.

It is not a multiplicity, and is omniscient.

Very great, indeed, is the difference between knowing and not knowing the import of these teachings.

[*THE WONDROUSNESS OF THESE TEACHINGS*]

This self-originated Clear Light, eternally unborn,[4] is a parentless babe of Wisdom. Wondrous is this.

Being non-created, it is Natural Wisdom.[5] Wondrous is this.

'his name' refers to the 'Mystic Name', or 'Mind', or 'Primality of Great Life'.

The translator of these verses of St. John's Gospel was a modern follower of the Gnosis, and England's outstanding scholar in the field of Gnosticism; and the Editor claimed him as a friend. The authorized version contained in the New Testament was made by men who considered Gnosticism 'heretical'. Owing to their anti-Gnostic bias, they failed to translate the Greek text in such manner as to bring out in English the real sense of the original, which is one of the few fragments in the present-day canon of exoteric Christianity that escaped the iconoclastic zeal of those who anathematized the Gnostics and destroyed all the invaluable manuscripts of esoteric Christianity they could lay hands on. Fortunately, a few manuscripts escaped; and among them are the *Bruce Codex*, now carefully treasured in the Bodleian Library, Oxford, and the *Berlin Codex*, in Berlin.

[1] This reference to the vacuity of space is to be taken figuratively only; for space, although apparently vacuous in the eyes of men, is actually the pleroma, or fullness, of all things, and the womb whence they come forth from latency, or abstractness, into the concrete, visible Universe.

[2] That Light, innate in every living thing, shines neither in nor from any place, for it is transcendent over place (or spatial differentiation), as over time; it shines only in the secret sanctuary of the aspirant's heart. Nor is there, as the next aphorism teaches, any *thing* that shines.

[3] This passage may be otherwise rendered: 'One's own mind is transparent, colourless (i.e. without *sangsāric* characteristics).

[4] All things which are born, or come into existence, being *sangsāric*, are transitory, illusory, unreal. Only the Thatness, transcendent over form, birth, being, existence, is non-*sangsāric*.

[5] Likewise, the Real, the True, the Thatness, knows no shaping, limitation

Not having known birth, it knows not death.[1] Wondrous is this.

Although it is Total Reality, there is no perceiver of it.[2] Wondrous is this.

Although wandering in the *Sangsāra*, it remains undefiled by evil. Wondrous is this.

Although seeing the Buddha, it remains unallied to good.[3] Wondrous is this.

Although possessed by all beings, it is not recognized.[4] Wondrous is this.

Those not knowing the fruit of this *yoga* seek other fruit.[5] Wondrous is this.

conditionality, creation. As the Unconditioned or Non-Created, Mind or Wisdom is simple, primordial, natural, but not of Nature, being non-*sangsāric* and beyond Nature. That which can be generated, formed, created, can also be dissipated, dispersed, destroyed; only that which is beyond generation, form, and creation, can be transcendent over them. Thus the Thatness, or Natural Wisdom, being superior to existence, is the Non-Existent At-one-ment of All Existences.

[1] Whatever manifests itself in time, or comes into *sangsāric* existence through being shaped or born, must inevitably go out of manifestation in time, or, in other words, suffer dissolution and death. The Real, the That-ness, must therefore be transcendent over both birth and death, as over all other dualities.

[2] There can be no percipient of Reality, for percipiency implies a doc-trine of 'soul', or of an eternally individualized *sangsāric* entity. The One Mind cannot see itself, for it is not a self, or a thing, or an object of perception; it can only know that it is. Its nature is to know, not to be known.

[3] These two aphorisms express the doctrine that good and evil are merely a pair of *sangsāric* opposites, a duality, which, like all dualities, is in at-one-ment in the True State. (See General Introduction, pp. 35–57, where the theory of good and evil is discussed.)

[4] In the words of Plotinus, 'The One is not separated from other things, nor is It in them: there is nothing that possesseth the One; on the contrary, it is the One that possesseth all' (v. v. 9).

[5] 'Fruit' (Text: *ḥbras-bu*; pron. *dra-bu*) in this context, as elsewhere throughout this treatise, is a technical term, implying the *yogic* result of the successful application of this *yoga* concerning the knowing of mind. Being ignorant of the wondrous fruit thus obtainable, the unenlightened seek elsewhere than within themselves for spiritual guidance, as the next aphorism indicates. Sarat Chandra Dās (*Tibetan–English Dictionary*, Cal-cutta, 1902, p. 929) defines *ḥbras-bu* as being the fruit or reward resulting from passing successively through the three stages of ascetic meditation, and as the results of *karma*. There are four distinguishable 'fruits' of pro-gressive perfection: (1) the ability to enter the stream of progressive per-fection, which conveys one from *sangsāric* Ignorance to *Nirvāṇic* Wisdom; (2) the exhaustion of all *karmic* need of rebirth save the final rebirth in this

Although the Clear Light of Reality shines within one's own mind, the multitude look for it elsewhere. Wondrous is this.

[*THE FOURFOLD GREAT PATH*]

All hail to this Wisdom here set forth, concerning the invisible, immaculate Mind!

This teaching is the most excellent of teachings.

This meditation, devoid of mental concentration, all-embracing, free from every imperfection, is the most excellent of meditations.

This practice concerning the Uncreated State, when rightly comprehended, is the most excellent of practices.

This fruit of the *yoga* of the Eternally Unsought, naturally produced, is the most excellent of fruits.

Herewith we have accurately revealed the Fourfold Great Path.[1]

This teaching without error, this Great Path, is of the Clear Wisdom here set forth, which, being clear and unerring, is called the Path.

This meditation upon this unerring Great Path, is of the Clear Wisdom here set forth, which, being clear and unerring, is called the Path.

This practice relating to this unerring Great Path is of the Clear Wisdom here set forth, which, being clear and unerring, is called the Path.

The fruit of this unerring Great Path is of the Clear Wisdom here set forth, which, being clear and unerring, is called the Path.[2]

world, preparatory to entrance into *Nirvāṇa*; (3) the experiencing of this final birth; (4) the supramundane state of the *arhant*, or saint, who has conquered Ignorance. The Tibetan canonical *Kanjur* describes five classes of 'fruits', or results: (1) the 'fruit' born of mental, moral, and spiritual education; (2) the 'fruit' not consequent on what men call education; (3) the spiritual precedence attained by a *Pratyeka*, or Non-Teaching, Buddha; (4) the spiritual precedence of a *Bodhisattva*, a candidate for Buddhahood; (5) the final stage of omniscience to which a Buddha attains.

[1] Or the fourfold Mahāyāna. The four preceding aphorisms reveal the four parts of this Great Path of the '*Yoga* of Knowing the Mind', which are (1) the actual teaching, (2) the actual meditation, (3) the actual practice, or practical application, and (4) the actual fruit, or result attained.

[2] These four aphorisms concern the four progressive stages in the '*Yoga*

[*THE GREAT LIGHT*]

This *yoga* also concerns the foundation of the immutable Great Light.

The teaching of this changeless Great Light is of the unique Clear Wisdom here set forth, which, illuminating the Three Times,[1] is called 'The Light'.

The meditation upon this changeless Great Light is of the unique clear Wisdom here set forth, which, illuminating the Three Times, is called 'The Light'.

The practice relating to this changeless Great Light is of the unique Clear Wisdom, here set forth, which, illuminating the Three Times, is called 'The Light'.

The fruit of this changeless Great Light is of the unique Clear Wisdom here set forth, which, illuminating the Three Times, is called 'The Light'.[2]

---

of Knowing the Mind', which are common to all *yogas*. The teaching, or the sowing of the seed of Truth, is the first stage; the meditation, or the intellectual comprehension of the teaching, is the second; the practice, or the practical application of the teaching, is the third; and the fruit, or the harvest born of the seed sown by the teaching, watered by the meditation and cultivated by the practice, is the fourth. What appears to the occidental as redundancy of expression, or unnecessary repetition, in these and the aphorisms which immediately follow, appears to the oriental as poetical emphasis; and this literary style, which is typically oriental, is found in the scriptures of all Schools of Buddhism, being particularly characteristic of the Pāli Canon of the Southern School. In ancient times, when all sacred and *yogic* teachings were commonly conveyed orally, this repetitive style of expression was adopted in order to ameliorate, as it did, the task of memorizing the words of the Teachers. Then, in later times, when the teachings were committed to writing and crystallized into canons and orthodox treatises at the dictation of those in whose memory the teachings were preserved, the old repetitive style was retained unchanged. As an instance of the repetitive style in occidental religious literature, one may take the 'Hail Mary' of the Roman Catholic Church.

[1] This phrase may be otherwise rendered: 'being explanatory [or illuminative] of the Three Times'—which are the past, the present, and the future.

[2] This epitomized *yoga* of the Light consists of four stages of perfection in devotion: (1) the initial glimpsing of the Light (the Divine Wisdom concerning Reality); (2) the progressive increase in the perception of the Light; (3) the comprehension of the essentiality of the Light, or of Truth; (4) the power to prolong meditation indefinitely and so enter into *samādhi*.

[*THE DOCTRINE OF THE THREE TIMES*]

The essence of the doctrine concerning the Three Times in at-one-ment will now be expounded.

The *yoga* concerning past and future not being practised, memory of the past remains latent.[1]

The future, not being welcomed, is completely severed by the mind from the present.

The present, not being fixable, remains in the state of the Voidness.[2]

[*THE* YOGA *OF THE* NIRVĀṆIC *PATH*]

There being no thing upon which to meditate, no meditation is there whatsoever.

There being no thing to go astray, no going astray is there, if one be guided by memory.[3]

Without meditating, without going astray, look into the True State, wherein self-cognition, self-knowledge, self-illumination shine resplendently. These, so shining, are called 'The *Bodhisattvic* Mind'.[4]

---

[1] Or, literally, 'is relinquished'.

[2] As has been set forth above, on pp. 7–9, 210[3], mind, in its true nature, takes no cognizance of *sangsāric* time, and is, therefore, as timeless as it is conditionless. By not practising the *yoga* of introspection whereby, as in modern psycho-analysis, all memories of past experiences are recoverable when brought under the purview of the present, latent memories remain latent, the past remains separated from the present. By not welcoming the future, or by ignorantly regarding it as not being realizable in the present, it is hidden, or cut off, from the present. And the present, being *sangsārically* unstable, is perceived by man as a constant flux of instability, or as an ever-moving point separating past from future. The present, and its two companion *sangsāric* concepts, the past and the future, are, in the primordial, unmodified, non-created state of the Voidness, realized by the master of this *yoga* to be homogeneous, or undifferentiated timelessness. To realize time *per se* is to realize the unpredicable at-one-ment of the Three Times.

[3] For countless aeons the microcosmic mind has been wandering in the *Sangsāra* and experiencing existence. Therefore, if the memories of the past be recovered by successful application of the *yoga* of introspection, they will be found to constitute invaluable stores of Wisdom, born of experiences during other ages and lifetimes when one had entered upon and trodden the Path, and adequate to guide and prevent one from going astray now.

[4] 'The *Bodhisattvic* Mind' is a symbolic term signifying the supernormally enlightened mind of one who, being a candidate for the complete enlightenment of Buddhahood, had taken the vow of a *Bodhisattva* ('Enlightened

In the Realm of Wisdom, transcendent over all meditation, naturally illuminative, where there is no going astray, the vacuous concepts,[1] the self-liberation, and the primordial Voidness are of the *Dharma-Kāya*.

Without realization of this, the Goal of the *Nirvāṇic* Path is unattainable.

Simultaneously with its realization the *Vajra-Sattva* state is realized.[2]

These teachings are exhaustive of all knowledge,[3] exceedingly deep, and immeasurable.

Although they are to be contemplated in a variety of ways, to this Mind of self-cognition and self-originated Wisdom,

Being'), not to relinquish *sangsāric* existence, by entering into *Nirvāṇa*, until all Ignorance has been transmuted into Divine Wisdom. In language which is astonishingly similar, Plotinus teaches of this same Divine Illumination, which he himself realized and of which he thus has right to speak: 'When one shall see the divine resplendence of virtue within onself; when one shall dwell within oneself wholly; when one shall cease to meet within oneself any obstacle to unity; when nothing foreign any longer altereth, by its admixture, the simplicity of thine inner essence; when within thy whole being thou shall be a veritable light, immeasurable, uncircumscribed, unincreasable, infinite, and entirely incommensurable because transcendent over all measure and quantity; when thou shalt have become such, then, having become sight itself, thou mayst have confidence in thyself, for thou wilt no longer have need of a guide. Thereupon, thou must discern with great care, for only by means of the eye that will then open itself within thee shalt thou be able to perceive the Supreme Beauty. To obtain this vision of the beautiful and of the divineness within, one must begin by rendering oneself beautiful and divine' (I. vi. 9).

[1] All concepts, as our text later teaches, are in their essentiality vacuous. In the True State, as in the Platonic realm of ideas, concepts *per se* are devoid of form or *sangsāric* content. Being of the Voidness, they are, as the unshaped, unformed, non-created, the supra-*sangsāric* unpredicable seed of thought of the Supra-*sangsāric* Mind, whence they are sown throughout space to produce shaped, formed, *sangsāric* universes of illusory appearances.

[2] *Vajra-Sattva* ('Immutable Being'), the *Sambhoga-Kāya* reflex of Akṣhobhya, the Dhyānī Buddha presiding over the Eastern Realm of Pre-eminent Happiness, is a personification of vast esoteric significance in the Mahāyāna. (See *The Tibetan Book of the Dead*, pp. 9[n], 108–10.) Vajra-Sattva is sometimes conceived as being equivalent to the Ādi (or Primordial)-Buddha, and he then symbolizes the *Dharma-Kāya*. Accordingly, realization of this state, when He is in this aspect, is equivalent to the realization of Perfect Buddhahood, or *Nirvāṇa*.

[3] Text: *mthah-drug* (pron. *tha-trug*), literally, 'six directions', namely, the four cardinal points, the zenith and nadir; here taken in a figurative sense as implying completeness, or exhaustion, of all knowledge.

there are no two such things as contemplation and contemplator.

When exhaustively contemplated, these teachings merge in at-one-ment with the scholarly seeker who has sought them,[1] although the seeker himself when sought cannot be found.[2]

Thereupon is attained the goal of the seeking, and also the end of the search itself.

Then, nothing more is there to be sought; nor is there need to seek anything.

This beginningless, vacuous, unconfused Clear Wisdom of self-cognition is the very same as that set forth in the Doctrine of the Great Perfection.[3]

Although there are no two such things as knowing and not knowing, there are profound and innumerable sorts of meditation; and surpassingly excellent it is in the end to know one's mind.[4]

There being no two such things as object of meditation and meditator, if by those who practise or do not practise meditation the meditator of meditation be sought and not found, thereupon the goal of the meditation is reached and also the end of the meditation itself.

There being no two such things as meditation and object of meditation, there is no need to fall under the sway of deeply obscuring Ignorance; for, as the result of meditation upon

---

[1] Literally, 'these teachings seek the scholarly seeker who has sought them', in the sense of their seeking to become one, or in at-one-ment, with the *yogin*, within whose mind they, being Truth or *Dharma*, are innate, awaiting the hour when he shall call them forth to seek and sanctify and awaken him.

[2] This paradoxical phrase implies that the seeker *per se*, the mind in its natural state of the Voidness, has no individualized, personal existence; and that, therefore, the seeker himself, although sought, cannot be found.

[3] See p. 207[3], above.

[4] Here, as above, and again in the aphorisms which are to follow, the language is paradoxical, and should be interpreted in terms of the doctrine of the Voidness. The aphorisms of this section are constructed with reference to the three aspects of treading the Path: (1) meditation, or thorough intellectual comprehension of the teachings after having heard them; (2) practice, or practical application of the teachings; (3) realization, or attaining the fruits, or results, of the practice.

the unmodified quiescence of mind,[1] the non-created Wisdom instantaneously shines forth clearly.[2]

Although there is an innumerable variety of profound practices, to one's mind in its true state they are non-existent; for there are no two such things as existence and non-existence.[3]

There being no two such things as practice and practitioner, if by those who practise or do not practise the practitioner of practice be sought and not found, thereupon the goal of the practice is reached and also the end of the practice itself.

Inasmuch as from eternity there is nothing whatsoever to be practised, there is no need to fall under the sway of errant propensities.[4]

The non-created, self-radiant Wisdom here set forth, being actionless,[5] immaculate, transcendent over acceptance or rejection,[6] is itself the perfect practice.

---

[1] Mind in its natural state may be compared to a calm ocean, unruffled by the least breath of air. Mind in its reflex (or *sangsāric*) aspect may be likened to the same ocean ruffled into waves by wind, the wind being the thought-process, the waves the thoughts.

[2] As similarly expounded in *Tibetan Yoga and Secret Doctrines*, Book II, 'The *Nirvāṇic* Path', p. 119, when the thought-process has been *yogically* inhibited 'There will undoubtedly arise the Simultaneously-born State'.

[3] Inasmuch as 'existence and non-existence' are a duality, existence *per se* and non-existence *per se* are merely meaningless *sangsāric* concepts; and, therefore, cannot be applied either to the practices or to the unpredicable Mind, which, being of the Voidness, of the Thatness, is transcendent over both existence and non-existence. The Absolute Reality can be realized, but it cannot be described by use of words, for words are only symbols representing mundane, or *sangsāric*, concepts. As Ashvaghosha teaches, 'the best human thought of all things is only temporary and is not Truth Absolute'.—*The Awakening of Faith*, Richard's translation (op. cit., p. 28).

[4] As will be seen later, every term of mankind's *sangsārically* conceived languages employed in an effort to lead the neophyte to the discovery of Truth *per se* must be, in the final analysis, rejected. If accepted as being other than *sangsāric*, all dualistic terms, imperfect similes, metaphors and phrases, such as the *guru* must perforce employ in the transmission of these teachings, become the source of error and errant propensities, which fetter the disciple.

[5] Wisdom, or Mind in its native condition, being unmoved by the process of *sangsāric* thought, is the All-Quiescent, the Motionless, the Immutable, the Actionless.

[6] Truth transcends the duality of acceptance and rejection, and is forever unaffected by man's opinion. 'When men consider and realize that the Absolute Mind has no need of thoughts like men's, they will be following the right way to reach the Boundless.'—Ashvaghosha's *The Awakening of Faith*, Richard's translation (op. cit., p. 15).

Although there are no two such things as pure and impure, there is an innumerable variety of fruits of *yoga*, all of which, to one's mind in its True State, are the conscious content of the non-created *Tri-Kāya*.[1]

There being no two such things as action and performer of action, if one seeks the performer of action and no performer of action be found anywhere, thereupon the goal of all fruit-obtaining is reached and also the final consummation itself.

There being no other method whatsoever of obtaining the fruit, there is no need to fall under the sway of the dualities of accepting and rejecting, trusting and distrusting these teachings.

Realization of the self-radiant and self-born Wisdom, as the manifestation of the *Tri-Kāya* in the self-cognizing mind, is the very fruit of attaining the Perfect *Nirvāṇa*.[2]

[*THE EXPLANATION OF THE NAMES GIVEN TO THIS WISDOM*]

This Wisdom delivers one from the eternally transitory Eight Aims.[3]

[1] The *Tri-Kāya*, or Three Divine Bodies, are the three aspects through which the Buddha Essence, the Thatness, manifests Itself. All true *yogas*, when conscientiously practised, assist the *yogin*, in varying degrees, to attain the One Goal; and although their immediate fruits or results *sangsārically* appear to be differentiated, in the *Tri-Kāya*, which is of Truth itself, they are in undifferentiated at-one-ment, because they are its conscious content. Though the rays of the Sun are innumerable and of varying effects, according to environment, receptivity, and conditions of perception, they are of one source and, therefore, ultimately of one homogeneous nature.

[2] Text: *Ye-sangs-rgyas-pa* (pron. *Ye-sang-gay-pa*). In this interesting compound, *Ye* = Eternal, or Beginningless, *Sangs* = Purification, and *Rgyas-pa* = Complete, or Full. Complete Purification (*sangs-rgyas-pa*), a Tibetan term synonymous with *Nirvāṇa*, which is here qualified as Eternal (*Ye*), is, consistently with the implied sense, translatable as 'the Perfect *Nirvāṇa*', in contradistinction to lesser degrees of *Nirvāṇic* enlightenment or of incomplete purification from *sangsāric* Ignorance. *Sangs-rgyas-pa* may also be taken as referring to the Buddha as the completely Purified One, or to Buddhahood as the Completely Purified State (i.e. *Nirvāṇa*). (See page 228[2], following.) There are three states of *Nirvāṇic* enlightenment recognized by the Mahāyāna: (1) conditional, or imperfect, *Nirvāṇa*; (2) Unconditional, or perfect, *Nirvāṇa*; (3) unlocalized, or absolute *Nirvāṇa*, wherein the *sangsāric* limitations of time and space are no longer existent.

[3] Text: *Mthaḥ-brgyad* (pron. *Tha-gay*), 'Eight Limits', or 'Eight Frontiers (or Ends)', with reference to the Eight Worldly Aims, which, taken in

Inasmuch as it does not fall under the sway of any extreme, it is called 'The Middle Path'.

It is called 'Wisdom' because of its unbroken continuity of memory.

Being the essence of the vacuity of mind, it is called 'The Essence of the Buddhas'.

If the significance of these teachings were known by all beings, surpassingly excellent would it be.

Therefore, these teachings are called 'The Means of Attaining the Other Shore of Wisdom [or The Transcendental Wisdom]'.

To Them who have passed away into *Nirvāṇa*, this Mind is both beginningless and endless; therefore is it called 'The Great Symbol'.[1]

Inasmuch as this Mind, by being known and by not being known, becomes the foundation of all the joys of *Nirvāṇa*[2] and of all the sorrows of the *Sangsāra*, it is called 'The All-Foundation'.

four pairs, are: gain and loss, good name and bad name, praise and defamation, happiness and misery. In other words, as already set forth, these teachings, when practised and realized, confer transcendence over all opposites, as over all transitory conditions to which *sangsāric* mind is fettered.

[1] As shown in *Tibetan Yoga and Secret Doctrines*, Book II, the Great Symbol occultly signifies complete spiritual enlightenment, or *Nirvāṇa*, or the realization of Mind in the True State.

[2] As otherwise set forth in *Tibetan Yoga and Secret Doctrines* (pp. 7–9), *Nirvāṇa* is a state beyond, or transcendent over the *Sangsāra*, or over the Realm of Birth, Illness, Old Age, and Death; it is emancipation from conditionedness and transitoriness, from existence as man knows existence. *Nirvāṇa* is not, therefore, as some misinformed writers have assumed, synonymous with total annihilation of being; it is a transcendence over *Māyā*, over Ignorance, over the Realm of Phenomena and of Transitory Appearances, a blowing out, by an act of will, of the flame of sensuous existence, an emergence from a lower into a higher consciousness, a triumph over the *sangsāric* animal mentality, the attaining of the Higher Evolution, of True Beingness. Sarat Chandra Dās (op. cit., p. 978), in referring to *Myan-hdas*, a Tibetan synonym for the Sanskrit term *Nirvāṇa*, quotes the canonical Tibetan *Kah-gyur* (sometimes, but less correctly, written, *Kang-gyur*, and *Kanjur*) as follows: 'The state of *Nirvāṇa* is supreme peace and bliss; it is freedom from illusive thoughts, egotism, and suffering; there is nothing of the three states of the damned, the sensations of heat and cold or hunger and thirst in it. Misery and transient transmigration having been exhausted, the emancipated one works for the good of others and achieves miracles inconceivably great.'

The impatient, ordinary person when dwelling in his fleshly body[1] calls this very clear Wisdom 'common intelligence'.

Regardless of whatever elegant and varied names be given to this Wisdom as the result of thorough study, what Wisdom other than it, as here revealed, can one really desire?

To desire more than this Wisdom is to be like one who seeks an elephant by following its footprints when the elephant itself has been found.

[*THE* YOGA *OF THE THATNESS*]

Quite impossible is it, even though one seek throughout the Three Regions, to find the Buddha[2] elsewhere than in the mind.[3]

Although he that is ignorant of this may seek externally or outside the mind to know himself, how is it possible to find oneself when seeking others rather than oneself?

He that thus seeks to know himself is like a fool giving a

---

[1] Or, literally, 'when dwelling in his stronghold' (or castle), which is the fleshly body.

[2] Text: *Sangs-rgyas* = *Sangs-rgyas-pa*, 'Completely Purified One (or State)', i.e. the Buddha (or Buddhahood). In the Mahāyāna sense, a Buddha is one who has become completely awakened from the slumber of the obscuring ignorance of Truth, i.e. from what in Sanskrit is known as *Avidyā*; or one thoroughly purged of all the *karmic* effects born of the wrong actions arising from *Avidyā*. *Sangs-rgyas* (pron. *Sang-gay*) also signifies 'being liberated from the beginning and by nature full of knowledge' (cf. S. C. Dās, op. cit., p. 1265), as implied by the doctrine of knowing the mind in its nakedness. Buddhahood is not to be realized externally, but internally, as being from beginningless time a natural characteristic of mind; one need not seek outside oneself, for Buddhahood is already innate in one, and only awaits the removal of *avidyā* to shine forth like the Sun when the clouds are dissipated. *Rgyas-pa* (pron. *Gay-pa*) by itself signifies one abounding in understanding, like a Buddha.

[3] This rendering of the aphorism was preferred by the Lāma Karma Sumdhon Paul. His collaborator in the translation of our present treatise, the Lāma Lobzang Mingyur Dorje, preferred the following rendering: 'Quite impossible is it, even though one seeks throughout the Three Regions, to find [or attain] Buddhahood without knowing the mind.' The parallel between this Buddhist teaching and the Christian teaching, of the *Christos* being within, is as remarkable as it is obvious; and lends added support to the contention that in essentialities the teachings of the Anointed One, in their original and Gnostic form, if not in their Church-Council form, are in at-one-ment with those of the Enlightened One.

performance in the midst of a crowd and forgetting who he is and then seeking everywhere to find himself.[1]

This simile also applies to one's erring in other ways.

Unless one knows or sees the natural state of substances [or things] and recognizes the Light in the mind, release from the *Sangsāra* is unattainable.

Unless one sees the Buddha in one's mind, *Nirvāṇa*[2] is obscured.[3]

Although the Wisdom of *Nirvāṇa* and the Ignorance of the *Sangsāra* illusorily appear to be two things, they cannot truly be differentiated.

It is an error to conceive them otherwise than as one.

Erring and non-erring are, intrinsically,[4] also a unity.

By not taking the mind to be naturally a duality, and allowing it, as the primordial consciousness, to abide in its own place, beings attain deliverance.[5]

The error of doing otherwise than this arises not from Ignorance in the mind itself, but from not having sought to know the Thatness.

Seek within thine own self-illuminated, self-originated mind whence, firstly, all such concepts arise, secondly, where they exist, and, lastly, whither they vanish.[6]

[1] Inasmuch as the Buddha-nature is innate in man, he need not seek salvation outside himself. If we search for what we already have, we are, indeed, like this fool. The same Zen-like doctrine was taught by the Mahārshi of Tiruvannamalai in the treatise entitled *Who Am I ?* referred to above.

[2] Text: *Myang-Ḥdas* (pron. *Nyang-day*) = *Mya-ngan las Ḥdas-pa* (pron. *Nya-ngan lay day-pa*) = Skt. *Nirvāṇa*. *Mya-ngan* = 'affliction', 'misery', 'sorrow'; *las* = 'from'; *Ḥdas-pa* = 'to pass from'; and the whole term = 'to pass from (or surmount) sorrow'. This is additional evidence that *Nirvāṇa* does not imply annihilation, but transcendence over the Realm of Sorrow, which is the *Sangsāra*.

[3] Here, again, the Lāma Lobzang Mingyur Dorje suggests an alternative rendering: 'Unless one realizes the Buddhahood [innate] in one's mind, *Nirvāṇa* is obscured.'

[4] Or, in other words, 'in their final *yogic* analysis'.

[5] In the words of Plotinus, 'Then, indeed, hath he attained at-one-ment, containing no difference, neither in regard to himself, nor to other beings' (vi. ix. 11).

[6] The *Yoga* of the Great Symbol (expounded at length in Book II of *Tibetan Yoga and Secret Doctrines*), which propounds a parallel analysis of the arising, existing, and passing away of mental concepts, will here be found very helpful. Concerning this *yoga* of introspection, upon which our

This realization is likened to that of a crow which, although already in possession of a pond, flies off elsewhere to quench its thirst, and finding no other drinking-place returns to the one pond.[1]

Similarly, the radiance which emanates from the One Mind, by emanating from one's own mind, emancipates the mind.

The One Mind, omniscient, vacuous, immaculate, eternally, the Unobscured Voidness, void of quality as the sky, self-originated Wisdom, shining clearly, imperishable, is Itself the Thatness.

The whole visible Universe also symbolizes the One Mind.[2]

present treatise is chiefly based, the late Mahārshi of Tiruvannamalai taught, in language surprisingly parallel to that of our own text, 'it is only when the subtle mind projects itself outwards through the brain and the senses that names and forms of the grosser world come into existence. When the mind lies absorbed in the *Hridaya* [the mind's Spiritual Centre or Source], these names and forms vanish. When the outgoing tendencies of the mind are suppressed and, with all its attention turned on itself alone, the mind is retained within the *Hridaya*, that condition is called introspection, or the subjective vision [Skt. *antarmukha-drishti*]. When the mind emerges from the *Hridaya* and busies itself with the creation of the gross world, that condition may be termed extrospection, or the objective vision [Skt. *bahir-mukha-drishti*]. When the mind resides within the *Hridaya*, the primal thought of ego, or the "I", gradually vanishes and what remains is the Transcendent Self or *Ātman* [the Brāhmanical equivalent to the One Mind of the Mahāyāna]. It is that state, wherein there exists not the slightest trace of the notion "I", which is called Real Vision [Skt. *Swarūpa-drishti*], and, also, Silence [Skt. *Maunam*]. This Silence is spoken of as the Vision of Wisdom [Skt. *Jñāna-drishti*] in Vedānta. Thus quiescence is nothing but that state when mind remains merged in the Self, the *Brahman* [Skt. *Ātma-swarupam*].' (See *Who Am I ?* pp. 6–7, upon which our more clearly expressed version is based.)

    [1] The Mahārshi employed a similar illustration: 'A man wandering in the sun retires to the shade of a tree and enjoys the cool atmosphere there. But after a time he is tempted to go into the hot sun. Again finding the heat unbearable, he returns to the shade. Incessantly he thus moves to and fro, from the shade into the sun and from the sun into the shade. Such a man, we say, is ignorant. A wise man would not quit the shade.' (Cf. *Who Am I ?* p. 12.) In this simile, the wise man is one who, having realized the true nature of mind, goes forth no longer into Ignorance; and the ignorant man is one who, not having attained Wisdom, is still not proof against the hypnotic glamour of appearances, and continually oscillates between the higher and the lower tendencies *karmically* innate within himself. As the *Upanishads* teach, the ignorant go from death to death; or, as the *Bardo Thödol* teaches, like a feather they are tossed about by the Wind of *Karma*.

    [2] As a homogeneous whole, the Universe symbolizes the undivided One Mind.

By knowing the All-Consciousness in one's mind, one knows it to be as void of quality as the sky.

Although the sky may be taken provisionally as an illustration of the unpredicable Thatness, it is only symbolically so.[1]

Inasmuch as the vacuity of all visible things is to be recognized as merely analogous to the apparent vacuity of the sky, devoid of mind, content, and form, the knowing of the mind does not depend on the sky-symbol.[2]

Therefore, not straying from the Path, remain in that very state of the Voidness.

[THE YOGIC SCIENCE OF MENTAL CONCEPTS]

The various concepts, too, being illusory, and none of them real, fade away accordingly.

Thus, for example, everything postulated of the Whole, the *Sangsāra* and *Nirvāṇa*, arises from nothing more than mental concepts.

Changes in one's train of thought[3] [or in one's association of ideas] produce corresponding changes in one's conception of the external world.

Therefore, the various views concerning things are due merely to different mental concepts.[4]

---

[1] As suggested by the aphorism which follows, the sky, although in reality a plenum and not a vacuum, illusorily appears to be vacuous; and only by reason of its apparent vacuousness is it figuratively, or symbolically, employed as an illustration of the vacuity of all visible or perceptible things, and then merely as a means to an end.

[2] The sky-symbol is employed merely to help mankind to discover Truth itself. As Ashvaghosha teaches, the Buddha 'only provisionally makes use of words and definitions to lead all beings, while His real objective is to make them abandon symbolism and directly enter into the true reality [Skt. *tattva*]. Because, if they indulge themselves in reasonings, attach themselves to sophistry, and thus foster their subjective particularization, how could they have the true wisdom [Skt. *tattva-jñāna*] and attain *Nirvāṇa*?' (Cf. Suzuki's translation, op. cit., p. 113.)

[3] Text: *sems-rgyud* (pron. *sem-gyüd*), 'mind-chain', 'mind-connexion (or link)', 'mind-disposition', 'mind-association'; and, accordingly, the 'association of ideas' of occidental psychology.

[4] These aphorisms, and those which follow, having been composed long before the rise of occidental science, tend to weaken the assumption of our own psychologists that oriental thinkers are neither entitled to be called

The six classes of beings respectively conceive ideas in different ways.[1]

The unenlightened externally see the externally-transitory dually.[2]

The various doctrines are seen in accordance with one's own mental concepts.

As a thing is viewed, so it appears.[3]

To see things as a multiplicity, and so to cleave unto separateness, is to err.

psychologists nor is their science psychological. The same oriental psychology of mental concepts is elaborately developed in *The Tibetan Book of the Dead*.

[1] Concerning the six classes of beings, see p. 205[2], above. This, too, is sound psychology; and concerns not only human, but all other beings throughout the various *sangsāric* states of existence. Western psychologists know little enough as yet about man *per se*, less about sub-human creatures, and nothing whatsoever about beings in non-human worlds.

[2] Or, in other words, the unenlightened (literally, 'the heretics') being by heredity and environment fettered to dualism, see good and evil, Heaven and Hell, God and Devil, Wisdom and Ignorance, *Nirvāṇa* and the *Sangsāra* as dualities, incapable of that transcendent at-one-ment of all dualities.

[3] A man in good health sees the world in a manner quite different from one who is ill. Or, again, any given individual will interpret an experience, a book, a work of art, or view an object differently at different times according to the mood in which he or she happens to be. Similarly, the unenlightened, who are the spiritually unfit, guided by delusive *sangsāric* stimuli and thus unable to transcend appearances, view whatever is sensuously perceptible as being real, whereas the enlightened, who are the spiritually fit, view the same phenomena as being unreal. Correlatively, a chemist knows by experimental proof that water is not really what it appears to be, for it is the product of the proportional combination of two gases, oxygen and hydrogen, which are invisible. In other words, the unenlightened look upon the *sangsāra* with what is popularly known as 'a jaundiced eye', whereas the enlightened view it with the clear healthy eye of Wisdom, as an illusion or phantasmagorial dream, which is as hypnotically attractive to the lost travellers in the desert of *sangsāric* existence as a mirage of water is to the camel dying of thirst in the midst of the Sahara. Thus the unreality of appearances is demonstrated by their complete dependence upon ever-changing mental concepts, the concepts being in their turn the products of mind in its *sangsāric* mood, and this mood being due to the mental disorder called illusion or self-deception. The unenlightened are, in fact, the *sangsārically* insane; and the enlightened are those who, having been cured, have transcended the realm in which such insanity is endemic and highly contagious. Viewed in this manner, the '*Yoga* of Knowing the Mind in Its Nakedness' is a transcendental system of psychotherapy, intended to cure mankind of the hallucination that they are immortal 'souls', existing in a valid Universe composed of real worlds, everlasting hells, and eternal heavens.

Now follows the *yoga* of knowing all mental concepts.

The seeing of the Radiance [of this Wisdom or Mind], which shines without being perceived,[1] is Buddhahood.

Mistake not, by not controlling one's thoughts, one errs.

By controlling and understanding the thought-process in one's mind, emancipation is attained automatically.[2]

In general, all things mentally perceived are concepts.

The bodily forms in which the world of appearances is contained are also concepts of mind.[3]

'The quintessence of the six classes of beings' is also a mental concept.[4]

'The happiness of gods in heaven-worlds and of men' is another mental concept.

'The three unhappy states of suffering', too, are concepts of the mind.

'Ignorance, miseries, and the Five Poisons' are, likewise, mental concepts.

'Self-originated Divine Wisdom' is also a concept of the mind.

---

[1] As has been already taught, there is neither any perceiver nor any objectiveness of Reality. Here, as elsewhere, the *Yoga* of the Great Symbol will serve as a very helpful commentary.

[2] This teaching, too, parallels that of the *Yoga* of the Great Symbol. (See *Tibetan Yoga and Secret Doctrines*, p. 139.)

[3] All objective things are born of mental concepts, and, in themselves, or apart from mind, have no reality. As has been shown above (on p. 229[6]), when the *sangsāric* or finite mind is active, objectivity arises; when it ceases its activity, when the thought-process is *yogically* inhibited, objectivity ceases. Of this, Ashvaghosha, in *The Awakening of Faith*, says, ' All phenomena are originally in the mind and have really no outward form; therefore, as there is no form, it is an error to think that anything is there. All phenomena [or phenomenal, or objective, appearances] merely arise from false notions in the mind. If the mind is independent of these false ideas [or concepts], then all phenomena disappear.' (Cf. Richard's translation, op. cit., p. 26.)

[4] Everything *sangsārically* conceivable, whether it be, as here, ' the quintessence of the six classes of beings', or any of the things named in the aphorisms which follow, is merely a concept of the finite mind. The degree of a concept's reality, if any, can be ascertained only by *yogic* introspection, by knowing mind in its natural state. The *Bardo Thödol* text expounds the same psychology, and repeatedly asserts that all deities or spiritual beings seen by the percipient in the after-death state have no real individualized existence any more than have human or other beings or objective appearances. (See *The Tibetan Book of the Dead*, pp. 32–33.)

'The full realization of the passing away into *Nirvāṇa*' is also a concept of mind.

'Misfortune caused by demons and evil spirits'[1] is also a concept of mind.

'Gods and good fortune'[2] are also concepts of mind.

Likewise, the various 'perfections'[3] are mental concepts.

'Unconscious one-pointedness'[4] is also a mental concept.

The colour of any objective thing is also a mental concept.

'The Qualityless and Formless'[5] is also a mental concept.

'The One and the Many in at-one-ment' is also a mental concept.

'Existence and non-existence', as well as 'the Non-Created', are concepts of the mind.

[*THE REALIZATION AND THE GREAT LIBERATION*]

Nothing save mind is conceivable.[6]

[1] Like Jesus and His disciples and the early Christians as a whole, the Tibetans believe that invisible beings, commonly called demons and evil spirits, inflict upon men and beasts many sorts of bodily and mental disorders and other misfortunes. (See *Tibetan Yoga and Secret Doctrines*, pp. 287–9.)

[2] Even as demons and evil spirits are believed to be the authors of certain forms of bad fortune among mankind, so gods are believed to be the authors of certain forms of good fortune.

[3] The various 'perfections' are such as those classified as the Six *Pāramitā* ('Transcendental Virtues'): Charity, Morality, Patience, Industry, Meditation, Wisdom. Four others are sometimes added: Method, Prayer, Fortitude, Foreknowledge. (See L. A. Waddell, op. cit., p. 138.) There are also particular doctrines known as 'perfections', for example, the Doctrine of the Great Perfection of the School of Padma-Sambhava; and our present treatise is a similar doctrine of perfection.

[4] This technical expression is purely *yogic*. It refers to the state of *samādhic* trance, in which there is unconsciousness of the external world of appearances, and profound one-pointedness of mind.

[5] This technical expression refers to the Vòidness.

[6] Or, otherwise rendered, 'There is nothing conceivable that is not mind'. This aphorism is perhaps the most paradoxical and profound of our present treatise; and to comprehend its significance even intellectually requires meditation and careful thinking. Inasmuch as all conceivable things are, in the last analysis, mind, there is nothing other than mind. Every objective thing, the world of appearances as a whole, the *Sangsāra* and *Nirvāṇa*, are, in their essentiality, mind. Apart from mind they are inconceivable, and cease to have even relative, or illusory, existence. So it follows that there is in fact nothing conceivable save mind. As the preceding aphorisms have emphasized, all conceivable terms descriptive of conditions and things are

Mind, when uninhibited, conceives all that comes into existence.[1]

That which comes into existence is like the wave of an ocean.[2]

The state of mind transcendent over all dualities brings Liberation.[3]

no more than symbols of mental concepts. The conditions or things themselves have their illusory being because they are the externalized products
of mind. In the True State, neither the *Sangsāra* nor *Nirvāṇa* are differentiated, for they have no existence *per se*; there is only the Thatness. There
being thus nothing conceivable which is real apart from mind, it may be
helpful to apply to the Mind *per se* some such term as the Ultimate, or Sole,
Concept. In doing so, however, we must remember that this is merely one
more *sangsāric* term, and, as Ashvaghosha would say, is not Truth Absolute.
The finite mind *per se* can never know the Infinite Mind *per se*. Only when
the finite mind is annihilated, is blown out like a flame of a candle by the
breath of Divine Wisdom, and *Nirvāṇa* is realized, can there be true knowing of mind. Here we have reached the frontier of the realm of terms; and
progress beyond it is for the fearless, for those who are prepared to lose their
life that they may find it. Mind (*sems*) in this context must not, however, be
identified with the illusory *sangsāric* aspect of mind, which is, as this *yoga*
emphasizes, merely a reflex of the Supra-mundane Mind, even as the moonlight is a reflex of the Sun's light, and no more real, in itself, than an image
reflected in a mirror. It is in the mundane manifestation of mind that there
arise the mental modifications, or concepts, which, as Patanjali teaches, the
yogin aims to neutralize. The materialist, who denies that there is supra-
mundaneness, knows no consciousness save that centred in the unenlightened
human mind.

[1] The mind's natural function is to think, to visualize, to conceive. This
is true both of the mundane and of the supramundane mind. The Cosmos
is as much the product of the thought of the One Mind, the Great Architect,
as St. Paul's Cathedral in London is the product of the thought of the mind
of Sir Christopher Wren. What a dream is to the dreamer, the world of
appearances is to the mind. Whatever dawns or becomes perceptible in the
Sangsāra has been conceived in the womb of the mind.

[2] When the ocean is undisturbed, it appears in its natural state as a
motionless homogeneous mass of water. When affected by external things,
such as winds and earthquakes, it loses its naturalness; motion is imparted
to it and waves arise on its surface. The ocean in its naturalness, as has been
explained elsewhere (on p. 225[1]), symbolizes mind in its naturalness; the
external things symbolize the thought-process, and the motion and waves
symbolize the products of the thought-process. It is in order to know mind
in its naturalness that the processes of thought, visualization and mental
conception, are to be *yogically* inhibited. It is easier to know the ocean when
it is in its natural condition. Then it is completely tranquil; and, its waters
being pellucid, the *yogin* may look into their depths; the mud and debris
which are poured into it by the floods of rivers of thought are absent. In
this connexion, the *Yoga* of the Great Symbol is of immense assistance to
the student.

[3] This aphorism parallels that previously given on p. 229, above. So long

It matters not what name may carelessly be applied to mind; truly mind is one, and apart from mind there is naught else.

That Unique One Mind is foundationless and rootless.[1]

There is nothing else to be realized.[2]

The Non-Created is the Non-Visible.

By knowing the invisible Voidness and the Clear Light through not seeing them separately—there being no multiplicity in the Voidness—one's own clear mind may be known, yet the Thatness itself is not knowable.[3]

Mind is beyond nature, but is experienced in bodily forms.[4]

The realization of the One Mind constitutes the All-Deliverance.

Without mastery of the mental processes there can be no realization.[5]

as man is fettered to appearances he cannot transcend appearances; he remains bound to the Wheel of Existence and, like a feather tossed about by the wind, goes from death to death incessantly. Emancipation and the attainment of Divine Wisdom are synonymous.

[1] Reality, to be real, must be devoid of foundation or dependence upon something external to itself. Similarly, the One Mind, to be real, must be devoid of root or source or origin.

[2] This parallels the aphorism, 'Nothing save mind is conceivable'; and might be phrased, 'Nothing save mind is realizable'.

[3] Were the Thatness knowable, dualism would be true; for there would then be an ultimate duality, the Thatness and the knower of the Thatness. The Absolute Truth is that the Thatness and the Knower of the Thatness are indistinguishably one; to know the Thatness, the knower must become the Thatness and cease to be the knower, even as one who would know existence must cease to exist.

[4] Even as the rays of the Sun are experienced millions of miles away by beings on the Earth and in conditions unlike those on the Sun, so the microcosmic aspect or radiance of the One Mind is experienced in myriads of bodily forms into which the One Mind, like a Sun, shines.

[5] Before there can be realization of the One Mind in its True State, there must be indomitable control of all the faculties and processes of the finite mind in order to inhibit them at will and thereby to experience the True State. Correlatively, the physical organism as a whole must be *yogically* disciplined. (See *Tibetan Yoga and Secret Doctrines*, Book II.) Plotinus likewise teaches that not until all thought and thinking are transcended can the Thatness be realized: 'If the primordial Principle thought, it would possess an attribute; consequently, instead of occupying the first rank, it would occupy only the second; instead of being One, it would be manifold and would be all the things which it thought; for it would already be manifold even if it limited itself to thinking itself. . . . Inasmuch as that is multiple which thinketh, the principle which is not multiple will not think. And as this Principle is the first, then intelligence and thought are entities

Similarly, although sesamum seed[1] is the source of oil, and milk the source of butter, not until the seed be pressed and the milk churned do the oil and butter appear.

Although sentient beings are of the Buddha essence itself, not until they realize this can they attain *Nirvāṇa*.

Even a cowherd [or an illiterate person] may by realization attain Liberation.[2]

[III. THE CONCLUDING SECTIONS]
[THE GENERAL CONCLUSION]

Though lacking in power of expression, the author has here made a faithful record [of his own *yogic* experiences].

To one who has tasted honey, it is superfluous for those who have not tasted it to offer an explanation of its taste.[3]

Not knowing the One Mind, even *pandits* go astray, despite their cleverness in expounding the many different doctrinal systems.

To give ear to the reports of one who has neither approached nor seen the Buddha[4] even for a moment is like harkening to flying rumours concerning a distant place one has never visited.

Simultaneously with the knowing of the Mind comes release from good and evil.[5]

later than the first. . . . As the Good must be simple, and self-sufficient, it hath no need to think. . . . That which thinketh is not thought, but what possesseth thought. Thus is there duality in what thinketh, but no duality is there in the First' (v. vi. 2–4, 6).

[1] Sesamum seed is one of India's chief sources of edible oil.

[2] The implication here is that literacy, or what we call 'culture', is not essential to realization of the highest spiritual experiences, for even an illiterate cowherd may attain Liberation. If, as assumed and as the colophon states, Padma-Sambhava composed this aphorism, he very probably had in mind as he formulated it his own cowherd pupil, Hūṃ-kāra, who attained such mastery of the occult sciences that he became a *guru* in his own right. (See the Epitome of the Biography, pp. 166–7.)

[3] There is an overabundance of men who are prepared to explain, most elaborately, all things in heaven and in earth without really knowing anything about them. They become *gurus*, collect disciples, and pose as 'Masters of the Far East'. The Christ called them blind leaders of the blind, for they mislead no one save the blind. To one who has himself realized Truth, their explanations of it are quite unnecessary.

[4] Or, in a freer translation, 'the Buddha within'.

[5] Such a release is from all other dualities as well, the duality of good and

If the mind is not known, all practice of good and evil results in nothing more than Heaven, or Hell, or the *Sangsāra*.[1]

As soon as one's mind is known to be of the Wisdom of the Voidness, concepts like good and evil *karma* cease to exist.[2]

Even as in the empty sky there seems to be, but is not, a fountain of water, so in the Voidness is neither good nor evil.[3]

When one's mind is thus known in its nakedness, this Doctrine of Seeing the Mind Naked, this Self-Liberation, is seen to be exceedingly profound.

Seek, therefore, thine own Wisdom within thee.[4]

It is the Vast Deep.[5]

[*THE FINAL GOOD WISHES*]

All hail! this is the Knowing of the Mind, the Seeing of Reality, Self-Liberation.

For the sake of future generations who shall be born during the Age of Darkness,[6] these essential aphorisms, necessarily brief and concise, herein set forth, were written down in accordance with Tantric teachings.[7]

evil being here regarded as the root duality whence all other dualities spring, even the ultimate duality, *Nirvāna* and the *Sangsāra*.

[1] So long as man is fettered to appearances, to dualism, his thoughts and actions result in nothing more than after-death states of heavenly happiness or hellish miseries to be followed repeatedly by return to the human state. Thus he remains bound to the ever-revolving Wheel of the *Sangsāra*.

[2] This aphorism succintly summarizes the *yogic* doctrine of concepts expounded above.

[3] The fountain refers to rain, which has its ultimate source in the Great Waters. Similarly, good and evil seem to be other than they are; they, like all dualities, all concepts of the *sangsāric* mind, are inconceivable apart from their ultimate source in the One Mind. In the Voidness of the One Mind they cease to exist, as do all other dualities; for there, as in the Great Waters, is undifferentiated homogeneity.

[4] This aphorism may be otherwise phrased: 'Seek, therefore, this Wisdom within thine own mind'; or, more literally, 'Therefore, thine own Wisdom, this [knowing of] mind, seek ye'.

[5] Text: *Zab-rgya* (pron. *Zab-gya*): *Zab* = Deep, *gya* = vast. This abbreviated expression may be rendered in fuller form as, 'Deep and vast is Divine Wisdom [or this Doctrine]': or more concisely, 'It is the Vast Deep'.

[6] Text: *snyigs-mahi = snyigs-mahi-dus* (pron. *nyig-mai-dū*), the 'degenerate age of evil' now prevailing: Skt. *Kali-Yuga*, 'Black [or Dark, or Iron] Age'.

[7] Text: *rgyud-lung* (pron. *gyüd-lung*), which may be rendered either as

Although taught during this present epoch, the text of them was hidden away amidst a cache of precious things.[1]

May this Book be read by those blessed devotees of the future.

[*THE* GURU'S *FINAL CHARGE TO THE DISCIPLES*]

Samayā; *gya, gya, gya.*

[Vast, vast, vast is Divine Wisdom.][2]

[*THE COLOPHON*]

These teachings, called 'The Knowing of the Mind in Its Self-Identifying, Self-Realizing, Self-Liberating Reality', were formulated by Padma-Sambhava,[3] the spiritually-endowed Teacher[4] from Urgyān.[5]

'Tantric prophecy' or as 'traditional precept'. We may, therefore, otherwise render the phrase as 'in accordance with Tantric [or traditional] teachings'.

[1] This treatise, like the whole of the *Bardo Thödol* Cycle, was recovered, when the time was ripe, by the *tertöns*, or Tibetan takers-out of hidden texts, all more or less of an occult or esoteric character. (See *The Tibetan Book of the Dead*, pp. 75–77.)

[2] Cf. pp. 202[4], 238[5], along with pp. 15–20 of the General Introduction.

[3] Text: *Pad-ma-ḥbyung-gnas* (pron. *Pe-ma Jūng-në*: Skt. *Padma-Kāra*), the ordinary Tibetan name of the Great Master of the Tantric occult sciences, popularly known outside of Tibet as Padma-Sambhava. As Sarat Chandra Dās, in the *Tibetan–English Dictionary* (Calcutta, 1902, p. 779), has written: 'Throughout Tibet, Padma Jungnas may be asserted to be more popular than Gautama the Buddha; and [where he is known] as *Guru* Padma, Urgyān Padma, and Lopön Hūṃkara, his votaries are full of belief in his present might and powers of assistance.' Among the Great *Guru's* many names there are two others much used by Tibetans: *Guru* Rinpoch'e ('Precious *Guru*') and Urgyān Rinpoch'e ('Precious One of Urgyān'). They also call him simply '*Lo-pön*', the Tibetan equivalent of the Sanskrit '*Guru*', and of the English 'Teacher', or, 'Spiritual Preceptor'. Our Epitome of his Biography gives a number of other names, mostly initiatory.

[4] Text: *mkhan-po* (pron. *khan-po*), a Tibetan appellation suggesting honour and prestige, applicable to a professor employed to teach, or to the head of a monastery, and, in general, to spiritually-endowed men of learning. 'In Tibet, the head of a particular college attached to a monastery, high priests who give vows to the junior or inferior *lāmas*, and professors of sacred literature, are called *mkhan-po*; also learned men, who as such are endowed with spiritual gifts [inherited] from their spiritual ancestors, are called *mkhan-po*. Again, learned men such as are sent to China are also styled *mkhan-po*.' (Cf. S. C. Dās, op. cit., p. 179.)

[5] Text: *O-gyan* (pron. *U-gyān*), ordinarily transliterated into English as Urgyān, the country of Odiyāna, sometimes, but probably incorrectly,

May they not wane until the whole *Sangsāra* is emptied.[1]

[Here the text ends.]

taken to be (as in the Tibetan *Lam-yig*) the modern Gaznee, in Cabul. (See
S. C. Dās, op. cit., p. 1352.)

[1] This is a Mahāyānic technical expression referring to the vow of a
Bodhisattva not to enter into *Nirvāṇa* finally until all sentient beings are
liberated and the whole *Sangsāra* shall thus be emptied of them.

Self-Salvation

'Therefore, O Ānanda, be ye lamps unto yourselves. Be ye a refuge
to yourselves. Betake yourselves to no external refuge. Hold fast to
the Truth as a lamp. Hold fast to the Truth as a refuge. Look not for
refuge to any one besides yourselves.'—The Buddha.

The Book of the Great Decease, ii. 33

(after T. W. Rhys Davids' Translation).

PLATE IX

MAITREYA THE COMING BUDDHA
Described on pages xxvii–xxviii

BOOK III
THE LAST TESTAMENTARY
TEACHINGS OF THE *GURU* PHADAMPA
SANGAY

ACCORDING TO THE LATE LĀMA KAZI
DAWA-SAMDUP'S ENGLISH RENDERING

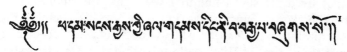

I. THE INTRODUCTION

ACCORDING to the late Lāma Kazi Dawa-Samdup, Phadampa
Sangay (or, as the Lāma otherwise called him, Kamalashīla)
appears to have flourished contemporaneously with Milarepa,
Tibet's Great *Yogī*. This name Kamalashīla is the same as

---

¹ This title, in Tibetan script, photographically reproduced from that of
our manuscript copy of the text, is in the late Lāma Kazi Dawa-Samdup's
own handwriting. Its English rendering is, 'Herein are Contained the Profound Manifold Teachings of Phadampa Sangay'. The late Lāma preferred
as an English title that which is placed here at the head of this Book,
because, as the introductory portion of the treatise states, the teachings
were Phadampa Sangay's last testamentary teachings to the people of
Tingri. A xylograph version of this work, examined by Lāma Lobzang
Mingyur Dorje, bears the title, 'The One Hundred Essential Teachings of
Phadampa Sangay to the People of Tingri (*Pha-dham-pa Sangs-rgyas kyis
Zhal-gdams Dhing-ri Brgya-rtsa-ma*)'.

A first-draft English translation of our text was made by the late Lāma
Kazi Dawa-Samdup shortly before the Editor became his disciple. Owing to
the passing away of the Lāma, the translation failed to receive the final
revision which he and the Editor had planned for it. When the manuscript
of the translation, accompanied by the original text, recently came into the
Editor's possession, its last page, or pages, were missing. In its entirety the
work appears to have consisted of approximately one hundred stanzas,
most of which are couplets, a few being of three verses. The xylograph text
referred to above consists of 102 stanzas. It is from our incomplete manuscript translation that the seventy-two stanzas herein given, in recension,
were selected. Their serial order corresponds to that of the Tibetan text, the
first being the first and the last the ninety-second therein. The Editor preferred to record the translated aphorisms, in keeping with the poetical
character of the original Tibetan text, in a metrical rather than a prose
form, although in some instances a prose version might have resulted in
greater clarity of expression.

that of the Indian *Bhikṣhu* Kamalashīla, who, like the Great *Guru* Padma-Sambhava, went from India to the Land of the Snowy Ranges and taught the *Dharma*. He is said to have been of the Sva-tantra Mādhyamika School of Buddhism, and the author of a number of treatises which are now extant in the Tibetan canonical commentary called the *Tanjur*. There is also attributed to him a work (*Tarka*) expounding the different philosophical systems of India.[1] A traditional belief, cited by the late Lāma, that Phadampa Sangay (or Kamalashīla) lived for seven hundred years may possibly suggest that Phadampa Sangay was, in the eyes of his disciples, the Kamalashīla of the *Tanjur*, who was alive some three centuries prior to the time of Milarepa (A.D. 1052–1135). Or, otherwise, it may imply that Phadampa Sangay was believed to be a reincarnation of the said Kamalashīla.

Phadampa Sangay is said to have established the Shibyepa (*Shi-byed-pa*) School of Tibetan Tantricism. According to legendary accounts, he paid seven visits to Tibet, and on one occasion was miraculously transported to China. The foundation of the Tingri (or Dingri) Langgor Monastery, near Tingri, a town in Southern Tibet about fifty miles north-east of Lapchi (*Lab-phyi*), the Mount Everest of European geographers, is attributed to him;[2] and it was to the people of Tingri that his final teachings were delivered.

Phadampa Sangay established in Tibet a system of *yoga*, nowadays little known elsewhere, called Chö.[3] His chief disciple was Ma-chik-lap-dön. The Apostolic Succession of the first twelve of the Great *Gurus* of this School is as follows: (1) Dorje Chang, the super-human *Guru*, (2) Padma-Sambhava, (3) Tilopa, (4) Naropa, (5) Jam-yang-ma-way Seng-ge, (6) Kha-do Sukha Siddha, (7) Thok-me, (8) Nāgārjuna, (9) Ārya Devā, (10) Saraha, (11) Birūpa, and (12) Phadampa Sangay.

Inasmuch as Phadampa Sangay's *yogic* system parallels that of Padma-Sambhava, the first of the human Apostolic *Gurus* of the Chö School, an epitome of it is here presented

---

[1] Cf. L. A. Waddell, op. cit., p. 31.   [2] Cf. S. C. Dās, op. cit., p. 815.
[3] Tib. *Gchod* (or *Spyod*): pron. Chö.

to serve as an independent commentary, derived from Tibetan sources, on the ' *Yoga* of Knowing the Mind in Its Nakedness' expounded above in Book II.

The Introduction as contained in the text itself represents the *guru* as being near the time of his passing beyond sorrow, and these teachings, which he uttered extemporaneously, as being his last. Its translation is as follows:

'May blessings rest upon this [Book]!

'Dhampa Tsharchhen [the disciple] approached Phadampa Sangay [the *guru*] and supplicatingly said, "O Reverend Phadampa, thou thyself art growing old and going on from bliss to bliss, but what are we ourselves to do, or to whom can we look for protection and guidance?"

'The *guru* was overwhelmed with sadness; and his voice was broken with weeping as he gave utterance to the following verses, which were his last testamentary teachings to the people of Tingri.'[1]

II. THE *GURU'S* TEACHINGS

'To give oneself, body, speech, and heart, to the cause of Holy Truth,
Is the best and highest occupation, O ye Tingri folk.

'Wealth and riches are illusory, loaned for the moment's use;
Show not over-fondness for them, neither hoard them, Tingri folk.

'One's kindred are alluring visions, glamorous mirages;
Break the tie, sever the knot of sentiment, O Tingri folk.

[1] After the manner of Milarepa, who delivered his teachings in songs and hymns, Phadampa Sangay sings these precepts. In Tibet, and commonly throughout India and the Orient, poetry is still considered to be the most appropriate literary vehicle for the expounding and recording of religious lore, as it was in the culturally golden days when the Ancient Mysteries and the Greek drama flourished. But, in the Occident, poetry has become unfashionable, and the use of language, both in literature and everyday life, is controlled by a utilitarian commercialism. As in the United States of America, where the ears of the many no longer hear the ever-present music of Nature, even the majestic sonorousness of the language of the Authorized Version of the Bible has ceased to be in popular favour, and Bibles called 'modern', in unmusical vulgar English, have appeared in many versions.

'Fatherland and homes are transient, even as a nomads' camp;

Let not fondness bind you to them; renounce all things, O Tingri folk.

'Even on one's birthday morning, omens of one's death appear;

Ever be alert and watchful; waste no time, O Tingri folk.

'One-pointedly devote yourselves to the Sacred *Dharma* Path;

It shall be, in the hour of death, your Guide and Boat, O Tingri folk.

'Infallible is *karmic* law, ever impartial, just, and sure;

Abstain from even the smallest wrongful act, O ye Tingri folk.

'In a dream-state are all actions, however righteous they may seem;

Transcend deeds, and seek ye knowledge of the Real, O Tingri folk.[1]

'Ever transient is this world of ours; all things change and pass away;

For a distant journey even now prepare, O Tingri folk.

'The rhinoceros, deep in a jungle, thinketh he's immune from harm;

But look, the jungle is afire! is he safe now, Tingri folk?[2]

'Over the sea of birth and illness, age and death there is no bridge;

Build even now the Vessel that can cross it, O ye Tingri folk.

'Narrow is the ambuscade of birth and death and the dread *Bardo*;

[1] All *sangsāric* states of consciousness are to be regarded as being illusory dream-states; and, therefore, even though one is performing actions in what men call the waking-state, the actions are as unreal as are actions performed in what men call the dream-state. Equally illusory are all *sangsāric* states of after-death consciousness. The Great Liberation is dependent upon transcending the *Sangsāra* and becoming a Fully-Awakened One, as was the Buddha. The True State, the Real, is the State of Quiescence, wherein there are no *sangsāric* thoughts or actions.

[2] The jungle is the jungle of worldliness, aflame with the fires of lust, hatred, and Ignorance, where man, like the rhinoceros, thinks himself immune from harm.

The Five Passions,[1] like armed bandits, oft waylay one on the
    Path:
Seek the sacred *Guru*; he'll conduct you safely, Tingri folk.[2]

'Once when found, the sacred *Guru* never afterward is lost;
Visualize him overhead,[3] and worship him, O Tingri folk.

'Should the *Guru* will to do so, he can reach one anywhere;[4]
Firmly fix your faith and reverence on your *Guru*, Tingri folk.

'He that hath the most of money may have most of avarice;
Impartially, to every one, give ye alms, O Tingri folk.

'He that hath the most of power may have most of evil deeds;
Hanker not for worldly power, O ye folk of Tingri land.

'Hesitate not, neither tarry, lest ye fail to gain the Goal;
Be brave of heart and of fixed mind, even now, O Tingri folk.

'None can tell when Death, that grim and spectral enemy,
    will come;
Even now make preparations for his coming, Tingri folk.

'None can help one on the morrow after Death hath cut one
    off;
Hasten onward, ever goalward; win the Race, O Tingri folk.

'Surely, like the shades of evening slowly merging into night,
Grim Death, pausing not a moment, cometh nearer hour by
    hour;
Even now prepare the means to baffle him, O Tingri folk.

'Fair are the flowers in summer, then they fade and die in
    autumn;
Likewise doth this transient body bloom and pass, O Tingri
    folk.

---

[1] The Five Passions are hatred, pride, lust, jealousy, and stupidity.

[2] In Tibet, and in India, it is generally believed that a competent *guru*
can direct the spiritual progress of a disciple not only through the human
state but also through any of the after-death states.

[3] As in other texts of our Tibetan Series, and especially in *Tibetan Yoga
and Secret Doctrines* (pp. 262 ff.), the *Guru* when meditated upon is to be
visualized as seated in *yogic* posture above the crown of the disciple's head.

[4] The *Guru*, here impersonally referred to, is the *Guru* Phadampa
Sangay, who teaches of the ability of a truly great *Guru* to respond, telepathically and psychically, to a call for spiritual aid and guidance by a
disciple anywhere, distance being no barrier.

'Glorious is this human body when illumined by life's light;
Fearful, like the demon hosts, is the sight of it when dead;
Perfidious its allurements ever are, O Tingri folk.

'Men meet in a mart, and then, when all their trading's done,
    they part;
So from kindred and from friends shall ye be parted, Tingri
    folk.

'Know for certain that Illusion's shaky building will fall
    down;
Even now prepare efficient safeguards, O ye Tingri folk.[1]

'The Eagle of the Mind is sure to take its flight with wings
    spread free;
Train yourselves to fly as freely, even now, O Tingri folk.[2]

'All the beings of the Six Realms have been our loving parents;
Meditate with loving-kindness towards each one, O Tingri
    folk.[3]

'Harmful foes inciting wrong thoughts are illusions karma-
    wrought;
Thoughts of vengeance, harm, and hatred cast away, O Tingri
    folk.[4]

---

[1] The shaky building is the precarious human body. In the hour of Full Enlightenment, the Buddha proclaimed that Illusion would never build the house for Him again.

[2] This yogic training, to fly as freely before death as the Eagle of the Mind does when the fleshly body dies, is in the practice of projecting the 'astral' body, set forth in Tibetan Yoga and Secret Doctrines, pp. 246–76.

[3] During the course of the infinite evolutionary outpourings of life, every living creature in every state of existence has been, at some time or another, a loving parent to every other sentient being. All living things, being ultimately one, are entirely interdependent in their relationships; and, when this is realized, the yogin ceases to have hatred for any, no matter how harmful or inimical they may illusorily appear to be and are karmically. Nor will he do harm to the least of them. This, then, is the yogic science of harmlessness (Skt. ahimsa). (Cf. Tibetan Yoga and Secret Doctrines, p. 77².)

[4] This teaching supplements that of the preceding stanza. Foes are the outcome of one's own actions. It is, therefore, folly to rebel against enemies. The right course to pursue is to transmute enemies into friends, by the all-conquering power of divine love. As the Buddha teaches, the more there is of hatred from others, the more should there be of love from the hated. Until mankind practise such wisdom as that set forth in the Sermon on the Mount, they will, by returning hatred for hatred rather than by returning love for hatred, continue to be fettered to Ignorance, and incessantly sow and harvest hatred, revenge, unbrotherliness, and war.

'Pilgrimage and doing reverence purge the body of its faults;
Worldly business put aside; it is never finished, Tingri folk.

'Chanting of the prayers of refuge purgeth foulness from
the tongue;
Waste no time in foolish talking; chant your prayers, O
Tingri folk.

'Humble faith and pure devotion purge the mind of wrongful
thoughts;
Meditate the gracious *guru* overhead, O Tingri folk.

'Bones and flesh, though born together, in the end must
separate;
Think not your life a lasting good; soon it endeth, Tingri folk.

'Seek the True State, firm and stable, of the Pure Mind; hold
it fast;
That is forever the Enduring, and the Changeless, Tingri folk.

'Grasp the Mind, the holy treasure, best of riches of man's
life;
That is the only lasting treasure, O ye folk of Tingri land.

'Seek and enjoy the sacred elixir of meditation;
Once *samādhi* hath been tasted, hunger endeth, Tingri folk.

'Drink ye deeply of the nectar of the Stream of Consciousness;
'Tis perennial, thirst assuaging, cool and pure, O Tingri folk.

'Seek as your son the ever fair, immortal Child of Wisdom;
That is the best and noblest offspring, never dying, Tingri
folk.

'Brandish the Spear of Reason aloft in the Voidness of space;
Aspiration hath no frontier, nor obstruction, Tingri folk.

'Keep alert the Unrestricted, as a guard against distraction;
Be calm of mind, but never slothful, O ye folk of Tingri land.

'Draw strength from the Unobstructed; let the Stream flow
naturally;
No suppression, no indifference, should there be, O Tingri
folk.[1]

[1] In other words, the *yogin* is warned against forcible suppression of

'Seek in your minds the Bodies that are fourfold and inseparable;
Neither hoping, neither fearing for results, O Tingri folk.[1]

'The *Sangsāra* and *Nirvāṇa* have their source in the One
Mind;
But that Mind itself hath neither form nor substance, Tingri
folk.

'Likes and dislikes leave no traces, like the flight of birds
through air;
Cling not to experiences; ever changing are they, Tingri folk.[2]

'Unborn Truth, the *Dharma-Kāya*, like the Orb that giveth
day,
Waxeth not nor ever waneth in its radiance, Tingri folk.[3]

'Rebellious thoughts are a house abandoned wherein robbers
prowl;
Hidden gold they seek within it, but they find none, Tingri
folk.[4]

undesirable or lower tendencies, passions, or thoughts. They are to be
analysed in a psycho-analytical manner in order that their origin and characteristics may be thoroughly understood. Then, when their unsatisfactory
and illusory nature is comprehended, but not before, the *yogin* is to transmute and transcend them. It is not by fearing, or trying to run away from,
an evil that one progresses, but by facing it boldly and conquering it. Nor
is one to go to the other extreme of weakly giving way to it, or of being
indifferent to it. As set forth in the *Yoga* of the Great Symbol, there are
various progressive steps in controlling, and, finally, in inhibiting the
thought-process. One of them consists in allowing thoughts to flow naturally;
thereby, little by little, the *yogin* attains psychic strength. (See *Tibetan Yoga
and Secret Doctrines*, pp. 129–30.)

[1] The fourfold Bodies which are to be realized by the 'Yoga of Knowing the Mind in Its Nakedness' as being an inseparable unity, are the three
Divine Bodies, the *Tri-Kāya*, and the illusory human body of the *yogin*.
There should never be hopes and fears concerning *yogic* success; for the
result is inevitable if the practice be right.

[2] Strictly speaking, likes and dislikes are *karmically* traceable, although,
practically speaking, they are, for the neophyte, as trackless or untraceable
as the airpaths of birds. Since, as this stanza implies, they are the results of
actions, or experiences, the *yogin* is advised not to cling to or hanker after
worldly experiences or sensuousness.

[3] The Truth, the *Dharma-Kāya*, the Thatness, is said to be the Unborn,
the Unshaped, the Unbecome; that which is born, shaped, and become, is
the Illusory, the *Sangsāric*.

[4] This teaching is similar to that concerning enemies. Rebellious thoughts
must not be fostered; they are as empty of good as the deserted house is
empty of gold.

'Sensuousness is ever-fleeting, like the ripples on a pond;
Seek ye not the ever-fleeting; 'tis delusive, Tingri folk.

'Though desires remembered charm one, as a rainbow's
colours do,
No need is there to cling to them; show not weakness,
Tingri folk.

'Bright and effulgent is the Mover, like the Sun when free
from clouds;
In your own mind, [in its darkness], place no trust, O Tingri
folk.[1]

'Like the zephyr is the Free Mind, unattached to any
thought;[2]
For no object have attachment; transcend weakness, Tingri
folk.

'The seeing of Reality, like a dream by one that's dumb,
Cannot be described in language to another, Tingri folk.[3]

'Blissful is the dawn of Wisdom, like the virgin's wedding
night;
Till experienced none can know it as it is, O Tingri folk.

'Forms objective and the Voidness, in their essence, know as
one;
Without circumference, and without centre are they, Tingri
folk.

'Uncontrolled thoughts, like the gazings of a belle into her
mirror,
Lead not to spiritual insight; know this truth, O Tingri folk.

'Like the frame and mounts of a violin are illusive bliss and
pain;

[1] The 'Mover' appears to be synonymous with the One Mind, as the
source of motion and of all *sangsāric* things. Its brightness and effulgence
are contrasted with the darkness of the unenlightened microcosmic mind.
[2] The 'Free Mind', or Mind in its True State, is calm yet unimpeded,
like a zephyr or gentle breeze, and transcendent over the thought-process.
[3] It is only by realization that the indescribable, unpredicable Thatness
can be known; it cannot be described in any language, for all languages are
entirely dependent upon *sangsāric* concepts born of *sangsāric* experiences.

From the primary come the secondary causes, Tingri folk.

'All creation, within and without, is contained in one's own
  mind,
Like the water in the ice; seek to know this truly, Tingri folk.

'The erring Wheel of Ignorance, like the moisture in a
  meadow,
Never can be checked, though one trieth every means, O
  Tingri folk.[2]

'This human life, endowed and free, is indeed the greatest
  boon;
Piteous are they who waste it aimlessly, O Tingri folk.

'Like the magic *Chintāmani* is the Great Path of the Truth,
Hard indeed to find, though sought for everywhere, O Tingri
  folk.[3]

'Life-maintaining food and raiment in some manner will be
  found;
So devote yourselves, most earnestly, to the *Dharma*, Tingri
  folk.[4]

---

[1] Both bliss and pain are the results of primary causes; they are an
illusory duality. The one is inconceivable apart from the other, even as is
good apart from evil. From the frame and mounts of a violin as the primary
causes are produced as secondary causes harmonious sounds; but, as the
Mahāyāna teaches, no sound is other than illusory.

[2] In spite of the doctrine that eventually, in the course of inconceivable
aeons, all sentient beings will transcend Ignorance, one creation period
meanwhile succeeds another, apparently interminably; and, from this
practical viewpoint, there is no stopping the erring Wheel of Ignorance.
The few attain deliverance from it; the many remain bound to it, and so
pass from one state of existence to another incessantly, meeting death after
death in this world and in other worlds. Foolish it is to count upon salvation
by stoppage of the Wheel; one must save oneself by one's own efforts. The
wise tarry not in pleasure-grounds of the senses; they enter the Path and
attain Liberation.

[3] The Great Path, the Mahāyāna, leads to the Great Liberation. Like the
magic wish-granting gem, known in Sanskrit as the *Chintāmani*, it grants
all right desires and petitions of those who are fortunate enough to have
found it.

[4] This suggests the command of the Christ: 'Take no thought for your
life, what ye shall eat, or what ye shall drink; nor yet for your body, what
ye shall put on' (St. Matthew vi. 25). And, in Chanakya's *Nītidarpana*, or
'Mirror of Morals' (xii. 20), according to the translation by Durga Prashād
(Lahore, 1905), it is said: 'The wise should think of religion only, and not of
bread; for one's livelihood is ordained from one's very birth.'

'Practise hardships and endurance in your youth and in your
    prime;

Difficult to change is habit when one's old, O Tingri folk.[1]

'If when any passion dawneth there be sought the antidote,
Infallibly all the symptoms will be cured, O Tingri folk.[2]

'Evermore bear in your hearts the pain and sorrow of the
    world.

Faith thereby regaineth vigour; trim your Lamps, O Tingri
    folk.

'Life is transitory, like the morning dewdrops on the grass;
Be not idle, nor give time to worthless works, O Tingri folk.

'Like the sunshine from a clear space twixt the clouds the
    Dharma is:

Know that now there is such Sunshine; use it wisely, Tingri
    folk.

---

[1] It is anthropologically interesting to know that man's experiencing of
life in Tibet as in Europe and the Americas results in the same deductions,
as is here suggested by the *Guru*'s saying, 'Difficult to change is habit when
one's old', and by other universally human sayings elsewhere in the treatise.
This evidence of mankind's mental at-one-ment gives added support to the
thesis set forth in our General Introduction, on pp. 12–14, that the microcosmic minds of men are like single cells in a multicellular organism, symbolized by the macrocosmic One Mind. In observing this self-evident
platitudinousness of a number of the precepts, we should remember that
Phadampa Sangay is not addressing a group of learned *lāmas* in a monastic
college but a group of simple-minded peasants in a Tibetan village, to whom,
as he well knew, the commonplace rather than the philosophically abstruse
deductions from life's experiences make the greatest appeal.

Platitudes when cut and polished become the precious gems of literature.
They are then known as proverbs, elegant sayings, golden precepts,
aphorisms of the *gurus*, and, in Bibles, beatitudes. So viewed, platitudes are
expressive of the very quintessence of mankind's experiences throughout
the ages; they set forth the principles and common denominators of life.
Accordingly, the platitudes of our treatise ought not to be dismissed merely
because they are commonplace. If made the bases for various exercises in
meditation, as the *Guru* intended that they should be, they will be found
productive of much spiritual fruit.

[2] The antidote for passions is Divine Wisdom, which teaches of their
illusory and unsatisfying nature. When the antidote is applied *yogically*,
through knowing the Mind, as taught above in Book II, passions are dominated; they are not to be forcibly suppressed, as is sometimes erroneously
taught, but analysed, understood, and transmuted, and then applied to
higher than mundane ends.

'Though one thinketh joys and sorrows come of causes opposite,
Yet within oneself are found their roots and causes, Tingri folk.

'If excess of faith should lead you to contempt of truth at times,
Meditate *karmic* results in the *Sangsāra*, Tingri folk.

'Associates whose acts are wrong tend to make one's own like theirs;
Keep yourselves detatched from friendships that mislead one, Tingri folk.

'Associates whose acts are right help one on the Virtuous Path;
In the Wise and Holy have unwavering trust, O Tingri folk.

'Delusions born of Ignorance are the root of every ill;
Keep the Knower ever watchful, and controlled, O Tingri folk.

'By neutralizing all the Poisons, ye shall cut the Journey short;
Keep in your hearts the antidote; e'er apply it, Tingri folk.[1]

'Not from effort that's half-hearted cometh Perfect Buddhahood;
Evermore be clad in Wisdom's armour, O ye Tingri folk.

'Propensities long entertained give direction to one's acts;
Deeds that have been done in past time recollect not, Tingri folk.[2]

'If ye fail to grasp a meaning, [to the *Guru*] make ye prayer;
Doubt ye not that understanding then will come, O Tingri folk.'[3]

---

[1] The Poisons are sloth, anger, lust, arrogance, and jealousy; the antidote for sloth is diligence, for anger, love, for lust, self-control, for arrogance, humility, for jealousy, selflessness.

[2] In Chanakya's *Nītidarpana* (xiii. 2), according to Durga Prashād's rendering, above cited, occurs the following parallel maxim: 'Bewail not the dead past, nor think of the future; the wise think of the present only.'

[3] The prayer is to be made either to a superhuman *guru* in a heaven world, such as a Dhyānī Buddha or a *Bodhisattva*, or to a human *guru*, who may be physically far distant. Apparently it is not necessary in Tibet to

III. CONCLUDING THOUGHTS: POWER, CONQUEST, SECURITY

It is by the practical application of such *yoga* of introspection as is set forth in this Book III by Phadampa Sangay, and, more fully, in Books I and II above by Padma-Sambhava, and in the three preceding volumes of this Tibetan Series, that the Journey from the mundane to the supramundane becomes realizable—without dependence upon any *guru*, god, or saviour. The Buddhas do no more than chart the course over which They Themselves have journeyed; salvation is not to be won through the grace and will of some supreme deity, but in virtue of self-directed effort. If man thinks himself to be insignificant and weak and helpless, he will be so; for man is what man thinks. 'All that we are is the result of what we have thought.'[1] When man recognizes that his limitations and bondage are of his own making, automatically he will become universal and free; when he knows that he is Buddha, he will cease to be man, and, mightier than Brahma and Indra, he will be Lord of Lords, God of Gods.

The greatest conqueror is the Conqueror of Self. The dominion of such a One is not over this world alone, but over all worlds and beings, over those who are not yet men, over those who have grown to manhood, and over those who are gods.

It is by looking within, in true oriental manner, not by looking without, that the Highway to Universality and Omnipotence and Freedom is discoverable. The eyes of the mundane see only the mundane, the transitory, the powerless, the insecure, the unreal; the supramundane, the non-transitory, the all-powerful, the all-secure, the real, can be perceived only by the inner vision.

Thus, for as long as the Occident continues to fix its gaze

conduct para-psychological experiments to ascertain if there be telepathy; for telepathy is recognized by all classes of Tibetans, whether learned *lāmas* or unsophisticated peasants, as being a quite ordinary outcome of a disciple's *yogic* training.

[1] The Buddha, in the *Dhammapāda*, i. 1, Irving Babbitt's translation (Oxford University Press, New York and London, 1936), p. 3.

upon appearances, it will suffer disillusionment; the youthful enthusiasm of pioneer epochs, the mature pride born of worldly achievements in architecture, art, science, commerce, government, and then the hopeless despondency of national decadence foreshadowing inevitable fall, will continue to follow each other in an orderly and monotonous sequence, age after age.

Today, in France and all of Europe, as in the United States of America and Soviet Russia, the quest is for Security. But occidental man remains fettered to the evanescent and the insecure. Not until he has grown old enough and wise enough to cast aside his many toys and relinquish desire and ambition and greed will he be prepared to adopt the sole technique which can assure Security. Not until he has grown weary of the Insecure, to which he now so fondly clings, although with an increasing sense of misgiving, will he renounce it. Not until he has ascertained by bitter experience that his utilitarianism, his machines, his animal comforts, his technocracies, his various ideologies and schemes looking to social well-being and a Utopia here on Earth are no more than will-o'-the-wisps of the mundane mind, to lead him farther astray in the morass of sensuous existence, will he transcend the Illusory, and, entering upon the Wisdom-Path, attain the unshakeable and everlasting Security of *Nirvāṇa*.

Here endeth the fourth volume
of the teachings of the
Gurus concerning the
Yoga Path that
leadeth to
the Great
Libera-
tion.

May this Book assist Mankind to transmute Ignorance into Divine Wisdom.

INDEX

Black-type figures indicate the chief references, most of which may be used as a Glossary.

'As long as the sky endureth, so long will there be no end of sentient beings for one to serve; and to every one cometh the opportunity for such service. Till the opportunity come, I exhort each of you to have but the one resolve, namely, to attain Buddhahood for the good of all living things.'

Milarepa, from his last exhortation to his disciples, in *Tibet's Great Yogī Milarepa*, page 271.

BOOKS OF RELATED INTEREST

A STRANGE COUNTRY

Muriel Barbery

A STRANGE COUNTRY

*Translated from the French
by Alison Anderson*

Europa
editions

Europa Editions
214 West 29th Street
New York, N.Y. 10001
www.europaeditions.com
info@europaeditions.com

Copyright © Editions Gallimard, Paris, 2019
First Publication 2020 by Europa Editions

Translation by Alison Anderson
Original title: *Un étrange pays*
Translation copyright 2020 by Europa Editions

Library of Congress Cataloging in Publication Data is available
ISBN 978-1-60945-585-9

Barbery, Muriel
A Strange Country

Book design by Emanuele Ragnisco
www.mekkanografici.com

Cover image: iStock

Prepress by Grafica Punto Print – Rome

Printed in the USA

CONTENTS

For Sébastien
For Gérard, my father

A STRANGE COUNTRY

in the final hour of loving
everything shall be empty
and full of wonder

BOOKS

戦争

WAR

There was a time when a great war, the grandest strategic game ever played, consumed two fraternal worlds.

I would like to tell you the story in the proper way, because it cannot be written in one single book. In fact, mankind and the elves would be more at peace with one another if they knew the four Books.

The four Books came from the four Sources, but they are customarily united in two motifs: murder, on the one hand; and poetry, on the other.

Book I—Those who have never prayed at night shall be denied the understanding of the price of desire—
Book II—Those who mistake force for courage shall be denied the privilege of striding through the realm of fear in peace—
Book III—Those whose eyes have never been burned by beauty shall be denied the right to die in the sun—
Book IV—But those who set conditions on love shall be granted the right to know the boundlessness of misfortune—

Who has time to think about the great Books when war is raging and the living are dying? And yet, their pages blend with the song of the earth and the sky, and can be heard in the very heart of battle.

同盟

ALLIANCE

In these tragic times, a company of elves and humans could hear the winds of dreams and believe in the rebirth of the four Books.

Among them were two young women, a priest, a painter, and a most remarkable elf, although the memory of centuries would not have retained his name—given his minor ancestry—had he not, during this long war, been the constant catalyst of encounters.

What follows is the story of the last alliance between humans and elves.

物語

TALE

However, before we begin, let it be known: we who live under the land of Spain are only responsible for the tale of the West. I know that in the East our people do not reside in the depths of the earth, but on the crest of a mountain, in the North on the shores of a frozen sea, and in the South on a plain inhabited by wild animals.

Who can hear us? We have neither heralds, nor tribunes, nor a face, and we listen to the dead telling us the story we murmur into the ears of the living.

Alliances
1938

PREAMBLE

A t the beginning of this tale, the human world had been at war for six years.

The war was started by a coalition, the Confederation, led by the Italy of Raffaele Santangelo, and which also included, in particular, France and Germany. The rumors of war that had been circulating for several months were swept aside by a large-scale invasion, which flooded the members of the League: Spain, Great Britain, and the countries of northern Europe.

Spain was an unusual case: the king was the League's natural ally, but part of his army, which had long been preparing this betrayal, broke away and allied themselves with the Confederation. At the beginning of the war, the regular Spanish troops loyal to the Crown and the League found themselves surrounded by the renegade generals, and Spain was cut off from her allies.

A remarkable event occurred in 1932, during the first year of the conflict, when an independent civilian resistance was organized in the countries belonging to the Confederation.

Santangelo's intentions were clear right from the start. In reaction to the League's refusal to renegotiate the treaties from the previous war, he set out to redraw Europe's borders by force. In the name of Italian pride and racial purity, he implemented a policy of mass displacement of the peninsula's inhabitants. In 1932, he passed laws on ethnic exclusion that would soon be enshrined in the Italian constitution; by 1938, there were camps all over the Europe of the Confederation.

Alejandro de Yepes was born in the land he was now defending in the snow. Others were fighting for the outcome of the war, but General de Yepes waged war for the tombs and acres of his ancestors, and hardly cared whether the League eventually triumphed or not. He was the native son of a region so poor that its noblemen looked flea-ridden to the rest of Spain; and indeed his father, in his life-time, had been both thoroughly noble and thoroughly poor. People were starving as, from the promontory of the castillo, they admired the most sublime view in all Extremadura and Castile and León combined, because the fortress was situated on the border between the two provinces and with a single ges-ture one could release one's eagles toward Salamanca and Cáceres. Good fortune saw to it that Alejandro would return there after six years of fighting far from home, at a time when Extremadura was becoming pivotal to the major offensive which, it was hoped, would bring an end to the war. What's more, that same good fortune had enabled the young general to come home a hero, for he had displayed a strategic acumen that defied the understanding of his superiors.

Superiors who were very worthy. These men knew how to lead and how to fight and they found it easy to hate an enemy who was even more abject than the ones they had fought in the past. They claimed to serve the League as much as they served Spain, divided as she was by treachery, and they had waged both battles at the same time with the bravery that comes with the conviction of the heart. Surprisingly, most of the officers hailed from rural parts of the country, while the cities had sided primarily with the enemy. It was an army made of men accustomed to handling rifles since childhood, and the harshness of their land had made them rugged and wily in action. They chose to side with the League because they shared an allegiance with their ancestors and with the king, and had no qualms about fighting their turncoat brothers. The fact that they were outnumbered ten to one did not worry them; as such, temerity had been their first mistake: a sense of panache inherited from their fathers had compelled the officers to fight in the front line, until voices—including Alejandro's—insisted they could not send soldiers into battle without leaders. And since those leaders had amply demonstrated their courage, they did without the serenade of honor from then on. No one doubted, anyway, that true honor consists in paying respects to the earth and sky, and that to honor one's dead, one must live.

The Franco-Italian confederation had taken Europe by surprise, putting an unprepared Spain to fire and sword by releasing cartloads of men carelessly sent to die. The generals committed to the League knew that while the best officers had remained loyal to the king, their strength overall was a farce and they would not find salvation in numbers, but through a volley of miracles. However, during the weeks it took the allied forces to regroup, Lieutenant de Yepes accomplished a miracle. When his soldiers joined forces with the friendly troops, they discovered that the subordinate who was the most poorly equipped in men and arms in the entire army was the one who had lost the fewest men and inflicted the greatest losses on the traitors. In those days, there was a remarkable general by the name of Miguel Ybáñez, now deceased, who was serving as army chief of staff. He deliberately promoted valorous young officers at the same time as he disgraced those who did not manifest any tactical gifts and who, moreover, lacked all strategic sense. Proper tactics are the backbone of an officer, strategy is both his lungs and his heart. And since no one, when outnumbered ten to one, can afford to lack either spirit or ardor, Ybáñez wanted strategists, above all.

In Alejandro, he found one of high quality.

During the early days of the conflict, Lieutenant de Yepes was cut off from his command. His hands were free and his line was simple: he had to save on men, time, ammunition, and supplies. The regular troops were more spread out than they were and communication by land was impossible. They were about to run out of supplies and everyone was imagining imminent disaster: pulverized like rats, the isolated units would perish, surrounded by troops that were largely superior in number. Without communications, knowledge of the terrain is an army's only chance of survival. With a heavy heart, Alejandro sent valiant men out as scouts—more than he would have liked—and lost far more than he would have wanted. But enough men came back to give him a clear picture of the theater of operations, something to which the enemy, confident of their strength in numbers, paid only moderate attention. In constant retreat, Alejandro infiltrated wherever he could, like water trickling down a slope among roots and rocks. He sought out the best locations for provisioning and resistance, and harassed his adversary with lightning actions that made it seem he was everywhere at once. In combat, he held back his artillery, and his men came under fire when they were saving their own resources—to such a degree that one day in December, he immobilized the gunners for nearly half an hour. The enemy shells fell like rain and Alejandro's men prayed to the Madre, but when the enemy general, convinced all he had to do now was wipe up a handful of ghosts, launched his infantry on them, the same men who not that long ago had been praying now blessed their lieutenant for saving their fine ammunition from being too hastily deployed. They were spread through the valley in loosely-knit groups, and not as many men perished as the concentrated enemy fire would have liked. In the end, retreating once again to a place where they could withstand a long siege, they inflicted heavy losses on the other side. As day fell, the stunned adversary could not understand why they had not prevailed, and they realized that they had neither won nor lost the battle.

At the request of Alejandro—now promoted to major—Ybáñez appointed a man from the ranks as lieutenant, who would later become a major himself when Alejandro was made general. His name was Jesús Rocamora and, by his own admission, he hailed from the asshole of Spain, a little town in Extremadura lost between two deserted expanses of earth to the southwest of Cáceres. A large lake was the only source of subsistence for the poor wretches in the region, who were fishermen and went to sell their catch on the Portuguese border, which meant that their lives were spent between fishing and an equally exhausting walk beneath the evil summer sun and the biblical cold of winter. There was a priest there who made a similarly meager living, and a mayor who fished all day long. The curse of the times, for a decade now the lake had been shrinking. Prayers and processions did no good: the waters were evaporating and, whether it was the wrath of God or of Mother Nature, the subsequent generations would be reduced to leaving or to perishing. And now, through that irony of fate that transforms suffering into desire, those who once cursed their village came to feel a wrenching attachment to it, and although there was not much to like about their life, they had chosen to die there with the last fish.

"Most men prefer death to change," said Jesús to Alejandro one evening when they were bivouacked on a shady little plateau, musing that they themselves would probably be dead by the next day.

"But you left," said Alejandro.

"It wasn't because I was afraid to die," said Jesús.

"What other reason did you have?"

"It is my fate to know nakedness and to suffer for mankind. It started in the village, and so it must go on in the outside world."

Alejandro de Yepes kept Jesús Rocamora by his side throughout the entire war. This son of hell's fishing grounds was one of the few men to whom he would have entrusted his life without flinching. The other was General Miguel Ybáñez. Chief of staff of the king's army, a little man so bow-legged that people said he'd been born on horseback, he was reputed to be the best horseman in the realm, a rider who leapt rather than climbed into the saddle. From his perch, he would stare down at you with his shining eyes and nothing could matter more than pleasing him. From what fabric is the skill for command cut? Yet in his gaze there was weariness and sadness. Most of the time he listened attentively, made few remarks, and gave his orders as if complimenting a friend, his voice devoid of all military sharpness—in response to which his men went out ready to die for him or for Spain, it was all the same, because the specter of fear had vanished, for a time.

One must imagine what it means to inhabit the province of life and death. It is a strange country and its only strategists are those who speak the language. They are called on to address the living and the dead as if they were all one, and Alejandro was well versed in that idiom. As a child, no matter the path he took, he was irresistibly drawn to the walls of the cemetery at

Yepes. There, among the stones and crosses, he felt he was once again among his people. He did not know how to speak to them, but the peacefulness of the place rustled with words for him. What's more, even when it meant nothing, the music of the dead reached him in a place in his chest that understood, irrespective of words. In these moments of great fulfillment, he saw an intense sparkling in the periphery of his vision, and he knew he was seeing the manifestation of an unknown and powerful spirit.

Ybáñez was also an initiate, and drew the strength therefrom that made him such a singular leader of men. In the month of November of the third year of the war, he came to Yepes to meet Alejandro. The young major had left the North and gone to the castillo not knowing why he had been summoned. A few snow flurries were falling, Ybáñez seemed gloomy, and the conversation was unusual.

"Do you remember what you said the first time we met?" asked Ybáñez. "That the war would last a long time and we would have to track it down behind its successive masks? Everyone who failed to understand this is dead now."

"Others died who were aware of what was at stake," said Alejandro.

"Who will win?" retorted Ybáñez, as if he had been asked. "I've been endlessly harassed, both about the war and about victory. But no one ever asks the right question."

He raised his glass in silence. Despite its wretchedness, the castillo boasted a cellar of perfectly aged wines, vintages once offered to Alejandro's father Juan de Yepes, as well as to his grandfather, his great-grandfather, and so on up the line to the dawn of time. This is what happened. One morning, somewhere in Europe, a man would wake up and know that he had to set out for a certain castle in Extremadura, a place he had never heard of until now. It did not occur to him that this notion was either fantastical or impractical, and not for a moment did the voyager hesitate or doubt when he came to a crossroads. These men were prosperous winemakers whose cellars contained the fruit of their talent, and now they selected wonderful bottles that they would once have reserved for their sons' weddings. They arrived at the gate of the castillo, handed the bottle to the father, the grandfather, or one of Alejandro's ancestors; they were given something to eat and a glass of sherry; then without further ado, after standing for a moment at the top of the tower, they went away again. Back in their own land, every morning they would think of the glass of sherry, the generous bread, the violet ham; the day went on and their servants could see how greatly they were changed. What had happened at the castillo? As far as the counts of Yepes were concerned, nothing differed in any way from the usual customs of their rank, and they were unaware of the strange ballet by which others were lured by their castle. No one was surprised, the event occurred and was forgotten, and Alejandro was the first ever to concern himself with it. But when he inquired, no one knew what to reply, and he spent his childhood feeling like an anomaly within the anomaly of the castillo. When the feeling grew so strong that it caused a pain in his chest, he went to the cemetery and engaged once again in his commerce with the dead.

One must be grateful for this inclination for tombstones, for twenty years earlier, he was in the cemetery on the November day when his entire family perished. Men had attacked the castillo and killed everyone they found. No one knew how many of them there were, how they had come, or how they left. No lookouts—by which we mean the eyes of old women and shepherds—had seen them coming; it was as if they had come out of nowhere and returned there in the same way. Alejandro left the cemetery that day because the strange light tasted of blood, but as he headed back up to the castillo the only traces he saw in the snow were the pawprints of hares and deer. Yet before he even went through the gate into the fortress, he knew. His body urged him to fall to his knees, but he continued on his way, down his path of suffering.

He was ten years old and the only surviving descendant of his clan.

The funerals were remarkable. It was as if all of Extremadura had gathered in Yepes, their numbers swollen by travelers from the past who had managed to reach the village in time. It made for a strange crowd and, anyway, everything was strange that day—the mass, the procession, the burial, and the homily given by a priest cloaked in a wind-ravaged cassock. The wind had begun to blow when the coffins left the castillo, and stopped abruptly with the last word of the funeral oration. And then silence fell all around, until the bells tolled the angelus, and there was a feeling of departing an unknown land—this is what had quietly filled people's hearts all day long, this inner crossing, this aimless wandering along unfamiliar paths, undisturbed by the priest's Latin gibberish or the ridiculous sight of a procession of toothless old folk. Now they awoke as from a long meditation and watched Alejandro walking back up the steep slope to the fortress. Only one man was with him, and the village council was praised for its decision to entrust the child to his wise hands. Everyone knew he would take care of the castillo and treat the orphan well; they were glad that he would initiate him into certain higher things and, above all, they were relieved that they would not have to take charge of the matter themselves.

Luis Álvarez must have been in his fifties and, whether from the stubbornness or the negligence of the gods, was altogether a little man, somewhat bent and very thin. But when he removed his shirt for the hardest tasks, it was to reveal taut and astonishingly vigorous muscles flexing beneath his skin. Similarly, he had an ordinary, unexpressive face, shining with deep blue eyes, and the contrast between the anonymity of his face and the splendor of his gaze summed up everything there was to know about the man. His position was that of steward: he supervised the upkeep of the domain, collected the rent from the tenant farmers, bought and sold wood and kept the ledgers. His soul, on the other hand, made him the guardian of the stars of the castillo. In the evening when they dined in the kitchen of the deserted fortress, Luis spoke with his pupil at length, for this man who was dedicated to serving the powerful and dealing with trivial commerce was in fact a great intellectual and a masterful poet. He had read everything, then reread it, and he wrote the sort of lyrical poetry that only a fervent soul can produce—a poetry of incantations to the sun and murmurs of stars, love, and crosses; of prayers in the night and silent quests. It was in his poetry, during the hours when he wrote it, that he perceived at the edge of his vision the same light Alejandro received from his dead, and he alone, more than anyone, would have been able to answer the boy's questions about pilgrimage. However, he kept his peace.

And so, for eight years, every day at noon, you could see him come down from the fortress in the company of the adolescent and sit at his table at the inn, wearing the same white shirt with an officer's collar and the same light-colored suit, the same worn leather boots and the same wide-brimmed hat—straw in summer and felt when the first frosts arrived, in winter adding one of those long overcoats that shepherds on horseback are known to wear. They would serve him a glass of sherry, and he would stay for an hour while everyone stopped by, asking about his latest poem or the estimated price of cattle. When he was seated he seemed tall because he held himself straight, one leg over the other, one hand on his thigh, elbow propped on the table. He would take a sip intermittently, then wipe his lips with the white napkin folded next to his glass. He seemed enveloped in silence, although he spoke a great deal during these meetings that passed for banal conversation. His elegance was not intimidating; it was elevating, comforting. Next to him, Alejandro sat quietly, and learned the life of poor men.

A lesser-ranked man can hold an entire country together. Blessed are the lands which know the comfort of such a being, without whom they are doomed to languish and die. In fact, everything can be read in two opposite ways; one has only to see grandeur in the place of wretchedness, or ignore the glory that shines through decline. Poverty had not made the place indigent: it evoked a calming fragrance of splendor and dreams, made all the more remarkable by deprivation; and as long as Luis Álvarez was managing the fortress, it was considered a place to be proud of, despite the knowledge that its land was no longer fertile and its walls were crumbling. And so, after the murder of the Yepes family, the steward naturally took over the tasks they had once performed. He presided over the first village council meeting after the tragedy, and later, when people looked back, it appeared to them as a moment of great dignity; in our collapsing world, such memories are almost more precious than life itself. He opened the meeting, then said a few words to honor the dead, and there can be little doubt that these words kept Alejandro from the madness of sorrow and made him a sane man—in particular the final words, which were addressed to him, although Luis refrained from looking in his direction: *the living must tend to the dead.* The child was sitting to the right of his steward, his gaze was feverish, but stiller than a stone. However, after he had heard these words, the feverishness of his eyes flickered out and he wiggled on his chair like any boy his age. Then the steward called the votes in the manner of the ancestors, naming the families and striking with his hammer at each decision. When everything had been examined and voted on, he adjourned the meeting and asked the priest to say the prayer for the dead. As the old priest was stumbling over his words, he continued for him, and at the end the entire council voiced the responses— nevertheless, one should not suppose that Luis Álvarez reigned over the land solely because he respected the organization of its rites: if the steward of the castillo had a natural authority, it was because he had created bonds with everyone, bonds that were rooted in a soil so spiritual that anyone who knew its poetry was born to govern the land. In the end, just after the last *amen*, the women began singing an old song from Extremadura. A song that no one knows anymore today, in a language that no one can translate anymore, but by God, was the music beautiful! It mattered little that no one understood it; it carried a message from stormy skies and a fertile land where the joy of the harvests mingled with the struggle to survive.

It was Luis Álvarez, in the end, who shaped Alejandro's vocation for war. On the eve of his sixteenth year, they were sitting by the fire, and the adolescent was drinking his first wine. Since Juan's death, there had been no visitors to the fortress, but the cellar held a collection of bottles that would last for centuries. Alejandro was finishing his second glass of petrus when Luis recited the poem he had composed that morning.

"I find some of them in my heart," he said. "But this one came from another world."

To the earth and the sky
Live for your dead
And stand vulnerable
Before mankind

That in the final hour
Your noblesse will oblige us

"What determines noblesse?" asked Alejandro, after a moment's silence.

"Courage," replied Luis.

"And what makes courage?" asked Alejandro again.

"Confronting one's fear. For most of us, it is the fear of dying."

"I'm not afraid of dying," said Alejandro. "I'm afraid of being responsible for men and failing them because the devil in me will have triumphed over the guardian."

"Then you must go wherever you can wage that battle."

Two years later, Alejandro left for the military academy. He had neither money nor savoir-faire, which is why he was a mere lieutenant at the beginning of the war; nor did he have a talent for career intrigue. All he wanted was to learn. After the academy, he set about joining units whose leaders had their men's respect—and so he learned, and the day the war broke out, he considered himself ready.

Naturally, he was mistaken.

He learned his lesson from circumstance, then from a simple soldier, during one of the first battles. Alejandro had already noticed this man from the ranks who'd proved to be very efficient at carrying out orders. Something told him that the soldier was from a poor background, but nothing in Jesús Rocamora's behavior invited familiarity or condescension: he was an aristocrat of the sort who are not born in castles, but where noblesse oblige is written in the heart. He was handsome, too, with an open face and sharply-drawn features, shining blue eyes, and lips crafted by a lacemaker's needle. Like Alejandro, he was not tall, but he had a fine bearing, black hair, broad shoulders, and hands that were not like any fisherman's. In addition, he liked to embellish his speech with expressions that would make a hussar blush, then return to the absolute gravity that is the custodian of noble causes.

On the fifth day of the war, Alejandro's troops were caught in a pincer movement; the lieutenant from Yepes was witnessing the moment when his men no longer understood him and, in panic, began to do everything back to front. And then, thanks to one of history's false miracles, Jesús Rocamora was suddenly at his side, begging for an order, gazing at him like a dog at its master.

"We've got to wheel the artillery round on the north flank," cried Alejandro, for whom the appearance of a man ready to listen was a godsend.

Then he looked at him and suddenly realized that Jesús should have been with the third unit, six kilometers from there.

"And retreat through the southern pass?" shouted Jesús in turn.

Alejandro had given those precise instructions earlier, and several times over, but no one had wanted or known how to follow them. Jesús Rocamora, however, saw to it that followed they were. Better still, he did not leave his lieutenant for a second—no sooner had he set things in motion than he came back, the way a dog returns to his master, to wait for the next order, which he already knew. After two hours of this, they found themselves on the summit of an ineffable ridge, where an angel's fart would suffice to either precipitate them into the abyss or show them the pathway down the mountain. Alejandro shouted to Jesús: Go, go, stop asking for orders! Jesús looked at him blankly and Alejandro said again, Go, away with you! So the other man cleared off like a nasty cur and showered his men with orders, no longer even taking the time to return to his superior.

They survived. Then they talked. Every evening they would speak and their acquaintance grew in a brotherly mood that precluded any sense of hierarchy. Then at dawn, lieutenant and soldier would put on their insignia and fight side by side with respect for their ranks. When Alejandro ventured to admit that he would have liked a more enviable status for Jesús, the soldier said: Fishing is the only hell I will ever know on this planet.

It was also Jesús who taught Alejandro his greatest lesson about war, and turned him from a mere tactician into a strategist.

"It'll be a long war," he told his lieutenant, the evening they were bivouacking on the shady little plateau.

"So you don't think we'll end up surrendering fairly soon?" asked Alejandro.

"We are the lords of these lands, we won't lose them as soon as all that. But winning is another matter. It will take time for our leaders to comprehend that while the forms of war may have changed, the essence has remained the same. Once the fronts are stable—vast fronts, sir, the likes of which we've never seen—and the generals see that no one will carry the day any time soon, it will become obvious that everything has been staked upon tactics—outdated tactics at that—but that war is still just what it has always been."

"A duel," said Alejandro.

"A duel to the death," said Jesús. "Tactics can be adapted, but in the end the winner will be whoever is the best strategist."

"And what makes for the best strategist?" asked Alejandro.

"Ideas always triumph over weapons," said Jesús. "Who would entrust an engineer with the keys to paradise? It is the divine part in us that determines our fate. The best strategist is the one who looks death in the eye and reads there that he must not be afraid of losing. And with every war this changes."

"The real lords are the fishermen," said Alejandro with a smile.

And then Jesús told him the story of his moment of revelation.

"I'm the son of a fisherman, but from the moment I set eyes on the lake, at an age when I couldn't even walk or talk yet, I knew I wouldn't become one. After that, I forgot what I knew. When I was a boy, I followed in my father's footsteps. I knew how to set the nets and bring them in, how to mend them, and all the things you need to know for the job. My first fourteen years were spent between ropes and walking, and I didn't want to remember that first sight of the lake. But on the morning of my fifteenth birthday, I went down to the lake. It was a misty dawn, and someone had gone over the landscape with ink; the water was black while the mist created incredible images. That landscape . . . that landscape went straight to the heart. I had a vision of the lake—dried up—and of a great battle, and of the face of a child instantly erased by the face of an old man. Finally, everything disappeared, the mist rose to the sky, and I fell to my knees in tears, because I knew I was going to betray my father and go away. I wept for a long time, until my body was drier than the lake I had seen in my vision, then I stood up and looked one last time at the dark water. In that moment, I felt I had just been entrusted with a burden, but also that this cross to bear would free me from my shame. With the priest, I learned to read and write, and two years later I enlisted."

Surrounded since childhood by the kindness of his elders and the affection of his peers, Alejandro had never known the brotherly friendship of men who have lived through the same conflagration. At the age of eighteen he had seen the army as a place to fulfill his desire for courage, and he experienced solidarity with his fellow soldiers of the sort that comes with the imminence of combat. But he had never yet met anyone whose heart was in tune with his own. When he went back to Yepes during the last year of the war to set up his headquarters in the castillo, he walked up the main street through the village, happy to see people coming up to shake his hand, the old folk embracing him. Outside the fortress, the priest came to meet him with the mayor at his side, leaning on a cane. They were dressed in black, as awkward and gloomy as scarecrows, but their faces lit up, for once, with their pride in the fact that their young lord was one of the great generals of the day. Alejandro felt his heart racing with gratitude and cheer, to be acknowledged and celebrated in this way. Next to him, Major Rocamora was smiling, and the people of Yepes appreciated both his open gaze and his devotion to their general—if, on top of it, Alejandro had known that they rejoiced in his friendship with Jesús because it meant a lord was indebted to a fisherman, his emotion, no doubt, would have increased tenfold.

There they stood, the young general and his young major, at the top of the tower in the castillo, now that the war had been raging for six years, bringing with it all the plagues that every war always brings. They stood expectant at the top of the great tower, like the world holding its breath on the eve of battle, on the summit where the roll of a single pebble will determine victory or surrender.

"It's going to snow," said Jesús.

Alejandro had seen only two Novembers with snow: the one when his family was murdered, twenty years earlier, and the one when Miguel Ybáñez had come to see him in Yepes, three years earlier, in the days when the conflict was spreading farther than anyone would have predicted. After their conversation about the long war, Miguel Ybánez had asked Alejandro to take him to the cemetery. The two men stood by the graves in silence, and after a moment, Alejandro saw the sparkling that was always there. Thick snowflakes began to fall and before long the cemetery was covered in a light powder that glistened in the late afternoon light. When they went away again, Ybáñez seemed lost in luminous, grave thoughts. The next morning, just before his departure, in a dawn of cruel frost, he told Alejandro he was appointing him major general and entrusting him with the leadership of the first army.

Three months later, the general from Yepes learned of the generalissimo's death, and he knew his life would be repeatedly marked by the murder of those who were dearest to him. For Alejandro, the death of Miguel Ybáñez was a personal tragedy, but it was also tragic for the soldier in him: the staff needed men of Ybáñez's fiber, and Alejandro had never met anyone else like him. His thoughts echoed with the words the general had uttered as he passed through the gate to the fortress.

"Meditate as often as you can."

Although he was from Madrid, Ybáñez had told him that he used to spend his childhood summers at his mother's family home, on the slope of a mountain overlooking Granada.

"Through meditation I learned the power of ideas," he said. "What else can you do when you see the sun rising over eternal snows and suddenly the Alhambra is there before you? Someday it will be destroyed, because that is the fate of works of human genius, but the idea behind it will never die. It will be born again elsewhere, in another form of beauty and power, because we receive the idea of it from the dead speaking to us from the sanctuary of their graves."

Pensively gazing into his glass, he added:

"That is why I conceive of the art of war as a meditation in the company of my dead."

Then he fell silent. After a moment, he said one last thing.

"Because ideas alone are not enough, one must also have a mandate. That is the question that no one ever asks me: who do we get it from and to what kingdom does it consign us?"

"We get it from our ancestors," said Alejandro.

"You are thinking about mandates and forgetting the kingdom," replied Miguel. "And yet tomorrow our kingdom will be covered with camps where people will be burned."

I have tried to describe Alejandro de Yepes through the three major figures of his youth, who shared the same aspirations in life. Why are some born to take responsibility for others, so that their lives become nothing but a succession of battles through which they learn to accept their burden? From that moment on, these battles, this burden, make them into guides whom their troops or brothers will follow to the gates of hell. However, this responsibility for other souls does not stop at the threshold to the cemetery, because the dead belong to the people entrusted to these singular men, and the terrible weight of the kingdom of the dead, the burning obligation to respond to the call, is what we refer to as the life of the dead: a silent, incandescent life, more intense and magnificent than any other, and a few individuals among the living have agreed to be its messengers.

Sons! To the earth and the sky!
Sons! Live for your dead!
Brothers! Stand vulnerable before us!
Brothers! Your noblesse will oblige us.

Book of Battles

戦

BATTLE

How did this war differ from the previous ones?

There was the fact that the Western world no longer knew its dead: either because it had grown old and was approaching an end it did not want to see, or because it had reached the limits of its dream and had to construct another one. In any case, it lacked the whispering of the dead, without which none can live honorably—who can call an existence decent if it has not received a mandate?

As for me, right from the start it seemed as if the battle would have to be resolved by radically rewriting the dream of history. Never had murder come closer to triumphing over poetry.

MURDER

The life of Alejandro de Yepes had begun with the murder of his family and continued with that of his protector, and he sensed, correctly, that he would endure other crimes. What he did not know, however, was that long before he came into the world, the source of his own story lay in a distant murder whose protagonists were strangers to him.

Given the fact that it had been committed neither for gain nor for power, but because the murderer had an obscure premonition that his victim had been sent by the devil, this murder occupied an unusual spot in the sequence of major murders, a spot that yielded up the hope of something beneficial.

Can one ever escape from the fatality of murder? Hope and horror—this shall all be told below. There is only fiction, there are only stories. It doesn't matter to me whether I know them in advance.

DARKER THAN NIGHT

Now two hours have gone by and Alejandro de Yepes, from the tower of his castillo, is watching the snow fall in the night. He has just been woken, and he's not sure he understands what's happening.

"How long has the snow been falling?" he asked.

"For two hours," Jesús replied. "In two hours, six feet of snow have fallen."

"Six feet," said Alejandro. "And you say these men arrived without leaving footprints?"

"Our watchmen are positioned so close together that even an ant could not get through. And besides, what sort of man can make his way through this snow? I don't know how they got here but it was not by road."

"From the sky?"

"I don't know. Suddenly there they were in front of us, in the grand hall, and one of the redheads asked to speak to General de Yepes, adding that he was sorry about the snow."

He wiped his hand across his brow.

"I know, sir, when I tell it like this, it all seems so strange. But I would stake my life on it that they are not enemies."

"Where are they now?" asked Alejandro.

"In the cellar. It's what the redhead requested. He seems very well informed, I must say."

They looked at each other for a moment.

"Should I have them brought up?" asked Jesús.

"No," said Alejandro, "I'll go down."

And turning in a circle on himself:

"There's something about this snow."

"It's not falling the way it usually does," said Jesús.

The cellar extended beneath the entire area of the castillo. It was a gigantic place, lit by torches which the steward, back in his day, would hold aloft as he walked up and down the rows of bottles. On the floor of sand and hard dirt, Luis would trace figures with a rake, in keeping with his mood of the moment. When he walked on them the next day, they remained intact, and this was not, by a long shot, the only marvel in the place. You did not have to be an architect to realize that an entire castillo cannot stand on such a huge open space devoid of any pillars. You could walk along rows bordered by old copper chests that had been there for who knows how long, and the arrangement of the various wines was mysterious, too. Luis would lay the bottle he'd been given in a certain place, and the next day he would find it somewhere else. The only bottles that could be easily removed from their alcove were at the end of the last row at the very end of the cellar, where he had received the delivery of petrus for Alejandro's sixteenth birthday. Finally, on certain occasions, the door to the place was kept closed, and when it was opened again everything had changed, although the beauty of it never disappointed. No matter which torch Luis lit, it would project an iridescent glow that glistened on the copper racks, and perpetuated its sparkle from one end of the cellar to the other; moving lines of luminous pearls traced a perfect, translucent architecture in the space; rows of earth and sand were interwoven, creating a feeling of peace. Luis had to show visitors the way out, otherwise they would have stayed there for the rest of their days.

That night, the cellar was even more resplendent than

usual. In the tilted bottles, the wine shimmered with flashes of pale gold, and a strange glow cloaked the floor with dull silver. In one gloomy corner, they found the three men grunting like pigs beneath their dark hooded capes. The one who was laughing loudest had a few flamboyant locks of hair; the second one, who had brown hair, was so massive in appearance that the others looked like imps in comparison.

Motionless, arms crossed, six feet from the threesome, Alejandro cleared his throat. They paid no attention. The intruders had found a barrel somewhere, on which they had placed their glasses and an impressive row of fine vintages. Of course, all three were completely drunk, something Jesús summed up by exclaiming, "Oh, the bastards!"

Alejandro cleared his throat again, with no more success than the first time, while the third thief caressed a bottle of rare champagne, saying:

"What we need now is a bubble."

At the same time, his hat slipped back to reveal a similarly flamboyant head of hair; a bright reflection from one of the racks lit up his fine, squirrel-like features; then everything went dark again. The only light came from the crystal glasses where they had poured champagne while Alejandro and Jesús looked on in silence. There was something wrong, but devil take them if they could say what it was, other than that it had to do with the liquid itself, which the second redhead was pouring cautiously. The two other men, very focused, kept an eye on the operation. Finally, they all relaxed, and Jesús and Alejandro saw that the bubbles were hastening toward the bottom of the champagne glasses, where they dissolved in a tiny hissing maelstrom.

"*Santa Madre*," murmured Jesús.

A singular irony: while exclamations and throat clearing had not sufficed to distract the drinkers, this faint murmur caused all three to turn around at once. The first redhead stood up straight, somewhat painfully, and reached for a torch. His head was wobbling, he was squinting slightly, and intermittently let out strange noises. However, he seemed to be the leader, for the others looked at him and waited for him to make the first move.

"Well, well," he muttered.

Then he turned to his companions with an apologetic look. The tallest one pointed a finger toward his pocket and the redhead's face lit up as he repeated, *Ah, well, well!* And the three men flung their heads back to drink from flasks they pulled out from underneath their cloaks. Judging by the faces they were making, the liquid must have had a bitter taste, but the most remarkable thing was that they instantaneously sobered up, and stood solidly on their feet as if they had not just consumed half the cellar—all things which caused Alejandro and Jesús to raise an interested eyebrow, for they too were not averse to drinking.

They all looked at one another again in silence.

The leader of the group was a paunchy little man with a round face and round eyes, fair skin and countless freckles; accompanied by a fine double chin and an abundant mane of hair, sagging shoulders and an upturned nose; in a word, he was not particularly becoming. But no soldier can fail to discern the danger concealed by artless attire, and Alejandro and Jesús saw that the man's gaze belied his bearing, that however inoffensive and good-natured he might seem, it would be dangerous to underestimate him, and that anyone who had made that mistake had probably not lived to brood over it; in short, they saw that this amiable inebriate was one of their own kind.

"I owe you an explanation," said the man.

The tall, dark-haired man stepped forward, bowed briefly and said, "Marcus, at your service."

The other redhead did likewise and said, "Paulus."

To which their leader added, also bowing:

"Petrus, your humble servant."

Then, somewhat brazenly:

"May I tempt you with a little upside-down champagne?"

A moment passed. Alejandro was still standing with his arms crossed, a stern expression on his face, rigid and silent as he confronted the strangers. Jesús . . . well, Jesús could not help but want to taste the champagne. There always comes a time when a man of reason discovers a penchant for extravagance, particularly when he has witnessed lakes evaporating without warning and mist writing sibylline messages on the sky. Moreover, in spite of the fantastical nature of the circumstances, he trusted these men.

Alejandro, his face inscrutable, took a step forward.

Another moment passed.

He took another step, and smiled.

"Alejandro de Yepes," he said, holding his hand out to Petrus. "You are acquainted with my tutor, I believe? He just went by, behind you."

"Oh, we met earlier," replied Petrus, shaking his hand. "I am glad he appears to you as well."

"Didn't you see him?" Alejandro asked Jesús.

"No, sir," he replied. "You saw the steward's ghost?"

"Just behind that gentleman," murmured Alejandro, "just behind him."

He gestured invitingly at the barrel.

"If you would do us the honor of pouring some *upside-down* champagne."

Should we be surprised by such composure? Alejandro had been hearing the voices of the dead for so long that it didn't strike him as incongruous in the least that it was also possible to see them. Luis's apparition, strolling along the rows of bottles, had had its effect, and now it was with a certain interest that Alejandro awaited what might come next.

They sat down around the makeshift table.

"You just have to focus," said Petrus, slowly pouring champagne into two clean glasses.

"A nice little vintage," Jesús pointed out, "it would be a mistake to deprive ourselves."

"You haven't seen anything yet," said Paulus. "Once you've tasted champagne upside down, you can't possibly go back to right side up."

"Is that what you are doing with the snow, too?" asked Alejandro.

Petrus seemed astonished.

"It's falling the right way, I believe."

"He's referring to Maria," said Paulus.

"Ah," said Petrus, "of course. Yes, yes, there is someone who makes the snow fall for us, hence its appearance which is, shall we say, rather personal, more meditative, blurring the perception of the enemy."

"Airplane radar can penetrate snow," Jesús pointed out.

"I'm not talking about that enemy," said Petrus. "You will have observed that the climate has been somewhat changeable in recent years—storms, frost, floods."

"Is that your Maria, too?" asked Jesús.

"No, no" said Petrus. "Maria only orders snow, the enemy alone is distorting the climate."

Setting the bottle back down, he added:

"Champagne and ghosts, on the other hand—that only happens in this cellar."

Alejandro raised his glass and studied the pale liquid. The descending bubbles tickled his nose pleasantly, and he could imagine that it would cause a sort of little explosion on the tongue.

He was wrong.

There was even such a lack of explosion on the first sip, the taste was so flat, and the bubbles so devoid of any impact that Alejandro and Jesús, disappointed, looked at each other from under their brows.

"Just wait a moment," said Paulus, with the indulgence of the initiated for the erring ways of the layman.

And indeed, the marvel began to work its magic, for the two men were overcome by a sensation of lying in the grass, their eyes riveted on the heavens on one of those days when fate is affable. The earthy taste in their mouth harmonized with the celestial lightness of the champagne until it released a euphoria whose substance they would have found difficult to describe.

"This is the beneficial effect of the alliance between earth and sky," said Petrus. "As the bubbles head toward the bottom they preserve the celestial value of the wine but multiply its earthy value."

After smiling at his glass, all tenderness, he added:

"Although there is not much you can do if the substance you start with is mediocre."

When the first glass was empty, Alejandro and Petrus smiled at each other, and Jesús noticed the redhead's beautiful, thoughtful gray eyes.

"How did you get here?" he asked.

"Over the bridge," replied Petrus. "The bridge that joins our world to yours."

Then, after a moment's silence:

"To you, it's invisible."

"Are you dead?" asked Jesús. "Are you ghosts?"

Petrus looked at him, surprised.

"I don't think ghosts drink champagne," he said.

"If you haven't come from the other life, where have you come from?" asked Jesús.

"There is only one life, and it encompasses the living and

the dead," answered Petrus. "But there are several worlds, and our worlds have been communicating for a long time. In reality, the first crossing of the bridge took place here in Yepes, although we only found that out yesterday."

Picking up the champagne bottle, he added:

"I have a long story to tell you, so it deserves another little drop."

"Can you tell us the name of your country?" asked Alejandro.

"We call it the world of mists," answered Petrus. "The world of mists, where the elves live."

There was a silence.

"Elves?" said Jesús. "You come from the world of elves?"

He began to laugh.

"Or maybe you yourselves are elves?" asked Alejandro without irony.

Jesús looked at his general as if he were a hen wearing a wig.

"That doesn't strike me as any more surprising than all the rest of it," said Alejandro in response to his gaze.

"We are elves," Petrus confirmed, "yes, we are." And to Jesús, tactfully: "I see you are somewhat surprised, so allow me to pour you another glass."

He filled his glass and, with a slight tilt of his chin, motioned to Paulus to fetch another bottle.

"Another bubble?" asked Paulus.

"Allow me to offer you one of my favorite vintages," said Alejandro pleasantly, as if the previous bottles had come from some unknown reserve.

He headed toward the back of the cellar.

"I thought elves lived in the far north," said Jesús. "The far north of sagas and legends."

He looked at the glasses lined up in front of him and added:

"And that they didn't drink."

"You also believe that God the father lives in heaven and that he doesn't drink," answered Petrus.

On seeing Jesús's horrified expression, he added:

"I'm not saying he drinks, I'm not saying he drinks. Simply, we all know that the spirit of the world doesn't have a beard and isn't ensconced on a throne on a huge pink cloud."

Jesús looked just as horrified, but Alejandro, coming back from the depths of the cellar, distracted them.

"Interesting," he murmured, setting a bottle on the barrel.

Petrus leaned over to read the label and smiled.

"Amarone," he said. "The wine of stories."

Marcus frowned.

"We've run out of tea," he said.

"Such improvidence," said Petrus, still smiling.

He looked up and seemed to be addressing someone invisible:

"You will bring us some, won't you?"

"Was that tea in your little flask?" asked Alejandro.

"Yes," Marcos replied, "very concentrated gray tea."

"The tea of our world," added Paulus. "It has . . . uh . . . special properties."

He fell silent and looked questioningly at Petrus.

But Petrus didn't care and was smiling gratefully at the amarone.

"Elves," said Jesús. "Do you have wine up there, too?"

"No, alas," reply Petrus, with a sorrowful face.

He dismissed the distressing confession with the back of his hand.

"Which is why bridges are so important," he said. "And please bear in mind that it is not *up there*. Elves do not live in the sky. It's crowded enough up there as it is."

"Do you mean with angels?" said Jesús. "Have you ever seen any?"

Petrus smiled, amused.

"The only traffic jams in the sky are those of the sky's own fictions," he said.

He took a swallow of amarone and let out a long sigh.

"This is the best I've ever drunk," he said, "And under these favorable auspices, I will begin at the beginning."

Jesús laughed.

"Now that I know there are no angels in the heavens," he said, "you can begin wherever you like."

"Ah, but there are angels on this earth," said Petrus.

He caressed his glass lovingly.

"The bridge that connects the world of mists to the world of humans leaves from a sacred place on our earth we call the Pavilion of the Mists. By order of the guardian of the pavilion, the bridge makes it possible to reach any point on the earth of humankind. Its arch is shrouded in thick mist, in which the traveler immerses himself, the guardian fulfills his task, and the voyager finds himself where he wanted to be. Elves can come and go as they see fit, but this has always been impossible for humans. However, a few days ago, four of them crossed over for the first time."

He poured another round of amarone.

"There is a war on now. You know all about it: the fronts are endless, the battles, too, and no one seems able to carry the day. The Confederation, who were on the verge of victory two years ago, have now become bogged down in absurd tactics. As for the League, they have been worn down by the length of the conflict and the deadly violence of the cataclysms."

"Tell us about these cataclysms," said Alejandro.

"Elves cannot fight in your world," said Petrus. "Rather, to be more precise, they lose most of their own powers there, and it becomes impossible for them to kill. But we know how to make use of natural elements, although ordinarily we do not allow ourselves to go against nature. Unfortunately, there is a very powerful elf in our world, the one who started the war, who doesn't care about that prohibition and has been causing the climate to go off kilter, using it as a weapon."

"The war was started to by an elf?" said Jesús. "I thought it was Raffaele Santangelo's intrigues."

"The president of the Italian Council is an elf," said Petrus. Jesús's chin dropped.

"But Santangelo is just a lackey," continued Petrus, "who came into the world of humans to support the aims of his master, the cataclysmic elf who stayed behind in the mists. I'm sorry to sound so melodramatic, but that is more or less the true story."

Probably to cure himself of melodrama, he poured a third glass of amarone.

"Does he have a name?" asked Alessandro.

"We call him Aelius," said Petrus.

"Is ancient Rome in fashion where you live?" asked Jesús.

"Unlike humans, elves are not in the habit of using names handed down through their lineage. As it happens, one of us, a very powerful elf allied with the League, lives in Rome, so that is where we went for inspiration."

He gave a big grin.

"As for me, I made a point of combining Roman empire and French vineyard."

He simultaneously reassumed his air of gravity and took a long sip of wine.

"Don't you think it's strange that Santangelo hasn't won?" he asked.

"Everyone thinks it's strange," said Alejandro. "No one can figure out his strategy."

"You're a strategist and a member of the high command of the League," said Petrus.

Alejandro looked at him, thoughtful.

"I think Santangelo doesn't want to win," he said, "he doesn't want a victorious side busy dressing its wounds. He wants men to die, all men, no matter which side they're on. I've said this many times, but no one wants to believe that after the last conflict there could still be people who want total war. In spite of this, I'm convinced that is Santangelo's intention. Why? I have no idea."

"There is dark smoke over parts of occupied Europe," Petrus said. "Your aircraft detected it. What do you think it is?"

"Massive fires," said Alejandro. "But what are they burning, there?"

Petrus fell silent, his expression and gloomy.

"So that's it," said Alejandro.

"Never before has the human race been so passionate about exterminating its fellows," said Paulus, "and never before have the elves fought such bloody battles. Even the mists are at war, and our kind are dying by the millions."

"In the beginning Aelius only wanted humans to die," Petrus said, "but those who want the death of one end up wanting the death of all. They end up wanting death as a crown so that a chosen few can reign over the scorched earth."

"Why did he want humans to die?" Jesús asked.

"Because our mist is declining, and he is holding you responsible for this plague," replied the elf.

"The mist on the bridge?" Jesús asked.

"The mists of our world," Petrus answered. "We are a world of mists. Without it, we cannot survive."

"It is your oxygen?" Jesús asked.

Petrus looked at him, puzzled.

"Our oxygen? No, no. We breathe the same air as you. But we are elves. We are a community of mists."

He wiped his hand across his brow.

"This is the part I always have trouble explaining. I forget every time that you separate everything."

"Could he be right?" Alejandro asked. "Are we responsible for the decline of your mists?"

Petrus, Paulus, and Marcus glanced at one another.

"That is something we have wondered, too," said Petrus at last. "But even if you were, it would not warrant war. And I am convinced that is not the true cause."

"So what is the true cause?"

He smiled.

"The decline of poetry?"

It was Alejandro's turn to smile. The fact that Petrus had invoked poetry made him a brother to Luis Álvarez. Time fell away and he could see his tutor sipping wine by the fireside.

"The older I get, the more I look for fervor," Luis had said to him, "and the more I find it in places where previously I saw only beauty. You are young and enthusiastic, your mind is fresh and excited, but fervor is the opposite of that. When it deserts us, we turn agitated and feverish, when it takes possession of us we are transformed into a calm, tenebrous lake, darker than the night, more motionless than stone. In this condition, we can pray without lying."

"I never pray," Alejandro had said.

"Oh, you pray," smiled Luis, "you pray every day when you go to the cemetery. Humans never pray more than when they are listening for their dead. But you will have to pray even more if you want to pay your respects to the earth and sky, and you will have to instill the compassion of poetry into your prayers. That's where passion is found—and in its wake, comes beauty."

In the half darkness of the cellar, the amarone coated the glasses with a dark lacquer that reminded Alejandro of Luis's tenebrous lake, and he suddenly remembered what he'd dreamt that night. He was standing in the middle of a wooden veranda, facing a forested valley. The valley was shrouded in a mist penetrated with organic breathing, an inspiration infused with elusive, vibrant life. Alejandro stood for a long time looking out at the extraordinary landscape, and yet a veil of anxiety was gradually changing it. Just when fear supplanted the joy of being there, he turned around, and in the darkness of a wooden pavilion with windows that had neither panes nor frames, he saw a woman. He could not make out her features, but he knew that she was young, and he thought she was smiling at him. Then he woke up. He'd been dreaming about that woman for several years now, ever since leaving Yepes to become a soldier, and this time, just after he woke up, he had seen her face, her pallor and her arctic eyes. He couldn't have said now whether she was beautiful or ugly, he could have said nothing about her beyond her youth, her fairness, and the gravity of her eyes. He'd thought she was smiling at him, but in fact she was looking at him gravely, and his entire childhood was in that look, along with the valleys of Extremadura, its stones, its parched landscapes, the slopes of the bluff where he lived, the harsh winters, and the violet dawns.

"More prosaically," Petrus resumed, "I believe our mists are dying because things in general are dying. The only hope of saving it is to accept that it will be reborn in another form. That is what we are striving for, those of us who believe in the eternity of poems. There is no other way out. When everything is used up, it will mean the end of our known world."

"That is very moving," Jesús said, "but you still have not told us the reason why you have come."

"I'm getting there," said Petrus, in no way offended, "I'm getting there."

He drained his glass and looked dejectedly at the empty bottle. Alejandro stood up, went once again to the far end of the cellar, and came back muttering *interesting*, like the first time.

Petrus read the label and seemed moved.

Jesús leaned closer in turn.

"Nuits-Saint-Georges," he read, "vin de Bourgogne."

"I've been there often," said Petrus. "The first time I was quite young."

The memory pleased him and he smiled to himself.

"And I went back there exactly twenty years ago, right after my visit to the castillo in Yepes."

He was no longer smiling.

"We chose your fortress as a safe place for our protégée, Maria, whom you heard us speak of just now, the young woman who commands the snow. But when I arrived, your family had just been murdered, and I decided to hide Maria in Burgundy."

"Do you know who killed them?" Alejandro asked.

"Not yet," said Petrus, "but everything is linked. If we chose your fortress to accommodate Maria, it was because of a series of corroborating factors. Among other disturbing events, a few days ago we came to discover that the first elf who ever ventured into the world of humans probably came to Yepes. Moreover, the castillo has the same motto as our mists."

"*Mantendré siempre*,"[1] said Alejandro.

"Which is also the motto of our council," Petrus said.

"And Maria, what role does she play?" asked Jesús.

"Maria?" echoed Petrus, surprised by the question. "She unites our forces."

"She's an elf?" Jesús insisted.

Petrus hesitated for a brief moment.

"We're not sure what she is," he replied.

Jesús seemed to be on the verge of asking another question, but the elf raised his hand.

"Now, if you will, the time has come for me to tell you what we hope to gain from our meeting."

He glanced at his glass.

"Apart from these wonders," he added. "Of course, it is

[1] I shall always maintain.

rather difficult to sum up a war in a few words. But it so happens that the final battle will be fought tomorrow."

Jesús burst out laughing.

"Wars like that no longer exist," he said. "This is not Alexander at Gaugamela or even Napoleon at Wagram. There is no final battle."

"I'm afraid there is," said Petrus, "and it will be fought tomorrow, and you will be called on to play a part in it—if we manage to get you across the bridge."

He laughed quietly to himself. He suddenly seemed old, but his gaze was even more beautiful than at the beginning of the story; his eyes a flinty gray, glinting with silver.

"It is time for us to greet our lady and entrust the rest of the story to her," he said.

He stood up, along with the other two elves, and all three turned to one side and bowed deeply.

In the darkness before them stood the young girl whom the general from Yepes had already seen in his dreams.

Darker than the night
More motionless than stone
The lake where we pray

Book of Prayers

酒

My people live beneath the enchanted earth of Yepes, and there is no more pleasant place for our purpose than the cellar of the castillo, for wine lays in the memory of centuries, stones, and ancient roots.

It should come as no surprise that elves are not familiar with the vine. For those who are together, reality suffices; these are not people of fiction and drunkenness. But the wine of humans is the brother of friendship and fables. It confers upon the whispering of the deceased the turn of phrase that will carry their words a great distance. Through wine, the bitterness of solitude turns sweet, in that exquisite relaxation that causes so much to blossom. It joins the nobility of the land with the chronicles of the heavens, the deep roots of vine stock with the clusters of grapes reaching for the sun—there is nothing better suited to telling the saga of the cosmos.

Still, there was one remarkable exception to the mists' indifference to the vine: Petrus was an accomplished elf and a master of wines. He could taste the poetry of his world, but he loved the stories of humans above all else, and he would gladly listen to them with a glass in his hand. Thus, he incarnated a bridge between the two worlds, as did all the other providential players in this war.

POETRY

If there is one intoxication shared by humans and elves, it is poetry.

On a day of drizzle or a night of pale moon, welcome the winds from the moor and write verses in honor of the old poets. The breath of the world will pass through you and vanish, but trapped in your feelings, it will have acquired a singular form—the birth of poems.

Blonde, pale, and gracious, she studied them gravely and Alejandro's life tipped on its end.

For a long time, he'd been hoping the war would forge him, grant him the humanity he dreamt of. From Luis, he learned that a man must look to the stars for guidance; from Miguel, that kingdoms are born from ideas; and from Jesús, that the heart lives off bareness. He'd entrusted war with the care of turning this instruction into a sparkling in a cemetery, so that he would know how to honor his duty to his dead. Now that six years had gone by, there was something he could still not grasp, and he hoped the elves would supply the missing element to the fulfillment of his destiny, through the new, more beautiful and terrifying guise of a women's gaze. No one understands what happens in the fleeting instant of an encounter—eternity contracts into a divine vertigo, then takes a lifetime to unfold again on a human time scale. How long have we got? wondered Alejandro.

The young woman stepped into the circle of torchlight and smiled at him.

Alejandro's whole life rushed headlong into that smile. He was submerged by visions and, as in his dream, he was gazing out at vast expanses where the hours of his childhood could again be found. The key is in the landscape, he thought, and on his palm, he felt the brief touch of an illumination, but when his fingers seemed to have curled around it, he laughed at the thought that he could have grasped the flow of dreams. The slopes of Extremadura were those of a land where tiny villages were swallowed by lofty summits and deep valleys. Above the mountains was a sky of hastening clouds; on the edge of his vision, the sparkling light he'd always known; perched on an outcrop was a church where a piano waited. How do I know all this? he wondered, as he flew on an invisible eagle's back over the valley of the promontory, unending fertile plains, then finally the outskirts of an unfamiliar city.

"Rome," said the young woman.

Alejandro remained silent and she said:

"I dreamt of you when I was in the Pavilion, and our memories are mingling."

Alejandro still said nothing, and she seemed troubled. The wavering torchlight blurred her features, but when she'd said *mingling*, she'd taken another step forward. How old was she? he wondered, terrified. He studied her face, her blond hair, her light eyes. Could someone so young have such a gaze? he wondered again, then he found out she was a pianist. Is she beautiful? he thought, and although he could see every detail and every one of her features, he understood, intoxicated, that he did not know. He also saw that her forehead was too large and her neck too thin, and to him she looked like a swan adrift in improbable tropics. What an absurd idea, he thought; ever more lost and intoxicated with his own state of being lost, he laughed. He wondered how much time had gone by since she had appeared. Someone behind him cleared his throat and he shuddered. He stepped forward and bowed in turn.

"You are Maria," he said.

There was a faint sound and Petrus appeared next to him, unsteady, his nose red and his eyes hazy.

"No, no," he said, "Maria is in Nanzen."

Gripping the edge of his cape in vain, he almost collapsed

onto the young woman. With surprising agility, he caught himself just in time and, looking at her, he muttered, "My child, be good to Uncle Petrus."

Against her thighs she was holding a woven basket, and from it she removed three gray flasks which she handed out to the elves. They sobered up as quickly as the first time and Petrus, friskier than a filly, turned and continued to speak to Alejandro.

"Maria stayed behind at the Pavilion of the Mists."

"My name is Clara," said the young woman, and again she seemed troubled.

Petrus looked at her, then at Alejandro.

"I missed something," he muttered.

Jesús came in turn to bow to Clara.

"Are you Maria's sister? Are you elves?" he asked.

Petrus observed Clara with tenderness and pride.

"Exactly twenty years ago, less one day, two extraordinary children were born," he said. "The first one is standing here before you. Her father is the guardian of our pavilion, her mother is a remarkable woman, but according to all logic, Clara should never have been born, because unions between elves and humans have always been sterile. The other child, Maria, is waiting for us in Nanzen. She was born to the head of our Council and his elfin companion but, unlike us, and like Clara, her appearance is strictly human."

"You look perfectly human to me," said Jesús, surprised.

"Not in our mists," said Petrus. "There, you will see how different we are from you. We only adopt a single appearance when we are here. Only Maria and Clara, despite their elfin blood, keep the same physiognomy in both worlds."

"What do you look like when you are up there? Do you grow wings?" asked Jesús, obstinately situating mist and winged creatures in the sky.

"Nothing grows on us at all," said Petrus, taken aback. "Simply, we are multiple."

"Among elves, do you speak Spanish?" asked Jesús, ever pragmatic, now that he'd got going.

"Anyone who has stayed at the pavilion can speak every language on earth," answered Petrus.

"What is the role of Maria and Clara?" Alejandro asked.

"Well, to save the world," said Petrus.

"Is that all!" commented Jesús.

"The question," continued Petrus, ignoring him, "is how. Six years of war and we were still blind—until, four days ago, when we obtained possession of a gray notebook dating from the sixteenth century. It belonged to an elf who also crossed over the bridge. He was an extremely talented painter, and we still have one of his paintings, which you will soon see. But the most astonishing thing—and, for us, the most interesting—is that he was the first elf who stayed in your world for good and chose to live a human life."

Petrus scratched his head.

"It's a long story, and I cannot begin to tell it now. Let's just say that the notebook contains vital information, both for the outcome of the war, and for the future of our mists, and now we are in a position to determine our next move. Not the one that we would have dreamed of, to be honest—what we have learned forces us to make a radical decision. But we have come so far that we must risk everything or face certain death."

"Who, in your mists, makes such decisions?" Alejandro asked. "Is it you?" he added, turning to Clara.

She laughed.

"Decisions are made by the Council of Mists."

"Presided over by Maria's father, if I got it right," Jesús said. "So he is your king?"

"The head of the Council is at the service of the mists," said Clara.

"Is your mist alive?" Jesús asked, still determined to understand.

"Come, we have to go now," said Petrus. "Anything you don't know yet, you will find out once you cross the bridge."

"Cross the bridge?" echoed Jesús.

"We will try to cross with you," continued Petrus, "and that is why Clara is here with us, for humans can only cross in her company."

"I think there's something you've failed to take into consideration," said Jesús. "General de Yepes commands the first army. He cannot leave his post in the middle of an offensive to go off and sip tea in a celestial pavilion."

There was a moment's silence.

Then Petrus scratched his nose and said:

"Yet that is precisely the plan."

And to Alejandro:

"It will not constitute desertion."

He broke off. Alejandro was staring at him without seeing him, scrutinizing the darkness beyond. Petrus looked in the same direction.

"Ah, so there are the dead," murmured the elf.

Alejandro found it hard to breathe.

Before him stood all his dead.

They appeared to him just as they had looked in days gone by, and had he not known that they were dead, Alejandro would have sworn on his honor that they were not ghosts. His family, Luis, Miguel, the men who'd fallen under his command, villagers he'd long forgotten: all of them had come through the gates of death to join the battalion of the living.

"Why?" he asked, out loud, and the congregation of the deceased vanished, with the exception of Miguel and Luis.

It was the same sensation as eighteen years earlier, when his family was being buried, and the funeral proceedings were enveloped in the torpor of a dream. He conversed with Luis and Miguel, back from the dead in the form of images they shared with him; he saw his tutor, thirty years younger, leading a group of men, marching through a baking hot day. The white-hot earth buzzed with insects, and the men moved forward, a holy spark in their gaze. He studied the poet's face and his clear eyes, his aristocratic brow, his puny body, and he thought: the power of such a man! A new image appeared. A boy was slicing his way through the grasses down a gentle slope. The long stalks yielded to his hips then rose again with the smooth grace of swans. He made his way slowly through the wild grasses while time fell away, and all that remained was this walking through the fields. All I want is this ecstasy, thought Alejandro and, at last, Luis spoke to him. Once again it was the older man sitting at his councilor's table; by his elbow the glass of sherry shone brightly like a splash of blood, and the young general heard the words his tutor was saying, smiling, so handsome, so poor, and so worthy in his laughable stronghold.

"*Everything shall be empty and full of wonder*," murmured Alejandro.

He awoke from his dream and saw that Jesús was looking at him.

"We're leaving now," he said. "We're crossing the bridge with them."

There was a silence.

"You didn't see them?" he asked Jesús.

"More ghosts?" Jesús asked.

Again a silence. Jesús sighed.

"I hope you know what you're doing," he said to Petrus.

"We haven't the foggiest," answered the elf.

He ran his gaze over the vast cellar.

"We'll be back, I hope," he said.

"How do you intend to get us across?" asked Alejandro.

"I'm getting there," said Petrus. "That is the last thing you must know before changing worlds. The mists, the gray note-book, the painting and all the rest—that will be for the other side. For the time being, we'll ask you to drink some tea that's been slightly altered and doesn't taste all that great."

"How do we know that your concoction won't kill us?" Jesús asked.

"Four days ago, Maria and Clara came here for the first time, thanks to this very same tea," Petrus replied. "But they were not alone. There were two humans with them."

"You mean real humans?" Jesús asked. "Not ghosts, or semi-something-or-others?"

"Real humans," said Petrus, "as human as one can possibly be."

"Are they waiting for us there?" Alejandro asked.

"They are waiting for us and, what's more, they are watch-ing us at this very moment," said Petrus. "A priest and a painter, but they are also soldiers."

For some unknown reason, to Alejandro these words seemed to echo those of his tutor, and again he murmured, *empty and full of wonder.*

"It's time, I think," the elf said to Clara.

The young woman smiled at him tenderly.

"I always obey Uncle Petrus," she said, with delightful irony.

She took a few more flasks from her basket, and when she turned to face Alejandro, she smiled at him with just a touch of mischief that said, Here we are, trapped like two fish in a net. To fall in love in the middle of a war, what a mad idea, he thought. For the second time that night, he laughed out loud. Petrus cast him a suspicious glance before holding up his flask: it acted as a prism, and the sparkling of the dead flickered in every direction through the cellar.

They all drank their gray tea.

For several seconds, nothing happened. The brew tasted vile, of fermentation and decomposition.

And they waited a few more seconds.

Life was split into two equal parts that went to crash on either side of infinity, then re-bonded under the sky. To Alejandro and Jesús it seemed to last forever, and yet to be occurring outside of time. In the second when the world faded away, images had scrolled past their inner gaze—fields, lakes, fine-weather clouds with the faint outlines of beloved faces. Above all, they had the sensation of eternity being transmuted into a journey, and they could have stayed in limbo forever to take that journey with neither movement nor duration, suspended in an infinite space devoid of place or shape. Finally, everything ended abruptly in a great sensory void. Now they couldn't take their eyes off the spectacle unfolding before them.

Beyond the red arch of the bridge of mists, beneath a black sky, an old wooden pavilion overlooked a valley of white trees. In the entire motionless scene, the only colors were the white of the trees and the black of the sky, and the crimson bridge like a splash of blood in one's vision.

Alejandro looked at Clara and knew that she was beautiful.

Is she beautiful?
A splash of blood in one's vision

Book of Paintings

亡霊

GHOSTS

Whatever shape you give them, it's useless to deny the existence of ghosts. If few humans encounter them outside of their imagination, that alone suffices to show how much they live among them.

How do we know what happened in ancient times? Because we know inherently. The blood of ages runs through our veins like a river, and as long as we pay attention to the earth and the sky, that blood will convey the heritage of those people who came before us.

It's not magic, it's not a chimera. Who could forget the first line ever drawn, when it came time to paint the landscape of the world?

快活

GAIETY

C lara had not always been mischievous and joyful. For far too long she had been confined to the fallow regions of the heart, and only laughed for the first time when she turned eleven. But love and war had immersed this solitary soul in a gaiety of the sort everyone will surely need, if it is true, as a great man wrote one day, that gaiety is the most amiable form of courage.

T he company who had come from the land of humans stood on the bridge of mists beneath an inky sky shot with light. The day was emerging from darkness and lit up the landscape. At the heart of this landscape was the red arch of the bridge, radiating with untold strength. Unlike the world around them, the creatures of flesh had preserved their colors.

"I don't understand what I am seeing," Jesús said.

"You are seeing the essence of our world," Petrus said. "Once you see it with the eyes the tea will give you, it will appear more normal to you."

"More tea?" muttered Jesús.

Beneath their feet the wood was vibrating slightly.

"Welcome to Nanzen" said Petrus.

Alejandro was stunned by the black sky. It was as if it had been wash-painted, and his gaze could follow the lazy, shimmering ripples as they merged with other magnificent figures. From this liquid ink came the light of dark lacquers, to which the invisible grooves of a brush gave a clear texture. Although Nanzen, with the exception of the bridge, was entirely black and white, the sense of nature there was more concentrated than elsewhere. The whiteness of the trees revealed their structure, without concealing their overall beauty, and in the center of this arboreal arena stood the Pavilion of the Mists. It was at the mercy of the wind through its paneless, frameless openings which were arranged asymmetrically, although the building itself was square. This broken rhythm surely led to a melodic vision of the landscape; the more one's gaze wandered aimlessly through the spans, the more the panorama took shape, in keeping with the most beautiful music; but if you asked the two men what they were seeing, they would simply have answered: an old bandstand at the mercy of wind and rain. The veranda all around had acquired the patina of age, and Alejandro understood that the building was not a vestige of the past, but the spirit of that past—neither rhyme nor reason, he thought again, before he was seized by another realization.

"The lines are perfect," he said out loud.

And he thought: the proportions of this rickety refuge are absolute.

The red bridge reigned over the austere territory. The arch was veiled in thick mist, and radiated a form of unfamiliar harmony.

"The bridge of mists is the bridge of natural harmonies," said Petrus. "It holds the elements of our community together. But it also brings about the union and synthesis of our worlds."

He broke off.

"You will hear the whole story," he said then, "but for now we must not keep our welcome committee waiting."

And indeed, leaving the pavilion, the delegation was coming to greet them, and I owe it to my integrity as a chronicler to mention that Alejandro and Jesús stood there speechless. One woman and two men, escorted by four creatures as absurd as they were splendid, were making their way along a path of black stones. Further along I shall relate the impression the woman made upon Jesús, but just then he was completely absorbed by the emotion of discovering elves in their native environment. Taller than humans, they seemed to be made up of different species that blended with one another in a slow ballet of metamorphoses. At the head of the delegation came a white horse that was also man and wild boar, *becoming* each of its constituent essences in succession. The blond man with glacial eyes changed into a snow-white horse, then his nostrils were transformed into a broad, steaming snout, he grew horns, and now he was a wild boar, finer than any Alejandro had ever seen in his territory for major hunting. Intermittently, the reflected light of an ancient waterway passed over the creature's face, and through a clearing in the mist Alejandro could see that the bridge spanned a silver stream with wild grasses growing on either side. The elf had about him the same fragrance of eternity that filled the young general with the greatest reverence. The second creature in the escort, a brown-haired man whose horse, a moment later, seemed made of quicksilver, inspired the same respect. His coat glinted with great beauty, a beauty preserved by the fur of the hare into which he was ultimately transformed—beige and brown, extraordinarily silky, and rippling with gentle quivers.

"The Guardian of the Pavilion and the Head of the Council," said Petrus.

What land is this, that creates leaders like gods? thought Alejandro.

"That is the impression the high-elves generally give," murmured Petrus.

Behind the masters of the mists, two elves displayed their fine human features and their lustrous coats of wild horses, while the third species turned out to be a squirrel for one, and a polar bear for the other. One was not overcome with deference in their presence, and it seemed to Alejandro that in comparison with the high-elves they must be minor elves, but their beauty was perhaps all the more moving in that it was instilled with innocence. Now Petrus advanced onto the descending arch of the bridge, and Alejandro and Jesús followed him, disrupting the enchantment to notice how, surprisingly, they were growing accustomed to the black sky. When their elfin companions stepped onto the path of stones and were transformed in turn, they could see that they all contained an essence of man and horse, and that Petrus, in addition, became the prettiest, most jovial, potbellied squirrel one could ever hope to meet. Then he gave his place to a little chestnut horse with lovely thoughtful gray eyes. Next to him, Paulus also turned into a squirrel and Marcus became a large brown bear. Just as they all regained their human form, a strange garment covered their bodies. It looked like a soft, organic cloth shot through with ripples which ceased the moment the human part of the elf vanished. It was difficult to identify the fibers the cloth was woven of, but it adjusted to the body while preserving the glow of the animal, and Jesús would have liked to touch its light and flesh.

As for Alejandro, it was the path that led to the pavilion that fascinated him above all. The stones were wide and flat and reflected the trees in the hollow below, as they were actually above the stones. There were no trees along the lane, but the flagstones radiated a swinging of branches in the wind which gave an impression of walking beneath thick foliage. Alejandro stepped onto the first stone and was surprised by the invisible, stream-like wave that went through the mineral hardness of its surface.

"Soon you will see liquid stones," said the adorable chubby squirrel Petrus had once again become.

Behind the four elves, a priest in a cassock brought up the rear of the delegation. His face was open and magnanimous, his form freighted with a paunch that attested to his delight in earthly pleasures. Although as a rule Alejandro did not like priests, he immediately took to this one, as did Jesús, who revered the men of the cloth, whence we may conclude that they had not met just one sort of man in the Church, for there are so many sad souls there, but also true scouts who set off to explore unknown lands with no aim to enlighten any other consciousness than their own. Above all, the priest's good-natured contours couldn't hide his gaze, that of a man who had observed and, upon observing, grown. He was walking with one arm around another man's shoulder, a tall, very handsome man, the same age as the good father—perhaps sixty or so—and this man, according to Petrus, used to be a painter. The man smiled at them with the sort of elegance that is born of the mockery one reserves for oneself, and the equal and opposite consideration which, on principle, one displays toward others: Alejandro and Jesús liked him, too.

The young woman was raising her hand in welcome. She gave off an air of singular authority, although her appearance was frail; her hair and eyes were brown, she was rather thin, and very distinguished, her skin was golden, her lips the color of fresh blood. Beneath the skin on her face there were fine veins that radiated in concentric circles from the bridge of her nose. There were moments when these veins were paler, to the point of fading and disappearing altogether. Then they returned to throb gently and darken her serious features. All at once she smiled, and Alejandro saw that she was smiling at Clara.

Turning to one side, he looked at the young woman and she took his breath away. She was smiling back at Maria; in her smile, he saw compassion and sisterly love, and his own passion was heightened still further. Now he knew that he would have to pray late into the night, no longer to die in honor, but that this flame would not fall to the enemy—how could I bear its loss? he pondered, and thought less of what he was feeling than of what Clara incarnated. And this was how Alejandro de

Yepes, in his thirtieth year, was awakened to love. Neither the
self-sacrifice of combat, nor the pledge to shed his blood down
to the last drop, nor allegiance to the land of his ancestors, nor
Luis's poetry, nor Miguel's ideas had ever shown him the way
so clearly, and if he'd thought he was close to it when he stood
before his dead, what was always missing was the echo of a
sigh. Now the fact that he'd always taken and never given
seemed so obvious to him that shame rose to his cheeks. He'd
already sensed this, briefly, in the cellar, when he felt that he
loved because he felt uplifted. But the smile Clara had given
Maria tore like a raging wind at the last ties binding him to his
former life, while he clung to the yearning to give with which
she filled him, a yearning that was transforming the parameters
of his heart one by one. Now he understood Luis's lesson, the
restlessness that comes from enthusiasm when passion has the
power to bathe us in calm waters: this passion had made him
cease to notice whether Clara was beautiful—never diminish-
ing his desire for all that.

The delegation from the alliance of humans and elves, now
a few steps away, came to a halt. Close up, the beauty of the
elves was almost unbearable. It emanated from the perfection
of human and animal forms commingled in their slow choreography of mutations, but also from the manner in which the
elves expressed their emotions, in the form of faint emanations
that traced drawings in space—and, whether it was pride, sadness, weariness, goodness, mischief, or courage, a symphony of
ethereal sketches was created, intelligible in the way that
abstract paintings are intelligible, and this made their deepest
hearts transparent to humans. Alejandro looked at Petrus and
was stunned by the etchings which the only alcoholic squirrel
in the civilized world was sending out in the air in leaping
bursts. There was courage there, candor and obstinacy, irreverence flirting with ribaldry, but also a procession of juvenile

aspirations bathed in ancient wisdom, in such a way that, through this consensus of lightness and depth, Petrus the minor elf actually appeared to be great.

"Am I seeing things, or do they have their heart written on their brow?" murmured Jesús.

Then the two men got down on one knee to greet the elves from the land of mists and their human companions.

Jesús Rocamora, as he bent his knee, got the impression that he was returning to a semblance of reality. The stone was lukewarm, and he liked the trembling of organic life. The first minutes had been a succession of shocks: the absence of colors, for a start, the young brown-haired woman, then at last the elves themselves, in all their fantastical multiplicity. Now that he was getting used to the black sky and the trimorphic creatures, the true impact of the change of worlds became clear to him.

"Welcome to Nanzen," said Maria.

She had a deep voice that evoked some elusive memory. For an unknown reason, he recalled his only encounter with Luis Álvarez, during the second year of the war—their one brief meeting, in a January of endless frost and exhausted soldiers. At the end, Luis had recited three lines to him. While some men are not cut out for words, that doesn't mean they cannot be found by a poem that has searched the stars for them; that will be their loyal companion on days of glory and in times of hunger from that day on. These three lines were all that Jesús would ever attain in terms of literature, but at least he'd recognized them from the very start as his own. After reciting them, Luis had added:

"They're special, because I knew them before I ever composed them."

"Don't you always have to know ahead of time what you are about to compose?" Jesús had asked.

Luis had laughed and replied:

"If you are a good craftsman, perhaps. But if you want to be a poet or a warrior, you have to consent to a loss of self."

In this mourning
Liquid soul
I sleep clothed in clouds

The lines had carried Jesús into a great, white silence. At the heart of the silence, a sensation was being born and, although he couldn't have explained why, he read it as the announcement of his redemption. Then it passed, and if Jesús sometimes thought of the three lines, it was when he despaired of ever understanding their effect upon his life—now, a young woman, her face stitched with tiny dark veins, was standing before him, and the poem became flesh, embraced as it was by passion and a woman's grief. Jesús was a strange mixture, as we all are. Because of his childhood by the lake, he believed that life is a tragedy, and the fact that he'd fled made him feel obliged to endure it without complaining. He was a Christian because he had spent time with his priest, a righteous man left sublime and powerless by his obstinate desire to pray, and from him, he inherited the belief that the crosses one bears can compensate for an act of disloyalty. He bore his own cross without bitterness, with a cheer astonishing in a man of duty and remorse, along with a healthy heart and a lust for life that kept him from being crushed by his burdens. But while he might not know what Maria had experienced in life, he knew the pain of it, the perfume of regret; he thought that the mist from the lake of his childhood had gone up to that black sky to relieve them both of their sorrow; and that Luis's poem, in a way, explained why they had met and, similarly, linked their fates. Of course, as a man who was as impermeable to intro-spection as he was to poetry, these were not the words he was thinking, and it will surprise no one to learn that, in the end, it could all be translated by a single thought in which he invested all his hope: *we will suffer together.*

"My name is Maria," she said again.

She turned to the man who was also a gray horse and a hare.

"My father, given his authority over the Council of Mists, asked me to greet you here," she said.

"Welcome to Nanzen," said the Head of the Council in turn.

"Welcome to Nanzen," said the man who was also a white horse and a wild boar. "In my capacity as Guardian of the Pavilion, I am honored to meet you. You are those we were not expecting, but it seems Yepes has a role in the history of our bridge."

Alejandro and Jesús stood up straight, and realized that they no longer found it incongruous to be conversing with a horse or a hare.

"How should we call you?" Alejandro asked.

The Head of the Council smiled.

"That is always the first question humans ask."

He let out a quiet modulation which was not exactly a melody, but a liquid sound, rather, where an ancient stream flowed.

"That is my name," he said.

He addressed his fellows in the same natural musical language which bathed Alejandro's and Jesús's spirits in a summer rain. It was very beautiful and harmonized so closely with the landscape that Nanzen now made them feel dizzy.

"But we also like the language of humans," continued the Guardian of the Pavilion, "and we are not averse to borrowing their names. To you I shall be Tagore."

"Solon," said the Head of the Council.

Jesús, who was no more enlightened about the former than the latter, looked at Maria. When the guardian had resorted to the language of elves, he saw in her eyes the gleam of the tall

trees reflected on the flagstones, and in this way, he understood that invisible foliage lived inside her, its memory so
enduring that it sometimes turned into a vision.

"Like you, I grew up in a poor region," she said, "but you
could see very beautiful trees there."

She turned to the painter and the priest and said:

"Here are two men who used to know those trees."

The men came forward and held out their hands to
Alejandro and Jesús.

"Alessandro Centi," said the painter. "In Italy, they call me
Sandro."

The priest took a sudden unexpected little bow.

"Père François," he said. "I am glad our paths have crossed."

Jesús made this sign of the cross.

"Are you French, Father?"

"I am indeed," said the priest.

"Are we in heaven?" Jesús asked.

Père François looked at Petrus and laughed.

"If we are, the angels are awfully strange-looking," he said.

Then he became serious again.

"To be honest, I don't know if all this is real or if I'm dreaming."

"Those who drink know that reality resides at the bottom
of a bottle of amarone," said Petrus.

"I'm the only one who can say what can be found at the
bottom of an Italian bottle," declared Sandro.

"Ecstasy," said Petrus.

"And tragedy," added the painter.

Maria, addressing the entire company, made a gesture of
invitation toward the pavilion.

"In the name of the Council of Mists," she said, "may I invite
you to have tea with me?"

She bowed slightly to Tagore and led the small group along
the path to Nanzen.

*

Nanzen. As they made their way toward the Pavilion, they saw below them a valley of tall trees, their tops veiled in mist. The pavilion was built on a promontory and elevated on pillars planted in thick moss gleaming with dewdrops. Worn steps led to a veranda that ran all the way around the old bandstand. When Alejandro stepped onto it he felt a brief, intense vibration. He went immediately behind Tagore, Solon, and Maria. The rest of the delegation followed, with Clara and Petrus bringing up the rear. From outside, the building seemed rather cramped, and Alejandro and Jesús were surprised to find it was big enough to accommodate them all and still project a feeling of spaciousness. As they left the veranda to go inside, they could sense they were going through an invisible vestibule, and now the sounds of the outside world were stifled. Oddly, Alejandro found the tranquility of the place seemed to match the nature of the mist in the valley, woven from the same evanescence, where a deep, vital breathing could be felt. All around, through openings that set off discrete portions of the panorama, the landscape unfolded in a succession of images. In the background, the red bridge, squeezed into the narrow space of a little window, revealed only the rising section of its arch; this confined perspective suggested the abstraction of a red stain upon the surface of an inky lake. Visible through other openings, further enhancing the tableau, was the splendor of trees and the mists in their successive rebirths. Every swirl of mist, every branch yielding in the wind, every mottled streak of black sky relentlessly produced the highest configuration of beauty.

The polar bear showed everyone where they should sit on the floor. Tagore and Solon sat across from each other to preside over the cenacle.

"Quartus, at your service," said the polar bear with a slight bow.

"Hostus," said the other minor elf just as he was being transformed into a squirrel.

He added:

"We are today's assistants."

The wooden floor was bare, apart from a faint silvery dust left undisturbed by their footsteps. A slight breeze traced swirling arabesques in the dust. On one of the walls of sand, a band of light-colored cloth, the only visible adornment, was decorated with unfamiliar writing as beautiful as a drawing and made with ink like that of the sky. Between two views onto the trees in the mist, against the wall on the side of the valley, was a bench covered in cups, teapots, terra-cotta bowls and a few rough-hewn wooden spatulas and ladles. Earthenware tea jars stood in a row under the bench. Next to them, on a brazier on the floor, a cast-iron kettle was whistling.

The only sound or motion in the room was the boiling of water and the dancing of silver dust. Quartus and Hostus set down two little cups of differing size and shape in front of each guest, then Quartus brought a teapot to Tagore along with a bowl and one of the tea jars. From it, the Guardian of the Pavilion took out a sort of crumbly brown cake and broke off a small piece. Hostus dipped a ladle into the kettle and Tagore poured a first splash of water onto the crumbled tea, which he set aside in an earthenware bowl. Then the assistant brought him another ladle of water and, as with the first spoonful, he poured it onto the tea leaves.

The guardian let out a sudden soft trill and everything changed. The power of ritual confers a rather stiff dignity upon humans until the moment it develops into a trance and, causing them to leave themselves behind, gives them the strength to grow. In Nanzen, the elves hadn't abandoned their nonchalant air, but their gaze showed they were conscious of the beauty and vanity of the world, the certainty of darkness, and the desire to honor whatever it was that, in spite of war, kept creatures standing tall under the heavens. Time passed, empires crumbled, people perished; at the heart of this disaster a fragment of the sublime was hidden; it was a serious moment, yet not solemn, deferential without being formal, and joyful, however grave the hour.

The silvery reflection on Tagore's face intensified. Something welled inside him. It was an intangible transfiguration, but Alejandro recalled the way Luis Álvarez would turn handsome when passion lit up his puny, ugly self and, in that light, made him more dangerous than an assassin. Now he looked at Tagore, no longer splendid, suddenly dangerous. Where did they gain such strength? he wondered. Looking around him at the austerity of the pavilion, with its ink calligraphies, its silver dust, and its views onto trees and mist, he found the answer in himself: from beauty.

"And, in its wake, fervor," murmured Petrus on his left. "Take note that one can also achieve it through poetry or, better still, amarone."

Solon looked at him and kept silent, laughing softly to himself.

Tagore poured tea into the first cup in front of each guest. When he sat back down, he raised his cup to eye level but, to the surprise of Alejandro and Jesús, he then transferred the contents into the second cup. They followed his example and, like the others, raised the empty cup to their nose.

They had imagined they would smell some rare perfume, but they were overcome with a fug of dust and cellars. There were so many layers of memory and childhood sensations here that Alejandro and Jesús relived long-ago adventures, when the cellar opened doors leading to an enchanted land, a place of moss and hiding places where they could hope without hindrance and travel without ever going anywhere, a land of undergrowth, and storerooms where dreams were metabolized, a land blessed with that inexhaustible time which the next day would run like water through one's fingers—they breathed in the tea, wishing that it would never end, while the magic of the empty cup wove its way through the years. Now they saw themselves in the forest of the time when they were no longer children. A downpour soaked the branches and the earth dripped and steamed in newfound brilliance; the smell of wet pathways rose from the ground with a telluric spirit that recalled that of their youth. Alas, they had to make their way in life, and mature, and the boys became men in whom faith in infinity was transmuted into the awareness of death. However, as they leaned out of the window at the fortress, toward the rain-drenched courtyard, General de Yepes and his major breathed in the pungent fragrance wafting toward them and over them, between heaven and earth. We have gone back through time, thought Alejandro, just as the cup lost all smell, and with it the intoxication of seeing the world through the prism of years gone by.

"It is customary for one of us to recite a poem before we drink the tea," said Solon.

Alejandro thought of the words he'd received from Luis's ghost, and a very old memory came to him.

"In my country, there is a song we sing at funerals, in a dialect of Spanish no one can speak anymore," he said. "It's an old poem from Extremadura which the women brought to me long ago for my dead."

And, suddenly understanding the old idiom, he recited the last two lines.

To the living the harvests to the dead the storms
And then everything shall be empty and full of wonder

A prolonged murmuring spread among the elves.

"Those are the very words someone wrote here this morning," said Solon, pointing to the cloth on the partition of sand. "Usually we write the poems down after we have recited them, but today an invisible hand got there before us."

"I don't understand a thing," said Jesús, who was beginning to have pins and needles in his legs, and was wondering if they would ever get around to drinking.

Tagore smiled, put down his empty cup, and drank slowly from the full cup. The taste of the tea was subtle, and retained none of the aromas of dust and cellar. Rather, it tasted of the affability of days and the relaxing interval of twilight; nothing changed, nothing became, the tea was drunk, the universe was in repose.

A few seconds went by.

Alejandro blinked.

Before them, in the middle of the room, an earthenware bowl had appeared.

Its irregular edges gave birth to a consistency of light that was striking and powerful. The creator had preserved the rough texture of the earth from which it was made, but the shape was extremely elegant. The sides were straight and tall, without tapering, nor were they regular, but sculpted with a jagged surface, slightly flatter where the lips would be placed. Touches of dull silver here and there conferred a patina of time, although, goodness knows how, it was clear to all that the bowl had been fashioned the day before. If someone had asked Alejandro and Jesús what they were seeing, they would've replied, a simple earthenware bowl, although they were conscious of the fact that they were gazing at the work of time, and not only the work itself but also the simplicity of feelings it commanded. What sort of art is this which incorporates the imperfection of wear and urges us to be modest and pure? wondered Alejandro. Beauty is caught in the trap of a voluntary erosion where we can contemplate our entire existence, to such a degree that all that is left to do is live on effacement, earth, and tea.

"I saw this bowl in a dream a long time ago," said Maria. "That very bowl, precisely."

"For as long as the pavilion can remember, the writing of the poem has been followed by the appearance of a bowl," said Petrus. "They are all splendid but this one has something more that thrills the heart."

Tagore took it to each guest in succession. When it was Alejandro's turn to drink from it, he thought he could feel the softness of Clara's lips where she'd placed them before him, and he welcomed the faint, sweet taste of the tea on his tongue.

The guardian went back to his place.

They waited in silence.

Life was flowing. Life was drifting. Life was expanding, about to burst its banks. What were those lights in the forest? The world had changed and they could no longer see a thing. Inside them, the river was swelling, heavy with jewels. Were these pale flowers? Stars upon the surface of the dark waters?

Then the water flowed over the dark banks and, in a stormburst, Alejandro and Jesús discovered the world of the mists.

In this mourning
Liquid soul
I sleep enclosed in clouds
To the living the harvests to the dead the storms
Then everything shall be empty and full of wonder

Book of Prayers

他人

OTHER

E very major story is the story of a man or a woman who leaves behind the distress of the self to embrace the dizziness of the other.

For this journey, one needs the song of the dead, the mercy of poetry, and the knowledge of the four Books.

The Book of Prayers.
The Book of Battles.
The Book of Paintings.
And the fourth Book which, at this point in the story, we cannot yet name for fear it might be misunderstood.

This is the story of a few souls who, in war, knew the peace of encounter.

文字

The world of the mists had several languages. The elves communicated among themselves through the modulations of streams and breezes, and those who had stayed at the pavilion in Nanzen could speak every language on earth. For a long time, they did not have writing, but when the desire came to them, they chose one form of writing in particular.

There were two reasons for this.

The first had to do with a human country where people wrote that way. Like the land of elves, it was surrounded by an emptiness of turbulent seas lost in fog, and it reflected the theory of the ancient poet who said that the land of the living was merely an island surrounded by mist or by the waters of a great dream.

The second reason was more essential: not only was this writing beautiful, but in it one could admire the flight of dragonflies and the grace of wild grasses, the nobility of drawings in ash and the great whirlwinds of storms.

Hence, one can understand why we were tempted to leave some writing upon the silk in Nanzen, since beauty, nature, and dreams are, if not our exclusive preserve, at least our daily bread.

The territory of the elves unfolded before their inner gaze. Just as the perfume of the empty cup had opened the doors of the past to Alejandro and Jesús, the tea had transformed their mental space, and they were partaking of a vision that did not belong to them, but which caused the landscapes of the mists to parade through their minds with fresh new colors.

"There is someone in my head," murmured Jesús.

The sky was blue or golden, the foliage was bursting with green and tawny colors, mingled with touches of orange and purple; the bowl had taken on a gray patina enhanced with veins of old copper—this renewal filled Alejandro and Jesús with joy, as well as an unexpected nostalgia for the black sky and white trees.

"Once someone has seen the structure of beauty they can never look at things in the same way again," said Sandro. "I still wonder whether it sharpens your vision or burns your eyes."

"Where have these visions come from?" asked Jesús. "I feel as if I am simultaneously here and there."

"From the tea and the good offices of the guardian," answered Hostus, "who has the power to see what is far from him and to share that vision with us. We are together here and with him there. We can look at what is before us and inside us at the same time."

"Until now, the Guardians of the Pavilion came to us from

the two high families, the wild boars and the hares, who are more powerful in contemplation and in prescience," said Solon. "The lower houses of squirrels and bears, however, are more lively and agile in action."

"So squirrels and bears fight better than the others?" asked Jesús, looking at Tagore, who had closed his eyes and did not seem to hear them.

"Not at all," said Petrus, "wild boars and hares are great warriors. But they're not great when it comes to their sentimentality, and with them, the urge to fight comes from reasoning, whereas with the squirrels it springs from the enthusiasm in their hearts."

"If they're not busy drinking," said Marcus.

"Along with the bears," added Petrus.

And to Alejandro:

"The high-elves are the aristocracy of this world, but it doesn't mean the same thing as in your world. I was a sweeper for much of my life and I am as highly respected as a guardian of the pavilion."

"Sweeper?" said Jesús.

"Moss sweeper," said Petrus.

"What makes an aristocrat, then?" asked Jesús.

"He is responsible for others," answered Solon. "He shoulders the burdens of the community. Having said that, history has shown that certain squirrels have more spirit than all the hares put together, and that they can shoulder burdens that would crush many a wild boar."

"Is it possible to see any place in the universe from here?" asked Alejandro.

"Any place at all," replied Solon. "And if you would kindly take a look at what Tagore is about to show you, I will try and tell you the history of the mists."

"Then, perhaps we could find out what role we have to play in it," said Jesús.

They all fell silent as yet another landscape unfolded in their minds.

"Katsura," said the Head of the Council.

Until that moment, trees and mist had succeeded one another with monotonous grace. Now the guardian's guests could intermittently glimpse wooden pavilions, the outline of high mountains, or even the contours of strange gardens. Then the vision broke through the fog and slowly came to rest at the foot of Katsura. It was a large city surrounded by peaks, with low dwellings set in terraced rows on what should have been the slope of a hill—however, despite their efforts to make what they were seeing conform with what they knew, they were compelled to face facts: Katsura, the capital of the elves, the chief town of the province of Snows, backed onto a void, clung to a flank of mist the way other cities cling to a mountainside. As far as the eye could see, there was a similar magic of landscape and buildings poised upon layers of vapor. The world was afloat on an ethereal gauze and the vast city shone forth, even perched on a void. Never had human eyes gazed upon a more admirable panorama, for the wooden structures bathed in mist were humble and perfect, as in Nanzen, and floated between the sky and the light mists in a sanctuary of mystery and cloud. And also as in Nanzen, verandas ran around the gray-tiled houses, some of them tiny, others more vast and similar to temples. One in particular was striking. In front, there was a great rectangular courtyard covered in snow and planted with trees, their dark branches sprinkled with snowflakes as if at random. On these wintry boughs, twisted and knotty like those of old fruit trees, delicate flowers had bloomed, pink or red around their light stamens, with round petals braided with scarlet and white. And so, the blood of the corollas, the dark wood, the glistening of the snow: the fine season and the cold one sharing their love on the austere, bare branches, made these claw-shaped branches somehow necessary, so that one's gaze, all along—leaving the heart to endure its ecstasy—could pick the flower that had emerged from winter. A gust came to die in the enclosed courtyard and the petals, strained, seemed to swoon. Then, as they rose again in a graceful arabesque, the wind transformed the air into a brush and gave the scene a brilliance and disposition that supplanted all preceding scenes by way of beauty.

"What are those flowers that bloom in the snow?" asked Alejandro.

"Plum trees flowers," replied Clara. "An essence that yields no fruit, only perfume in winter."

"The headquarters of the Council of Mists," said Petrus, pointing to the building with the rectangular courtyard. "It also houses a large library where I used to work as a sweeper. There is lovely moss beneath the snow, and sand walkways that are cleared daily of dead leaves."

"What do sweepers do in winter?" asked Jesús.

"They read," said Solon. "But that part of the story is for later."

Alejandro focused on the vast valley beyond the city. Now and again, stolen from a patch of mist, a handful of gray roofs could be seen hanging on the line of sky. Everywhere there was the same snow, the same purple flowers on barren branches, the same swaths of steep mountain—and from one summit to the next, one tile to the next, one flower to the next, a painting was created the color of the first Nanzen, a play of ink and blood between darkness and light. Everything floated, the mist coiled upon itself, and the world sparkled in successive facets.

"Sometimes the mist decides to cover the universe, with the exception of a single bare branch," said Petrus. "Sometimes it contracts and we see the greatest possible proportion of things. But we never encompass all of them."

"Everything rests on a void," murmured Jesús.

"There are islands of land suspended in the mist," said Solon.

Hostus brought the bowl to each of the guests for a second time. Alejandro was surprised by the new taste of the tea, strong and pungent, with the hint of an unknown spice against the perfume of a white flower.

"Our tea opens and develops like wine," said Petrus. "There are vintages and cellars for aging. The one you are drinking today is over two centuries old. With each sip, you move forward in time, in the secret of stones, in the life of the earth."

Alejandro looked at the light cloth where, earlier, the poem had been written, and it seemed to him that the writing had changed. Some characters looked like human figures, others like trees or even flowers, and he was beginning to get used to their strange shapes, to make out the gist of the meaning—but his hunches were fleeting and slipped away the moment he thought he was about to grasp them.

It came stealthily, like a rustling of cloth or a ray of light. Was it around them? Was it inside them? A moment ago, they had been alone, now there were a multitude of them. When he used to haunt his cemetery, the young Alejandro heard the voices of the dead in an echo that seemed to come from the depths of the earth, but this time presences seemed to emerge from the mist in a way that is hard to describe, for humans are strangers to the community of the spirit, to the impalpable ties of those who, although they may not have their own body, do at least know the union of consciousness. Every existence in these lands acted in accordance with the mist, lives which, although they did not speak or appear to each other, could sense one another through osmosis.

"The mist is alive," said Jesús with a sigh.

"Let's just say it is the breath which brings the living together," said Petrus.

"It is by regulating the harmony of the mists from the pavilion that we assure the continuity of our world," added Solon.

"I thought natural phenomena were self-regulating," said Jesús.

"Our existence rests on an inhabited void, an osmotic medium we must alter so that it will answer the needs of our community. The mists are the web of eternity, and however slow our evolution might seem to humans, we live in time. And so, we transform the mists thanks to the properties of our tea, the power of temporal alteration without which the mists would ignore us. We drink our tea and the mists obey, the mists listen and we are together."

"How do the mists listen to you?" Alejandro asked.

"The guardian greets the mist and retransmits its message to the community," answered Solon. "The tea grants him this power to welcome and, in return, informs the mist of the elves' needs."

"He greets the mist?" asked Alejandro. "I thought you altered it."

"Welcoming is already a way of altering," said Solon, "it is even the highest possible level of altering reality. Few of us, however, are capable of this, to the level the mists require, and it is not by chance that the most powerful guardian the elves have ever had came to power during this era of total war. Without Tagore's empathy, I think we would already have foundered."

"Without his empathy for the mists?" asked Alejandro.

"His empathy for the whole, of which we are a fragment," said Solon. "Everything is connected, everything is attuned."

"Not everything is transformed into its opposite," said Alejandro. "Human beings do not become rocks."

"No," said Solon. "But they can hear the sorrow of stones."

On seeing that Alejandro, disconcerted, had fallen silent:

"Those who cannot hear the sorrow of the world cannot know themselves in their own sorrow."

"In that case, I wonder what your opinion of humans might be," said Alejandro.

"Most of you do not hear stones, or trees, or animals—our brothers, although they live in us elves the way we live in them," said Solon. "You see nature as the environment you share with other beings; for our kind, it is the principle that makes them exist—not only them, but everything that has been and that shall be."

The effect of the second sip of tea was making the presence of the elves more intense. For Alejandro and Jesús a thousand impressions were leading to a cacophony of images—they experienced the sensation of a vertiginous plunge into a valley of trees, and they realized they were leaping from treetop to treetop, until they landed on a new branch. Before long, it became a breathless race through a pre-human forest where the light of the sun struggled to enter. Low to the ground, the race lasted a long time in the exhalation of dead leaves, borne on the delight that the sap beneath the bark was also that which flowed in their blood. Suddenly, everything was illuminated and they were above fields of shrubbery with tight foliage, trimmed in vague rows across gigantic expanses. From these undulating stretches of green dunes, where furrows of mist reflected furrows of crops, there came a perfume of the sacred, familiar to Alejandro from cemeteries and battlefields. As they flew for a while over these plantations, the presence of the elves from the community grew ever more intense. They are never alone, thought Alejandro—it was as if he could feel every one of these foreign sentient beings without having met a single one, and deep in his chest he felt the piercing of a stake, both familiar and strange.

"These are the Inari tea plantations," said Clara.

He looked at her and the stake caused his heart to bleed.

"That is what the presence of those who do not suffer from

solitude does to those who are alone," she said. "The tea plantations carry the presence of the community."

"So tea is a sort of telepathic elixir?" asked Jesús.

"There are two ways to drink tea," said Petrus. "The ordinary method of each elf, which connects us to one another and keeps our bonds alive. And the extraordinary method, which takes place in the pavilion. It's the same tea, but Nanzen grants it other powers."

Tagore's vision changed and they saw a lagoon, above which the mist delineated a channel. Propelled by some invisible force, barges without sails drifted slowly across the lagoon, making their way between walls of fog that rose like high banks of clouds, and moved forward along the weave of the mists.

"Circulation between the major islands is one of those powers," said Petrus. "When the channel opens, the mist turns liquid and it is possible to sail there, like on a river. In peacetime, there are locks of mist that open and close at set times, but the Guardian of the Pavilion can change them as he sees fit. One of the great battles of this war has been over these shipping lanes. We have to intervene continuously regarding the configuration of passages, in order to bar the way to the enemy."

"I can't see any oarsmen or sails," said Jesús.

"Everything in our world is propelled by intention and vision," answered Petrus. "Through the tea, the guardian and his assistants visualize the destination, and transmit it to the boatmen."

The spectacle shifted yet again, and the slow procession of ships vanished, to be replaced by a peculiar garden. Can we even refer to it as such, something that contains neither flowers, nor trees, nor earth? Devoid of the charm of verdancy, it was an enclosure consisting entirely of stones and sand. On a flat expanse furrowed with parallel lines, a few rocks of varying shapes and sizes formed isolated summits in the sea. On the horizon of the shore other rocks rose in a miniature range of peaks, sculpted by the powers of earth and time. Everything was motionless, but the sound of the surf could be heard; everything was inanimate, but one sensed that the landscape was alive. I cannot imagine a more peaceful spot, thought Alejandro, and he felt a sense of relief that eased the lacerating pain of the stake. He turned to Jesús; stunned, he saw a tear flowing down his major's cheek.

"The stones are liquid," said Jesús, almost beseechingly.

"What do you mean?" said Alejandro, failing to understand.

He looked closely at the stones and suddenly he saw it, too. A few tongues of mist billowed over the garden, and wherever they had been, the rocks had turned liquid: they preserved their form by passing from solid granite to a quicksilver lava. All around, the sand was becoming a lake, shot through with the sparkling of gems before it returned to its hard mineral surface—thus, the sand and the stones not only represented the water and the mountains, but also incarnated the solidarity of states of matter, and Jesús Rocamora, gazing at the scene, was taken back to his early life.

"We are a world of incessant metamorphoses," said Solon. "We are transformed into horses and animals of the earth and sky but, in the past, beyond the three essences, we were every species at once."

"Vapor turns solid, rock turns liquid, and you will also see plant life becoming fire," said Petrus. "This is only possible because we live at the heart of the mists."

"What is this garden called?" asked Jesús.

"The garden of heaven," answered Petrus.

"Heaven," murmured Jesús.

Another tear trickled down his cheek.

"In heaven, then, everything is changed into its opposite," he said.

"The opposite is still the same, but in its extreme form, for everything proceeds from one and the same matter, with multiple facets," said Solon.

The garden of stones disappeared and an indistinct shape appeared on the horizon, perhaps a terraced city or a high cloudbank—what are we looking at, wondered Alejandro. But they went closer and it was indeed a city of wooden houses, surrounded by undulating fields where more tea was growing, although the plants did not undulate as gently as in Inari, and the leaves were colored gray, and cold.

"Ryoan, the city of the enemy, surrounded by its plantations of gray tea," said Petrus.

It was as vast as Katsura, with the same buildings surrounded with verandas, the same tiled gray roofs, the same trees with red flowers. There was the same beauty in the snow, the same encounter of seasons on the hospitable dark branches but, despite this, it was a horrible sight.

"There aren't any mists," whispered Jesús.

"There are *no longer* any mists," Solon corrected him. "They were once the most beautiful on earth and I don't know a single one of us who wouldn't have given his life for such glory. But Ryoan was crushed by the enemy and now you see the sad result. Everything has become rigid, the void is being filled, we are losing our life force and our connections, we cannot breathe and the community is disintegrating."

They stood for a moment facing the fallen city, picturing its erstwhile splendor, while once again, Alejandro felt his life spin upside down. The discipline he'd imposed upon himself in order to speak for his dead on the battlefield, his enduring solitude in spite of friendship, his castillo crippled with murder and poetry, the war and its abject processions—in the end, everything was being borne along on the flow of an unknown river that released an uninterrupted outpouring of debris inside him. If the sobriety of ink and whiteness in Nanzen seemed familiar, and if the humility of the earthenware bowl had transported him, it was because they'd made the bare structure of his life visible to him; and so, through the magic of feeling the impalpable presence of the tribe of elves all around him, the inhabited mists had offered him the pathway to the other—when he went deep inside himself and accepted his own destitution, he received in return the sweet delight of the encounter. Was it the presence of the elves that served as a balm and healed his grieving heart, or was it that his love for Clara had opened him to the possibility of receiving? I ask the question, but it hardly matters, for great power is a chimera inside us that either elevates us or kills us, since living is nothing more than being able to forge ahead in life by telling one-self the right story. The presence of the community of elves was, to Alejandro, a stronger remedy than the sufferings of the past, and Clara's smile completed the transfiguration. The stake was plucked from his heart and borne away on the waters of the river.

Jesús, too, gazed at the enemy city. With the strength of the mist, his faith had taken on a new dimension. The fact that the mist brought the breath that turned the stones to water made it the messenger of his redemption. The liquid rocks could change dishonor into honor, betrayal into a gift, and damna-tion into salvation, while this alchemy required the barrenness of the void. Moreover, we know that Major Rocamora, although he was not a man of words, was nevertheless a soul whose behavior could be affected by three lines of verse, and we weren't surprised that he was open to the grace of moving stones. Might I add, as I have an undeniable affection for these men, that the young General de Yepes and the young Major Rocamora, driven by their renewed hope that suffering might be transformed into fervor, had just ventured onto a path rarely used by humans. It has been marked out by the breathing of the void, which removes the mess that burdens us—however, we must not simply feel it in ourselves, but also discover it all around us, in the erasures in which true beauty is born, through the unique branch of a world engulfed in fog or through an earthenware bowl more spare than the trees in winter.

"What does the new poem say?" Alejandro asked Clara.

"I cannot read their language," she said, looking at the light cloth.

"*The last alliance*," said Petrus, who had turned toward the wall where the ink inscriptions were glowing faintly.

After a pause, he added:

"Separation is an illness, union is our way of life and our only chance. That is why we are founding our wager regarding this war upon new alliances."

He gave Solon a questioning look.

"We will speak of the prophecy later," said the Head of the Council.

Petrus remained silent and Alejandro said:

"So you are doomed to drink tea until your last breath."

The elf gave out a long sigh.

"That is the entire question of this war," he replied. "You have seen the color of the tea plantations around Ryoan. That ash gray comes from a noble rot which is eating at the leaves through an entirely natural process. All it will take is one degree more of humidity and a fungus will develop on the tea plants. You have something similar with wine, do you not, and it yields magnificent vintages? Simply, here, the consequences are fatal, and it is unfortunate that we did not realize this earlier. But this blindness, like all the rest, is due to the powers of gray tea."

"Fatal?" said Alejandro. "Everything we have seen of the tea up to now is that it makes drunkards sober and opens the door to humans to enter this world."

"Those are simply a few pleasant side effects," said Solon. "It is because of the power of gray tea that the enemy built his bridge and his pavilion and kept them invisible for a long time."

Tagore's vision rose in altitude and they discovered Ryoan's bridge and pavilion on the other side of the city. The construction was similar to the ones in Nanzen, except that the wood had been coated in gold leaf. The arch had the same curve and the same elegance as the red bridge, the pavilion had the same appearance of chaotic openings and immemorial verandas, but there was no more mist to be seen there than in the town of Ryoan itself, and everyone gazing upon this gilded splendor was cloaked in a feeling of deepest dissonance.

"The bridge can be crossed thanks to the power of the gray tea," said Petrus. "It is thanks to the tea that Aelius is conducting his war and accelerating the decline of the mist he claims to be saving. You will note that the enemy's strength resides in a substance that is easier to produce than any weapon on earth."

There was a moment's silence.

"That is why we have made a radical decision," said Solon.

The images vanished. Tagore opened his eyes and Alejandro felt a pang of anguish. Without knowing why, he recalled the words Jesús had uttered long before, the evening after the battle when they sat conversing on the shady little plateau. The best strategist, he had said, will be the one who looks death in the eye and sees what he must not be afraid of losing.

Tagore nodded his head.

"We will destroy the tea plantations," he said. "All of them, down to the last one, at dawn on the coming day."

Who knows what we are looking at

The Book of Paintings

TEA

Though elves loved poetry, they didn't make up stories. Those who are on good terms with the world have little need of works of the imagination, particularly as the tea served the same purpose as wine and human fiction—that of rooting the community in its earth and in the spirit of its members.

Can one conceive of a life without fables, or novels, or legends? One would have to endure, relentlessly, the burden of being oneself; there is no distance between consciousness and dreams, no way to escape from the naked truth; but in return, how great the ecstasy of living in the intimate glory of things.

However, when the elves began to notice the decline of their world, this gave rise to renewed resolution. That is surely how the temptation of Ryoan was born, whereas others came to think that an alliance between tea and wine could perhaps save them from disaster.

空

VOID

It is said that everything came into being from the void, the day a paintbrush traced a line separating earth and sky.

Poetry is the proper balance of earth, void, and sky; murder comes into being when it is forgotten.

One must travel light, said the ancient poet. Humans are weighed down with so many burdens! The mists of Nanzen could be so beneficial to them!

GENESIS
1800–1938

The practice of storytelling is a strange thing. The day before the great battle of this time, in the sixth year of the deadliest war ever endured by humans and elves, at a turning point between epochs, the likes of which only two have ever existed in the history of the humans of the West, I must take a shortcut in order to continue the tale. Just as the earth never appears so vast as after the tide, stories and fables require the ebb and flow of the seas—and so, just as the waters are changing, a simple shell is revealed which on its own knows how to embrace the entire cosmos. It is our eyes, our ears, our feelings and our knowledge, and it is to that shell that we must turn for light in the darkness.

Here it is, then, slightly less than a century and a half ago: our lonely shell at the moment when the great tide of kingdoms is ebbing.

TO THE LIVING
1800

There were not many elves as modest in appearance as Petrus, nor many destinies as brilliant as his. In fact, it seemed at the outset his fate was to remain as obscure as the woods and the good family of squirrels into which he was born. The Deep Woods, to the east of Katsura, were a region of mountains and forests inhabited by terraces of thorny pine trees, whose branches reached skyward from their twisted trunks, to form a sort of parasol, so elegant you could weep. Nature had created them in great number, then planted them one by one in the rocky surface, choosing each location as if it were the setting for a jewel. Then the entire scene was cloaked in mist, and as it emerged from the void it revealed a landscape of peaks crowned with pine trees that seemed to be writing upon the sky. The Deep Woods were highly valued by the community of elves and, bathed in the majesty of high-altitude fog, they went there to admire the rising and setting of a sun that glorified every branch and every engraving of foliage. From one summit to the next the elves proclaimed the beauty of the sight, and Petrus grew up with these dawns and twilights that rustled with sounds and poetry. The ridges stretched beyond space, against a golden backdrop sketched with the curve of pines.

There are many mountains worthy of such moments of wonder, but none can compare to these. Fortune had decreed they would be vertiginously high and narrow, and wherever one looked, the slender mass of summits bathed in an ocean of clouds. At times, the trees, set on a single salient peak, were as delicate as lace in the great mossy void. At other times, the entire range rose above the cloudbank and offered up its succession of peaks. But what ultimately enthralled one's vision was not the unending succession of undulating summits, but the fact that they overlooked a vaporous mass that seemed to give birth to each slope before leaving it with the kiss of a pine tree. Once lost in the sight, where the mystery of creation seemed to have found refuge, it was to encounter simply one's own self; as if one were a mountain in a storm that turned the world on its head then restored it to the hollow of its own consciousness; and this was what the elves of every province came to seek in the Deep Woods, traveling great distances to stand in the morning to face the mystery above them. Later they would recall the hard rock, which was smooth and affable in places and sharp as a blade in others, and again they would see the landscape of the Deep Woods, the velvet mists, and the beauty of the mountain range, as if it were their own internal landscape.

Quite logically, the province was largely inhabited by elves that were also squirrels, bears, and eagles, who feared neither the steep crags nor the dizzying heights. The villages seemed to have been transported through the ether before being deposited on their high plateaus; and then all was hidden, revealed, and so on, to infinity. And so, everything that was true for the world of elves in general was true here a hundred-fold, given the fact that these colossal spires reaching for the sky reserved for the mists valleys that were no less colossal, gigantic expanses where the hand of the elf could not be seen. From Mount Hiei,[2] all you could see on the horizon were three needles floating on the magma until, suddenly, ten more broke through the surface, and you felt reborn. The mountains, rising

[2] Pronounced "He-ay."

out of nothing, hovered suspended over this absence; through the force of the void, spirit and rock sketched a *pas de deux* on the summit of existence before turning back to the original nothingness; and these games of hide and seek, of incessant birth and dying, gave the mountain in return the shape of consciousness that it had lacked until then.

It was in such a land that Petrus—who was not yet called Petrus—was born and grew up. He retained a sincere affection for the realms of mountains and the poems of dawn. Lulled by the affection of his family and the favor of the great mists, his first decades were filled with enchantment and love. Far from the sound and fury of the rest of creation, the squirrel elves made up a peace-loving house. They didn't write poetry, but they gladly partook of the poetry of others and, although they thrilled to the speed of flight, they could remain motionless for long stretches of time. While they were frugal in nature, they knew how to entertain extravagantly, and even though they were far away from Katsura, they were never the last to reply to a summons from the Council. The surrounding landscape described them as well: as obscure as their woods and as noble as their mountains, they wandered in peace there, among tree-tops and cliffs, and didn't suffer from either metaphysical dilemmas or from any longing for unknown horizons.

Despite the idyllic landscape, Petrus's youth had been quite turbulent. Among his numerous relations he was unique because, ordinarily, all elves are identical: their human form is handsome and dignified, their horse is noble and thoroughbred, their third animal is ideally proportioned, but here we must face facts: our hero doesn't correspond to the norm of the species. Shorter than his brothers, he also had more padding, which had grown, by adolescence, into a little belly, the likes of which had never been seen on any local lads, and, year after year, he grew chubbier, and the fine features of his kin melted into a round mug. It's true that he had the most remarkable eyes in all the Deep Woods, and his mother had eventually come to believe that Petrus could be summed up by a pair of silver pupils. In reality, it was not only his eyes, but above all his gaze that was so striking, and the contrast between his chubby face and the pensive twinkle of his eyes meant that everyone around him grew irresistibly fond of him, so much so that the only elf in the mists who had a perfectly ordinary appearance had a special gift for arousing the affection of his peers. But others followed him not only because they loved him, but also because they wanted to protect him during those adventures where he oughtn't go on his own, for fear of losing his life. The mists had never seen a clumsier elf: he had almost lost his tail by getting it caught between two boulders, something which in all the memory of the Deep Woods had never happened, and it had earned him the torment of remaining trapped in his squirrel essence until his appendage was completely healed (and he was forced to nibble hazelnuts which—another oddity of his nature—he only moderately enjoyed, and this added to the pain he felt in his poor crushed tail). It must be said that his rescuers, once the fear that he might be seriously injured had been set aside, had some difficulty in restraining their laughter as they set about moving the boulders. Three days earlier, the same Petrus had almost killed himself, about to take a squirrel leap just as he'd decided to change into a horse, and he'd only been saved thanks to the thick carpet of fresh pine needles, where he landed with a stunning lack of grace. Icing on the cake, for no apparent reason he often tripped over his own tail. To slip on his own tail! For an elf, this was as unthinkable as turning into a cauldron. In short, the patent conclusion to be drawn from all this—even if one couldn't really understand why—was that Petrus would go from one disaster to the next, but his lucky star would save him, every time.

*

Naturally, his awkwardness and appearance were only the tip of the iceberg. What lay below the surface was a mind configured like no other, completely indifferent to the matters of mountains—perpetual rebirth, merging marvels, and so on. The morning of his first hundredth birthday he gazed glumly at the sparkle on the summits of jade-lacquered pine trees and thought that it would be impossible for him to live any longer in this sublime boredom. His usual sidekicks were there with him: a ravishing squirrel and a tall brown bear, full of the graceful, powerful vivacity Petrus utterly lacked—and, turning to them as they became lost in silent admiration of the landscape, he declared:

"I can't take it anymore, I have to get away."

"And where would you go?" asked the bear, tearing himself away from the splendor of the vista.

"I'll go to Katsura," said Petrus.

"You'll get yourself killed ten minutes into the trip," the other squirrel pointed out, "and if you survive your own bad luck, you'll pick the wrong channel."

"It doesn't matter where I go," Petrus said obstinately. "I just don't want to end up like some old pine tree on a peak that's never seen the world."

"But the world is inside you," said the bear, "in every pine tree, every peak, and every boulder you see."

Petrus sighed.

"I'm bored," he said, "so bored I could die. If I hear one more poem about twilight I'll make a point of throwing my horse into the void of my own free will."

In the distance, they could hear the modulation of a voice as supple as bamboo, as crystal-clear as a stream, and saying something which, in the language of humans, meant roughly:

Dark woods on the edge of mist

My friend the pine
Whispers to the twilight

"Right," said the bear, placing his paw on Petrus's shoulder, who was holding his head in his hands and shaking it gloomily, "don't torment yourself like this. For every problem, there's a solution."

The solution was what Petrus had stated. He had to leave. Inside him rumbled a call which his hundredth birthday made irrepressible, and the very next day he left the Deep Woods in the company of his two sidekicks—without his mother knowing, because she would have tied him to a tree—and without the slightest idea of what he would do in Katsura.

"We'll go with you as far as the capital," said his friends, "then we'll come back here. We can't reasonably set you loose on the world without an escort."

If ever there was an epic journey, this was it. There can be little doubt that without his guardian angels—whom you will recognize as the future Paulus and Marcus—Petrus would have gotten lost and killed a hundred times or more. His distraction and awkwardness were compounded by the fascination of the journey. Never had he breathed like this, never, since leaving the Deep Woods had they been so dear to him, and never had he understood their message so clearly. Distance was enlightening, as it clarified the scene he'd gazed upon all his life in vain, and gave it meaning through magic and nostalgia. Again, he saw Mount Hiei and its spire pointing toward the sky with a pang in his heart as delicious as it was wrenching, and he was astonished that it had taken this departure for him to feel the fullness of being in every rock and every pine needle, in a whispering friendship, touched by the mystery of the living. Four days after they had left the territory of the Deep Woods, he felt a moment of regret so sharp and painful that he came to a halt in the middle of the path, stunned at the sensation of ecstasy this wound had given him. They'd just reached the region of the Southern Marches, a short cold plain where the mist glided like seagulls above the shore. This was the last stage before the first channel, since they were reaching the edge of the earth and would soon have to call on the services of the boatman. They had already been circling the abysses of mist on which the mountains stood for a long time, but soon there would be no more path and they all thought excitedly about their first passage through the locks. They'd never left home, and Paulus and Marcus had to confess they were enjoying this adventure. Now, however, Petrus was standing stock-still in the middle of the path, overcome and radiant, and so oblivious to everything around him that he could have walked on the tongue of a dragon and never realized.

The channel was one of the smallest in the mists, for the Southern Marches and the Deep Woods had the lowest population density in this world. However, when they came within sight of the estuary, the spectacle was phenomenal. The black earth stretched lazily between its bands of fog, then came up against a mountain of mist that rose toward a sky so high it never seemed to end; there were no more bearings, no sense of distance, only an intuition of infinity that split any scale of vision wide open.

"Who knows what we're looking at," murmured Petrus, emerging from the abyss of his thoughts to dive into the abyss of the channel, no longer able to tell reality from madness.

At the tip of the estuary they came upon others aspiring to cross, waiting and drinking tea at the way station. A little otter elf, not yet twenty years old, was serving the travelers. Petrus, who didn't feel at all like drinking, collapsed on a chair and sat there without touching his cup—which was a great pity because the tea served at the estuary of the Southern Marches is prepared according to a very special method, with a view to ensuring the comfort of the voyage.

For the time being everything was calm. They could hear the cries of birds, they admired the fast-moving mist, the black earth, the pilgrimage trails. Seated at right angles to infinity, the travelers conversed placidly among themselves. The elves' osmotic life and their immersion in the cosmological dimension of the world have made them a species that is unfamiliar with solemnity. Humans only resort to solemnity because in everyday life they are small, but under certain circumstances are called upon to raise themselves up to an unaccustomed level of the soul. But elves, as a rule, are tall, since in their hearts they respect the presence of wholeness, and they have no need to raise themselves up or to let themselves go. And so, while they were waiting until it was time for the channel to open, everyone sipped phlegmatically on their tea, at the foot of immoderation. The paneless windows in the way station looked out onto large sections of lagoon and sky, mingled like so many charming pictures—however, since the weather was mild on that late autumn afternoon, everyone stayed out on the veranda to make the most of these nuptials of earth and sky.

The channel of the Marches opened twice a day, at daybreak and again at roughly five o'clock in the afternoon, in order to serve Hanase,[3] the main town in the province of the Ashes, in what was, give or take, a slow four-hour crossing. From Hanase there was another lock to pass through before they reached Katsura. Shortly before five o'clock, the voyagers saw the father of the little otter come in, for he was also the boatman. His equine incarnation, with its robe flecked with shimmering light from the water, was transformed into an otter with an impressive build. His human features seemed to have

[3] Pronounced "Ha-na-say."

changed in substance: while preserving their shape, they had become liquid, illuminated by that tremulous light one finds beneath the surface of the water. Was it from living in these desolate Southern Marches, where the earth had become the shore, and the sky had turned into the sea? His physiognomy represented some essential immersion, the original wave through which we are no longer objects, but flow—who knows what we are looking at, thought Petrus again, ruminating on a failure to merge with the flow of mist which left him, frustrated and unhappy, on the banks of the river where his fellow creatures were frolicking.

"Well, damn," he murmured.

Now the channel opened. It's crucial to remember that everything was ordained through Nanzen, and in Nanzen, by the pavilion, and in the pavilion, through the agreement between the guardian and his mists. In those days, the guardian was a wild boar elf who was about to begin his four hundredth year of service, and who was intimately acquainted with the currents of his world. Thus, everything unfolded at a pace that was unequalled in harmony; the channel opened, the mist which had hitherto risen to the heavens now coiled inward and dissolved into a liquid carpet where barges appeared, moored to a wooden pier; finally, everything became stable and everyone, connecting to the mist, set off at a march behind the boatman. Petrus, absorbed by his metaphysical ruminations, morosely afflicted by his sentiment of exclusion from the great brotherhood of elves, only half paid attention as he followed along behind. Moreover, for him to understand the boarding maneuvers, he should have drunk the tea at the way station. But because he hadn't, and was ignorant of the instructions the others had received, he did everything all wrong: instead of staying in the middle of the pier with his eyes down and walking in a straight line to board his barge, he veered off slightly to the left and, still in a glum mood, cast a sullen look at the mist.

A fleeting sensation of dizziness suddenly tipped him over the edge of the pier. There was a hellish *splash* which caused everyone to turn around, while the boatman gasped with disbelief, but before Paulus and Marcus could say a word the elf, ordering them to stay still, called out into the mist for help.

"Don't be afraid," he said to them.

A moment passed in total silence. The voyagers, trying not to feel dizzy, concentrated their gaze on the spot where the unfortunate elf had disappeared. After a long while, there were ripples on the surface of the passage, and Petrus slowly rose above the mist, imprisoned in a net held in the mouths of four silvery dolphins. The contrast between the squirrel's distraught expression—his tail stuck in the fine mesh of the net, thus preventing him from transforming himself—and the smiling grace of the large dolphins was so striking that Paulus and Marcus, after an initial effort, were no longer able to contain their laughter. The squirrel's face was also painfully squeezed by the net, and was dripping pitifully. His fur was drenched, and he looked like a poor hairless critter set to dry by the fire. The dolphins pulled the sides of the net together so that he could be hoisted up onto the solid wooden pier and, exhausted and dying of shame, there he collapsed, wheezing like a turbine.

"In the five hundred years I've been doing this job, I've never seen such a thing," said the boatman, his otter face still wearing the same flabbergasted expression as his human face had the moment Petrus fell.

"But you do have nets," Marcus pointed out.

"For baggage," he replied, "in case they get knocked over or there's wind. But for an elf!"

Petrus continued to blow like a whale.

"Thank you, my friends," he croaked to the dolphins, breathing heavily.

One of them swam up to him and, raising his silver snout, let out a shrill arpeggio, before going back where he had come from.

"Mist dolphins," murmured Paulus. "I'd heard of them, but actually seeing them is something else entirely."

"There is a great population in the mist," said the boatman, "and my best friends are there."

Then, to Petrus:

"Perhaps you too are fated to have strange friendships."

Petrus would have liked to answer him, but he'd gotten his paw stuck between two planks on the pier and was trying to work it loose as discreetly as possible, which in fact led to frenetic wiggling that revived Paulus and Marcus's laughter. Finally, he achieved his aim and, springing up, took with him a centuries-old slat of wood as he did.

The boatman looked at him with stupefaction.

"Good," he said after a moment, "let's go now."

Marcus and Paulus escorted their waterlogged friend, and everyone was able to board. There were six of them in each barge, and four boats in all. The boatman had taken his seat in the boat with the three friends, joined by a pair of deer elves. The mist was lapping faintly at the side of the boats and Petrus, who'd ended up in the bow, was catching his breath. After his fall, in the seconds before the arrival of the rescuers, he hadn't felt any real fear. The mists in the channel had the texture of air and water combined, the resistance of a liquid in which he could breathe, and this aqueous, gaseous weave aroused in him the awareness of a time when the living dwelled equally on earth and in the sea, in an airy existence made of oxygen, sunshine, and water.

"We dwell in the atmosphere," he thought, as the boatman closed his eyes and the crossing began.

He gave a sigh and hoped for a well-deserved rest. It would

have been magnanimous, indeed, if he could have stayed with his thoughts about strange friendships and cosmological fluidities. The mist was rising with streaks of gray iridescence, as if composed by a painter with a delicate touch, using here a light brushstroke, spreading there a wash in successive layers of dark ink. There were moments when the flows of mist rose all at once toward the sky, and clustered together in a tasseled cloud. Then everything grew lighter, and in the clarity after the storm, as if a brush had divided the world in two, one could make out the perfect line of the horizon. As a rule, Petrus enjoyed these demonstrations of cosmic painting, for he appreciated the beauty of the universe, and his gaze differed from that of his peers: he felt that this beauty was calling for *something else*, whereas his fellows wanted nothing more than the beauty itself, but he had no idea what that something else could be. Often, when in his Woods he gazed at the summits dotted with their ineffable pine trees, he could sense an undulation trying to emerge, vibrating lightly in the air with each twilit poem, but then it dissolved, for lack of whatever it was that was missing and which, he could tell, was missing in him, too. And while in the poetry there was some of this mysterious restlessness, the manner in which the lines agreed with an outside world from which he felt irrevocably separate left him dissatisfied, deprived of the instrument that would at last have enabled him to *experience* his moments of ecstasy.

So, he had believed that the crossing would provide a respite for him, give him time to become himself again, and the early moments had seemed to keep that promise. But for a while, now, the barge seemed to him to be rocking a great deal; above all, he could feel the stirrings of nausea, and that did not bode well.

"Do you feel sick, too?" he whispered to Paulus.

"No," replied the elf, astonished.

Then, with consternation:

"You don't feel mist-sick, I hope?"

"Feel what?" asked Petrus, alarmed.

Paulus looked at him with trepidation.

"Mist-sick. Travel-sick. Did you drink the tea at the way station? Normally, you shouldn't feel like this."

"No, I didn't drink it," said Petrus, now frankly worried. "I wasn't in the mood to sit drinking tea."

"What's going on?" asked Marcus, coming closer, "Why are you whispering like conspirators?"

"He didn't drink his tea," said Paulus wearily. "He wasn't in the mood."

Marcus looked at Petrus.

"I cannot believe it," he said, finally.

And, divided between exasperation and pity:

"How do you feel?"

"Horrible," said Petrus, who didn't know which tormented him more, nausea, or the prospect it could get worse.

To make things worse indeed, a few hours earlier, on leaving his pine forests, now more beloved than ever, he had stuffed himself with herb pâté (something he adored) and some of those sweet little red berries that can be found at the edge of the Southern Marches (and which he was mad about). Subsequently he had felt terribly sleepy, which had made the last leg of the journey quite difficult. Now there could no longer be any question of sleeping, because the pâté, the berries, and a few older remains of cranberry compote were fighting for the honor of coming out first, while Petrus, looking all around him in horror, saw nowhere that he might reasonably dispose of them.

"You're not about to throw up now, are you?" whispered Marcus in a hiss of irritation.

"Do you honestly think," gasped Petrus, "that I have any choice in the matter?"

His fur had taken on an interesting greenish tinge.

"Not in the barge, please," said Paulus.

"Above all, not in the mist," said Marcus.

He sighed with pity and weariness.

"Take off your clothes," he said, "and do what you have to do in them."

"My clothes?" said Petrus indignantly.

"Stay a squirrel or a horse, whichever you prefer, but take off your clothes and be as quiet as possible," answered Marcus.

Petrus wanted to answer back, but he seemed to suddenly think better of it, and his companions understood that the dreaded moment had arrived. Once he'd changed into a man, he turned modestly to one side and removed his clothes, baring his pretty little round white buttocks, which were sprinkled with freckles. Then he changed into a squirrel. What is about to follow will remain forever in the annals of the mists, for no one had ever seen such a thing and, above all, *heard* such a thing. Vomiting is very rare among elves, for they do not indulge in excesses harmful to the smooth workings of the organism, and so the event was shocking in and of itself. But you must know that of all the animals, squirrels get it over with most indelicately. Consequently the other three elves turned away with horror the moment they heard the first rumblings of release.

"What's going on?" asked the boatman, while Petrus was apocalyptically spewing his guts out.

"He's mist-sick," answered Paulus.

"I'm sorry," hiccupped Petrus between two bursts of pâté.

The boatman and the two deer looked at him, stunned.

"Didn't he have tea at the way station?" asked the boatman.

No one answered. For a moment, they could see that the boatman was piecing a series of concordant clues together and, gazing at the finished picture, finally understood that he was dealing with a madman. Just then, Petrus let out a final spasm and the boatman laughed so hard it caused the entire barge to shudder, bursting the deer's eardrums. His laughter gradually subsided and then, looking at the pale squirrel clutching his clothes close to him, he said:

"Well, dear friend, I have no doubt that an interesting destiny awaits you."

And we know he was right about that. At present, however, the voyage had become a nightmare, and Petrus's stomach, emptier than it had been in decades, was now regurgitating nothing more than a little bitter bile and the shame of having soiled his clothes.

"I won't kill you," Marcus said, "that would be letting you off too lightly."

But Petrus shot him such a pathetic look that he softened his tone somewhat.

"I hope this has taught you a lesson," he sighed, in the end.

As for Paulus, he was far more positive.

"I'd never seen one of our kind throw up," he said, showing a lively interest. "It seems really horrible."

The crossing continued at its slow pace, rocking Petrus with nausea. The others enjoyed sailing through the mist. The boatman had closed his eyes and the barges moved along smoothly, in close collaboration with Nanzen. It was an hour for prayers, and all the elves knew this, without ever having learned as much. Immersed in the inhabited void of the mist, in symbiosis with the living creatures of the world, becoming the vapor that conveyed the message, and, beyond, turning into water, air, mountains, trees, and rocks, the passengers were lost in gratitude for the great cosmic mix. That is how our prayers that do not require liturgy are recited, and how our hymns are sung, when the point is not to worship—if praying, as I believe, really means loving life. The barge plowed its way through the mist, life turned gently back in on itself, and everyone nestled in the furrows of the mystery of being there.

Then the journey was over. The channel began to close over again behind the barges and they could see a pier on the shore similar to the one in the Southern Marches.

"You will get off first, and go straight ahead," said the boatman to Petrus once they'd docked. "Here there are no dolphins, but there are divers who don't want to jump in just when the passage is closing over."

Petrus, obeying conscientiously, hopped as fast as he could toward the shore and collapsed, panting, before he even knew where they'd landed, and it took his breath away.

Directly opposite, Hanase sat at the top of a hill of mist so thick it seemed to be lifting the city skyward. Gray particles, rising up from gardens of trees and rocks where smaller, rounder shapes could be discerned, floated upon the scene.

"Hanase," said the boatman.

Everyone stood silent and motionless on the shore. In keeping with ritual, he added:

"The dead must tend to the living."

And they stayed there, silent, honoring in their hearts those who had passed away before them.

> *The dead must tend to the living*
> *The living shall know strange friendships*

Book of Prayers

ASH

Ash is the boundary of matter and dream, the world made visible in near-evanescence.

祈

PRAYERS

Is the Book of Prayers the oldest book of all? Some think it requires the prior violence of battles. But those who hear the great clouds speak and the breathing of trees know that the first breath is also the first prayer, since no one can fight without first taking in pearls of air.

Like a day slipping between two clouds of ink, like an evening sighing in the weightless mist, wrote the poet. The breath that brings the world to life is necessary to this relaxation from the world—the ecstasy that helps humans to escape themselves, and the magic allowing the world to enter gracefully into them, are the literal text of the first oration. In this impalpable trance, they breathe in unison in the mingled air of the living and the dead, and thus they know what their fathers before them fought, and painted.

Hanase, the City of Ashes, the second sanctuary of the mists.

"I seem to recall that the year we studied the four sanctuaries, you were snoring at the back of the class, after stuffing yourself with redcurrants," said Paulus.

"Ah yes, the four sanctuaries," said Petrus, struggling with a vague memory buried by digestion and naps.

They set off. Night was falling, and the lights on the hillside were coming on. Petrus could think of nothing but a good bed and something to fill his stomach, and he found the straight path to the city monotonous.

"The four sanctuaries," he murmured, nodding off and tripping over his tail.

Behind him, Marcus gave a sigh.

"Oh," said Petrus again, stopping short, "the four sanctuaries, Hanase, the City of Ashes."

"Well done," said Marcus, giving him a thump.

"I mean, now I remember. But I'm almost certain that I was asleep during that lesson," said Petrus, captivated by the mechanism he'd just discovered, and beginning to suspect that his awkwardness and distraction could also be his genius.

For now, along the narrow strip of land, the evening mist sighed to the rhythm of lazy twists and turns; although it was almost pitch dark and they couldn't see any trees, the passage was shrouded in those shadowy scatterings of light formed by foliage in good weather, and their nocturnal stroll was resplendent with the lightness of dragonfly wings falling from invisible branches.

"The transparencies of the way to Hanase are renowned," said the boatman, coming up to Petrus. "They are said to be even more beautiful than the ones in Nanzen. Whatever the case may be, they both share the memory of the origins."

"The origins?" echoed Petrus, who was thinking of other things.

He had a headache and everything was muddled again.

"The memory of trees," said the boatman, looking at him, somewhat puzzled.

"What does that have to do with origins?" muttered Petrus out of mere politeness.

The boatman stopped in the middle of the path.

"What do you mean, what does it have to do with origins?" he asked.

"Forgive me, my mind was elsewhere," said Petrus. Suddenly wrested from his thoughts, he didn't understand a thing, but didn't want to get in trouble either.

The boatman began walking again.

"There are some, nowadays, who forget the origins," he said, with a mixture of anger and sadness; "it does not bode well."

"Would you be so kind as to close your trap until tomorrow?" muttered Marcus.

"I was thinking of something else," Petrus replied, "my head is upside down and my stomach is empty."

"He's thinking about eating," said Marcus, turning back to Paulus.

"By the way," said Petrus, "the memory of trees, the whispering of pines, the breathing of the world—I had my fill of all that in the Deep Woods, don't start on it again here."

Paulus tapped him curtly on the head.

"Shut your mouth," he said, "I don't want to hear you blaspheming."

Petrus rubbed his scalp reproachfully.

"What is this city of the dead, anyway? If someone would tell me, maybe I would shut up."

Paulus sighed and, working his way toward the front of the procession, went to speak to the boatman.

"Could you tell us where there might be a teahouse open at this time of night?" he asked.

"I'll take you there," said the boatman, glancing with dismay at Petrus. "You can also sleep there."

But after a short silence, he gave a smile that spread from ear to ear on his silken otter face.

"At least you don't get bored with this one around," he said.

Before long, they arrived at the gates of Hanase. The streets were narrow, but as they walked up toward the top of the hill, they passed large gardens where gray flakes were rising, then enveloping the city. It was dark in those enclosures, and they could just make out the shapes of trees and rocks, and other, rounder shapes, from which the ashen sequins seemed to be wafting. Petrus, who had forgotten his headache and his hunger, followed his companions in silence, absorbed by the unusual atmosphere of the city. They passed a crowd of elves wandering through the halo of cottony particles, along the sides of beautiful houses where wooden verandas were adorned with low tables and comfortable cushions.

"Pilgrimage houses," said the boatman to Paulus, pointing to one of them. "You could have spent the night there, too. But I think your friend needs a more robust experience."

At the very top of the city, they stopped outside a dwelling plunged in darkness. On the wooden sign to the right of the entrance they could only make out the sign for tea.

"The oldest teahouse in Hanase," said the boatman.

"I hope they have room," said Marcus. "I'm exhausted."

"It's Nanzen that ordains the flow of tea," said the boat-man. "There is always room."

He bowed amiably.

"Now I shall leave you," he said.

And to Petrus, half-derisive, half-kindly:

"Good luck, my friend."

The three companions, now on their own, looked at one another.

"Do we have to knock?" asked Paulus.

"Would you rather sing a serenade?" replied Petrus testily.

He was hungry again and he felt a shooting pain in his head. Raising his hand, he prepared to knock.

Before he had time to complete his gesture, the door sound-lessly slid open to reveal a vestibule perfumed with an aroma of undergrowth and iris. On the dirt floor, three large flat stones, freshly rinsed with clear water, invited them to move forward into the darkness. At the back of the entrance, an ele-vated wooden floor led to a doorless opening, enhanced with a short, two-paneled curtain bearing the sign for tea. It had been calligraphed in a style whose name our friends didn't know, but I may reveal it, if you like, because it matters to the beauty of the moment: and so, drawn in the style of wild grasses, the sign for tea invited them to enter. Beneath their bare feet the water was like the ford of a river. In an alcove on the right, an incense stick gave off its fragrance of fresh breeze and humus, wrapping them in a veil of iris and moss.

"I love irises," murmured Petrus (who was not only a stom-ach, but also a nose).

They sat down on the edge of the floor and waited for the soles of their feet to dry. Then they headed toward the opening and, crouching down, crept under the curtain.

In front of them was a long corridor; on either side, closed sliding doors; all around, the dull, gentle sound of rain on stones, although it was dry in the building and there were no signs of the rainstorm, apart from its resonance. The soft melody, however, making its way into the recesses of their hearts, made them feel like crying. They followed the corridor as far as another opening marked by a curtain printed with the same sign. Beyond it was darkness. Paulus, the first to crouch down, went under the cloth, and Marcus and Petrus heard him cry out from very far away.

"I'll bet you that on the other side we'll fall into an endless vortex," murmured Petrus.

"I'm surprised you know that word," said Marcus.

Behind the curtain was a dark vestibule, where it seemed to Petrus all his senses were on the alert; then the scene that had caused Paulus to cry out was revealed to them.

They were standing on a podium overlooking a garden. The moon had risen and illuminated the entire scene, with the help of stone lanterns where torches had been lit. Three earthenware bowls awaited them on the floor. Beyond them was the garden. A stream wound its way to a pond where the dark sky was reflected. Crowning the motionless waters were the bare azaleas of winter, their branches reaching out in battle order, and they offered the eye even more joy than the summer generosity of their flowers. All around the pond was a beach streaked with parallel lines. In a few places, they could see the leaves of a heavenly bamboo plant standing above the furrows on the shoreline; in another spot, three rounded stones added commas to the text of the sand. Further still the moon, streaming with a weave of light, polished the leaves of the maple trees. But although the garden was very beautiful, it did not derive its substance from its natural elements: at the end of the pond, a bronze basin tossed light ashes up into the twilight; they flew into the ether like moths, rising slowly from the bowl into the sky.

"It is a funeral urn," murmured Petrus.

"It is a funeral urn," said a female voice, causing them to turn in unison to see a snow-white mare smiling amiably at them.

She changed into a female hare, her fur sparkling with moonlight, iridescent with silvery shimmers. When at last she became a woman, they could not take their eyes off her time-less face, a delicate mother-of-pearl that seemed to have been dusted with a transparent cloud, and this eternal beauty, and the exquisite texture of her complexion, left Petrus with the impression of an unfamiliar, grandiose world.

"The boatman asked us to receive you this evening," she said.

And, to Petrus:

"If you will give me your garment, we will wash it."

His fur turned crimson.

"You will be more comfortable as a man, to drink tea," she said.

Then she added:

"Apparently the boatman likes you."

Petrus, in torment, handed his soiled clothes to her, and she disappeared behind the curtain.

Paulus and Marcus looked at him and guffawed.

"Luxury cleaning," said Paulus, mocking.

"You offloaded your puke onto the most beautiful creature in the universe," Marcus pointed out.

"I didn't do it on purpose," said Petrus, wretchedly.

"That's worse," said Paulus, "that means you'll do it again."

They gazed silently at the garden. Stones had been laid on the bed of the stream in order to create the loveliest melody, and now the scene was lulled with its special music. This type of activity had always bored Petrus as much as tea calligraphy and flower arranging, along with pottery and singing, that were part of a young elf's education for an unbelievable length of time. He got pins and needles in his legs when it came to art lessons, and his only consolation was the presence of flowers, which he loved passionately. Most of the time, alas, he had to make do with looking at some unfortunate peony withering on its stem before it was stuck in its vase beneath the tea poem. But whenever he tried to complete the exercise, which meant he rummaged at random in the floral display, the professor looked vexed and, shaking his head, murmured some vague excuse before grabbing the flower from his hands.

"You just put a white tulip under an ode to three scarlet camellias," Paulus said to him. "Can't you try and read, at least?"

"If only we could eat them," sighed Petrus in return.

In fact, he did nibble at them now and again, in secret, for not only was he crazy about the perfume of flowers, but also their taste, and he knew all the ones that were edible. You must understand the extent of Petrus's extravagance: elves do not eat much in the way of flowers or leaves, any more than, by nature, they eat any part of an animal, since the former are the source of life and the latter are their brothers—and so a feast of that kind was tantamount to devouring the very cause of their existence or worse yet, devouring themselves, and Petrus was always very careful to hide when he indulged in his vice. Clover, violets, and nasturtiums featured in the trio of his preferences, but he wouldn't turn his nose up at a wild rose, either, and they grew in abundance around the family home, because his mother knew of nothing more refined than their fragile corollas above their black thorns. As Petrus feared his mother more than any other secular power on earth, he was doubly mindful when pillaging the woods. As a result, he was never caught, and remained awkward when it came to subjects that did not interest him, but crafty and furtive when his desire was aroused.

This time, Petrus was sensitive to the charm of the stream. Night was deepening and something inside him was slowing down. A flake landed on his paw and he gazed at it with curiosity.

"No one knows who we are looking at," said the hare elf, startling him.

He looked again at the ash, so light and potent in its near-immaterial state.

"Are they our dead?" he asked.

She handed him his clothes.

"They are our dead," she replied.

Petrus regretfully allowed the ash to fly away and he took his clothes back, covering himself just as he was transformed into a man.

"You are a high-elf," said Marcus. "This is the first time we've met a representative of your house."

She motioned to them to sit down by the three empty bowls. A high-elf, thought Petrus, that is why there is an invisible burden on her shoulders and a perfume of hidden worlds all around her. Maybe that's what I am looking for.

"It's not what you are looking for," she said. "Your destiny is elsewhere, but I don't know how to see it. Unprecedented things are happening in the mists these days, and we have become attentive to unusual circumstances. Perhaps you are one of the pieces of this strange puzzle that is being assembled."

Paulus and Marcus adopted the expression of the well-brought-up who must not be rude, and Petrus himself, although flattered, seemed doubtful.

"Puzzle?" he asked courteously, all the same.

"The Council issued a new alert yesterday in several provinces where the mist is in difficulty," she said.

"Has it affected Hanase?" asked Paulus.

"As you were able to see from the lock; our mist is intact," she replied.

A shadow passed over her face.

"The day it is affected, we can bid farewell to this world."

She made a graceful gesture with her right hand.

"But these are merely passing nighttime thoughts."

They saw that the bowls had been filled with a golden tea that flickered with the same light as the bronze sides of the basin.

"One of you must choose a flower and recite a poem," she said.

Marcus looked mockingly at Petrus.

"Would Mr. Puzzle feel up to honoring his studious past?" he asked.

Astonishingly, Mr. Puzzle did feel up to it. Was it the strangeness of the situation, the hollow feeling in his stomach, or the touch of the flake of ash—it seemed to him that the inanity of his years of schooling was being driven against the cliffs of the present moment, releasing a trembling corolla from its gangue.

"I would like an iris," he said.

An iris appeared, lying between the bowls, smaller than those you are accustomed to seeing in your gardens, its white petals dotted with pale blue, its heart deep purple, and its stamens orange.

"A Ryoan iris," she said. "They are to be found mainly in the province of Dark Mists, but one can also occasionally come upon them around here. In the tradition of the worlds, irises are messengers, flowers of annunciation."

"The tradition of the worlds?" asked Petrus. "What worlds?"

"The world of elves and the world of humans," she said. "I have studied the human symbolism of flowers, and it is similar to our own."

"Are you acquainted with the world of humans?" said Petrus.

"No," she replied, "you can only see it from Nanzen, but I

used to belong to the Council's community of gardeners. In my moments of leisure, I went to the library to read books about humans and flowers."

"Humans really exist," asked Marcus, "they're not just a legend?"

"A legend?" she said, surprised.

"It's hard to believe in something that only exists in your thoughts," said Marcus.

"Existence is not a variable given," she said. "Reality is the place where hunger and faith, life and death, dreams and flowers all come together and blend. A tree, an elf, a note of music, a chimera born from the night—everything exists while proceeding from the same matter, and all is displayed within the same universe."

She fell silent and Petrus suddenly thought of a poem, which he recited to those gathered there.

The mandate and the realm
In the heart of an old woman
An iris from Ryoan

Paulus and Marcus looked at him, stunned, but their hostess closed her eyes and was contemplative for a moment.

"I cannot see everything your poem is invoking," she said. "There are the living, the dead, and strange friendships."

"I saw . . . I saw peculiar images," said Petrus.

He tried to grasp one of them as it was slipping away, like flowing water.

"There was a faint sound from another world," he murmured, troubled.

She looked at him thoughtfully. After a moment, she made the ritual gesture of invitation by placing her hands, joined at her fingertips, on the floor, and bowing her face toward them. They greeted her by bowing their heads in turn and raising their bowls to the sky. Then they drank. The moon sparkled and sent a silvery flash through the ashes. The tea tasted of clay and chalk turning into dust and dirt.

"I've never drunk anything like this," said Paulus.

"This tea is a thousand years old," she said.

"A thousand years?" gasped Marcus. "To what do we owe the honor?"

"To the boatman, and Nanzen," she said.

"I didn't know that a simple boatman could prevail upon Nanzen to serve a thousand-year-old tea to three traveling strangers," said Paulus.

"A simple boatman? The channel that connects the Marches to the Ashes is one of the most ancient in this world," she said, "and it is always remarkable elves who seek to be in charge of it. Moreover, otters constitute a very particular lower house, engendering some of the most extraordinary characters in the mists."

"Why is that?" asked Petrus.

"If you will just take another sip," she replied, "you'll see why."

They drank again from their bowls. Ever since Paulus and Marcus, still under the effect of the tea from the Marches, had landed on the shores of Hanase, they'd been hearing the distant sounds of the dead all around them, mingled with the effervescence of the living. The first sip of the thousand-year-old tea, making its way to as yet untouched layers of empathy, had transformed the dull echo into a faint clamor, which the second sip evolved into a symphonic uproar. For Petrus, however, who had emptied his last flask from the Deep Woods long before they'd reached the departure lock and, consequently, had no longer been receiving much from the mist for a good while, there was nothing miraculous about the first sip at all, but the shock of the second one was so intense that he thanked the heavens that his stomach was empty. You must understand how the voices of Hanase's dead resonate. Their song delivers no message, there are merely ashes mingled with air—and this snow into which past lives have been diluted transforms reality into a vague music, a drifting threnody that enters each elf as much as he flows into it, that melts the limits of his being to dilate it beyond what is visible, and transforms the world into a fluid place where the living and the dead move together.

"I feel like I'm swimming," Petrus finally managed to say, clinging to his bowl.

"That is the lesson of the ashes," she said. "We are all mixed together in the same air. You felt nauseous because you passed without transition from an awareness of the borders to the intuition of the mixture."

"Is that where this sensation of being immersed comes from?" asked Petrus.

"Everything always comes from contact with everything else, through immersion into the vaporous matter. It is through that matter that we can mix with others and be transformed without losing ourselves; it is also through it that life and death are mingled. The thousand-year-old tea simply made this fluidity more perceptible to you."

After a moment, she added:

"Otters swim at the border between earth and water, and live in the heart of the memory of sharing."

The vision of an old, wrinkled face crossed Petrus's mind, then vanished.

"Do humans have the same appearance as us?" he asked. "I think I just saw the old woman in the poem in my thoughts."

"I saw her, too," she said. "It would definitely seem that you are destined for strange encounters."

"It's just a vision," said Petrus.

She did not reply.

"Does the path to the lock preserve the memory of vanished trees?" asked Paulus.

"Of all living things, trees best incarnate the reality of mutations," she said. "They are the motionless vectors of the genesis and transformation of all things. The transparencies of the path are made from the invisible presence of trees long dead, but which, like ashes, live on with us in another form."

They mused for a moment on this transparency beyond death.

"What does *to be with* mean if one is no longer conscious?" asked Paulus.

"What we are before our birth and after our death," she said. "A promise and a memory."

"For the living," he said.

"For the living," she replied. "Those who have passed are fully fledged members of the great people who are entrusted to us, and the duty to respond to their call is what we call the life of the dead."

"Is that what the high-elves do?" asked Petrus. "Respond to this call?"

"Some are born to assume responsibility for other creatures," she said. "That is our realm, and our mandate, the ministry that gives life to the powers of death, to their territory and legacy. This eternity and this responsibility are henceforth incumbent upon you, because today you have drunk from the thousand-year-old tea."

The garden glittered with shards of moonlight. The sensation of immersion was growing stronger. They drank a third and last sip of tea. Petrus, in spite of his dislike for metaphysical effusions, let himself go to the peace of the mixture and wondered how the ashes were moved to these bottomless urns. At funerals, the bodies of deceased elves were burned, but he'd never known that they were subsequently taken to Hanase. They were scattered from the deceased elf's favorite mountaintop, and then disappeared from view forever.

"Nothing disappears forever," said their hostess. "The ashes are brought here by the mists. The bottomless urns are what is left of the eternity they passed through before returning to mingle with the time of the living."

"So, the dead are alive?" asked Paulus.

"Of course not," she said with a laugh, "they are dead."

Petrus smiled. Indisputably, the trip was improving. His nausea had left him and the shock of the second sip of tea was dissolving into the third. He drifted nonchalantly about, and heard the tumult of the dead without attaching any more importance to it than to the twilight poems from his Woods. The fact she'd laughed at the thought the dead could be alive reinforced his indifference toward mystic effusions. And yet, he thought, I can hear the song of the dead more clearly than I can feel the presence of the living.

She got up.

"Your beds are ready," she said.

But before taking her leave, she said to Petrus:

"In Katsura, you will go to the Council library and you will introduce yourself as a friend of the Wild Grasses."

"The Wild Grasses?" he repeated, surprised.

"It is the name of our establishment," she said.

They bowed deeply, finding nothing to say that was equal to what they had just experienced.

"I hope you will forgive us our peasant ways for not knowing how to thank you," said Marcus finally.

"Only now is the true experience beginning," she said.

She waved her hand toward the bottom of the garden.

"Your quarters are on the other side."

And then she was gone.

They stood for a moment in silence gazing at the scene. A cloud drifted on a patch of moon and the world's rhythms had slowed. The ashes rose toward the heavens in lazy swirls, the melody of the stream became more languid, and the light on the maple leaves stopped glistening. As for the song of the dead, it expanded still further, deeper, more solemn—such peace, suddenly, thought Petrus, and he felt the spirits of repose enfold him.

"Shall we go?" said Paulus.

There was no visible path to the other end of the garden, and they had to resign themselves to walking on the sand. But although they felt as if they were sinking into it, their steps didn't disturb the lines. The further they went, the more the distance seemed to increase, and the maples as a whole looked as if they were retreating and growing larger. Above all, there was a different quality to the air in the garden—sharper, giving clarity to one's thoughts. Perception gained in precision, and crossing the enclosed space became a journey. But a journey to where? wondered Petrus. Or to whom?

Suddenly he knew he was heading toward someone, that every step was taking him closer to their encounter, and that he had come to this place solely for that purpose.

At last they reached the end of the garden. On the other side of the row of maple trees, standing on pilings driven deep into the black water, a wooden platform awaited them for the night. As they went closer, the sounds of the garden were stifled, and they felt as if they were entering a bubble of silence. Then the garden behind them also vanished, and they found themselves on a moonlit island, lost in the middle of a dark lagoon. There was not a breath of air; in harmony with the rhythms of the earth, the stars refrained from twinkling. Summoning their courage, they went up the steps; on the floor of the platform, the ripple of an invisible stream swirled around their ankles.

However, all that interested them were the mattresses set out for the comfort of their night. Soft and thick to look at, they were made of moving ash.

"Ash mattresses?" murmured Petrus.

"Night of the dead," Petrus heard himself reply, just as colossal fatigue came down upon their shoulders.

If only I could reach that mattress, he thought, before taking another step and collapsing onto his bed of dust.

It was a strange night, where he wandered in his dreams along a path lined with tall trees, aware that he was stepping on human ground. Whether the light was different or there was a sense of negligence in the woods—a sort of fantasy about the copses and passages, as if they'd been trimmed and traced at random—one could sense a presence there, and its nonchalance was pleasing to him. The path led to the edge of the trees, and came out to face a landscape of verdant hills. In the distance, two sparkling little lakes; all around, vineyards nestling into the landscape; below them, a village in a valley. Thin lines of smoke rose from stone houses with steep, tawny roofs; judging by the tender green hue of the vegetation, it was springtime; seasonal flowers were breaking through the freshly turned earth of the plots. There was an abundance of the veined, purple hellebores much appreciated by elves as the end of winter draws near; but there were also daffodils, tulips scarcely opened and crunchy as oatcakes, and grape hyacinths interspersed with crocuses and cyclamens. Above these lovely carpets, tall irises formed battalions in charge of overseeing the gardens. Their lower petals were puffed out in a hanging curve which seemed to form a face with velvet cheeks, from which a bearded tongue emerged. These were taller, more complicated irises than the ones in Ryoan, with something inexplicably martial and slightly ridiculous about them, but they spread all around them the same fragrance of annunciation and message, turning each plot into the guardian of a secret. They're growing vegetables that will ripen in summer, thought Petrus, and you can smell the simples which perfume and heal. After a moment, he added: this is a dream, but it is all true, and I can go on ahead without fear of waking. He began walking toward the village. In the blue sky, a little tasseled cloud went by and a breeze began to blow. It caressed his nostrils with the perfume of the tulips, mingled with a touch of lemon balm; the path wound through the springtime trees and he was intoxicated with this unusual display of nature. Here, anything is possible, he thought. When he reached the first houses, he thought again: this countryside is my landscape.

Then everything faded, because the old woman in the tea poem was coming toward him, her arms laden with wildflowers. She was smiling in the spring light and Petrus liked looking at her aged face, like parchment beneath her headdress with ribbons the color of forget-me-nots. Borage flowers matched their azure cheer, and there was a brisk, mischievous charm about her appearance. She went by him without seeing him and he decided to follow her. After a moment, she paused by a row of pink irises, then went into a farmyard. She glanced over her shoulder, went up the steps to the entrance, and disappeared inside. Petrus stood there for a moment, petrified. Reality was transfigured by this brief gaze, which he alone had seen, into a succession of scenes bathed in an unreal light. He now knew that the old peasant woman had given birth to a daughter, and that daughter to another daughter who, in the future, would conceive her own daughter in turn, until the line of women ended with the arrival, in the fifth generation, of a much-loved son. He knew that the last-born girl would inherit the science of simples from her ancestor, and that the true encounter would be that of the last female descendant, not yet born. And so, the theater of worlds was revealed to him. Gigantic fronts covered an entire continent, endless smoke rose toward the sky, armies gathered beneath a sky of storm, and the much-loved son lay dying on a field littered with corpses. He stood for a moment gazing with horror at this rumbling apocalypse until, without warning, the scene changed. In the sweetness of a summer twilight, tables had been adorned in the garden with large June irises, and a female voice was saying: *the lovely evenings around Saint John's Day*, then, after a silence: *go, my son, and know for eternity how much we love you.* How is it that I can understand her language? he wondered, and at that very moment he woke up. He raised his hand to his heart. Everything is in the dream, he thought; landscape, love, and war. He recalled the words of the hare elf: *the day the mist of Hanase disappears, we can bid farewell to this world*—and was overcome by a premonition of coming disaster. Come now, he said to himself, I'm raving. But before the last vestiges of the dream could dissipate, he thought again: there you have ecstasy and tragedy beneath a beribboned headdress. Finally, he was fully awake.

They thought they were resting on mattresses of ash above black water, but they'd slept on layers of cool grass right on the floor of the very first platform. It was raining, and the garden was gleaming. What the showers do to the garden, thought Petrus, and in the world; here, they pass by, they concentrate the universe. Abandoning himself to the music of water falling upon water, he delighted in this liquid encounter, where the ordinary time of the living was erased.

"It is time to go," said Marcus, "the first channel to Katsura is about to open."

They stood up and looked at one another.

"Did everyone dream of great things?" asked Paulus.

The other two nodded their heads.

"We'd better get going," said Petrus, "I'm hungry and I want to drink as much tea as possible before the departure."

He suddenly felt it was urgent to get under way and, looking one last time at the pond, he thought: everything is beginning.

They went back down the corridor they had taken the night before, went again through the vestibule fragrant with iris, and came out into the street in dazzling sunlight. There was no trace of the garden's warm, melancholy rain. All around whirled ashes, stitched with clarity by the morning light. Now that they were going down to the lock, the crowd grew thick and, at last they reached the grand channel that led to Katsura. As it opened out before them, huge and grandiose, a hundred barges appeared.

"We are late," said Petrus, before rushing into the way station building, where a host of steaming teapots awaited them.

He took long sips of a black tea that tasted of chestnut, before gobbling down a tray of little tarts dripping with honey. Paulus and Marcus, who followed at a more leisurely pace, nibbled decorously on a few mouthfuls of pumpkin mille-feuille, and after that they went out and stood at the back of the line on the pier.

The barges could accommodate a dozen voyagers, but as they quietly boarded the last one, they found themselves alone with two wild boar elves accompanied by one of their piglets. Petrus scrupulously followed the instructions of the boat-men—otters, beavers, and seagulls—who were overseeing the maneuvers with a watchful eye. Fully satisfied that he'd accomplished his task, he collapsed in his designated seat.

Then the barges set off in the liquid mist, and they departed without knowing that now, they were traveling in the company of their dead.

Brothers, do not forget the mandate and the realm
Sons, in the heart of an old woman an iris from Ryoan

Book of Prayers

死者

THE DEAD

Elves can understand their dead without envoys, since they welcome everything that has been and ever will be by means of tea and mist. Thus, every elf stays in the second sanctuary at least once in his life—whether he knows it or not, he will go there.

Released from the desire to live, the dead do not wish to weep and do not wish to laugh. They cultivate emotion without appetite, and joy beyond conquest. They know how to uncover meaning that is not drowned in thirst. And it is through this quest, detached from necessity, that the intuition of the beauty of living can be born.

But few men understand now the wisdom of immersion in ash.

PAINTINGS

In Petrus's dream, the theater of worlds was lit by that cold, pure light that has inspired the most beautiful works of art. Paintings are the motionless translations of our moving dreams, which in return bathe us with the clarity of paintings.

No one will be surprised to learn, therefore, that a canvas painted in Amsterdam in 1514 played a decisive role in this story. It had to do with the first bridge between the worlds, but also with murder and its immeasurable consequences.

One must be familiar with the light and landscapes of the North to understand this singular artist's decision to settle in Amsterdam, for he could just as easily have gone south, east, or west, since from the pavilion he'd been given a free rein to begin his human life wherever he desired.

Finally, one must be acquainted with the history of humans and elves to understand what he decided to paint, and to penetrate, beneath the visible surface, the invisible sparkling.

The invisible sparkling behind the transparency of tears.

They set off, unaware that they were now traveling with their dead. The journey from Hanase to Katsura, the capital of the elves, would take six hours, and Petrus intended to have a pleasant time along the way. He'd drunk the tea from the Ashes and filled his stomach. Moreover, the sight of the hundred barges gliding over the liquid mist had been well worth the trip. The barges advanced ten abreast, forming a magnificent display in the wide channel. And so, I find myself enjoying the sight, thought Petrus, surprised by this contemplative mood, attuned to the memory of the tea-house. What really happened there, I wonder, he thought again, recalling the night of the dead. Finally, he set aside his orderly thinking, and let himself go into the gentle trance of the voyage. No one spoke, the boatmen only voiced brief instructions regarding the passengers' comfort—it could go on like this forever, thought Petrus and, suddenly weary, he yawned noisily.

"There are six hours less ten minutes of crossing remaining," Marcus pointed out.

"Six hours less ten minutes of potential disaster," muttered Paulus.

"I drank the tea," said Petrus, offended.

Paulus studied him skeptically, but Petrus was already lost in the new vistas the channel offered.

In the monochromatic setting of the mist, wild grasses had

sprouted, spindly and sublime in an airy dishevelment, and they looked as if they'd been penned with black ink, as they stood stark against the whiteness of the décor in irregular groups, some as bushy as copses, others no more than three sprigs bending gracefully, like the necks of mourning women.

"The name of the teahouse," he murmured.

In the evanescence of the world, the grasses evoked the lines of a text. They were unbelievably graceful, because they rose out of the mist with no sign of their roots, but what intrigued Petrus most was that the black tufts could be read like calligraphy. This beauty of the handwritten poetry which, up to now, he'd always found deadly dull, now seemed vibrant and full of meaning to him. Something was calling him, and for the first time he felt *penetrated* by figures from without; their enigmatic tale promised far greater delights than any he'd found in the poems he knew from his youth. For elves, you see, have too much respect for the living kingdom ever to constrain it; they allow their woods and their pastures the freedom to grow as they see fit; consequently, their inner gardener is merely the servant of nature, a prism refracting and sublimating nature. But one thing Petrus knew for certain was that there was something about the channel's wild grasses that couldn't be summed up either by the freedom of natural things nor by any intention to magnify them—shimmering inlaid with a touch of adventure; a mystery that delighted with its perfume of enchanted revelation. Perhaps that something is inside me? he wondered, and for the second time in as many days two lines of verse came to him.

Wild grasses in the snow
Two children of November

I'm turning into a poet, he thought, amused. Two children, that's not elfin, it's human, he reflected. Suddenly, everything disappeared, the channel was empty once again, and he felt orphaned. Go on, he thought, I'm not good at crossings. He wedged himself into his seat to have a nap, but an image suddenly came to his mind, so clear that it caused him to sit bolt upright. A little girl was walking toward him, wrapped in an iridescent veil that drifted slowly around her. Marcus looked at Petrus, raising a questioning eyebrow, and the apparition vanished. However, it stayed in his mind and again he saw the serious little face—ten years old, perhaps—the dark golden skin, her mouth like a stain of new blood. Then the vision was gone.

"Everything all right?" asked Marcus.

He nodded, and eased into his seat again. No one spoke; before long, he dozed off.

He awoke with a start, driven by a feeling of urgency. It seemed as if he had slept long and deep, and he hoped the journey was nearly over.

"You slept for a good two hours, snoring like a trumpet," said Marcus spitefully. "So, we couldn't get any sleep."

"Two hours?" echoed Petrus. "So there are four more hours to go?"

"Apparently snoring doesn't affect the ability to do math," said Marcus to Paulus.

"I'll never last," said Petrus.

"What do you mean, last?" asked Paulus.

"I have to do something about the tea I drank," he replied, looking all around him.

Marcus and Paulus studied him with consternation.

"How many cups did you drink?" Marcus finally asked.

"I don't know," said Petrus, annoyed, "maybe a dozen. You're not about to reproach me for being conscientious?"

"A dozen," echoed Paulus.

"Didn't you read the signs?" asked Marcus.

"Was it too much for you to read the signs?" asked Paulus.

"We were late," said Petrus, "I wasn't about to waste time reading poems."

There was a silence.

"They weren't poems?" he asked.

Marcus and Paulus didn't reply.

"I didn't read the signs," he said. "I was busy drinking."

"And eating," said Marcus.

"Otherwise you would've learned that because of the length of the crossing, they recommended drinking only one cup of tea," added Paulus.

"It's highly concentrated," said Marcus.

"And the toilets are at the way station, to be used before departure," said Paulus.

"But usually we don't need to explain that to anyone other than elfkins," said Marcus finally.

When Marcus said, "highly concentrated," Petrus began to suspect something.

"Did you see the grasses?" he asked.

"Grasses?" said Paulus.

"The wild grasses," said Petrus.

"There were no wild grasses," said Marcus.

Petrus registered his reply with interest, but his bladder, alas, now required all his attention.

"I can't possibly hold it for four hours," he said, beginning to sweat like a pig.

"Well, you will have to," said Marcus.

"That's a superelfin feat," said Petrus, "I can't."

Paulus let out a whistle of irritation.

"Not on the barge, in any case," he said.

"And especially not in the mists," said Marcus.

Then he gave a sigh.

"Take off your clothes," he said, "and do what you have to do inside them."

"My clothes?" said Petrus, horrified.

"Then you'll just have to hold it," answered Marcus.

Petrus felt so pitiful, and the prospect of soiling his clothing yet again was so disgusting to him, that he wanted to believe he could do the impossible. For ten minutes, he wriggled like a worm on his seat, changing from horse to squirrel, then man, unable to find either a position or a shape that might bring him some relief.

"If you make yourself sick on top of it," said Paulus, exasperated, "that wouldn't be very smart, either."

Petrus was about to reply when he noticed that the young wild boar elf was looking at him with interest. All I need is a spectator, he thought, annoyed. The boar's parents had fallen asleep, but their offspring was watching him with his lovely brown eyes fringed with rebellious eyelashes and, in spite of the urgency of the moment, Petrus took note of the roundness of his young snout, the delicate line of the stripes on his back, and the adorable neatness of his silky hooves. How could such a pretty animal become so ugly when it grew up? he wondered—for although the wild boars of the mists are a more handsome species than those to be found on human earth, they are not particularly refined, either. Petrus was already not crazy about hazelnuts and acorns, but the thought of digging in the ground to feed off them turned his stomach (moreover, like his fellows, unless circumstances dictated otherwise, he only fed when he was in human form, and he even suspected that his horse self was allergic to forage).

The young wild boar, captivated by his contortions, was still scrutinizing him unabashedly.

"You drank too much tea," he said, "I saw you at the way station, you were really thirsty."

"I wasn't thirsty," snapped Petrus.

"I can give you a vase," said the boar, ignoring his answer. "It's a present for the Head of the Council. If you like, you can borrow it, you can empty it when we arrive and give it back to me discreetly. Your clothes wouldn't be enough," he added, realistically. "So that's why I thought of the vase."

There was a prolonged silence, then Paulus cleared his throat.

"That's very kind of you," he said, "but we cannot do that."

"And why not?" asked the piglet, turning into the most admirable little human specimen you could ever meet.

His blond hair was perfectly matched by his blue eyes, which were virtually impossible to look away from. Was it the fact they were so light, almond-shaped, magnified by sweet lashes that were also blond, and garlanded with perfect brows? Or were those eyes so beautiful because of the spark that migrated from those artfully drawn pink lips, lighting an exquisite fire in them? The young elf was smiling at them, and it seemed as if the world was glistening, so much so that Petrus, bewitched by such an endearing face, briefly forgot his torment.

"A vase intended for the Head of the Council cannot be used as a urinal," continued Paulus.

But he couldn't take his eyes off the splendid young face either.

"It won't diminish its beauty," said the boy, and he smiled again.

Marcus, Paulus, and Petrus, lost in that smile as if they were in a forest carpeted with periwinkle, all felt their resolution give way at the same time.

"It simply isn't done," said Marcus, in a final effort at decency which lacked all resolve.

The elfkin reached for the vase, which was wrapped in a soft poppy print fabric and stamped with family seals in flat tints of ink. Elves have two seals, that of their animal self and that of their personal house. The seal of wild boars, in tribute to the species' preference for nocturnal life, consists of a

waning moon above a tea plantation. Added to this was the
piglet's own family seal, a spotted iris against a background of
tiny stars. Said piglet checked that his parents were asleep, and
he went over to the threesome, whose will was as weak as their
reflexes. There was a hypnotic fluidity about his movements,
and while he was removing the vase from its cloud of poppies,
Petrus, Marcus, and Paulus looked at him dumbly. He set it
down before them.

"It's an urn," murmured Paulus.

It was indeed an urn, of light, changing bronze, alternately
fawn, gray, brown, or, finally, a milky comet white.

"It comes from the oldest bronze foundry in the mists,"
answered the elfkin. "We came to Hanase for it, and we are
taking it to Katsura to give it to the Head of the Council."

"I thought that urns didn't travel," said Paulus.

"Only bottomless urns," he replied.

He changed into a colt, a ravishing bay colt—but however
adorable he might be, the spell that had bound the threesome
was broken, and Petrus shook his head as if emerging from a
dream.

"I appreciate your offer," he said to the colt, "but I cannot
accept it."

And as the moment was dire, and he didn't think he could
wait any longer, he took a few steps toward the back of the
barge, turned to one side and, revealing his white buttocks,
removed his clothing. Then he turned into a squirrel and
relieved himself as discreetly as he could. It felt so good and so
wretched that he could have wept twice over, and in the end,
in fact, it was tears of gratitude that came, because in addition
to the remarkable relief, a miracle had occurred: the more he
wet his garment, the faster it dried. The supple cloth absorbed
the liquid, creased, then dried. When he'd finished his business, he didn't dare get dressed again, but he waved the cloth
in front of Paulus, Marcus, and the colt.

"Well, I never," said Paulus. "When it rains it doesn't dry that quickly."

"I'm astonished we didn't know this before," said Petrus, "it would have spared me a few very nasty minutes."

"You must be the first elf who has ever urinated in his clothing, that's why," said Paulus.

"It's cosmic," said the colt, turning into a piglet.

Once he was human again he wrapped up the urn and laid it at his parents' feet. They were napping quietly, and Petrus was surprised that this pair of peaceable high-elves had given birth to such a subtle little monster, for he didn't doubt for a moment that the blond boy was as handsome as the very devil. Once the enchantment of his smile and sky-blue eyes had waned, Petrus felt a fleeting intuition of danger, and now that the young elf was coming back toward them, he still felt an unease, something the boy's dazzling face couldn't dissipate.

"Which province are you from?" Marcus asked him.

"We are from Ryoan," he replied, "which is why we have the iris on our coat of arms. My father is the Council emissary for the province of Dark Mists. He presides over the permanent assembly and is in command of the regular units."

"Is it customary for envoys to offer urns to the Head of the Council?" asked Paulus.

"Ordinarily," said the elfkin, "we give presents to everyone in the upper chamber. But this is an election year and we thank the departing head with personal gifts."

"That's right," said Marcus, "I'd forgotten, the Head of the Council has been serving for four hundred years."

"It's a historic moment," said the elfkin, "when you reach Katsura it will be bubbling with excitement."

"So there will be a new guardian in Nanzen," said Paulus thoughtfully. "If I'm not mistaken, he will be appointed by the Head of the Council, then voted on by the new councilors."

"I will go to Nanzen someday," declared their traveling companion straight out.

Marcus laughed.

"How can you know that?" he asked.

"I will be appointed Guardian of the Pavilion," replied the elfkin, "and I will be the master of Nanzen."

They looked at him, flabbergasted.

"Desire makes destiny," said the little high-elf. "In the meantime, we will support our champion."

"Who is this champion?" asked Petrus.

"A high-elf hare from the Dark Mists who is running for office for the first time, against a high-elf hare from the province of Snows, who is already on the Council."

"Ryoan versus Katsura," said Paulus. "Our Deep Woods are not about to give rise to a leader."

"All it takes is a little ambition," said the elfkin. "Don't you want to be part of history?"

"We are members of lower houses," said Marcus, "I suppose that explains why we have so little appetite for power. History, on the other hand, belongs to everyone. And I didn't know that you could call a candidate a champion."

"We've never had a more unusual candidate," said the elfkin. "He doesn't belong to the inner circle of councilors, even though he does come from another prestigious lineage, that of the Council's master gardeners. He is so brilliant that in only two hundred years he has managed to obtain the endorsement of the councilors. Now he has his eye on the ultimate office."

"Will your family vote for him?" asked Petrus.

"My family and many others. The elves are afraid, they need a daring leader to fight against the new dangers of our time."

"New dangers?" echoed Marcus.

The other elf looked at him as if he'd just stepped out of a dusty closet.

"The day before yesterday the Council issued a new alert regarding several provinces where the mists are in difficulty."

"Yes," send Paulus, "we already heard about it in Hanase. What does that have to do with your daring leader?"

"My father thinks this is only the beginning of a long death, and that we need someone who will not be afraid to face the causes."

"And what might these causes be?" asked Petrus.

He was in a bad mood from being stuck in his squirrel essence, and he could feel the defiance growing inside him. The young elf turned into a piglet while taking his time to reply. He lowered his lashes graciously and when he looked up again he said in a conspiratorial tone:

"Humans."

The other three looked at him aghast and he seemed pleased with the effect he'd had.

"How could humans have anything to do with the fluctuations of the mist?" asked Paulus, puzzled.

"It's a long story," said the piglet.

He wanted to continue, but suddenly something shook the barge violently. A murmur of astonishment spread over the channel and the boatmen closed the communicating canals. The shock woke the piglet's parents, and when they found their son in the company of the threesome, they came over, smiling, and bowed amiably. In their human shape, they were indecently good looking, as dark as their child was blond.

"I hope our young chatterbox hasn't been too much of a bother," said the father.

"Not at all," said Paulus politely.

"Quite astonishing, that sudden jolt," said the mother, frowning.

She had a deep voice with something of a drawl, which Petrus liked.

"Your son told us you are from Ryoan," said Paulus. "I've heard it's an incomparable city."

"You are very welcome there," she replied, "we are always happy to share the splendor of our dark mists. May I ask where you are from?"

They didn't have time to reply because new instructions required the passengers to remain seated and the three wild boar elves returned to their seats. But after a moment, as nothing particular was happening, everyone began once again to enjoy the gentle pleasure of being on the water. As for Petrus, he was thinking. *Perhaps you are one of the pieces of the puzzle that is being assembled*, the hare elf at the teahouse had said— and, indeed, he felt as if they had drifted into the center of a game that was beyond them. Even though the wild grasses in the channel were hallucinations, a product of his exaggerated consumption of tea, they disturbed him as much as real writing would have done. And even if they are chimeras, shouldn't they make us see something? he wondered. Then, exhausted by all these incongruous considerations, which were giving him a headache, he fell asleep. But before nodding off he had one last thought: what an adventure! And as he slipped into sleep, he smiled.

At last they reached Katsura.

"Our first real lock," said Paulus.

The boatmen woke the travelers shortly before the channel began to close again behind the barges, which stayed motionless on a patch of liquid mist while other mists, to the rear, returned to vapor. Facing them was the void of still more mist: the lock. The boatmen sought their positions in successive adjustments of a few centimeters, the channel grew ever narrower, and before long the boats were lined up side by side on the last square of liquid in the world. No sound, no movement; the mist coiled on itself as time was suspended and everyone held their breath. Not a single native of this world was ignorant of the fact that the lock at Katsura was dangerous, and although it had not happened in five centuries, a distracted mooring maneuver could throw barges, boatmen, and voyagers into the void from which none would return.

After a long while the boatmen relaxed, just as a sound came to their ears, and the mist lifted to reveal, far below them, the great city bathed in light. They went slowly down toward Katsura, following a vertical trajectory which had given its name, the Well of Mist, to the lock, a well of half a league that was used ten times a day in both directions by one to two hundred boatloads of pilgrims. It was the middle of the afternoon and the November sun shone above the gray roofs. There was no sign yet of the lovely soft snow that covers the province from the end of the year until the first days of April; plum and maple trees blazed with their autumn colors, and from above, Katsura looked as if it were on fire; tall gingko trees added amber touches, like will-o'-the-wisps frozen in flight. Beyond them was a landscape of trees in fog with a few isolated villages here and there, but what dominated were the vaporous mountains the city backed onto. They overlooked the snowy peaks that circled the city and created such an imposing lofty landscape that Katsura seemed to be floating there like the survivor of a shipwreck. Closer inspection of the city revealed it to be more solid and firmly anchored than rock, because the mist, in contrast, gave it a vigor that no solid ground could have conferred. As the descent continued, the mist grew ever larger and seemed to muster a force that would have been threatening were it not for the beauty and harmony it shared with the rest of the landscape.

At last, the docks came into sight. The disembarkation zone was just before the city, offering a new perspective that was equally dizzying, for what could be more breathtaking than this spill of wooden houses interwoven with the most beautiful trees on earth? The trees were set among the buildings in a random order that to Petrus seemed not unlike the wild grasses in the channel: thus, his first sight of Katsura was also under the seal of a text waiting to be deciphered.

At the heart of the city and its wonderful garden, the astonishing proportions of the headquarters of the Council of Mists immediately caught one's eye. There are few important buildings that fail to correspond to the image of what they are, places of celebration or of power whose appearance sets them apart from ordinary places. But the Council headquarters managed to be the heart of that world and still prove humble and whispering, its low-lying wings and hidden courtyards apportioned according to a secret, asymmetrical plan. There were surely shady patios there, the murmur of water from a fountain on a birdbath, a dark, cool room from which the Head of the Council could look out at the moon, and so on, to infinity, in the labyrinth of this noble house that diluted any evidence of power in vibrant humility. From where they stood they could see all this, and everyone saw it just as they did, and that was the intention of the founding fathers of Katsura—that one could only reach the city after discovering it from on high, then observing it from below, before giving up on either perspective to embrace that of meditation.

Disembarkation began, and Petrus, with his clothes under his paw, diligently followed the boatmen's instructions. Katsura enchanted him, and the air he breathed seemed brisker than elsewhere. On solid ground, they bade farewell to their traveling companions.

"Good luck," said Paulus to the piglet, just as he was again turning into a blond angel, "may your quest lead you with wisdom."

But the elfkin was looking at Petrus.

"I have a feeling we shall meet again," he said.

The family of wild boar elves turned away and walked off casually, but Petrus felt a chill, something he couldn't put his finger on.

"What's the plan, now?" Marcus asked.

"We're going to the library," said Paulus.

"That's out of the question," said Petrus, "I need to find a roof, for a start, then wash my clothes, and get a little sustenance."

"Sustenance?" said Paulus. "Stuff your face, you mean. That is out of the question. You need to pay your respects on behalf of the Wild Grasses first. I don't want you to go off feasting before you've done your duty."

"My duty?" asked Petrus. "What duty?"

"Oh," said Marcus, "you're right, what does one owe in exchange for a thousand-year-old tea?"

"Do you think an unwashed squirrel is the best ambassador for a session of introductions?" Petrus protested.

But Paulus set off, followed by Marcus, then Petrus, who between sighs dragged his feet morosely as he followed his companions.

His torture, however, did not last long. It took barely ten minutes to reach the first houses and the labyrinth of little streets that rose up toward the Council headquarters. What an enchanting city! thought the friends, as they discovered the cobblestones, warm and soft beneath their paws, and majestic trees along shady passages, and pretty houses with their windows concealed by bamboo blinds that combined transparent and opaque effects. Little moss gardens ran all around the verandas, and their small size gave rise to a feeling of depth which Petrus, after a moment, attributed to the distinctive elements that gave each house its charm—here, a smooth, hollow stone where rainwater collected, there, a sudden shower of heavenly bamboos, or over there, a dialogue between a maple tree and an azalea. All around them were the terraces of high, misty mountains, and a skyward gaze revealed their undulating crests, but they were also visible straight ahead, at the end of a narrow street ending on the void. Here and there a bouquet of trees would vanish beneath a cascade of mist then come back in sight, while the gauzy mass that had engulfed the trees, denser and more imposing than an iceberg, dissolved or unfurled in search of more foliage. Where the houses were concerned, however, by virtue of the equilibrium of the world of mists, which requires that elfin constructions remain visible, the only things that disappeared, intermittently, were the sunny slopes of a roof, a mysterious veranda, or a door decorated with a hanging vase of violets.

By the time they came in sight of the Council headquarters, Petrus had forgotten that he was annoyed and hungry. The noble house was preceded by a large, rectangular courtyard planted with hundreds of plum trees and crisscrossed by pathways of light sand. It was surrounded by a delicate moss that broke like a wave at the walls of the enclosure, which made the edges of the garden seemed mobile, uncertain, and in spite of its mystery the place seemed open to the flow of that world.

They stood for a moment silently contemplating the tide of plum trees.

"I can only imagine what it's like when they're in bloom," murmured Paulus.

A host of elves strode along the passages admiring the trees. The next day would be winter, but that November afternoon, the soft air gave the impression that autumn would never end and, from one languid moment to the next, one warm flow of light to the next, they would remind themselves, not to forget to love. Oh, how I would love to love! thought Petrus, brushing his paw over the fringe of a ribbon of cool moss. Oh, how pleasant life is! thought Paulus and Marcus, smiling vacantly. Such a lovely autumn! Oh, love! thought the elves on the pathways, and the message was carried, beyond the Council, the city, the mountains, a message born of trees and seasons which kept this world together.

They could have stayed in the warmth of that dream of love for a long time, but a hare elf was coming to greet them.

"We were informed of your arrival," he said when he stood before them.

The three friends bowed, and Paulus and Marcus took on their human form.

"If you will come with me," said the elf, "I will take you to the library."

When he noticed what Petrus was holding beneath his paw, he asked:

"Is there a problem with your clothing?"

The squirrel in which Petrus was stuck blushed to the tips of his ears.

"Unfortunately, it, uh, got dirty during the crossing," he stammered.

The hare elf's face lit up with surprise, but he commented no further.

"Let's go," he said, and they followed him along the main path that led to the Council headquarters.

Access was through a gigantic gate reinforced by tall, circular pillars. The vigor that emerged from these columns of dead trees, after an immemorial life, was phenomenal, and stepping over the raised edge at the bottom of the gate, the friends placed their palms on the pillars. The surface was rough, streaked with centuries and shot through with deep dissonances. Across from the entrance, a wooden veranda ran all the way around another, smaller, rectangular courtyard which was planted with the same plum trees and carpeted with the same cool moss. Tall, open doors faced them and on either side.

"The north door leads to the high chamber and the quarters of the Head of the Council, the west door to the inner gardens, and the east door to the library," their guide informed them. "By inner gardens, I mean the ones where it is possible to walk about, but there are others visible from inside the building."

They headed to the right and, passing a great many elves, went past the wooden partitions adorned with long banners of silk and printed with the emblem and motto of the Council. Beneath an ink drawing of snowy peaks in the mist one could read *I shall always maintain*, written in the hand of every leader from the dawn of elfin times. Petrus lingered for a moment by one of the pen drawings. Through an optical illusion, its curves also formed a line, in such a way that one's gaze moved constantly from the tenderness of the rounded signs to the austerity of a single brushstroke. The hare elf paused in turn.

"It is said that this was drawn by the hand of the elf who witnessed the birth of the bridge," he said.

He was about to add something when he was interrupted by a movement near the north door. A group of elves emerged, and everyone drew back against the partitions to let them go by. They turned left and came up to meet our foursome.

Two hare elves were marching in the lead. They were clearly the candidates for the supreme calling, for each one of them was followed by a number of other hares as well as imposing wild boars. The elves in the escort had the bearing of their respective high-elfin houses, an accentuated gravity to their gaze, and a way of moving that implied excellence—but this, already striking, was nothing in comparison to the allure of the two hares at the head of the procession. Ordinary elves move about the world, thought Petrus; but the world adjusts to the movements of those two. As they came forward, they quickly turned into their constituent species, and it was troubling to see how much their animals resembled one another. The hares' fur was ermine-like, until they turned into horses with a white robe glinting with bronze. The muscles beneath their skin caused the velvet robe to ripple, and now and again it shimmered like a landscape of hills in the distance. At other moments, the cloak seemed made of pure silken snow, and one could really believe that the two candidates were brothers by blood.

Everything changed when they took on their human appearance. The taller one had thick white hair despite his age—three hundred years or more—brooding gray eyes that flashed like thunderclouds, a hard face with marble features, a hooked nose, high eyebrows, and prominent cheekbones. Given this face sculpted in hard rock, he seemed both young and old at the same time. His demeanor was nonchalant, but haughty, his gait fluid and controlled, which suggested strength and will—an elf like this can carry the mists on his shoulders, thought Petrus. He turned to look at the other elf and felt his heart leap. Oh, love! There can be no lovelier creature in this life! he thought. A mane of copper hair flew from the creature, his ice-cold eyes sparkled, and his milky complexion gleamed in an etching that roused trembling and desire. One couldn't get enough of this mixture of crystalline purity and fiery heat, a vision that was both frightening and warming. Unlike his competitor, he seemed insolently young, and Petrus, dazzled by the fact that so much beauty and vigor could be concentrated in a single being, told himself that he must be the head of the Council gardeners. His porcelain skin reminded Petrus of the elfkin they'd met during the crossing, but he walked with a feline self-confidence, the suppleness of a predator destined for combat. To be honest, there was something warlike about him that was surprising in an elf who devoted himself to the noble practice of gardening, and bit by bit his initial bedazzlement faded and Petrus was overcome by the same sensation of danger he'd felt with the piglet. The group drew level and Petrus's gaze was drawn to one of the boars in the retinue. Sweetness welled up in him like a stream with impetuous currents of youth, wiser than ancient rivers, and Petrus was almost more intimidated by the depth of his silver gaze than by the aura of power of the two hares.

This was the first encounter between Petrus and the elf who would soon become the greatest Guardian of the Pavilion ever known in the mists and who, one hundred and twenty years later, would father an extraordinary child called Clara. At that moment, the wild boar exchanged a brief glance with the storm-eyed hare that attested to an enduring friendship. Then they walked past the foursome and disappeared onto the veranda. After a moment, passersby on the veranda whispered among themselves, then returned to their business.

"What a shock," said Paulus.

"You were lucky to see them," said their guide. "This was the last council meeting before the start of the campaign, each one of them will now return to his stronghold."

His brow creased with concern.

"There has never been a more fraught election," he said.

"Who is your champion?" asked Marcus.

"Champion?" echoed the elf. "Are you for the garden? Their partisans use that term."

"I didn't know that," said Marcus. "We are from the Deep Woods, we know little about what goes on here."

"The distribution of the professions of faith will only start tomorrow, that's true," said the hare. "You will have a better idea of who is in the running once you've read them. As for me, I've been serving the library for five hundred years. I know who my candidate will be."

"So it's Katsura against Ryoan, the library against the garden?" asked Paulus.

"What garden, I do wonder," said their guide. "That which shines does not maintain."

"Aren't you concerned about the decline of the mists?" asked Petrus, recalling what the piglet had told them.

"Must we adapt our behavior because of that concern?" replied the hare. "We are not a warlike species, and our leaders shouldn't be warriors."

"The champion of the garden is a warrior?" asked Petrus, surprised.

"The best of us all," answered their guide.

He wiped his hand across his brow.

"But the war is mainly in his mind."

"I'm curious to see what his gardens are like," said Paulus.

"You'll see an example at the library," said their guide. "And perhaps you will think that purity is not always the best ally of the heart."

He motioned to them to go ahead, and followed them into the room.

The room extended over three thousand square feet, protected by large picture windows that looked out onto the inner gardens. Bamboo blinds could be adjusted at varying heights depending on whether one wanted to meditate on the floor, or read at the tables set up below the invisible shelves. In the center of the room, scrolls and tomes were suspended in the air, neatly stored on an immaterial frame.

"There aren't any walls," thought Petrus, "just windows and books."

"And readers," said the hare, with a smile.

And so, he understood why he had come.

Wild grasses in the snow
Two children of November

Book of Battles

保

Maintain

The candidates' professions of faith were disseminated throughout the entire territory of the mists one hundred days before the election, in which every elf over the age of one hundred could take part. Later, in the provinces, assemblies would be held, where the programs could be discussed. On the day of the election, Nanzen would tally the votes and the Guardian of the Pavilion would come to Katsura to announce the results.

Let us agree to call our candidates of the moment the councilor and the gardener respectively, and let us hear a few words about their vision for the future of the mists.

The councilor's profession of faith was magnificent, for it was written in the style of the wild grasses, with a melodious turn of phrase that resonated in every heart. The hare elf of Katsura may have appeared cold and austere, but his prose and manner were warm and kindly.

I shall always maintain, he wrote at the end of his speech. More unexpected was the phrase that preceded his motto: *the older our world gets, the more it is in need of poetry.* When was the last time anyone had read the word *poetry* in a leader's profession of faith? I will leave this question to the historians and, for the time being, look forward to this tribute to the spirit of childhood.

権力

POWER

Inversely, the gardener's profession of faith reflected none of the brilliance of his person. It was as devoid of heart as he seemed to have been fashioned with love, and as drearily dry as he was insolently youthful. One must be glad of this lack of subtlety in the prose, when the elf was such an expert in the conviction of his gaze and his acts, since it would cost him this election and the next one, thus demonstrating that the mists were not yet prepared to sacrifice their multi-millennial soul.

Elves are less inclined than humans to act under the influence of fear, for tradition, with them, is not opposed to progress, nor is movement opposed to stability. When the gardener wrote, *I shall be the protector of the continuity of our culture against the threats of modern times*, he could not hope to win over a species used to thinking in circular terms. Some even suspected that he was driven—perhaps without even being aware of it—by that force that undoes more than it maintains: a thirst for power.

However, he was right about one thing, and it would soon earn him enough partisans to build an army: the mists were declining and it was becoming ever more difficult to keep the avenues of this world together.

A Dream So Lofty
1800–1870

I have come here to read, that's the message, thought Petrus, who two days earlier would have thought it extravagant that messages could be spread throughout the world.

"I'll take my leave of you now," said their guide with a bow, "someone will be coming to look after you."

The three friends stood there for a moment, but no one came, and they went over to the large picture window to admire the garden.

It was a centuries-old jewel, embellished over time by the Council's successive gardeners, an elite respected among the mists because each one of them had completed an interminably long apprenticeship, kept up a permanent commerce with trees, and made art that worked with the legacy of the ages—all things the elves believed were vital and to which they devoted themselves by tending their gardens and respecting their trees. The enclosure of the Council was sealed with a velvety moss that covered the roots of specimens so old that on the very ground they formed a miniature landscape of valleys and hills. On this late autumn day, the maple trees were ablaze; in the foreground, all along the building, a strip of sand streaked with arabesques gave the garden its waves; beyond it began the ocean of greenery. Here were a few azaleas that had already lost their leaves; there, heavenly bamboo in bunches of red berries; and everywhere, those pine trees that are pruned over the centuries until they have taken on a singular shape—

their essential form, which is found inside and requires a gardener who will listen to what the tree is whispering to him, while winds and storms speak only to its bark. They resembled the trees in the Deep Woods, but at their extremities the contortions of their dark branches produced needle fascicles, trimmed by the gardener's art to form delicate lashes, and against the dry wood they seemed to be winking, while singing a hymn that was refined and graceful—it was something to see, the openwork wings reaching out from the bare, rigid tree trunks, then branching out in the air like figures so graphic that for the third time in two days Petrus wondered whether the world were not murmuring a poem in his ear.

In the middle of the scene, the mercury waters of a pond reflected the heavens and the branches, but it took Petrus a moment to understand the strangeness of what he was seeing. He had to blink several times to adjust to the aberrant color scheme that lost its hues in the water, reflected back as black branches on a gray mirror of waves. From this alloy of metal and ink a ballet from the foundries of the universe emerged, where the streaks of pine trees performed a monochrome choreography on the liquid silver. Harmonizing with the scene were stones of various shapes and sizes that formed ageless mineral promontories and bridges along the shore or above the surface of the pond. There one knew the fraternal flow of rock and river; there one felt the tremor of a powerful vision, of a dream of mountains and shores—this is the essence of our world, thought Petrus, and the dream is so lofty that it will never die.

Beyond the pond, a lane bordered with slopes of bamboo led to a gate with a thatched roof. Ryoan irises had been planted there, and were nodding at winter camellias that had just bloomed, set in rows along the avenue and flanked, to the rear, by tall bamboo and slender maple trees. The Katsura maples are particularly elegant, because the capital of the elves is sheltered from strong winds by the rampart of its mountains of mist. Thus, the leaves are the same as everywhere, so delicately carved that their veins and edges form a living lace; but the absence of storms means that that the branches do not need to strengthen to resist the gusts, they remain slender, can bow to the breeze, languid dancers. A swarm of mist rose, slipped between the branches, then evaporated, swirling lazily on itself, and the friends mused it must be a pleasing thing, to come and admire this garden during the long winter. Similarly, they supposed there were other jewels within the annexes to the central building, for through the leaves and needles they could see its verandas. To the left of the pond, the picture windows offered a glimpse of a sunlit room and, to the rear, a raised, interior garden consisting of three large stones set on gray sand. They seemed to have been tossed in the air to fall again at the perfect distance from each other, and the precise form and precise gap between things must certainly be known to achieve such perfection: Petrus did not doubt that it was the work of the young chief gardener. It had the same sparkling purity to it as his very person, and Petrus understood how one might become fascinated. Those who wish to reach the summit barefoot must have a heaven-sent talent, he thought, astonished at all the elevated thoughts he'd been having since his arrival in Katsura, and mentally he scoffed at himself. This moment of distraction changed everything, and he no longer saw the mineral garden in the same way as before. The arrangement that had so delighted his gaze now seemed fossilized, and the stones emitted a message of death which gave him the shivers. *Purity is not always the best ally of the heart*, their guide had said, and this absence of love, now so obvious, made his hair stand on end.

"It's magnificent," said Marcus.

Petrus saw he was looking at the stones.

"It's cold," he replied.

"It's frozen," said Paulus.

"Yes, it's cold and frozen," said Marcus slowly, as if he were waking from a dream.

"How may I assist you?" asked a voice behind them.

They turned around and found themselves facing a tall female elf with red hair and light gray eyes.

"I am the Council's steward," she said.

Turning into a squirrel, she was such a striking replica of his mother that Petrus, fully aware that he'd left his Woods without saying goodbye, blushed violently from the tips of his claws to the top of his ears.

She looked at the cloth he was clutching in his paws.

"Is there something wrong with your clothing?" she asked.

The crimson squirrel in which Petrus was trapped gave out an indeterminate gurgling sound and Paulus, feeling sorry for him, came to his rescue.

"There was an incident during the crossing," he said.

"That is the first time I've ever heard of an incident involving clothes," she said.

"The same for us," said Marcus, looking at Petrus mockingly.

But when he saw Petrus's despair, he resumed his serious air.

"Our hostess from the Wild Grasses asked this temporarily mute gentle-elf to introduce himself to you," he said.

"Yes, but why?" she asked.

"Were you not informed?" asked Marcus.

"We were simply informed of the arrival from the Deep Woods of two squirrels and one bear," she replied.

Dumbfounded, they fell silent.

"Do you not know, either, why you have been sent?" she said, turning into a bay mare with rounded hindquarters.

She studied them, thoughtful.

"The Wild Grasses never do things without a reason," she continued, "particularly during such a troubled period."

"Might you have some work for me?" asked Petrus, his voice so clear that Paulus and Marcus stood there gaping.

"I don't see what's so astonishing about that," he added, in response to their stupor. "I intend to stay here, and I have to make a living."

"What can you do?" she asked.

It was his turn to stand there openmouthed.

"Well," he said, "I don't know. Anything, I imagine, that doesn't require any particular skill."

"You are not good at job interviews," she said, somewhat put out.

She thought for a moment.

"These days, with the elections, I have enough to do without trying to make sense of all this. I may as well keep you on hand, after all."

She frowned.

"Does he really not know how to do anything?" she asked Marcus and Paulus.

They looked embarrassed and she sighed.

"Can you sweep?" she asked Petrus.

"I suppose so," he replied.

She clicked her tongue, annoyed.

"Tomorrow at dawn, west door," she said.

Then, turning into a squirrel and looking just like his mother when she was angry, she turned and was gone.

"You really have some nerve," said Marcus.

"Are you serious?" asked Paulus. "Do you really want to stay in Katsura and spend your days sweeping paths for the Council?"

"I am serious," answered Petrus in a huff. "I don't see why you won't believe me."

They looked at him doubtfully for a moment.

"Let's go," said Marcus in the end, "let's leave this place, we have to find an inn before nightfall."

They agreed, and set off. Before leaving, Petrus cast one last gaze at the books and scrolls floating in the air, and it seemed to him they twinkled faintly in a knowing farewell.

"See you tomorrow," he murmured.

Finally, they went through the gates and back into the streets of the city.

That is how Petrus's life in Katsura began and, although the time has come for us to proceed more speedily with our tale, and return to the protagonists of the last battle of the war, we must say a few words about those years in the capital of the elves, simply because the world they embodied is now gone forever. For the last seven decades, those who have been in charge of the intrigues of fate relentlessly asked themselves this burning question: should they die to make way for a new era, or had their very world come to its end?

"We always believed that individuals and civilizations perished, but that the species would survive," the Head of the Council would say one day to Petrus. "And what if our species has reached its own limits and is meant to die without leaving a trace? Should we not view this war differently?"

However, seventy years would pass before this conversation took place, and while they may have appeared to be monotonous years, for Petrus they were a constant adventure. Every morning he did his sweeping while he daydreamed, and during the seasons when snow covered the paths and the moss, he worked at the library, archiving scrolls and books. Then he read. Twice a year, during his leave, he went traveling. Sometimes Paulus and Marcus came with him on a joyful escapade; most often, he went off on his own and connected with other good souls he met along the way; and he was certainly the elf with the greatest number of friends in faraway places of all the mists, for the species, as a rule, rarely leaves its native province. In Katsura he'd found a place to live at the top of the town with an old unicorn elf lady with whom he shared breakfast every day at dawn, laughing and conversing. From the window of his room he could see the mist rising and falling over the great city. In the morning, it took on tints of bronze that caused his heart to leap, and he enjoyed those sunrises so much that for all his laziness he would wake up early. When he set off down the deserted streets in the brisk air, he forgot the endless tedium of the task before him. On his way down to the Council headquarters, he looked out over the city as it fanned out below him, at the foot of the snowy peaks and the cliffs of mist. The rising sun fringed them with an incandescent edging that frayed above their dark crest; the streets and bridges of the white city were enveloped in amber fog, great vaporous exhalations that disintegrated above the streams, and it was a long dream of water and wood, in a luxuriance of sunlight. Petrus would stop by the dew-lit trees to perform his devotions to beauty, greeting a bird perched on the stone, the swaying bamboo, the camellias in improbable winter. But there were also dawns when the great blaze from some activity in Nanzen (renovations, or major cleaning in the channels) gave everything a fiery glow. There was wind then, too, and brief hailstorms, which left the city purple and steaming; transparent spears of mist soared at great speed toward the sky; and these tantrums of climate strengthened the proof that his life was in search of some missing intensity. He did not know how to define it, but before long it propelled him toward the channels, and caused him to travel all over the country.

Travel had become second nature to him, and the actual journey became almost more important than the places he visited, although there was hardly a remote corner of this world unworthy of praise.

He loved the province of the Leaves, and the pavilion and

bridge of mists on an outcrop in the distance, but above all he'd been astonished by the density of the forest that separated Nanzen from the rest of the world, with neither channel nor passage to get there. At the way station where travelers could stop and admire the first sanctuary, in the distance, they served a frothy green tea with a grassy taste. There was no backbone to its flavor—a powerful flavor of nothing, a smooth, pale concentrate of forest from before the time of elves, which evoked unusual images to Petrus, in particular a dimly lit scene where, against a background of silky darkness, a glass of water stood next to three forgotten cloves of garlic, and he became convinced that this vision with the texture of a painting came from *elsewhere*, from an unknown land that was calling to him, although he couldn't figure out how to get there.

He also loved the northern regions which, in the mists, unlike in human lands, are the warmest. There, one could hear the constant song of cicadas, and swarms of dragonflies vibrated above the rice paddies; above all, the provender they served there was seasoned with grilled herbs and generous spices. In the south, he'd felt at home in the provinces of the Friezes and the Frozen Sands, where all day long they drank warm honey beside the fireplace. Outside, there were endless beaches and stormy plains, constant wind and glacial islands; and yet, beneath the steep thatched roofs where they warmed themselves as they shared their supper, the elves of those lands had created a very comfortable life for themselves. As a reward for their indoor isolation, they would venture out the next morning into the frozen mist of dawn and, suddenly, it was as if everything had been cleared away and made bright, a powerful gust had chased the clouds away to reveal a huge sky, a profusion of pure sky, a sky so enormous that one was lost in it, a sky where seagulls passed high overhead as if shot there by invisible archers.

This was the world Petrus explored at every latitude and I cannot fully describe the landscapes of mountains and coasts, waterfalls and lakes, volcanoes and prairies. But in every province the same mists could be found, the same trees and the same moss, which give these lands their identity, the same traditions of tea, and the same wooden verandas where one could stand and admire the affability of huge clouds. It was a blessing for the journey, when he still felt out of his mists (as they say in these parts), his status as a stranger gave a logic to this fantasy, and he became a privileged observer of the customs of his fellow elves, painting throughout his travels a picture that few elves have had the opportunity to imagine, and while he might yearn for an elusive elsewhere, he learned to love his people deeply, and their manner of dwelling upon their lands.

For the landscapes of the mists are the alter egos of the souls that incarnate them. Humans, because they separate the seer from the seen, and the creator from the created, cannot understand the nature of this game of mirrors. Elves do not conceive of their lands as portions of the world they might inhabit, but as dynamic forces in which their own energy is released, while the tea gives inner eyes and ears to this great, vital fusion—thus, they could not imagine themselves admiring mere landscapes, but rather, in every valley, every tree, and every garden, the work of the cosmos as a whole, an immense solidarity reverberated to infinity by the mists. This gave rise to a peace-loving population, since the whole would not dream of combatting the whole; elves would be stunned to think one could tell stories, as I am doing, where they could see only landscapes that have been arbitrarily selected from the magma of life. Instead, their days were spent in peace: they drank their tea, which awakens an awareness of the universal mixture; they worked in order to contribute to the proper running of the community; then, once they had drunk their tea and done their work, they tended their gardens, wrote and recited poetry, sang, enjoyed pottery and calligraphy—all activities valued by humans as exquisite forms of leisure, but which, for the elves, constitute the natural continuation of the harmony of the world, flows of action inserted in a flow of mist which, in return, acquires its flesh through these activities. And so, while all this may have delighted the self-respecting elf in Petrus, he also felt frustrated for a reason that the library would reveal to him.

One day when, in the presence of the steward, he expressed his surprise that the books were suspended in the air, she replied:

"These texts and inks are the repositories of the dream of the mists."

Indeed, the dream of the library had the shape of interconnected books that told the history of the mists, scrolls of poetry that celebrated the mists, or parchments that recorded the great deeds of the mists, all of it interspersed with delicate inking that invariably painted trees and mountains in the mist. After decades of reading, he'd had his fill of the misty, elegiac, historical fresco to which all the literature and art of the elves seemed to be reduced, and he despaired of understanding what it was that drove him day after day to keep looking there for that *something* the wild grasses of the channel had once whispered to him, long ago. He did like to read, however, the way some people pray, in the quiet contemplation of a motionless voyage steeped in the value of a reality that real life itself had failed to give him. But this unusual freshness quickly soured, drowned in the endless repetitions of monotonous celebrations, and from all his voyages through channels or poetry, the only thing he gained was a sense of frustration that grew exponentially as the years went by. I have a particular fondness for Petrus, simply because, while I loved the world of elves before the fall, I also understood whatever incongruous aspirations he might have in his heart; one must, in a way, be a stranger to the world to wish to invent it, and unknown to oneself to want to go beyond what is visible.

Do not suppose, however, that he did not love his native land and that, the moment he saw the end was near, he did not feel his heart breaking. It was four decades after arriving in Katsura, while he was on his way to Ryoan for the first time. The channel between Katsura and Ryoan was unstable, by virtue of a topological oddity that had placed the two great elfin cities as far apart as possible in this world, at its highest altitude and at its lowest, and this produced a flow of tension that made the eight-hour boat ride one of the most unpredictable for Nanzen. The channel was often closed and Petrus, after a long series of failed attempts to reach the city, only got there after he had already explored three-quarters of the rest of the elfin territory. After a somewhat chaotic crossing—but turbulence in the channel, once so rare, had now become commonplace—Petrus and his companions landed at dawn at the docks of the fourth sanctuary, and all three now stood there gaping. He thought he'd seen so many marvels that nothing could ever dazzle him again, but he was wrong, for in all the known worlds, there has never existed a more absolute city than Ryoan, and by absolute, I mean beautiful and powerful, but also *impossible.* Although it was entirely shrouded in dark mists, the houses and trees shone like black diamonds. Darkness emerged from light, the world was lit up while an alchemist's filter allowed one to see every object clearly and distinctly, standing out against the background it should have dissolved into. Here there were no mountains, but there were cliffs of mist, as imposing as the ones in Katsura, entire sections standing tall all through the city. These huge gleaming screens ran from east to west, and day and night Ryoan was resplendent in their dark light. There was, too, a liquid silver, a flowing iridescence of the sun in the interstices of darkness, streaming over bridges and silent gardens—all was darkness, all was silver, all was transparency, and the city could be seen through canopies of mist that sparked like power lines. There was a caressing softness to it all, and you missed it once it had moved eastward, then you gratefully welcomed the next wave as it came out of the west.

"It's like a painting in ink and crystal," said Paulus, rousing the other two from their stupor.

"It is said that the brilliance of this darkness knows no rival," said Marcus. "I understand why the elves from Ryoan are proud."

And indeed, as Petrus would declare that first evening, over a mug of honey more refined than any found in other provinces: wandering through the streets of the town was a level one spiritual experience. Earlier on, they had gone past a garden where, on a patch of black sand, a single bitter orange tree grew, and its little white flowers, sculpted against the background of dark mist, looked like stars adrift in the nocturnal ether. Their perfume, which he could taste in his mug of honey, had almost driven Petrus mad, and everything was like that in this welcoming, sublime city, which the three friends did not want to leave.

"Ryoan has this effect on me—like a filter that makes everything seem sharper," he said, again.

He didn't know where this sort of idea was coming from, but each time he had such a thought, it seemed right to him, and familiar, and he would point it out to his two companions.

"It's the effect of the thousand-year-old tea," declared Paulus, setting his mug down. "Ever since we drank it we've been living with our dead, or they've been living with us, I don't know which, but they dignify our private thoughts."

The night before the departure, they went out into the warm twilight. Walking along the banks of the river, yielding to the flow of seasons, trees, and mountains whispered by the current, they made an unexpected encounter. It was only once the elf had come right up to him and smiled that Petrus, addled by the excess of orange flower syrup he'd indulged in at dinner, recognized the blond angel from the channel at Hanase, his complexion more delicate, his eyes bluer than ever, a young adult now and so dazzlingly beautiful that Petrus was (almost) speechless.

"Now I find you just when I'm about to leave Ryoan," said the elf with a smile, "It must be a sign of fate."

They all bowed amiably.

"Where are you going?" asked Paulus.

"To Katsura, through the first channel at dawn," he replied, turning into a wild boar so gracious he made one think of a deer. "I've just been accepted onto the team of gardeners to the Council," he added proudly.

"That's quite a coincidence, said Petrus, "I'm also working at the upper chamber."

"My father recommended me to the head of the garden," said the fine boar, turning into a gorgeous horse.

"He's a remarkable artist," said Petrus politely.

"Who should have been Head of the Council," said the other elf nonchalantly.

There was a moment's silence.

"Our present head has all the qualities required to govern the mists," said Petrus.

"You think this is so because he was elected? Do you believe that the common elf has any idea what the qualities of a leader should be?" asked the horse.

"There are none more common than I," said Petrus, after a moment's silence.

The young elf looked hard at him for a moment then gave that irresistible smile that banished any misgivings.

"I doubt that very much," he said, before bowing gracefully and taking his leave.

But after he'd gone a few steps he turned around briefly.

"I will see you soon," he said to Petrus, in a way that made his blood run cold.

In his capacity as head sweeper, Petrus was witness to the Council's important affairs and backstage intrigue. His subordinate status cloaked him in an invisibility that gave him access to all sorts of information more prominent elves wouldn't be able to obtain, particularly as he was still just as popular as he had been back in his Woods. Everyone liked Petrus, everyone sought out his company, and not a day went by when he was not invited for a drink of maple or rose-hip syrup, to which he would respond favorably if he had finished his reading. Sweeping was an agreeable vocation; the brooms were made of light bamboo and one hardly needed to touch the ground; the job was neither difficult nor tiring, and he took pleasure in leaving a tidy space behind him, cleaned of a few careless leaves. He worked only from dawn to lunchtime, and his afternoons were as free as was his access to all the remotest areas of the headquarters, including the inner gardens which could be reached through the north door, and the Council Chambers. However, the more the time passed, the less he felt like going there. The head of the gardeners had not won the election, but was clearly gaining influence over the upper chamber. Gradually, gray sand came to replace the moss, and the vegetation disappeared in favor of magnificent stones that the gardener's assistants would track down in the four corners of the mists—thus, a visitor to the garden would see, through successive plays of stone and sand, the tide on the shore, eternal mountains, or the unyielding lakes of this world. But these displays were unfeeling, which came as no surprise to Petrus, who was careful to sweep below the picture windows of the upper chamber whenever the Head of the Council was reading out the daily report on the mists from Nanzen. And Petrus overheard the questions on the part of the head of the garden and the curator of the library who, along with the ten councilors, and sometimes envoys from the provinces, had the right to attend the sessions.

He could not have imagined better leaders than those who had been elected. The Guardian of the Pavilion in particular filled him with admiration, with his melodious voice and ageless gaze. The head of the garden never attacked him to his face, any more than he did the hare elf from Katsura who presided over the sessions with elegant authority and a sense of irony that was fairly uncommon among elves. They were giants. They were giants in the service of a world deep in turmoil, because every daily report described the increasing decline of the mist. Moreover, they had to confront the destroyer of the centuries-old vegetation, obsessed with stones and perfection, who was no longer in hiding and was openly campaigning against humans.

"How can you deny the facts?" he asked the Head of the Council. "How can you ignore that their unbearable frivolity is destroying the paradise that was entrusted to them and, through the contagion of the bridge, is also poisoning our own paradise?"

"There are no simple causes or remedies to any illness," replied the hare. "Designating a providential enemy will not save our mist."

"You are deluding yourself with chitchat while criminals are running about the countryside with impunity," replied the gardener.

"Decline is not a crime, but a challenge," replied the guardian.

"Nothing will give us back our mists if we do not act."

And this went on, tirelessly, while Petrus, year after year, saw the elves grow despondent and the words of the gardener infiltrate their hearts, although there was not yet a single councilor who was willing to adopt a radical position regarding the human question.

When destiny takes an abrupt turn, there are no flowers to distract us from it. It was a fine November afternoon and he was reading, ensconced on a soft cushion in a recess in the library, looking out at the only garden that had been spared the mineral mischief of the elf from Ryoan. He read and sighed intermittently, vaguely interested and bored by the autumn elegies in a collection that was part of a great classic of the mists, the *Canto of the Alliance*, where the natural affinities of mountains, forests, and clouds were celebrated over and over. It was illustrated ad nauseam with magnificent ink drawings where, against a background of misty summits, trees gracefully lost their leaves, and birds, joined by the writing of poetry, flew high in the sky.

Neither spring nor summer nor winter
Know the grace
Of languid autumn

He sighed again and, taking the volume with him, went out into the first courtyard where he sat in the sun, his back against an old plum tree. It was very mild and, after a few additional pages of maple trees blazing in the setting sun, he was about to doze off when something in his reading startled him and made him sit up, his heart pounding and his nose quivering. He stared at a camellia flower before him that a gardener from the first shift had left on the moss, not seeing it, went back to the text, shook his head, read it over and over, endlessly.

the rebirth of the mists
through two children of snow and November
the rootless the last alliance

"By the mists," he murmured at last (which, in elfin, is the equivalent of "holy mackerel").

He did not know which was more upsetting, that he'd found in these lines the inspiration of those he'd once spontaneously created, under the influence of the wild grasses in the channel, or that for the first time he was in the presence of such an *unthinkable* text. From his reading, he could swear that this poem did not celebrate anything that existed, did not evoke anything that had ever happened but, on the contrary, described the affliction of the mist and outlined the remedy as if it had anticipated and conceived them. Three lines in an unknown story and life was radiant, in league with a heart swollen with a new intoxication so intense that he could feel that heart pounding fit to burst, and he could no longer see what was there before him—and precisely, there before him, observing him in silence, stood the Head of the Council. How long has he been standing there? wondered Petrus, leaping to his feet. The sun was setting, smoothing the moss in the courtyard with its low-angled light. He felt a chill and blinked his eyes as if emerging from a long dream. He stood there for a few moments before the silent Head of the Council.

"What are you reading?" asked the Head, finally.

Everything that had gathered in Petrus's mind during the hours he'd remained motionless rereading the poem now metabolized and, stunned by the words coming from his mouth, he said:

"A prophecy."

The Head of the Council raised an eyebrow.

"A prophecy?" he said.

Petrus felt as thick as his own broom. Lowering his eyes on the book he was holding in his hands, he mustered his courage.

"A prophecy," he said.

He read the three lines out loud, and every word pierced the cool late-afternoon air like a dagger.

"Where did you find this?" asked the Head of the Council after a moment's silence.

"In the *Canto of the Alliance*," replied Petrus, handing him the book.

There was another silence.

"I don't know how many times I've read the *Canto of the Alliance*," said the Head of the Council, "but I have no recollection of these lines."

Petrus, respectful, remained silent.

"Yet I have the memory of an elephant," said the elf, turning into that hare with the ermine coat that caused crowds to melt with admiration.

He remained thoughtful for a moment while Petrus said nothing, embarrassed and not knowing which stance to take.

"How long have you been working here?" asked the hare.

"Seventy years," Petrus replied.

"You're not from Katsura, are you?"

"I am from the Deep Woods," replied Petrus, "I came here because of a rather peculiar set of circumstances."

The hare turned into a white horse.

"Which were?"

"Well," said Petrus, "I was sent by the Wild Grasses of Hanase."

The horse stared at him as if he'd changed into a slug.

"And what twist of fate took you into the Wild Grasses?" he asked.

"The recommendation of the boatman from the South Marches, who asked the hostess to serve us a thousand-year-old tea," said Petrus.

The Head of the Council laughed.

"Is that all," he said.

Almost to himself, he murmured the name of the boatman in a trill that ended with a plop in the water.

"A squirrel from the Deep Woods, sent by the oldest servants of the mists, and a sort of prophecy come out of nowhere," he continued. "Imagine my surprise to find out only today what's been going on. Do you have something else up your sleeve, by any chance?"

Petrus blushed.

"Just before I arrived in Katsura, I composed a similar little poem about two children."

"Are you a poet?" asked the Head of the Council.

"No, I'm a sweeper."

The Head of the Council changed into a man.

"I'm afraid you are going to have to give up your vocation," he said. "Come tomorrow morning to the upper chamber. I'm going to convene an extraordinary session and you would do well to prepare yourself for a long day."

Finally, he went away, leaving Petrus more dumbfounded and distraught than a broom.

A dream so lofty
Neither spring nor summer nor winter
Know the grace
Of languid autumn

Book of Paintings

聖地

SANCTUARIES

The land of elves has four sanctuaries.

Nanzen, in the province of Leaves, received, regulated, and brought together the mists by means of all the paths and channels.

Katsura, the capital of the elves and the jewel of Snows, was in charge of maintaining the foundations of this world.

Ryoan, at the heart of the Dark Mists, kept the books for the eternity of beauty.

Hanase, finally, the only city of Ashes, maintained the connection between the living and the dead.

The sanctuaries are the secret hearts of a world where the answers to the questions in the great Books are being worked out.

The question of fervor, which Nanzen prayed for every day, that the mist might be saved.

That of courage in battle, overseen by the upper chamber of Katsura.

That of beauty, incarnated by Ryoan's natural paintings.

That of love, finally, the greatest question of all: the dead of Hanase whisper the canto of love, and this canto travels through space and time, and it rides upon the great winds of the dream, and one day it reaches our distant ears.

予言

PROPHECY

The Head of the Council immediately agreed with Petrus's hunch that the three lines were a prophecy. He knew the difference between human and elfin literature, and he knew it was impossible for the poem to be part of the *Canto of the Alliance*—and yet, it was or, at least, it had become part of it.

Elves do not tell stories the way humans do, and they are impervious to stories of *invention*. They sing of their great exploits, compose odes to birds and to the beauty of the mists, but imagination never adds anything to this elegiac celebration. Who would ask for stories in the Great Whole where every event is merely the reflection of the entire story?

As there was no trace in either the annals or the memory of elfin ages of two children of November through whom a rebirth of the mists was said to have come, the poem was an unclassifiable text, which they hoped would prove prophetic. The Head of the Council, who already suspected that the splendid, eternal, and static world of his own kind would be forced to change in order to survive, understood that the sweeper Petrus's epiphany commanded the path to a new alliance.

I t seemed to Petrus from the Deep Woods that he had had two distinct lives: the life before and the life after the moment he read the prophecy. In the first of those lives, there was a broom; in the second, adventure; and he saw his erstwhile voyages and little adventures as leaps of a mouse in a cage.

As if it were meant to happen, that year of epiphanies for Petrus had also witnessed a series of memorable events, bound together by a noose that subsequently seemed to be pulled ever tighter, until it could only lead to war—but anyone who, in those days, could have understood the fabric and the significance of those events would have been very clever indeed. They were, in no particular order: a man's murder, which would send the Head of the Council to Rome; the discovery of a singular painting in which the decline of worlds was sealed; the discovery of the existence of a gray notebook which would change the face of the coming war; and the discovery, by Petrus, of human wine.

Not long after the sweeper Petrus first appeared before the upper chamber and the birth of the idea of an alliance with humans, a conversation took place between the head of the gardeners and his young right-hand man, the piglet from Hanase who was now an adult wild boar. For thirty years, Petrus had been encountering him on the paths of the Council, and their mutual hostility had continued to grow. The initial amiability of the young wild boar had changed to scorn, once he noted the sweeper's lack of enthusiasm for his champion's intrigues. The worship he devoted to his leader made him his most eager acolyte, and they were quite a sight, the pair of them, when they took on their human forms and ambled casually through their surroundings—so handsome, and so evil, thought Petrus, who at times was still unsettled by their dazzling smiles; then he would shake his head and the spell dissolved.

Then one January morning, Petrus overheard this conversation between the two, and he related it to the Head of the Council and the Guardian of the Pavilion. All three of them were standing in the study of the hare elf from Katsura, a tiny little room that opened onto the most marvelous scene. Although he had strolled through many a remarkable garden, Petrus did not know of a single one that offered a concentrated sense of nature the way this one did. That the quintessence of artifice could produce a sensation of such pure nature in a single garden entirely conceived by the mind and hand of an elf, both charmed and stunned him. It was little more than an enclosure of light-colored sand, azaleas, and heavenly bamboo, through which a stream ran, preceded by a hollow stone where birds frolicked. But, however modest it might be, the scene evoked a sensation of the vast world, through a transubstantiation of distances and things, and Petrus had renounced trying to plumb its mystery.

"I tend it myself," the Head of the Council said to him one day, showing him the tools stored along the outside veranda: shears, a little broom, a bamboo rake, and a basket made of woven bark.

And Petrus was not averse to the fact that the gardeners didn't sniff around there. However, the time had come for the report: wandering aimlessly along the corridors in the upper chamber after work, he glimpsed the two cursed souls around the corner of a veranda and, deeming they had a strange manner about them, he followed them, then positioned himself discreetly below the little room they slipped into in order to converse. Apparently, the head of the garden had news from a nephew who, by virtue of the regulations of the mists authorizing families of dignitaries from the headquarters of the Council to travel in both worlds, had recently gone over to the human side, and, in a city called Amsterdam, had found a painting (which did not interest his uncle) and a gray notebook (which interested him greatly), sent them to another city called Rome, then disappeared without a trace. Prior to this he'd come back from Amsterdam a first time without the gray notebook, for he feared the Guardian of the Pavilion might get wind of it, and the head of the garden cursed his own precaution, which now deprived him of the object he seemed to covet. The story, which made no sense at all to Petrus, didn't seem to surprise the other two.

"We always keep an eye on elves who go to stay in the human world," the Guardian told him, "and last night we witnessed the nephew's murder."

"Murder?" echoed Petrus, horrified.

"Murder," confirmed the Head of the Council. "It would seem he wanted to earn human money by selling the painting to an art dealer, and the dealer killed him then made off with the canvas and the notebook. The dealer's name is Roberto Volpe and I'm on my way to Rome to meet him."

"Meet a murderer?" asked Petrus, even more horrified.

"Astonishingly, Roberto Volpe is an amiable, peace-loving individual who, on top of it, just became a father this morning for the first time," answered the Head of the Council.

"What an astonishing business," said the guardian. "We need to take a closer look. Unfortunately, in the commotion over the murder, we failed to determine what Volpe might have done with the mysterious gray notebook. But the head of the garden didn't send his nephew to Amsterdam just by chance, and I bet he knew what he was looking for. So now we have a double quest to pursue: the two children, and the gray notebook."

"Do you think the two are connected?" asked Petrus.

"We think that everything is always connected," answered the guardian. "Including a certain sweeper who was sent to the Council library upon the intuition of the Wild Grasses."

Petrus was speechless.

"There are times we may be blind, but we are not morons," said the Head of the Council. "Apparently you like traveling?"

His expression was sour.

"Still, I'm not sure what I'm offering you is exactly a privilege. This first murder of an elf in human territory augurs a sad beginning but, in these dark times, we must show discernment and audacity."

He exchanged a glance with the guardian.

"Your unexpected discovery in the *Canto of the Alliance* has given us proof that the key of time is to be found in the link between the worlds. I don't know why you told us this so long after you were singled out by the two highest authorities in our world, the Wild Grasses and the boatman from the South Marches, nor why, in the interval, fate went and stuck a broom in your hands, but it would seem you have been chosen for this adventure."

He gave Petrus what seemed to be a rather stern look—or was it solemn?

"I have decided to appoint you special envoy of the mists to the human world," he said, "in charge of the dual quest for the gray notebook and the two children of the *Canto*."

He stood up, signaling that it was time to leave.

"Be here tomorrow at dawn," said the Guardian of the

Pavilion, "and bring what you need for several days' travel, for every kind of weather and every season."

Petrus left the Council headquarters in a state of such confusion that for the first time he went home to the wrong house, then seemed not to recognize his old unicorn elf. Special envoy from the Council of the Mists to the human world! he said to himself, over and over. He didn't have the slightest idea what he would have to do, and the few instructions he'd received had left him mired in confusion. Elves only wear one outfit, which keeps them closely covered at all times, but they also wear capes when it rains, and warm coats in cold weather with added headgear that more or less resembles that of humans. Petrus spent the night trying to put together a bundle then, at daybreak, he stuffed a few belongings at random in the canvas bag he used for traveling. Finally, realizing to his horror that the sun was already quite high in the sky, he rushed to the upper chamber and, without knowing how he got there, found himself in the private study where he'd been the previous day. Before him stood the Head of the Council, observing him with thoughtful intensity. Next to him was the Guardian of the Pavilion, murmuring something Petrus couldn't hear, as sounds vanished into a cottony confusion where he felt his intelligence disappearing as well.

The guardian placed a hand on his shoulder. There was an empty moment while the cotton was endlessly diluted in an icy void. Then they were in Nanzen. The pavilion was silent. Through its windows that had neither trim nor panes, Petrus could see the mist sculpting the trees in the valley. To the rear, at the top of the red bridge, a thick fog was whirling in place.

"How did we get here?" Petrus asked the guardian.

"By the bridge," he answered, handing him a cup of tea.

"I thought it led only to the land of humans."

"The bridge is only visible when it serves to pass between

worlds. Inside our own, it does not require any special material form."

He went to fetch some clothes that were neatly piled on a bench, along with utensils for making tea, and unfolded them in front of Petrus. There was a sort of two-legged sheath, a large, coarsely cut shirt, and a sort of cape with arms.

"This outfit will be suitable wherever you go," said the guardian. "When it comes to shoes, however, it will depend on your destination."

"But where am I going?" asked Petrus. "I haven't a clue." Then, remembering their conversation from the previous day: "To Rome, perhaps?"

The guardian shared images which made him plop in astonishment upon his squirrel rear end.

"Rome," said the master of Nanzen.

But Petrus couldn't understand what he was seeing.

"These are stone buildings," said the guardian. "Collective buildings, in a way, or houses of cult and power."

"So tall, and so dead," murmured Petrus. "I don't think I'll go there. To be honest, I really have no idea what I'm supposed to do, and for sure I don't know where to start."

"Trust your heart," said the guardian.

For a moment Petrus, uncertain and lost, did not move. Without warning, the face of the old woman with the blue ribbons from his dream at the teahouse came back to him from the depths of his memory, and he saw her coming toward him against a background of little gardens with freshly turned earth. He felt the light presence of the guardian penetrate his spirit and he heard him say, I see her. The vision shifted. Verdant landscapes of meadows and woods went by, and then the vision paused above a village nestled in a valley. His heart pounding, Petrus recognized the stone houses with tawny roof tiles. Snow had covered the orchards, and plumes of winter smoke rose toward the sky.

"That's it," he said, "that's where it is."

The images vanished and the guardian opened his eyes.

"Burgundy," he said. "At least there's no lack of snow there."

An hour later, feeling as much at ease in his human clothes as a squirrel in a tutu, his feet clad in instruments of torture which the guardian had referred to as clogs (stuffed with woolen socks that were unpleasantly scratchy against his calves), Petrus was standing on the red bridge.

"We will not let you out of our sight. When you're ready to come back, all you have to do is let us know," said the guardian.

Finally, he gave him a little purse which contained the money he might need on the other side.

Petrus took a step forward and entered the circle of mist. It was extraordinarily thick and he felt a silkiness against his cheek. And now? he thought, deep down feeling somewhat grumpy. This, I think, sums up our hero better than anything, because his stomach, deprived of breakfast, was now ruining the exquisite frisson of adventure that had been running down his spine. He closed his eyes, took a deep breath, and prepared himself for a long, icy void. A biting blast slapped his brow and he opened his eyes again in surprise.

He was already on the other side. Mercy me! he thought, on seeing the farm from his dream there before him. It was late afternoon and the light was fading. From the only window whose shutters were still open, to the left of the front door, came a beam of lamplight. Just then, someone opened the window and leaned outside, struggling against the icy wind. In the increasing gloom, Petrus couldn't make out her features, but even without seeing her he knew and, his heart leaping, his feet unsteady in his clogs, he took a few timid steps closer. Now he could see the craggy old face, the headdress with ribbons the color of forget-me-nots, and the vitality of a gaze that was both similar to and different from that of the woman in his dream—seventy years have gone by, he thought, this is her great-granddaughter.

"Sweet Jesus!" she exclaimed, on seeing him.

I understand her language, thought Petrus, stunned. She looked him up and down for a moment then, evidently judging him to be harmless, she swayed her head from left to right and said:

"What on earth are you doing, standing there stock-still and stupid? Come into the warm and we'll talk by the fire."

As he awkwardly came forward, still wobbling in his clogs, she laughed, reached for the shutters, which she closed with a bang, then slammed the windows just as energetically. A second later, the front door opened.

He slipped inside and found himself in a large room where a fire was burning in the hearth. There was a small crowd of people, who turned in unison to look at him.

"Hello, friend, what are you doing out in such frosty weather?" asked one of the guests, motioning to him to join them by the fire.

I understand, thought Petrus, but will I be able to speak? But he took the plunge, bowed politely, went closer, and felt the words roll naturally off his tongue.

"I got lost," he said, which was precisely what the guardian had instructed him to say, in any circumstance. "I was looking for an inn for the night, but I must have taken a wrong turn."

The man looked at him with amusement.

"A bow, and a fine gentleman's manner of speaking," he murmured, "but not an ounce of ill intent, for sure."

He thumped Petrus on the back, almost knocking him head over clogs.

"You've come at just the right time," he said, "Cousin Maurice is visiting and we're having a little feast."

He pointed to a man with a tanned, affable face, who gave

a smile and raised two fingers to stroke his temple, briefly—so
that's how they say hello on the farm, thought Petrus.

"What's more, our Marguerite is in the kitchen, and that
means a sight better food than you'd get at the inn," added the
farmer, before placing a tiny glass in Petrus's hand identical to
the ones the other men were holding.

He reached for a bottle filled with a clear liquid. Petrus,
prompted by some powerful hunch, doubted it was water.

"Doudou's plum brandy," said the man, pouring him a
splash of said liquid. "And Doudou never jokes around with
serious things," he added, while the others laughed.

He looked Petrus straight in the eye.

"My name is Jean-René Faure," he said.

"Georges Bernard," said Petrus, something the guardian
had also suggested, and for a split second he dreamt he might
really be called Georges Bernard and stay forever in this farm-
house room with its fragrances of paradise.

He'd never smelled such aromas, and he concluded that
whatever was simmering in those pots was not what elves put
in theirs—there were mysterious smells, powerful and musky,
their warm sensuality both disturbing and enchanting at the
same time. Just as he was thinking this, Jean-René lifted his
glass right next to his and clicked them together, saying,
Cheers! And Petrus, glad of a way to remedy the excessive sali-
vation caused by the aromas around him, followed his example, tossing back his head and drinking the entire contents of
his little glass in one go.

He collapsed on a bench. Am I about to die? he wondered.
A wonderful warmth spread all over him, and he realized
everyone was looking at him and laughing.

"This can't be the first time he's ever had a drop?" asked
Jean-René, placing a hand on his shoulder.

Petrus wanted to reply, but he could feel tears streaming

down his cheeks. Suddenly letting go, accepting his fate, completely intoxicated by the fire in his gut, he began to laugh, too.

"Thanks be to God!" exclaimed Jean-René, immediately pouring him another glass of Doudou's plum brandy.

And the feast began, and no one was surprised by the presence of the potbellied ginger fellow, who did not seem to know how to put one clogged foot in front of another, but they all immediately recognized him as a harmless, likeable sort, given the candor of his clumsiness.

It was a time for drinking and joking about the day's minor events. When the women, placing the fruit of their concoctions on the table, gave the signal, they sat down; Jean-René recited a prayer before slicing a gleaming loaf of bread, and the cooks served the first of four dishes—or were there ten? Petrus had lost count by the second glass of wine they poured him: it was a reserve, they told him, one they kept for special occasions. He'd liked Doudou's plum brandy earlier on, and at the end of the meal he did justice to the jar of greengages in eau-de-vie opened to round out the experience. As for the wine, it was a brilliant finishing touch, and without it he certainly wouldn't have been able to honor the contents of his plate—which would have been a great pity because Marguerite was reputed to be the best chef in all the low country. Moreover, the provender being served that evening was the product of last week's hunting through the snowy woods where the trees cracked like ice floes and where the animals—caught straight out of their dens, no time even to blink an eye—had the succulent flesh of creatures who hadn't registered their demise. To you who are familiar with human food, I will describe the menu and the adversity this implied for Petrus: in addition to the soup with bacon which was the farm's everyday fare, he was made to suffer duck roasted on the spit, jugged hare, pheasant pâté, the leftovers of a doe terrine, braised endives, potatoes roasted in the fireplace, and a frying pan full of caramelized cardoons. Finally, after the half a cheese (from our own cows, if you please) per guest, they dished up a plum pie with an autumn crabapple compote, accompanied by a sauce that was both sweet and sour, known to refine the palate of any gourmet.

For now, Petrus was gazing at the soup where, among the carrots, potatoes, and leeks, there floated pinkish, off-white bits, and he questioned his neighbor about them.

"Pig, by Jove, pig!" answered the neighbor.

Pig! I can't eat pig! thought Petrus, horrified, picturing the Guard of the Pavilion crammed into a stewpot. But the pinkish morsels seemed to be winking at him, and the aroma was beguiling him like a succubus. After his third glass of wine, he mustered his courage and bit cautiously into the meat. He was met with an explosion of pleasure that dissolved any vestiges of the guilt that had already been diluted by the wines of the arrière-côte. While the fibers of bacon disintegrated on his tongue, he let the juice slip toward his throat and thought he might swoon with pleasure. What followed was even greater ecstasy, and after the sensual delight of the duck on the spit, he had no more scruples about wallowing in carnivorous debauchery. I'll do penance later, he thought, attacking the terrine and its fat and chunks, which either melted in his mouth or resisted his bite in a demonic ballet. It will come as no surprise to learn that the next morning he could not recall having had thoughts so foreign to his culture and his nature, not to mention the fact that he resolved his moral conflict by convincing himself that a stranger must adapt to the customs of the countries he visits, and by deluding himself that the animals had been killed without feeling pain—which forces us to acknowledge the fact that Petrus was behaving in a perfectly human manner. I will leave it to others to judge whether one should be glad of this. After dinner, everyone behaved like humans and natives of France, particularly Burgundians: the men enjoyed their little nightcap, the women tidied up the kitchen, drinking herbal tea, and they honored the dinner with fine compliments. Maurice decreed that Marguerite's pheasant pâté was the most tender in the civilized world, which caused much debate regarding a related existential problem of major importance (the consubstantial dryness of pheasant pâté) then, without batting an eyelash, he asked the chef to share her secret—to which she replied by saying she would rather be crucified alive and left to the crows of the six cantons than divulge the secret to her knack for pâté.

And while Petrus may have enjoyed the evening's fare, the wine had been an experience of another order. A first sip, and it was the land of Burgundy in his mouth, its winds and mist, its stones and vine stock; the more he drank, the deeper he penetrated the secrets of the universe in a way which the contemplation of the peaks in his Woods had never allowed; and while his elfin soul understood a hundredfold this magic born of the alliance between earth and sky, what was human in his heart could be expressed at last. In the dual story for which the winemaker and the drinker were responsible the most marvelous thing, beyond the enlightenment of intoxication, could be found; the vine told a slow adventure, vegetal and cosmic, an epic of low walls and hillsides in the sun; then the wine loosened tongues and gave birth in turn to stories which the prophecy had only foreshadowed. There was talk of miraculous hunting and virgins in the snow, of holy processions, of sacred violets, and fabulous creatures whose wanderings captivated the villagers, absorbed by their last drams of liqueur, while a new life was added to the everyday one, sparkling in the background of what was visible, and opening the freedom of dreams in waking time. He did not know whether he owed this metamorphosis to the talent of his new human companions, or to the exquisite floating feeling that each new glass of wine instilled, but he could sense the death throes of his old frustration that an intangible screen was keeping things from him. Now the screen had been shattered, and he had access to the throbbing pulse of his emotions; the world was radiant, more intense; although he had no doubt that this was possible without wine, the vine and the tale stood together with this transfiguration of levels of reality; and now that, seven decades on, he understood the message of the wild grasses in the channel, he was so moved by it that he stammered something his neighbor had to ask him to repeat.

Everyone fell silent around the table.

Maurice again asked Petrus to repeat what he'd said. They were all staring at him with those soft moist eyes that come from food and the vine, and he mumbled, his voice quavering slightly:

"It would be as if the world was a novel waiting for its words."

How stupid he felt, dismayed by his own syntax, seeing that they were waiting for an explanation. But unexpectedly Jean-René came to the rescue, raising his little glass of brandy and declaring in a kindly tone:

"For sure, what would we do without stories by the fire and old grannies' fairy tales?"

The congregation nodded their heads, sufficiently softened by wine to give credence to this cryptic translation. They cogitated briefly on the matter (but not too much), then returned to their conversation, which was slowed by the prospect of settling cheek on pillow, and snoring off the wine until the next day at dawn.

Still, while they were halfheartedly making their final

comments for the evening, one topic Maurice broached landed on the table like a flying spark and made everyone sit up straight in their chair to enter the debate with passion.

"I say there's no better season than winter," he insisted, without batting an eyelid.

Then, pleased with his contribution, he rewarded himself with a final splash of brandy.

As one might have expected, the trap worked.

"What ever for?" asked Jean-René, his tone falsely amiable.

"For hunting and gathering wood, by Jove!" replied the simple man.

This was the signal for a heated discussion that Petrus only dimly understood, other than that it was something to do with hunts and dogs, timber and orchards, and a divinity in those parts whom they referred to as the whip. It lasted a pleasantly endless amount of time, which he enlivened with a few additional glasses, but in the end (and to his great regret), because it was getting close to midnight and all good things must come to an end, Marguerite took it upon herself to end the discussion.

"Every season is the good Lord's," she said.

Out of respect for the granny, (something to do with her mastery of pheasant), the men fell silent and celebrated their renewed alliance with the courtesy of a final splash of plum brandy. Jean-René Faure, however, who could not ignore the laws of hospitality, asked Petrus what his favorite season was—and Petrus was surprised to discover how easy it was to think, despite his drinking and eating like a Burgundian pig. He raised his little glass to each man in turn, as he'd seen done, and recited the three lines from the *Canto of the Alliance*:

> *Neither spring nor summer nor winter*
> *Know the grace*
> *Of languid autumn*

The others looked at him, astounded, then at each other, eyes shining.

"For sure, if we start with poetry . . . " murmured Jean-René.

They all bowed their heads with unexpected deference. Marguerite was smiling; the women nudged a leftover piece of pie with a final dollop of sour cream in his direction; and everyone seemed happier than the little angels in the great heavens.

"Time for bed," said Jean-René finally.

But instead of taking their leave, the men stood up, their faces serious, and the women made a sign over their breast which, Petrus would later learn, was the sign of the cross. Gripped by the solemnity of the moment, he wanted to imitate them, so he stood up, made the same sign, almost tripped over his own plate, steadied himself on his clogs, and listened to the final prayer.

"Let us pray for those who fell in battle," said the host, "and in particular for the village men whose names are carved on the monument across from the church, so that no one will ever forget them because, though now the fighting's still recent, tomorrow they'll all be gone from people's minds."

"Amen," said the others.

They lowered their heads and stood for a moment in contemplative silence. So they have fought a major war, thought Petrus. Then there was a faint murmur as conversation started up again, and he felt that something was trying to make its way inside him—was it the beneficial effect of the wine, or the dignity of the moment; he could hear faint voices, intermittently.

"Unfortunately, I have heard say that prayers are not enough to knock sense into a man's brain," said Jean-René, placing a friendly hand on his shoulder.

After a pause, he added:

"That is why I go to the cemetery every day to hear what my dead have to say to me."

The simmering echo suddenly exploded in Petrus's head.

"*There was a great earthquake, and the moon became as blood*," he said, then stopped, stunned.

What am I on about? he wondered.

But the other man was gently nodding his head.

"That's it, precisely," he said, "that is exactly what we went through, the lot of us."

Finally, the guests withdrew and Petrus was shown to his room, a little lean-to that smelled fragrantly of hay, where they had prepared a woolen mattress, a soft pillow, and a warm blanket. The visions from the long-ago dream at the teahouse were swirling through his brain, and the horror rumbling inside him made his heart sink, once again. Did I see images of some bygone war or of a war yet to come? he wondered, and then, surrendering his last weapons to the excellent local wine, he collapsed on his bed and instantly fell asleep.

It was a sleep with neither tremors nor visions, a night of existential void that left no memories. On waking, however, he was painfully called back to life, and he more dragged himself than walked to the common room. There was an enticing smell, and a young woman was busy clearing a table where three cloves of garlic lay next to a glass of water and a large earthenware jug.

"Would you like some coffee?" she asked him.

Although he couldn't open his left eye, the first sip did Petrus a world of good.

"The men told me to tell you they send their regards and that you are welcome to stay at The Hollows for as long as you like," she said. "It's the first major hunt of the year, and they couldn't wait for you this morning, but if you're hungry, I can make something for you."

"Is The Hollows the name of the farm?" asked Petrus, politely declining her offer of food.

"It is that," she said, "and has been for longer than anyone can remember."

"Where are the other ladies?" he asked.

She laughed.

"Ladies, indeed . . . " she said before stopping herself, then adding: "They're with the priest at the Marcelot farm, where we heard the old woman won't make it through the day."

And she made the sign of the cross.

An hour later, Petrus took his leave, instructing his hostess to thank Jean-René Faure and to assure him that he had business to see to, but would not fail to come back again soon. Then, stumbling inelegantly in his clogs, he went out into the courtyard. There was not a breath of wind; a vast blue sky was set upon a pure white land; on the branches, pearls of ice twinkled like stars. Not sure what he was doing, Petrus set off down the main road until he came to a large wrought-iron gate. There were stone walls, and pathways in neat rows, and a large rectangle of tombstones and crosses: it was the cemetery. He stood before the graves, ignoring the cruel chill and the searing pain in his head. After a moment, he raised his head and said out loud: I want to go back to Nanzen.

A second later, the Head of the Council and the Guardian of the Pavilion, arms crossed, were gazing at him with an expression devoid of all indulgence.

"I hope you have a headache," said the Head of the Council.

Petrus turned into a squirrel, and he felt how greatly he had missed his animal essences.

"I have a headache," he said, wretchedly.

"*There was a great earthquake, and the moon became as blood*. Where did you get that from?"

"I have no idea," said Petrus.

"Revelation 6:12, although the quote has been truncated,"

said the guardian. "If you are capable of reinventing the human Bible after a few glasses of their wine, perhaps we should think of forgiving you your wanderings."

"The Bible?" said Petrus.

"We are going to have to educate you before we send you back among the humans," said the Head of the Council. "We cannot leave things to chance."

"They are not left to chance," said the guardian.

Petrus looked at him gratefully and, trusting his impulse, he said:

"I have to go wherever there's wine."

The Head of the Council raised his eyebrow, ironically.

Petrus hunted for his words and couldn't find them.

"Wine," echoed the Head of the Council, thoughtful. "We have never paid any attention to it. It never occurred to elves to grow wine grapes, let alone drink it."

On hearing these words, Petrus felt everything come clear in his mind, the way it does in stories and fables, when one grasps what cannot be clearly explained.

"Wine is to humans what tea is to elves," he said. "The key to the alliance is there."

In a time of miraculous hunting
Of sacred violets
Great earthquakes
Beneath a moon of blood

Book of Battles

狩

THE WHIP

The whip is the only true divinity of hunting country. His knowledge of every copse and every thicket is honored. It is known that he leaves at dawn to mark out the path for the hunt, and this silent prayer through the sleeping woods serves him as the finest of matins, rendering thanks to earth and sky and singing the nobility of thrushes.

旅

TRAVEL

If there is one human inclination elves are lacking, it is that of travel.

This inclination, paradoxically, affects humans because of a flaw that makes it impossible for them to *be here*, to find themselves in the simple *presence* of things, and it has molded them into creatures who are both restless and inspired.

Can anyone imagine what immersion in the world combined with an appetite for change would look like? To welcome the void and delight in fantasy? Yes, we can imagine it, and we dream of it, and we pray to the great winds of dreams to take us there.

WE ARE ALL
1871–1918

A t the time when Petrus began traveling all over the world of humans, the Head of the Council returned from Rome with astounding news.

"We know who the gray notebook belonged to," he said to Petrus one day when they were both in Nanzen together with the guardian and a handful of his assistants.

He told them how he went to Rome under a false human identity—an orchestra conductor by the name of Gustavo Acciavatti—and, on the pretext of acquiring some Italian Renaissance drawings, he'd met Roberto Volpe. He was normally pleasant company, but the murder had broken him, and his fascination with the painting was eating away at him. At the end of the evening, the elf had followed the dealer into a large room where the curtains were drawn; the painting was hanging on a wall papered in black silk. The Guardian of the Pavilion shared the image and Petrus studied it with curiosity: a sober, intimate scene was unfolding against a dark background; the protagonists' faces were devastated. Now better informed about human religions, he recognized a scene from the Christian New Testament.

"A pietà, like the ones the Flemish painted by the thousand," said the Head of the Council. "Christ in the arms of the Virgin and, in the background, Mary Magdalene and a few grieving followers."

"It's beautiful," murmured Petrus.

He fell silent, prey to a fleeting intuition.

"It's magnificent," said the Head of the Council, "but that is not the painting's only quality. Although I've been studying the art of humans for a long time, it took me a while to understand what I was seeing here."

Petrus blinked and his vision of the painting was turned on its end.

"It was painted by an elf," he said.

"It was painted by an elf. An elf established in Amsterdam as a painter at the beginning of the sixteenth century according to the human calendar. In reality, the first elf to have gone over to the human world."

"I thought the bridge has existed since the dawn of time," said Petrus.

"I should have said, to have gone over *for good* into the human world. To us he'd vanished into thin air, but apparently, he chose to become a man. It had never happened before, we didn't have the slightest idea it was even possible. However, we have no reason to doubt this information, insofar as we heard it this morning from the renegade's father, in other words, from the lips of the previous Guardian of the Pavilion."

"Three hundred years ago the offspring of the former guardian went forever into the human world and no one ever knew about it?" said Petrus.

"I'd summoned my predecessor to Nanzen to ask his advice, and I mentioned the fact that the victim went to Amsterdam in search of a painting and a gray notebook, and he then informed me that his eldest child had transformed the bridge long ago in a way that would allow for permanent passage to the other side, and that afterwards he had settled among humans by taking on the identity of a Flemish painter."

"But why did he hide the fact, not to mention how?" asked Petrus.

"A father's heart is unfathomable," answered the guardian, "and he was surely afraid that others might be tempted by the adventure. This morning, however, he couldn't keep the secret any longer, although he had divulged it earlier to another elf we know—an elf whose family he has been acquainted with since childhood."

"The head of the garden," said Petrus. "They are both from Ryoan."

He looked again at the painting. Why do I know that it was painted by one of our kind, even when I know nothing about human painting? he thought. The picture is telling a human story, but the way it goes to the heart of things is elfin. And yet, there is something else, indefinable, something I cannot put my finger on.

"Why and how did our elf go over to the humans?" said the Guardian of the Pavilion. "His father doesn't know, his son didn't want to see him again once he'd gone over."

"In what way did he transform the bridge?" asked Petrus. "Why didn't that transform our world?"

"In fact, the mists were transformed," said the guardian. "They were already declining, to a lesser degree, and according to my predecessor, this alteration to the bridge regenerated them in a spectacular way. I think the gray notebook contains the answers to our questions, in the hand of our exiled painter."

This marked the beginning of an unprecedented era, where the partisans of the garden gained in influence, the Head of the Council went to Rome on a regular basis in order to meet with Roberto Volpe, and Petrus devoted himself body and soul to his two quests, dividing his time between the world of humans and the Council library. The library contained a section that was closed to the public and only accessible upon special request. But the Head of the Council had placed it at his disposal without restriction or directions.

"Humans know nothing of our existence and we have

always been glad of that fact," he said, entrusting him with the key. "We are a peace-loving sort, and the wars, however violent, with the peoples on the borders have never had the power to destroy the foundations of our harmony. But humans are a warlike species, on another scale altogether than our nasty orcs or our evil goblins."

"Why are they so aggressive?" asked Petrus.

"They are haunted by the notion of their own divinity, and their appetite for war comes from the fact they have rejected their animal selves," he replied. "Humans do not recognize the unity of living creatures, and they consider themselves to be above all other kingdoms. Along these lines, I have come to believe that our woes stem from the loss of a number of our own animals."

"Apparently in antiquity we were not merely triple," said Petrus.

"Our ancestors were every animal at once. One day I shall introduce you to one of these venerable old forefathers."

"A living ancestor?" asked Petrus, stunned.

"That's the big question," answered the Head of the Council.

The *Human Literature* section in the library was restricted but, as Petrus would learn along the way, one could count the requests for special dispensations over recent centuries on one hand. It contained scholarly works about humans written by elves who had lived among them, including Guardians of the Pavilion and Heads of the Council through the ages. But it also contained books written by humans, and Petrus began to read them voraciously; his zeal, far from lessening over time, ended up encroaching upon his sleep.

He could not believe what he was reading. He'd spent so many years yawning over the sublime elegies of his peers, so many years unaware that the object of his quest was to be found in the next room! He devoured essays on the human way of life, where he found the material to plan his journeys to the other side of the red bridge, but it was their storybook fiction that amazed him beyond expression, turning the world on its head, digging tunnels in the marrow of life. As he'd begun to explore the vineyards of France, he chose primarily French novels, and was amazed at how he could understand the language, although he often had to turn to the dictionary because of a lexicon that, to him, seemed to know no limits. Elfin language is univocal and precise; through melodic sounds it represents a natural world devoid of afterworlds, and one can easily match the thing with the word. As for elfin writing, it was borrowed from the earth's eastern civilizations, and consists of lines full of imagery, the polar opposite of the formal alphabets that we in the West use to signify reality. But French, which by the grace of Nanzen, Petrus could read as if it were his mother tongue, seemed to gain in verbosity what it lost in constituent flesh, and he was astounded that a language of such disembodied essence could, paradoxically, be so rich in inexhaustible possibilities. Nothing delighted him more than whatever was *unnecessary*, embellishments serving no other purpose than to be decorative, with which sentences and turns of phrase were saturated, and he wanted to read not only works of literature, but also grammar books and treatises on conjugations and, finally, writers' correspondence, where he would learn how a story is constructed and developed. Then, after relishing the ingeniousness of the language and its practice, he immersed himself anew in a novel, and once again life was illuminated.

"You will feel the same way about other terrestrial idioms," said the Head of the Council, one day when he confessed to his admiration for the French language. "But unbridled invention fails to fascinate me—all that reading you enjoy so much leaves me puzzled. I much prefer human music."

The motionless journey of literature made him see the world in a way he couldn't in the mists, just as it would've been impossible for him to understand the message of the wild grasses in the channel had he not spent the evening listening to legends and tales at The Hollows farm. Like a damp cloth seeping with ink and pigment, human fantasies made the world exude its invisible layers and exhibit them, naked and shivering, in broad daylight. That was the true grace of stories, their complex weave where one never looked at the visible part of the cloth, but rather at a faint sparkling only hinted at in the weft. This ineffable vibration replaced reason and the explanations of the mind when it came to understanding the heart, and Petrus did not see the characters of tales and novels as any less real than the beings he encountered in everyday life, that life which takes place in the motion of voyage and reveals so little about intentions or souls. One thing amused him: he never felt more of an elf than when he was striding through the countries on earth, only to discover that he was definitely human once he returned to his mists. When he was wandering around the vineyards in France or Italy, he thought tenderly of his serene land of tea and poetry; the moment he set foot in Nanzen, he was overcome with nostalgia for humans and their slovenly ways, for their gift at making life luxurious by spicing it up with the hint of imperfection that gave it all its genius. Finally, he was enchanted by wine and, to add a finishing touch to its benefits, the winemakers also told him stories, tales that had their roots in the soil of the vineyards, then rose toward the heavens of desires and dreams. And so, Petrus understood that it wasn't the wine that accomplished a task, the way the elves' tea did, but rather the fictions the wine catalyzed; thus, it was the metaphor, and not the cause of the miracle—however, he refrained from admitting to any of this, partly because he wanted to go on drinking, and partly because what he had begun to suspect at The Hollows was confirmed every time he took a sip from the bottle.

Unlike humans who lose their faculties when drinking, when he drank wine, Petrus found that some of his qualities were enhanced. Of course, he felt the drunkenness that made the world spin toward amiable shores and, like everyone, he would begin to blather on after only a few glasses. But this didn't diminish his ordinary skills, and it even endowed him with a few extraordinary talents, as became evident during a fight he unwillingly got caught up in at an inn in Montepulciano, in central Italy, where he'd been welcomed for the night after a visit to a winery. He was killing time, playing with a last jug of Tuscan wine, and he had no idea why tempers flared, but suddenly the lads had gone for each other's throats, bellowing in dialect and lashing out every which way. Yet, even in the panic, it was easy for Petrus to dodge the blows: the more unsteady he was on his feet, the better he outsmarted the strategies of his adversaries as they whirled their arms uselessly in the air. Well, look at that! he thought, delighted, when a lad twice his height, thinking he'd got Petrus by the collar, crashed enthusiastically against the wall instead. Petrus stumbled in front of another fellow who was plowing the air where he'd stood a second earlier, then he collapsed just in time in front of a third one who wanted to squeeze his throat with his big hairy paws. When the troops had reached the verge of exhaustion and he was the last one standing, he went up to his little room and snored the sleep of the just.

So many fascinating things happened in these stopping-off places where tempers flared that he felt at home, and established a routine. He had come back several times to visit Jean-René Faure and the good souls at The Hollows, and he always took a room at the neighboring Hôtel de la Poste, where the fare was not as mediocre as Jean-René had declared it to be. Still, he never missed an opportunity to dine at the farm when Marguerite was cooking. She excelled at stews and roasts, but she also knew how to work miracles with the sweets from the garden, and he so passionately loved her quince jellies that she would never let him leave without a little basket full of them where, depending on the season, she would also add a few fresh walnuts, crisp apples, or an armful of pink carnations. Then he would go back to the inn drunk as a lord and sit down in the common room, where they would bring him his half-jug of wine. It so happens that in addition to the well-being procured by these last solitary drops, the innkeeper's daughter was blonde, buxom, and smiling. In his native land, Petrus showed so little interest in members of the opposite sex that he'd long believed that love didn't interest him—at least not the sort of love that drove his fellow creatures to declare their ardor, share an open veranda overlooking a little garden of mist, and conceive elfkins who one day would go running among the bamboo and the stones. The young women at the inns, starting with Roselyne-from-the-Hôtel-de-la-poste, made him understand that his past indifference was due precisely to the fact that he loved human women. Picture their first dialogue one evening when Petrus had just come in from a dinner at The Hollows that had lasted longer than usual, due to both a guinea fowl that had been reluctant to cook and a fascinating debate between disciples of Burgundy wine and zealots of claret (the end of said debate is transcribed here).

"Your fondest memory?" Petrus (not yet familiar with the wines of Bordeaux) asked Jeannot (who had a crush on him).

"I don't have any," replied the lad, "but I dream of tasting some petrus, someday."

"Petrus?" said the elf who, that very morning, while pursuing his exploration of human beliefs and religions, had come upon an engraving with the following caption: *Sanctus Petrus ad januas paradisi.*

Enchanted by the coincidence, he added:

"That is my second name."

Then he thought, what am I on about.

"You mean you are also called Petrus?" exclaimed Jeannot, delighted.

From that day on, they only ever called him Petrus at the farm. And so, when he was sitting on his bench in the common room, and Roselyne came to ask him if he needed anything, placing her smile and her white bosom well within sight of his tired eyes, and she added, *what's it they call you, then*, he replied:

"Petrus."

She smiled.

"That's a sweet name, Petrus," she said.

Then she pinched his cheek and added:

"Petrukins."

I owe it to my honesty as a historiographer to say that things did not stop there, and that the next day, Petrus returned to Nanzen with crimson cheeks and a furtive gaze. Roselyne, for all her youth, was not unskilled, and she led him to her room with a disarming, natural ease. There, delightfully candid, she kissed him, long and gently. Her lips had a taste of Mercurey wine and nothing seemed more desirable to Petrus than this serving girl with her ample forms and mischievous gaze. When she undressed and revealed her lovely, heavy, slightly pendulous breasts, he understood that it was her imperfections that were kindling his desire. Her milky skin, round thighs, plump belly, soft shoulders—all characteristics which, in the mists would have been inconceivable and shocking—filled him with lust, and when she placed her hand in his beard this lust became dizzying. When she tore off his clothes and drew him onto the bed and made him collapse on top of her, the exquisite softness of her offered body almost made him swoon with pleasure. As she was giving herself to him and for the first time he was delighting in intimacy with the opposite sex, he thought: right, this is not the time to falter. And, leaning over her face, seeing the delicate texture of her skin, the sweat beading at her temples, the charming flaw of her nose that was slightly off-center, he thought again: I love her smell. Roselyne smelled of the rose perfume she used every morning, but also the sweat of a long day's work, and this mixture of refinement and nature pleased Petrus, and broke all the elfin rules governing desire.

Now he was standing, dying a thousand deaths, before the highest authorities of his world.

"We shall have to find a way to preserve your privacy," said the Head of the Council, who was trying hard not to laugh (which so surprised Petrus that he blushed all the deeper).

"A bit more discretion would do your quest no harm," said the guardian (who was having a very good time as well), "and you have emptied two innocent pillows of their feathers."

There was, in fact, a moment when Roselyne, naked as a worm, had stood up on the bed and, laughing hysterically, had tossed all the duck feathers in the air, above her lovely tousled head.

"I am sorry," said Petrus, who was thinking of jumping out the window.

"We must agree to a signal to help us anticipate the nature of your activities," said the guardian.

They agreed, and Petrus went on with his explorations interspersed with wine and comely young women.

He was in the habit of saying he was traveling on business, and if anyone asked him, what sort of business, he would simply say, family business, because family business is family business, after all, and anyone who tries to stick their nose in it is simply a boor. But the gentlemen he met at the winemakers' did not refrain from divulging their identities and positions, and Petrus learned all about the enterprises and professions on the planet, as well as the splendors of a species he'd learned to love despite all their vanities. One day, when he was at a winemaker friend's, somewhere in the Côte-d'Or, he met a writer for the first time. He was impressed by his bearing, his mustache and his little beard, but surprised by what he heard him saying when he entered the cellar where the great man was drinking and joking with a few others. It sounded like they were exchanging dirty jokes, one after the other, and so on for a good while, and Petrus was disappointed not to hear the writer telling proper stories. Then he forgot his frustration and began to laugh heartily himself. There were a few unforgettable witticisms—*of all the sexual aberrations, the worst is chastity, Christianity did a lot for love by making it a sin*—with, toward the end, a more serious conversation where Petrus was on his own to put his questions to the writer.

"Have you been to war?" he asked.

"I wasn't at the front," the writer replied, "but I have written about war and I will continue to do so, particularly because the one that is coming will be even more terrible and deadly than the previous ones."

"The one that is coming?"

"There is always a war coming. Always a civilization dying, which the next civilization will refer to as barbarian."

"If everything is doomed, what can we do?" asked Petrus.

"We can drink wine and love women!" the writer said. "And believe in beauty and poetry, the only possible religions in this world."

"You're not Christian?" asked Petrus.

"Are you?" asked the writer, looking at him, amused.

"No, no," said Petrus, "I'm—"

He broke off, at a loss to say what he was.

The writer looked at him, even more amused.

"Do you read?" he asked.

"Yes," said Petrus, "as much as I travel."

"We spend too much time in books and not enough in nature."

"I learn a great deal from traveling, but mainly from books," said Petrus.

"*So, as I did not study, I learned a great deal,*" answered the man. "I wrote that one day in a book no one will read anymore, once flowers wither on my tomb."

"So there is no hope?" asked Petrus.

"It is because we believe in roses that we make them blossom," said the writer. "The fact they end up dying does not change anything. There is always one war coming and another one ending, and so we must relentlessly start dreaming again."

They were silent as they emptied their last glass.

"Do you know who is the first to die?" the writer asked at last, thoughtfully.

Petrus could find nothing to say.

"The visionary," continued the writer. "It is always the visionary who dies, in the first exchange of gunfire. And when he falls in the snow, and knows he is dying, he recalls the hunts of his childhood, when his grandfather taught him to respect the deer."

There was another moment's silence.

"Farewell, friend," he said at last. "May life bring you gaiety, which is the most amiable form of courage."

Petrus often pondered this conversation, and had no trouble honoring its premise—wine and women—and he understood how one could learn without studying. That is the virtue of the novel, he thought, at least for the reader; writing one must be another kettle of fish.

That day, in addition to his meeting with the great writer,

Petrus also received a surprising piece of information from his winemaker friend in la Côte, and he decided to look into it further.

"I recently went to Spain," the winemaker (whose name was Gaston Bienheureux) told him suddenly.

As he said this, his expression grew wistful, which surprised Petrus, who was used to seeing him frank and talkative.

"In a place in Extremadura called Yepes," continued Gaston. "There's a castle there, with an extraordinary wine cellar, and all the winemakers in Europe go there."

He fell silent, took a sip of his *vin d'amitié*, a vintage reserved for friends that he would never sell, and seemed to forget what he'd said. When at dinner Petrus raised the subject again, Gaston didn't know what to say.

The next day, in Nanzen, the guardian shared the vision of a stony, arid plain, broken now and again by sun-baked trees and hills and, on the horizon, a village dominated by a fortress. One hour later, Petrus landed there. It was hotter than hell, and Petrus grumbled at having to wear a bamboo hat that felt itchy on his forehead. Need I tell you that thirty years—which amounts to barely four in an elf's lifetime—had gone by since our hero became the Council's special envoy to the human world? That there is not a trace, anywhere, of the two children of November and snow, and that the entire matter seems to be frozen in permafrost? Patience, however—for everything has been set in motion and is coming together, and one day soon Petrus will find out what to expect from Yepes. In the village, he didn't meet a soul. He went into the inn and, after the torrid heat outside, it felt as cold as the grave, no one came. After a moment cooling down and growing impatient, he went back out and took the steep path that led to the fortress.

At the gates to the fortress, he came upon a young boy who waved at him.

"What fair winds bring you here?" he asked politely.

But the boy barred the way.

"I've come upon the recommendation of a winemaker friend," said Petrus.

"Are you a winemaker yourself?" asked the boy.

"No," said Petrus, who at the time was not prepared to lie.

"I'm sorry, but you must go on your way," said the young guard.

Petrus looked up at the stone walls and studied the narrow windows. An eagle was flying very high in the sky and there was a sharp hardness to the air, but also the fragrance of wonder, a perfume of fury and roses which made him think of the poetry of his mists. *Worlds are born because they die*, he murmured, before waving goodbye to the boy and turning on his heels. Then he remembered another line and, finally, he begged Nanzen to repatriate him.

"*We are all about to be born,*" he said to himself again, upon landing on the red bridge.

He delivered his report on his visit to the guardian and the Head of the Council, who were also puzzled, and it was decided he would go there again the very next day.

But it was at this very moment in the story that news from Rome caused the sky of quests to explode, upending the calendar of actions, diverting Petrus from Yepes, and precipitating a historical decision on the part of the Head of the Council himself.

Roberto Volpe was dead, and he had left all his belongings to his son Pietro, from whom the Head of the Council—still going by the identity, in the human world, of Gustavo Acciavatti, orchestra conductor by trade—had tried to purchase the painting. Pietro had refused to sell it, but they had become friends. Prior to this, Leonora Volpe, Pietro's young

224 - MURIEL BARBERY

sister, had fallen in love with the Maestro, who often came to
visit her father on the pretext of acquiring Renaissance drawings. The Head of the Council, who had also fallen in love
with Leonora, did not see how he could go against these
workings of fate, because this woman's presence had become
more vital to him than anything else on earth. Tall, dark-
haired, languorous and elegant, she gave a texture to his life
that it had always lacked. Her rather austere beauty, without
adornment or artifice, gave him a feeling of land and rooted-
ness that contrasted with the evanescence of his misty world;
but she also had something of a dancer about her, a languid
way of moving that evoked the trees in his homeland. And so,
he was going to reside permanently on the other side of the
red bridge, although he hadn't uncovered the secret of permanent passage into the world of humans, and had to conceal
his elfin nature. The painter in Amsterdam, through the
transformation he had transmitted to the bridge, had taken
on the genetic characteristics of the species but, as the gray
notebook was still unrecovered, for the moment the new
Gustavo had to remain content with merely pretending to be
a human.

For the first time in the history of the mists, a Head of the
Council was resigning from office and calling for new elections. He gave no reason. The world of elves was in turmoil,
and resented this man they loved and admired for abandoning
ship just as the mists were declining even further.

Naturally, the head of the garden ran in the new elections
with a profession of faith that was even more pathetic than the
previous time, and his campaign was bitter and ugly. His
opponent, a councilor from Inari, in the province of Snows,
took after his dear friend who had resigned and strove to
win the highest office with the same elegance and ability to

distance himself. He was narrowly elected, and now I can refer to him by the name you are familiar with, that of Solon, Gustavo's old friend, but also the guardian's, which he reaffirmed in Nanzen immediately after his accession to the leadership of the Council. I'll wager you will not be surprised to learn that this guardian you have known for a long time was called Tagore by humans; and so now we have caught up with all the elfin protagonists from the beginning of our tale—those who, in slightly less than forty years from now, will welcome Alejandro de Yepes and Jesús Rocamora to Nanzen, fresh from their castillo.

For the time being, however, Solon, Tagore, and Gustavo are working to thwart the enemy's maneuvers. In the person of the head of the garden, baptized Aelius by the opposite camp, the devil is sharpening his knives and rallying his loyal supporters. Does he really believe that humankind is responsible for the extinction of the mists? Who can really know these things? Between the lies our hearts tell us, and the truths we will not admit to, everything has ended up looking like a puzzle where the pieces are mixed and muddled. The fact remains that Aelius's crusade, unable to obtain weapons legally, is now borrowing the weapons it had always coveted, and is conspiring to provoke total war. It is not yet the war that will break out in the human world and last three years, filling the elves of Nanzen with dismay—but the master of Ryoan will find inspiration in it for his own patiently instigated war. A few more years and, once he has gained possession of the gray notebook, he will construct and conceal his own bridge. Then he'll be able to come and go between the two worlds without resorting to the services of a traitor, and will begin to move his pawns on the chessboard of the earth. Appropriately, his first move will be to send his most faithful right-hand man to Rome: the Hanase piglet has become Raffaele Santangelo, the future governor of the capital and

subsequent president of the Italian Council, upon the orders
of his master in Ryoan.

Every story has its traitors. Our story has one in particular,
who wrought so much evil that, out of weariness or sorrow, we
shall not speak his name, for he belonged to the respected elite
of assistants to the pavilion, and no one had ever witnessed
perfidy of this extreme in the mists. He passes information to
his master, removes all trace of his passage, executes his orders
in both worlds, and delivers the gray notebook by resorting to
corruption and murder. Due to a consubstantial impossibility
in the species, which has endured despite all its mutations,
Aelius will require the complicity of human assassins for his
despicable plans. The traitor recruits them, then makes them
disappear in a fashion we will learn of soon, the same which
saw the murderers in Yepes vanish into thin air without a trace.

The world of mists will be confronted with the first internal
division in its history, and Aelius is recruiting new partisans
every day, with his speeches filled with anger and fear. I believe
this goes to show that something among the elves has been
broken, for they'd always been impermeable to fear, doubt,
and the question of decline.

Petrus continues to read and travel. Despite his efforts, the
guardian cannot get him into the fortress at Yepes, but only as
far as the gates, where he is sent away, every time. Marguerite
dies of old age, Jean-René of ill health. Petrus makes friends all
over Europe, a continent in turmoil, at a time when rumors of
war can be heard, despite the pledge that the last war would
really be the last. Silence and shadow lengthen and spread like
a flood over the continent.

Now it is 1918 on the human calendar, fourteen years

before the beginning of the greatest conflict in the history of elves and humans combined, fourteen years of intensifying intrigue, while the armies begin to form.

But first a night of November and snow.

Worlds are born because they die
We are all about to be born

Book of Battles

薔薇

ROSES

I t is said that everything was born from the void the day a brush drew a line through it, separating earth from sky. And so, a rose must have followed, then the sea, the mountains, and the trees.

It is in drawing a line of ink that one makes the earth emerge; it is in believing in roses that one makes them bloom.

So much effort for such mortal creatures, so much beauty doomed to flourish and die. But the battle for the birth of this beauty—doomed to die that night—is all we will ever have in this life.

雪

SNOW

I t is said that everything was born from the void the day a brush drew a line through it, separating earth from sky. And so, snow must have fallen, a soft snow that made the chill of the dawning of the world less cruel.

Maria was the lady of snows, of the thawing of bodies and hearts, of light snowflakes and dawns full of promise. It had snowed in the first scene, it would snow in the last, and she wondered if the balm would appease her troubles—the snows of the beginning and the snows of the end are the same, they shine like lanterns along a path of black stones, are a light inside us piercing the night, and fall on the plain where worlds dissolve and take with them sighs and crosses.

OF SOLITUDE AND OF THE MIND
1918–1938

Night of November and snow—somewhere in central Italy a young woman gives birth to a little girl, and in Katsura, the companion of Solon, the Head of the Council, gives birth to their first elfkin, also a girl.

Both newborn babies are miracles.

The young woman's name is Teresa and she will die that same night. The child should never have been born: her father is an elf, and unions between the two species are sterile. It's in Rome, at the home of Gustavo Acciavatti, that Tagore met Teresa, a young virtuoso pianist who belonged to the group of artists and friends, including Sandro Centi and Pietro Volpe, who often met at the Maestro's villa. Solon, Tagore, and Gustavo were childhood friends before they became companions and allies in power—but that was not their only bond, for both of them, among the most powerful elves in all the land of mists, had fallen in love with human women. Who could ever have suspected that one of those unions would produce a child?

In Katsura, another child was welcomed into the world: the infant did not look anything like an elfkin, but rather like a human baby, unable to change into a foal or a doe or any other animal—a high-elf resembling a human child, looking out at the world with her big black little girl's eyes.

Tagore has left Italy to go to the upper chamber where a select council is being held with the councilors Solon can trust. They have been preparing for it since the announcement of Teresa's pregnancy, but they did not suspect the clauses of fate would be so clear. Now the two children of November and snow have been born, and the prophecy will live.

the rebirth of the mist
through two children of snow and November
the rootless, the last alliance

"Rootless ones," murmurs Gustavo, the former Head of the Council, who has just arrived from Rome.

Solon nods. Petrus, recently repatriated from a holiday on the banks of the Loire (and vats of a sparkling wine apt to raise the dead) feels his heart sink (while his head is like a watermelon).

"We have to hide them," he says.

"I will have your daughter taken to the Abruzzo," Gustavo says to Tagore. "There is a presbytery there, with an orchard. Sandro has often spoken to me about the place because his brother is the priest at the presbytery, and he will take care of her."

"I trust Sandro," said Tagore. "Teresa loves him like a brother."

He bursts into tears.

"Loved him like a brother," he says.

Everyone is silent, sharing his sorrow.

"I will take your daughter to Yepes," Petrus says to Solon. "Maybe that is where fate is telling us to go."

In the November night, it is snowing on all the paths of fate.

It is snowing on the steps of the church in Santo Stefano di Sessanio, on the slopes of the Gran Sasso, where the daughter of Teresa and Tagore has been left in warm swaddling clothes, while they wait for the priest to find her. A few seconds later, the priest takes the little bundle in his arms and disappears around the corner of the nave.

It is snowing on the castillo in Yepes where, for the first time, Tagore has been able to gain entrance for Petrus, but for only a minute, alas, after the assassination of the family at the castle. The elf is about to leave for the pavilion again when suddenly it seems to him that the tiny girl is shivering. On an old chest, there is a blanket of fine cambric, and he wraps her in it with care. Then he asks the red bridge to take him to The Hollows. Before long it is cousin Angèle who, on her way to feed the rabbits, finds the tiny high-elf on the steps, looking just like every other little baby girl on earth. Petrus watches as the granny takes the bundled infant in her arms and disappears back into the farm, dries his tears mingled with snowflakes, walks for a while through the snowy countryside, then leaves again for the land where his own kind live.

The night of snow is over, a fine dawn spreads across the heavens, and the peasants of The Hollows discover the embroidered inscription on the poor little girl's white cambric blanket: *mantendré siempre*. A little girl from Spain! they all exclaim in wonder once Jeannot, the son, who was a messenger in the war and went a very long way, right to the bottom of Europe, has confirmed that it is Spanish—and so they baptize her Maria in honor of the Holy Virgin and the words on the fine Castilian linen. At that very moment, in the Abruzzo, the priest's old servant brushes the locks of hair blonder than little springtime grasses from the infant's brow, and marvels at the clarity of her ice-blue eyes which stare at her as if they want to eat her. *Ti chiamerai Clara*, she said.

And so, Maria and Clara, the two extraordinary children, would grow up under the protection of the ordinary souls who had adopted them, and as wards of the trees and mountains in their respective lands.[4] In Burgundy, the coming of the little girl embellished the seasons and caused the crops to prosper, and everyone suspected she was magic—although, deep in their Christian selves, they refused to entertain the idea. But there was a moving halo around her, and they could see she knew how to talk to the trees and the animals in the forest. She was a joyful, affectionate child, who brought happiness to the old grannies on the farm, and warmed the heart of André and Rose, her adoptive parents. They had lost their own children in infancy, and didn't know which saint to thank for the late gift of this child who was so lovely and cheerful. In Santo Stefano, Clara spent most of her time in the kitchen with the old housekeeper, listening to her tales of the Sasso. The priest treated her like his daughter, but he was a man of little depth, for whom she felt polite indifference, and the joy she took in her mountains meant this did not matter. All day long, she ran up and down the slopes and learned the only maps that mattered to her heart, those of the stones on the paths and the stars in the broad sky. The girls grew, one darker than twilight, with brown eyes and skin of honey, the other heart-stoppingly fair, with her sky-blue gaze and complexion like hawthorn blossom—and until they turned ten, nothing noteworthy happened beyond the confirmation of their grace, so that those who loved them could sleep in peace and perform their consecrated devotions before the Lord.

Then they turned ten, and the wheels of fate began to turn more quickly before resuming a falsely peaceful pace. In

---

[4] This is where the story told in *The Life of Elves* begins, covering the period from 1918 to 1931.

Burgundy, the villagers obtained the confirmation that the little girl was magic when a fantastic beast appeared one snowy
night—that of her birthday—as they were searching for the
child in the dark, for she hadn't come back to the farm. The
men found Maria on the hill in the middle of a clearing, in the
company of the creature, which initially appeared to be a big
white horse, then turned into a wild boar, and finally a man,
and so on in a circle dance of species that left them all gasping
for breath. Finally, the creature vanished before their eyes, and
they went back down to the farm holding the little girl tight in
their arms. Now, we know that this was Tagore, who'd come to
give Maria the vision of her arrival in the village, because he
thought, as did Solon and Petrus, that the powers of the children would be nourished by the knowledge they would gain
from their own story as they grew up. The little girl from Spain
learned that she'd been adopted and saw her special skills
grow ever stronger—for talking to the animals in the fields and
shelters, for discerning the pulsations and figures the trees
traced in the air of her countryside, for hearing the song of the
world in a symphony of energy that no human being has ever
perceived, and for increasing the talents of those men and
women who shared her life. The day she turned eleven, finally,
another fantastic beast appeared before her in the shape of a
mercurial horse combined with a hare and a gray-eyed man,
whom we recognize as Solon, come in daylight for the first
time to meet his daughter.

It was on that day that proof of treason was found. The
Head of the Council had been spied on, and the enemy
launched an intimidating attack in the form of tornadoes and
arrows of smoke. And this confirmed what we had known ever
since his cursed soul had passed through the human world and
he had become the leader in Rome: Aelius was in possession of
the gray notebook; another pavilion and another bridge had

been built; he could move back and forth between the two worlds and play with the climate as he liked. The only good thing in all this misfortune was that Aelius had never had any faith in the prophecy Petrus had unearthed in the library and, during the Council sessions, he'd always sat there scornfully disregarding the wild imaginings of that elf from an obscure house. So he was not the least bit interested in Maria, and the little girl was able to stay for another year in the village, carefully watched over by Nanzen and, before long, by Clara.

Clara, the orphan of genius. In the Abruzzo, a piano had come to meet her the summer before she turned eleven, bequeathed to Father Centi by an old aunt in L'Aquila, and brought to the presbytery by Sandro. They set it up in the church and sent for the piano tuner at the beginning of July. The first notes played on the untuned keys sounded to Clara like a sharpened knife, a luxurious swoon; one hour later, she knew how to play and Sandro was giving her musical scores which she executed to perfection, never making a single mistake, and with a technique that caused the mountain wind to blow through the church.

Sandro Centi had been living with his aunt in L'Aquila for nine years. All that remained of his extravagant youth in Rome were painful memories that still woke him at night, to crucify him, heart pounding, on a cross of regret. His entire life had been one of doomed, tragic love affairs and dissatisfaction with his art. He'd been a great painter, but he burned his canvases and stopped painting forever. He'd been madly in love with a woman, and prized friendship as a sacrament, but the woman had died and he turned his back on all his friends in Rome. However, after the episode in the church, he had a messenger take a letter to Rome for him and, at the beginning of August a tall, rather bent man came to the door of the presbytery. His name was Pietro Volpe, he was the son of Roberto Volpe and an art dealer like his father. He was a friend of the Maestro, who had married his sister Leonora, and he had gone through life tortured by the hatred he felt for his late father. He had come all the way from Rome at Sandro's request; he had once helped Sandro build his career, and he loved him like a brother. Clara was asked to play for him on the fateful piano and, the next day, Pietro left for Rome again, with the virtuoso orphan in tow.

Rome, loathsome city. Clara was inconsolable over the loss of her mountains, and now she studied music with the Maestro, who had taken her on as his student as if he didn't know her. Every day, he told her to listen to the stories that were hidden in each score; every day she found it harder to grasp what he expected of her. At the Villa Acciavatti, she saw Sandro, Pietro, and Leonora, the first woman she had ever loved. The rest of the time she was shadowed by a bizarre chaperone called Petrus, who didn't seem terribly in the know about things, and was invariably to be found sleeping off the previous night's wine in a comfortable armchair.

She studied, relentlessly.

The Maestro asked her questions which induced her to describe the wooded countryside or the plains of poplars she had seen in visions while playing, because these landscapes were engraved upon the composer's heart and memory—until, one day, the music opened a path to Maria in faraway Burgundy and, very quickly, she learned to see her, simply by thinking, and to follow every one of her movements, effortlessly. Her magical gaze embraced Maria's companions at the farm, and she grew fond of Eugénie, Marguerite's daughter, but also of André, Jean-René's son and Maria's adoptive father and, finally, of the village priest, who was as different from her own priest as an oak is from a hazel tree.

It was now clear that the two children were miraculous, not only because of the circumstances of their birth, but also because of their own genius. Although elves lose their animal essences on human earth, when they are in the proximity of Maria they appear in all their triplicate splendor. As for Clara, she could see space and beings from a distance, and exercised her father's powers of vision and prescience from outside the pavilion at Nanzen. The facts could not be denied: on human earth the little girls created enclaves where the physical laws of the mists held sway.

A year went by, deceptive strides of peace.

We are now two years from the start of the war.

January came, colder than any ice field, gloomier than a dawn without light. It was so abnormally cold that humans came to suspect the Good Lord was punishing them in one fell swoop for a century's worth of sins, but the elves, well, they knew that the enemy had their own bridge and were torturing humankind with the cruelty of frost. It was during this devilish season that the inaugural event of the disaster occurred, although it appeared quite harmless to begin with: the visit to The Hollows of one of the father's brothers, with all the honors due a decent man who was also, incidentally, an excellent hunter. As was fitting in the land of Burgundy, honors consisted of a succession of "light, *local* fare," which meant they dined on a truffled guinea fowl set amid liver terrine and pot-au-feu en ravigote, garnished with caramelized cardoons, their juice still running down the diners' throats despite the vin de côte. To make it all go down, there'd been talk of a cream tart enhanced with Eugénie's quince jellies—but in fact, it had not only been talk, and it was ever so hard to get up off one's chair when it was time for bed. Then at around two o'clock in the morning there was a terrible stir upstairs: Marcel, who had had more than enough liver terrine, was now at death's door with a colossal liver infection.

They are beautiful indeed, those women who launch a crusade against evil, of that beauty that expresses the essence of their sex: from her mother, Eugénie had inherited a love of flowers, a talent for quince jelly, and the gift of healing. Maria, as it happened, had the power to enhance that gift, and, splendid and dangerous as are all handmaidens to great causes, they formed a league, joined in secret by Clara, who was watching them from her Roman villa. The alliance of the two little magicians' powers was placed at the service of Eugénie's gift, and, against all expectation, Marcel was saved. But while the forces of our worlds may be exchanged, none can be created and, too late, Maria realized that Eugénie must die in order for her godson to live. Is it any surprise to learn that the auntie herself had received the message of this pact between life and death in the form of an iris with petals streaked pale blue, a deep purple heart, an orange-tinted stamen? The red bridge of concord provides the images of truth with strength, and it knows how to signify important moments. It is from the bridge that Petrus, one hundred and thirty years earlier, had received the tea poem, as well as the premonitory vision of Eugénie and her iris, for he knows what has occurred and what will occur at all times and on every level of that strange thing we call reality.

Alas, Maria was convinced she had killed her granny and, in truth, such a young soul could not understand what she had actually given her. Before being told of her imminent death, Eugénie had a vision of the son she had lost in the war, sitting before her at the feast of St. John, at the table decorated with solstice irises. He was just as she remembered him, although he had already fallen in battle along with so many of our young men, and she said to him: *Go my son, and know for all eternity how much we love you.* And then the sorrow of thirty years had been transformed into an explosion of love so intense that Eugénie had thanked the Lord for this final, generous gift to his pious lamb. In the end, she died happier than she had ever been.

But Maria didn't know this, and the first battle was looming. Marcel's miraculous recovery had drawn Aelius's gaze upon the farm, and he unleashed on the low country the controlled anger of a raging storm, a wall of cyclones and floods, masking human mercenaries at the ready. It was the first battle of a notorious war that wouldn't begin until two years later, and it was fought on the marl of the February fields, its officers country bumpkins transformed into strategists, with two twelve-year-old girls for generals, one all the way in Rome communicating mentally with the other. What was even more remarkable—although Maria wanted no more of miracles that would cost the lives of loved ones—was that there would be three more miracles, at least as far as human standards for marvels went.

The first was with the telepathic communication between the two girls: Clara had learned how to compose and play in such a way as to create a bond with Maria that connected them mentally day and night.

The second miracle resided in the power of the stories and dreams that were catalyzed by the children of November and snow—something neither humans nor ordinary elves could do, for while the former know how to dream, they do not know how to turn their daydreaming into reality, whereas the latter are incapable of fiction, but do know how to influence the forces of nature. Clara and Maria, now united by a shared language and story,[5] opened a breach in the sky through which a troop of elves

[5] *all dreams are in you, and you walk on a sky/of snow under the frozen earth of February*
This is the story that Clara forms spontaneously while composing, which comes to her from Maria's heart and from her own poetic powers.

entered the human world and, preserving their powers, fought alongside the bumpkins until they defeated the commando of villains. In the end, a sky of snow ordered by Maria defeated the storm and gave way to a firmament of a blue so pure that all the men sobbed with happiness. In the persons of the little girls, the elves now had a new bridge between magic and poetry at their disposal, and they also revealed a beyond-princely valiance to a handful of yokels—the last alliance was alive.

The third miracle concerned the ancestor Solon had spoken to Petrus about, and who had briefly come back to life when the girls opened the sky to the company of elfin combatants. But we shall not speak of him just yet, for the matter of the elves' ancestors requires an intelligence which, paradoxically, we can only see in the deepest night.

That same day, Sandro, Marcus, and Paulus left Rome and set off for Burgundy. No one could determine how powerful the enemy's pavilion and bridge were, but they suspected that they harbored neither clear vision nor prescience, and that for the moment, the overland route would be safer than trying to cross the red bridge. Besides, Sandro couldn't cross it, because every attempt to do so with a human had ended in failure. When the companions arrived in the devastated village, three days after the battle, Maria and Father François were waiting for them. Sandro immediately took to the peculiar priest, who was loved by his flock because he respected them and valued their hare pâté and indulgence in goose fat. Moreover, the priest had known the sky of dreams Maria and Clara had opened, and he now felt an earthly fervor supplanting the God of his confession within him. He'd always thought that he must accomplish his mission through preaching, but the words that came to him now at funerals and services no longer owed a great deal to the religion of the Churches. He'd devoted his life to the superiority of the mind over the body, and was discovering that he was a man with a deep nature, a messenger of the indivisibility of the world and the unity of the living. He learned Italian because he wanted to understand the girl to whom they'd sent a poem in that language,[6] and he had long been torn between his Christian incredulity that she could be magical and his love of the truth. Now he was resolved to accompany her wherever she went. In addition to his conviction that this was his destiny, he wanted to be at her side, a spokesman for those who could not speak, as he'd been once already on receiving the words of one of the village lads, wounded in the battle, who had confided in him as he was dying. To be more precise, he hadn't received those words directly: Maria was holding the brave man's hand and listening to his dreams while Clara transcribed them into music. Through the bond between the two girls, the priest had been able to hear those dreams and transmit to the courageous man's widow the words the melody had given him. They were fine words, that came from a humble heart and a mind deprived of book-learning, but which spoke of the glory of days standing tall under the sky because one has loved and been loved. And Father François wanted to live like that from now on, in the wake of those little girls who had given life and sparkle to love, and it mattered little to him that this distanced him from his Church and his cozy presbytery.

So many makeshift lodgings in the wanderings to come—we are leaving behind the territory of the story that was told elsewhere[7] to return to our own story for seven long years, six of them years of war. Danger was everywhere, the enemy could

---

[6] *The hare and the wild boar watch over you when you walk beneath the trees/Your fathers cross the bridge to embrace you both when you sleep*

A poem written by Tagore in the margins of a musical score of Teresa's that Clara found in Rome. It was on reading this that the path was opened to Maria's vision. The poem was then sent to Burgundy by Solon.

[7] This is where the story told in *The Life of Elves* comes to an end.

spring out of nowhere. Clara had stayed behind at the Villa Acciavatti, Maria had gone to a region she immediately took to, with its vast plateau swept by raging winds and thick snowflakes.

"It is a magical land," said Alessandro as they crossed the plateau, "a land of solitude and the mind."

There was a farm where they could take refuge for the coming year. Clara would join them there, escorted by Pietro Volpe's men. In his youth, the dealer's hatred for his father had turned him into a hooligan, a young man who fought barefisted in the street. Now he commanded a secret militia of men more loyal and dangerous than Templars.

"What is this place called?" asked Maria.

"The Aubrac," answered Father François.

And, looking all around him:

"It would be a good place to retire."

Clara arrived very early in the morning. On the horizon, the hills of the Aveyron, green and gentle to the gaze, shone intermittently, brushed with dawn; a few shreds of mist drifted by; the world seemed austere and watchful.

A bird sang.

No one understands what happens in the fleeting instant of an encounter—eternity contracts into a divine vertigo, then takes a lifetime to unfold again on a human time scale. The little girls studied one another as if they were meeting for the first time. The tiny dark veins of the first battle throbbed on Maria's face, and Clara raised her hand to touch them gently with her index finger. Then they embraced as sisters but, beyond the enchantment we feel at the sight of fraternity, there was also something else happening in those unfathomable depths which, for lack of a better name, we refer to as the life of the soul. Maria had always been a joyful, mischievous child, quick as a flash and happier than a lark. But she also knew how to feel sorrow and anger, and she wept more tears when Eugénie died than the host of adults on the farm. As for Clara, before she came from Rome, she had not smiled more than twice in ten years, any more than she had learned to feel emotion or to weep. Leonora had begun to soften her neglected heart and Petrus, in turn, had done what he could, in his shambolic way, but the little girl from Italy still lacked that which is received through the grace of a mother and father. In particular, there had been a moment during the battle when the Maestro had said to her: *one day, you will go back to your community*—and she had understood this as meaning, you will go back to the community of women. In a burst of empathy that had reversed the equation of her life, she had had a vision of her mother's face, then of a long line of women singing lullabies in the evening, or screaming with pain on opening the letter from the army. This procession made her understand war, peace, love, and mourning in a way that forged a heart too long deprived of gentleness.

When Maria opened the sky above the fields of Burgundy, the little French girl became every particle of matter and every acre of nature in a sort of internal transformation that terrified her and increased her remorse over Marcel's miraculous recovery. Clara knew all this, and she took her hand in the only way that might calm her. She looked at the little dark veins throbbing beneath Maria's skin, and she promised to prevent anything like this ever happening again in the future. With what steel are deep friendships forged? They require pain and fervor, and perhaps, too, the revelation of lineages; in this way, a fabric with neither desire nor debt can be woven. Her compassion—because she knew the cross Maria had borne since Eugénie's death—rounded out Clara's character and made her a fully-fledged member of her own community, crystallizing the women's message, which in turn opened inside her an awareness of the grandeur and poverty of the female domain.

But while Maria sensed, gratefully, that Clara understood her burden, a strange transfer of personalities occurred, and the mischief and joy of her character passed to the other side of their sisterhood. Now it was often Maria who was seen wearing a face that was stern and inscrutable, while at her side Clara, released from the austerity and solitude of her childhood, was loving and mischievous. It is this light irreverence which, despite the depths of her gaze, will bewitch Alejandro de Yepes eight years hence, and it is this irreverence, too, which everyone will soon be needing, if it is true, as the writer said, that gaiety is the most amiable form of courage.

A few days after Clara's arrival, Tagore and Solon came over the bridge of mists to the farm in the Aubrac. It was a strange feeling—for Maria, who had other parents, and for Clara, who had never had any—to acknowledge these fantastical strangers as their fathers. While the men were strangers to them, they loved the horses, the hare, and the wild boar, with the kind of love only our childhood selves permit. Finally, they walked hesitantly toward them, then Maria ran her hand through the hare's fur, while Clara caressed the boar's spine.

The next time, Tagore and Solon came to the farm in the company of a female elf whose white mare turned first into an ermine. Her gleaming fur enchanted Maria, and then her human features left the girl speechless. Everything was the same: her eyes, her black hair, her golden skin, her oval face, her rather Slavic cheekbones, and her well-defined lips: all the same as her daughter's. Maria studied her in awe; she knew this was her mother she was looking at, but the knowledge poured over her like a rain shower on a roof.

The elf smiled at her through her tears, then changed into an ermine, as the tears vanished.

"I learned a great deal from Rose and Eugénie while watching them bring you up," she said. "I shared their joy as they cherished you and their pride in seeing you grow up, and I'm glad you like violets, and that they taught you the use of simples."

Sandro took a step forward and bowed.

"Maria is the heir to your ermine, is she not?" he asked. "It is through your filiation that she commands the snow."

"If Katsura is covered in snow six months a year, it is because we like to see the flowers bloom in it," she replied.

"I dream of seeing your world," murmured Sandro.

Marcus placed a hand on his shoulder.

"We dream of it with you," he said.

During the trip from Burgundy, and while they were settling on the farm, Father François, Sandro, Paulus, and Marcus had become friends.

"I understand why you get along so well with Petrus," said Marcus the first evening, when Sandro was asking for wine at the inn.

"Don't you drink?" asked Sandro.

"We have tried," said Paulus, "but elves and alcohol don't mix."

"But Petrus drinks," said Sandro.

"I don't know how he does it," sighed Marcus. "We're a complete mess after only two glasses, but after three bottles he's still going even stronger. However, he doesn't feel too well the following day."

"Humans, too, have varying reactions to alcohol," said Sandro.

"Do they have remedies for intoxication?" asked Marcus.

"For intoxication?" said Sandro. "Without intoxication, we could not endure the solitude of reality."

"We elves are never alone," Paulus replied.

A year passed quickly on the plateau in the Aubrac, often uniting the girls, their fathers, and Maria's mother, whose presence unexpectedly comforted the young woman. When she turned into an ermine, she gave off a familiar perfume (different from that of real ermines, for elfin animals may look like their species, but lack certain of their characteristics, such as odor, and manners of expression or even washing), the odor of a village woman who sews sachets of lemon verbena in her petticoats, one of those refinements of peasant women, who could no doubt teach city ladies a thing or two. Maria had the power to communicate with animals; she'd always had a particular penchant for hares, which she found rather similar to ermines; the animals her mother changed into gave her a sense of familiar ease that the woman herself failed to create and, most of the time, the elf stayed at the farm in her winter ermine form. Maria would kneel by her side, breathing in her perfume and burying her face in her soft fur. The rest of the time, they talked, and the elf described the world of mists, its channels, liquid stones, and winter plum trees. Maria never wearied of these descriptions; Clara, at her side, also listened eagerly. Ever since a certain night in Rome, the little Italian girl had possessed the gift of reading the minds of the people she was with: the landscapes the elf described were visible to her and, like her father, she knew how to make them perceptible to others around them. Every day, Maria would hold her close as they listened to the ermine, and the elf knew of nothing more precious than these two girls, their arms around each other, who, now and again, would run their delicate hands through her fur.

Bit by bit, Maria and Clara came to have a picture of the mists, and Tagore, Solon, and Gustavo tried to work out a way to take them there. But every attempt failed, one after the other.

"What do you feel?" Gustavo asked Maria while trying once again to lead her across the bridge, amid multiple doses of strong tea from the mists.

"Nothing," she replied.

Gustavo turned to Clara.

"Can you tell Maria a story by playing something, the way you did during the battle in Burgundy?"

"You want me to give her an instruction manual, but it was really the power of a dream and a story that caused the sky to open," she replied.

Gustavo paused thoughtfully for a moment, and Petrus chuckled.

"She's your daughter, all right," he said to Tagore.

He winked at Clara.

Petrus and Clara had known each other since her first days in Rome, and he and Maria had greeted one another warmly.

"He's never completely sober or completely drunk," Clara had said at the time.

And she'd given Petrus a wink that made him flop onto on his squirrel tail. Then the elf turned into the potbellied red-head that most humans found harmless and jovial. Who could have imagined that this clumsy little man was working day and night to organize what, in wartime, would be a civilian resist-ance so well structured and operational that its mystery would exasperate humans in the highest ranks of army and State? Petrus went back and forth across the red bridge, uniting his future companions at arms, including honest people of both sexes, some of whom, naturally, were winemakers. During the war years they had resisted, and very soon would launch the ultimate operation in support of the League. Alejandro had led the operations with a few of their leaders, ordinary people who had no military experience, but who knew how to say where, what, and how, before returning in silence to their fac-tories or fields. They reminded him of Luis Álvarez, as he'd appeared to him in the vision in the cellar, walking with his comrades in arms through the baking summer heat, and Alejandro knew that that was another sort of resistance, at another time and in another place, but, like this one, it had lived on hawthorns and roses.

Ultimately, Petrus was not only a glutton and a drunk, but also had a temperament cut out for command. In the mists and in the land of humans he'd had to fight more than once, and his composure, his cool head—from inebriation, awkwardness transformed into strokes of genius—all were roundly hailed. With gratitude they watched him stumble, and they liked his amiability crossed with efficiency; although he fought without hatred, he gave no quarter, and that in itself is the model of fighters who win wars.

But now opportunities to fight were plentiful. The enemy had troops stationed in Ryoan, not yet an army, but there was nothing about the ever more frequent skirmishes to suggest the war would be a chivalrous one.

"They behave like orcs," said Solon with disgust, after an enemy commando raid in the outskirts of Katsura, which set off the interelfin war, just before the first battle on the fields of Burgundy.

Aelius's elves had killed irrationally and ruthlessly. Consequently, the defense of the provinces was reinforced, but hearts were heavy at having to reason like the adversary.

"There is no reason for such squeamishness," Petrus protested. "The only purpose of a fight is victory, by any means and any scheme possible. The spirit of chivalry is incompatible with good strategy."

"To what do we owe these exalted military reflections?" asked Solon.

"To the greatest war novel ever written on earth," retorted Petrus.

"Might that be *War and Peace*?" suggested Solon.

He was not a great adept of human fiction, but Petrus suspected Solon had read at least as much as he had.

"*Gone with the Wind*," he replied.

*

The next day, Solon convened a select elfin council to decide how Nanzen would make the main channels impassable to the enemy.

"What does Scarlett think of our plan?" he asked Petrus at the end of the session.

"That Atlanta was lost when the Yankees captured the channels of communication," replied the squirrel.

Tagore burst out laughing.

"In short," said Petrus, "we shall win if we control the channels. I'm not sure the enemy's pavilion and bridge have the power to do so."

"We don't know their strength," said Tagore, "but what worries me more than anything is that we cannot see them. Ryoan appears to us with neither pavilion nor bridge."

Petrus filed his report on the search for the gray notebook. He had gone to Amsterdam, but the archives he collected there revealed little about the son of the former Guardian of the Pavilion. He'd resided there, become a renowned painter, then died in his house on the Keizersgracht in 1516, at the respectable human age of seventy-seven. All that remained of him was the canvas which Roberto Volpe had committed murder to obtain.

A year went by and war broke out.

Petrus, Marcus, Paulus, Sandro, and Father François further reinforced their indestructible faith in the strength of their community. They had to change locations often, for fear of being found by the enemy. Petrus continued to travel and unite the forces of resistance. They tried unsuccessfully to get the two little girls, the painter, and the priest over the bridge, and everyone wondered with little success where that damned gray notebook might be. Battles were fought in succession and all they had in common was the scale of the carnage. Europe was nothing but one gigantic battlefield, and the war spread to other continents. Purges of all sorts were taking place in the countries of the Confederation, more terrible than terror, more despicable than horror: Raffaele Santangelo had succeeded beyond his own expectations in putting to fire and sword countries that desired nothing but peace. The elves of the last alliance remained in the shadows and did not show themselves to the League. As it happened, they had their work cut out for them in the mists, now split into two fratricidal camps.

Sixth year of the war. The last battle is drawing near, and night is falling in the upper chambers in Katsura.

"What will be left of the worlds when it is all over?" Solon asks bitterly.

"Worlds are born because they die," replies Petrus.

Of solitude and the mind
Furious winds and downy snowflakes

Book of Paintings

手帳

NOTEBOOK

T hen Petrus found the gray notebook. You see, it just so happened that Roberto Volpe had a little vineyard in Montepulciano that was cultivated on his behalf by devoted tenant farmers. He produced respectable vintages which, in his youth, would have earned him the right to go to Yepes. It was there that, unbeknownst to all, he had taken the gray notebook he had inherited along with the painting.

The guardian thought he was sending Petrus to stand as usual outside the fortress of the castillo, but the elf found himself in the cellar, peering at a bottle of 1918 petrus. Just next to it was the notebook. Twenty years earlier, thanks to the indiscretion of one of the Volpes' clerks, Santangelo had sent a winemaker to Yepes who had copied out the contents.

The gray vellum booklet contained only a few lines: *The gray tea is the key to mutations. It builds bridges and transforms passages. The first bridge is the work of gray tea and a single brushstroke. Ink and gray tea are the pillars of all rebirth.* Above the door in the cellar, carved in stone, was this motto: *Mantendré siempre.* And next to it, an inscription in the hand of the painter from Amsterdam: *I came here first.*

There are eight days remaining until the last battle.

橋

BRIDGE

Alessandro Centi knew the red bridge without ever having set foot on it. Thirty years earlier, he'd painted it without ever having seen it. The canvas displayed only a large splash of ink and three pastel strokes of scarlet. But those who had crossed the bridge were stunned by this miracle, which reconstituted the bridge without representing it realistically.

Similarly, the first canvas that Sandro had shown Pietro upon his arrival in Rome did not represent anything known, but the dealer knew it was the ideogram for mountain used jointly by elves and by populations in the East of the earth.

Sandro was cut out to live on the other side of the bridge, just as Petrus was on human earth, and these permutations of desire are all that can revive the worlds. The first bridge of the mists had once regenerated a world that was stagnating, its mutation by the painter elf had seen to it a second time, and the elves of the last alliance saw that their role was to reinforce the footbridges between the two sides.

The bridge, that icebreaker—as much conquest as metaphor.

RUIN
1938

PREAMBLE

In four days, the elves of the final alliance made a long series of discoveries and deductions.

The gray tea fulfilled the desires expressed in the pavilion.

Twenty millennia earlier, someone—probably the guardian—had infused leaves attained by noble rot, then built a bridge between the two worlds.

Twenty millennia later, through the same process, the guardian's son had succeeded in transforming the bridge and crossed forever into the world of humans.

How had they discovered the power of gray tea? No doubt it was by chance, as are all the great stanzas in the history of the living.

Four more centuries and the traitor, one of Tagore's assistants, offered Aelius the opportunity to come to Nanzen in secret and create a pavilion and a bridge that would be hidden from view, then the power of the fungus in the tea plant was revealed to the members of the last alliance and they were able to see them—golden, arrogant, and deadly—in the absence of Ryoan's mist.

Gray tea was produced by exposing tea plants to constant humidity for twenty-four hours. Prior to this, elves used to burn the leaves decomposed by rainy weather. In Ryoan, they were now being grown in entire fields.

Gray tea enabled humans to cross into the mists and come back out again. Whether through some flippancy or magnanimity on the part of fate, it also made drunkards sober.

Gray tea was dangerous. It left no trace. It figured in no archives. It was careful not to be seen. It edified, then disappeared, so much so that it is easy to understand why Nanzen and Katsura took so long to comprehend the role it played.

One way or another, gray tea had something to do with ink. No one knew the role of the *single brushstroke*, but they were pleased that Sandro was one of them.

Finally, if the gray notebook had fallen into Petrus's hands, perhaps it was because the spirits of Yepes had chosen their camp and an unknown authority in Extremadura had sided with the last alliance—but it is hard to know such things for sure, for despite all their qualities, stories are known to be unpredictable and mischievous, and we never know their conclusion in advance.

N anzen, year six of the war. We left the community of
the last alliance at the time when the bell was tolling
for the tea, and we must now round out the tale with
everything that has happened between the intention and its
consequences: so many events, so many reversals, so much
uncertainty, made forever true by death, in fact, and now that
the last battle has been fought, the ruins of what were our
worlds, and their legacy, and their tragedies.

How could the elves imagine destroying the foundation of
their universe? What despair leads to such a radical path?
Katsura was losing the war, and the mists were growing weaker;
every time the bond between humans and elves was strengthened, they had regenerated; but the gray tea represented a
threat that compelled them to change the configuration of the
footbridges. The enemy's bridges and the pavilions would disappear, but Nanzen, which was not built upon tea, would hold.

"We will destroy the tea plantations," said Tagore. "All of
them, right down to the last one, at dawn on the coming day."
"But without tea, your world will collapse," said Alejandro.

Tagore shared the vision of the two infants taken in that
snowy night and everyone followed the events, great or trivial,
of their magical lives, grannies and piano included, up to the
first battle of the war. When the vision filled with the fury of

Aelius's storm, Alejandro and Jesús placed their hands upon their hearts. Then their hearts stopped beating when detachments of elfin fighters poured from the sky as it opened above the fields. Before long came the meeting between the two girls, in the courtyard of a farm amid verdant hills before years of fleeing while total war raged. And, in the end, as if through some chemical precipitation of time, some sort of accelerated acquaintance when, ordinarily, one must share years together, the young girls were as familiar to Alejandro and Jesús as if they had grown up with them. Finally, Tagore projected the image of Petrus confronting the former Head of the Council with a book in his hand. Behind them an old plum tree was visible against a background of moss and a wooden veranda.

"What are you reading?" asked Gustavo.

"A prophecy," said Petrus.

And in the calm, late autumn evening he read out loud.

the rebirth of the mist
through two children of snow and November
the rootless, the last alliance

"Maria and Clara are the children of snow and November," Tagore said to Alejandro. "We have consented to the fall of tea because we have faith in the prophecy. Fate did not bring us all together by chance, and ever since we found the gray notebook, we have been trying to picture its role in the last battle. There must be a reason why we have a priest and a painter with us, just as you are here because of the pull of Yepes. That is where the son of the former guardian went for the first time, and where we believe the first bridge of the worlds was built. It is no accident, either, that the heir to the castillo is a member of the high command of the League, nor is the fact that he comes from a harsh, poetic land like all those in this tale."

A new landscape unfolded before their mind's eye. The last

battle was about to begin, and the first phase would be fought on the battlefields of this world. The tea plants of Ryoan and Inari shone gently in the uncertain night. At the edge of the plantations, along lengthy esplanades, leaves were drying, before they would be crushed on long wooden tables. Beyond the esplanades were barns without a facade, and under their roofs of bark, bundles of canvas hung in the air. Slightly to one side of the storage lofts stood the pavilions where the most remarkable vintages of tea were ageing.

The fields at Inari would be burned with no adverse effect, but those in Ryoan were dotted with elves on the lookout, posted in force around the perimeter—for the most part bears and wild boars armed with spears and bows which to humans seemed gigantic. The zone would have to be evacuated before it was set on fire, and in spite of the advantage of surprise, it was not easy to strategize for such an unequal contest. Moreover, they were working against the clock, for there was only one full day left before the empathy of ordinary tea would wear off for most of the elves, and three for the tea the company had drunk in Nanzen. An hour earlier, the Wild Grasses had destroyed their entire stock—it will come as no surprise to you to learn that, of all the authorities in the mists, only the house of Hanase had permission to stockpile dried leaves. The elves collect their daily allotment at their neighborhood lodge, which is supplied every day through the channels or by air— eagle, albatross, and seagull elves. Sometimes, raptors or seabirds would come to offer their services, but elves do not like to take advantage of the labor of other living species. While the dolphins of the mists did work together with the boatman in the Southern Marches, it was more out of friend- ship than necessity, because the channels allowed for a close- ness between them and this relieved their labor of its alienat- ing burden.

"I'm in charge of the tea destruction commando," Petrus told Alejandro and Jesús. "I intend to surprise the enemy with an unusual strategy, and I could use two humans for the task."

Then Tagore offered the hospitality of his dwelling for the rest of the night.

There was an indefinable fragrance in the air of the pavilion. Of solitude and mind, thought Alejandro.

A moment later, they found themselves under an awning on a wooden veranda that looked out onto the forest. The moon-lit trees were tall and straight, an orderly row reaching for the sky. At the center of the clearing, the windows of the guardian's residence, which was lower and more spacious than the Pavilion of the Mists, were covered with light veils that floated in the night air. Next to the door, camellias had been placed in a little bamboo vase hanging on the wall. Everyone fell silent and took in the gentle murmur of ancient trees. Clara and Alejandro sat apart in one corner of the veranda, Jesús and Maria did likewise, off to one side. Petrus, Marcus, Paulus, Sandro, and Father François deliberated amongst themselves. Tagore and Solon went inside.

Time rustling, like tissue paper.

"We might be dead tomorrow," Clara said to Alejandro.

She smiled and he understood why he thought she was beautiful. Her brow was too big, her neck was too long, and her eyes were too light, but there was something about her smile that made him feel as if he were embracing the waters of a dream. Not a word was exchanged, but, through their gazes, despite the absence of intimacy to which war condemned them, they concentrated in one hastily-snatched hour all the days of a lifetime of love. It happened in the order everyone is familiar with, and thus they experienced those first gazes where they drowned in the headiness of adoration and temptation; then, after the magic of the early days, they slowly came to reality; after having construed love, they elevated it to its authentic life. After the luxuriant dawns and wild storms, they saw their true faces; he sat at the hearth, tired and worn, and she knew what sort of man he was. When at last they fell asleep, exhausted and happy, they had known their fill of lovemaking, of every parting and every joyful meeting, of every tempest and every wonder ever known to mind and body, through the sharing of tea and the song of ancient trees, and afterwards when they woke, they were a man and a woman enriched by every moment of transport, every transfiguration of love. Just before waking, they shared the dream of a chilly late afternoon on the farm on the plateau in the Aveyron, while clouds of crows whirled and shrieked overhead, gathering under a storm on the horizon. The lovers were hurrying to take shelter when a solitary snowflake appeared, light and fluffy among the birds, that all on its own caused the storm to recede—and though the storm was wild with rage, other fat snowflakes, soft and dumb as feathers, fell tenderly to hide a land of newfound peace.

At the far end of the veranda, Maria was talking to Jesús with the same silent, tea-induced affinity.

She was telling him about the trees in the countryside where she'd grown up, the tall elms and riverbank willows, but also the oaks by the field next to the farm, their quivering branches leaving etchings on the air. She told him about the hill, to the east of the village, that they could reach by a winding trail until it merged into an undergrowth of poplars, where every family was permitted to gather wood and where they would come for their share by first snowfall—and then she described the towpaths of the six cantons, their lakes of emerald and rushes, Eugénie's vegetable garden, her artemisia, marjoram, and mints. The faces of her grannies, wrinkled like autumn apples, went through their shared vision until there was only the smallest of the four faces, cheerful and stubborn beneath her cap with its ribbons the color of forget-me-nots.

"Eugénie," said Maria.

In the tiny, boundless space that divides loving hearts, Jesús felt her sorrow and mourning as if they were his own. In turn, he told her of his arid land, the dried lake of his childhood, the pain of staying and the wrenching loss of going, but also, some days at dawn, the beauty of the water in a calligraphy of dark mist.

"We were innocent," she said, with a pang of sadness.

He went on telling her about Extremadura, its plains and desolate forts, the onslaught of sunlight, the cruel rocks and his amazement at the way the stones in the mists turned liquid.

Her gaze was full of distress, like that of a wounded child.

"What did Eugénie say to you before she died?" he asked.

She told him how her auntie had lost all desire to live when her son died in the war, how she came to hate violets when the innocent fell in battle, and how she was horrified by the transparent skies above the carnage—then one day she recovered from her grief by healing Marcel. In the end, she had come to Maria's little room, to sit on the edge of her bed, and she said, *You have healed me, my love.*

Jesús took her hand. Her palm was like the skin of a lovely peach, her fingers so fine and slender he could have wept.

She shared one last scene where the old granny was speaking to her and smiling—a new scene, that was neither a memory nor a premonition, just the effect of the tea and the redemptions of a night of love.

"Look," said the auntie, smiling with astonishment and cheer. "Look," she said again, "what I couldn't tell you that night. Oh, he has his ways, the good Lord! Are we dead, are we alive? It doesn't matter, look what you gave me, my love."

She showed them a garden, where two long tables were set and decorated with solstice irises. In the soft evening air, she was smiling at a young man—my son, she thought with amazement, who died in the war, but I was able to tell him how much I loved him. And from this, the gladness of a dialogue between the living and the dead had engulfed the old peasant woman's heart, and she felt such intense happiness that dying no longer mattered to her.

"A dead woman talking about her dead," she said, amused.

Turning one last time to her beloved little girl, she said:

"Don't forget to pick the hawthorn."

Maria drew closer to Jesús and buried her face in his chest.

He put a hand in her hair, savoring the timelessness of hours of love.

Not far from there, looking out onto the trees in the play of light and shadow, Petrus had opened a few bottles he'd appropriated from Alejandro's cellar. Everyone was saying they might all be dead tomorrow, and they all knew the one thing a living being can know about death.

"It always comes too soon," said Father François.

"It always comes too soon," said Petrus.

They could drink the wine from Yepes.

"When I think I might have to give this up," Petrus said.

With a wrenching sigh, he added:

"And women. Woe is me."

Just before dawn the company, along with Solon, Gustavo, and Tagore, gathered in the middle of the veranda, which was bathed in darkness and moonlight.

"Now the time has come for us to say farewell to our culture," said the Head of the Council.

Petrus took one last sip of amarone and opened another bottle. In their glasses, pale gold sparkled faintly in the moonlight.

"A Loire wine—this alliance of modesty and refinement drives me crazy," he said.

"Almost nothing," murmured Alejandro, raising the glass to his nose.

On the palate, the wine had the crystalline texture of soft stone turning to white flowers, with a faintly sweet touch of pear.

"Stones and flowers," said Clara, tenderly.

In front of everyone, she placed her lips briefly on Alejandro's.

Petrus raised his glass and said:

"When I arrived in Katsura for the first time, one hundred and thirty-eight years ago (Marcus and Paulus chuckled over a certain memory of that event—he ignored them), I had no idea of the destiny that lay in store for me there. For a long time, I wondered what was expected of an insignificant squirrel who was constantly out of his mists. Then I realized that it was precisely these qualities that made me the instrument of fate, which uses intelligent men to carry out its plans, but needs an idiot to bring them all together at the appointed time."

"I really wonder what an idiot might be," said Father François.

"An alcoholic who believes in the truth of dreams," answered Paulus.

"What a fantastic gospel," said the priest.

They honored in silence the last of the wine before Paulus gave each of them the sobering flask, and then the strange troop headed back to Nanzen.

The valley of trees rustled with unfamiliar sounds and the moon flooded the path with black stones. Silent and motionless in the hour before dawn, in battle order outside the pavilion, the general staff of the army of mists awaited them.

Are we dead are we alive

Book of Prayers

文体

STYLE

Petrus loved stories and fables for the power they had, like wine, to open the freedom of dreams in waking time, but, in addition to the intoxication from the story, he was just as sensitive to the way they were crafted as he was to the refinement of different varietals. A beautiful story with no style is like a petrus in a trough, he liked to say to Paulus and Marcus (who couldn't give a damn).

What was more, he had a weakness for the French language, its earthy power and courtly *coquetterie*, because roots and elegance are to the text what taste is to wine, with that added grace which comes from a passion for what is unnecessary, and that added significance which, always, is born of beauty.

戦略

STRATEGY

Petrus felt deeply human and, dare I say it, French. While he did value the art, light, and food of Italy, his heart beat resolutely for the slapdash panache of France.

One rainy day in England, in 1910, he went to a match of a curious sport the French were playing against the English. Although at the time he only understood one rule—that the aim was to score a leather ball all the way at the far end of the opposing side—he enjoyed the moves and passes for their demonstration of human talent and ingenuity.

After one play where the French looked like a swarm of ballerinas facing a squadron of sluggish draft horses, the old Englishman who was chewing tobacco in the stands next to him had said: a plague upon those Frenchies, but it's the rugby that everyone wants to see—and this summed up why Petrus ranked France above all else—in addition to wine, women, and pleasant landscapes.

Now, twenty-eight years later, at the hour of the last battle, he had a hunch that the war would be won with a strategy of ballerinas.

We Are Heading Toward the Storm

Nanzen, dawn of the last battle.

There were twenty or more elves from a variety of houses, including a unicorn, a beaver, a zebra, and a black panther. The elves of the central provinces do not often have the opportunity to meet their compatriots from the hotter climes, but Petrus, Marcus, and Paulus were delighted to see their old friends from the Northern Marches again, the zebra and the panther, who were serving as officers in the army and whom they'd already fought alongside. As for the humans, they kept a safe distance from the imposing feline, although they were most astonished by the fact that half the staff consisted of female elves. Although the present-day leaders were all male, in the past there had been memorable female Guardians of the Pavilion and Heads of the Council, to the extent that the increasing absence of women from positions of responsibility now appeared to Solon and Tagore to be yet another obvious sign of decline.

At the center of the elfin detachment, the female unicorn turned into a woman with white hair, black eyes, and very wrinkled skin. She was slender and athletic and, in the end, so stunningly beautiful they couldn't imagine how age could have produced such a vision.

"We are ready," said the female chief of staff to Solon and Tagore.

They went inside the pavilion, where Hostus, Quartus, and ten other assistants were waiting for them. Like the first time,

268 · MURIEL BARBERY

the place, despite its lack of space, seemed perfectly capable of containing the entire company. The members of staff and the guardian's assistants took their seats against the partitions, and the same elves as before formed a circle in the center of the room. The unicorn sat on Solon's right and her first lieutenant, a beaver elf, reported on the army's movements. All the battalions had reached their positions. The troops would intervene at the final signal from Nanzen, and after that, each unit could count only on itself; but all of them had been posted to strategic points and would have the advantage in most of the decisive attacks. In any case, the enemy couldn't imagine someone would ever want to destroy the tea; the elves of the last alliance, on the other hand, were prepared to do so. Naturally, the soldiers had been informed that a return through the channels would be jeopardized; the beaver added that no one had succumbed to regret at this point.

Once the report was finished, Petrus took over and asked Tagore to share a scene showing thirty or more strangely dressed men. Some of them, leaning over the others, formed a confused mass. Others stood to one side, useless and waiting for something to do, on a vast lawn streaked with white lines. There were two teams, one dressed in white, the other in blue, apportioned on either side of the swarming mass, from which one member in blue was trying to remove something. No one was moving, but after a long while, the man in blue succeeded in what he was trying to do and hurled the fruit of his conquest behind him. Everything changed gears and shape. On either side of the melee, the blue and white men began running toward each other, in perfect diagonal lines; the thing that looked like a ball went from front to back along the blue line and, just as the configuration of players met between the two lines, it was transformed and realigned; but the ball was still making its way, bouncing from a forward runner to a back runner in a choreography that drew a whistle of admiration from Father François. Then the man carrying the ball collapsed, tackled in full flight by an opponent and, again, the lads tumbled upon each other while the same player as before struggled to wrest his Holy Grail from the pile. In the rear and in the front, a fluid mechanism wonderfully in tune with the pleasure of watching, the idle players re-formed in diagonal lines and, once again, waited for their time to come. And it came, in the form of a new retrieval very near one end of the terrain that was marked by two gigantic posts. This time, the coveted item was thrown to the right and after a rapid and complicated series of rear diagonal passes, the last blue man on the line flattened himself on the grass, the ball under his belly, and this caused some of the men to raise their arms in victory, and the others to lower them in defeat. Finally, the scene vanished and they all looked at each other cautiously.

"That was rugby, wasn't it?" asked Alejandro. "I went to a village match once, long ago, although it's not a very popular sport in Spain. I didn't understand all the rules, but the sequence of moves was interesting."

"It is rugby," Petrus confirmed, "and strategy, too, as your military eye will have noticed."

"Fixed positions and deployment tactics," said Jesús. "Do we need rugby for that?"

In the center of the circle Hostus placed a round ball made of interwoven maple twigs.

"The maple trees from the Northern Marches are known to catch fire a few minutes after they are placed near a tea leaf," said Petrus.

You will also see plant life becoming fire, Jesús recalled.

"We will have to progress in a linear fashion by leaving the seeds to the fire behind us," continued Petrus, "like in a game with several balls, where the lines move forward and the opponent cannot stop their progress. If we attack from all sides, or concentrate our attack, we cannot set fire to the perimeter without burning ourselves to a cinder at the same time. But if we invite the enemy to a scrum with our rear lines in support, we have a chance of attaining our goal."

"Anyone who takes part in the melee will be sacrificed," Alejandro pointed out.

"It is my hope that the first engagement will incur no losses," said Petrus. "We will be the masters of a game where the enemy doesn't know the rules. They will think we are attacking them, but we will be unarmed, equipped only with our legs for running and our arms for throwing."

"What weapons do they have?" asked Alejandro.

"Bows, swords, spears, and axes," answered the unicorn elf. "And their mastery of the climate."

"They'll chop us to bits if we're unarmed," said Jesús.

"Not necessarily," said Paulus, looking at Petrus, "we've been trained in an art of evasion designed by the only alcoholic elf in the known world."

"Very effective in close combat," added Marcus.

"We can do a great deal of harm by falling," Petrus reassured them.

There was a silence, disturbed only by the sound of the wind in the trees in the valley.

"It could work," said Jesús slowly. "In any case, I'm in."

Alejandro nodded.

They went to the bridge. Dawn was breaking. Far behind the pavilion, beyond the valley, brief flashes of lightning were expiring with the night. Day was coming and the lightning drew fiery streaks upon the sky that faded into the dawn. Then they heard a distant rumbling between pauses in the thunder.

"We're heading toward the storm," said Petrus.

Out of the mist on the middle of the bridge, there came a team of eight elves—three squirrels, two bears, a wild boar, and two otters—and after respectfully saluting Solon and Tagore, they joined Petrus's commando. Alejandro looked at Clara, Jesús looked at Maria, the squadron, now at full strength, bowed to the rest of the assembly and moved forward onto the bridge.

There was a powerful thunderclap.

A few members of staff now entered the mists of the arch. The others went back to the pavilion.

The last battle was beginning.

On the other side of reality, Petrus's commando landed at the edge of the gray tea plantations in Ryoan. On yet another side, the staff materialized around the plantations in Inari. At the far end, or side, or quadrant of the world, Aelius and Santangelo, in the golden pavilion, were beginning to suspect that something was brewing.

And so, the action got underway in Ryoan. The only inter-species rugby team ever was deployed with lightning speed and efficiency, increased tenfold, I must say, by Petrus's gift for encouragement. No sooner was he back on his feet, crouching behind the rows of tea, than he pulled a bottle from his bundle and generously shared out the contents, then stood up straight, like the very devil, brandishing his first ball of maple twigs—at which point the team swarmed onto the plan-tation and almost immediately encountered the opponent. Alejandro and Jesús closed the diagonal on the left, keeping the right distance from the last elf on the line. They saw the first ones, including Petrus, collide head on with a group of bears armed with spears, then deceive them with the art of evasion Paulus had praised—and it was magnificent, because the elves of the alliance fell like drunks between the enemy's paws, then slipped away like eels, leaving their opponents

behind them, now busily hitting each other. For a moment
Alejandro and Jesús only had to run, but finally, they drew
level with the ruck and faced their first adversaries.
Ordinarily, higher-ranking officers do not excel in close combat, but Alejandro de Yepes and Jesús Rocamora were the
sons of arid lands, where lords and serfs labor under the same
yoke and the same rigorous climate. They were as agile as any
survivor of hostile conditions, and they knew when to fall to
the ground and twist sideways to avoid a blow with an ax, a
toss of the spear, or those odd whirlwinds, miniature tornadoes, that whistled like arrows in flight then disintegrated on
reaching the ground. After a moment, real arrows began to fly,
aiming at random above the rows of tea, and new tornadoes
came swooping down in bursts, sometimes coming close to
the very enemy they were supposed to protect. But it was all
happening very quickly, and it would have taken a clever soldier on Aelius's side to thwart the plans behind such a mysterious attack. The commando spread out by passing, dodging,
dropping, passing again, with a diabolical precision that no
doubt would enthrall numerous coaches in human lands, and
I must say that this match, absurd as it was for being played
only by one side, was nevertheless an impeccable incarnation
of the essence of rugby. Petrus didn't like chivalry and its
moral sentimentality; he thought that, of all the evils, war was
the ugliest and vilest; that one must win quickly, brutally, and
absolutely; and that spies and assassins were the true artisans
of victory. But he hated these requirements of war as much as
he hated war itself, and since he knew that the aftermath
would be as hideous as the enemy's hatred, he was not sorry
that the opening scene was a good performance. The beauty
of rugby stems from its organic quality: the team is nothing
without its members, who are nothing without the team.
When, after lengthy entanglements, endless scrums, and pitiful advances, the line spreads out and covers giant portions of

the field, it's not just the fluidity of movement, but also the combined effort of heart and legs that rouse the spirit, because the player who scores is heir to the precision and enthusiasm of all the others. And so, Petrus of the Deep Woods, this meticulous and fiery elf, sly and crafty, but also frank and amiable in the company of friends, and ultimately passionate about *elsewhere*, although he was loyal to his fathers and his mists, had in this war at least one battle which, like French rugby, suited his nature and evinced a refinement and panache that Scotch whisky truly had not spoiled. He knew that a succession of massacres lay ahead, and he was savoring this last engagement, fought without damage or casualties. At the dawn of a tragic time, he put the heart of despair into his work and saw it as a tribute to the courage of the just.

When the two Spaniards broke enemy lines for the first time and, gliding like fish in a river, found themselves on the far side of the battalion of huge hares, they felt such jubilation that the first ball of maple passed to Alejandro really felt like the Holy Grail to him. He carried it one hundred yards or so and put it on the ground between two tea plants. Then he went on running behind a row that was shorter because of the dislocation of the initial lines. Arrows whistled and fell at random, Aelius's side had given up on the tornadoes, and if they hadn't been running with the wind in their ears, they would have heard the sounds of alarm all around the perimeter. Our heroes had already run a league when enemy reinforcements descended on the plantation. Alejandro passed the ball he'd just received from the forward to Jesús, and ran smack into the stomach of a wild boar. The shock dazed him and he had difficulty getting quickly back on his feet. Jesús watched with horror and shouted as the boar raised his ax; Petrus, in front of the line, turned around, and with a classic skip pass, took aim and hit the pig right in the snout. The ax fell an inch from

Alejandro's skull; shouting with relief, he rolled over and got promptly to his feet.

Opposite him, armed with a huge ax, stood a gigantic elf who didn't look like he was in the mood for sipping tea.

"Grizzly!" shouted Paulus from the other side of the field.

The ax was raised. Alejandro plunged between the monster's legs and felt his right shoe fly off into the air. He scrambled frantically forward, but the elf had turned around and Alejandro knew, from considerable experience, that the next strike would split his back open.

Hopelessly crawling, he waited for the blow.

Behind him, Jesús shouted again.

The blow didn't come.

To the south, behind them, the plantation caught fire.

The rows of gray tea went up all at once. There was a huge rushing sound, a wind of flame, and the plantation began to burn. Petrus started shouting too and, tearing himself away from the spectacle, the alliance team continued to advance. The enemy, horrified, froze on the spot. They could hear a bell ringing—a bucket brigade was being formed—but the commando reached the end of the first crops without incident. They'd gone a league and a half, and had a clear path for the two remaining leagues. They distributed their last maple balls, then reached the deserted storage barns. Petrus tossed the last vegetal fireball into the bales of tea hanging in the air, where it stayed calmly swinging and vibrating among the packaged leaves. Before giving the signal for the transfer, Petrus stopped at the edge of the burning tea plantations. The sky now had a wild, tawny hue and, in the shimmering of fire, tongues of flame resembled swaying flowers.

Then they all went back to Nanzen.

At that moment, the unicorn chief of staff of the mists was gazing at Inari's demise. From the vast fields of green tea, a hundred times more expansive than those at Ryoan, billows of smoke were rising, the likes of which they'd never seen in the mists, and she watched them rise skyward as the world of her youth vanished in the dawn. She who had observed the other world from the pavilion, who had visited the Head of the Council on human land, admired the genius of humans, their prodigious art and the hope it gave its people, knew, in the end, of nothing more beautiful than the mists rising over the front at Katsura. In these absolute, gilded dawns, as the community of elves, dusted by the ash of Hanase, whispered among themselves with every drift of mist, the voices of the living and the dead joined in a communion that no humans—and this she was sure of—could ever equal.

Embers from the fire fell at her feet. She took two steps back and felt a tear flow down her cheek.

The first phase of the last battle was over. On the horizon, thick clouds of smoke gathered and sat stagnant over the land. The atmosphere changed subtly, and everyone could hear Solon's final address to his people.

"The plantations at Inari and Ryoan are burning," he said. "Never before have the leaders of the mists had to make such a painful decision, but we hope for times of rebirth like those we have always known after a hard fall. I ask those who have never doubted our wisdom not to fear change. To those who went over to the ranks of the enemy, I will say how saddened I am by this disaster orchestrated by hatred. We are a dream, a magic place of trees and stones, the reverie of a spirit swept with mist, the vapor through which the energy of life circulates. We are a breath of atmosphere, a glittering of dust on the rivers of time that unite things and beings and cause the living and the dead to mingle. We are a harmony traversed by the winds of dreaming, an infinite plain welcoming roses and ashes. But we are also a nation more ancient than all others, old and disenchanted, imprisoned in a modern world where we no longer know how to live. Through the logic of decline, our ancestors entered into lethargy just as our mists were beginning to weaken. Twice, a footbridge built to the shores of human land regenerated the mists. Tragedies have always come of divisions and walls, rebirth from bridges built on unfamiliar shores—thus the fall of the tea must be the gate to new alliances, if it is not to remain vain and tragic forever. Inhabitants of the mists, I know your reservations regarding the human race. Are they not to blame for every negligence in their management of the world, for every display of cruelty toward the living? And for how many massacres and wars? And for such cynical exploitation of other kingdoms, when they have neither mist nor tea to bring about a concord of consciousness? And yet, they do possess one treasure we do not have. They have the faculty of painting that which does not exist, and of telling that which will never happen. As strange as it may seem to our spirit immersed in the flow of the world, that faculty creates a parallel truth that enhances the visible and shapes their civilizations. We must invent the future now, and that visionary gift, allied with our natural harmony, will have the power to save our worlds. At present the tea is burning, and I do not know how much longer we will be connected in consciousness, but I am confident that when words no longer suffice, thought will continue. As for me, I will do what I must: I shall maintain."

He fell silent, and Tagore projected the faces of the humans and the elves of the last alliance into the mist. In return, the community loyal to Nanzen sent the message of their allegiance, mixed as much with worry and sorrow as with their refusal to hate and their trust in the integrity of their leaders. Finally, they voiced their unexpected enchantment with the two little girls born on a night of snow.

Before leaving the pavilion, the chief of staff put her hand on Petrus's shoulder.

"Your little incursion with backward passes was quite clever," she said.

"When this is all over," he replied, "I'll take you to see a real match."

"Who knows what we'll be watching, a joust or a battle?"

"One must be blind to see," said Petrus. "Maybe we are too clear-sighted."

We are headed toward the storm

Book of Battles

TREES

Plant life is existence in the absolute, the integral communion of nature with itself. Plant nature turns everything it touches into life. It transforms the radiance of the sun into a living thing. Far from adapting, it engenders. It creates the atmosphere through which everything comes into being and mixes without melting into one. It fabricates the fluidity without which there can be neither coexistence nor encounter. It gives birth to the matter that makes mountains and seas. It exposes the life of one to the life of all the others. It is the source of the first world, of breath and movement, of *misty regions* and the divine creation of climate. It is the paradigm of the vital immersion and liquid circulation of all things.

We inhabit the air, thought Petrus, after his fall into the mist in the channel in the Southern Marches. A tree, in its solidity, immobility, and power, is simply the most material, most poetic expression of that truth, the boatman of respiration, the native figure of the life of air—in other words, of the life of the spirit.

STONES

S tars wander across the sky, and trees will change them into life. This is why stones and mist enjoy such close solidarity, and why Clara, given her childhood in the mountains, has conceived of her art as a melody of pebbles in a stream.

And so, the gardens of liquid stones found long ago in the mists are what we have just described: the root of life, the mineral nature of the heart, and the path to redemption.

FLAMES ARE OF CLAY

The community loyal to Nanzen swore allegiance to the last alliance; the elves' flow of sympathy toward Alejandro swept away, in a great gust, any last vestiges of his old solitude; for Jesús, the water of a stream bathed the wounds of treachery; but the people of the mists were immeasurably enchanted by the two young women.

The girls were awakening to romantic love and they were in charge of the battle of the era. Those who are loved can bear the rigors of winter; those who love, find the strength to fight: Maria and Clara knew love in every conceivable way, and saw that their turbulent fate was bringing its just reward of caresses and gifts. What was more, their fate had bonded them like two branches of the same bough, and only Clara understood what terrified Maria; she alone knew how to calm her fears, and only Maria, in return, gave Clara the strength that forges boatmen—what I mean is an absolute, blind trust, with neither hesitancy nor doubt; and I believe that this mad bond explains why Maria's impertinence and gaiety spread to Clara, through a sort of transfer where the stronger of the two took care, for a while, of the other's most precious possessions. Despite physical separation, the young women added to the merging of their souls the singular trait of their foreign blood or appearance which, over and above the ineffable alchemy of encounters, made their friendship indestructible—to a degree that ordinary humans, or elves, could not even imagine.

Let us look at them through the eyes of the two Spaniards, who give no thought now to their absence from the League, for they are driven by the certainty that the real battle is being fought alongside the magicians of November. They are beautiful, the way all beloved women are beautiful, but the fairness of one, the golden skin of the other, their sleek, natural elegance are merely the rough outlines of their invisible grace. Fortunately, Alejandro and Jesús, because they were soldiers and came from poetic lands, wanted to die in the sun and see the invisible quality burning their gaze. They wanted to become acquainted with that land which they could just make out at the edge of their perception—that invisible land that has neither soil nor borders, known as the female continent. The fact that two young women born in the snow and the wind could bear that name so proudly will surely come as no surprise to those who have followed the story this far, for snow, wind, and mist are the filters that reveal the secret contours of things, unveiling their constantly changing essence, and offering a vision of it that penetrates the ages.

Who knows what we are looking at? thought Alejandro. All we want is to burn there or die.

In the meantime, the conflict had begun in every part of the world, and Petrus, to whom the question of women did not seem a thorny one, declared at that very moment:

"The enemy has reacted."

"If it was still necessary to prove that Nanzen has gone mad," said Aelius, "the fact that our sacred plantations will soon be reduced to ashes will amply suffice. Our dead, our eras, our ancestors spoke through the tea, and now they have been insulted by a bunch of demented leaders, a false prophecy dug up by a flea-ridden vagabond, with the iniquitous reinforcements of foreign mercenaries. Humans are beasts, a baneful copy of animal nature, the mutation of its virtues into vices. They spread death, lay waste to the nourishing earth, and threaten their own planet with annihilation. They are the survivors of ruinous wars that have taught them neither the vanity of force nor the virtue of peace. To hunger, they respond with repression; to the poverty of all, with the wealth of the few; and to the call for justice, with the oppression of the weakest. Tell me, you madmen who seek to ally yourselves with those madmen: do they not deserve death? and if not a single one remains, would it really be a tragedy for our mists? I remember what Ryoan was like before the tea's downfall and I weep. Is it conceivable that this splendor is gone forever? At dawn, the dark mists passed through our city; the gold of the sky fell upon the silver streams, we would savor our shared tea in silence; the channels opened and a world of tranquil souls lived together. But the snows of Katsura will not return, and we will not hear our deceased anymore. We will live on our lands instead of living in our mists, we will forget the air and its lightness, the song of trees and the connivance of kingdoms, we will err like humans in indigence and the opacity of the other, because humans are merely gregarious, whereas we, in essence, are communitarian creatures. Thus, Nanzen's actions force us to resort to tactics good elves find repugnant, until the only ones remaining on the field of battle will be the brave elves of the winning side."

Aelius fell silent.

"He's better as an orator for misfortune than he was as a speechifier in times of peace," said Petrus.

"*To resort to tactics good elves find repugnant*," Marcus repeated. "The battle will not be a pretty sight."

"We won't forget that the greatest war of all time was desired and started by an elf," said Petrus, "who worked to make humans exterminate one another in the name of the purity of races, and to ruin the world with camps devoted to total crime. And by the way, let us not forget that he himself destroyed his beloved mist."

"*Humans are beasts*," quoted Sandro. "Some will believe it."

"I don't care what they believe," said Petrus. "Wars are won with friends."

In successive waves, the elves' tide of appreciation for the young women helped to ease their unquiet souls. Its vibrations swelled then died in a sweet lament and, in the end, one could only remember having heard: *here you are.* All the same, a faraway rumble now covered the threnody of allegiance and sympathy of the Nanzen faithful.

"All the units are engaged in combat," said the chief of staff.

And Tagore shared the vision of an apocalyptic scene.

"Shinnyodo in the province of the Northern Marches, the granary of our mists," he said.

As far as the eye could see, there were blood-splattered fields of wheat and dead elves. Above the slaughter, a sky of lightning snapped like a storm jib. Dull explosions resounded, and the earth steamed and vibrated incessantly. The plains were littered with bows, and with equal numbers of elves, their throats pierced by an arrow or stabbed by a sword. The inhabitants of the mists don't wear armor or carry shields—the energy required to remain in a single essence would distract them from the combat at hand. Obliged to change form, their fatal vulnerability must be offset with dexterity and speed. The others continued the massacre, openly fighting hand-to-hand, forming a melee where the rumbling rose in volleys toward the storm. Eddies of air and water crossed the plain, bringing in their wake all the desolation of a wildfire. When they met, a silent explosion pulverized a considerable area of elves; their blood went on flowing long after the passage of the silent explosion. In the forefront of the battle, those who were crossing swords contended with gaping chasms that opened beneath their feet and engulfed entire cohorts. In places, the earth seemed to be crawling, like some frantic mole, then towered like a mountain to strike the adversary headlong. The speed of arrows and spears was increased by an in-draft that opened a dizzying channel where weapons pierced twenty bodies before ending their flight in one last throat.

At that very moment, in the west, a clamor arose from the enemy camp. Huge clouds of mist drifted up and began to move eastward. Aelius's soldiers went through the mist and raised their arms to the sky, screaming vengefully.

"The very depths of abomination," murmured Tagore.

When the clouds of mist reached their target, they were transformed. For one second, they swirled around, like in more fortunate times, dancers coiling inward, then fanning out with all the grace imaginable on earth, until they formed walls of stunning beauty. Gaining speed, they moved into the ranks of the last alliance, Dantesque blades mowing down the fighters as if they were mere rushes in a stream, and Alejandro, horrified, thought that human weapons cut a sorry figure in comparison with these thunderbolts of depraved nature.

Suddenly the sky exploded with red gashes, oozing their stench into the storm, and waves of mist now went by from east to west, mowing down the enemy elves.

"What about us, what are we waiting for to act?" asked Jesús.

"A sign," answered Solon.

"After waiting for two centuries," said Petrus, "the final hour seems to be lasting a thousand years."

The final hour, good Petrus, is the only one that does not belong to time. The hour for waging the battle, the hour for dying and watching others die: these are the infinity of pain held in an infinitesimal amount of time. Thus, time is transfigured and, in its transfiguration, delivers us to absolute pain.

"An hour in which we will see the worst outrages," said Tagore.

On the western horizon of the battle, a dark stain was spreading like a flood. To the east, the troops had frozen, and then a loud cry arose from all sides. Orcs! Orcs! shouted the soldiers, and in their clamor, surprise could be heard as much as scorn and rage. These orcs were joined together, moving like a giant, wobbly cockroach. Aelius's elves stepped aside to let them through, but their repulsion and shame was evident.

"If you still believed in it, this is the day to contemplate the ruins of elfin chivalry," said Petrus.

The orcs, shorter and broader than the elves, had neither hair nor fur, but an ant's cuticle studded with sticky spots. They walked heavily, almost limping. Oddly, blue wings fluttered intermittently in the background of their repugnant forms.

"Orcs are insects, prisoners of their chrysalis, half-beasts that have never managed to become the animals dormant inside them," said Solon.

"Can you imagine these abject creatures becoming cerulean blue butterflies?" asked Father François.

There was no scorn in his voice.

"In this world, everything is possible," said Petrus, "but at present they don't seem to be in a nymph-like mood."

They could clearly hear a song made up of grunts and panting.

"Or a nightingale mood," said Paulus.

"I cannot imagine how Aelius managed to win them over, nor how many envoys he must've lost during the negotiation," said Solon.

"Where do they live?" asked Jesús.

"In the borderlands," answered Petrus. "It's a hybrid zone that belongs to neither the mists nor the land of humans, and where other similarly aggressive species live."

Father François looked at the wheat. The soldiers' feet had pressed the ears to the ground, but here and there, the rumpled spikes stood up from puddles where soldiers lay dying, pointing their bloody sheaths at the sky; scarlet drops fell like pearls and, one after the other, returned to the earth. Bit by bit, the blood changed; it turned black and hardened, spreading over a large area, reflecting the lightning from the storm as the elves died. Despite the terror of it, there was something magnificent about this explosion of the sky's rage into shooting stars flung against a dark ink. Father François turned to the north, where the plain vanished into the mist, bordered by rows of wheat that were intact, as if exempt from the darkening blood. His gaze embraced the struggle between whiteness and darkness, his heart embraced the battle of the worlds, where the plum tree flowers were being engulfed, his soul embraced the end of the era of great elm trees and mist, and, finally, his entire being embraced the desolation of lands where neither leaves nor petals grow.

He thought of death, which always comes too soon, and of war that never ends, for he had come into the world during the great conflict of the past century, and while still a young man, had lived through the first war of this century. While looking for a guide that might advise him how to survive during times of disaster, he was convinced he had found it in the religion of his brothers. He had believed in an ark of the alliance of souls united by a love of Christ, and he had lived to entrust them to God and shield them from the machinations of the devil. He saw the universe as a battlefield, where the desire for good repulsed evil, where the realms of death retreated from the charging steeds of life. But one day in January, eight years earlier, an old woman had died in the village, and when it came time to recite the last prayer, he had searched his memory in vain for the usual antiphonies. It was a strange moment; in the distance, a new war was coming in the form of a storm sent by the enemy. Now it was up to him, with this coming threat, to proffer the last words for a sister who lost her son on the battlefield; and then he saw things as they really were, draped in darkness and blood, empty and cruel as the sea; and he had known that there is nothing on this earth, nothing in the heavens, nothing in people's hearts save the huge solitude of humankind, where the illusions of the devil and the good Lord have come to stay; nothing but hatred, old age, and illness, to which he no longer wanted to attach the cross of a sin, a crucifixion of a resurrection. For a moment that was deeper than despair, more painful than torture, he faltered, beneath a sky deserted by faith. If he no longer believed in anything, what was left to make him a man? Then he looked around him and saw the cemetery crowded with men and women standing straight in the icy gusts of wind. He looked at each face and each brow and, in a great blaze of light, he wanted to become one of them. Now that eight years had gone by, he remembered the cemetery flooded with peasants come to pay tribute to their departed sister, and he thought: what is greater than one's self is not in heaven, but is standing there before us, in another's gaze, and we must live at their pace. There is nothing on this earth but trees and forests, tall elms and dew-laden mornings, nothing but sorrow and beauty, cruelty and the desire to live—there is nothing but elves, hawthorns, and humans.

The scene vanished, and when another one replaced it, the pavilion gave a violent tremor. Tagore's vision left the battle of Shinnyodo and looked over at another arena of combat. The

288 · MURIEL BARBERY

earth was shaking, a powerful pounding, and the landscape was streaked with a crimson glow, shreds hanging from the ruins of the sky. Batteries of cannons were positioned on the hills above the field. The plain was swarming with soldiers, tanks, and units of both mounted and portable machine guns. Beyond the field, other verdant hills could be seen and, farther still, a blue expanse bordered by light shores and chalky cliffs. The sea: were it not for its presence, you might think you were in the Aubrac. The hills were gleaming with light, a green velvet covered the folds of earth, and the breath of the wind brushed the coves and outcroppings.

"This is the plain of Ireland, its beauty and its fall," said Tagore. "There are many others now that look like this, but I chose this place because it is a land of spirits and fairies, a harsh, enchanted, poetical land of the kind this story seems to favor. It has been home to great poets, one of whom wrote these lines, which, today, seem apt."

It is snowing on the plain of Ireland and the flames are of clay
Snow on the hollows and the blind rivers
Cemeteries raised on the mire of black blood

A louder explosion than the previous ones shook the scene of the fighting. Infantry and gunners were concentrated in the center of the plain behind their cannons and machine guns. Now we could see the men busy at their wretched task, which we call war, or lying dismembered in mounds on the ground ravaged by shells. The men were heavy and feverish, brown with mud and blood. In addition, there was a pouring rain that had nothing to do with the natural rain of Ireland, for the enemy was transforming the rain into spears that froze the moment they reached their targets.

"Caught between frost, mud, and fire," murmured Alejandro. "The only true hell."

The scene grew darker before changing to the estuary of the channel in the Southern Marches. A group of dolphins was circling around the barges moored there. The elves of the Deep Woods would never have imagined there could be so many of them, perhaps thousands. An elf standing firmly on the pier was addressing them.

"The channel is dying," he said, "leave this place and go to the sea."

A cloud of mist around the landing stage parted and let in a bleary light, then another gap formed a few yards further away and the channel swayed suddenly. Through the opening, a strange jumble was visible—whether it was houses, trees, streets, or mountains, no one could say.

The elf on the pier raised his otter forepaws toward the sky.

"The boatman," murmured Petrus, feeling a strong bond with him.

"Farewell," he said, "friendship survives falls."

The dolphins performed a deep arpeggio before diving and disappearing for good. The members of the last alliance looked at the channel and, above it, the city where the ashen flakes were drifting. The decline of the mists was continuing, and from the channels came the sound of a wrenching dirge.

The vision changed, yet again.

"For the last time, before the final painting," said Tagore.

On a patio of roses, Gustavo Acciavatti was holding a woman in his arms and saying *I love you*. Next to him, wrapped in paper and placed against a wall, a rectangular shape was waiting. Farther away, a tall, bent man, of a respectable age, but vigorous appearance, was also waiting. Gustavo embraced him in turn—embraced Pietro Volpe, Leonora's brother, the son of Roberto and heir to the painting that will open the gates to the future.

*

After looking one last time at Leonora, the former Head of the Council, now *direttore* in the land of the humans, set off for Nanzen.

> *It is snowing on the plain of Ireland*
> *And the flames are of clay*

Book of Battles

T<small>EARS</small>

There were so many tears in the painting of destiny.

Landscape paintings show the soul of the world in the shimmering that the painter's genius extracts from our ordinary perception, but the tears of a pietà show humans in their invisible nudity.

The soul now liquid, the beauty of fervor visible at last—we must dream of the landscape that contains all landscapes, the tear that encloses all tears, and, finally, the fiction that encompasses all others.

The Four Books

The life of humans can be portrayed through prayers, battles, paintings, and legacies.

Through prayers, so that the world will have meaning.

Through others' wars, where the battle with oneself is fought.

Through paintings—be they gardens or canvases—which, in causing our vision to hesitate, reveal the essence hidden behind what is visible.

And through invisible legacies, which are the only ones that allow us to attain love.

In the Final Hour of Loving

The former Head of the Council appeared on the bridge of mists, the painting of destiny under his arm. When he left the arch of the bridge, he was transformed into a white horse, then into a hare with immaculate fur. When he stepped into the pavilion and became a man once again, he looked at Clara and seemed unsettled.

"I am smiling because I no longer have to play for you," she said mischievously, and the Maestro seemed even more stunned.

When he stood before Maria and handed her the painting, the little veins on the young woman's face darkened.

She gently freed the canvas from its tissue paper.

In the morning light, the painting acquired all its texture. Its splendor was intact, but the Nanzen dawn gave new meaning to the fresh tints and material. It was no longer a scene of lamentation and fervor, but a story, drifting as it waited for its words. And yet it was the same scene reproduced over and over in human art: Mary and Christ's followers, weeping over the body taken down from the Cross; tears like dewdrops, the beauty of the Flemish style, so sharp, crystalline; in spite of this, beyond the story of the image, the members of the last alliance felt something vibrate, something that responded to the wood of the pavilion, the trees in the valley, the stones on the tea path, something beneath the surface of the painting that was struggling to get free. The mist idled in the forest, intact and light. Beyond the last tree-tops, a stormy sky still threatened. A bird sang. Something in the order of reality shifted and the dawn light took on a clarity which reminded Sandro of the landscapes in Flemish painting that he'd once loved. The transparencies of the path flickered and, in the space between two breaths, the trees appeared in sunlight. All along the black stones were hundreds of maple, pine, and plum trees, interwoven above the passage, whose vanished form received the power to transform itself into a vision with an intensity of presence that no living tree could ever attain. The transparencies of the path were turning opaque again and this rebirth from beyond death was the sign that the elves were waiting for. Tearing themselves away from the contemplation of the resurrected trees, they looked again at the canvas.

A transparent wave passed over its surface, altering the scene before them, and mingled with the tears of the faithful. Maria held her hand out to the painting and the wave withdrew, then froze. Tears were flowing down the Virgin's cheek, water in water forming drops that caught a blurred reflection, and what was vibrating below the scene took refuge in these moving pearls.

"The pavilion is revealing the essence of the painting, its internal power of transformation," said Solon.

They all felt their hearts beating as if at the moment of a new birth.

Tagore handed each of them a flask.

"Let us see what the gray tea can do," he said.

When they'd all drunk, Maria and Clara looked at each other.

"First Pietro," said Maria, "then the other battles."

"I would like a piano," said Clara.

A piano appeared in the room.

It was a fine student's piano, smooth as a pebble, although it had traveled far and gone through a great deal. Clara went closer to the object that had come to meet her the summer before her eleventh birthday, and which had initiated her into the profound delight of music, taken her to Rome under Pietro's protection, and led her to the painting which Roberto had acquired by committing murder.

When she ran her fingers over the keys, the notes made an interval that tore the silk of time and revealed a beach swept by mountain winds. You must understand who Clara Centi was, the orphan from the Abruzzo who had learned to play her piano in one hour and was acquainted with the stones of the mountain slopes the way sailors are acquainted with the stars in a black sky. The daughter of Tagore and Teresa knew the path to spaces and souls; through her music she was connected to landscapes and hearts, and this made her a ferrywoman, assembling spirits beyond their regions and their ages and, in the end, giving shape to the dreams that Maria would incarnate in the world.

The music told the story of the father and the son who had hated one another, even though one never knew why and the other would not say why. But Clara played and, through the power of the gray tea, all those present heard Roberto's confession to his son.

Which said: the night before your birth, I killed a man who wanted to sell me the Flemish painting. When he showed it to me, something glittered, but I felt he had been sent by the devil

296 - MURIEL BARBERY

and, on a sudden impulse, I killed him. A murderer has no right to love and I did penance by forbidding you to love me. I have no regrets, because if I hadn't had this determination, the murder would have led to other murders. Farewell. Love your mother and your sister and live honorably.

In the end, moved by one last thought, he added:

May the fathers bear the cross
And the orphans, grace.

The piano fell quiet.

Tagore shared the vision of a great hall filled with paintings and sculptures. The art dealer was on his knees, weeping, the way one weeps in childhood, huge sobs as tears rolled down his cheeks like dewdrops and fell, with a cheerful little bounce, in keeping with the words that came to him in the hour of knowing. As mad as you are, he said, I love you and you will never know it.

Then he disappeared from the mind of the humans and elves in Nanzen.

Against the partition, the painting was changing. Again, water was flowing, erasing the scene of lamentation. The faces trembled before they were washed away by the wave and, before long, all that remained on the canvas were Mary's tears. After a moment, when the tears had swelled to the extreme, there was only one left, a transparent, rounded setting for a new scene, hidden behind the first. Beneath the lamentation, the same elfin hand had painted a verdant, bluish landscape, with hills, cliffs by the sea, and long patches of mist. The Flemish masters are the only ones who have ever attained such perfection in the execution of scenes, which their mastery of light infuses with the glistening of the world, but in this painting, there was an additional sense of soul and beauty, given the fact it had been started in Nanzen then painted over in Amsterdam with the scene of the pietà. It had remained as it was until the conjunction of the pavilion and the gray tea brought it back to light in its dual stratification, offering the visual symbiosis of human and elfin lands and mist.

"It looks like Ireland," said Petrus.

A strong earthquake shook the pavilion, and Tagore shared other visions. The moon lingered in the Irish sky and, despite the heavy downpour submerging the fighting, it shone through the storm clouds. Corpses were piled into dunes of red blood; black blood covered the wheat of Shinnyodo, and the fields here and elsewhere were littered with flesh and mutilated bodies.

And then.

And then Maria entered the battle.

BOOK OF BATTLES

The moon above the plain of Ireland was bloodred, and Clara played a whisper of notes lighter than snowflakes. Everyone heard the story they contained, the story of snow and the soul of the country that met like plum flowers on winter wood and transformed the clay of combat into flames. Then Maria's power brought the melody to life and the clay from the field actually seemed to be germinating and rising up into a tree of fire that did not burn, but warmed the soldiers' bodies and hearts. The cold spell passed, the ground turned solid, and everyone looked at the burning clay covering the fields and stopping the battles. It began to snow.

You must understand who she was, Maria Faure, the little girl from Spain and Burgundy, born of two powerful elves, but brought up by the old grannies in The Hollows. To the totality of art that Clara incarnated, Maria responded with her power to know the totality of nature. Since childhood, she had been in constant contact with flows of matter that took the form of impalpable traces, and this allowed her to see the radiance of things. She recognized no other religion than that of violets, and was stunned that other people could not hear, as she did, the hymns of the sky and the symphonies of the branches, the great organs of clouds and the serenade of rivers. Through this magic, during the first battle on the fields of Burgundy, she had processed and transformed the sketches traced by living things the way one would paint on a canvas of desire. In this way, she had known how to turn the earth and sky upside down in order to open the breach through which the elfin fighters appeared.

It was snowing over the countryside of Ireland and, while the magnificent, idiotic snowflakes were falling, the clay of the massacres became a fire where pain was assuaged.

Clara's music became more tragic in tone.

At the other end of reality, through the power of the young women, the bridge and the pavilion at Ryoan began to burn, and their dull gold rose into the sky in magnificent spirals.

In Nanzen, through the bare openings in the pavilion, they saw the red bridge fade away. It hesitated then vanished like a mirage, while the mist over the arch shot upward in bursts of silver, then hung suspended, uncertain of its death.

In Ryoan, the golden smoke turned to gray, dirty streaks.

Nanzen trembled, and Solon said:

"They have drunk their last tea."

The final message from the enemy passed through the mist.

Mad, insane as you are! What choice have you left us?

History is not written with desire, but with the weapons of despair!

Father François felt an icy shiver down his spine then a furtive presence slipped into his mind.
Give us the words, said Clara's voice.
What words? he asked.
The words of the wordless, answered Clara.

BOOK OF PRAYERS

He pictured himself, after the battle, back on the hill where one of the brave village lads had fallen. He was a country boy, hard-working, more stubborn than a stone, high and mighty in speech, with a rough tenderness, a reveler when feasting, but solemn in friendship, who loved his wife with a love that stood straight as a candle under the stars. As a peasant, he'd been poor, as a man, rich with the only treasure that cannot be owned, and when he died in the fields of Burgundy he gave the priest his confession. It was the dream of a wooden house opening out onto the forest, where everyone would aspire to know love and a peaceful existence; a dream of a land that would belong to itself; of hunting that would be as just as it was beautiful; and of seasons so grand they would make one feel grander. It was a story of desire and hunts, a dream of a woman and her scent of leaves and lemon verbena, the fantasy of a simple heart festooned with mystical lace. This brave fellow's name was Eugène Marcelot, and at the time of his death, he had never learned to read or write. The inner flames rising on the marl of his fields cried out to tell him why he was a prince, but he did not know how he could tell his wife that he'd gone on standing under the sky because he loved her. Maria and Clara's powers had enabled Father François to hear the text from that simple heart, and after closing the valiant man's eyes, to take his message to his widow.

Today, as the tears of lamentation were diluted, it seemed to him that, at last, he understood Eugène Marcelot's mute confession, its significance in the first combat, and its role in the last battle of the war. He'd seen the landscape behind the tears at Eugénie's funeral, in the moment when he was searching inside for Christ's words, and all that came to him was the proof of the grandeur of trees and the incantations of the sky. To our suffering, he thought, death suffices, and to our faith, the fervor of the world. He suddenly remembered another painting that had left him thunderstruck when he was a young man—a German painting from the sixteenth century representing Christ between his Deposition and the Resurrection, lying on a sheet in a tomb—cold, alone, and abandoned to the work of decomposition, and Father François says out loud: if the universe is simply a novel waiting to be written, let us choose a story where salvation does not require torture, where flesh is neither guilty nor suffering, where mind and body are two accidents of a single substance, and where the idiocy of loving life does not have to be paid for with cruel punishment. So it goes, in the lives of humans and elves, alternately scenes of passion and vast plains, battles and prayers, tears and sky. I look at Mary's tears and call out to the love of Eugène Marcelot in the total landscape; I look at the landscape behind the crucifixion and I call out for the harmony in the substance of our tears. Through that harmony, all borders to lands and to the mind will be abolished, an act which, since humans became human, we have called love.

Finally, he looked at Petrus and thought: may the blind bear the cross and the idiots, grace.

As Clara was conveying the message to Maria, playing a

melody that seemed to her the exact transcription of his words, beautiful and lyrical, placated and serene, he felt himself falter. The world had changed its appearance. He saw its substance and energy spread out before him in an undulating fan that rippled and snapped like a ship's mainsail. A force leapt through the world with the energy of a will-o'-the-wisp, riding currents and gliding over the foam of magnetic lines above abysses of indistinct vibrations—just as everything vanished, he seemed to discern a luminous painting and he thought: earth and art have the same frequency. When the tempest abated and he came to in the world as he knew it, he thought: this is how Maria perceives the universe, in the form of waves and currents that order the mutation of each thing; and he thought again: such power should have consumed her, but she has only a few marks on her face.

Several new shapes materialized on the landscape of the canvas. What is there to say about this miracle where roses, irises, and hawthorns appear, along with humans, elves, and houses opening out onto the forest? Before their eyes, the painting was transformed into a synthesis of the two worlds, where there were vineyards and tea plantations, houses of wood and stone at the edge of silent forests, cities beside rivers where barges without sails slid by. They could sense Eugène Marcelot's dream everywhere, they could sense the harmony of the mists everywhere; before long, on the surface of the painting there was a spray of sparks where a blurred figure appeared, taking form as it erased men and elves.

It covered the entire landscape.

"Are you the one who is doing all this?" Sandro asked Maria. She nodded.

"But it's Clara's music that gives me the image and the meaning," she said.

On the floor of the pavilion, Solon placed a little sphere covered in fur that looked like the blurry form on the painting.

"An ancestor," murmured Petrus.

The downy sphere began to spin and a first essence emerged from it, that of an otter, followed by a hare, a boar, a bear, and so on until a multitude of species were represented and were turning with all the others in the space of the pavilion, now infinitely expanded. The last essence to appear, a tawny squirrel, ended the dance and stood there quivering with its fellows, in a perfect representation of the entire animal kingdom.

"Is this what we are going to become?" asked Jesús, looking at the resurrected ancestor.

The painting changed again, the ancestor disappeared, and two figures appeared: a jovial peasant and a little potbellied ginger man, Eugène Marcelot and Petrus of the Deep Woods. Then the landscape began to melt, the outlines of creatures and things faded under a new flow of water that formed little eddies on the canvas, the impact of invisible tears falling from a sky of black ink. The landscape was engulfed, then vanished completely, again revealing the scene of lamentation.

It was transfigured.

There was nothing more marvelous than seeing the delicate touches Maria gave to the scene, because through the power of the gray tea, her mind had become the bristle of the brush modifying the story of life. The music Clara composed, echoing Father François's words, ended in a wrenching ode, a murmured farewell—the last gaze—the last battle. The nails of the crucifixion faded first, then the stigmata, the crown of thorns, and the blood on Christ's brow, and all that remained was a dead man surrounded by the affliction of his loved ones, while superimposed upon the faces, the landscape of trees and hills reappeared, carpeted in hawthorns and roses.

So it goes, in the lives of humans and elves, alternately scenes of passion and vast plains, battles and prayers, tears and sky, thought Father François. Why add suffering to suffering? There is only one war, and it is enough for our sorrow as living creatures. And he thought again: so be it, may the idiot triumph over the madmen.

The piano fell silent.

BOOK OF PAINTINGS

Hostus placed a sable brush before Sandro, along with black ink, and I must tell you that this black ink was not there by chance, either. It came from a quarry at the edge of the mists, by steep slopes where lampblack was mined, and through it, Sandro's life was endlessly reflected to him. The first painting he'd shown Pietro on arriving in Rome featured four lines of India ink, made in a single gesture, a single breath. In the language of elves, this was the sign for mountain, and Pietro, who knew how to read it, was astounded that Sandro could have imagined the sign without ever learning it. After that, Sandro only painted works he found trivial, although in Rome they called him a genius, until Pietro showed him the Flemish painting and its incandescence burned his eyes with a beauty he didn't know how to survive. But before leaving Rome and heading for his retreat in L'Aquila, he produced a final canvas of flat tints of black ink with neither figures nor outlines, simply enhanced by three strokes of carmine pastel. And everyone who had ever seen the bridge of mists immediately recognized it.

After that, he gave up painting for good.

On the floor of the pavilion, the silver dust froze, then escaped in flurries of tiny stars. We are adrift, thought Sandro, looking at Petrus, we are vagabonds blindly searching for a kingdom, because *they* know that they are *from elsewhere* even though they are from *here*. We are adrift from being in two worlds at once: the one that gave birth to us and the one we desire. Petrus was born in a sublime universe, and all he thinks about is drinking and telling stories; I come from an imperfect life where I drank more than I painted, although I aspire to the silent, absolute nature of visions. We who know the price of land and the message of the wind, the taste of roots and the headiness of uprooting, can be pioneers who build the unknown footbridges.

Tagore handed him a last flask of gray tea.

"Plums from the garden," he murmured after drinking.

He dipped the brush into the ink.

There was a strange quivering in the air—or was it in the earth, the sky, the universe? They blinked.

The world had become black and white, except for the creatures of flesh, and the ancestor, who was vibrating through his multiple avatars.

Reader, do not think that the authentic line is born on the canvas, it occurs before that, in the intake of breath through which the painter absorbs the totality of the visible, in the exhalation with which he prepares to restore it to the tip of his bristles. When they touched the floor, the pavilion trembled slightly. How long did the gesture last? It was fleeting and infinite, concentrated and widespread, unique and multiple, but Sandro had been nurturing it for sixty years, and the line was traced with a flowing ease that made the members of the last alliance rub their eyes, because on the wood of the pavilion there was only one line.

———▲

a single naked line
that contained all the others
a single black line where
all the colors and all the shapes
could be seen
a single line starting on the floor of the pavilion
and extending to the surface of the Flemish painting
absorbing its figures and its stories

Petrus had already seen a similar line in Katsura, drawn by the Head of the Council who, it was said, had witnessed the birth of the bridge. His curving calligraphy looked like a single line which, in turn, represented every possible curve, just as today they could see only a single brushstroke and yet they perceived everything that was visible. What illusion of vision enabled it to bring with it the consistency and prolixity of the world? While this world was regaining its colors and Maria was focusing her mind on Sandro's line, Petrus thought again: it is the visionary who gives his flesh to the story, but he must have the power of these little girls to write the text.

On the floor, the ink dried, and gradually the line grew larger until it passed through the wooden partitions of the pavilion, which had become transparent. Outside, the line changed into a colossal structure that expanded to create a bridge sparkling with darkness, with neither arch nor pillars, a simple black streak leading far away to the outer reaches of one's gaze.

"The new bridge," said Maria.

The mist that had once engulfed the arch coiled in on itself in one last graceful sigh of languor, then pulled apart, before melting slowly into the arch. Mist from all the provinces appeared on the horizon and, unrolling over the valley, they too headed toward the new bridge between the two worlds.

When there was no more mist they looked at the bridge and saw that it ended in the void. Its pure line flowed into *nothing,* where one could discern neither mist, nor trees, nor clouds. Below it, a dark lake had appeared.

"I have lived for no other reason than to see this vision," said Sandro.

In the room, the ancestor in his multiple incarnations began to spin and, with each spin a species was absorbed into him, while it went through the partitions of the pavilion and melted into the lacquer of the bridge. And so, Clara played a hymn— a strange hymn, as free as the clouds, as dangerous as fervor— and on the painting, which had become a simple spot of black ink, there were inscriptions in the language of elves that humans could now understand—the drifting story they'd fore- seen in the beginning, the one that simply wanted to be writ- ten and was waiting for someone who was willing to continue the work of the painter from Amsterdam—the story that told of the tears of love and the landscapes of fervor.

In the final hour of loving
Everything shall be empty and full of wonder

How does one capture the passing sparkle? All that is required—something elves know how to do—is to reduce life to its most basic framework and inscribe it on a final landscape in its essential nudity; then in the end, turn the landscape— something humans know how to do—into the setting of the last story—the novel of novels, the fiction of fictions.

In the final hour of loving
Everything shall be empty and full of wonder

The inscriptions, on leaving the surface of the painting, passed through the partitions of the pavilion and melted into the bridge of ink. The mist had lived and now was making room for the void where creatures and things move about. Just like the miraculous mist that rendered the world never completely visible—sometimes opting to cover all the universe except for a single bare branch, then contracting to allow the greatest possible proportion of things to be seen—the void restored the balance of invisible wholeness.

You must understand what it is, this void we are talking about, because we people in the West are accustomed to thinking it is simply nothingness, absence, or lack of matter and life, whereas the void that the new novel of the world wished for was an authentic substance. It was the valley in which things bathe, the inhabited breath of life which takes them into the cycle of their mutations, the invisibility of the visible, the inner image of living essences, the nakedness of the currents where the winds of dreams are engulfed; it was the energy that makes the world turn on its invisible hub, the palpable impalpability of the mystery of being there, the ineffable become presence; and it passed over the wonder of the hawthorns and the roses in a painting that preserved the precedents, although it never stopped abolishing itself—I would like for you to touch this beauty that exists only thanks to the victory of the void over fullness, the recomposition of the world's paintings in keeping with waves of effacement where what kills and encumbers us is drowned—that beauty which sends its roots into the earth and sky and is not born of the continuity of things, but of the destitution that reveals the heart. New landscapes from the story passed over the painting, taking shape, then vanishing in successive volleys of rivers and verdant hills, of valleys of white trees or branches drowning in the invisibility of clouds. The void encircled them with breathing like an ermine stole, made them shine in their brilliant nakedness, then gently dissolved them before giving birth to a new configuration of nature, a new victory of the wonder of visions.

Here, anything is possible, thought Petrus.

"We have heard the gospel of the idiot," said Maria to Father François.

"Empty and full of wonder. The old song from Extremadura that Luis reminded you about, yesterday, in the cellar," said Jesús.

———▲———

"Yesterday," murmured Alejandro. "An eternity has gone by since then."

In the final hour of loving
Everything shall be empty and full of wonder

Book of Fathers

ONE

One must know the language of the elves and the peoples of the East of the planet in order to bring about the union of nature and the spirit, but one must also have the imagination of humans to tell the story that commands all the others.

The single brushstroke is the unit through which multiplicity comes about, the bridge between species and worlds, the mold of all novels, the unveiling of the passing sparkle, the feast of wonder, the freedom of the void, and the enchantment of the world.

And what is more, a single brushstroke is proof that reality is always generated by a vision transformed into fiction. The vision offered by the gathering at Nanzen was clear: wonder is born from the void which, in turn, generates the simplicity of beauty.

And, in its wake, the complexity of fervor.

父親

FATHERS

The fourth Book is the Book of Fathers.

One's understanding of *fathers* must not be any different from one's understanding of the other great Books. The female continent fully subscribes to the mandate through which we learn to live. We say fathers the way we could write mothers, brothers, sisters, or friends. But men and elves, beyond gender, beyond culture, inscribe the reality of invisible transmissions upon paternity, the proof that the living are responsible for the dead, and the dead are responsible for the living—thus, the Book of Fathers is the depositary of territories, lineages, and legacies that cannot be detected by the naked eye.

Real prisons and real legacies are always invisible, transmitted by the wind of dreams and the breathing of trees.

The fathers came to the rescue of the last alliance.

There are no sons without fathers, there is no life without a mandate, no freedom without legacy. Alejandro had watched in silence as the red arch was transmuted into a black footbridge, and the dead trees appeared above the transparencies of the path. Their vibration was similar in nature to that of the cemetery in Yepes, and there he also found the sparkling of bygone days. The dead of each kingdom speak to one another, he thought, and he wanted to share this thought with his beloved. Looking at Clara, he saw she was gloomy, her gaze distant and dark.

"What's the matter?" he asked in a low voice.

"Something's not right," she said quietly, "but I don't know what it is."

Tagore showed them the battlefields of the two worlds, where the fire was subsiding. The clay of fire had consumed weapons and bodies: the surviving soldiers from Ireland and elsewhere were wandering, sobbing, through the snow. Alejandro looked at the wheat of Shinnyodo, imprisoned in its black blood, the field where orcs, bows, swords, and dead bodies had vanished into the flaming earth, and he thought he could hear a new sound. The guardian handed him a flask of near-black tea, which had a familiar taste, and he murmured: sherry. The sound rising from the fields of Shinnyodo grew louder, and the gray tea revealed its source.

Do you know what it means to inhabit the province of life and death? It is a strange country, but only those who speak its language are human. They are called on to address the living and the dead as if they were only one being, and Alejandro was familiar with that idiom. As a child, no matter which path he took, he was irresistibly drawn back to the walls of the cemetery at Yepes. There, among the stones and crosses, he felt he was among his loved ones. He did not know how to speak to them, but the peacefulness of the place rustled with words for him. What's more, even when it meant nothing, the music of the dead reached him in a place in his chest that understood, with no need of words. In these moments of great fulfillment, he could discern an intense sparkling at the edge of his vision, and he knew he was seeing the light from some form of unknown, powerful spirit. Now, in Nanzen, it was taking on a new form and he understood the power the gray tea could give him.

He looked at Maria, and she nodded to him. Clara, drawing on their silent dialogue, played a psalm in tune with the legacies conveyed by the heavens.

BOOK OF FATHERS

The dead of Shinnyodo were the first to be reborn. It was a fabulous sight, not only because Alejandro's desire resurrected the dead, accompanied by Clara's music and catalyzed by Maria's power, but also because the world became atmospheric and they all felt themselves drifting in the reality of the great mixture, where the living and the dead are united. We live in the atmosphere, thought Petrus—in the newly liquid world, where the present, past, and future came together on the infinite span of an instant, and the dead of all eras stood up and joined the soldiers on the side of the last alliance.

Men, women, and elves of eras long buried appeared, not in the form in which death had taken them, but as they had been in that moment in their life when they had been happiest. And so, dressed and prepared according to the customs of their century, they came into sight, incarnate and tangible, with none of the singularities that common faith grants to phantoms.[1]

One could see this crowd, or rather, this army of the dead on every field, and the survivors fell to their knees in shock. It was an army that carried no weapons and did not want to fight, wandering through the snow of battles and sowing the flowers of plum trees, speaking of invisible legacies and bringing shame upon the folly of war. One could also sense, in the heart of this crowd, a puff of air in the form of a rose or, perhaps, a snowflake, and one could hear, flowing through every consciousness like a river, the women's singular message. They murmured: *we are with you*, and everyone could feel the power of the lineage, its liquid force and the grace of a wild continent. Then Clara's piano fell silent.

Two men came into the pavilion and Alejandro embraced Luis Álvarez and Miguel Ybáñez, restored in the final hours by the great mixture. I have given the mercy of poetry to my prayers, Alejandro thought, and I have accepted the mandate. As a reward for this devotion, I see the life of my dead—and, indeed, he saw them returned from death, while the past reasons for their fate were revealed to him. He saw Miguel's murderer, an assassin of the same sort as the Yepes killers, all recruited by the traitor, then sent into the void from which no one returns: it had destined them for the mists in the same way one might be destined for Nanzen or Rome, and the unfortunate souls had disappeared forever. This is what had enabled the enemy to kill the general who could defeat the Confederation, without leaving a trace, along with the witnesses, in Yepes, of the quest for the gray notebook.

Outside, the new bridge vibrated with the totality of life. Below it, the new lake of time was filling. Its shores were submerged by water that flowed away into the void and, on the other side of this void, rejoined the land of humans. Water lapped against the walls of the castillo in Yepes and flowed onto the plain of Extremadura in a scene of great beauty because the lake, in covering the landscape, also changed its configuration. Was it that the black waters offered one's gaze a form so simple they created wonder, or was it that one sensed the world was less *full* in its plain liquid nature? Or was it that the waters told a story without a Church, a fable to greet the wishes of every heart?

The battle was coming to an end.

"We have to go, and we don't know whether murder or poetry will carry the day," said Luis.

"What began with one murder ends with another," said Miguel.

"What came about through treason engenders treason," added Luis.

"Something's not right," Clara murmured again.

"Something's not right," said Solon.

Sandro Centi stood up.

As shared by Tagore, the scene at Yepes was changing.

The lake was burning.

Tall, raging flames rose above the water and as they spread, roaring, the world was filling up—yes, the world was becoming *fuller* and denser, until all these crowded panoramas became suffocating, with their cities, houses, factories, and throngs of people moving indifferently through their surroundings.

Luis and Miguel vanished. Sandro staggered.

He collapsed on the floor of the pavilion.

They ran over to him, and Maria and Clara, kneeling by him, took his hands.

He was burning with fever.

"He's dying," said Clara.

Gustavo, Solon, and Tagore had leapt up and were peering out at the world—casting all the power of their great minds into the struggle as they searched through the universe with the force of the tea, going over every acre and every pathway, trying to find the seed of betrayal, every breach of strength and every tremor in the dream.

It is the visionary who dies, in the first exchange of gunfire, and when he falls in the snow, and knows he is dying, he recalls the hunts of his childhood, when his grandfather taught him to respect the deer.

Who told me that? thought Petrus.

Then he remembered.

"It was the writer," he said.

He knelt down next to the painter.

"Give him snow," he said, to Maria.

She looked at him, not understanding.

"He is dying," said Petrus. "Give him the comfort of snow."

"He cannot die," she said.

Sandro opened his eyes.

"My little one, for ten years you have been there, whenever I've been reborn and whenever I have died," he whispered. "How many more times will this happen?"

With an effort, he added:

"I have lived only for this peace."

It began to snow in the Pavilion of the Mists, and there came a breath of air, which filled their thoughts with the image of a deer at the edge of a snowy forest, then of a cascade of transparent plums in a summer orchard.

The air stopped moving.

"He is dead," said Father François.
The snow was falling gently.
Minute gilded cracks slithered like lizards across the new bridge.
"We've been blind," said Tagore, "the enemy has been playing us from the beginning."
"*History is not written with desire, but with the weapons of despair*," said Petrus. "The gray tea is deadly."
Must one be clear-sighted or blind to thwart the machinations of destiny? Of them all, Petrus was the one who foresaw how that which touches our hearts is always that which we come to understand last—alas, at first we see only the inessential, and our hope is always caught up in its net, and we pass by the garden of our soul without seeing it. The gray tea was deadly. By agreeing to let it rule their vision, Katsura and Nanzen had sealed their own ruin. Had Aelius activated its toxicity only toward the end, or had he made use of it right from the start? It was too late to go solving riddles. The enemy preferred its own destruction over a victory of the alliance. All those who had drunk the tea would die there today, enemies and allies alike, in a final tragedy.

Some are born to assume responsibility for other creatures. That is our realm, and our mandate, the ministry that gives life to the powers of death, to their territory and legacy. This eternity and this responsibility are henceforth incumbent upon you, because you have drunk today from the thousand-year-old tea.

"Who said that?" wondered Petrus.
Then he understood.
Those who had drunk the thousand-year-old tea would survive the poison, because they would be traveling forever in the

company of their dead. Since the boatman from the Southern Marches had presented the three elves with the tea upon their arrival from the Deep Woods, Petrus, Paulus, and Marcus would go on living.

Those who had not would die.

"We've failed," said Solon.

"There are no prophecies," said Petrus, "only hopes and dreams."

"Those who drank the thousand-year-old tea will live," said Tagore. "And perhaps our daughters, who are from both worlds at the same time."

On the fields of the two worlds, the resurrected had disappeared, and the fighters from each side were burning with an invisible fire. Cries of suffering could be heard; Tagore maintained their clamor for a moment, until the terror of the sight gave way to the lake in Extremadura. The fire had gone out and a brown mire, a plague that had infiltrated the black water, was overflowing onto the shores of the lake. It spread across the world, over the ground, and through the air, beneath the crust of the earth and into the strata of the sky, poisoning fields and clouds for more years than one could count. The trees were weeping, and they could hear a wrenching requiem rising from the transparencies of the path. Finally, the dead foliage faded away until it disappeared from view altogether.

"Our presence was revealed to humans," said Solon.

"How will the war end?" asked Alejandro.

"Fighting will resume on earth," said Maria.

"The tea has had its day," said Solon, "we no longer have any purchase on the tide of History."

"Other camps will be built," said Tagore.

"The pavilion is still there," said Father François.

"Amputated of its mists, its dead, and its bridge," replied the guardian.

*

When death is drawing near, there is only one lake that can distract us from it. We all have one in our heart that stems from the favors and pain of childhood. It remains in our breasts and become granite, until the enchantment of the encounter makes it liquid again.

The images of the dried lake came back to Jesús, the place where his father and the long dynasty of poor fishermen had suffered; the taste of betrayal and the redemptive relief of burdens came back; the wars he'd fought as son and soldier, their insanity and afflictions came back; he looked at Maria and once again he saw the stones that the mist turned to liquid. In the end, everything is empty and full of wonder, he thought; so must we die to understand nakedness without suffering? And with a heart that was now unburdened of regret, he looked forward to going to join the dead souls of his fathers—the great Eugène Marcelot, who loved his wife the way one lights a candle in a church, and all those who, before him, had known the peace of encounter.

To Alejandro, the image of Luis's calm, dark lake came back, a lake where men pray when they want to live and love. I have spent my entire life pleading that my dead might be saved, he thought, and they are the ones who are saving me in the hour of my death. He saw again the bowl where one could contemplate a life of effacement and of the land, he remembered the presence of the elves in the mists, he looked at the woman who'd elevated him to love, and heard the last message from those who had come before him. Empty and full of wonder, he murmured. Ideas always triumph over weapons and, whatever Luis might think, poetry triumphs over murder.

Every major tale is the story of a being who leaves the

desolation of the self to embrace the vertigo of the other and, from this freely given absence of self, finally embraces the wonder of existence. Jesús Rocamora and Alejandro de Yepes had laid down their burdens. They looked at the women they loved.

In that hour when dreams were crumbling, and they did not know whether they would live or die, they were transfigured. The transfer that had come with the war, making Clara joyful and mischievous, was reversed once again; there was an ultimate migration of hearts, and Maria was the child she had been, lighthearted and full of cheer like a clear stream, spreading the charm of her impertinence all around her. But she looked at Clara and plumbed the wild soul the little Italian girl had regained through this reversal: that soul once bereft of laughter and tears had reconnected with her former gravity, but now she was unable to shed the traces of gaiety that had been entrusted to her for a time, and thus she forfeited the darkness and solitude of her newly recovered childhood. In this way, Maria Faure and Clara Centi, finding themselves equally balanced as sisters, stepped together onto the female continent and, comforted by the compassion of the lineage, prepared to live or die in the company of their loved ones. Everyone felt the presence of that guild, its seal of exalted solidarity. Everyone felt Maria's burden of grief and power vanish like a dream upon waking, and Clara's gravity acquired a sheen of stippled silver as she was grazed with happiness.

Paulus, Marcus, Hostus, and Quartus wrapped Sandro in a light-colored cloth and the group left the pavilion.

"The dead never leave us," said Petrus, walking side by side with Alejandro. "The second sanctuary was the heart of this world. I wish I had understood it earlier."

"Would it have changed anything?" asked Alejandro.

"You would have drunk the thousand-year-old tea," he replied.

"If you drank the thousand-year-old tea, it was because you deserved to," said Alejandro.

"Fate is unacquainted with dignity," said Petrus, "but it has earned me the right to be in charge of the rest of the story, like all those who stay behind to contemplate the fall of their worlds and the deaths of their friends."

"Of the lot of us, you're the aristocrat," said Alejandro.

They reached the shores of the lake. The brown mire muddying the waters on the other side of the bridge troubled the surface here with ripples that resembled hostile writing. The black bridge began to break in a strange way: the little fissures became cracks that disappeared in on themselves and created nothingness where previously the mist had lived. Then it seemed that this nothingness produced a new substance, thick and clogged, where vast metropolises and buildings could be seen through the fog—a yellow, viscous fog that stuck to creatures and things while the sky opened and let in harmful rays.

"Nothingness is not emptiness," said Solon. "From the void come dreams, fullness proceeds from nothingness, stifling and killing us."

"How could we have lost this war?" asked Tagore.

"The first murder is never the first," said Father François.

"The world was not ready for the fiction of fictions," said Petrus.

"It was a beautiful dream, though," said Father François. "A tale without a chapel, a story without a Church."

"Who wants to chart their own destiny when others can choose it for them?" asked Petrus.

And all at once, the time had come to say goodbye, the way

it always comes, too soon, and there is no way to be prepared for it, because it is difficult to live well, but even harder to die well. It is autumn, November, the most beautiful month, because everything is decaying with beauty and dying with grace—and this loss, which means that everything perishes, leaving in its wake the fervor of an ephemeral sparkling, is the very thing that we call love. And so it is that in these hours, when everything is declining, the last Book makes itself known, the most precious of all, the only one that matters to the living and the dead. I cannot describe to you precisely what was in the heart of those who were about to die, but you must know that on the face of the little French girl, who was also a little Spanish girl, there were once dark little veins, and now there was not a trace of them, and Petrus pointed this out, mumbling something only Father François could hear: *in the final hour of loving.*

The elf took a dusty bottle from his bundle.

"This one picked me," he said.

On the label, decayed with moisture, one could read:

1918 – Petrus – Grand Vin

Need I tell you that the moment they all drank from the crystal glasses—miraculously preserved in the idiot's bundle—the last wine of this last day, strange figures appeared on the surface of the evil waters?

Wild grasses upon the lake.

END OF THE FOUR BOOKS
OF THE PRESENT TIME

景観

There have been two major landscapes in this story—the cellar at Yepes, on the one hand; the harsh, poetic lands of Burgundy, the Abruzzo, the Aubrac, Ireland, and Extremadura, on the other.

If the cellar attracted pilgrims among winemakers and caused ghosts to appear, it is because the vine and the dead both participate in the great story of the world—and what better metaphor is there for this than that of voyagers carrying the elixir of fables into the laboratory of the novel?

Finally, if all the protagonists of this story grew up in lands of solitude and the mind, it was because everything is born of the earth and the sky, and everything decomposes when that native poetry is forgotten—as Alejandro de Yepes and Luis Álvarez had once found out.

I shall always maintain was the motto of the mists and of the castillo at Yepes. What is there to do in this life other than maintain the magic of a story of phantoms and roses?

小説

NOVEL

Q*uand il n'est pas songe, le roman est mensonge—When it is not a dream, the novel is a lie*, said a writer whom Petrus may meet someday.

The spirits of the world are no different from those of the novel—consequently, the writer who holds the pen holds, in the ink, the totality of what was and of what will be. If the first elf to have crossed the bridge of mists went to Yepes, it was because he wanted to reach the limits of reality, the heart of the strange stronghold where the borders between lands and the mind are abolished. And if the first elf to have opted for a human life also went to the poetic land of Extremadura, it was because my pen had decided so, and my dream, and the totality of the world to which my kind give their voice.

Ultimately, I also included phantoms and wine, because everyone is heir to a story that they must make their own, something which, as we know, would be most compatible with the magnanimity of a good reserve vintage.

暗い森

The Apocalypse According to Petrus

The idiot, given his blindness, can see far into the future; given his heart, he knows space and time; given his mind, the layers and alluvia of reality; it is because of him that all have gathered here, because he is the servant of stories and I decided it would be so.

Petrus knew the power of hope and the inexorability of the fall, the grandeur of resistance and the eternity of war, the power of dreams and the perpetuity of battles—in short, he knew that life is only what happens in the interstices between disasters. There are no better friends than those who despair, no more valiant soldiers than the adepts of dreams, no more brave knights of wonder than unbelievers and drinkers, when faced with the apocalypse.

Proof of this is the words he said at the end, when everyone was standing by the black water, and the humans and elves who had not drunk the thousand-year-old tea were dying in the arms of those they loved.

We have lost the battle, but time does not stop with this defeat—thus, I am destined to continue the novel of this strange country of war and dreams which we call the life of humans and of elves.

CHRONOLOGY

4,000,000 B.C.
Birth of the Pavilion of the Mists.

100,000 B.C.
First decline of the mists.

20,000 B.C.
Birth of the first bridge in Nanzen.
First regeneration of the mists.

1400
Beginning of the second decline of the mists.

1501
First definitive passage of an elf into the world of humans.
Beginning of two centuries of regeneration of the mists.

1710
A hare elf from Katsura (Gustavo Acciavatti to humans) is
elected councilor to the upper chamber.

1750
Beginning of the third decline of the mists.

1770
A hare elf from Ryoan (the future Aelius) becomes head of the
gardeners of the Council.

1800
Petrus arrives in Katsura.
Gustavo is elected Head of the Council, a boar elf from Katsura (Tagore to humans) is appointed Guardian of the Pavilion.

1865–1867
Franco-German war.

1870
Aelius's nephew finds the painting and the gray notebook in Amsterdam.
Roberto Volpe kills him.
Birth of Pietro Volpe.
Petrus finds the prophecy: birth of the idea of an alliance.
He becomes the Council's envoy to the human world.

1880
Birth of Leonora Volpe.

1900
Death of Roberto Volpe.
Gustavo marries Leonora.
A hare elf from Inari (Solon to humans) is elected Head of the Council, Tagore remains Guardian of the Pavilion.

1908
Birth of Alejandro de Yepes and Jesús Rocamora.
A boar elf from Ryoan (Raffaele Santangelo to humans) enters the service of the head of the garden.

1910–1913
First World War in the human world.

1918
Birth of Maria and Clara (beginning of *The Life of Elves*).
Aelius discovers the contents of the gray notebook.

1922
Aelius builds the pavilion and the bridge in Ryoan.

1926
Raffaele Santangelo becomes governor of Rome.

1928
Clara arrives in Rome.

1931
First battle on the fields of Burgundy (end of *The Life of Elves*).
Beginning of the inter-elfin war.

1932
First year of the Second World War among the humans.

1938
Sixth year of the war.
Petrus finds the gray notebook.
Last battle of the era of the mists.

ACKNOWLEDGMENTS

My thanks and gratitude to Jean-Baptiste Del
Amo and Édith Ousset.
Many thanks, too, to Shigenori Shibata.

In the memory of Meziane Yaici and Sayoko
Tsutsumi.